7.95

CHILD DEVELOPMENT

McGRAW-HILL SERIES IN PSYCHOLOGY

HARRY F. HARLOW, *Consulting Editor*

BARKER, KOUNIN, AND WRIGHT · Child Behavior and Development
BEACH, HEBB, MORGAN, AND NISSEN · The Neuropsychology of Lashley
VON BÉKÉSY · Experiments in Hearing
BLUM · Psychoanalytic Theories of Personality
BROWN · The Psychodynamics of Abnormal Behavior
BROWN AND GHISELLI · Scientific Method in Psychology
CATTELL · Personality
CRAFTS, SCHNEIRLA, ROBINSON, AND GILBERT · Recent Experiments in Psychology
DEESE · The Psychology of Learning
DOLLARD AND MILLER · Personality and Psychotherapy
DORCUS AND JONES · Handbook of Employee Selection
FERGUSON · Personality Measurement
FERGUSON · Statistical Analysis in Psychology and Education
GHISELLI AND BROWN · Personnel and Industrial Psychology
GRAY · Psychology Applied to Human Affairs
GRAY · Psychology in Industry
GUILFORD · Fundamental Statistics in Psychology and Education
GUILFORD · Psychometric Methods
GUILFORD · Personality
HAIRE · Psychology in Management
HIRSH · The Measurement of Hearing
HURLOCK · Adolescent Development
HURLOCK · Child Development
HURLOCK · Developmental Psychology
KARN AND GILMER · Readings in Industrial and Business Psychology
KRECH AND CRUTCHFIELD · Theory and Problems of Social Psychology
LEWIN · A Dynamic Theory of Personality
LEWIN · Principles of Topological Psychology
LEWIS · Quantitative Methods in Psychology
MAIER AND SCHNEIRLA · Principles of Animal Psychology
MILLER · Language and Communication
MISIAK AND STAUDT · Catholics in Psychology: A Historical Survey
MOORE · Psychology for Business and Industry
MORGAN AND STELLAR · Physiological Psychology
PAGE · Abnormal Psychology
REYMERT · Feelings and Emotions
SEASHORE · Psychology of Music
SHAFFER AND LAZARUS · Fundamental Concepts in Clinical Psychology
SIEGEL · Nonparametric Statistics: For the Behavioral Sciences
STAGNER · Psychology of Personality
TOWNSEND · Introduction to Experimental Method
VINACKE · The Psychology of Thinking
WALLEN · Clinical Psychology: The Study of Persons
WATERS, RETHLINGSHAFER, AND CALDWELL · Principles of Comparative Psychology
ZUBEK AND SOLBERG · Human Development

John F. Dashiell was Consulting Editor of this series from its inception in 1931 until January 1, 1950. Clifford T. Morgan was Consulting Editor of this series from January 1, 1950 until January 1, 1959.

From Child Development, a McGraw-Hill Text-Film.

Child Development

ELIZABETH B. HURLOCK, Ph.D.

Associate in Psychology, Graduate School
University of Pennsylvania

THIRD EDITION

New York   Toronto   London

McGRAW-HILL BOOK COMPANY, INC.

1956

CHILD DEVELOPMENT

Library of Congress Catalog Card Number 56-6963

VII

31416

To my husband
Irland McKnight Beckman

PREFACE

Each year more and more studies of children appear in scientific journals. These studies are being made, not by child psychologists alone, but by sociologists, educators, anthropologists, social workers, and members of the medical profession. To include all or even a fraction within the two covers of one book can be done either by reporting all of them in detail or by mentioning only the high points of each.

If the former approach were used, the book would be so large that no student could be expected to cover it within a college year, let alone a semester. Furthermore, he would very likely become lost in the forest and come out so dazed that he would not know what it was all about.

If, on the other hand, the latter approach were used, the student would become familiar with the general principles of child development and the different research studies in each area. In addition, he would have ample references for further research in any area in which he had a special interest. This, it seems to the writer, is the more scholarly approach, and for that reason, it has been adopted in writing this second revision of the book which first appeared in 1942.

This is not a revision of the original text or of the second edition. It is a complete rewriting within the framework of the original text, using the major areas of the child's development as the topics for each chapter. To keep within the limits of the usual college semester of fifteen weeks, the chapter on the history of child psychology, which appeared in the original text and in the second edition, has been replaced by a chapter on social adjustments.

Because good social adjustments are so basic to mental health, not only in childhood but throughout life, it seemed justifiable to devote more space to this aspect of social development than would be possible if it were included in the chapter on social development. Furthermore, it seemed more important to the student's understanding of the child than a historical study of research in child development, and therefore has replaced it. That is the only change made, so far as chapter headings are concerned.

Within each chapter, however, there is new material combined with the important studies reported earlier. Tables have been removed to make way for graphs, not because tables are valueless, but because graphs present the material more clearly and emphatically. A number of graphs from recent studies have been added, and some of the original ones have been retained. All the pictures which appeared in the first two editions have been replaced by those from the *Child Development* films which are correlated with this book.

Throughout, emphasis has been placed on cultural influences and the role they play in determining the pattern of the child's development. Much of this material, which has appeared since the second edition of this book was published, is now included in the different chapters where it is related to the main topic of the chapter. As the student reads, it is hoped that he will become increasingly aware of the importance of culture as a determinant of the individual's behavior.

The bibliography has been greatly expanded to cover the important earlier studies of children and as many of the newer studies as possible. It is hoped that this bibliography will prove to be especially useful to those students who are anxious to delve further into different areas of the child's development than space has permitted in this book. While not every reference reported has been quoted from directly, all have been consulted, and the material contained in them has been used in one form or other.

The author is greatly indebted to her many professional colleagues, especially those who are members of the Division on Developmental Psychology of the American Psychological Association, for their suggestions and criticisms. She is also indebted to those who have written her suggestions and criticisms, based on their classroom experience with the second edition of this book. These suggestions and criticisms have proved to be most helpful in planning the new edition. Finally, the author is greatly indebted to all who have graciously given their consent for the use of their material in this book.

ELIZABETH B. HURLOCK

CONTENTS

TEXT-FILMS

The nine films listed below and five follow-up filmstrips correlated with *Child Development* are available singly or as a complete series. Several illustrations from the films appear in the text.

Principles of Development (17-min. motion picture with follow-up filmstrip). This film outlines the fundamentals of growth from early infancy through the period of childhood. Development follows a pattern which is continuous, orderly, progressive, and predictable. Within this pattern there is considerable correlation between types of development. For example, physical growth affects motor development. Often one type of development waits on another. If a baby concentrates on walking, he may learn no new words for months. Development goes from general to specific responses. The baby likes people in general before he prefers mother. Each child passes through each stage, and each stage has its characteristic traits. The pattern will vary for each individual depending on his development. All development is caused by maturation and learning. The interrelation of these two factors is the key to all child training. In common human skills like sitting or walking, training is of no particular help. The baby will learn when ready. Special skills are best learned when the child is ready for them. The variables which make each child different from every other one are: sex, intelligence, race, glands, nutrition, health, fresh air and sunlight, position in the family, incentive, heredity, and parental attitude. Correlated with Chaps. 1 and 5.

Heredity and Prenatal Development (21-min. motion picture with follow-up filmstrip). The development, subdivision, and eventual union of male and female sex cells is shown. First, the development of the sex cells in the male is explained. The function of the chromosomes and genes in influencing hereditary traits is shown. The development of the male sex cell from primary spermatocyte to spermatozoa or mature sex cells is followed. Next, the development of the female sex cells in the ovaries is traced. This includes the elements of the ovum, how it subdivides and, if fertilized, divides again. The chromosomes and their genes determine such traits as sex, color of hair, and other physical and mental characteristics. Training and environment will shape the development of certain of these characteristics. The fertilization of the ovum by the sperm cell is described, and then the development of the fetus is traced until delivery. The influence of environment starts in the mother's body after fertilization. The cause and develop-

xiii

ment of identical and similar twins is shown. In live photography, the first moments and days of a newborn baby are explained. Basic physical actions of the newborn baby are breathing, eating, and eliminating. The close connection between physical and emotional sensitivity of the very young child is emphasized. Correlated with Chaps. 2 and 3.

Child Care and Development (17-min. motion picture with follow-up filmstrip). It is the habits of daily physical care that ensure a child's being happy and healthy. The children of one family, ages 9 months, 3, 6, and 9 years, are observed. A proper diet is important for good health. The influence of emotions on the child's appetite is noted. Playing outdoors is beneficial. Play helps develop and coordinate both small and large muscles. Clothes should be comfortable and practical for the weather and purpose. Specific suggestions on what to look for in each article of clothing are given. Attractive clothing can give a sense of confidence to a child. Cleanliness, by washing and bathing, and good grooming are to be encouraged. Good sleeping conditions should be coupled with the development of a desirable attitude toward sleep. Throughout, the film stresses the importance of the attitudes of both parents and children in establishing good routines of daily living. Correlated with Chaps. 4, 8, and 14.

Children's Emotions (22-min. motion picture with follow-up filmstrip). The major emotions of childhood are curiosity, fear, anger, jealousy, and joy. A baby's reactions are intense because he has had little experience in meeting new situations. Early emotions are from internal causes, later emotions from external causes. Curiosity is a natural state for a baby confronted with so many new, interesting things. Curiosity is largely satisfied by touching and tasting. This curiosity should be encouraged. Fear is natural too, but should be kept from becoming habitual. Sudden, strange, and loud are the qualities of sights and sounds which cause fears in children. How the common causes of fear change from age six to age ten is shown. Later, the fears will usually disappear. Careful teaching can prevent or lessen most childhood fears and most childhood anger as well. Anger is caused by frustrating experiences. These experiences are seen in the film from the child's point of view. The best antidote for a baby's anger is diversion, understanding the baby's inability to do things for himself and the intensity of his desire to try, and allowing some initiative. Jealousy can be caused by having to share his mother's affection with others. Privileges and affection given other siblings are a common cause of this emotion. Jealousy may be allayed by a fair share of attention and affection, equal rights, an understanding of the child's needs, and consistency in discipline. Joy should be an emotion often experienced. Pleasurable experiences come from play, playmates, and family. It is the result of physical well-being from reasonable discipline and loving understanding. Correlated with Chaps. 7 and 15.

Social Development (16-min. motion picture with follow-up filmstrip). The reasons underlying the changes in social behavior at different age levels are analyzed. The way in which children play with one another has an important influence on their later happiness. At one and a half, the baby is a passive bystander in the social scene. He enjoys being alone, experiments with his surroundings, and starts to assert his independence. Obedience should not be insisted upon. At two, he enjoys parallel play, during which he likes to be with someone but playing by himself. At age three, cooperative play starts. There are no social distinctions among children yet. Quarrels are frequent but quickly pass. Three- and four-year-olds use imagination in play increasingly. Fours are active and develop increasing muscular control. Differences in play due to sex start. At five, play is more organized and competitive. Leadership becomes evident. At six, separate gangs are formed by both sexes and the influence of the group is strong. Popularity as a personality trait becomes evident at this age. All these patterns mix and overlap, but at each age level there is a definite organization to children's social behavior. As children grow older they seek out natural leaders, and with this development comes the conflict of gang loyalties versus family loyalties. While the child must meet and solve his own social problems at each age level of his growth, understanding parents can make the inevitable adjustments much easier and smoother. Correlated with Chaps. 8 and 15.

Children's Play (27 min). Play is a dynamic factor in a child's development, as well as a requirement for good health. This film points up the changing form of children's recreation, portraying play at each age level. It describes the differences in free spontaneous play, make-believe play, constructive play, collection, amusements, games, and sports. The film demonstrates the important contributions parents can and should make to give their children the best possible chance for healthy play. It emphasizes the need for play time, ample space for play both indoors and out-of-doors, proper equipment, companions, learning in play geared to the child's ability, and the health needed to enjoy play. Correlated with Chap. 10.

Children's Fantasies (21 min). To children all fantasies, useful or destructive, are very real. Because fantasies have an effect on development, understanding the reasons for fantasies is a necessity for parents and educators. This film discusses such common problems as how to stop excessive daydreaming; how Santa Claus should be presented; what to do about imaginary friends; why some children imagine that they are adopted; how to combat fear of the dark. It points up the effect of parental discipline, television, comic books, and fairy tales on a child's fantasies. Fantasy or daydreaming is seen in this film as a pastime that can be either an escape from reality or, when properly channeled, an impetus to artistic, creative living. Correlated with Chaps. 11 and 15.

Sibling Relations and Personality (22 min). In a series of case studies, this film demonstrates the importance of the kind of relationships a child has had with his brothers and sisters throughout the developmental years. This relationship is seen to be an important factor in personality shaping. The film shows personality influences on the oldest child of a large family, the middle child, the girl who has been reared to be the model child, the girl who feels that her parents would have preferred a boy. Differences in siblings are seen in the cases of the boy whose brother is more talented, the girl whose sister is prettier and more popular, the boy who feels his grandparents prefer his sister. Illness or weakness of one child can effect another in a family as it did the child whose brother is overprotected and the child whose sister was cared for at home during a long and serious illness. Knowledge and understanding of these complex influences are important aids in helping a child through childhood and adolescence. Correlated with Chaps. 14 and 15.

Sibling Rivalries and Parents (11 min). In any family one encounters a certain amount of rivalry among the brothers and sisters—rivalry for attention, esteem, and love. The film describes the reasons for this rivalry, the varied manifestations of it, and means of holding natural friction to a minimum. It answers such questions as: Should parents forbid quarrelling? Is it better to reason a child out of anger? Will training children to separate feelings from action help curb home quarrels? What can the family council do for this problem? This film shows that, with proper guidance, a family can move through the years of childhood with only a normal amount of quarrelling. Correlated with Chap. 14.

Chapter 1

PRINCIPLES OF DEVELOPMENT

From the moment of conception until death, the individual is constantly changing. He is never static. Throughout the childhood and adolescent years, he develops into the physical and mental structure that characterizes the adult. Even then, changes do not cease. Instead, they continue, but at a slower rate, until the deterioration that characterizes senescence sets in. Thus development is a continuous process which starts even before birth. Birth is merely an incident in a long succession of changes, not the beginning.

The individual may not always be aware of the changes, both physical and psychological, which are constantly taking place. In the early years of life, when the changes are rapid in rate and pronounced in degree, attention is focused on the changes because of the constant adjustments the individual must make to them. Furthermore, these changes are welcome to the individual because they signify that he is "growing up." This contrasts markedly with the attitude of the individual toward changes in adulthood, when each change proclaims to him and to the world that he is "growing old" (Kahn and Simmons, 1940).

Meaning of Development. Development is not limited to growing larger. Instead, it consists of a progressive series of changes of an orderly, coherent type toward the goal of maturity. The term "progressive" signifies that the changes are directional, leading forward rather than backward. The terms "orderly" and "coherent" suggest that development is not of a haphazard, casual type, but rather that there is a definite relationship between each stage and the next in the developmental sequence. Each change is dependent upon what preceded it, and it, in turn, affects what will come after.

According to Gesell (1952), "Development is more than a concept. It can be observed, appraised, and to some extent even 'measured' in three major manifestations: (*a*) anatomic, (*b*) physiologic, (*c*) behavioral. . . . Behavior signs, however, constitute a most comprehensive index of developmental status and developmental potentials." Development results in new characteristics and new abilities on the part of the individual. It consists of a transition from lower to higher stages of activity or function. While there is some development at every stage in the life span of the individual, more

1

development occurs in the early years of life than after maturity has been attained.

Studies of Development. Two methods have been used to trace the course of human development. The first consists of measuring different large groups of children at different age levels to get norms, or standards, of development for these ages. The second method of studying development consists of the reexamination of the same individuals at certain intervals of time throughout the childhood and adolescent years. While this method unquestionably gives a more accurate picture of the typical child's development, it is not always practical to use it. From studies made by both methods, we have today norms of the typical pattern of development from the moment of conception until maturity has been attained.

There are three important advantages to be derived from knowing what is the normal development of the child. It enables one to know what to expect of a child at every age and to know, in a general way, at what age different forms of behavior will emerge into more mature forms. Because the pattern of development is approximately the same for all children, it is possible to judge each child in terms of the norm for his age, thus showing if his behavior is typical or atypical for his age. And, finally, since all development requires guidance, knowledge of the normal pattern of development enables those in charge of the child to guide his development into desired channels.

TYPES OF CHANGE IN DEVELOPMENT

Development consists of changes, but not all changes are of the same sort. Nor do they influence the process of growing up in the same way. The changes which occur in development may be divided roughly into four major classes, which are as follows.

1. Changes in Size. Changes of this type are especially obvious in physical growth, though they can be observed readily in mental growth if a standard test of intelligence is used. Each year, as the child grows older, his height, weight, and circumference measurements increase unless some abnormal condition interferes with normal growth. Likewise, the different internal organs and structures, such as the heart, lungs, intestines, and stomach grow larger to take care of the increasing needs of the body. Mental development shows similar changes in magnitude. The child's vocabulary increases annually; his ability to reason, remember, perceive, and use creative imagination, all normally expand during the growth years.

2. Changes in Proportion. As may be seen from the accompanying diagram (Fig. 1), physical development is not limited to changes in size. The child is not merely a "miniature adult," as was formerly believed, but his whole body shows proportions different from those of the adult. This is especially evident when the baby's body is magnified to adult size. It is not until the child reaches puberty, around the age of thirteen years, that the proportions begin to approximate those of the adult body.

Changes in proportion are also apparent in mental development. In early childhood, imagination is predominantly fantastic, with little reference to reality. Gradually, as the child grows older, the fantastic element gives way to a very realistic, matter-of-fact, common-sense sort of imagination, so harnessed and controlled as to be useful in planning and in all forms of creative work. A change also occurs in the interests of the child. At first, his interests are concentrated on himself and his toys. Gradually, his interest shifts to other children of his acquaintance and the activities of the neighborhood gang. Then, in adolescence, the interests are focused on members of the opposite sex, clothes, and all that is closely bound up with courtship.

3. Disappearance of Old Features. A third important type of change which occurs in the development of the individual consists of the disappearance of certain features. Among the physical features, the most important ones to disappear gradually as the child grows older are the thymus gland, often called the "gland of babyhood," located in the chest; the pineal gland at the base of the brain; the Babinski and Darwinian reflexes; "baby hair"; and the first set of teeth, the "baby teeth." Among the mental traits which gradually outlive their usefulness and then disappear are babbling and all other forms of baby speech; childish impulses to act before thinking; babyish forms of locomotion, such as creeping and crawling; and sensory keenness, especially in regard to taste and smell.

4. Acquisition of New Features. In addition to the discarding of features which have outlived their usefulness, a fourth type of developmental change is to be observed in the acquisition of new physical and mental features. Some of these are acquired through learning, but many of them result from the maturing or unfolding of native traits not fully developed at birth. Among the physical features, the most important ones which are acquired during the growth period are first and second teeth and primary and secondary sex characteristics, the latter making their appearance during the early months of adolescence. Among the mental traits acquired by the individual are curiosity, especially about sex matters, the sex urge, knowledge, moral standards, religious beliefs, different forms of language, and all types of neurotic tendencies.

Fig. 1. The bodily proportions of the newborn infant and adult. (*After Stratz, from K. Bühler, Mental development of the child,* Harcourt, Brace, 1930. *Used by permission.*)

CAUSES OF DEVELOPMENT

Development of the physical and mental traits of the individual comes partly from an intrinsic maturing of those traits and partly from exercise and experience on the individual's part. By *maturation* is meant the development or unfolding of traits potentially present in the individual resulting from his hereditary endowment. According to Gesell (1952), "maturation may be defined as the net sum of the gene effects operating in a self-limited life cycle. Here lies an important key to his constitutional individuality." The appearance of a trait through maturation is frequently characterized by a striking suddenness. In the case of walking, for example, one of its most characteristic aspects is the sudden appearance of each successive stage, often after one had believed that the child would be far behind the usual age for attaining this particular skill.

Development likewise is brought about partly by a second cause which results from the activities of the child himself. This type of development is generally referred to as *learning* because it requires exercise to bring about changes in the physical structure and behavior of the individual. Not all learning is of the same type. It may result from practice or the mere repetition of an act which, in time, brings about a change in the individual's behavior. Or it may come from training, which is a selective, directed, and purposive type of activity. Whether it be caused by practice or training, the changes which take place in the child's behavior are due to the activities of the child.

The plasticity of the human physical and nervous structure makes it possible for the human being to be molded into patterns that would be impossible in animals where the neuromuscular equipment is nearly ready to function at birth. The human child, because he is capable of learning, can make more varied types of adjustment than is possible among animals. This, in turn, makes it possible for him to make greater progress and to rise to a higher level than is possible among animals (Punke, 1950). The period of greatest plasticity, when learning plays its most important role, is in childhood. At this time, attitudes, habits, and patterns of behavior are established, and the individual's personality is molded. What is learned at this time will determine largely the future successes or failures in the individual's adjustments to life (Freud, 1920).

Interaction of Maturation and Learning. Maturation and learning are not separate and distinct causes of development. Instead, they are closely interrelated, and one influences or retards the other. Maturation is stimulated and influenced to some degree by the different environmental factors with which the individual comes in contact. Without effort, traits potentially present will not develop to their maximum, while with effort, properly directed and applied at the time when those traits should normally begin to mature, the development will be more nearly complete. If, on the other hand, a trait is limited in its potentialities for development, no amount of effort or exercise on the individual's part will be adequate to bring it up to a desired standard.

Maturation provides the raw material for learning and determines to a large extent the more general patterns and sequences of the individual's behavior. As the body structure changes and matures, behavior dependent upon it appears. It is an error to suppose that maturation is limited to the prenatal and learning to the postnatal periods of the individual's life, for some learning takes place before birth, just as some maturation occurs after birth. It is true, however, that development during the prenatal period is due mostly to maturation and is very little dependent upon exercise.

Studies of Maturation and Learning. Many experimental investigations of the role played by maturation in the development of the individual have been made. The main purpose has been to discover the relative importance of maturation as compared with learning, or, expressed in other terms, how much of the child's development will occur of its own accord and how much will have to come about as a result of the child's experiences. This is far from an easy problem to solve, and it has been investigated from different angles, with the use of different methods. The most important of the methods are the following:

1. *The Method of Isolation.* The method of isolation for the study of maturation has been used much on animals. The fundamental principle of this technique consists of isolating the young individual from older members of the same species, to see if certain traits of behavior, characteristic of that species, will appear without an opportunity for learning on the animal's part. Studies of human babies, using the isolation technique, have been very infrequent because of the practical difficulty of getting babies for such a study, and because of the objection raised by parents and others that it is unfair to the child (Dennis, 1936, 1941; Dennis and Dennis, 1938).

2. *Method of Co-twin Control.* The second method of studying the relative importance of maturation and learning in the child's development is the method of co-twin control, used first by Gesell and Thompson (1929). In this method, identical twins serve as subjects. One twin, Twin *T,* or Trained Twin, is given practice in learning different functions, while the other twin, Twin *C,* or Control Twin, is given no training. After a certain time, the results of training are compared with the achievements of Twin *C* to determine how effective the training has been (Gesell and Thompson, 1929, 1941; Strayer, 1930; Hilgard, 1932; McGraw, 1935, 1939, 1940; Mirenva, 1935; Thompson, 1943).

While the co-twin control method is a good one from the point of view of scientific accuracy and control, there are practical obstacles in the way of applying it, especially after the early years of life. It would be almost impossible to carry out a series of tests on a large number of identical twins, because of the difficulty of getting free rein over these twins for experimental studies. Again, because Twin *C* may be retarded in development by eliminating training, even though it be only along certain lines, it would be difficult to use this method after the early years of babyhood.

3. *The Matched-group Method*. Because of the practical difficulties in using the method of co-twin control to study maturation, a third method, the *matched-group method*, has been used. This is an offshoot of the co-twin control method in that it uses two similar groups, matched in traits definitely related to the behavior study, instead of two matched individuals, as used in the case of identical twins. Like the method of co-twin control, this method studies the relative influence of maturation and learning through the training of one group, while the second group is allowed to develop of its own accord without any opportunity to learn (Gates and Taylor, 1926; Hicks, 1930, 1930a, 1931; Hilgard, 1932, 1933; Jersild, 1932; Wells and Arthur, 1939).

4. *The Genetic Study of Large Groups.* The fourth method that has been used to study the relative importance of maturation and learning in the development of the child consists of a genetic study of large groups of children, to see whether a pattern of development appears, regardless of differences in environment. If children from different environments, who have been subjected to different opportunities for learning, show behavior that is similar in its fundamentals, even though differing in specific details, it is apparent that this behavior has not been learned. Thus, it is argued, the behavior must be due to the natural unfolding of traits potentially present or to maturation (Terman, 1925, 1926, 1930; Gesell, 1930; Shirley, 1931a; Terman and Oden, 1947).

Regardless of the method used, the studies of maturation and learning have all emphasized the interaction of these two factors of development. Maturation provides the necessary foundations for learning, but without practice, development would not take place through maturation alone. As Dennis (1941) has pointed out, "Maturation in and of itself seldom produces new developmental items, but maturation of structures when accompanied by self-directed activity leads to new infant response." In *phylogenetic* functions, or functions common to the race such as crawling, creeping, sitting, and standing, training is of little advantage. In *ontogenetic* functions, or functions specific to the individual such as swimming, roller-skating, tricycle riding, or scaling inclines, training is necessary. Without it, development will not take place (McGraw, 1935, 1939, 1940).

According to Gesell (1952), it is "unnecessary to make a rigid distinction between maturational and environmental factors. The physical endowment and the cultural environment interact. . . . There is evidence of a ground plan of development governed by an inherent dynamic morphology, imposed by a combination of racial and familial inheritance. For this reason a child of a given stock in a given culture tends to exhibit at advancing age levels maturity traits which are more or less typical for the group as well as representative of his constitutional self."

Implications. Because development is dependent upon both maturation and learning, it makes variation possible. Were development due to maturation alone, as is true of many of the animal species, there would be no such thing as individuality. Among humans, on the other hand, even though there is a uniformity of growth, there is also "extraordinary" variation in the growth pattern (Washburn, 1950; Wishik, 1950). "Every infant," according to Gesell (1952), "has a unique pattern of growth which expresses itself ontogenetically in his behavior characteristics. The entire course of ontogenesis is ballasted by intrinsic maturational determiners."

Maturation, which depends upon the hereditary endowment of the individual, sets limits beyond which development cannot go even when learning is encouraged. This is seen more in the case of animals than in humans because in the former maturation plays a more prominent role in development than it does in humans. However, limitations are present in human development also. In physical and mental development, as well as in the development of aptitudes, the limiting effects of heredity have been found to exist. As Gesell (1949) has pointed out, "All educability is dependent upon innate capacities for growth. This intrinsic growth is a gift of nature. It can be guided, but it cannot be created: nor can it be transcended by an educational agency."

The effectiveness of learning depends upon maturity. A child cannot learn until he is ready to learn. The necessary physical and mental development must be present before new skills or new abilities can be built upon the foundations. Learning a conditioned-reflex action, it has been reported, is impossible even with excessive drill, until maturation has laid the foundations. This occurs usually during the third month of life (Morgan and Morgan, 1944).

From the many studies that have been made of the interrelationship of maturation and learning, we have the beginnings of an inventory of normal development which suggests at approximately what age to expect behavior of different types and hence when to begin training. Phylogenetic functions will develop without specific practice. Even interferences and restraints from the environment will retard the functions only slightly. Given an opportunity to do so, the baby will exercise spontaneously in ways that will improve his development. In the case of ontogenetic functions, on the other hand, systematic training is needed. This is most advantageous if given when the basic motor coordinations are already developed. Even in the case of phylogenetic functions, none of which unfolds at a high level of development, practice and training, either spontaneous or forced, cause them to develop to a higher level.

Knowing the role played by maturity has a practical bearing on the education of the child. It suggests at what age training should begin and in what sequence the training should occur. If the child is not old enough or mature enough to profit by the teaching, it has little value for him and can be regarded as wasted time and effort on the teacher's part (Jersild and Bienstock, 1935). In addition, premature forcing of the child to learn results in negativistic, resistant behavior which militates against successful learning and may even retard learning. If, on the other hand, the necessary maturation has been attained, time and effort are saved in teaching and the attitude of the child toward learning is more favorable. Should the child not be permitted to learn, even though ready, his interest is likely to wane. Later, when he is expected to learn, his interest may have reached such a low ebb that he will be unwilling to put forth the effort needed for successful learning.

Developmental readiness, according to Blum (1952) is the

individual's state of preparedness with respect to some one or more areas of functioning. Synonymous with maturity, developmental readiness appears primarily influenced by laws or principles which tend to be on nature's side rather than dependent upon the nurture to which the young child is exposed. Thus a state of readiness may be thought of as having been achieved largely through the child's responses to internal stimuli pressing him toward growth. . . . A factor, however, which necessarily has to be taken into account is timing, with the recognition that learning, whether in the intellectual, social, or motor sphere, is best achieved when what is offered educationally is timed to the child's state of readiness or maturity.

Havighurst (1953) has called this the "teachable moment." According to him,

when the body is ripe, and society requires it, and the self is ready to achieve a certain task, the teachable moment has come. Efforts at teaching which would have been largely wasted if they had come earlier give gratifying results when they come at the *teachable moment,* when the task should be learned.

If education is to be effective, then it must be related to the maturation levels of the child. There are, however, two reasons why this is frequently not done. In the first place, the age at which the maturation of different mental and physical functions occurs is not fully established. Because of individual variations, it would be difficult, if not actually impossible, to set any specific age and be certain that it was correct for all individuals. Then, too, there are misconceptions and biases which have set the pattern for educating a child. In the case of reading, for example, it has been assumed for generations that all children are ready to begin reading when they enter school, while, in reality, some are ready before they enter school and others are not ready for varying lengths of time after they have entered school. Educators often underestimate the child's abilities and delay the teaching of "difficult" subjects. Yet, studies of the development of mental abilities have shown that the child's intellectual capacity is pretty well matured by the time he is twelve years old (Wechsler, 1950).

How, you may wonder, can one determine when the child is ready to learn? There are three criteria which are generally used to indicate the child's state of readiness. These are (1) the child's interest in learning, (2) how sustained his interest will remain over a period of time, and (3) what progress he makes with practice. When the child's interest wanes quickly or when he seems to make no appreciable improvement, in spite of continued practice, there is reason to question whether he is ready to learn.

RATE OF DEVELOPMENT

Development, whether "physical" or "mental," is not a uniform process in which equal amounts of growth take place annually each successive year. For one thing, it is extremely rapid during the prenatal period, when the individual grows from a microscopically small germ cell to an infant weighing approximately 8 pounds and about 20 inches in length. At birth, the baby is three-tenths of his height at the age of eighteen. In other words, in 9 months his growth is approximately one-third of what it will be eighteen years hence. From fertilization to birth, increase in weight is estimated at 11,000,000 times, and from birth to maturity, the increase is 22 times. This means that 99 per cent of the increase in weight is completed before birth (Scheinfeld, 1950).

This accelerated rapidity of development continues throughout babyhood, to the age of three years, except for the first two weeks immediately following birth, when a "plateau" stage occurs during which the newborn infant is becoming accustomed to his new environment. To realize how rapidly the changes have occurred, all one has to do is to compare a three-year-old with a newborn infant. During this period, one can almost see the baby grow. Moreover, the physical development is closely paralleled by an equally rapid mental development.

From three to six, the growth rate continues to be rapid, though not so rapid as in the preceding three years. From birth to five years, growth equals that of the years five to fifteen. But, toward the age of six, growth begins to slacken, and from then until just before adolescence, the rate of development is somewhat retarded. Then, in preadolescence and early adolescence, at approximately twelve to fourteen years, the rate of development is once more accelerated, only to slow down again in two or three years, as the individual approaches the level of maturity.

Or, to compare six-year periods: the rate of development during the first six years is proportionally three times as great as during the next two six-year periods. In general, the third of the six-year periods, which begins during the adolescent years, is the slowest from the point of view of rate of development. Studies of different animal species have shown that there is a high correlation between the rate of development and the brain weight. This, likewise, holds true for the human species (Hofstaetter, 1951).

While it is true that the limit of the child's physical and mental development is determined by the structure of the germ cells from which he has developed, nevertheless, the activity of the child, plus such environmental factors as food, exercise, and education, influence the rate and extent of the changes as the child approaches the limit of his development. No two individuals develop at exactly the same rate, though the pattern of development is similar for all. Frank (1950) has expressed the individuality of development thus: "The life career is a broad highway along which every individual must travel. Each individual with his unique heredity and nature (including prenatal) will travel along that highway at his own or her own rate of progress and will attain the size, shape, capacity, and developmental status which are uniquely his or her own at each stage in the life career." Studies of babies have revealed that those who are slow in creeping are also slow in climbing and prehension (Ames, 1940). Among the mentally retarded, the pattern is retarded, while among the gifted, there is acceleration of the developmental pattern.

CHARACTERISTICS OF DEVELOPMENT

There are certain features which are characteristic of human development and which influence greatly the form it takes. It is impossible to evaluate these fairly in every respect so as to list them in the order of their importance. Nevertheless, an attempt will be made to list first those which seem to be most influential. The characteristics of development are as follows.

1. **Development Follows a Pattern.** Every species, whether animal or human, follows a pattern of development peculiar to that species. The rate and the limit of development are similar for all members of the species. In the case of the human being, development is not of a haphazard, unorganized type. Rather, it occurs in an orderly, patterned fashion. Even the prenatal development is like that of other fetuses, in that there is a genetic sequence, with certain traits appearing at each month. The same is true of the postnatal development. Each stage is the outcome of the one preceding it and the prerequisite of the one following it. The baby, for example, cuts

his molars before he cuts his incisors, can stand before he walks, and can draw a circle before he can draw a square.

On the basis of evidence obtained from genetic studies of groups of children over a period of years, Gesell (1941) contends that behavioral development follows a regular pattern that is relatively little influenced by experience. He likewise states that "although no two individuals are exactly alike, all normal children tend to follow a general sequence of growth characteristic of the species and of a cultural group. Every child has a unique

Development follows a regular and predictable pattern that is similar for all children. (*From Child Development, a McGraw-Hill Text-Film.*)

pattern of growth but that pattern is a variant of a basic ground plan. The species sequences are part of an established order of nature" (Gesell, 1949).

Cephalocaudal Sequence. In both prenatal and postnatal life, development follows the *cephalocaudal sequence,* which means that control of the body, as well as improvements in the structure itself, develops first in the head and progresses later to regions farthest from the head. At the end of the second fetal month, the length of the head rivals that of the trunk (Gesell, 1954). In the newborn infant, skin sensitivity comes in the uppermost part of the body before it appears in the lower (Sherman and Sherman, 1925).

The cephalocaudal sequence is illustrated also in motor functions. When the baby is placed in a prone position, he can lift his head by his neck before he can do so by lifting his chest or before he can sit up. He can control the muscles of his trunk before he can those of his arms and legs, and those of the arms and legs before he can the muscles of his feet and hands. At the age of twenty weeks, for example, the baby has control over the muscles of his eyes, head, and shoulders, but his trunk is still so flaccid that he must be propped or strapped in a chair to be able to maintain a sitting position. At this age, the pelvic zone and the extremities are very immature (Gesell, 1954).

In the cephalocaudal sequence, the development not only extends from head to foot in the direction of the longitudinal axis, but it also proceeds from the central to the peripheral segments of the body. In the early developmental stages, the arms and legs tend to react as wholes. Gradually, control appears in the elbow and wrist joints, and later, in the knee and ankle joints. In a study of grasping, the elbow and digits were found to participate in reaching movements with increasing effectiveness from the sixteenth to the fortieth week of life (Halverson, 1933). Control over the legs and feet for standing and walking do not occur until about the age of sixty weeks (Gesell, 1954).

The general pattern of development is not altered by the speed of the development. All children pass through the same fundamental forms, at approximately the same times. Gesell's (1930) studies of premature and postmature infants showed that the growth course follows a genetic sequence, irrespective of irregularity of birth. Retesting of an infant born two months prematurely showed growth curves similar to those of full-term infants. While prematurely born babies may lag behind the pattern of development for babies born at full term during the first three to five months of postnatal life, they then conform to the pattern of the average individual of the same age as they (Melcher, 1937).

General Pattern of Development. Genetic studies of babies from birth, by frequent observations and examinations, have revealed that there is a general pattern that all babies follow. This pattern is as follows:

From 4 to 16 weeks, the baby gains control of his 12 oculomotor muscles.

From 16 to 28 weeks, he gains command of the muscles which support his head and move his arms. He then begins to reach out for things.

From 28 to 40 weeks, he gains control of his trunk and hands. This enables him to sit, grasp, transfer, and manipulate objects.

From 40 to 52 weeks, he extends control to his legs and feet, to his forefinger and thumb. He can now stand upright, poke, and pluck.

During the second year, he walks and runs; articulates words and phrases; acquires bowel and bladder control; and acquires a rudimentary sense of personal identity and of personal possession.

During the third year, he speaks in sentences and uses words as tools of thought. He displays a propensity to understand his environment and to comply with cultural demands.

During the fourth year, he asks innumerable questions, perceives analogies, and displays a tendency to generalize and conceptualize. In the routines of home life, he is nearly self-dependent.

At the age of five years, the child is well matured in motor control. He can hop and skip. He talks without infantile articulation and can narrate a long tale. He prefers associative play and feels socialized pride in clothes and accomplishments. He is now a self-assured, conforming citizen in his small world (Gesell, 1954, condensed from p. 339). The general pattern of prenatal and postnatal development is illustrated in Fig. 2.

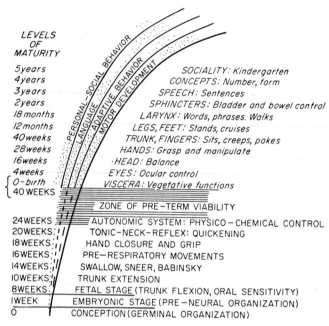

Fig. 2. Ontogenetic trends and sequences of behavior. (*From A. Gesell, The ontogenesis of infant behavior, in L. Carmichael, Manual of child psychology, 2d ed., Wiley, 1954. Used by permission.*)

Specific Phases of Development. Not only does total development follow a pattern, but specific phases of development, such as motor, social, and play, follow a pattern also. In the area of physical development, there is a pattern not only in height and weight but also in the growth in breadth of the bones and muscles (Lombard, 1950). Patterns in different aspects of motor development have been found in the case of prehension (Halverson, 1931; Castner, 1932), in block building (Johnson, 1933; Ames, 1948), and in writing (Ames, 1948; Ames and Ilg, 1951). Patterns in the development of speech from the birth cry to the ability to speak in an adult manner have been reported (Irwin and Chen, 1946; Irwin, 1948; McCarthy, 1952, 1954).

Patterns in behavioral development have been reported by Bühler (1935) and Ilg et al. (1949). There are patterns in the development of the emotions (Spitz, 1949; Banham, 1950, 1951) and in smiling (Ames, 1949). Patterns in the development of social behavior have been observed by Friedman (1951) and Ames (1952). The child identifies himself with different people at different ages and uses these as models for his behavior (Winker, 1949; Havighurst, 1950, 1953). The baby's reaction to his image in the mirror develops in a predictable manner (Gesell and Ames, 1947), as does the child's ability to read (Ilg and Ames, 1950) and to compute mathematical problems (Ilg and Ames, 1951). Patterns in the development of the understanding of the meaning of time (Ames, 1946; Springer, 1952), the meaning of money (Schuessler and Strauss, 1950; Strauss and Schuessler, 1951), and the meaning of self (Ames, 1952) have been found to be predictable. All these areas of development will be discussed in subsequent chapters.

2. Development Proceeds from General to Specific Responses. In all phases of development, whether motor or mental, the child's responses are of a general sort before they become specific. In both prenatal and post-natal development, general activity precedes specific activity. At no time and under no conditions is the reverse the case. This is apparent first in muscular responses. The newborn infant moves his whole body at one time, instead of moving any one part of it. The baby waves his arms in general, random movements before he is capable of so specific a response as reaching. Likewise, his legs are used for random kicking before he can coordinate the leg muscles well enough to crawl, creep, or walk.

The baby can see large objects before he can see small ones, because his eye movements are not coordinated enough at first to focus on small objects. The same pattern is seen in handedness. When the baby first reaches for an object, he not only uses both hands, but his legs and whole body are thrown into the response simultaneously. Around the sixth month, the reaching response is restricted to the two hands, and later, at approximately one year of age, to one hand. In learning a new task, such as dressing, the whole body wiggles and is thrown into activity. With improvement in this skill, the activity is limited to the hands. Children do simpler things first and more complex ones later (Ames, 1940).

In other aspects of development, the same sequence is seen. The baby produces general, babbling sounds before he can say words. In building a vocabulary, he learns general words before specific. For example, he uses "toy" for all playthings before he learns to call each toy by its name. All dogs are "doggie" at first and then are designated as "Rowdy," "Inky," or "Scottie." Concept formation follows the same pattern. The baby first distinguishes living from inanimate objects, then human beings from animals, then different types of human beings, as white, colored, American, or Chinese. In emotional behavior, the baby first responds to strange or unusual objects with a general fear, which is the same in all situations. Later, his fears become more specific and are characterized by different types of behavior in different situations. All his emotional patterns develop from general states of excitement and quiescence as he grows older (Spitz, 1949; Banham, 1950, 1951).

3. **Development Is Continuous.** From a superficial study of the growth of one feature, such as height, it may seem that the individual grows by "fits and starts" rather than at a continuous rate. Likewise, the use of such terms as "babyhood" and "adolescence" suggests that there are definite periods when growth takes place and implies that at other times growth has ceased. This, however, is not the case. On the contrary, growth continues from the moment of conception until the individual reaches maturity. It takes place at a slow, regular pace rather than by leaps and bounds. The development of both physical and mental traits continues gradually until these traits reach their maximum growth during the period of late adolescence. The use of certain terms to designate growth stages has been accepted to stress the fact that a particular type of growth is occurring at that particular time.

No traits, whether physical or mental, develop suddenly. On the contrary, they are all the product of a growth which started before birth. Several examples will illustrate this point. In physical growth, the appearance of the first teeth during the first year of life suggests that they developed suddenly. This, however, is not true. Teeth begin to develop as early as the fifth fetal month, though they do not cut through the gums until about five months after birth. Speech does not come overnight, but is gradually evolved from the cries and other sounds made by the baby at birth.

Because development is continuous, what happens at one stage carries over and influences the following stage or stages. For example, malnutrition in babyhood will produce physical and psychological damage which cannot later be entirely compensated for. Emotional tension caused by unfavorable environmental conditions in the child's home will leave its mark on the developing personality of the child. Unhealthy attitudes about himself and his relationship to others, established during the early years of life, are rarely eliminated completely. Their influence on the individual's outlook on life is seen even in maturity and old age.

4. **Individual Differences in Rate of Development Remain Constant.** The common belief that the baby who is physically or mentally below average will "catch up" to the average has not been substantiated by scientific evidence. On the contrary, there is plenty of evidence to show that the rate of growth is consistent. Those who developed rapidly at first will continue to do

so, while those whose development was slow will continue to develop slowly. Curves of height have shown that children who are tall at one age are tall at other ages, while those who are short remain short (Baldwin, 1922). Weight and height measurements at half-yearly intervals for boys and girls up to thirteen years who had been grouped according to birth weight revealed that the direction of difference noted at birth tended to be maintained during childhood (Illingworth et al., 1949). In the prepuberty growth spurt, girls who grow much in one year grow much during the whole of that period while girls who grow little in one year grow little during the entire period (Muhsam, 1947).

In behavioral patterns, the same principle holds true. Individual movements, whether of simple or advanced patterns, have been found to remain remarkably constant over a period of time (Ames, 1940). Growth curves for mental age for bright, average, and dull children have shown a constancy that is found in curves for physical growth. Accelerated mental growth continues to be accelerated (Gesell, 1928). Terman's (1926, 1947) study of men of genius showed them to be precocious during childhood. Children who are mentally deficient do not, except in unusual cases, "catch up" to the normal child. What is more likely to happen is that they will become more and more retarded as they grow older.

5. Development Occurs at Different Rates for Different Parts of the Body. Not all parts of the body grow at the same rate, nor do all aspects of mental growth proceed equally. At birth, the different parts of the body vary in relation to one another. If the body is to attain adult proportions, inequalities in growth must take place. The different phases of mental and physical growth occur at their own individual rates and reach maturity at different times. In some areas of the body the growth may be rapid, while in others, the growth may be slow or even interrupted by intermittent pauses (Wishik, 1950). Thus, the pattern of relative size of the organs of the body changes from time to time.

The brain attains its mature size around the age of six to eight years, but gains much in organization after that. The feet, hands, and nose reach their maximum development early in the adolescent years. This accounts, in part, for the awkwardness, clumsiness, and self-consciousness characteristic of these years. The heart, liver, and digestive system grow much during adolescence. In Fig. 3 are shown curves of growth for different types of body tissue.

Measurements of different intellectual capacities have revealed that they develop at different rates and reach maturity at different ages (Wechsler, 1950). Creative imagination develops rapidly in childhood and seems to reach its peak during youth. Reasoning, on the other hand, proceeds at a relatively slow rate of development. Rote memory and memory for concrete objects and facts develop more quickly than memory for abstract, theoretical material. General intelligence for the average individual reaches its peak around the age of fourteen years.

There may be any combination of acceleration and retardation in the development of height, weight, and intelligence, maturation of the emotional processes, or sexual maturation. This irregularity of the rates of development of the various aspects of structure, function, social adaptation, and intelligence has many psychosomatic implications. A bright child, for example, may be out of step with his contemporaries in his interests and activities but be socially unacceptable to an older group. This, in turn, may affect his social adjustment, his sense of personal adequacy, and the development of drives and motivation (Sontag, 1946).

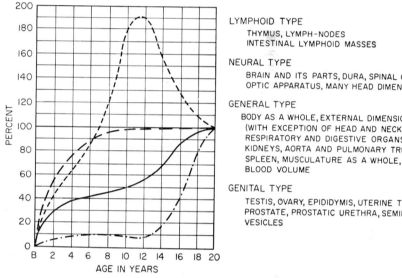

LYMPHOID TYPE
  THYMUS, LYMPH-NODES
  INTESTINAL LYMPHOID MASSES

NEURAL TYPE
  BRAIN AND ITS PARTS, DURA, SPINAL CORD,
  OPTIC APPARATUS, MANY HEAD DIMENSIONS

GENERAL TYPE
  BODY AS A WHOLE, EXTERNAL DIMENSIONS
  (WITH EXCEPTION OF HEAD AND NECK)
  RESPIRATORY AND DIGESTIVE ORGANS,
  KIDNEYS, AORTA AND PULMONARY TRUNKS,
  SPLEEN, MUSCULATURE AS A WHOLE,
  BLOOD VOLUME

GENITAL TYPE
  TESTIS, OVARY, EPIDIDYMIS, UTERINE TUBE
  PROSTATE, PROSTATIC URETHRA, SEMINAL
  VESICLES

Fig. 3. The major types of postnatal growth of the various parts and organs of the body. The curves are drawn to a common scale by computing their values at successive ages in terms of their total postnatal increments (to twenty years). (*From J. A. Harris, The measurement of man, University of Minnesota Press, 1930. Used by permission.*)

6. Most Traits Are Correlated in Development. The popular assumption that compensation is a general rule in the development of a child is not borne out by experimental studies. It is not true that the child who is above average in one trait will be below in others, and vice versa, as a means of equalizing his capacities. As Gesell (1954) has pointed out, "The products of growth are envisaged as a fabric in which threads and designs are visible." This correlation of development is illustrated in Fig. 4. True, the rates of development for different parts of the body differ, but they are compensatory in that above-average growth in height during one period may be accompanied by below-average growth in weight, but in subsequent periods the reverse will be true (Muhsam, 1947).

The child whose intellectual development is above average is generally above average in size, sociability, and special aptitudes. The child whose intellectual development, on the other hand, is below average, does not compensate for this by having very superior health, highly developed special aptitudes, great sociability, or superior physical structure. Mental defectives tend to be smaller in stature than the normal child. Idiots and imbeciles are the smallest of the feeble-minded group. Similarly, high-grade intelligence has been found to correlate highly with early sexual maturing, and low-

Fig. 4. The interrelatedness of a child's life. (*From M. E. Breckenridge and E. L. Vincent, Child development, 3d ed., Saunders, 1955. Used by permission.*)

grade intelligence with late sexual maturing, though there are climatic, racial, and other determinants that have to be kept in mind.

7. Development Is Predictable. Because the rate of development for each child is fairly constant, the immensely important consequence is that it is possible for us to predict at an early age the range within which the mature development of the child is likely to fall. X rays of the bones of the wrist of a child will tell approximately what his ultimate size will be (Bayley, 1946). This may prove to be very important, especially in cases where either the parent or the child is concerned about his present size.

Knowing what the ultimate mental development of a child will be is of outstanding value in the planning of his education and in helping him to train for the type of work he is best fitted to carry out. It has also proved to be of great value in the choosing of babies for adoption. Methods of determining the ultimate mental development of a child are more reliable than those used to predict his ultimate physical development. In the re-examination of babies during the first two years of life, for example, it was found in 80 per cent of the cases that the developmental rating made on the first examination corresponded to the final rating, made when the babies were two years old (Gesell, 1928). Among those rated as mental defectives, only one did not rate the same at the age of two years as he was rated on the first examination (Gesell, 1930).

Following the same group until they were in their teens, Gesell (1954) reported that in "no case did the course of growth prove whimsical or erratic." In only one case was there a marked alteration in trend. Only when there are unfavorable conditions does the ultimate development of the individual become less predictable. Goodenough (1954) has pointed out that when large changes in IQ scores occur at later ages, it is usually found that it is generally in the case of those whose initial scores showed large deviations from what one would expect on the basis of ancestral intelligence. Terman's (1926) study of the early mental traits of geniuses who lived between 1450 and 1850, as revealed in the reports of their achievements, showed them to have been eminent as children.

8. Each Developmental Phase Has Traits Characteristic of It. At each age, some traits develop more rapidly and more conspicuously than others.

According to Feldman (1941), "Human life proceeds by stages. The life periods of the human individual are no less real and significant than the geological ages of the earth or the evolutionary stages of life. . . . Each stage is distinguished by a dominant feature, a leading characteristic, which gives the period its coherence, its unity, and its uniqueness." Up to the age of two years, for example, the baby is concentrating on investigating his environment, gaining control over his body, and learning to speak. From the ages of three to six years, his development is concentrated on making him a more social creature (Podolsky, 1953).

Studies of groups of children tested at different periods during the growth years have revealed that

not only does each child appear to have a characteristic constitutionally determined individuality which first expresses itself in infancy and which continues to appear consistently throughout the preschool years (and presumably thereafter) but that in addition *each age level* has a characteristic pattern of its own which is consistent from child to child. Thus the behavior of any given child at any given age is colored partly by his own basic individuality and partly by the pattern of his age level. The pattern does not consist so much of what the child can accomplish as it does of the way in which he behaves (Ilg et al., 1949).

Furthermore, in the developmental pattern, there are phases which are characterized by "equilibrium" and others characterized by "disequilibrium." In the former, the child is making good adjustments and is easy to live with. In the latter, by contrast, his adjustments appear to be disrupted by conditions within himself or by environmental factors, and, as a result, he is difficult to live with. At this time, there are tensions, indecisions, insecurities, and similar behavior problems. These periods of equilibrium and disequilibrium, according to Gesell (1941), alternate in accordance with the principle of reciprocal neuromotor interweaving. In a period of disequilibrium, the child's behavior may appear to be "problem behavior." Such behavior difficulties are not individual aberrations but are characteristic of his age level and, hence, predictable.

Genetic studies have revealed the predictable ages of disequilibrium as well as those of equilibrium, when the child is "in focus." In the early years of life, for example, the periods of disequilibrium have been found to occur at the ages of 15 months, 21 months, 2½ years, 3½ years, and again just before puberty changes make their appearance, between the ages of 10 and 12 years (Furfey, 1926; Bühler, 1927, 1935; Gesell, 1939; Gesell and Ilg, 1946; Ilg et al., 1949; Stendler and Young, 1950). Between these periods of disequilibrium are periods of equilibrium when the child is "in focus" and when his behavior shows signs of better adjustment. There are, of course, individual differences in the actual ages at which these periods of equilibrium and disequilibrium appear.

9. Many forms of So-called "Problem Behavior" Are Normal Behavior of the Age in Which They Occur. Each developmental age has certain undesirable forms of behavior which are normally found at that age and are outgrown as the child passes on to the next stage of development. A detailed study of the characteristic behavior of 3½-year-olds has revealed the following forms of behavior that are characteristic of a state of disequilibrium: physical incoordinations; fears of falling and of high places; excessive tensional outlets, such as eye blinking and nail biting; stuttering; "psychological deafness"; visual difficulties; emotional insecurity; problems in adult-child relations, such as demanding attention and shyness; easily hurt feelings; emotional extremes; and marked expressions of affection. At this time, there is a developmental spurt, especially in boys who have been slow in starting. The behavior then becomes well organized, well rounded, and up to age expectations, which characterizes the beginning of a period of equilibrium (Ilg et al., 1949).

By contrast to this difficult behavior is the five-year-old who is "in focus." At that age, he is cooperative, friendly, sympathetic, affectionate, and helpful. This period of equilibrium is followed by a period of disequilibrium which is a "trying age," when the child is difficult, aggressive, explosive, demanding, fresh, nasty, insulting, argumentative, bratty, impudent, and rude (Gesell and Ilg, 1946). After the child enters school, his behavior generally improves (Stendler and Young, 1950) and he remains in equilibrium until the physical changes accompanying puberty begin (Furfey, 1926; Bühler,

1927; Leal, 1929; Wickman, 1929; Hurlock and McDonald, 1934; Hurlock and Sender, 1930; Stone and Barker, 1937; Long, 1941; Stolz and Stolz, 1951; Stouffer, 1952).

Lack of understanding of the normal behavior of children at different ages is responsible for much of the parent-child friction. Even teachers are often annoyed by behavior which is perfectly normal for the child's level of development. In one study, for example, many of the forms of behavior

Many forms of so-called "problem behavior" are normal for the age at which they appear and are often bids for attention. (*From Child Development, a McGraw-Hill Text-Film.*)

of their pupils which teachers reported as especially annoying to them indicated that they were interpreting normal behavior as problem behavior. The child's carelessness about his work and his appearance and vocal aggressiveness such as name calling and shouting were normal for the children of their ages, especially for those of the lower social classes. The child's indifference to his school work and his daydreaming instead of working indicated that the child regarded his lessons as of little practical value to him, and hence he had little motivation to study. It was concluded that "teachers need to understand, accept and tolerate the normal behavior patterns of children and they must accept children in terms of the social and behavioral standards of childhood and not attempt to mold children into the teacher's image of proper behavior and deportment" (Kaplan, 1952).

It must be recognized that certain forms of problem behavior cannot be overlooked on the grounds that the child will "outgrow" them as he grows older. Behavior that is not typically found at the child's age level is a danger signal of future trouble. From birth to eighteen years are trying years for a child. The child who shows major or minor disturbances is likely to maintain or develop handicapping personality disturbances in adulthood unless the disturbance is discovered and remedied before it is too late (Topp, 1950).

10. Every Individual Normally Passes through Each Major Stage of Development. While it is true that the time required to complete the development characteristic of each stage differs from one individual to another, nevertheless, except in unusual cases, the development will be completed at approximately twenty-one years of age. Inability to pass through all the developmental stages is correlated frequently with low-grade intelligence. Poor health, unfavorable environment, lack of incentive to develop, and many other factors may also retard the normal rate of development, but their influence is only temporary.

Implications. Knowledge of the principles of development is important for three reasons. First, it helps us to know what to expect and when to expect it. Otherwise there would be a tendency to expect too much or too little of the child at a given age. Both of these are bad. In the former case, the child is likely to develop feelings of inadequacy because he does not measure up to the standards his parents and teachers have set for him. Expecting too little gives him too little incentive, with the result that he does not do as much as he is capable of doing.

The second advantage of knowing how development occurs is that it gives the adult information as to when to stimulate and when not to stimulate growth in the child. It gives a basis for planning the environmental encouragement that must be offered and the correct timing of this encouragement. When the child is beginning to walk, for example, he must be given opportunities to practice walking and the necessary motivation. Absence of either one may delay the onset of walking beyond the time when it would normally occur.

Finally, knowing what the normal developmental pattern is makes it possible for parents, teachers, and others who work with children to prepare the child ahead of time for the changes that will take place in his body, his interests, or his behavior. While this psychological preparation will not eliminate all the tensions that normally accompany adjustment, it will go a long way toward minimizing them. The child who is prepared for what will be expected of him when he enters school, for example, makes better adjustments to school and is happier there than is the child who had no foreknowledge of what to expect. Similarly, the child who learns to co-operate in the family adjusts better to the social group outside the home than does the child who has been permitted to be the center of attention at home.

Because patterns of development follow one another in so fixed a sequence and appear so consistently at certain ages for the majority of children, it is possible to set up standards of what to expect at each age. We therefore have height-age scales, weight-age scales, mental-age scales, social development–age scales, etc. Most children conform to the standards given in these scales, with only slight variations.

One of the most comprehensive standards has been given by Havighurst (1950, 1953) in his series of "developmental tasks" for different age levels. According to Havighurst, a developmental task is a "task which arises at or about a certain period in the life of an individual, successful achievement of which leads to his happiness and to success with later tasks, while failure leads to unhappiness in the individual, disapproval by the society, and difficulty with later tasks." Developmental tasks are set by inner and outer forces. There are three sources of such tasks: physical maturation, cultural pressures, and personal values and aspirations which are part of the personality, or "self," of the individual (Havighurst, 1950, 1953).

The major developmental tasks for childhood are as follows:

INFANCY AND EARLY CHILDHOOD (BIRTH TO 6 YEARS)

Learning to walk
Learning to take solid foods
Learning to talk
Learning to control the elimination of body wastes
Learning sex differences and sexual modesty
Achieving physiological stability
Forming simple concepts of social and physical reality
Learning to relate oneself emotionally to parents, siblings, and other people
Learning to distinguish right and wrong and developing a conscience

MIDDLE CHILDHOOD (6 TO 12 YEARS)

Learning physical skills necessary for ordinary games
Building wholesome attitudes toward oneself as a growing organism
Learning to get along with age-mates
Learning an appropriate masculine or feminine sex role
Developing fundamental skills in reading, writing, and calculating
Developing concepts necessary for everyday living
Developing conscience, morality, and a scale of values
Achieving personal independence
Developing attitudes toward social groups and institutions (Havighurst, 1953)

FACTORS INFLUENCING DEVELOPMENT

The rate and pattern of development can be changed by conditions within and without the body. Physical growth depends partly upon food and general health conditions and partly upon such environmental factors as sunlight, fresh air, and climatic conditions. Personality patterns may be influenced more by attitudes than by social relationships, or the reverse may be true.

As has just been hinted, development is not due to one factor alone but to many, each related to the others and all interdependent. The relative importance of the different factors has never been determined, though it is evident that some play a more important role than others. These factors, as nearly as possible in the order of their importance, are as follows.

1. Intelligence. Of all factors influencing the development of the child, intelligence seems to be the most important. High-grade intelligence is associated with a speeding up of development, while low-grade intelligence is associated with retardation. Several examples will be sufficient to illustrate this point. The age of first walking and talking has been carefully studied in relation to the child's intelligence, and it has been found that, in the case of walking, very bright children first walk at 13 months, average children, at 14 months, morons at 22 months, and idiots at 30 months. In talking, very bright children talk first at 11 months, average children at 16 months, morons at 34 months, and idiots at 51 months (Terman, 1926).

2. Sex. There is ample evidence available at the present time to show that sex plays an important role in the physical and mental development of the child. Differences in the rate of physical growth are especially apparent. At birth, boys are slightly larger than girls, but girls grow more rapidly and mature sooner than boys. Girls, on the average, mature sexually a year before boys, and at this time they are larger than boys. This is definitely apparent at the prepuberty age, from nine to twelve years. Girls also attain their full size sooner than boys. In mental growth, as measured by intelligence tests, there is a slight difference in favor of girls. Girls develop mentally earlier than boys and reach their mental maturity slightly sooner.

3. Glands of Internal Secretion. In recent years, studies in the field of endocrinology have shown the importance of the role played by certain of the glands of internal secretion in the physical and mental development of the child. These glands affect the development in both the prenatal and postnatal stages of growth. A few of those that are definitely known to influence growth will be used as illustrations.

The level of calcium in the blood is regulated by the parathyroid glands, located in the throat, near the thyroids. Deficiency of these glands results in defective bone growth and hyperexcitability of the muscles. Thyroxin, produced by the thyroid glands, is essential to physical and mental growth. Deficiency of thyroid activity, during the growth years, stunts the physical and mental development of the child, producing the "cretin," or deformed idiot.

A too active thymus gland (located in the chest), or a too active pineal gland (located at the base of the brain), will retard normal development and keep the child physically and mentally childish too long. Deficiency in the activity of the sex glands delays the onset of puberty, while hyperactivity brings about a precocious sexual development. Extreme cases of gonad hyperactivity are known as *puberty praecox*, or early sexual maturity, in which the child may be sexually mature even between the third and fourth years.

4. Nutrition. At every age, but especially in the early years of life, feeding is of great importance to the normal development of the child. It is not only the amount of food eaten that is important; the vitamin content is as important as, if not more important than, the quantity. Defective teeth, rickets, skin diseases, and innumerable other disturbances can be traced directly to incorrect diet during babyhood and early childhood. The larger stature of the children of today, as well as that of children of the higher economic classes, is due in part to improved feeding in the early years of life.

5. Fresh Air and Sunlight. The size, general health condition, and maturing age of the child are influenced by the amount of fresh air and sunlight the child gets, especially during the early years of life. This is very evident when comparisons are made between children from good and poor environments. Whether they affect the mental development as well as the physical is yet debatable.

6. Injuries and Diseases. Any injury to the child, such as head injuries, toxic poisons from diseases and drugs, bacterial poisons from diseased tonsils, adenoids, or typhoid fever, will retard to a certain extent the child's development. Except when these conditions are very pronounced, the effect is limited almost exclusively to the physical development.

7. Race. Racial differences in development show that children of the Mediterranean races develop physically sooner than do the children of the countries of northern Europe. Likewise, children of the Negro and Indian races are slower in their development than are the children of the white and yellow races. Comparisons of white and Negro babies during the first year of life revealed that the developmental level achieved by the Negro babies was about 80 per cent as mature as that of the white babies (McGraw, 1931). When environmental factors are taken into consideration by comparing white and Negro babies of approximately equal socioeconomic status, it was found that by the third half year, the Negroes began to be slightly lower in their developmental trend than the whites (Pasamanick, 1946).

8. Culture. In an attempt to determine what influence culture has on the young child's development, Dennis (1939, 1940) studied a group of Hopi

Indian babies. He found that, in spite of the differences in their culture and that of typical American babies, the Hopi babies showed the same social and motor responses as did the American babies. Positive social responses were found to appear at the same age in both cultures. Shyness and fear of strangers appeared at the same age levels. Other reactions were likewise found to be entirely comparable.

When comparisons were made with the material reported in 40 biographies of white babies (Dennis and Dennis, 1937), it was found that every response of the white babies was observed among the Indians and that no response was observed among the Indians that was not commonly noted among the white babies. Dennis concluded his study with the statement that "present evidence shows clearly that the general picture of infancy in the two cultures is the same in spite of the diversity of the customs surrounding child care. . . . This corroborates the view that the characteristics of infancy are universal and that culture overlays or modifies a more basic substratum of behavior."

9. Position in the Family. The position of the child within the family may influence his development more through environmental than through native factors. The second, third, or fourth child within a family generally develops more quickly than the first-born, not because of any pronounced intellectual difference, but because of the fact that the younger children learn from imitating their older brothers and sisters. On the other hand, the youngest child of the family, especially if distinctly younger than the other children, is apt to be slower in his development because he is "babied" and given little incentive to develop his latent abilities.

DEVELOPMENTAL PERIODS

Lawton (1943) has pointed out that "Our life span is divided into periods, each with its own problems of adjustment. These age periods are not related in surface story since the problems change; it is the method of attacking these problems which is likely to remain the same. Throughout the life span, people develop techniques of handling each of their difficulties. Some of these techniques are suitable and efficient, others are inappropriate and wasteful, or a method may be suitable for one age period and not another." What changes take place will depend upon the needs of the individual at that particular stage of his development (Rubinov, 1933).

Scientific studies of children have shown that at different ages certain general forms of development are taking place which distinguish that age from the ones which precede and follow it. As the child emerges from one developmental period to another, there is a gradual shift in emphasis on the dominant form of development taking place at that time. While there is no clear-cut dividing line between the different periods, nevertheless it is possible, on the basis of evidence derived from the study of large groups of children, to mark off major developmental ages, each characterized by its own specific form of development, which overshadows in importance the rest of the development occurring at that age.

The five major developmental periods, with their characteristic forms of development, approximate ages, and names commonly applied to them, are as follows.

1. Prenatal Period. This period extends from conception, when the female ovum is fertilized by the male spermatozoon, to the time of birth, roughly 9 calendar months, or 280 days. While the prenatal period is a short one, it is nevertheless one of extremely rapid development. Developing from an organism microscopically small to an individual weighing 6 to 8 pounds and measuring approximately 20 inches in length is without question rapid growth. The primary development taking place at this time is physiological and consists of the growth of all the bodily structures.

2. Infancy. Beginning with birth and extending to the age of ten to fourteen days is infancy, the period of the *neonate,* or the *newborn*. This is a plateau, or resting stage, in human development. It is at this time that adjustment to a totally new environment, outside of the mother's body, must be made, and thus the infant learns to be self-dependent. During this time growth, for the most part, comes to a standstill temporarily and is not resumed until the infant is able to cope successfully with his environment.

3. Babyhood. The third developmental age in the child's life is babyhood, a period extending from the age of two weeks to approximately two years. This is the age of helplessness because of the baby's necessity for depending on others for his every need. Gradually the baby becomes more independent through learning to control his muscles so that he can feed himself, walk, dress himself, talk, and play. Accompanying this self-reliance is an attitude of independence, which is apt to make the child resent being "babied."

4. Childhood. Strictly speaking, the childhood years include the years from age two to puberty, though the entire period of immaturity, from birth to maturity, is often called *childhood*. Development at this age is characterized first by growth of control over the environment. The child who, as a baby, learned to control his body, now seeks to gain control over his environment so that he can make himself a part of it. When he is not able to do this, he relies upon the use of speech to gain the information he seeks. As a result, he is often a "living question mark." In addition to this, the child learns to make social adjustments at this age. From approximately the sixth year, socialization is of paramount importance. The name "gang age" is sometimes given to this period because group activities of all sorts play so important a role in the child's life.

5. Adolescence. The adolescent years extend from the onset of puberty, between the ages of eleven and thirteen years in the average child, to the age of maturity, twenty-one years. Because this is such a long developmental age and because different forms of development occur at different times within this age, it may be subdivided into three shorter periods, (*a*) preadolescence, (*b*) early adolescence, and (*c*) late adolescence.

a. Preadolescence. This is a short period, approximately a year long, immediately preceding adolescence proper. In girls it generally occurs between the eleventh and thirteenth years, while in boys it comes approximately a year later. Charlotte Bühler of Vienna has called this the "negative phase," because there is normally a negative attitude or an "about-face" in behavior at this time. Rapid physiological development of the sex life of the child seems to upset, temporarily, the emotional and social control developed in earlier ages.

b. Early Adolescence. This period follows preadolescence and extends to the age of sixteen to seventeen years, thus coinciding with the high-school age. Very often it is called the "awkward age," because of the awkwardness, clumsiness, and accompanying self-consciousness which so frequently occur. During this time, physical and mental growth are completed.

c. Late Adolescence. This last developmental age, coinciding roughly with the college age, is often referred to as the "smart," or "show-off," age because of the keen delight which the normal boy or girl in this phase of development shows in being the center of attention. The most important forms of development which occur are adjustment to a mature form of life, in which the child learns to be independent of adults and plan his life according to his own wishes. In addition to this, there is adjustment to members of the opposite sex, in which the adolescent gradually learns to get along with members of the opposite sex in work and social activities.

In general, late adolescence may be looked upon as the last step in the long period of development which begins at the time of conception. By the end of late adolescence, development has reached a point where the individual is legally and socially regarded as mature, and thus capable of living an independent life, free from supervision and guidance.

Chapter 2

PRENATAL DEVELOPMENT

Life does not begin at birth, as many believe, but at the time of conception, approximately nine months before birth. Growth during the prenatal period is very rapid, resulting in the development of an organism capable of a large number of complex activities in the short span of nine months. Birth is therefore merely an interruption in the normal development of the individual, caused by a change in environments from that of the mother's body to that of the world outside the mother's body.

Speculation about the origin of life occurred in ancient times among primitive peoples and among civilized peoples. Because primitive peoples did not associate intercourse between the sexes with the birth of the child, many theories of a mystical sort grew up to explain birth. Greek philosophers, on the other hand, recognized the fact that sexual relationship always precedes the birth of a baby and, with this knowledge in mind, evolved a theory which maintained that the woman was the receptive soil in which the seed from the male was planted. This theory held that the role of the mother was to supply nourishment for the developing baby, and the source of this nourishment was believed to be the menstrual blood which ceased flowing during the period preceding the child's birth. Never, in ancient times, was there any recognition of the fact that the mother produced a seed, which, when united with the male seed, gives rise to a new individual.

It was not until the seventeenth century that the woman's contribution to the fertilization of the male seed was recognized. During that era, de Graaf, a Dutch physician, suggested that the woman supplied an egg. A few years later, a Dutch spectaclemaker, van Leeuwenhoek, reported that "little animals," or what are now known as *sperm cells,* were found in the male semen, and these, he contended, were the male contribution to the new human being. During the nineteenth century scientists recognized that the union of the egg and the male cell was essential to the creation of a new organism. Since this discovery, a lively interest in embryology has arisen, with the result that our knowledge of prenatal development is not only more extensive but also more accurate with each succeeding decade.

Methods of Study. Study of the development taking place before birth is extremely difficult and, in some cases, almost impossible, in human subjects. Our knowledge of the growth occurring at this time is of necessity

29

limited by the difficulties involved in the study itself. Information about development during the first two months of life comes from studies of animals or from human embryos operatively removed from the mother's body (Carmichael, 1954). To date, no embryologist has been able to devise a technique to enable him to observe the progress of the fertilized human ovum down the Fallopian tube or the process of becoming embedded in the maternal uterine wall (Corner, 1944; Carmichael, 1954). Information about the living fetus comes from three sources: (1) the mother's report of fetal movements; (2) sounds of fetal heartbeats and movements detected by instruments used on the mother's abdominal wall; and (3) direct observations of fetuses operatively removed because a diseased condition of the mother necessitated the artificial termination of pregnancy.

Reports given by mothers in regard to fetal movements are, like all introspective reports, subject to error. How accurately the mother will be able to report will depend, in large measure, on her interest in the subject and on her training in scientific techniques. For the most part, the only information of importance to be derived from this technique is the fact that the prenatal activity is pronounced enough for the mother to be able to feel it and localize it. Furthermore, mothers may vary in their uterine sensitivity, owing to such physical factors as their size, the position of the fetus in the uterus, and muscular tension. These individual differences in the threshold of sensitivity are bound to have a profound influence on the mother's introspective report.

Technical aids and special apparatus, such as the stethoscope, cardiograph, string galvanometer, and X ray have been used to study fetal heartbeat, fetal activity, position of the fetus, and whether or not there will be twins. Fetal movements have been measured by placing a tambour on the mother's abdomen through which fetal movements may be recorded (Ray, 1932; Sontag and Wallace, 1933, 1934, 1935a; Kellogg, 1941; Bernard, 1946; Carmichael, 1954).

Direct observations of a human fetus are impossible except in the case of fetuses from miscarriages, abortions, and premature births. These fetuses are rarely "normal" but are defective in one aspect or another, which has led to the early termination of pregnancy. The procedure used by Minkowski (1921–1928a) illustrates the third method of studying the fetus. It consisted of taking the fetus alive from the mother's body by Caesarean section under a local anesthetic. The fetus was then placed in a bath of physiological salt solution at normal blood temperature to prolong its life and make experimental study possible. This technique involves cutting off the fetus from normal oxygen supply, and the movements observed are thus the movements of an increasingly asphyxiated organism with increasing metabolites in the blood, which results first in hyperactivity and then hypoactivity.

CARRIERS OF HEREDITY

What the individual is and what physical and mental traits he possesses are determined by the type of parents, grandparents, and other ancestors he had. What is transmitted from parent to offspring is not the trait itself but the *gene* which will determine the form the trait will take in the off-spring. To understand fully the role played by the gene in heredity, one must know what the gene is, where it is located, and how it acts as a trans-mitter of hereditary traits.

Chromosomes and Genes. The individual begins his existence as a single cell, the fertilized germ cell, or *zygote.* This cell is formed by the union of two germ cells, one from the male and the other from the female parent. The outer ring of the cell is the *cytoplasm,* which consists of a mass of relatively undifferentiated protoplasmic material. The function of the cytoplasm is still unknown. Within the cytoplasm is the *nucleus,* the "life-giving" part of the cell. This contains the *chromosomes,* of which there are 24 pairs in the human sex cell. Each chromosome consists of a string of minute particles, the *genes.* The genes are the physical substances passed on from parent to offspring and thus are the true carriers of hereditary traits. Each chromosome contains about 3,000 genes (Thoms, 1954).

Except in the case of pairing of X and Y chromosomes (see section on Determination of Sex), chromosomes are always arranged in pairs, with the two members of each pair exactly alike in size and appearance. Each contains the same number of genes arranged in the same order. One of the chromosomes in each pair comes from the father and one from the mother. They remain distinct, and each chromosome contains genes from the parent from whom it originated. In the fertilized germ cell of the human being, there are 24 pairs of chromosomes, half of which have come from the mother and half from the father. This is illustrated in Fig. 5.

From his two parents, the child thus receives a new combination of parental genes, made up of genes which the parents themselves have received from their parents, and they, in turn, from their parents. Which 24 chromosomes the child receives from each parent may come from either or both grandparents. Thus a child may not have many traits in common with one or both of his parents but may resemble one of his grandparents or greatgrandparents.

Some characteristics are associated with the sex of the individual. These "sex-linked" characters are produced by genes carried by the chromosomes responsible for determining sex. Traits known to be sex-linked are, for example, color blindness, hereditary baldness, and hemophilia. Sex-linked traits rarely appear in both father and son. They generally skip a generation and are transmitted from a man, through his daughter or daughters, to one or more of his grandsons (Spencer, 1955).

Maturation of Sex Cells. The maternal and paternal germ cells, which later unite to form the fertilized cell, have been developed in the reproductive organs, the *gonads*. The male gonads, the *testes*, produce the male germ cells, the *spermatozoa* (singular—spermatozoon), while the female

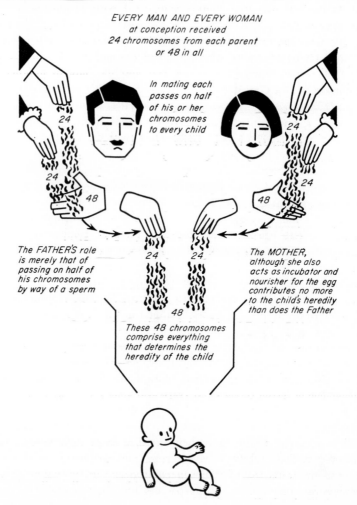

EVERY MAN AND EVERY WOMAN
at conception received
24 chromosomes from each parent
or 48 in all

In mating each
passes on half
of his or her
chromosomes
to every child

The FATHER'S role
is merely that of
passing on half of
his chromosomes
by way of a sperm

The MOTHER,
although she also
acts as incubator and
nourisher for the egg
contributes no more
to the child's heredity
than does the Father

These 48 chromosomes
comprise everything
that determines the
heredity of the child

Fig. 5. The heredity process. (*From A. Scheinfeld, The new you and heredity, Lippincott, 1950. Used by permission.*)

gonads, the *ovaries,* produce the female germ cells, the *ova* (singular—ovum). Before these sex cells can fertilize or be fertilized and thus give rise to a new individual, they must become mature, or go through a process known as *maturation*. This takes place after sex maturity has been attained by the boy or girl, following the onset of puberty.

Maturation consists of chromosome reduction through cell division, in which one member of each pair of chromosomes is lost. The result is a *haploid cell,* or a cell with one-half its usual number of chromosomes. This has come about because every immature sex cell, whether male or female, has divided into four mature cells, each with 24 chromosomes. In the process of division, the 48 chromosomes of each cell arrange themselves into 24 pairs on opposite sides of the nucleus, each pair containing one chromosome from the father and one from the mother. When the pairs separate, one chromosome goes to one cell and its mate to another (see Figs. 6 and 7).

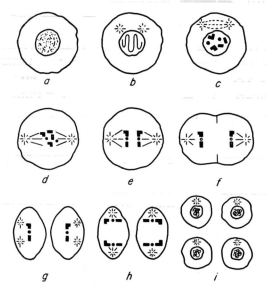

Fig. 6. Maturation of sperm. (*From F. M. Teagarden, Child psychology for professional workers, rev. ed., Prentice-Hall, 1948. Used by permission.*)

The male cell, the sperm, divides into four cells, or *spermatids,* each of which is capable of fertilizing a female cell. The spermatids are known as *gametes,* or "marrying cells." When division occurs in the female cell, one chromosome from each pair is pushed outside the cell wall. These are known as the *polar bodies,* and they cannot be fertilized. In the process of division, three polar bodies are formed, smaller in size than the *ovum,* or gamete, which is capable of being fertilized. The polar bodies are soon absorbed and secreted. The ovum, unless it is fertilized, later disintegrates and passes from the body with the menstrual flow. Each sperm cell and each ovum, when mature, contains 24 chromosomes.

Implications. There is no specific scientific knowledge in regard to the way the pairs of chromosomes of either the male or female cell divide.

Division seems to be a matter of chance. In one cell, after division has occurred, there may be 20 chromosomes from the female and 4 from the male, or 8 from the female and 16 from the male, or any other combination. For that reason when one cell combines with another in fertilization, it is possible and probable that more traits will be inherited from one side of the family than from the other. This explains the "skipping of a generation" in a given trait.

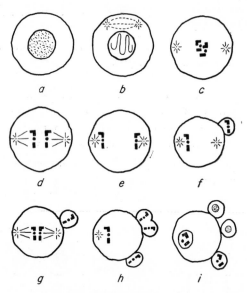

Fig. 7. Maturation of ovum. (*From F. M. Teagarden, Child psychology for professional workers, rev. ed., Prentice-Hall, 1948. Used by permission.*)

If one considers the different possible combinations of 24 chromosomes from the male and 25 from the female germ cells, it has been estimated that there are 16,777,216 possible arrangements (Scheinfeld, 1950). Under such conditions, it is understandable why children of the same family are often so different that one would not suspect they were related. Only in the case of identical twins do children have the same genetic make-up. Because the combination of genes is a matter of chance, one cannot predict with any degree of accuracy what the physical or mental characteristics of a child will be from knowing his parents.

Ovum versus Spermatozoon. There are several outstanding differences between the ovum and the spermatozoon:

1. The ovum is large as compared with the other cells of the body, while the spermatozoon is among the smallest cells of the body. The ovum is approximately 0.1 millimeter in diameter, weighs about one-millionth of a gram, and is about the size of a period on a page. The spermatozoon

is even smaller, measuring 50 microns (a micron is one-thousandth of a millimeter) in length, with the head alone 5 microns long (Scheinfeld, 1950). How small a sperm cell is can be appreciated when one realizes that it has been estimated that it would take 300,000,000 sperms to fit into a teaspoon (Thoms, 1954), or that if all the sperm cells from which the approximately two billion people now living over the face of the globe developed were put together, they could easily be packed into a mass the size of an aspirin tablet (Spencer, 1955). The cause in the difference in size of the sperm cell and the ovum is the yolk, or food material for nourishment of the new individual, which the ovum contains in addition to its chromosomes. Should the ovum be fertilized, it could exist with the nourishment from the yolk until it attaches itself to the wall of the uterus and becomes a parasite.

2. The ovum is round in shape and nonmotile, with no means of locomotion within itself. It therefore has to depend entirely upon the contractions of the tissues by which it is surrounded for its movements. The spermatozoon, on the other hand, is elongated in shape and very motile. It is made up of a head consisting chiefly of the nucleus, which is composed primarily of bundles of genes, as is true of the nucleus of the ovum. Back of the head is the body, an elongated portion, to which is attached a cilium, or fine, hairlike tail, which, by lashing back and forth, enables the spermatozoon to swim forward through the semen in which it is released. It has been estimated that a fast sperm goes an inch in about an hour and that it can continue to swim at this speed for as long as 2 days (Thoms, 1954).

3. While normally only one ovum is produced in each menstrual cycle, approximately 28 days, the spermatozoa are very numerous, with as many as 200,000,000 found in 3 cubic centimeters of seminal fluid in one ejection. Several hundred million sperm cells develop every 4 or 5 days as compared with one ovum every 28 days (Thoms, 1954).

4. The ovum carries a large bulk of cytoplasm, containing the nucleus, which is made up almost entirely of bundles of genes, and some yolk which assists in nourishing the embryo. The spermatozoon, on the other hand, has a minimum of cytoplasm.

5. The ovum contains 24 matched chromosomes, while half of the spermatozoa contain 23 matched and 1 unmatched, and half, 24 matched chromosomes. The significance of this difference in number of chromosomes in the spermatozoa will be discussed in the section on Determination of Sex.

HOW LIFE BEGINS

How life begins, and the sources from which the new organism develops, must be clearly understood if the picture of human growth is to be complete. The early stages of growth and the approximate times at which they occur are as follows.

1. *Ovulation* is the process of maturing and escape from an ovary of one ovum during each menstrual period. The female ovary is made up of a mass of follicles containing ova which, if and when they develop, will be capable of being fertilized by male germ cells. It has been estimated that at birth there are approximately 200,000 ova, many of which will atrophy during childhood, leaving only about 30,000 when the girl reaches puberty. Of these, approximately 400 mature between the onset of puberty, between thirteen and fifteen years of age, and the onset of the menopause in the middle forties. There is also a belief, though not yet definitely proved to be true, that the ova which mature during the woman's fertile period of life are not those which were present in an immature state during her childhood, but are newly created ova, only a few weeks old (Thoms, 1954).

During every menstrual cycle of about 28 days each, one of the follicles swells, is pushed to the surface of the ovary, ruptures, and expels a ripe ovum. This is brought about by a hormone from the pituitary gland at the base of the brain. When the follicle is swelling, this is not due to increase in the size of the maturing ovum but to the development of a hormone that will play a very important role in reproduction, *estrogen*. When the supply of estrogen reaches a certain point, the follicle ruptures and both the estrogen and the ripe ovum are released (Ratcliff, 1950; Thoms, 1954; Davis, 1955; Potter, 1955). Though not definitely proved to be true, it is generally believed that the two ovaries alternate in this function, with one ovary producing a ripe ovum one month and the other ovary, the next month.

After being released from its follicle in the ovary, the ripe ovum enters the open end of the nearer Fallopian tube and is propelled along the tube. This is done by a combination of factors: fluids composed of estrogen from the ovarian follicle and a mucus from the lining of the tube; cilia, or hair-like projections which line the tube; and rhythmic, progressive contractions of the walls of the tube. By the combined efforts of these three factors, the ripe ovum makes its way down through the tube and into the uterus or womb which is connected with the lower end of the tube (Ratcliff, 1950; Thoms, 1954; Davis, 1955).

Just when ovulation will occur during the menstrual cycle and how long the ovum will remain in the Fallopian tube is difficult to determine because of the wide variations, not only in different women, but also in the same woman at different times. The average time at which ovulation occurs is on the 11.8th day of the menstrual cycle, with variations from the 5th to the 23d day. In the same woman, a variation from the 5th to the 16th day in consecutive cycles is not an exception to the usual pattern (Altmann et al., 1941). Once it enters the Fallopian tube, the ovum moves rapidly down to the uterus. As is true of ovulation, there are marked individual differences from one woman to another and in the same woman from one menstrual cycle to another, in the time in which the ovum remains in the tube. It has been estimated that the ovum takes from 2 to 7 days to pass down the tube and into the uterus, with an average of 3 days (Ratcliff, 1950; Thoms, 1954; Davis, 1955).

2. *Fertilization*, or conception, consists of the formation of a fertilized egg, or *zygote*. Before the sperm cell reaches the ovum, it has to travel a long and hazardous path from the male sex glands, the *testes*, to the female ovary. In normal fertilization, the ovum is in the Fallopian tube on its way from the ovary to the uterus. Fertilization is believed to take place within 12 to 36 hours after the ovum enters the tube, usually within the first 24 hours (Thoms, 1954; Davis, 1955; Potter, 1955). As a result of coitus, spermatozoa are deposited at the mouth of the uterus and make their way toward the tubes. They are attracted to the ovum by a strong hormone attraction which draws them into the tube.

The sperm must reach the ovum before it loses its energy. It is believed that a healthy sperm cell can wait in the female sex organs for 24 to 36 hours before losing too much of its energy to be able to penetrate the outer wall of the ovum (Potter, 1955). If the ovum is not fertilized while in the Fallopian tube, it will die before or right after it leaves the tube and be expelled from the body. This means that fertilization can occur only during a period of 1 to 2 days in approximately the middle of the menstrual cycle.

After one sperm enters the ovum, the surface of the ovum is so changed that no other sperm cells can penetrate it. Thus, the fertilized ovum is completed when contact with one sperm has occurred. When the sperm cell penetrates the wall of the ovum, the nuclei from the two cells approach each other. In time, there is a breakdown in the membrane surrounding each, and this allows the two nuclei to merge. The new cell, thus formed, has the original number of chromosomes, 24 pairs, one-half of which came from the male and one-half from the female cell.

Significance of Fertilization. The moment of fertilization is unquestionably one of the most important, if not actually the most important, moment of the individual's entire life. Three decisive things now happen which will shape the entire course of his future life. At this time, not only is a new individual created, but his entire *hereditary endowment* is determined. As Kuhlen and Thompson (1952) have stressed, "Every individual's supply of genes, the bearers of hereditary factors, is given him once for all and inalterably at conception."

Because each human being, whether male or female, produces many more germ cells than will ever be used, and because in each of these cells are genes from both parents in varying numbers, two important points must be remembered: (1) it is impossible to predict with any degree of certainty what the offspring will be like, since the genes are assorted by chance; and

(2) the genes carry the traits of the ancestors of the individual and may produce in the offspring traits that are traceable to one or more of the ancestors, even though they may not be found in either parent. To be a given kind of person, according to Scheinfeld (1950), involves the union of a particular ovum with a particular sperm. The probability of this particular union occurring is but one chance in 300,000,000,000,000.

The second thing of importance that happens at the time of fertilization is the *determination of sex*. How this occurs will be explained in detail in the section of this chapter that deals with determination of sex. Suffice it to point out at the moment that, contrary to popular beliefs, there is no known way of changing the sex of the newly created individual after the moment of conception. That the individual's sex is a factor of major importance in determining the entire pattern of his life will become more and more apparent in subsequent chapters of this book.

Finally, whether the individual will be a *singleton* or one of several children born at the same time will likewise be determined at this time. The whole matter of multiple births, their causes, their different forms, and the effects they have on the life patterns of the individual will be discussed in detail in the section of this chapter that relates to multiple births.

Difficulties of Fertilization. When a healthy sperm meets a healthy ovum at the right time in the life cycle of the ovum, the chances are that the sperm will fertilize the ovum. But conditions are not always favorable to fertilization. Should this condition remain month after month, the woman will be "sterile" and not able to produce offspring. At the present time, medical science knows how to control or cure most of the causes of sterility, and as a result, there are fewer childless marriages among those who want children than was true in the past when the causes of sterility were less well known than today.

Failure of fertilization of an ovum may be caused by many conditions, the most important of which are:

1. Unfavorable conditions in the female reproductive organs, such as a too acid condition of the vaginal secretions which kill the sperms or an obstruction in the Fallopian tubes, due to inflammation or some foreign substance.

2. An unfavorable condition of the ovum due to poor health, vitamin or glandular deficiency on the woman's part, or old age. A deficiency of thyroid or pituitary secretions will, for example, slow down the maturation and release of the ovum, with the result that it does not have enough yolk to survive until it becomes implanted in the uterine wall.

3. An unfavorable condition of the sperm cells. Even in healthy males, it has been estimated that about 12 per cent of the sperm cells are the wrong size, the wrong shape, or deformed in some way. In less healthy

males, or in those suffering from some disease, from some glandular or nutritional deficiency, or from the debilitating effects of old age, the chances are that a far larger percentage of the sperm cells would be defective. There would be, also, under such conditions, a much smaller quantity of sperm cells produced than under normal conditions. Or the sperms may be slow and sluggish in their activity, as happens when the male is in poor health or very old. To reach the ovum, the sperm must travel up the Fallopian tube where the ovum is being pushed down by muscular contractions of the tubal walls and by the current of liquids in which it is immersed. This requires great strength on the part of the sperm cell. Then, when the sperm meets the ovum in the Fallopian tube, it must have enough strength left to penetrate the outer wall of the ovum. Only healthy sperm cells can accomplish the ultimate goal of the sperm's existence (Thoms, 1954; Dickinson, 1955).

PERIODS IN PRENATAL DEVELOPMENT

The prenatal period, which extends roughly over 9 calendar months, or 10 lunar months, is approximately 280 days long. However, there are marked individual variations in the length of this period, ranging from 180 days, which is the shortest time when a fetus has been reported to be born alive, to 334 days, the legal limit of postmaturity (Carmichael, 1954). This period may be divided roughly into three subdivisions: (1) *the period of the ovum,* or the "germinal" period, which extends from the moment of conception to the end of the second week; (2) *the period of the embryo,* which extends from the end of the second week to the end of the second month, or six weeks in duration; and (3) *the period of the fetus,* which extends from the end of the second month to birth. Of the three periods, the period of the fetus is the most variable in length and may range from 18 to 40 weeks, depending on whether the fetus is dislodged from the uterine wall ahead of schedule, at the average time, or after the average time.

The period before birth, short as it is in relation to the life span, is characterized by growth and development more rapid than at any period of similar length in life. Growth from a single cell, microscopically small, to an individual composed of about 200 billion cells of different types (Corner, 1944), measuring approximately 20 inches in length and weighing, on the average, 7 pounds, is phenomenal in the short period of 9 calendar months. Equally great development is seen in the change from a single cell with no power of its own to an individual composed of muscles, bones, skin, and organs that are ready to function at birth or even before birth.

Growth and development in the prenatal period are not only rapid, they are orderly and predictable. From scientific studies it has been found that development follows a pattern not only in the development of the different parts of the body but in their functioning as well. This pattern follows the law of developmental direction (see pages 11-12), which holds that the direction of development is from head to foot, from the axis to the periphery of the body. The head, for example, develops sooner than the legs, the arms sooner than the hands, and the fingers before the toes. At no time during the prenatal period is the developing organism just a miniature adult in proportions, as may readily be seen in Fig. 1, page 3.

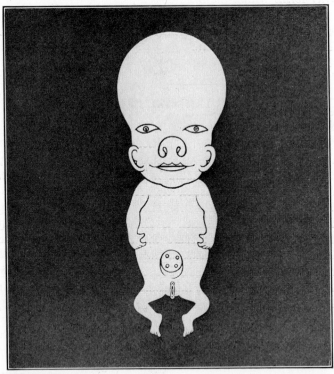

In the early stages of prenatal development, the head develops first. (*From Child Development: a McGraw-Hill Text-Film.*)

Because the development in the prenatal period is orderly and predictable, it is possible to give a "timetable" of the development of structures and functions at different stages in the prenatal period. Each of the subdivisions of the prenatal period, the periods of the ovum, of the embryo, and of the fetus, is characterized by development peculiar to it. In making a survey of the prenatal development of the human individual, this subdivision into three periods will be followed.

The Period of the Ovum

The period of the ovum extends from the moment of fertilization to the end of the second week. During this time, the individual retains an egglike organization. Its size remains practically unchanged because it receives little or no external nourishment. Marked changes, however, occur in the internal structure of the *zygote,* or fertilized egg. The single cell divides and subdivides many times until a globular cluster of many cells is formed. A small cavity forms within the mass of cells, thus resulting in an outer and separated inner cluster of cells. The outer layer develops later into accessory tissues that protect and nourish the embryo. Part of the inner cluster of cells develops into the embryo.

This cell division takes place as the fertilized ovum is carried down the Fallopian tube to the uterus. By the time it reaches the uterus, it is about the size of a pinhead, though its size varies according to how long it has been in the tube after being fertilized. During the first week of this period, the fertilized ovum is unattached and free-moving.

After a mature ovum has been released from a follicle in the wall of the ovary, the lining of the uterus begins to undergo changes in preparation for receiving the ovum, should it be fertilized. This preparation is brought about by two hormones, *estrogen,* which was present in the follicle in which the ovum matured and was released when the follicle ruptured, and *progesterone,* which is also produced in the wall of the ovary. These two hormones prepare the uterine wall by increasing the blood-vessel and glandular systems of the wall, so that it becomes a thick, soft cushion to house the fertilized ovum and secretes material which the fertilized ovum can use as its first source of nourishment (Ratcliff, 1950; Davis, 1955; Potter, 1955). Should this preparation be unnecessary, as is true when no ovum is fertilized, there is a breakdown of tissue in the uterine wall, which is eliminated from the body in the menstrual flow.

When the fertilized ovum reaches the uterus, it floats about unattached for several days. For nourishment, it must rely upon the small amount of yolk within the ovum itself. Normally, this is adequate to keep the ovum alive until it attaches itself to the uterine wall, becomes a parasite, and derives its nourishment from the mother. When the ovum finds a place in the uterine wall, it shoots out feelers which push their way through the blood vessels in the uterine wall, thus tapping a new source of nourishment (Potter, 1955). This process is known as *implantation* and occurs about 10 days after the ovum has been fertilized.

While many fertilized ova follow this pattern, others do not. If the ovum remains unattached for too long—and this is believed to be due to a deficient supply of hormones from the thyroid and pituitary glands of the mother, which slow down the entire pattern of reproduction—it will die when it has used up all its yolk. Or it may attach itself to a small fibroid tumor in the mother's uterine wall and fail to get nourishment. Occasionally the ovum does not move down through the Fallopian tube after it has been fertilized, but remains and attaches itself to the wall of the tube. This is known as a *tubal pregnancy*. Because complete fetal development is impossible in the tube, it is then necessary to remove the fertilized ovum surgically. Even more occasionally, fertilization occurs in the abdominal cavity, which likewise necessitates surgical removal.

THE PERIOD OF THE EMBRYO

The period of the embryo extends from the second week to the end of the second month. It is a time of rapid change. By the end of this period, the embryo represents a miniature individual in his development. From then on, the major changes that take place consist of changes in actual or relative size in the parts of the body already established, rather than the appearance of new features.

After implantation, the cell mass which started to develop immediately after fertilization differentiates into three layers, the *germ layers*, from which all parts of the body develop. These layers grow unequally, with folding in and out of the portions of the layers, and thus give rise to the different body structures. The outer layer, the *ectoderm*, produces the epidermis of the skin, hair, nails, parts of the teeth, skin glands, sensory cells, and the entire nervous system. The middle layer, the *mesoderm*, gives rise to the dermis, or inner skin layer, the muscles, circulatory and excretory organs. From the innermost layer, the *endoderm*, come the lining of the entire digestive tract, the Eustachian tubes, trachea, bronchia, lungs, liver, pancreas, salivary glands, thyroid glands, and thymus.

During the period of the embryo, special structures form to provide nourishment and protection until the baby is born. Where the fertilized ovum embedded itself in the uterine wall and sent out threadlike structures to tap a source of nourishment, the *placenta* develops. As the villi, or threadlike structures, become more and more branched and intertwine, they form a fairly solid looking mass, somewhat pie-shaped. This mass is the placenta. Eventually, the placenta grows to be about 1 inch thick and 8 to 10 inches in diameter, covering about half of the uterine wall. After reaching a certain thickness, the placenta tends to increase in area rather than in thickness (Dow and Torpin, 1939). Figure 8 shows the relationship between the mother and the developing child.

The connecting link between the embryo and the placenta is the *umbilical cord*, which is attached to the embryo's abdominal wall at one end and the placenta at the other. The umbilical cord is composed of blood vessels united in a single ropelike structure. There are no nerves in the cord, thus making transfer of thoughts from the mother to the embryo impossible.

In time, the cord becomes the thickness of a man's thumb and measures 10 to 20 inches in length. This length is important because it makes fetal activity possible.

The third structure which develops during the period of the embryo and which serves a useful purpose until birth is the *amniotic sac.* This is a water jacket, or bag, in which the embryo is protected from possible injuries to his delicate tissues until the time of birth. The sac, made up of four membranes, is attached to the placenta and contains a watery fluid, the *amniotic fluid,* in which the embryo develops. As the baby grows larger during the period of the fetus, the sac increases in size to adjust to the changing size of the fetus. Just before birth, the sac breaks, releasing the amniotic fluid which helps to lubricate the passageways for birth. Within

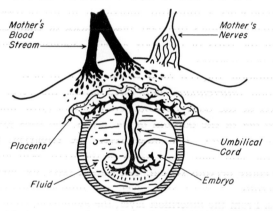

Fig. 8. Relationship between mother and developing child. (*From A. Scheinfeld, The new you and heredity, Lippincott, 1950. Used by permission.*)

a few minutes after birth, the sac, placenta, and cord are expelled from the mother's body as *afterbirth.* Their usefulness ends when the baby arrives in the world.

Once the accessory apparatus of the cord, placenta, and sac have been established, the embryo is protected and nourished so it can grow and develop. The maternal blood flows into the placenta from arteries in the uterine wall, thus permitting oxygen, water, and food materials in the mother's blood stream to be transported through the umbilical cord to the embryo. There is no direct connection between maternal and embryonic blood streams. The only connection is in the placenta, where certain elements from the mother's blood are sucked into the cord and carried to the embryo. Through this same cord, embryonic waste products are filtered back through the placenta into the maternal blood and are removed from her blood through the organs of excretion. The embryo develops its own circulatory system, but must rely upon the placenta, which acts as a filter, for its source of nourishment and its elimination of waste products (Gilbert, 1939; Corner, 1944; Gesell, 1949; Carmichael, 1954; Potter, 1955).

End of Second Lunar Month. By the end of the second lunar month, the embryo is approximately 1¼ to 2 inches long and weighs about 2 grams, or ⅔ ounce. This is an increase of about 2,000,000 per cent since fertilization occurred. Its form is so well developed that it is distinctly human and would not be mistaken for an animal. The head development is the most pronounced of the entire body. The *eyes* are now in front of the face, with *eyelids* in the form of folds of skin above the eyes. The *ears* closely resemble those of a human being, but are low on the side of the embryo's head. The *mouth* opens, and the lower *jaw* is small, so that the embryo is almost chinless. There is a single broad *nose* and a large, bulging *forehead*. The *body proportions* differ from those of the newborn in that the head of the embryo is enormously large while the arms and legs are tiny.

The *trunk* is no longer potbellied, but is elongated and rounded, so that it resembles that of a human. Most of the internal organs are apparent. The *heart* structure begins to appear about the eighteenth day, and by the end of the third week, it starts to function as a result of independent muscular contraction. The *liver,* which is one-tenth of the entire body volume, crowds the rest of the organs. Bile is secreted from it at this time. The *intestines* are shoved into the umbilical cord, and the *appendix* appears. The *diaphragm* is a sheet of tissue which divides the chest from the abdominal cavity. The *sex organs* are now differentiated in both the internal and external structures, so that it is possible to distinguish the sex of the embryo in a large percentage of cases.

The *arms* have elbows and webbed fingers, while the *legs* have knees and webbed toes. The *tail* of the embryo reaches its maximum development at this age and then regresses. Most of the *muscles* of the body are formed, and some of them, especially the muscles of the arms and legs, are capable of functioning. No bone is deposited at this time. There is a *cartilage* formation of backbone, ribs, collarbone, arm, and leg bones which have the shape of the bones they represent. Around the middle of each cartilage is a narrow sheet of hard bone which, in succeeding months, spreads nearer to the surface as the cartilage degenerates and disappears.

The development of the nervous system begins even as early as the period of the ovum when the beginnings of nervous structures are apparent. During the early part of the period of the embryo, the first groove in the ectoderm folds inward to form the neural tube, the lower part of which develops, eventually, into the spinal cord, and the upper part into the brain. By the fifth week, the principal structures of the brain, the cerebellum, medulla, midbrain, and end brain, can be distinguished at the top of the neural tube. These higher brain centers do not, however, function effectively until the time of birth. During the second month, neurones appear in the form of neuroblasts, or cells without nervous extensions. The major part of neural development, it is thus apparent, comes during the period of the fetus. The *umbilical cord* shows regular spinal twists, owing, it is believed, to the turning of the fetus in the uterus. In operatively removed fetuses, *spontaneous movements* can be observed. These movements are wormlike contractions of the arms, legs, and thorax. They are ideomuscular in character and not evoked by external stimulation. *Peristaltic* movements may begin as early as the seventh week.

Hazards. The period of the embryo is a critical period of the prenatal span, not only because it is the time when all the fundamental structures of the body are formed and when the accessory apparatus needed for protection and nourishment until the time of birth are developed, but also because there are certain hazards which may influence the future of the embryo. Of these, two hazards, miscarriages and malformations, are the most serious.

A *miscarriage* is a spontaneous abortion brought on by natural causes as distinguished from induced abortion brought on by instrumentation either illegally or for therapeutic purposes (Guttmacher, 1955). It has been estimated that approximately one out of every three fertilized ova do not survive until birth and that the most critical period for the ending of their lives is during the second and third months after fertilization. Of the fertilized ova that miscarry, approximately 72 per cent do so before the fourth month of pregnancy begins (Ratcliff, 1950; Guttmacher, 1955).

There are many old wives' tales to explain the ending of pregnancy, and like most old wives' tales, these rarely hold up in face of medical evidence. According to these beliefs, miscarriages come from a physical shock, a fall, overexcitement, overexertion, smoking, drinking, or an unfavorable attitude on the mother's part toward her developing baby. Other old wives' tales maintain that a woman who has once experienced a miscarriage has little chance of being able to carry subsequent pregnancies to full term. To ease the distress of parents who have lost a baby through a miscarriage, the belief has grown up that this is a "blessing in disguise" and that the miscarriage was nature's method of eliminating an unfit cell which would develop into a physically or mentally deformed individual, should its development continue (Ratcliff, 1950; Guttmacher, 1955).

Modern scientific investigations have thrown light on the causes of miscarriages and the times when they most frequently occur. Of the many causes, the following have been found to be the most important, though no attempt has been made to date to discover the frequencies of miscarriages due to each cause: *defective germ plasm,* due to chromosome abnormality of the sperm or ovum, to some physiochemical mishap in fertilization, or to some environmental factor connected with implantation or the early development of the fertilized ovum; some *abnormality of the female re-*

productive organs; multiple pregnancies; severe maternal illness, such as pneumonia; the *RH factor; vitamin deficiency; severe malnutrition; thyroid deficiency;* and *progesterone deficiency.* If miscarriage is due to a defective fertilized ovum, it generally occurs early during the prenatal period. If, on the other hand, the fertilized ovum is normal but the environment in which it is developing is abnormal, for one reason or another, the miscarriage comes later, generally in the third or fourth month of pregnancy, with the most frequent numbers of miscarriages in the tenth or eleventh week of pregnancy (Ratcliff, 1950; Guttmacher, 1955). See Fig. 9 for the usual times of miscarriage. Of all the abnormal environmental conditions that result in the dislodging of a normal embryo or fetus from the uterine wall, it is now believed that *deficiency of progesterone is the most common.*

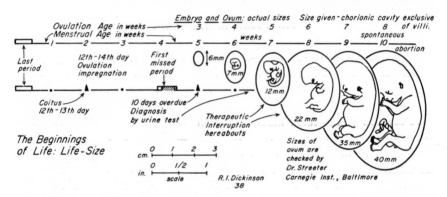

Fig. 9. Early pregnancies and embryo development. (*From E. L. Potter, Pregnancy, in M. Fishbein and E. W. Burgess, Successful marriage, rev. ed., Doubleday, 1955. Used by permission.*)

Progesterone is a hormone produced by the ovary and released in large quantities, together with estrogen, at the time of ovulation, when the ripe ovum is released from the follicle in the wall of the ovary. The two hormones prepare the uterus for receiving the fertilized ovum when it passes through the Fallopian tube to the uterus. The function of progesterone is to make the uterus lie quietly so that the ovum can lodge in the uterine wall and not be dislodged. However, as the ovum enlarges, during the period of the embryo, and later, in the period of the fetus, increasingly large amounts of progesterone are required to maintain quiet in the uterine walls. The ovary alone is incapable of producing sufficient quantity, and as a result, the work is taken over by the placenta. The uterus itself, thus, takes over the work of producing the hormone that makes it lie quietly.

If the placenta does not produce enough progesterone to maintain the state of quiet required for normal development of the embryo or the fetus, and if the uterus begins to contract, it frequently results in dislodging the embryo which is not yet safely anchored to the uterine wall by the thread-like structures attaching it to the placenta. The result is that it breaks loose from the placenta and is discharged from the mother's body in a miscarriage. For some unexplained reason, approximately 160 male embryos are lost through miscarriage for every 100 female embryos (Ratcliff, 1950).

The second major hazard that faces the developing embryo is the possibility of *developmental irregularity,* or abnormal development of minor or major severity. While irregularities in development may occur at any time during the prenatal period, they most often occur during the period of the embryo because this is the time when the major parts of the bodily structures are being formed (Gilbert, 1939). The causes and common forms of developmental irregularities will be discussed in detail in the section of the chapter dealing with developmental irregularities (see pages 53–56).

THE PERIOD OF THE FETUS

The period of the fetus extends from the end of the second month to the time of birth, which normally occurs at the end of the tenth lunar month. It is characterized chiefly by the growth and development of the parts of the body established in the second period, the *period of the embryo,* rather than by the appearance of new parts.

At the end of the third lunar month, the fetus measures approximately 3½ inches long and weighs about ¾ ounce. Two months later, it measures approximately 10 inches and weighs about 9 to 10 ounces. By the end of the eighth lunar month, the fetus is from 16 to 18 inches long and weighs from 4 to 5 pounds. At the age of 10 lunar months, the end of the prenatal period, the fetus is about 20 inches long and weighs from 7 to 7½ pounds. It is thus apparent that the period of most rapid growth is in the early part of the period of the fetus (Gilbert, 1939).

Measurements of fetuses from the third lunar month to birth have revealed that their development follows the law of developmental direction. The *body length* shows a rapid increase in the beginning of the fetal period and a steady decline in growth rate. The body-length increase is a little over sevenfold between the third month and birth. The *head* is nearly one-third of the total body length at the third fetal month; one-fourth at the sixth month; and slightly less than one-fourth at birth (Scammon and Calkins, 1929).

The *face* becomes relatively a little broader during the fetal period. There are many changes in the structure of the nose, mouth, and throat, and sockets for the teeth appear. Typically, the *skin* of the fetus is much wrinkled during midpregnancy, owing to the comparative absence of subcutaneous fat. The hair on the scalp is short and poorly pigmented. At the end of the fetal period, the skin is very red, owing to the visibility of the vascular system just beneath it, and is covered with *lanugo hair,* or soft, woolly hair that is shed shortly after birth, which appeared for the first time in the middle of the prenatal period (Carmichael, 1954).

The external dimensions of the *trunk* increase between sevenfold and ninefold from the third fetal month to birth. The trunk becomes more slender in relation to body length in the latter part of the fetal period. The girth of the abdomen increases more rapidly than the girth of the thorax (at the level of the nipples). At the third fetal month, the length of the *arms* approximates one-third of the total body length and two-fifths at birth. Between the third fetal month and birth, the length increases about eightfold; the hand length, eightfold; and the circumference, fifteenfold. Before the third fetal month, the arms are longer than the legs. After that, the reverse is true. In the fourth month, the toe and finger patterns are established and the nails grow gradually at the end of the fetal period (Carmichael, 1954).

The *internal organs* are not only well developed, but they begin, in some instances, to function at the end of the third lunar month. By the end of the fifth lunar month, they assume positions nearly like those of an adult. By the fourteenth or sixteenth week, *fetal heartbeat* can be detected by a stethoscope. The heart rate declines as the fetal period progresses, though it is still higher and less variable than the heart rate of the newborn infant. During periods of fetal activity, heart rate shows tremendous variations, with an increase of 30 to 40 beats within a minute, then subsiding as quickly (Sontag and Richards, 1938). It is twice as fast as the mother's heart rate (Gesell, 1949). There are *circulatory* changes, and *chest* movements supplement the action of the fetal heart (Carmichael, 1954). Movements occur in the *digestive* organs as a result of internal stimulation during the early part of the fetal period. During the third month, the *kidneys* begin to function and the waste products discharged by them pass through the placenta and are excreted by the mother. The *adrenal glands* are relatively the largest during the fourth fetal month, while the thyroids increase steadily after that (Ekholm and Niemineva, 1950). Before the end of the fourth fetal month, most of the primary ossification centers have appeared (Noback and Robertson, 1951).

The *nervous structure* necessary for reflexes, including the peripheral nerves, spinal ganglia, medullary area, anterior and posterior roots, is present, but in an embryonic state, at the end of the third lunar month. Short, threadlike prolongations appear which later become the axons and dendrites of the *neurones*. By the fifth prenatal month, it is believed, the complete number of neurones to be possessed by the mature individual is present, though many of them are still in a very immature state of development.

From the fifth month to the end of the prenatal period, development of the nervous structures consists of extension of the axons and dendrites, modifications of the synapses, and acquisition of a myelin sheath or covering. This makes possible the establishment of patterns and systems of organization of the paths, some of which are functionally mature before birth, some at birth, and others not until after birth. The earliest to mature are the ones involved in the fundamental reflexes and vegetative control, as in the case of the heartbeat. The maturing occurs first in the spinal cord, then in the midbrain, and last, in the various regions of the cerebral cortex. Not all parts of the brain develop at the same time. The regions controlling motor activities develop far in advance of the other areas of the brain (Carmichael, 1954).

By the end of the third lunar month, the *muscles* are well developed and spontaneous movements of the arms and legs may be observed. These movements are asymmetric, uncoordinated, and arhythmic. A month later, the muscles are capable of spontaneous movements. They are more rhythmic and coordinated than before. With continuing development of the nerve centers and muscles, it has been demonstrated that the fetus can be conditioned to respond to tactile vibration by movement, even in the absence of loud noises, between the seventh and eighth lunar months. Such conditioned movements are controlled by the spinal cord and lower brain centers, as the cerebral cortex is not yet functioning at that time (Spelt, 1948).

A number of studies of the state of development of the different *sense organs* during the fetal period have been made (Forbes and Forbes, 1927; Sontag and Wallace, 1935a, 1936; Preyer, 1937; Gilbert, 1939; Kellogg, 1941; Corner, 1944; Gesell, 1946; Bernard and Sontag, 1947; Carmichael, 1954). These studies have revealed the following facts about the state of the sense organs during the fetal period.

1. *Cutaneous Sensitivity.* This begins in the oral-nasal region, involving the mucous membrane of the nostrils and the red of the lips. Skin sensitivity develops by spreading over the head region and then progressively over the whole surface of the body.

2. *Temperature.* In prematurely born infants, the temperature sense is much the same as in normal, full-term infants. They react less strongly to stimuli warmer than the body than to stimuli cooler than the body at the time the stimuli are applied.

3. *Pain.* The pain sense is little developed during the prenatal period. Even when a prematurely born infant is stimulated until blood comes, little or no response is made.

4. *Taste.* The taste buds begin to develop during the third fetal month and are more widely distributed in fetal than in adult life. They are to be found not only on the tongue but also in the hard palate, the tonsils, and parts of the esophagus. Later they are limited to the tongue. Even though

the taste mechanism is present before birth, there is no adequate stimulation of this sense until after birth. In prematurely born infants, sweet is
distinguished from salt, sour, and bitter.

5. *Smell.* So long as the nasal cavity is filled with amniotic fluid, as it is
during the entire prenatal period, there can be no adequate olfactory stimulation, and olfaction does not occur in its normal form until the nasal cavity
is filled with air. Smell reactions in the premature, however, show that the
smell mechanism is well developed.

6. *Vision.* The eye begins to develop during the second or third week of
embryonic development. No stimulation, however, is possible before birth.
In the prematurely born, specific reactions to light and pupillary reflexes
occur. Eyelid reactions and eye movements occur before birth.

7. *Hearing.* The auditory mechanism is well enough developed so that
it could function before birth, but the infant remains partially deaf until
the Eustachian tube of the ear is opened and the gelatinous liquid of the
fetal middle ear is drained out. This occurs shortly after birth, owing to
breathing and crying, which help to drain the passage. The fetus, as is true
of the newborn, is deaf to sounds of normal intensity. Only strong sounds
that can pass through these mechanical blocks can bring forth reactions.

8. *Balance.* The semicircular canals, in the inner ear, attain their adult
size by the end of the prenatal period. They begin to function early in the
period of the fetus.

Fetal Activity. Individual differences in fetal activity have been noted and
reported by mothers. Some fetuses are active as much as 75 per cent of the
time, others as little as 5 per cent. There are differences in the type of fetal
activity, as well as in amounts. Some fetuses constantly turn and squirm,
while others keep the same position but kick and thrust with their hands
and feet. Some have hiccups almost every day, others not at all. In the first
month of perceived motility, there is the greatest increase in strength and
number of fetal movements. From then until the ninth lunar month, there
is a regular increase in movements, though large variations in the amount
of movement occur from day to day (Newberry, 1941; Harris and Harris,
1946; Hooker, 1951). During the last lunar month before birth, lack of
increase in movement may be explained by the fact that there is increased
pressure on the fetal head, thus inhibiting bodily movement, or the crowd-
ing of the entire fetal body in the amniotic sac, thus decreasing the space
available for movement (Newberry, 1941).

In the early part of the fetal period, there is more activity in the head than
in the leg region. Gradually, as the fetal period draws to a close, the amount
of activity in the leg region almost equals that in the head region. This
shows the operation of the law of developmental direction (Kellogg, 1941;
Hooker, 1951). The fetus is usually more active at the close of the day
than in the morning, thus indicating that the mother's fatigue may play

a role of some importance in amount of activity (Harris and Harris, 1946). With increase in fetal age, the number of periods of fetal activity tend to decrease, but they increase in length from about 4 seconds, on the average, at the 170th day to an average of about 33 seconds on the 256th day (Kellogg, 1941).

Causes of variations of fetal activity have been studied, and the reports indicate that there are certain factors that are associated with variations in fetal activity. Following maternal activity, the number of fetal movements is smallest during the first 5 minutes, gradually increasing until, after 30 minutes, there are approximately as many movements as after sleep. The explanation given for decrease in fetal activity after maternal exercise is that there is an increase in supply of oxygen available to the fetus at that time (Schmeidler, 1941). Maternal fatigue seems to increase rather than decrease fetal activity (Harris and Harris, 1946). More frequent and more violent fetal movements occur when the mother is severely fatigued (Sontag and Richards, 1938). Fetuses are equally active when the mother is occupied in any activity but eating. The fetus is significantly less active when the mother is eating (Richards et al., 1938). Sudden feelings of fear or anger on the mother's part produce immediate and marked increases in the number and violence of fetal movements (Sontag and Wallace, 1936).

Excessive activity of fetuses may cause them to be considerably underweight for their body length because energy-producing foods are not stored as fat (Sontag, 1940). Infants who had been most active as fetuses have been found to show certain motor performances earlier than the average age. Individuals who had been least active as fetuses, on the other hand, were found to be slow in acquiring motor skills postnatally (Richards and Newberry, 1938).

Fetal activities are of two types, specific *reflexes* and mass activity or *generalized movements* involving most of the body. Most of the basic reflexes, as swallowing, the palmar, plantar, flexion, and Babinski reflexes, are established between the fourth and fifth prenatal months. By birth, all the others are present. Owing to the maturation of the nerves and muscles, generalized activity to external stimuli occurs as early as the third month. This appears first in the head region. Later, generalized movement becomes spontaneous and does not have to be stimulated by external stimuli. Between the fourth and fifth month, this activity becomes more differentiated, thus allowing the head to move independently of the trunk, or the arms and legs to move without movements of the head (Gilbert, 1939; Barker et al., 1943; Gesell, 1949; Carmichael, 1954).

Newberry (1941) recorded three types of generalized movements in fetal activity. These were (1) slow squirming, stretching, pushing, and turning movements; (2) quick kicks, jerks and thrusts of the extremities; and (3) hiccups, or rhythmic series of quick convulsive movements. Kicking activity was found to be the largest component of the total, and hiccuping the smallest. In Fig. 10 are shown the curves for these three types of activity from the fifth month before birth to the month before birth.

Hazards. Like the periods of the ovum and the embryo, the period of the fetus is not without its hazards. There is no guarantee, because development has progressed without any complications up to now, that it will automatically continue to progress without complications of any sort until

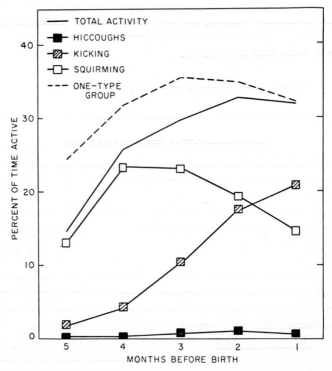

Fig. 10. Developmental trends in three types of fetal activity. (*From H. Newberry, The measurement of fetal activity, J. comp. Psychol., 32, 521–530, 1941. Used by permission.*)

the normal, full-term period has been attained. As was pointed out in the section of this chapter relating to hazards of the period of the embryo (pages 45–47), many of the miscarriages of healthy embryos do not occur until the fourth or the fifth month, in the early part of the period of the fetus. In such conditions, the miscarriage is more likely to be due to a deficient supply of progesterone than to any one other cause (Ratcliff, 1950; Guttmacher, 1955).

Toward the end of the period of the fetus, development is sometimes interrupted and the fetus arrives in the world ahead of schedule. This is known as a *premature birth.* When the fetus reaches the end of the seventh lunar month, he is at the *age of viability*. He has a chance of living if born at that time because of the greater development of the nervous system than during the previous month. Sometimes an infant who has passed only 6 lunar months, or 180 days, in the mother's body is born and survives successfully. But 180 or 181 days is usually considered the average lower limit below which viability cannot be maintained (Carmichael, 1954).

In terms of size, the border line between viability and nonviability is 2 pounds 3 ounces. As Guttmacher (1955) has emphasized, "This does not mean that all infants weighing less are foredoomed to death—an occasional infant weighing a pound and three quarters has been known to survive— nor does it mean that all weighing more than 1,000 gms. are certain to be reared. It simply means that the 1,000 gm. fetus has more than an obscure chance for living." What effects prematurity have, how severe these effects are, and how permanent or temporary they are will be discussed in detail in the section on prematurity in the following chapter (see pages 98–104).

DEVELOPMENTAL IRREGULARITIES

Most individuals develop according to the pattern just described. There are, however, exceptions where a deviation in development, either minor or major, occurs. Since the beginning of history, people have attempted to explain the causes of these deviations, and as a result, a number of old wives' tales have grown up, have been passed down from generation to generation, and are even today accepted by a large portion of the population as the true reasons for the deviations from the normal development.

Traditional beliefs about the causes of developmental irregularities may roughly be divided into two categories: those that emphasize heredity as the cause and those that emphasize the role played by maternal impressions. For many years, such deviations as a cleft palate, clubfoot, or idiocy were explained as hereditary and, in many instances, due to bad heredity from the mother's side of the family. Then there are many tales about the effects of the mother's markings of her baby by her thoughts, emotions, or her cravings. Marking the baby was believed to be the result of "thought transference" or some mystical relationship between mother and fetus.

There are many accounts of terrors due to black cats or burglars or over-indulgence in certain favorite foods told as conclusive proof of the cause of birthmarks or other forms of disfiguration on the infant's body. A person born with a harelip was said to have a mother frightened by a hare when she was pregnant. But as Fasten (1950) has remarked, "If the body of the developing child were strongly influenced by all the cravings, desires, worries, and frights of the pregnant mother, it would bear hardly any resemblance to a normal human being."

Our present-day medical knowledge of the relationship between the body of the fetus and that of the mother furnishes us with evidence to disprove these traditional beliefs about maternal markings. There are two lines of evidence to show that maternal impressions cannot cause abnormalities. The first is that the same types of abnormalities are found in most of the lower animals where, because of the low level of development of the nervous system, maternal impressions do not exist. The second line of evidence comes from knowledge of the fact that there is no direct connection between the mother and the fetus—only an indirect connection through the umbilical cord and placenta, where there are no nerves, only blood vessels—and hence the mental, emotional, or nervous condition of the mother can have no direct effect whatever on the fetus.

Even though science has gone far in clearing up these superstitions about maternal markings, many of them still persist. They influence the thinking of many women, and this often interferes with medical care during pregnancy and at the time of birth. Of equal seriousness, believing that the mother is primarily responsible for any developmental irregularity that may appear in her baby may lead to feelings of guilt on her part and an unhealthy attitude toward the baby which may influence the whole pattern of the baby's future life. This belief may likewise lead to friction with the husband, stemming from his attitude that the wife was wholly responsible for the physical or mental abnormality of their baby.

Studies of Developmental Irregularities. Most information available at the present time regarding developmental irregularities comes from the abnormal development of the fetus itself or from experimentally induced structural changes in lower animals. It is impossible to study the normal human fetus experimentally by changing environments to see what effects these changes have on the development of the fetus. This technique has been used with animal objects and has thrown light on certain problems up to now misunderstood or about which there was no available information. By the use of changed environmental conditions involving the use of cold water, chemicals, insufficient oxygen, or ultraviolet rays, *monsters*, or individuals departing greatly in form or structure from the usual type of the species have been experimentally produced.

Two-headed monsters among tadpoles can, for example, be produced through the use of chemical or mechanical stimuli. By adding magnesium chloride to water, the eyes of minnows can be displaced. Changed environmental conditions change the rate of development, thus altering the balance of growth among the different parts of the organism. In an experiment on mice, Ingalls (1950) induced specific physical defects in the young by a systematic reduction of oxygen at different periods in pregnancy. The nature of the deformity in the offspring was determined by the intensity, duration, and timing of oxygen deficiency, or "anoxia." Deprivation of oxygen on the eighth day of pregnancy, for example, resulted in incompletely formed skulls, while deprivation of oxygen on the twelfth day resulted in a hare-lip. By depriving pregnant rats of vitamin A, deformities in the eyes of the young were produced. Riboflavin-deficient mothers had offspring with skeletal deformities. A vitamin D-deficient diet of the mother also pro-duces skeletal deformities in the offspring, but of a different nature than those resulting from riboflavin deficiency (Warkany, 1944).

The results of such experimental studies as those referred to above have brought out three facts of importance that throw light on the cause or causes of developmental irregularities. These facts are the following.

1. Developmental irregularities may be due to defective genes owing to heredity or to disturbance or disease of one or more of the endocrine glands, or to a defective prenatal environment. As Corner (1944) has pointed out, structural abnormalities may be the result "either of a good egg in a bad environment or a bad egg in a good environment." Many of the develop-mental defects formerly attributed to heredity, such as a cleft palate, harelip, clubfoot, or Mongolian idiocy, are now shown to be the result of prenatal environmental factors, especially *anoxia*, or insufficient oxygen resulting from a disease or injury suffered by the mother during pregnancy (Ingalls, 1950).

In concluding his study of environmental effects, Ingalls (1950) has em-phasized, "Contemporary research has clearly demonstrated that environ-mental factors account for a substantial fraction of all congenital anoma-lies and crippling defects. The important consideration is the prenatal en-vironment. It is a man's environment that is susceptible to manipulation, not his genes and chromosomes." Thus, as time goes on and research throws further light on the specific environmental factors responsible for produc-ing developmental defects, it may be possible to prevent many of them (Rusk, 1955).

2. Developmental irregularities are due to an environmental disturbance which occurs at the same time as the formation of a particular organ. Experimental studies have revealed that the period in the prenatal de-velopment at which the agent is introduced, rather than the agent itself, is the determining influence in producing abnormalities. The rate of develop-ment, when changed by some foreign agent, alters the course of growth in the different parts of the organism, and abnormalities result (Rusk, 1955).

As Stockard (1931) has pointed out, there is a special time in the time-table of prenatal development for the development of each organ. If some-thing interferes to keep an organ from developing at the proper time, it will never be able to express itself fully, since the moment for the rapid outgrowth of some other part will have arrived. The *timing* of the dis-turbance is thus the crucial factor, rather than the disturbance itself. Ingalls' (1950) experiments on rats indicated that particular defects are caused by disturbances in the prenatal environment at particular moments of pregnancy and *at those moments only.*

While the number of studies in which it was possible to determine the times when a particular condition occurred in the prenatal environment that was associated with a particular developmental irregularity have been somewhat limited, they are still numerous enough to emphasize the importance of the timetable of abnormalities. Rickets, which are frequent in prematurely born children, result not from postnatal dietary deficiencies, but from the fact that they did not spend the last months *in utero* when mineralization of the skeleton is most active. In Mongolian idiocy, the parts of the body which are usually deformed are those which are just "budding" around the eighth week of pregnancy. An abnormal condition of the prenatal environment at this time produces these abnormalities in the child's development (Benda, 1949; Ingalls, 1950).

Rubella, or German measles, which in childhood is a mild disease, has been found to produce such defects as cataracts, deafness, anomalies in the structure of the heart, defective teeth, microcephaly, mental deficiency, stillbirths, and neonatal deaths when it occurs *during the first three or four months of pregnancy* (Shock, 1947; Beswick et al., 1949; Hopkins, 1949; Levinson, 1949; Wesselhoeft, 1949; Ingalls, 1950; Schall et al., 1951; Lundström, 1952). Of these defects, deafness is most frequent (Beswick et al., 1949). Rubella occurring at a critical period in the development of the end organs of the ear produces vascular changes. The vessels are the first to suffer, and lack of nutrition is then followed by developmental arrest in the ear, causing deafness (Schall et al., 1951).

Developmental irregularities may occur at any time during the prenatal period, though they are most common during the periods of the ovum and the embryo (Corner, 1944). At these times, any disturbance to the normal course of development is more serious than later on, because, in these early stages, the different parts of the human organism are taking form. Only those which develop during the period of the fetus, as is true of mineralization of the skeleton, will be markedly influenced by unfavorable conditions in the prenatal environment.

3. Unfavorable factors in the prenatal environment do not produce developmental irregularities when they occur before a certain part of the body has started to develop or after it is formed. After the fifth month of pregnancy, rubella was found to have no more effect on the offspring than was true of a control group where the mothers did not suffer from rubella (Lundström, 1952). In the case of Mongolian idiocy, the parts of the body fully formed by the eighth prenatal week and those which have not begun to develop at that time are usually normal (Ingalls, 1950). *Timing,* thus, is the critical factor.

THE DETERMINATION OF SEX

For centuries, two outstanding problems have existed in relation to the determination of sex: the first consists of an attempt to *predict,* early in pregnancy, the sex of the unborn child; and the second, to *control* the sex desired. Because so many superstitious beliefs and practices have grown up as a result of the desire to meet these problems, a brief survey of the most common superstitions will serve to show how important a role they have played in the past.

Predicting Sex. Attempts to predict the sex of the developing fetus have been numerous and, for the most part, ludicrous. A coin tossed over the shoulder of a pregnant woman would, if it came up "heads," foretell the arrival of a boy baby, while "tails" meant a girl. In German folklore there is the superstition that if barley and wheat are soaked in the urine of a pregnant woman and then planted in the ground, the sex of the fetus can be detected by the one that grows first. Should it be barley, the offspring would be a girl, while wheat would forecast the arrival of a boy.

Recently, more scientific techniques have been used to predict sex. The *heartbeat test* maintains that if the fetal heartbeat is 125 or less per minute, the fetus is a boy; 144 or more heartbeats per minute means that the fetus is a girl. Unfortunately this test is not accurate because of the individual differences that occur in the rate of the heartbeat. More recently an attempt has been made to use X ray in the *ossification-of-bones test.* This is based on the knowledge that comparable bones ossify earlier in girls than in boys. But, once again, individual variations from one fetus to another make this test far from accurate.

Based on evidence that the maternal hormone levels change in accordance with the fetal sex, a smear test has been developed to determine the amount of the estrogenic and androgenic hormones present. This, however, has not proved to be too successful (Neiburgs, 1947; Neiburgs and Greenblatt, 1949). The most recent and most widely publicized method of predicting sex is a test of the maternal saliva. This test is based on the assumption that a certain chemical substance in the maternal saliva, the precise nature of which is not yet known, is related to the male sex hormone. The presence of this substance has been found to be associated with the later birth of a boy, while its absence has been related to the birth of a girl. In a preliminary sampling of this test, an accuracy in the predicting of boys was reported in 98.6 per cent of the cases, while in the case of girls, there was accuracy in 95 per cent of the predictions (Rapp and Richardson, 1952, 1952a). To date, this has proved to be the most accurate method of predicting the sex of an unborn child.

Controlling Sex. There have been countless theories about how sex can be controlled in the human offspring. An early superstition was that if a man went to bed on his wedding night wearing his boots, a boy would be conceived. Some theories stress that fertilization just after menstruation is supposed to result in the female offspring. Others claimed that the food eaten by the mother during pregnancy would determine the sex of the child. A girl child, it was believed, could be produced if the mother ate large amounts of sugar. The month of the year when conception occurred was likewise supposed to determine sex (Gilbert, 1939). Then there is the belief that if a pregnant woman drinks certain potions regularly, she can influence her child to be either a boy or a girl. To produce a boy, the potion must be alkaline, while to produce a girl, it must be acid (Fasten, 1950). Recent experimental investigations have disproved all the old theories and have, at last, given accurate scientific data regarding a problem that man has striven for years to solve.

X and Y Chromosomes. Discovery of sex chromosomes has shown that the factors that actually determine sex are internal and that the sex of the fertilized ovum is fixed at the time of fertilization. In every species in which sexual reproduction occurs, one of the sexes has a pair of chromosomes represented by a single member like the other chromosomes and one that is different. In the human being, the unmatched chromosomes appear in the male, while in the female all pairs are matched. Sex is determined by the presence or absence of a pair of unmatched chromosomes, the X and Y chromosomes, in the matured spermatozoon. This is illustrated in Fig. 11, which shows how male and female chromosomes combine to determine the sex of the new offspring.

When the sperm cell divides during the maturation process, half the spermatozoa thus formed contain an X, or matched, chromosome and half an unmatched, or Y, chromosome, the latter differing somewhat in size and shape from the matched chromosomes. There are thus, at the time of maturation of the spermatozoon, 23 pairs of matched chromosomes and an extra pair made up of one X and one Y chromosome. When division occurs, there are, as a result, two kinds of spermatozoa, one with 23 matched, or X, chromosomes and one unmatched, or Y, chromosome. The second type contains 24 matched or X, chromosomes. These two kinds of sperm cells occur in equal numbers. In the case of the female ova, on the other hand, all have an equal number of matched chromosomes.

When the ovum is fertilized by the spermatozoon with the Y chromosome, a male offspring results; when fertilized by a spermatozoon with all X chromosomes, on the other hand, the result will be a female offspring. Whether the ovum will combine with a spermatozoon with a matched or an unmatched chromosome, no one can tell ahead of time, and no one can influence the combination in any way. After the fertilization has occurred, nothing can be done to change the sex of the fertilized cell. Determination of sex is therefore obviously a matter of chance. It is not something that can be controlled or influenced by human endeavor.

Sex Ratio. Statistics show that there is an excess of male births in the ratio of 105 to 106 males for every 100 females. This excess of males is seen also in abortions and premature births (Bernstein, 1948, 1952; Myers, 1949a; McKeown and Lowe, 1951). The chances of being a boy are thus 5 or 6

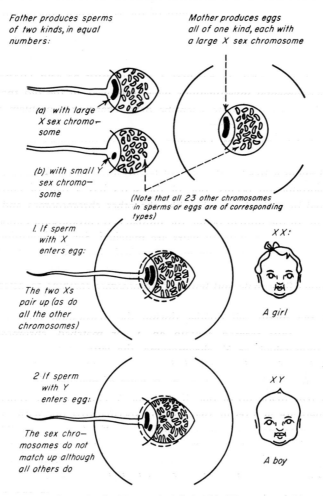

Father produces sperms
of two kinds, in equal
numbers:

Mother produces eggs
all of one kind, each with
a large X sex chromosome

(a) with large
X sex chromo-
some

(b) with small Y
sex chromo-
some

(Note that all 23 other chromosomes
in sperms or eggs are of corresponding
types)

1. If sperm
with X
enters egg:

The two Xs
pair up (as do
all the other
chromosomes)

X X :

A girl

2 If sperm
with Y
enters egg:

The sex chro-
mosomes do not
match up although
all others do

X Y

A boy

Fig. 11. How sex is determined. (*From A. Scheinfeld, Women and Men, Harcourt, Brace, 1943. Used by permission.*)

per cent greater than those of being a girl. What is responsible for the larger percentage of boys than girls is still unknown. It has been explained in many ways, the most credible explanation being based on the belief that because the 23 X and 1 Y chromosome spermatozoon (the one that produces a male offspring) is slightly lighter and hence swifter in movement than the 24 X chromosome spermatozoon (the type that produces female offspring), it is likely to reach the ovum sooner. As a result, the chances of producing a male offspring are slightly greater than the chances of producing a female one. As Scheinfeld (1950) has pointed out, "a canny Nature starts the sexes off with a surplus of males to partly provide for the greater drain upon their number later."

According to tradition, more boys are born in wartime than the normal 105 or 106 boys for every 100 girls. Data from the United States, Great Britain, Canada, Australia, and New Zealand, however, showed that the sex ratio did not appreciably increase during the war years as compared with the years immediately preceding and following the war. Thus there was no evidence that war significantly increases the number of boy babies (Myers, 1949a; Scheinfeld, 1950). There is also a traditional belief that there is a relationship between age of parents and sex of offspring, with young fathers producing more male offspring than older fathers. Once again, there is no evidence from scientific studies that such is correct. Evidence seems to point to the fact that there is no relationship whatever between the sex of the offspring and the age of either the mother or of the father (Bernstein, 1953).

Another tradition is that "boys run in some families" just as other families have only girls. As Spencer (1955) has pointed out, "Of course the sex distribution among the children of a given family will be subject to the usual chance fluctuations observed when small samples are used. Even in large families, a certain small proportion of these will be expected to be all of one sex purely by chance." Studies of sex distribution in families have shown that, in two-child families, there was an excess of unisexual sibship, and this held true also for three-child families. This study, based on a sample of 6,000 cases, may have been subject to a sampling error and thus does not mean that families can have only children of one sex (Myers, 1949; Bernstein, 1952). In the upper socioeconomic groups, a study of American and German families has revealed that since 1928, in both small and large families, there is a sex ratio of 120 to 125 males for every 100 females (Bernstein, 1948; Scheinfeld, 1950).

Sex Preferences. As all indications point to the fact that the sex of any child is purely a matter of chance, over which no one has any control, it would seem logical for parents to have no preference for one sex or the other in their children. Instead, they should be happy if the child is normal and healthy, regardless of its sex. However, such is not the case in many families. Studies of sex preferences for offspring have revealed that the traditional preference for male offspring still persists.

When expectant parents were asked if they wanted a girl or a boy, it was found that the answer depended almost entirely on the sex of the older child or children in the family. If all or most of the children were of one sex, then 90 per cent of the parents questioned said they hoped the new baby would be of the opposite sex (Dahlberg, 1948). In another study, college students were questioned about the preferred sex of their future children. Their answers showed that the male child was strongly preferred. If there were only one child in the family, 92 per cent of the men and 66 per cent of the women students said they would prefer the child to be a boy. Thirty-four per cent of both the men and the women said that if the children in the family were predominantly of one sex they preferred them to be male, as contrasted with 6 per cent who preferred predominantly female children. Over half of the group, 55 per cent, wanted the family to be composed of one-half male and one-half female children (Dinitz et al., 1954). How seriously preferences for children of a given sex can affect parental attitudes and, in turn, parent-child relationships will be discussed in the section of the chapter on Parent-Child Relationships dealing with parental preferences.

MULTIPLE BIRTHS

Multiple births, or the birth of two or more offspring within a few days of one another, are the result of an asymmetrical cell division or of several simultaneous fertilizations. When the fertilized ovum divides, early in the prenatal period, cells may split away from each other, and each group thus formed grows independently of the others. Monovular twinning may result from hormonal disturbances, such as the slow secretion of folliculin, which would prevent ovulation. Or it may be due to an inherent tendency of the egg to divide. If this tendency manifests itself before the reduction division, then two separate eggs are formed (Dahlberg, 1952).

The larger the number of offspring born at one time, the rarer is the occurrence. It has been estimated that twins occur once in every 87 births, triplets in every 7,000, quadruplets in every 550,000, quintuplets in every 57 million births (Fasten, 1946). Only 47 cases of quintuplets have ever been recorded and 6 of sextuplets (Newman, 1940). Multiple births occur more frequently among Negroes than among whites, and among whites more often than among members of the yellow race (Newman, 1940). Maternal age has been found to have no effect on multiple births coming from the division of one egg. Up to the age of thirty-eight years, however, there is a definite liability to two-egg twinning, followed by a rapid decline after that age. For a mother who has produced multiple births, however, there is ten times greater probability of later multiple maternity than for a woman who has not had twins or other forms of multiple births (Stocks, 1952). There is no evidence that twins "run in families," nor is there any evidence of weather or seasonal effects (Scheinfeld, 1950).

There are many superstitious beliefs about multiple births among both civilized and primitive peoples. To some primitive peoples, twins are regarded as a good omen and the twins are given special honors and privileges by the other members of the tribe. Among other primitive peoples, the reverse is true. In some cases, multiple births are regarded as such bad omens that the babies are destroyed at birth. Civilized peoples, likewise, have different attitudes toward multiple births. Some regard them as "animallike," while others look upon them as having special hereditary endowments. Still others consider them as "scientific curiosities."

Twins. It was formerly believed that all twins (two individuals born at the same time) were of the same type. Scientific studies have revealed that there are two distinctly different types of twins. The first type, the *identical,* or uniovular, twins, come from a single ovum fertilized by a single sperm; the second type, the *nonidentical,* biovular, or fraternal twins, are the product of two ova fertilized simultaneously. Nonidentical twins occur more frequently than identical twins, though there are no statistics available to show exactly what the difference in frequency is. It is estimated that approximately one-fourth of all twins are of the one-egg type. Figure 12 illustrates the two types of twins.

Identical Twins. When one ovum is fertilized by one spermatozoon, it occasionally happens that at the time of the first division of the cell, when the ovum divides to form two, these new cells separate instead of remaining together. Why this division takes place, no one knows. The result is that each part develops into a complete individual. Twins formed thus are called "identical" because they have exactly the same assortment of genes. For that reason, they resemble one another very closely in all their hereditary traits. They have the closest degree of kinship possible for two distinctly separated individuals. They are always of the same sex; they have one placenta and are enclosed in one chorion coat. When the division of the fertilized ovum is incomplete, the result is a pair of *Siamese twins.* They are always identical in sex and, like other identical twins, will be closely alike in physical and mental traits. Whether or not they will remain joined together throughout their lives or can be separated depends upon where the joining of their bodies occurs.

Nonidentical Twins. In the human female, only one ovum normally matures at a time, and thus only one child develops. Occasionally, two or more ova may develop simultaneously and be fertilized at the same time. The individuals who develop from these two ova are known as *fraternal, biovular,* or *nonidentical* twins. The name "nonidentical" suggests lack of similarity in the physical and mental make-up of the twins. The explanation of this fact is that, when the chromosomes of the two ova divide, the grouping is not likely to be the same for both. One ovum may receive a preponderance of chromosomes from the maternal grandfather, and the other from the maternal grandmother. In addition to that, both ova are fertilized by individual spermatozoa, each with its own assortment of chromosomes. The offspring, as a result, are certain to be unlike in many traits, as is true of

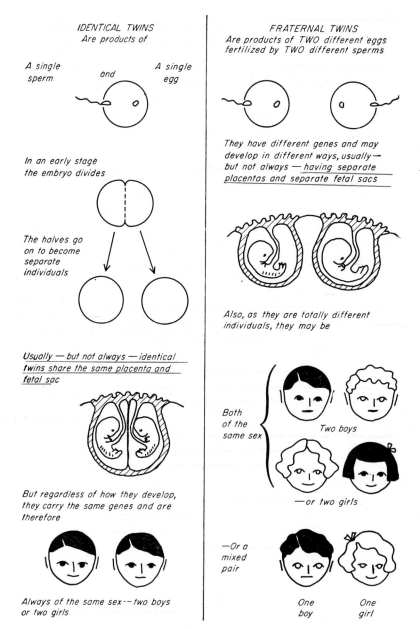

IDENTICAL TWINS
Are products of

A single
sperm

and

A single
egg

In an early stage
the embryo divides

The halves go
on to become
separate
individuals

Usually — but not always — identical twins share the same placenta and fetal sac

But regardless of how they develop, they carry the same genes and are therefore

Always of the same sex — two boys
or two girls

FRATERNAL TWINS
Are products of TWO different eggs
fertilized by TWO different sperms

They have different genes and may develop in different ways, usually — but not always — *having separate placentas and separate fetal sacs*

Also, as they are totally different individuals, they may be

Both
of the
same sex

Two boys

— or two girls

— Or a
mixed
pair

One
boy

One
girl

Fig. 12. Two types of twins. (*From A. Scheinfeld, The new you and heredity, Lippincott, 1950. Used by permission.*)

ordinary brothers and sisters. Nonidentical twins may be of the same or of opposite sexes. During the prenatal period, two distinct placentas are formed, and each ovum thus has its own prenatal environment. Nonidentical twins are not really twins, but rather are simultaneous pregnancies.

Characteristics of Twins. There have been many studies made of twins, both identical and nonidentical, to determine how similar they are in physical and mental make-up, how they differ from ordinary siblings, and how long their similarities persist, even when marked changes occur in their environments as they grow older. In general, these studies have revealed that twins are more likely to miscarry, to be born ahead of schedule, to suffer from birth injuries, or to be stillborn than are singletons (Newman, 1940; Gesell, 1954; Jones, 1954). Those who do survive are, on the average, slightly inferior, both physically and mentally, to singletons (Newman, 1940; Jones, 1954).

In *physical characteristics,* identical twins are much more alike than are nonidentical twins, who often show no greater resemblance to one another than do ordinary siblings (Newman et al., 1937; Newman, 1940; Gesell and Thompson, 1941; Jones, 1954). Even in senescence, and in spite of marked differences in environment over a period of years, this physical similarity in identical twins persists, as shown in similarity in graying and thinning of the hair, senile wrinkle formation, and teeth deficiencies (Kallman and Sander, 1949). *Mental similarities,* as revealed by intelligence tests and educational achievement, are striking in identical twins as compared with nonidentical twins. On the whole, twins are found to be slightly below the average level of siblings in intelligence-test scores (Hilgard, 1933; Newman et al., 1937; Carter, 1940; Newman, 1940; Gesell and Thompson, 1941; Woodworth, 1941; Troup and Lester 1942; Gesell, 1954; Jones, 1954). Mental similarities in identical twins persist beyond the age of sixty years (Kallman and Sander, 1949).

In *language ability,* twins are markedly retarded in all aspects of language ability as compared with singletons. This retardation is not due so much to intellectual differences between twins and singletons as to the fact that twins develop a language of their own consisting of deformed words which are often even unintelligible to members of their own families (McCarthy, 1930, 1954; Day, 1932; Davis, 1937b; Carter, 1940; Gesell and Thompson, 1941; Lézine, 1951). Day (1932) has explained language retardation in twins thus: "One surely could not learn as much or as rapidly from companionship with an individual so nearly on his own plane as from one in advance. . . . Satisfactions from this companionship may be adequate to the twin . . . whereas the single child . . . may be motivated to gain his satisfactions from a wider field."

How twinship affects the *social development* of the individual has been subjected to extensive study. Because identical twins spend more time together, have more interests in common, and are more self-sufficient so far as outside companionship is concerned than are nonidentical twins or regular siblings, it is not surprising that they have been found to enjoy similar reputations among their peers and to show a marked similarity in social competence as measured by a scale of social maturity (Troup and Lester, 1942). Even during the preschool years, twins are competitive for attention, and in their achievements they copy one another and show similar feelings toward others because of their dependency on one another (Burlingham, 1949, 1952).

As twins grow older, sibling rivalry and feelings of competition and inferiority become more pronounced. To the twin, his twin represents a rival not found to such a marked degree in ordinary sibling relationships. In spite of the fact that the twin is also an ally, there is a strong feeling on the part of many twins that they lack independence and that they are constantly being compared with their twins in all their achievements. If they do not measure up successfully, they feel frustrated (Kent, 1949). Being dressed alike because it is "cute" helps twins to retain their dependence on each other and interferes with their establishing social independence (Stains, 1951). In a study of pairs of identical twins sixty years of age and older, it was found that their marital history differed markedly from those of nonidentical twins and of ordinary siblings. Many more of the identical twins were celibate than were the nonidentical twins, and fewer of them had children. The explanation given was marital disharmony, which is particularly common among identical twins, owing to the closeness of the twin relationship (Kallman and Sander, 1949).

The closeness of twins and their dependence upon one another affects their *personality development*. It is difficult for twins, especially identical twins, to distinguish between themselves and their twins (Lézine, 1951). This does not help them to develop individual personalities (Stains, 1951). The rivalries and antagonisms arising from frustrations (Kent, 1949) are likely to leave their mark on the patterns of their personalities. The dominant twin in a twin relationship will develop a personality pattern that differs from that of the dominated twin. Only in personality traits are identical twins not much more alike than are nonidentical twins (Newman et al., 1937; Carter, 1940; Newman, 1940; Gesell and Thompson, 1941; Gesell, 1954; Jones, 1954). However, in spite of different social and marital histories, senile twins were found to develop similar senile psychoses (Kallman and Sander, 1949). The *life span* of identical twins has been found to differ by an average of 36.9 months as compared with a difference of 78.3 months for nonidentical twins (Kallman and Sander, 1949).

Triplets. Scientific studies of triplets are few in number. However, there is some information of value relating to the abilities of triplets, especially as they compare with twins and singletons. Triplets may be of three types:

identical, in that all three have come from the same fertilized ovum; two identical and one sibling; or three siblings, each having come from a separate fertilized ovum (Anderson and Scheidemann, 1933). Because triplets are less frequent than twins, most of the studies have been limited to a few sets of triplets who have been studied extensively to determine what are their physical and mental characteristics. Only in the case of Howard's studies (1934, 1946, 1946a, 1947) of triplets, where 69 sets ranging in age from two to fifteen years were studied, have the investigations used more than 7 sets.

In *physical development,* there is a lag in tempo of development as compared with twins and singletons. The mean age of erupting the first tooth, for example, is a month later than has been reported for twins. In *developmental traits,* such as sitting alone, standing alone, and walking, there is also a developmental lag. Triplets are slower in saying their first words and in forming sentences than are twins and singletons. *Mental development,* as measured by intelligence tests, shows a developmental lag likewise. However, among older triplets, this lag is less pronounced than among younger triplets, suggesting that the developmental lag may affect only the early development. Tests of *emotional* and *personality* development indicated that triplets behaved socially and temperamentally like single-born children of the same age and had interests and attitudes normal for their sex (Sanders, 1932; Anderson and Scheidemann, 1933; Lund, 1933; Howard, 1934, 1946, 1946a, 1947; McCarthy, 1954).

Quintuplets. Numerous reports of the famous Dionne quintuplets have appeared from time to time since their birth. One of the most authoritative of these is that of Blatz (1938). According to Blatz, the quintuplets did not begin to walk until they were about fifteen months old. They used gesture language, as is true of twins, and did not catch up to single children until about the fifth year. At the age of three years, they had a vocabulary of 110 words, which is retarded for that age. Annette, who was the most advanced of the five in language, began to use words at the nineteenth month, while all the others were using a few words by the time they were twenty-one months old (Blatz et al., 1937). McCarthy (1954) maintains that it is difficult to explain their language retardation entirely in terms of the social situation since they had much individual attention from adults during this time. Intelligence tests were given only until the quintuplets were about 3½ years old. These tests showed them to be backward as compared with norms for single children.

FACTORS INFLUENCING PRENATAL DEVELOPMENT

There are many traditional beliefs about the mother's activities and about the different conditions within her body which are believed to influence either mildly or seriously the child developing within her body. To date, there has been little scientific research along these lines. While it is generally believed by scientists that variations in the diet, health, and glandular secretions of the mother during pregnancy, which influence the chemical condition of her blood, have a marked effect on the developing fetus, present information regarding these influences is slight. It is difficult and, at times, impossible, to tell whether an effect apparently produced by one factor actually comes from that factor or from some other factor.

There is, however, evidence to suggest that the fetal environment is very important. This includes hormones, drugs, toxins, food, sounds, pressures, emotional states and many other factors (Sontag, 1941). Any disturbance in the fetal environment may cause a modification of the bodily functions and overt behavior patterns both before birth and during the period immediately following birth (Sontag, 1946). How seriously or how permanently these factors will influence fetal development will depend not so much on the factors themselves as on when they occur (see pages 55–56). The following factors have been found, to date, to have the most influence.

1. Food. As the growth of the fetus is most rapid during the latter part of pregnancy, the mother's food is most important at that time and should be selected to fill the requirements of the fetus. The fetus needs proteins for tissue building and repair, fats to form tissue fats, and fuel for the body, as well as a surplus to store in body fat as a reserve, and carbohydrates for strength and energy. Mild amounts of qualitative or quantitative hunger are not serious, but severe amounts are (Smith, 1947; Sontag and Wines, 1947; Burke et al., 1943, 1949).

When the mother is seriously malnourished or undernourished, so that the fetus does not receive from the maternal blood stream the needed elements of nourishment, prenatal growth is hindered. Malnutrition, resulting in vitamin deficiency, is more serious than insufficient food. The effect is either some physical abnormality such as rickets, nervous instability, general physical weakness, or mental deficiency of a more or less pronounced sort (Sontag, 1941). Vitamin deficiency in the diets of expectant mothers, especially a deficiency of B-complex, has been found to affect the intelligence of the child in the early years of life. Whether this effect will eventually be compensated for has not yet been determined (*New York Times*, 1955a).

Serious malnutrition may result from poverty or from war conditions. When the diets of pregnant women during the last 3 to 6 months of pregnancy were rated as poor, fair, or excellent, it was found that those whose diets had been above average had babies whose physical condition was predominantly excellent or good. By contrast, mothers whose diets had been rated as poor had only 5 per cent of the babies in good or excellent condition, while the others were in poor condition, were stillborn, or died in early infancy (Eblis et al., 1941; Burke, 1949). The weight and length of the fetuses decrease as maternal diet becomes poorer (Burke et al., 1949).

There is no question about the fact that the "ravages of faulty maternal nutrition fall with tragic emphasis on the mothers in poor homes and their children" (People's League of Health Report, 1942).

The severe hunger women of all economic groups suffer from during war periods has been found to take its toll on their unborn children. During the siege of Leningrad by the Germans from 1941 to 1943, the stillborn rate doubled and the rate of premature births was abnormally high. Generally lowered vitality and frequent congenital softening of the skull bones were also common (Antonov, 1947). Much the same effects were reported during the period of German occupation of Holland in the winter of 1944 to 1945. When the maternal food supply was increased, birth weight and length returned to their previous normal levels and there was a decrease in the numbers of premature births and stillbirths (Smith, 1947).

2. **Maternal Health.** Any diseased condition of the mother that affects her general metabolism will influence to a certain extent the development of the fetus. The diseases believed to be the most serious are: (a) *Syphilis,* which is often called "the great slayer of the unborn." This frequently causes miscarriages, still births, congenital mental deficiency, blindness, or deafness. Toxins of syphilis in the blood of either parent may injure parts of the germ cells before fertilization, or the fetus may become infected before or at the time of birth. The result is likely to be a physically or mentally defective child. (b) *Gonorrhea,* which is frequently called "the great sterilizer," because it is a very potent cause of sterility in both men and women. This disease may infect the baby's eyes when it passes through the birth canal and thus cause "congenital blindness." Because of this, most states have laws requiring the use of some prophylactic for all babies, usually one drop of 1 per cent solution of silver nitrate in the eyes of the newborn. (c) *Endocrine disorders,* which are thought to have pronounced influence on the development of the fetus, but medical information of a reliable sort is still very scanty. When there is a thyroid deficiency, the younger the fetus the more pronounced the symptoms of abnormal development. Bones and cartilage, except the skull, fail to develop; the abdomen protrudes and becomes large and flabby, the skin is rough and coarse; the hair is shaggy; and the intellectual development is subnormal. A pronounced condition of thyroid deficiency is known as "cretinism." (d) Prolonged or *wasting* diseases of the mother, such as tuberculosis and diabetes, have effects on the fetus similar to those of malnutrition. (e) *Toxins,* or poisons in the mother's blood, coming from lead or phosphorus from certain occupations, such as paint and pottery manufacturing, and bacteria from certain diseases are known to influence detrimentally the developing fetus. Lead poisoning causes abortions, deaf-mutes, and other deformities. The heavy use of quinine during the malaria season by mothers brings an increase in the number of cases of congenital deafness due to the

effects of quinine on the fetal inner ear (Sontag, 1941). (*f*) *Rubella*, or German measles, as was pointed out on page 56, has been found to bring about serious physical and mental malformations when it occurs during the first four months of pregnancy, but to have no effects when experienced later in the pregnancy period. (*g*) Recently the Rh blood factor has been found to result in abortions, stillbirths, or low-grade intelligence (Shock, 1947; Potter, 1948, 1955; Gerver and Day, 1950). (*h*) *X ray and radium*, when used in too small amounts to end the growth of an animal fetus, nevertheless bring about changes in the offspring and affect the succeeding generation. The use of X ray or radium on the maternal pelvis during the childbearing period may produce, according to Murphy et al. (1942), no effect on ovulation, temporary sterility, or permanent sterility. No harmful effects to the health or development of the children subsequently born occur in cases of temporary sterility. When irradiation is used during pregnancy, the effect depends partly on the strength of the radium or the X-ray exposure and partly on the age of the fetus. When exposures are used early in pregnancy for therapeutic purposes, they are generally of greater strength. This is likely to have severe effects on the fetus, the most common of which is microcephaly, or an abnormally small head and brain, with accompanying mental deficiency. If used at the end of pregnancy for diagnostic or measurement purposes, the exposures are of short duration and have no effect on the fetus. A preliminary report of the effects of exposure to the atomic bomb have indicated that stillbirths, malformations, and decrease in birth weight were common (Neel, 1953).

3. Alcohol. Because of the present social tendency for women to drink, there are many theories but little scientific evidence regarding the effect of alcohol on the offspring. Even if it is not used by the mother, the male germ cell may have been weakened by alcohol before fertilization occurs. Owing to the fact that the fetus obtains nourishment from the maternal blood stream, it is obvious that the constant introduction into the blood stream of chemical substances which impose a burden of accommodation on the physiological mechanism of the mother must, in one way or another, impose a burden on the fetus. When the limits of accommodation are exceeded, there are certain "danger signals," such as nervousness, wakefulness, or irregular heart action, which show that as the mother is being affected detrimentally, the fetus is likewise affected. Even a moderate intake of alcohol is apparent in minimal quantities in the milk secretion of the mother.

Pearl (1930) maintains that "alcohol acts as a definite but not too drastic selective agent upon both germ cells and developing embryos, eliminating the weak and leaving the strong." Pearl quotes an investigation by Polisch in which he says that "in a group of very heavy, steady drinkers there was not the slightest evidence of demonstrable germinal injury of the offspring." According to Jennings (1930), "The genes show a very great resistance to alcohol. Either it does not alter them at all, or it kills them; in either case no modified descendants result."

4. Tobacco. Tobacco contains nicotine, a powerful narcotic poison. When inhaled, its effects are more injurious than in ordinary smoking because of the disturbance of blood pressure and heart action. General resistance to infections is lowered, especially in the mouth and throat. Sontag and Richards (1938) reported that, during the last 6 months of pregnancy, cigarette smoking by the mother was followed by an increase in fetal heart rate. The maximum effect appeared from 8 to 12 minutes after the cigarette was begun. In animals, such as the cow and the cat, nicotine has been found to lessen milk secretion. There is no definite scientific evidence at this time to show that this is true for the human mother.

5. Emotional Experiences of Mother. There are many traditions relating to the effect of the mother's emotional experiences on the growth of the fetus. Some of them go so far as to hold that, if the prenatal period is predominantly a happy one for the mother, the disposition of the baby will be made cheerful and happy. A prenatal period, on the other hand, marked by emotional disturbances, fears, and worries will, it is believed, result in a morbid, sad, introverted personality for the baby. If the emotional experiences of the mother influence the developing fetus in any way, it is through the glandular changes which take place in her body during the prenatal period. These "blood-borne" anxieties affect the fetus and carry into the period of the newborn (Sontag, 1946).

Women who are not happy about their pregnancy usually experience more nausea and vomiting than those who are happy (Roberston, 1940; Squier and Dunbar, 1946; Wasman, 1947; Wallin and Riley, 1950). The mother who resents the coming of her baby, either because it will interfere with the pattern of her life or because of her economic situation, experiences continued emotional tension which affects the activity of the fetus and the later adjustment of the infant to its postnatal environment (Wallin and Riley, 1950).

6. Age of Parents. Whether the age of the parents has any influence on the development of the fetus has never been proved scientifically. Studies relating to the age of the parents and the intelligence of the child show that older parents have more intelligent children than have younger parents. This, however, may be due to the social level of the parent and not to age. In the higher social classes, where the average intelligence quotient is highest among the children, there is a tendency to marry later because of the long period of training necessary to prepare both men and women for their life occupations (Terman, 1925; Steckel, 1931). There is a tendency for parents of approximately the same age to have more intelligent children than there is for those who are widely different in age (Steckel, 1931).

Chapter 3

THE NEWBORN INFANT

After approximately 10 lunar months in the protection of his sheltered prenatal environment, the newly developed individual is now equipped to adjust to an environment outside the mother's body. In preparation for this change of environment, the structures in the lower part of the mother's body become soft and relaxed, ready to dilate and permit the passage of the fetus to the outside world. As a signal of this state of readiness, there are rhythmic contractions of the uterus which are defined by the mother as abdominal cramps. They come infrequently and irregularly at first, beginning in the back and spreading to the abdominal area of the mother's body. If they are "false pains," they soon subside. When, however, they are a true signal of the beginning of birth, they increase in frequency, intensity, and duration with the passage of time.

The second signal of the approaching birth is the escape of fluid from the vagina. This is the amniotic fluid which has come from the rupturing of the amniotic sac in which the infant has been housed throughout the prenatal period. The escape of the amniotic fluid is a slow dripping at first, followed by a flow as the contractions of the uterine wall rupture the sac. This is generally followed by the appearance of a thick, mucous, bloody discharge from the vagina, known as the "show." By this time, the muscular contractions are more regular, more frequent, and more severe.

Periods of Labor. The process of giving birth, or "labor," is usually divided into three periods. In the *first period,* preparation is made for the emergence of the fetus from the mother's body. At this time, the contractions of the uterine wall force the lowermost part of the uterus, the *cervix,* to dilate. This takes from 12 to 16 hours, the length of time varying markedly from individual to individual, though it is usually longer for first-born than for later-born children. When the cervix is completely dilated, the uterine contractions become stronger and the fetus is pushed downward through the cervix and vagina and expelled from the birth canal. The period of expulsion is the *second stage* of labor and lasts from 1 to 3 hours for first-born as compared with 15 to 30 minutes for later-born children.

Birth is not complete until the infant has been detached from the umbilical cord. The *third,* and *final, stage* of labor is when the placenta, the remnants of the ruptured amniotic sac, and the umbilical cord are separated from the wall of the uterus and expelled from the body as

71

"afterbirth." This usually takes from 5 to 30 minutes. The umbilical cord is compressed with two clamps and then cut between the clamps. The end attached to the infant's abdominal wall is then compressed with a piece of tape or metal clip to avoid bleeding from the blood vessels in the cord which have been cut. The entire time needed for the total birth process ranges from an average of 15 hours for later-born children to over a day for first-born. However, there are marked variations in these times (Greenhill, 1955; Potter, 1955). The time when the physical discomforts are most acute will be in the latter part of stage 1 and throughout stage 2 of the birth process.

The normal position of the body of the fetus during birth is head downward. In 96 per cent of all births, the *vertex presentation* occurs in which the head of the fetus is in the mother's pelvic cavity and its buttocks are up near the mother's ribs. The most favorable position is head downward, with the face pointed downward toward the mother's back and with the top of the fetal head directed upward toward the mother's abdomen. When the fetal face is pointed upward instead of toward the mother's back, there may be complications in birth. Normally, the infant's head emerges from the mother's body first, followed by the emergence of first one shoulder and then the other as the body slowly rotates in the birth canal. This is followed by the emergence of first one arm and then the other, then the trunk, and finally the legs.

When versus How Born. There are many traditional beliefs about the most favorable times to be born. These are expressed in the old rhyme which states that "Monday's child is fair of face, Tuesday's child is full of grace," etc. There are also beliefs about the most favorable seasons of the year in which to be born. Whether or not the months of birth have any influence on the abilities of the individual has been the subject of many scientific investigations as well as of speculation. Studies of eminent men have revealed that more of them were conceived during the first half of the year than those conceived during the last half of the year (Peterson, 1936). In another study, it has been reported that the largest number of eminent men are born in October, with the lowest number in the spring months (Pintner and Forlano, 1934).

No personality differences have been found that are correlated with season of year in which the individual is born. However, those who are born in the spring, summer, or autumn months have been reported to be decidedly more sociable than those who are born in the winter months (Pile, 1951; Middleton and Sumner, 1953). A number of studies have been made to see if there was any correlation between IQ scores or school achievement and the month or season of birth. While most of these indicate that bright individuals are born more often in the summer and fall months than in the winter or spring months, others have found the reverse to be true.

The differences found, however, have been too small in most cases to be statistically reliable (Blonsky, 1929; Pintner, 1931; Pintner and Forlano, 1934, 1939, 1943; Peterson, 1936; Pintner and Maller, 1937; Fialkin and Beckman, 1938; Huntington, 1938; Gordon and Novack, 1950). The general conclusion about the studies reported to date could be the same as the conclusion Gordon and Novack (1950) drew from their study, which was, "There is nothing in the data reported above that denies a slight I.Q. ad-

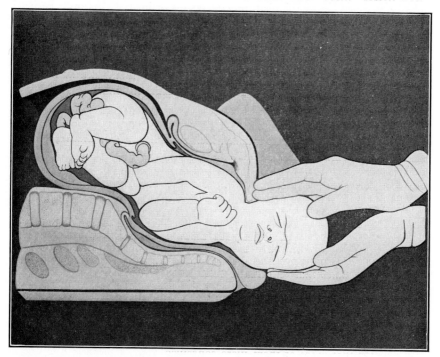

In normal childbirth, the baby emerges from the mother's body headfirst. (*From Child Development, a McGraw-Hill Text-Film.*)

vantage for cold-weather conceptions; on the other hand, there is nothing that would warrant long vacations for the country's obstetricians for the first half of each year." Seasonal variations in the relationship of intelligence to month of birth may come mainly from the influence of the health factor (Pintner and Forlano, 1933; Pintner and Maller, 1937).

Studies of *type of birth,* on the other hand have indicated that *how* the individual is born is important. As Pratt (1954) has emphasized, "The effects of birth on the infant may be inconsequential and transitory or they may greatly affect the course of subsequent development." In general, there are three types of birth. The first is the *natural,* or spontaneous, type in which the position of the fetus in the mother's uterus and the size of the fetus in relation to the size of the mother's reproductive organs make it possible for the fetus to emerge into the world in the normal, head-first position.

Should the size of the fetus be too large for the mother's organs, or should the position of the fetus be such that a *breech birth* would occur (a birth in which the infant's buttocks appear first, followed by the legs and finally the head), or should the position of the fetus be crosswise in the mother's uterus, *transverse presentation,* then either the position of the fetus must be changed before the birth process begins or instruments must be used to aid the delivery. By the use of the X ray several weeks before the anticipated birth, doctors today can usually determine if there will be any difficulties in delivery which will necessitate the use of instruments, and if so, they deliver the fetus surgically by *Caesarean section,* in which the fetus emerges into the world through a slit in the maternal abdominal wall instead of through the birth canal.

While birth in any of the types of delivery just described may be dangerous, there are more hazards associated with instrument births or Caesarean sections than with normal births. In a breech birth, for example, there is always the possibility that the fetus will suffocate before its head emerges. A transverse presentation inevitably requires the use of instruments, which, if applied to the head of the fetus, may result in injury to the brain tissue, which in turn may result in poor motor coordination, paralysis, or mental deficiency. The fetus delivered by Caesarean section has less chance of being injured in birth than has the fetus delivered by instruments, but he frequently has difficulty in establishing respiration.

Birth Effects. Studies of the effects of different types of birth have revealed that even the natural, spontaneous form of birth is not without its hazards. Difficulties may start even before the birth process begins with the premature separation of the placenta or abnormalities in circulation which interfere with the fetal supply of nutrition. This may be especially serious if the brain does not receive an adequate supply of oxygen and other nutritional substances. During the birth process, *anoxia,* or interruption of the oxygen supply of the brain, compression of the brain as the fetal head passes down the birth canal, and hemorrhages in and around the brain may occur (Benda, 1954). Pressures on the bones may cause the fracture of a bone, there may be temporary or permanent damage to some of the nerve centers or to the sense organs, especially the eyes and ears (Pratt, 1954). To determine whether the rigors of the ordinary birth process produce any evidence of brain damage or temporary malfunctioning as revealed by electroencephalograms, records were made of the brain waves of newborn infants. These revealed a minimum of disturbance, suggesting only temporary brain damage (Ellingson and Lindsley, 1949).

Difficult births, many of which necessitate the use of instruments to aid delivery, have been reported to produce more damage and more severe damage than natural, spontaneous births. The damage may not be apparent until months or even years after the birth, and it may be temporary or permanent (Benda, 1943; Usdin and Weil, 1952). Anoxia, brain damage, and damage to the other parts of the nervous system, as well as damage to the sense organs and fractures of the bones, are more common in difficult births where instruments must be used than in normal births. Motor disabilities, cerebral palsy, and low-grade intelligence are frequently reported as aftermaths of difficult births (Doll et al., 1932; Benda et al., 1951; Benda, 1954; Pratt, 1954).

Studies of older children and adolescents who have been born with the aid of instruments have revealed that they have more unfavorable personality characteristics than those who have been born spontaneously. General hyperactivity, restlessness, irritability, distractability, anxiety, speech defects, especially in the form of stuttering, and poor concentration have been reported as more common among those born with the aid of instruments than among those born spontaneously (Wile and Davis, 1941; Despert, 1946; Boland, 1951).

Caesarean babies, by contrast, have been reported to be the quietest, to cry less, and to make better adjustments to their postnatal environments than either the spontaneously born or the instrument-delivered babies (Fries, 1941; Ruja, 1948). They do, however, experience more difficulty in establishing respiration, and this may, in turn, affect their brains. Studies of Caesarean babies have been too few to date to know just what effects this type of birth has on their later development.

In conclusion then, it is apparent that *when* the individual is born is of slight importance. On the other hand, *how* he is born is of major importance. Not only does the actual process of birth affect him temporarily or permanently, to a slight or to a major degree, but the type of birth affects the attitudes of his parents toward him. A baby who emerges into the world with a minimum of discomfort to the mother will arouse emotional reactions on the part of both parents of a very different sort than those experienced by parents when the birth of their baby has been accompanied by prolonged and difficult labor, especially when this labor has resulted in some form of damage to the baby. How seriously parental attitudes resulting from the type of birth can affect the whole pattern of the individual's life will be discussed in the section of this chapter that deals with premature births.

PERIOD OF THE NEWBORN

According to medical standards, the period of the newborn extends from birth to the end of the second week, or until the navel is healed. Infancy is generally subdivided into two periods, the *period of the partunate* and the *period of the neonate*. The *period of the partunate* consists of the first fifteen to thirty minutes of life, including the time during and immediately after parturition or birth. It covers the time when the infant ceases to be a parasite, with the cutting of the umbilical cord, and becomes for the first time a separate, distinct, and independent individual. The *period of the neonate* covers the remainder of the infancy period and is characterized by the making of adjustments essential to a life free from the protections of the intrauterine environment. (The term "neonate" is derived from the Greek word *neos,* meaning "new," and the Latin verb *nascor,* meaning "to be born.")

Before making a survey of the outstanding characteristics of the newborn, it must be understood that in different infants the state of development at birth differs greatly. The greatest differences are to be found in abnormal cases and premature births. At birth, many infants show capacities which in others do not develop for weeks or months. For that reason, one is justified in assuming that entrance into the world does not signify the same starting point of development for all human beings. It is only logical to suppose that, as the premature infant is smaller than the mature or postmature one, his mental development is also below the average. The description of the newborn, given in this chapter, will therefore refer only to the normal, 10-lunar-month infant.

Period of Adjustment. Throughout the entire span of life, the individual is required to make adjustments to new environmental conditions and to new conditions which take place in his body. At no time, however, are the adjustments as pronounced or must they be made as suddenly as at the time of birth when there is a change from an intrauterine to an extrauterine environment and from the state of being a parasite to being an independent individual. While these adjustments are being made, the newborn infant usually loses weight and shows, by his behavior as well as his appearance, that he has lost ground since he emerged into the world. Usually this condition lasts approximately a week, after which he begins to regain the lost weight as he becomes adjusted to his new environment. As a rule, it takes about a week to regain the weight lost in the week following birth. The period of the newborn is thus a *plateau stage* in development, because no marked development occurs until the weight lost after birth has been regained.

The four most important adjustments the newborn infant must make when he is born are as follows: (1) Adjustment to *temperature changes.* In the sac in the mother's uterus, he is accustomed to a constant temperature around 100°. After birth, the temperature will be between 68° and 70° and will vary, especially after he leaves the hospital nursery. (2) Adjustment to *breathing.* In the amniotic sac in the uterus, the fetus is surrounded by a fluid environment and all oxygen comes from the placenta through the umbilical cord. When the cord is cut, after birth, the infant must inhale and exhale air. The birth cry normally comes when breathing begins and thus serves to inflate the lungs. At first, breathing is imperfect and irregular. The infant yawns, gasps, sneezes, and coughs in his efforts to regulate the amount of air he needs.

The other two major adjustments the newborn infant must make are: (3) Taking of *nourishment* through the mouth by sucking and swallowing, both of which are reflex activities often imperfectly developed at birth and which frequently make it impossible for him to get the nourishment he needs, thus resulting in loss of weight. This is in direct contrast to the constant supply of nourishment he has been accustomed to receive from the placenta through the umbilical cord. And (4), Adjustment to *elimination*. Within a few minutes or hours after birth, the excretory organs begin to function, thus eliminating waste products from the body which formerly were eliminated through the umbilical cord and the maternal placenta.

How quickly and how successfully the newborn infant will make these four major adjustments will depend partly upon the type of birth experience he has had, the length and severity of labor, and the type of prenatal environment he has had, especially during the last few months of pregnancy. Infants born spontaneously or by Caesarean section usually adjust more quickly to their new environments than do those who have experienced a long and difficult labor where instruments have had to be used to aid their emergence into the world.

The prenatal environment likewise plays a role of major importance in their early adjustments to life. Intense and prolonged nervous and emotional disturbances of the mother during the last months of pregnancy have been found to cause a hyperactive state in the fetus. This persists after birth and manifests itself in various body functions such as feeding difficulties, gastrointestinal dysfunction, sleep problems, hyperactivity, and general irritability (Sontag, 1941, 1946; Thompson, 1942; Dunbar, 1944; Fries, 1944). In describing the effects of unfavorable prenatal environmental conditions, Sontag (1946) has pointed out that "as a newborn infant, his mascular activity level is high, as is the level of certain other of his physiological functions. He is the infant who is prone to have an exaggerated bowel activity and a higher fluctuation of heart rate. Such disturbances of somatic function may include cardiospasm. Infants who do not tolerate their feedings, regurgitating them or passing them as undigested curds, often have a history of such disturbing prenatal environment."

Critical Period. Because birth itself is an ordeal for the human infant as well as for the mother and because the adjustments that must be made to the postnatal environment are difficult, not all newborn infants are capable of survival. While the percentages of stillborn infants and of deaths immediately following birth and during the period of adjustment after birth have been declining in recent years owing to improved medical techniques of prenatal care, childbirth, and postnatal care, the death toll is still high.

This is evidence of how critical this period of life is. Government statistics for all areas of the United States have revealed that of the 31.8 individuals out of every 1,000 who die during the first year of life, 70 per cent die in the neonatal period (Federal Security Agency Report, 1950).

The most critical time during this period is on the first day of life, when 29 per cent of all the neonatal deaths occur (National Office of Vital Statistics Report, 1947). The next most critical days are the second and third days after birth (Takahashi, 1954). There are many causes of neonatal deaths, the most common of which are prematurity, congenital debility, malformations, injuries at birth, pneumonia, influenza, diarrhea, and anoxia, or deficiency of oxygen resulting from the drugs used to relieve pain during delivery (National Office of Vital Statistics Report, 1947; Mengert, 1948; Benda, 1954; Mayer and Marks, 1954; Takahashi, 1954).

There are a number of factors that influence the mortality rate during the neonatal period. *Sex differences* have been found to exist, with more boys dying than girls, even when the boys and girls are the same birth weight (Gibson and McKeown, 1951, 1952; Takahashi, 1954). *Racial differences* are marked, with nonwhites showing a higher mortality rate than whites (Mayer and Marks, 1954). In neighborhoods which are predominately Negro, the mortality rate is greater than in neighborhoods predominately white. Mortality rates increase as the number of Negroes in the neighborhood increases (Yankauer, 1950). The *economic level* of the family is likewise a factor of importance, with the highest mortality rate in families of the poorest economic levels (Mayer and Marks, 1954). The prenatal diet of mothers is poorest in the poor economic groups, and this contributes to the high neonatal mortality rate (Eblis et al., 1941; Burke et al., 1943, 1949). The greater the *birth weight* of the infant and the longer the *gestation period*, the lower the mortality rate in the neonatal period (Gibson and McKeown, 1952, 1952a). Finally, neonatal mortality has been reported to increase with increasing birth order (Gibson and McKeown, 1952).

STAGE OF PHYSICAL DEVELOPMENT AT BIRTH

No two newborn infants are exactly alike in size, in appearance, or in the stage of development they have reached in all areas of their physical, mental, and behavioral growth. However, the pattern of development is similar for all, with variations of a quantitative rather than of a qualitative nature. These variations are generally traceable to length of the gestation period, factors in the prenatal environment, or type of birth the infant has experienced.

Size. The average weight of the newborn infant is 7.5 pounds, and the average length 19.5 inches. Weight ranges from 3 to 16 pounds, and length from approximately 17 to 21 inches. Male infants are generally slightly larger than female infants, but the differences are not as great between the sexes as within the sex group (Meredith and Brown, 1939).

Variability in birth size is dependent upon many factors, the most important of which are: (1) *Maternal diet,* especially during the last months of pregnancy (Burke et al., 1949). There is a significant relationship between the protein content of the mother's diet and the size of the infant at birth. A diet containing less than 75 grams of protein daily during the latter part of pregnancy has been found to result in an infant who is short and light in weight (Burke et al., 1943). The poorer the mother's diet, the smaller the infant will be (Smith, 1947; Sontag and Wines, 1947; Burke, 1949). (2) *Economic status* of the family affects the quantity and quality of the maternal diet, and this, in turn, affects the infant's size. In the poorer districts, the average size of infants is slightly but significantly smaller than in the better districts (Gibson and McKeown, 1951). Negro infants are usually smaller than whites, owing mainly to economic factors (Scott et al., 1950). (3) *Ordinal position* affects the birth size of the infant, with first-born infants averaging less than later-born. A comparison of first-born with fifth- and later-born infants revealed that the first-born were 1 per cent shorter and 9 per cent lighter than the later-born (Meredith, 1950). (4) *Fetal activity,* especially when excessive, may cause the infant to be considerably underweight for his body length (Sontag, 1940, 1941, 1946).

Loss of weight during the first few days after birth usually occurs. Heavy infants lose more and for a longer time than light infants. First-born infants generally lose less than those born later. The minimum weight is generally reached between the third and seventh days, after which there is a gradual regaining of lost weight. How quickly the lost weight will be regained depends upon many factors, especially sex, size at birth, order of birth, and type of birth. Infants born in the summer and autumn regain their birth weight slightly sooner than those born in the winter and spring (Meredith and Brown, 1939; Salber and Bradshaw, 1953, 1954). There has been found to be a relationship between the loss of weight and the time of first feeding. Infants fed for the first time 6 or more hours after birth lose less than infants fed earlier. Second- or later-born infants can be fed sooner than first-born, and boys earlier than girls (Salber and Bradshaw, 1954).

Physical Proportions. The physical proportions of the infant differ greatly from those of the adult (refer to Fig. 1, page 3). The infant's head is about one-fourth of the entire body length, while in the adult, it is one-seventh. The part of the head where the greatest disproportion exists is in the area above the eyes, the cranial region. In the infant, the ratio between the cranium and face is 8:1, while in the adult it is 1:2. The infant's face appears to be broad and short because of lack of teeth, the undeveloped condition of the jaws, and the flatness of the nose. The arms, legs, and trunk are small in relation to the head. The abdominal region of the trunk is large and bulging, while the shoulders are narrow, just the opposite of the adult proportions.

Infantile Features. The eyes of the newborn are bluish gray, but this color gradually changes to whatever the permanent color may be. Though almost mature in size, they are uncontrolled in motion and roll in a meaningless fashion without relation to one another. The tear glands are inactive, and therefore crying is not accompanied by a flow of tears. The neck is so short that it scarcely exists, and the skin covering it lies in deep folds, or creases. A heavy growth of fine-textured hair often covers the head.

The muscles of the newborn are small, soft, and uncontrolled, with those of the legs and neck less developed than those of the arms and hands. The bones are composed chiefly of cartilage, or gristle, and consequently are soft and flexible. The flesh is firm and elastic, while the skin is soft, deep pink in color, and often blotchy, especially in the head region. Sometimes a soft, downy growth of hair is found on the body, mostly on the back, but this soon disappears. Approximately once in every 2,000 births, the infant is born with a tooth or even two teeth. They are usually the lower-central incisors. Because this condition occurs with significant frequency in certain families, it suggests that some genetic factor is contributory (Massler and Savara, 1950).

Physiological Functions. The physiological functions of the infant differ greatly from those of a child or an adult. The *basal pulse rate* of the infant at birth has been reported to range from 130 to 150 beats per minute immediately after birth and then to drop to an average of 117 beats several days after birth. The average adult basal rate is 70 beats per minute. The capillary resistance is less right after birth than later, especially among prematurely born infants, and this may be related to the frequency of hemorrhages during the birth process (Pratt, 1954). There are marked variations in the pulse rate. According to Halverson (1941), in profound sleep the mean rate is 123.5 beats per minute as compared with 218.2 during crying.

The *respiration rate* during the first week of life is 35 breathing movements a minute and 38 to 40 a minute during the second week. This contrasts with a mean number of 27.8 at one year, 19.1 from ten to fifteen years, and 18 at adulthood (Pratt, 1954). Breathing is rapid, irregular, and abdominal in type in the newborn infant. It gradually becomes more regular, more rhythmical, and deeper, as the thorax is more involved when the child assumes an upright posture and begins to walk (McCarthy, 1952; Pratt, 1954). There are marked variations in breathing rate and type of breathing from infant to infant and in the same infant under different conditions. In sleep before awakening, the mean rate was found to be 32.3 as contrasted with 133.3 respirations a minute during crying (Halverson, 1941).

As compared with the arteries, the *heart* is small and must therefore beat more rapidly to maintain normal *blood pressure.* In a healthy infant, the *temperature* is higher and more variable than in an adult and is maintained between 98.2 and 99.0° F. The infant's *stomach* empties in 4 to 5 hours, the *small intestines* in 7 to 8 hours, and the large intestines within 2 to 14 hours (Pratt, 1954). When cow's milk is used in the infant's formula, the passage through the stomach requires 3 to 4 hours as compared with 20 minutes to 1 hour for breast milk (Trainham and Montgomery, 1946). The *hunger contractions* of the infant are more vigorous than those of an adult. Small quantities of milk or water, however, will bring about a temporary inhibition of these contractions (Pratt, 1954).

When *self-demand feeding* is used, there will be an average of 8.6 feedings during the first six days of life, then declining to an average of 7.9 on the seventh day. This shows a definite pattern of feeding behavior even as early as the first week of life (Olmstead and Jackson, 1950). There are marked individual differences in the spacing of feedings from infant to infant and from feeding to feeding in the same infant (Gesell and Ilg, 1937). *Defecation* occurs most frequently during the first half hour after feeding, with a median number of defecations in 24 hours of 4.7. Most defecations occur during waking periods, and the infant is quiet during and after the act (Halverson, 1940). The average number of *voidings* in a 24-hour period is 18.6, with most of them occurring during periods of wakefulness and when the infant is quiet, generally within an hour after feeding (Halverson, 1940).

The newborn infant *sleeps* or dozes from 15 to 20 hours daily as contrasted with 8 hours or less in the case of adults. He is not, however, immobile most of the time (Pratt, 1954). There is a decline in the amount of sleep from 84 per cent on the day after birth to 68 per cent on the fourth day (Pratt et al., 1930). The infant's sleep is broken by short waking periods which occur on the average of every 2 hours. The waking periods are generally fewer and shorter during the night than during the day. Gradually, the length of the unbroken sleep periods increases (Bühler, 1930; Pratt et al., 1930).

The infant is wakened by hunger, pain, and internal sources of discomfort. The only environment stimuli that will disturb him are changes in temperature and very loud noises. In contrast with older children, the infant sleeps more lightly and can be awakened more quickly and easily. He is able, also, to fall asleep more readily. The sleep of the infant reaches its greatest depth during the first hour, while during the second hour the sleep is lighter and can be broken more easily. External stimuli are less effective immediately after feeding than later (Richards, 1936). In deep sleep, the infant is generally more quiet than in light sleep (Wagner, 1938; Reynard and Dockeray, 1939). Figure 13 shows two typical sleep curves for infants, with deep sleep in the middle of the curve.

The characteristic method of falling asleep and awakening has been described by Bühler (1930) as follows: "The newborn child twitches in that moment when he falls asleep. . . . Awakening, the newborn child throws his head backward, stretches his arms and body" (p. 119). When placed in a prone position, the posture of the newborn is similar to that of the fetus during intra-uterine life (Shirley, 1931a). Movements during sleep increase with age throughout the first two weeks, as is true of the waking period. The infant often smiles during sleep. More variations in sleep posture from one infant to another occur than is generally believed.

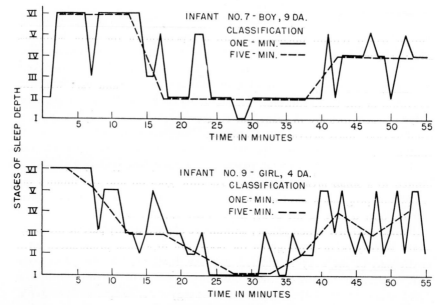

Fig. 13. Typical sleep curves for infants with records of 50 minutes or more. (*From M. C. Reynard and F. C. Dockeray, The comparison of temporal intervals in judging depth of sleep in newborn infants, J. genet. Psychol., 1939, 55, 103–120. Used by permission.*)

MOTOR ACTIVITIES

At birth, the infant is not an inert bundle of skin, bones, and flesh, but is a moving, acting creature. Indeed the movements made are so rapid, varied, and diffuse that at times, especially during waking periods, it is difficult to record every movement of the infant's body (Gilmer, 1933). Because the fetus has few opportunities to learn, it has been contended that "most of the behavior of the infant at birth is unlearned and that fetal development is almost entirely a matter of maturation" (Dennis, 1943).

Mass Activity and Specific Activities. The first activities of the human infant are random, imperfect, and uncoordinated. And yet, within a period of a few years, these movements will, for the most part, be harnessed and controlled to form the basis for the coordinated skills needed in everyday life. In spite of their apparent lack of organization, the motor activities of the newborn may roughly be classed into two descriptive categories, suggested first by Irwin (1930). These are (1) *mass activity* and (2) *specific activities.*

Mass activity is activity which includes general movements of the whole body. It occurs independently of specific external stimulation, is highly uncoordinated, and is due to the neurological immaturity of the infant. *Specific activities* are activities which involve certain limited areas of the body. This classification includes (1) reflexes, definite responses to specific sensory stimuli which remain unchanged with a repetition of the same stimulus, and (2) general responses, which may arise from either external or internal stimulus and which involve larger groups of muscles than are used in reflex responses. They are less specific than the reflexes and vary with the repetition of the same stimulus. This is not true in the case of the reflexes.

Specific activities are in reality an outgrowth of mass activity. In the prenatal period, mass activity predominates. When one part of the body is stimulated, the whole body responds. At birth, the same is true. Even in the case of crying, the infant's entire body is active, though crying itself is limited to a small area of the body. As time goes on and the infant's development progresses, local activities, which are more specific in form, involving only a part of the body, make their appearance.

1. Mass Activity. When sensory stimuli are applied to any part of the body, motor activity occurs throughout the body, but in a most pronounced form in the part of the body stimulated. Movements limited to one part of the body are relatively infrequent, because the immature condition of the nervous system results in a diffusion of energy when a specific stimulus is applied to one area of the body. When, for example, a tactual stimulus is applied, a response usually occurs first in the stimulated area, followed by responses in other areas of the body (Delman, 1935).

The energy expended by the infant is thus great because the activity is diffused. It is estimated that the energy expended is $2\frac{1}{2}$ times as great in the infant as in the adult, when pound-to-pound comparisons are made. Likewise, it is estimated that in crying the infant expends three times as much energy as in sleep because of the greater amount of mass activity in the former compared with the latter activity (Gilmer, 1933). Muscular activity raises heat production. When very active, crying infants were compared with inactive infants, a significant increase in heat production was found (Richards, 1935).

Not all parts of the infant's body are equally active. Observations of newborn infants during the first ten days of life have revealed that the greatest amount of movement is in the trunk and legs and the least in the head (Gatewood and Weiss, 1930; Irwin, 1930). A significant difference between movements of the right and left arms has also been reported, with the motility of the right arm typically exceeding that of the left arm throughout the first ten days after birth. It has been suggested that this laterality difference in the frequency of arm movements may be regarded as the basis for later handedness (Stubbs and Irwin, 1933; Valentine and Wagner, 1934).

Individual Differences. Individual differences in mass activity are pronounced. The more complex the type of activity, the more pronounced are the variations. Infants who were most active during the fetal period are most active in the period of the newborn (Sontag, 1941, 1946). There is less

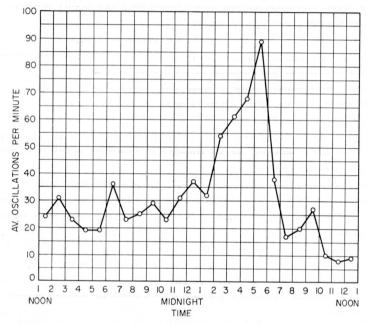

Fig. 14. Variations in mass activity at different times of the day. (*From O. C. Irwin, The amount and nature of activities of newborn infants under constant external stimulating conditions during the first ten days of life, Genet. Psychol. Monogr., 1930, No. 8. Used by permission.*)

difference in activity between the sexes than within each sex group (Pratt, 1932). Negro infants are less active than white infants (Pratt, 1930). In individual infants, there are variations in activity at different times of the day, with peak activity coming in the early-morning hours and the least activity at noon (Irwin, 1930). These variations are shown in Fig. 14.

Mass activity is influenced by the *bodily condition* of the infant. The most pronounced activity occurs during crying, hunger, pain, and general bodily discomfort, while the least activity comes when the infant is asleep or after he has been fed. Infants who are wet, insufficiently nourished, or uncomfortable are likely to be restless and "fussy." With the approach of feeding

time, activity is increased and is then followed by a period of relative inactivity after feeding, when the infant drops off to sleep (Pratt et al., 1930;
Irwin, 1932b; Richards, 1936, 1936a). Body temperature does not seem to
have any effect on the amount of mass activity the infant experiences
(Irwin, 1933).

Environmental conditions likewise influence the amount of activity of
the infant. Light is disturbing to an infant and becomes increasingly so with
added intensity. Least activity occurs in dim light and greatest activity in
intense light. Darkness, on the other hand, increases bodily activity, especially when the infant passes from light to darkness (Irwin and Weiss,
1934; Redfield, 1939; Irwin, 1941). Auditory stimuli bring about an increase
in general activity in infants. The pitch of the stimulus is less important
than the intensity or the duration of the sound. Crying infants respond least
to sound stimulation while awake, and inactive infants respond most
(Pratt, 1934a; Stubbs, 1934). Activity of the infant is hampered by clothing
and covers. When these are removed, activity increases (Irwin and Weiss,
1934a). Bodily activity does not seem to be affected by changes in temperature between 74° and 88° or by changes in humidity between 22 and 90
per cent (Pratt, 1930).

2. Specific Activities. Specific activities of the newborn have been divided
into two types, (a) reflexes and (b) general responses, for convenience; the
distinction is one only of degree. Studies of reflexes have been especially
numerous.

a. Reflexes. The outstanding reflexes present at birth or shortly afterward
may be summarized as follows: pupillary corneal, conjunctival, lip, tongue,
chin, breathing, Darwinian (grasping), Achilles tendon, patellar, triceps,
biceps, abdominal, cremasteric plantar, Moro, sucking, visceral, flexion, knee
jerk, pharyngeal, heart action, sneezing, Babinski (fanning of toes), and
others. Only a few of the reflexes seem to be related to age. Changes to
greater or less reaction occur between the seventeenth and the seventy-fifth
hour after birth (Chaney and McGraw, 1932). The sucking reflex can be
aroused by stroking the lip or cheek or by a gentle pat if the infant is asleep
(Norval, 1946). Breast-fed infants develop a stronger sucking reflex than
do infants fed by bottle or cup. However, the breast-fed infants show a
slightly poorer appetite on the first three days of life than do bottle- or cup-
fed infants (Davis et al., 1948).

The first reflexes to make their appearance are those which have distinct
survival value. The patellar, pupillary, and digestive reflexes are all ready
to function several months before birth, as may be seen in the case of the
prematurely born. Heart action, breathing, and sneezing begin at birth.
Sneezing sometimes occurs as the infant is taken from the mother's body
and precedes the birth cry. The other reflexes listed above can be aroused
within a few hours or days after birth.

The Babinski, Moro-embrace, and Darwinian reflexes appear shortly after birth, but disappear within the first months of life. The *Babinski,* or fanning of the toes, which follows a gentle stroking of the sole of the infant's foot, is generally gone by the age of six months and is never present in normal children after the age of 2½ years. At first, this reflex involves movements of the entire leg. Later, the response is limited to movements of the ankle and toes (McGraw, 1941). The *Darwinian,* or grasping, reflex is distinctly weakened by the end of the second month of life. The ability to suspend the entire body weight attains its maximum strength by the end of the first month of postnatal life, after which there is a rapid decline of the ability (McGraw, 1940b).

The *Moro-embrace* reflex occurs when the infant is placed flat on his back and the mattress or table on which he is placed is struck with a forcible blow. The infant throws out his arms in an arc movement, resembling an embrace. At first there is marked general bodily response, with bowing and clutching movements of the arms and legs. Accompanying or following this is vigorous crying. As time goes on, the amount of general bodily activity is reduced, so that by the eighth month the Moro reflex takes on the mature form, which consists of a quick, fine body jerk, accompanied by crying (McGraw, 1932a).

Hunt (1939) has differentiated the "startle pattern" from the Moro reflex. The startle pattern is typified by flexion. The eyes blink, the head moves forward, the shoulders come up and in, the arms flex at the elbows, and there is flexion of the fingers. The leg movements resemble those of the Moro reflex, though the two patterns can be clearly differentiated in the upper limbs. The startle pattern is elicited mostly by sudden loud noises, though it does come in response to other stimuli of a sudden, intense nature (Hunt and Clarke, 1937). By the twentieth week, this pattern changes markedly (Clarke, 1939).

b. General Responses. What are often called "general responses" are those that involve larger portions of the body than the so-called "reflexes" but, like the reflexes, are present at birth. They too are direct responses to stimuli, whether external or internal. The most common of these are:

1. Visual fixation on light. During the first day of life, the infant can focus his eyes momentarily on a light held in front of him. Eye movements are, on the whole, very uncoordinated at first.

2. Spontaneous eye movements. These consist of opening the eyes and rolling the eyeballs from side to side, with little or no coordination.

3. Shedding tears. Occasionally, tears are in the eyes at birth. Generally, however, the first show of dampness around the eyes appears from the thirteenth to the sixteenth day after birth.

4. Feeding responses, such as sucking, swallowing, tongue, cheek, and lip movements. The feeding reactions are called forth by a direct stimulation in the region of the mouth, whether it be the touch of a nipple or some object unrelated to food.

5. Sucking fingers. This form of reaction appears as early as 20 minutes after birth.

6. Yawning. This often occurs within the first hour after birth and can be aroused by touching the lips or chin.

7. Hiccuping. This reaction often appears during the first few hours of life.

8. Rhythmic mouthing movements. Often, during sleep, the infant will open and shut his mouth rhythmically, and in many instances, the tongue will protrude for as much as half an inch.

9. Slight frowning and wrinkling of the brow. This response generally occurs during sleep.

10. Turning and lifting the head. When placed either in a prone position or on their backs, infants can lift their heads slightly on the first day of life. This enables them, when prone, to free their noses for breathing.

11. Sitting. When the infant is placed in a sitting position, the flaccidity of his body results in a fall forward into a closed-jackknife position. Several days later, he shows slight resistance to the forward fall.

12. Turning movements. The infant can turn his body slightly by kicking and squirming, but this is not strong enough to enable him to turn from back to side or from face to back.

13. Hand and arm movements. When the infant is asleep, as well as when he is awake, the arms and hands are in almost constant motion. The arms are waved around in a random, aimless fashion, and the hands are opened and shut for no apparent purpose.

14. Prancing and kicking. If the infant is supported at the axillae, so that the body weight can rest on the feet, "prancing" movements occur. When the infant is given something to kick against as he lies on his stomach, a few vigorous kicks will push him forward an inch or so.

15. Leg and foot movements. The infant often stretches his toes for no reason other than the mere enjoyment he derives from it. Kicking is very pronounced during infancy and is usually alternate and rhythmical.

16. Body jerks. This is any sudden jerk or tensing of the trunk, plus limb movements. They vary so markedly from one infant to another that they cannot be classified into any well-defined pattern. Body jerks are most frequent during the first few days of life and during deep sleep (Wagner, 1938).

As can be seen from the above list, the infant is capable of a large repertoire of activities. What is characteristic of these activities is that, in varying degrees, they are undefined, aimless, and uncoordinated. They are, however, the basis from which we shall see skilled actions of a highly coordinated type gradually developing as a result of baby's and child's learning.

VOCALIZATION OF THE NEWBORN

The Birth Cry. The birth cry, which appears at the birth or shortly afterward, marks the beginning of vocalization. This is purely reflex at first and is caused by air being drawn rapidly over the vocal cords, thus setting up vibrations in them. Many fantastic interpretations have been given to the birth cry. Kant referred to it as "a cry of wrath at the catastrophe of birth"; Adler has explained it as an indication of the infant's sudden and overwhelming feeling of inferiority at being placed in so new and complex an environment. In reality, of course, the significance of the birth cry is primarily physiological. It serves two purposes: to supply the blood with suffi-

cient oxygen and to inflate the lungs, making breathing p
first time the individual hears his own voice and, thus, is in
pattern of language development (McCarthy, 1954).

The birth cry is not a true precursor of speech. Once the lu
come inflated, crying comes from internal or external stimula
part of the pattern of generalized behavior characteristic of th
infant. It is related to breathing and follows closely the rhythm of
(Pratt, 1954). When the newborn infant cries, the mouth is open

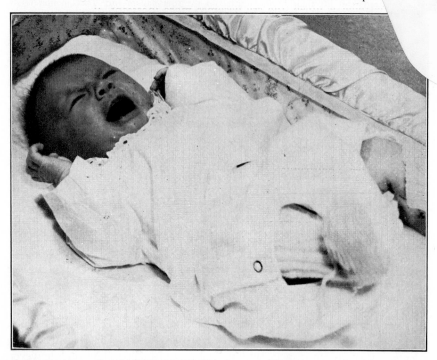

Crying in the newborn infant is accompanied by mass activity. (*From Child Develop-ment, a McGraw-Hill Text-Film.*)

usually in a rectangular shape, the tip of the tongue is elevated, the muscles
of the face are strongly contracted, and the eyelids are tightly closed. The
sound made by the infant is uttered with force and loudness (Irwin and
Chen, 1941). When the infant is swung or rocked, when he is sucking, or
when auditory stimuli are presented to the infant, the crying ceases (Pratt,
1954). The birth cry differs from infant to infant and is, to a certain extent,
influenced by the type of birth, as well as by the physical condition of the
infant. In the quick, expulsive form of delivery, the cry is sharp and deep.
On the other hand, in cases of premature birth, or in cases of infants who are
in poor condition, a little moan generally accompanies each inspiration. Pro-

longed labor, resulting in the exhaustion of the infant, is generally accompanied by a weak, short, intermittent cry. Infants damaged at birth or prenatally have cries that differ from those delivered normally in pitch, rhythm, volume, and accentual character (Palmer, 1940).

Changes and Developments. During the first 24 hours after birth, the infant's cry may take on different meanings according to the pitch, intensity, and continuity of the cry. In general *discomfort,* the cry at first is monotonous in pitch, staccato-like, and intermittent; then gradually, unless some relief is given, the cry becomes more incessant. *Pain* is characterized by a cry which rises in pitch. If pain is accompanied by increasing physical weakness, piercing tones give way to low moans. In *rage,* the cry is longer, the breath is held, and the infant's face often becomes purplish. Gulping sounds, which generally accompany the rage cry, result from the opening of the infant's mouth, with the resultant closing of the air passages of the throat. Intermittent sobs usually continue even after rage has subsided. When a recording was made of the *hunger* cries, it was found that they were one octave above an adult female and two octaves above an adult male speaking voice. For the next six months, the development was toward higher pitches (Fairbanks, 1942).

The cries of the newborn infant are almost exclusively vowel sounds, with few consonants heard (McCarthy, 1954; Pratt, 1954). To determine what vowel sounds appear in the crying of the newborn, Irwin and Curry (1941) studied the crying of 40 infants. Front vowels, or vowels produced by the front mouth parts, were found to be almost exclusively used. Older children and adults, by contrast, use all mouth parts. No sex or age differences within the first ten days of life were noted.

Stimulation of Cries. The stimuli which arouse the infant's cries come from the immediate environment or from the physiological condition of the infant. (Contrast with this the reasons why an older child or adult cries!) Conditions under which crying occurs during the infancy period are as follows: (1) hunger; (2) pain or discomfort from noxious stimuli, such as rough handling, circumcision, sores, and so on; and (3) occasionally fatigue or lack of exercise. No uniform cries for the different situations are necessarily found among different infants. The cries that occur under such circumstances differ in intensity and duration, depending partly on the vocal strength of the infant and partly on the internal or external stimuli which aroused them.

Starting with the assumption that the crying of the newborn is a reflex protective mechanism, Aldrich et al. (1945, 1945a, 1945b) made continuous observations of the crying of newborn infants. These observations revealed that infants cry more often for unknown reasons than for any other cause. When the total number of minutes of crying was calculated, it was found that hunger cries occupied 35.5 per cent of the crying time, and crying for unknown reasons 35.1 per cent. The hunger cries were of longer duration than the cries for unknown reasons. Wet diapers proved to be the third most common cause of crying, and vomiting the least common.

Bodily Accompaniments of Crying. The crying of an infant rarely occurs without bodily activity of some sort, and this generally begins when crying begins. In the case of vigorous crying, every part of the body is thrown into action. The infant squirms; kicks; flexes and extends his arms, legs, fingers, and toes; rolls his body and turns his head from side to side. See Fig. 15.

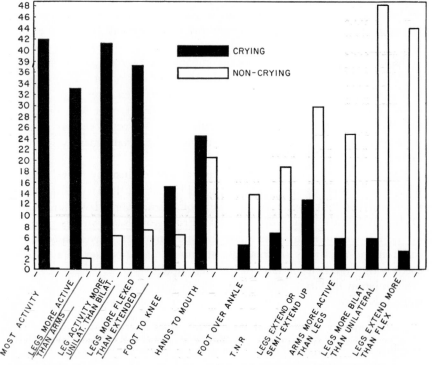

Fig. 15. Differences between bodily activity in crying and noncrying. (*From L. B. Ames, Motor correlates of infant crying, J. genet. Psychol.,* 1941, **59**, 239–247. *Used by permission.*)

The kicking is usually fairly rhythmic, but varies somewhat, according to the conditions which aroused the crying. In anger, for example, the kicking is more vigorous and abrupt than during other emotional states, and the feet are generally thrust out simultaneously instead of alternately. This activity is a signal that the infant needs attention, and it thus serves as a form of language (Irwin, 1930).

Amount of Crying. How much the newborn cries is an individual matter. Among the newborn babies observed by Aldrich et al. (1945b), the baby with the least crying activity cried 386 minutes during the first eight days of life, or 48.2 minutes per day. This compared with a total of 1,947 minutes for the baby who cried the most, an average of 243 minutes per day. For the group, the average crying amounted to 936 minutes during the eight days, or 117 minutes per day. In Fig. 16 is given a frequency distribution of the different causes of crying of an average infant on an average day. When changes are made to individualize the nursing care of the infant,

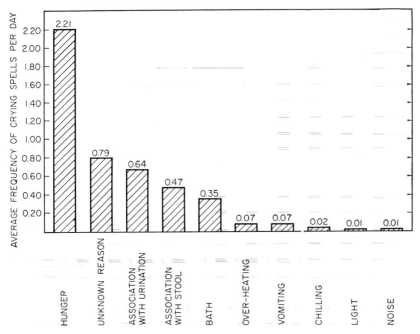

Fig. 16. Frequency distribution of the different causes of crying spells of an average baby on an average day. (*From C. A. Aldrich, C. Sung, and C. Knop, The crying of newly born babies, III, The early home period, J. Pediat., 27, 428–435. Used by permission.*)

the crying has been found to be reduced 51.4 per cent (Aldrich et al., 1946). There is no indication that the amount of crying of the infant is influenced by crying of other infants. Community living, in a hospital nursery, does not increase the amount of crying of an infant (Blanton, 1917; Aldrich et al., 1945). There is also no evidence that the amount of crying is influenced by the length of labor (Ruja, 1948).

Explosive Sounds. In addition to crying, the infant is capable of another type of vocalization, *explosive sounds,* which are not unlike heavy breathing. These are very commonly referred to as "coos," "grunts," and "gurgles." They are uttered without intent and without meaning and occur purely by chance whenever there is a contraction of the vocal muscles. Since these sounds are low in pitch and weak, compared with cries, they are often overlooked entirely or are regarded as unimportant.

From the long-term point of view, explosive sounds are far more important than cries, which are used less and less as the child grows older. The explosive sounds, on the other hand, are gradually strengthened and develop, during the second half of the first year, into babbling, which in turn develops into speech. When one realizes that the explosive sounds are in reality the fundamentals of speech, their true significance at once becomes apparent.

Other Sounds. In addition to cries and explosive sounds, the newborn infant is capable of making other sounds. *Sneezing* is a reflex type of explosive sound which occurs within the first few hours after birth and occasionally before the birth cry itself. As a rule, the healthy infant sneezes several times a day and thus cleans his nose of any foreign matter. *Yawning* is likewise a type of explosive sound. It may be heard as early as five minutes after birth. *Whining,* which may be reliably discriminated from crying, occurs during irregular breathing. The mouth is partially opened, the tongue tip is not elevated, the muscles of the face are only slightly contracted, the lids are usually open, and the sounds made are feeble (Irwin and Chen, 1941).

Hiccuping is another explosive sound of the reflex type. This may be observed from the seventh day, but occasionally it occurs before then. Hiccups range from a few seconds to over a quarter of an hour, with a mean length reported as 5 minutes, 34 seconds. The onset of the hiccup period is always sudden, but the ending is less abrupt. Hiccups vary from barely audible inspirations to loud, sharp sounds. The loud sounds never persist throughout the entire period of hiccuping. Usually groups of them are interspersed with groups of relatively quiet inspirations. Single, isolated hiccups rarely occur (Wagner, 1938a).

SENSITIVITIES OF THE NEWBORN

It is difficult to determine what sensations the infant is capable of experiencing at birth. Inasmuch as sensation is best studied by the introspective method, a method that cannot be used in the prespeech level of development, it is impossible to determine accurately what the sensations of the newborn are and how they compare with the sensory experiences of older children and adults. In experimental studies of the newborn, the criterion generally used to determine the presence or absence of a given sensory capacity is some motor response to the sensory stimulus which normally would arise from the sense organ stimulated. There are evidences at birth or shortly afterward the sense organs are ready to function. While the reactions of the infant to sensory stimuli are not necessarily similar to those of an adult, nevertheless a selective reaction is made. Some of the sense organs are more highly developed than others, and the resultant sensations are consequently stronger and more nearly like those of adults. Of all the sensitivities, reactions to the stimuli of touch upon the skin are found to be the most numerous. Even prematurely born infants respond to the different sensory stimuli in much the same manner as those who are born at full term (Peiper, 1924; Gesell, 1949a).

1. Sight. At birth, the retina has not reached its mature development. It is thinner than in the adult eye, and the cones in the fovea are short and ill-defined. The area of the retina is smaller than in the adult eye, but the number of cones per unit area is the same. At thirty hours of age or shortly afterward, the pupillary reflex is well established. Before that, there is only a sluggish response to light. The protective responses of turning the head, closing the eyelids, and crying appear shortly after birth. Optic nystagmus, the ability to follow moving objects and then move the eyes backward in the opposite direction, comes several hours after birth. Ocular pursuit of a moving object is poor unless the object moves slowly. Horizontal, vertical, and circular pursuit with both eyes develops markedly during the first ten days of life (Beasley, 1933; Gesell, 1949; Pratt, 1954).

The question of whether or not the infant sees color has not yet been experimentally determined. Studies of the development of cones in the eye of the newborn have given no clue as to sensitivity to color. Any attempt to determine color sensitivity at birth must be based on the manner of functioning of the eye and not on its anatomical condition. Studies of infants have revealed that, as early as the seventh or ninth day of life, they respond in a slightly dissimilar way to different colors of the same physical energy. Blue has the most marked effect, and red the least. Girls are more affected by colors than are boys, who seem to be partially color-blind and incapable of seeing red (Smith, 1936).

2. Hearing. There seems to be no agreement among scientists as to whether or not infants respond to sound stimuli by auditory sensations immediately after birth. Some report that reactions occur within ten minutes after birth, while others report that deafness exists during the first few days of life. At birth, hearing seems to be at the lowest stage of development of all the sensitivities. Many infants are totally deaf for several hours or days after birth, owing primarily to the stoppage of the middle ear with amniotic fluid. Very often, loud noises near the ear of the newborn produce little or no reaction. There are, however, individual differences in infants in their sensitivity to sound stimuli (Bryan, 1930; Pratt et al., 1930; Pratt, 1954).

3. Taste. Studies of the sensitivity to taste stimuli have revealed that the newborn infant has a more highly developed sense of taste than of sight or hearing. Distinctive reactions to different taste stimuli are made during the first week of life. The reactions to sweet stimuli are primarily positive, in the form of contented sucking, while those to salt, sour, and bitter stimuli are mainly negative, in the form of discomfort reactions. Respiration and circulation are least influenced by sweet stimuli, slightly disturbed by salt, and considerably affected by sour and bitter stimuli. There are, however, wide individual differences in taste thresholds (Pratt et al., 1930; Shirley, 1931a; Dockeray, 1934; Pratt, 1954).

4. Smell. Using such stimuli as asafetida, oleum dippelii, acetic acid, ammonia fumes, petroleum, compound spirits of orange oil and geranium, and mother's milk have shown that the sense of smell is well developed in the newborn. This high sensitivity is shown in such reactions as squirming, crying, grimaces, and sucking movements and may be observed within the first hour after birth. Reactions to olfactory stimuli are made when the infant is asleep as well as when awake, and refusal to take the breast occurs whenever the breast has been rubbed with such an odor as petroleum. Ammonia and acetic acid prove to be the most effective stimuli in arousing definite responses in infants, though they respond to weaker stimuli such as valerian and cloves, indicating an ability to smell them also. Wide individual differences, however, occur in infants, as well as in the same infant from one day to another (Pratt et al., 1930; Disher, 1933; Pratt, 1954).

5. Skin Sensitivities. The skin sensations of touch, pressure, temperature, and pain are present at birth or shortly afterward. Sensations of touch are present at birth in all parts of the body. This may be seen whenever the stroking reflex occurs. Some parts of the body, however, are more sensitive than others. The mucous membrane of the lips, for example, is hypersensitive, while the skin of trunk, thighs, and forearm is hyposensitive. Cold stimuli produce prompter and more pronounced reactions than do heat stimuli. This is observed also in the differential sucking reactions to changes in the temperature of milk (Pratt et al., 1930; Jensen, 1932; Pratt, 1954).

Sensitivity to pain is weak during the first day or two of life. The places of highest sensitivity are the soles of the feet, the lips, eyelashes, mucous membrane of the nose, and skin of the forehead. The body, legs, underarms, and hands are hyposensitive as compared with the adult. Pain responses not only appear earlier in the anterior end of the body, they also develop more rapidly than those in the posterior end. This is seen by the fact that the infant's face is more sensitive to painful stimuli than the legs, and this holds true for the first four days of life. Sleep increases the threshold of sensitivity, which results in more nonlocalized and diffuse than localized responses during sleep (Sherman et al., 1936; Crudden, 1937; McGraw, 1941a; Pratt, 1954).

6. Organic Sensitivities. It is difficult to tell specifically whether the organic sensations of hunger and thirst are developed at birth. Crying may indicate only general discomfort, or it may be the result of specific discomfort arising from hunger and thirst. Hunger contractions appear to be

fully developed at birth. They differ from those of an adult only in that they occur at more frequent intervals. These internal sensations are responsible for most of the activity of the infant (Pratt et al., 1930; Richards, 1936; Pratt, 1954).

EMOTIONS OF THE NEWBORN

Experimental studies of the emotions of the newborn infant have been limited in number, but extensive in scope. Following the theory of Watson (1925, 1925a) that at birth or shortly afterward, only three distinct emotional reactions occur and these may be aroused by only a very few specific stimuli, many attempts have been made to determine whether the newborn infant is capable of any emotional behavior as definite as the patterns of fear, rage, and love that Watson described. In general, these studies have revealed that the infant's behavior is best characterized as generalized activity, with no definite emotional pattern and lacking the "stirred up state of the organism" which is characteristic of emotions (Sherman and Sherman, 1929; Irwin, 1930, 1932, 1932c; Pratt et al., 1930; Pratt, 1932, 1934a, 1954; Taylor, 1934; Hunt et al., 1936; Hunt and Clarke, 1937; Dennis, 1940a).

According to Bakwin (1947), the newborn is equipped with a well-developed set of emotional responses. Even among infants born several months prematurely, emotional reactivity is present. These responses he divided into two groups, the "pleasant," or positive, responses and the "unpleasant," or negative, responses. Pleasurable responses are elicited by patting, rocking, warmth, snug holding, and allowing the baby to suck. Unpleasant responses, on the other hand, are elicited by changing the infant's position abruptly, by sudden loud noises, by hampering the infant's movements in an uncomfortable position, by a cold object applied to the skin, and by a wet diaper. To disagreeable stimuli the infant responds by crying. Spitz (1949) is unwilling to recognize the pleasurable responses as beginnings of emotional patterns. According to him, at birth there is only a state of diffuse excitement in the nature of displeasure. There is no pleasurable emotion present, only a state of quiescence.

The outstanding characteristic of the infant's emotional make-up is the "wholeheartedness," or complete absence of gradations, of response to stimuli of different degrees of intensity. Regardless of the stimulus, the resultant emotion is intense in character and sudden in appearance. As the emotional life develops, through the childhood years, this "all-or-none" condition gradually gives way to a controlled system of well-graded and controlled emotional states. As Pratt (1954) has stressed, "Upon the acquisition of the responses depends the adequacy of the adjustment to the stimulating situation."

CONSCIOUSNESS OF THE NEWBORN

How does the world appear to the newborn, and of what is he conscious as he first observes the environment into which he is born? For years, interest of a speculative sort has been concentrated on this problem; but because of its highly subjective nature, it is impossible to do more than guess from the infant's behavior as to what goes on in his mind and what he perceives during the first days after birth. The limited information we have comes from our knowledge of the conditions of the sense organs at birth and from observations of the infant's behavior in different situations.

Many attempts have been made to describe infant consciousness. One of the earliest of these is the oft-quoted statement of James (1890) that the "baby, assailed by eyes, ears, nose, skin, and entrails all at once, feels it all as one great, blooming, buzzing confusion" (p. 488). And, in his analysis of sensations, he says that "prior to all impressions of the sense organs, the brain is plunged in deep sleep and consciousness is practically nonexistent. Even the first few weeks after birth are passed in almost unbroken sleep by human infants. It takes a strong message from the sense organs to break this slumber" (pp. 7–8).

Stern (1930), while stating that the newborn infant is mainly a "creature of reflexes," nevertheless grants that the first traces of consciousness may be present at birth. According to him, "all that we are possibly justified in assuming is the presence of a dull, undefined foreshadowing of consciousness in which the sensorial and emotional elements are so inextricably intermingled that they may be designated either as 'sense-emotional states' or 'emotional-perceptive states.' The presence of feelings of comfort or discomfort is evinced from the very first day by the bodily habit as a whole, by the expression of the face, and by the active expression of screaming." Koffka (1925) believes that the "newborn infant experiences the world differently from us adults, just as an unmusical person hears a symphony differently from one who is musical."

CONDITIONING IN THE NEWBORN

The ability to learn on the part of the newborn has been denied by the Pavlovian school of Russian physiologists and psychologists, on the grounds that the formation of conditioned responses is impossible because, during the first few months after birth, the cerebral cortex functions very incompletely. A number of attempts have been made to see if conditioning can be achieved during the period of infancy. In the case of feeding reactions, the association with the sound of a buzzer resulted in significant changes in the infants' reactions after the buzzer was sounded (Marquis, 1931). Changing infant feeding schedules may result in frustration, which indicates that conditioning has taken place (Marquis, 1941, 1943).

Application of the conditioning technique to other situations than feeding has not resulted in evidence of a conclusive sort. In fact, a conditioned response has been found to be difficult to elicit during the first ten days of life, and when it does appear, it is unstable. On the whole, it appears that many infants cannot be conditioned and that those who can are unstable in their responses even when it appeared at first as if they had learned to respond successfully to the substitute stimulus (Kasatkin and Levikova, 1935; Wenger, 1936; Wickens and Wickens, 1940; Pratt, 1954). Because of the cortical immaturity of the newborn infant, not only is conditioning limited, but also what little conditioning there is, is of little permanent value (Merry and Merry, 1950).

Whether it will be possible to condition the emotions of the newborn, as can be done easily and quickly during the first year of babyhood, has not yet been investigated. Likewise, since the infant's food is limited in variety, the problem of conditioned taste likes and dislikes is not important and, as a result, has not been investigated. The infant's complete unawareness of the individuals present in his environment does not offer an opportunity for the study of conditioned social likes and dislikes. Therefore, what learning there is through the conditioning technique is apt to take place in connection with feeding and emotions alone.

BEGINNINGS OF PERSONALITY

Differences in personality are apparent during the first few days of life, just as differences in appearance are. Some infants are "good as gold," while others are fussy and troublesome. These differences may be due partly to age (premature as compared with full-term infants), circumstances of delivery, or health conditions. Shirley (1933a) studied the personalities of babies from data obtained in connection with periodic tests. Personality tests were found to be constant enough over a period of time to justify the assumption that a "nucleus of personality exists at birth and that this nucleus persists and grows and determines to a certain degree the relative importance of the various traits. Some change is doubtless wrought by environmental factors, but this change is limited by the limitations of the original personality nucleus." Irritability, for example, was found to be greater during the first fourteen days of life than it was as the baby grew older. This trait, Shirley maintains, is fairly well established from birth on.

Birth Trauma. As was pointed out in the beginning of this chapter, birth is a physiological shock to the infant great enough to require a period of time before he recovers sufficiently to continue the steady process of development that began at the time of conception. According to the psychoanalytical school, there is also a psychic trauma resulting from the rupture of the fetal relations with the mother. This brings about a state of anxiety which can have a lasting effect on the pattern of his personality (Rank, 1929,

1932; Freud, 1936; Sadger, 1941; Ribble, 1944). There is, however, little evidence that the newborn infant is capable of understanding the change that occurs in the pattern of his life or that he is capable of experiencing any emotions well enough developed to have a lasting influence on his personality (Despert, 1946; Anderson, 1948; Ruja, 1948; Pratt, 1954).

There is, however, the possibility that the mother's emotional reactions will influence the infant, even though he does not comprehend their meanings. Infants who are separated from their mothers do not make as good adjustments to their postnatal environments as those who are with their mothers (Menzies, 1946; Spitz, 1949). Emotional tension of the mother before birth which frequently carries over to the postnatal period has been found to influence the infant's postnatal adjustments and thus, to some extent, affect his early relationship with his mother (Sontag, 1941, 1946; Dunbar, 1944; Fries, 1944). If the mother is not happy about having a baby, or if the baby is not of the desired sex, this is bound to influence her behavior and will be sensed, if not understood, by the infant (Wallin and Riley, 1950; Levy and Hess, 1952).

The mother's attitude toward the new baby is often confused and unstable. Her emotional reactions shift from day to day, even from hour to hour, especially if she suspects there is something wrong with the infant (Carithers, 1951). It would seem logical, therefore, to conclude that the maternal attitude as reflected in the mother's relationship with the infant is a more important factor in the personality development of the infant than the psychic trauma that the infant is supposed to experience when his life as a parasite ends and he must adjust to an independent life.

PREMATURE BIRTHS

Prematurity means a condition in which the newborn infant is relatively unfit for extra-uterine life because his prenatal development has not been completed. There is a lack of development or a retardation in development which has been caused by a shortening of the period of the fetus during prenatal life. The more premature the infant is, the more poorly equipped he is for extra-uterine life.

Criteria of Prematurity. There are two criteria which are generally used in determining whether or not the newborn infant is premature. The first is the *length of the gestation period*. When the gestation period is estimated to have been between 28 and 38 weeks long, the infant is considered to be premature. The second criterion of prematurity is *birth size*. This is judged either in terms of weight or in terms of relation of weight to length. This criterion is more commonly used than the length of the gestation period, which cannot always be estimated accurately. When the infant at birth weighs 2,500 grams (5 pounds 8 ounces) or less, he is considered to be premature. The lighter the weight, the less chance there is for survival.

Should the head circumference be less than 33 centimeters and the crown-rump length less than 32 centimeters, these are taken as additional proof of prematurity (Ellis, 1951).

Seriousness of Prematurity. Survival is relatively rare when birth weight is 1,000 grams (2 pounds 3 ounces) or less. For those infants whose weight is above this, the chances of survival vary according to birth weight (Crump et al., 1952). If the infant weighs more than 1,500 grams (3 pounds 5 ounces), its chances of survival are estimated to be four times as great as if its weight were 1,500 grams or less. Separate norms must, however, be used for infants of different races and for the two sexes. Infants whose gestation age is 29 weeks or less have a mortality rate of 63.3 per cent as compared with 21.5 per cent for those whose gestation age is 34 to 37 weeks. When weights are the same, those with a younger gestation age have as good a chance of survival as those who are older, emphasizing the fact that weight is more important than age (Steiner and Pomerance, 1951).

The ratio of male to female deaths in the postnatal period among prematurely born infants is 2 to 1 (Crump et al., 1952). Prematurity is more common among first-born than among later-born children, and this accounts partially for the higher mortality rate among the first-born (Jones, 1954). Of all neonatal deaths, 46 per cent have been found to be due to prematurity (Reardon et al., 1951). Furthermore, more prematurely born infants die during the first year of life than is true of those born at full term (Alm, 1953). The most common time for death among the prematures, however, is on the first day of life. More than half of the deaths of prematurely born infants occur then (Reardon et al., 1951).

In spite of medical progress in caring for prematurely born infants, the mortality rate is still very high. One-third of the deaths in the first year of life are among babies whose birth weight is less than 5½ pounds. In the United States, mortality statistics show that, although only one out of every 15 to 20 births are premature, approximately 40,000 premature infants die annually. It is estimated that a premature infant has only one-ninth the chance for life that a full-term infant has. The reason for this is that he is less capable of making the difficult adjustments to the postnatal environment than the full-term infant is. He breathes in jerks and gasps and requires almost three times as much oxygen as a nine-month-old baby. He is often anemic and requires blood transfusions. Because the sucking and swallowing reflexes are weak, the premature infants must usually be fed artificially, through a tube or intravenously. His ability to withstand changes in temperature is poor, and this necessitates keeping him in an incubator, where the temperature can be kept constant as it was in the prenatal environment. And because he is extremely susceptible to infection, he must have careful medical attention to avoid developing an illness that may prove to be fatal (*Newsweek* Report, 1950).

Traditional Beliefs. From the beginnings of history, among civilized as among primitive peoples, beliefs about the prematurely born infant have been unfavorable. These beliefs center around the assumption that, because the individual has been deprived of the normal development before birth, he will be physically weak throughout life and will develop into a dullard. Among many primitive peoples and among civilized peoples in ancient times, before the dawn of Christianity, it was a common practice to put prematurely born infants to death at birth or to put them on a mountainside, with other defectives, and allow them to perish. These practices were based on the beliefs that the premature infant's chances of growing up to be normal were slim and that, for the good of the rest of the population, they should be done away with to avoid becoming social dependents.

Even today, many of the traditional beliefs about the ultimate outcome of the prematurely born individual are still held and have a marked influence on the treatment the child receives throughout his childhood years. He is likely to be overprotected by overly solicitous parents and to be deprived of the normal environment of full-term children of his age level. As a result of these beliefs, the prematurely born infant who survives is at a disadvantage from the start, and the pattern of his personality is likely to be seriously influenced by the effect these beliefs have on his home environment (Knehr and Sobol, 1949).

While most of the studies of newborn infants have been limited to an investigation of the effects of prematurity during the first few years of life, there are a few which have attempted to discover the long-range effects of prematurity by follow-up studies of prematurely born infants into childhood and late adolescence (Gesell, 1946; Drillien, 1948; Beskow, 1949; Knehr and Sobol, 1949; Howard and Morrell, 1952; Alm, 1953). These studies have revealed two important facts about prematurity: what effects prematurity have and how long these effects will persist.

In commenting on the effects of prematurity, Gesell (1946) has said, "The healthy premature infant does not acquire any unnatural precocity from his head start. Neither does he suffer any setback. This should be a great comfort to his anxious mother. She should be assured that the healthy premature infant follows the basic sequence of normal mental growth, making due allowance for his spurious age." When, however, the prematurely born infant is not healthy, or if he suffers some injury at birth, the long-term effects will be serious in proportion to the unfavorable birth conditions.

The second fact that has been revealed about the effects of prematurity is that infants prematurely born, as a rule, develop faster in their early postnatal environment than do infants who are born at full term. The premature infant, for example, at the age of nine months from the time of conception is more mature than the infant of full term who has just been born. The premature, however, is generally judged in terms of age from the time of birth, and this puts him at a decided disadvantage in comparison with full-term infants.

The necessity for corrected age for the premature has been stressed by Gesell (1946), who states that "The developmental status of the premature infant must always be appraised in terms of corrected age rather than in those of his spurious chronological age. Born or unborn, the infant cleaves to the inherent sequences of behavior maturation. He remains faithful to his fetality, even when birth has made him an infant" (p. 143). If the infant's actual age is considered, Gesell (1933a) maintains that he suffers no appreciable retardation in his development.

Characteristics of Premature Infants. Studies of prematurely born infants have been numerous. These studies have brought out a number of characteristics of the development present at birth of the premature as compared with full-term infants. For the most part, they show the behavior repertory characteristic of the newborn, though in a less developed form.

1. *Physical Development.* The time needed to regain the weight lost at birth among infants born prematurely has been found to be inversely related to the length of the gestation period (Steiner and Pomerance, 1951). The greatest gain comes between the fourth and sixth months after birth, which is later than the growth spurt for full-term infants. Smaller infants, however, start to gain later than heavier infants (Glaser et al., 1950). In the preschool period, there is less difference in height, weight, and general physical development between prematures and full-term infants than during babyhood (Drillien, 1948). At twenty years of age, however, those who were born prematurely have been reported to be slightly smaller, as judged by height and weight, than those born at full term (Alm, 1953).

Premature infants have more illnesses during the first year of life than do those born at full term. This is true especially in the case of respiratory and nasopharyngeal disturbances (Drillien, 1948). As they grow older, they suffer slightly more from such physical defects as malnutrition, dwarfism, and obesity than do full-term children. The most serious defect found among prematures is related to their eyes. Otherwise prematurity does not seem to affect physical growth to any appreciable extent (Howard and Morrell, 1952).

A recent report of eye defects associated with prematurity stressed the fact that the use of oxygen for premature infants frequently results in *retrolenthal fibroplasia,* the formation of scar tissue that makes the lens of the eye opaque and leaves damage ranging from mild impairment of vision to blindness. Frequently, however, oxygen is essential to save the life of the prematurely born infant whose respiratory mechanism does not function as adequately as that of the full-term infant (*New York Times* Report, 1954). The prematurely born infant is highly sensitive to sounds and noises. As babies, they are not only more keenly aware of sounds than are full-term babies, but they also are more interested in their meanings. They are, however, easily distracted by voices, traffic noises, and sounds made by other babies (Shirley, 1939).

2. *Developmental Status.* The developmental status of prematurely born individuals, as measured by developmental schedules, has been found to be somewhat retarded for the first five months of life. After that, the retardation becomes increasingly less until the age of two years, when the gap between the full-term and the prematurely born children closes (Melcher, 1937; Benton, 1940). In measuring development, if the starting point is taken from conception, rather than from birth, less difference is noted between the premature and the full-term baby. This is, however, less important as the child grows older (Knehr and Sobol, 1949). There is a significant difference in the ages at which prematures sit, stand, and walk as compared with full term-babies (Drillien, 1948). Babies whose birth weight had been under 4 pounds have been found to be retarded by a month or more through the first eighteen months of their lives. Those whose birth weight was 4 to 5 pounds, on the other hand, catch up to the norms for their ages by the time they are nine months old (Shirley, 1938a). Babies who were smallest at birth have been found to be most retarded in sitting, standing, and walking (Drillien, 1948).

3. *Motor Control.* Prematurely born infants have been found to be somewhat backward in motor performances as compared with full-term infants. They are retarded in the use of the index finger for pointing, in the pincer grasp, in postural control, locomotion, and in manual control. They are less graceful in their movements than full-term babies, they have poorer posture, and have a tendency to be awkward and clumsy. They are either very active or sluggish and slow in their movements (Melcher, 1937; Shirley, 1939; Drillien, 1948).

4. *Speech.* Prematurely born babies are retarded in speech, they persist longer in using baby talk and use more letter substitutions, such as "pray" for "play" and "tix" for "six," and they have more speech defects, especially stuttering, than do full-term babies (Hess et al., 1934; Shirley, 1939; Drillien, 1948; Davis, 1952).

5. *Intelligence.* When testing intelligence in young children, if the amount of prematurity is taken into consideration, premature children as a group are not intellectually inferior to full-term children. Unless this age differential is taken into consideration, premature children are somewhat retarded in their intellectual development during the first two years of life. After that, no significant difference is apparent (Gesell, 1928; Hess et al., 1934; Benton, 1940; Beskow, 1949; Knehr and Sobol, 1949; Schachter and Cotte, 1951; Howard and Morrell, 1952). There are, however, more cases of serious mental defects among the prematures than in the general population. For the most part, these defects are found among those who suffered

from cerebral hemorrhages at birth or immediately after birth (Benton, 1940; Beskow, 1949; Knehr and Sobol, 1949; Schacter and Cotte, 1951; Howard and Morrell, 1952). The smallest prematures contribute more than their share of the ranks of the mental defectives (Benton, 1940).

6. *Emotional Behavior*. Conflicting reports about the emotional behavior of prematurely born infants have been given. Shirley (1939) found the premature babies she studied to be more petulant, shy, irascible, and negativistic than children whose prenatal development was normal. In addition, she noted a marked aesthetic appreciation accompanied by a desire to create artistically. Melcher (1937), on the other hand, noted a rather moderate affective reaction among the prematurely born and described them as "gentle babies."

7. *Social Adjustments*. How prematurely born children react to people and social situations and what sort of social adjustments they make as compared with full-term infants has been extensively investigated. In general, these studies indicate that in the early years of life, the adjustments are superior to those made as the child grows older. In babyhood, there are some indications that the personal-social behavior is superior (Mohr and Bartelme, 1930) and that they are more advanced in this area of their development, as shown by smiling and noticing people, than in their motor development (Jersild, 1954). Other reports indicate that as babies, prematurely born children are shy, are much attached to their mothers (Shirley, 1939), and show more dependency reactions, such as hiding the head in the mother's lap, clinging to the mother, or turning to her for help and approval, than are observed in full-term babies of the same ages. This is explained by the fact that, owing to their physical weakness at birth, there is a tendency for their parents to overprotect them, and this is reflected in certain aspects of personality (Hess et al., 1934).

In the preschool years, more problem behavior has been reported among the prematures than among the full-term children. This is reflected especially in feeding problems (Drillien, 1948). While Alm (1953) contends that at twenty years of age there is no significant difference in the social adaptability of boys born prematurely as compared with those born at full-term, Howard and Morrell (1952), who studied both boys and girls up to the time they were nineteen years old, give another picture. According to them, the prematures do not make as good adjustments as those born at full term. Over half of the group they studied had made poor adjustments, as shown by the fact that 12 of the group of 22 were of the submissive, passive type, and 8 were unusually aggressive. Contributing factors, they claimed, were a poor physical endowment, deprivation of immediate postnatal maternal tenderness, and later overprotectiveness on the part of their parents.

8. *Nervous Traits*. Nervous traits or behavior disorders have been found to be definitely more numerous among prematurely born than among full-

term children (Hess et al., 1934; Shirley, 1939; Benton, 1940; Beskow, 1949; Howard and Morrell, 1952). Many indications of behavior disorders have been given, including thumb and finger sucking, nail biting, masturbation, psychosomatic difficulties (poor sleep, fatigability), emotional difficulties (irritability, shyness, temper outbursts, extreme irascibility, and a tendency to burst into tears at the slightest provocation), disturbances in the intellectual field (concentration and attention difficulties, forgetfulness), shyness, dogged determination not to comply with directions, peculiar gestures with the hands, and hypersensitivity to sounds (Hess et al., 1934; Shirley, 1939, Benton, 1940). Even among older adolescents, nail biting, habit spasms, and chronic masturbation are more commonly found than among adolescents who were born at full term (Howard and Morrell, 1952).

Explanations for the greater number and variety of nervous traits among the prematurely born have, for the most part, laid the blame on environmental conditions. Jersild (1954) suggests that prematurely born children are overprotected at first, then pushed to enable them to catch up to children born at full term. This tends to make them nervous. According to Benton (1940), the greater frequency of nervous traits among the prematures is caused by hereditary factors, birth injuries, faulty nurture, and initial feeding habits. Shirley (1939) states, "Possibly the environmental milieu of the premature is entirely responsible for their development of nervous mannerisms." When the babies are young, their mothers are anxious about them and hover over them with great solicitude. Later, they overurge the child in an attempt to close the gap between him and the child who was born at full term.

Chapter 4

PHYSICAL GROWTH

Physical growth influences behavior, and behavior, in turn, influences physical growth. As Carrel (1935) has pointed out, the individual is "a compound of tissues, organs, fluids, and consciousness." The interrelationship between physical growth and behavior is so important that an understanding of how the human child grows and develops is essential to an understanding of the similarities and differences *between* different individuals and the changes that take place in the *same individual* with increasing age. As Anderson (1942) has pointed out, "As soon as one works with children, he becomes aware that behavior of the moment is an end product determined by many factors, some of which are clearly related to the physical make-up and physiological state of the child. He . . . quickly becomes concerned with the problems of physical growth, body form, physiological adjustment, appetite, etc., all of which affect the adjustment of the child."

Normal Physical Development. The popular idea is that the relationship between physical and mental growth is one of compensation. Physical superiority is supposed to be accompanied by mental inferiority, the "beautiful but dumb" type, while the brainy person is thought to be a physical weakling. There is, however, no scientific evidence to support this theory. On the other hand, there is plenty of evidence to show that the relationship is one of correlation rather than compensation. Superior children are slightly superior in physical development, just as dull children are backward in physical development or have some physical defect.

There are four major areas in which normal physical development influences behavior (Kuhlen and Thompson, 1952). With the development of the *nervous system* there is an increase in intelligence which brings about new patterns of behavior. The emotional behavior of the child is directly related to his ability to perceive meanings in situations, just as the degree of social acceptance he enjoys is related to his ability to understand the thoughts, feelings, and emotions of others. Growth of the *muscles* brings changes in motor capacities and strength, which are reflected in changes in activities engaged in by the child and the degree of his participation in these activities. The child's play at all ages is largely dependent upon his muscular development, especially in the case of games and sports.

Changes in the functioning of the *endocrine glands* result in new and shifting patterns of behavior. At puberty, for example, there is a shift from

105

dislike for members of the opposite sex to a liking for them, from activities with one's own sex to activities with members of the opposite sex, and from lack of interest in personal appearance to preoccupation with looks and dress. And, finally, changes in the gross physical structure, his *physique*, in terms of height, weight, body proportions, and general physical appearance, affect the child's behavior.

As Thompson (1954) has pointed out, "The toddler whose eyes are at the level of an adult's knees sees a far different world from that envisioned by an adult; a child whose center of gravity is relatively low will have less difficulty in balance than one whose center of gravity is high. The mechanics of picking up an inch cube present a different problem to the tiny hand of the 1-year-old from the one presented to the hand of the 5-year-old." Babies who expand rapidly in physical size develop more slowly in their ability to sit, creep, and walk than do those with a slower rate of gain (Weech and Campbell, 1941). Body build is one of the important factors in determining the child's interests (Bayley, 1951).

The influence of the child's *physique* on his attitude toward the social group is very great. Because of his inferior size, the little child feels shy in the presence of adults, while in the presence of bigger children he feels inferior. The child's physique affects his reaction to himself as well as to others. Realization of how others feel about his size or general appearance has a marked influence on his concept of self. As Thompson (1954) has pointed out, "Children may suffer emotionally from being a 'Shrimp,' 'Tubby,' 'Redhead,' or 'Bucktooth.' The taunt, 'Brown eye turn around and tell a lie' can leave permanent personality scars."

Because what a child can do, say, think, or feel at a given age depends to such a large extent upon the stage of physical development he has attained, the child may rightly be said to "behave in accordance with his physical age." The stage of the child's physical development is thus more significant than his chronological age in determining his behavior.

Deviant Physical Development. Physical development that varies enough from the norm for the child's age to be noticeable, the malfunctioning of any physical organ, or physical defects, all influence the pattern of the child's behavior. *Body size and shape* have been found to influence the child's physical performances. Thin boys of average size, for example, perform better than boys of medium physique or average height. Those who are large and obese are the poorest performers of all (Bookwalter, 1952). Marked deviations in size not only affect the child's behavior but also his social acceptance by his peers. The obese child loses out in active play and, as a result, lacks the necessary opportunities to learn social skills which are essential to social success.

Because of his lack of social acceptance, the child often turns to overeating as a form of compensation (Bruch, 1940, 1941, 1943; Bruch and Touraine,

1940; Bronstein et al., 1942; Spock, 1953). The close relationship between obesity and personality has been explained by Bruch (1943) as follows: "Overeating is frequently used to combat anxiety and to satisfy aggressive impulses in children who had grown up under circumstances that had failed to give them adequate acceptance and emotional support from those persons on whom they were most closely dependent." How markedly deviations in body size can affect the child has been emphasized thus by Sontag (1946): "The unconscious cruelty of children toward anyone of them whose body does not conform to theirs in size, form, and function may be an important factor in the emotional adjustment of children lacking this conformity."

Dietary deficiencies lead to *loss of energy,* which, in turn, makes the child behave in a manner that suggests he is lazy or dull (Merry and Merry, 1950). He frequently whines, is fretful, and makes poor social adjustments (Thompson, 1954). His energy level is often very important in determining how he will react to what he interprets as a hostile environment (Sontag, 1946). Society expects certain behavior at certain ages. The child who does not come up to these standards, because of lack of energy or some other physical condition, is likely to be regarded as "maladjusted" (Merry and Merry, 1950). Studies of *enuresis,* for example, have shown that parents' ignorance of the ages when a young child can be expected to control his bladder causes them to scold and punish the child when he becomes wet, thus leading to a psychosomatic problem (Sweet, 1946).

Endocrine disorders result not only in body defects, but they also influence the intelligence and personality development of the child. In the case of *pituitary dwarfism,* for example, there is a deficiency of the growth hormone from the pituitary gland. The individual is a perfectly formed and proportioned miniature adult. The mental development is normal, as only the growth-promoting factor is absent. Any psychological effect will be indirect, as it affects the individual's attitude toward his dwarfism. In the case of *hypothyroid dwarfism,* on the other hand, the whole development of the child is affected. In severe cases, this is known as *cretinism.* Since the thyroid hormone is responsible for cell development, all the cells of the body are affected unfavorably by a deficiency of this hormone. The bones grow slowly, and their ossification is retarded. The brain cells develop inadequately, and this causes mental deficiency. How seriously thyroid deficiency will influence the child's development depends partly upon the seriousness of the deficiency and partly upon the period in the growth cycle when it occurs. The most serious time is the period of prenatal development, when growth and development are most rapid (Morgolese, 1948).

Deafness, blindness, or a *weak heart* keeps the child from entering into the play activities of other children. The result is often the development of unfavorable attitudes which color the child's whole behavior. The child who suffers from some physical defect is often neglected or even ridiculed by other children, or he may be sympathized with by them, depending on the severity of his defect, and this affects his attitude toward himself. The effects of prolonged illness and physical defects will be discussed in detail in the section of this chapter which deals with health conditions (see pages 128–133).

GROWTH CYCLES

Growth is rhythmic, not regular. A child does not grow a given number of pounds annually or a given number of inches in height. Growth comes, on the contrary, in cycles or waves, the "periods," or "phases," of growth (Scammon, 1942; Krogman, 1948; Thompson, 1954). This growth is not random or haphazard. As Krogman (1948) has pointed out, "The child grows in obedience to certain biological laws inherent in his phylogenetic history. . . . This means that man has a *growth pattern* which is at once generalized—his phylogeny—and specialized—his ontogeny. Research has enabled us to analyze this twofold pattern and to ascertain the part of it that is uniquely human. In fine, we have a pretty good idea of what constitutes normal human growth."

Studies of the growth cycles have revealed that there are four distinct periods, two characterized by slow growth and two by rapid growth. From birth to two years, there is rapid growth. This is followed by a period of slow growth up to the time of puberty or sexual maturing, beginning usually between the eighth and eleventh years. From then until fifteen or sixteen years, there is rapid growth, and this is followed by a period of fairly abrupt tapering off of growth to the time of maturity (Meredith, 1935; Scammon, 1942; Krogman, 1948; Thompson, 1954). Because growth is an energy-consuming process, it is important that the work burden of the child be adjusted, whenever possible, to meet the demands of growth (Krogman, 1948).

These growth cycles are so universal and predictable that clothing for children is sized accordingly. The rapid growth in the first year necessitates two sets of clothing, the *infant* size for the first six months and the *first* size for the last six months. The next larger size is adequate for the child from his first to his second birthday, while the size larger serves for two years, from the second to the fourth birthday. Sizes suited to the development of older children and adolescents likewise take into consideration the growth and the resting periods.

Variations in Growth Cycles. There are variations in the normal pattern of growth cycles. But as Krogman (1948) has stressed

with few exceptions, the variation follows an orderly progress; there is a range which we have learned to expect. Growth is not a narrow path; it is, rather, a broad highway. We do not so much stray from the path of growth as we meander along the highway of growth. Variation is in and of itself an unequal factor, for some children are more variable than others, and variability, in general, increases with age. The excessive variability of some children may be explained in part by their hereditary background, and in part by their food and health habits, as well as their health vicissitudes. As a rule, a markedly erratic growth progress in a child is a signal for more intensive investigation, for health problems seem to be correlated with extreme deviates. A growth item, i.e., length of a limb segment, which is less variable than, say, weight, will be more significant in its deviation.

A number of factors have been reported to influence the amount of variability that accompanies the growth pattern. *Family* and *ethnic background* influence the rates of growth for different children. Similar growth patterns within families in height, bone development, age of sexual maturing,

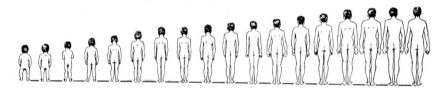

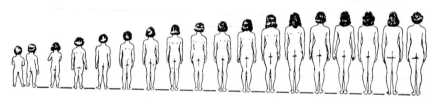

Fig. 17. Characteristic sex differences in growth. (*From N. Bayley, Individual patterns in development, presidential address, American Psychological Association, Division on Developmental Psychology, Sept. 5, 1954. Used by permission.*)

and eruption and decaying of teeth have been reported (Gould and Gould, 1932; Boas, 1935; Reynolds, 1943; Klein, 1946; Krogman, 1948; Thompson, 1954; Breckenridge and Vincent, 1955. There are *sex* differences in growth with boys growing faster than girls at certain ages and girls faster than boys at other ages (see Fig. 17). Variability within the sex group is usually greater for boys than for girls (Norval et al., 1951). For both boys and girls, however, variability in growth rate increases with age (Krogman, 1948).

Body size influences the rate of growth and is responsible for some of the variations that occur. A small child grows over a longer period of time than a large child who has a greater period of initial growth (Muhsam, 1947; Krogman, 1948; Norval et al., 1951). *Body type* likewise influences variations in growth patterns. Ectomorphs, for example, grow in height over a longer period of time than do mesomorphs, while mesomorphs grow faster at each age level, especially in weight (Dupertuis and Michael, 1953). *Emotional tension* may seriously curtail growth rate, though it has a greater effect on weight than on height (Widdowson, 1951).

  Season of the year is responsible for some variations in growth rates, just as there are variations from one year to another. July to middle December is the season most favorable for increase in weight, with the most rapid gains from September to December. At this time, the average gain is four times that from February to June. The least growth comes from the beginning of May to early July. Growth in height, on the other hand, follows an entirely different cycle. The greatest increase comes from April to the middle of August, paralleling the slow period of increase in weight, while the least increase comes from August to the end of November, the period of greatest increase in weight (Marshall, 1937; Reynolds and Sontag, 1944; Krogman, 1948; Dale, 1950; Thompson, 1954). Because seasonal variations are most marked in weight, it suggests that this may be merely a seasonal difference in water content of the body rather than a true growth trend (Thompson, 1954). Or it may reflect differences in time of day when the weighing is done (Krogman, 1948).

  Growth Cycles for Different Organs. The human body does not grow as a whole, nor does it grow in all directions at once (Thompson, 1954). Each organ and each part of the body follows its own laws of development. The different parts of the body have their own individual periods of rapid growth, and each reaches its mature size at its own individual time. However, as Merry and Merry (1950) have stressed, "All phases of growth are continuous and take place concurrently. For example, the individual's skeleton does not grow on one particular day, while the rest of his structure lies dormant, nor does his nervous system develop at one time and his muscles at another; but all are developing at the *same* time, each in its own way and at its own rate."

  Studies of growth curves for height and weight have shown that they converge until about six years, run parallel until ten years, and then diverge. Height is gained at a constantly *decelerating* rate, while weight is gained at a constantly accelerating rate. As Krogman (1948) has expressed it, "We get taller faster, heavier slower." The lower part of the face grows more rapidly than the upper, especially from ages five through eight years (Allen, 1948). In muscular growth it has been found that increase in breadth of the muscle in the calf of the leg comes with increasing age. Growth occurs at a rapidly decelerating rate in the second year, at a slowly decelerating rate to the onset of puberty, then at an accelerating rate during puberty, and at a decelerating rate thereafter until growth ceases (Lombard, 1950).

  Studies of age changes in head hair from birth to maturity have shown that the shape of the hair shaft changes from a more nearly round to a more nearly oval form during the first two years of life. After that, there is no consistent trend. The shaft increases in size at a rapid and uniform rate during the first three years of life, then less uniformly and at a slower rate (Trotter and Duggins, 1948). Scammon and Calkins (1929) maintain that there are four main types of growth, each with its own sequence and tempo. These types are *general,* or skeletal, *nervous, lymphoid,* and *genital.* The muscles, bones, lungs, and genitals increase approximately twenty times in size during the growth years, while the eyes, the brain, and some other organs increase much less because they are relatively more developed at birth. The eyeball, for example, completes most of its growth during the first 5 years and the brain during the first 10, while the heart and some other organs require more than 20 years to reach their mature size.

In general, growth of the parts of the body follows the *law of developmental direction,* referred to in Chap. 1 and explained in more detail in Chap. 5. This means that, for the most part, development occurs first in the upper part of the body and later in the lower part of the body. Changes in body proportions are relatively slight during the first half year of postnatal life. From then until puberty, however, head growth is slow, limb growth rapid, and trunk growth intermediate (Thompson, 1954). The brain and facial features attain maturity in size and development before the organs and features of the trunk and limbs.

BODY SIZE

Body size is determined by measurements of height and weight. While these measures follow a pattern of development that is markedly similar, with slow gains in weight being paralleled by slow gains in height and rapid gains in height going hand in hand with rapid gains in weight, the total growth in height from birth to maturity is less than the total growth in weight. It has been estimated that the total increase in height is 3½-fold and the total increase in weight twentyfold (Merry and Merry, 1950). Increases in body size for boys and girls at different ages are shown in Fig. 17, page 109.

Height. While marked variations exist in the height of children of the same age, there is a pattern of growth which is similar for all children. Expressed in terms of averages, the pattern gives a picture of the typical growth for the typical child. The baby at birth measures between 19 and 20 inches. During the first two years of life, there are rapid increases in height. At four months of age, his height is, on the average, 23 to 24 inches; at eight months, 26 to 28 inches; and at one year, 28 to 30 inches. At two years, he is 32 to 34 inches tall, and by five years, his height should have doubled, making him 40 inches tall. From then until the onset of puberty, growth is at a slower rate. At 12 years, children are 2¾ times their birth height, or approximately 55 inches. From ten to fourteen years in girls and from twelve to sixteen years in boys, there is a rapid growth spurt followed by a period of slow growth until eighteen or twenty years, when mature height is attained.

Predicting adult height can be done with relative accuracy today. X rays of the bones of the wrist and the hands give an accurate assessment of the maturation of the skeleton (Gruelich, 1950). Because there has been found to be a high correlation between the skeletal age of the child, as determined by X rays of the bones of the hands and wrists and the proportion of adult stature achieved at the time the X rays are taken, it is now possible to tell with reasonable accuracy how tall the child will be when his full growth has been completed (Gray, 1948; Bayley and Pinnau, 1952). Furthermore, because the child's height shows a general tendency to increase in correlation with the parents' height, owing to the manifestation of inherited similarities, this may likewise be used as basis for prediction of adult height (Bayley, 1951, 1954). Predicting adult height during infancy and during the pre-adolescent growth spurt is not only difficult but is less accurate than at other ages (Simmons, 1944).

Weight. Weight is more variable than height at all ages. While the average baby may weigh between 6 and 8 pounds at birth, there will be some babies whose weight is only 3 or 4 pounds, and others whose weight is nearly double the average. The pattern of increase, however, is much the same for all. By the end of the first month of life, the average baby has not only regained the weight lost after birth, but has begun to show a weight increase. At four months, he should have doubled his birth weight and, at the end of the first year, trebled it. During the second and third years, the average increase is 3 to 5 pounds annually. After the third year, gains in weight are at a slower rate until the onset of puberty. At five years, the child should be approximately five times his birth weight, and at the onset of puberty, between 70 and 90 pounds. As is true of height, there is a marked increase in annual gain in weight for three or four years, followed by a slowing down in increase until mature weight has been attained, late in the adolescent period.

The weight of the child at every age is dependent to a certain extent upon his *body build*. While there are many types of body build, roughly body builds fall into three major categories: the *endomorph,* characterized by a tendency to store up excessive fat; the *mesomorph,* characterized by a heavy, hard, and rectangularly outlined body; and the *ectomorph,* characterized by a long, slender body, slender muscles and long, thin bones (Sheldon et al., 1940). In judging the "normal" weight for a child, his body build must be taken into consideration. A mesomorph, for example, would be expected to weigh more for his height than an ectomorph. The relation of weight to body build is illustrated in Fig. 18. To discover the "normal" weight for a child, it has been suggested that the most accurate indicator is to use calf width and height (Massler and Suher, 1951).

Many children are *obese* in that their weight is proportionally too great for their height. Very rarely is this due to a glandular condition. On the contrary, it generally stems from psychological factors of an unfavorable sort, such as overdependency, feelings of rejection, and feelings of inadequacy (Bruch, 1939, 1940, 1941, 1941a, 1943; Bruch and Touraine, 1940). Bad family eating habits and constitutional factors are likewise responsible for obesity (Tolstrup, 1953). Among older children and pubescents, appetite increases and habits of overeating may develop (Wolff and Bayer, 1952). While most obese children derive their overweight from fat, others are too heavy because of their bone and muscle development (Reynolds and Asakawa, 1948).

Variations in Body Size. Variations in body size are present at birth. These variations become more pronounced as the child grows older and are

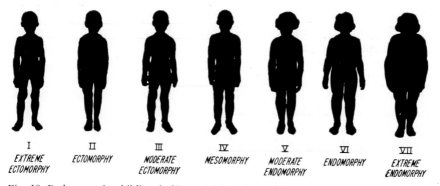

I	II	III	IV	V	VI	VII
EXTREME ECTOMORPHY	ECTOMORPHY	MODERATE ECTOMORPHY	MESOMORPHY	MODERATE ENDOMORPHY	ENDOMORPHY	EXTREME ENDOMORPHY

Fig. 18. Body types in childhood. (*From M. Massler and T. Suher, Calculation of "normal" weight in children, Child Develpm., 1951, 22, 75–94. Used by permission.*)

especially great in late childhood because of differences in ages at which different children begin the growth spurt that accompanies puberty. Variations in weight are greater at all ages than variations in height because weight is more susceptible to environmental influences than is height. Because each child has his own growth pattern, influenced by his body build, any variation from averages for his age group should take into consideration his "type." One method of measuring his variations that has proved to be successful is the Wetzel Grid (1944, 1948), which has seven channels for seven body types. Because a child's growth normally progresses in a particular channel, any deviation from this channel is indicative of his health status. When, for example, the curve moves to the left, it means the child is changing to a stocky physique which may lead to obesity. Should the curve move, on the other hand, to the right, this is indicative of a change to a more slender physique and a loss in nutritional status.

Variations in *birth weight* are maintained through the growth years and remain constant. For example, in girls at the age of seven years, a mean difference of 11.2 pounds was found between those whose birth weight was 9 pounds 9 ounces or more and those whose birth weight was 5 pounds 8 ounces or less. At eleven years, the difference was 12.8 pounds. This was true of boys also. Variations in birth length likewise remain relatively constant throughout the childhood years (Illingworth et al., 1949, 1950). While some change in relative heights may occur in late childhood, at the time of the puberty growth spurt, tall children do not become short nor do short children become tall (Meredith, 1938). *Family* influences are responsible for variations in body size throughout childhood as children tend to resemble members of their families as growth progresses (Howells, 1949; Bayley, 1951, 1954).

Birth order has little influence on variations in body size. There is, however, greater correlation in height than in weight measurements for brothers (Howells, 1948). *Sex* differences in favor of boys are present from birth until eleven or twelve years in both height and weight. Then girls are slightly larger than boys until the fifteenth year, after which boys again surpass girls (Simmons, 1944; Krogman, 1948; Thompson, 1954). Variations due to *racial* stock have been reported for children of all ages. While Negro babies during the first year of life do not differ in size significantly from white babies of comparable economic levels (Bakwin and Patrick, 1944; Scott et al., 1950), differences become greater with age as the Negro child typically is of a more slender build than the white child (Royster, 1936). Children of Finnish ancestry are larger than those of Italian ancestry at all ages (Matheny and Meredith, 1947), as is true of those of Mexican ancestry (Meredith and Goldstein, 1952). Children from Okinawa are smaller in both height and weight than are children from France, South Africa, or the American Indians (Meredith, 1948). Japanese children are smaller, age for age, than white children (Krogman, 1948).

Size varies with level of *intelligence.* Children of high levels of intelligence are taller and heavier for their ages than are children of lower levels of intelligence (Hollingworth, 1926; Katz, 1940; Thompson, 1954). Variations in size according to the socioeconomic status of the family are marked, especially in weight. These differences are due to differences in diet, especially during the early years of life, housing conditions, health practices, and occupational demands (Bowles, 1932; Meredith, 1941; Hopkins, 1947; Meredith and Meredith, 1950; Greenberg and Bryan, 1951). Children whose fathers belong to the professional or managerial class are larger in every body measurement than children of skilled or semiskilled workers. These differences become greater as the children grow older (Ames and Flory, 1944; Meredith, 1951). Children suffering from nutritive deficiencies, due to family poverty, are smaller and their speed of growth is retarded as compared with that of children of the same ages whose economic status is better

(Dreizen et al., 1953). *Prolonged heat* retards growth and the onset of puberty (Mills, 1950).

PHYSICAL PROPORTIONS

At birth, the proportions of the body are very different from those of the adult (see Fig. 1). The child's growth therefore results not only in an increase in size but, of equal importance, in a marked change in the proportions of the different parts of the body. Likewise, not all parts of the body attain mature proportions at the same time. Some areas attain their mature size at one age, while others attain maturity at earlier or later ages. But, by the age of sixteen or seventeen years, the different parts of the body have, for the most part, assumed their mature proportions, and the individual is similar in appearance to an adult.

In general, changes in proportions follow the law of developmental direction. Early changes in proportions are in the head and later in the trunk. The arms and legs are the last areas of the body to attain mature proportions. For example, the child at 5½ is 65 per cent as tall as he will be at 17½ years, but he weighs only 33 per cent as much as he will then. After 5½ years, there is an increase of over 50 per cent in arm span, but the increase in head circumference is less than 7 per cent (Garrison, 1952). From a chubby, top-heavy infant with proportionally too short limbs, the individual becomes a child with a head and trunk still too large for his limbs. At puberty, the growth of the limbs is greatly accelerated, and thus adult proportions are finally attained. Throughout childhood, there are no marked sex differences in body proportions.

Proportions of the Head. The *head* grows proportionately less after birth than do most other parts of the body, because it has to grow less to attain mature size. At birth, the length of the head is 22 per cent of the total body length. If these proportions remained constant, a mature man of 6 feet would have a head of about 16 inches in length instead of the average of 8 or 9 inches, thus resulting in a real monstrosity. From birth to maturity the length of the head doubles, but the total stature is 3½ times that at birth. The surface area of the head decreases from 21 per cent of the total surface area of the body at birth to 13 per cent at five years, 10 per cent at twelve years, and 8 per cent at eighteen years (Boyd, 1935). At ten years, the head is 95 per cent of its adult size, and at fifteen years, 98 per cent (Davenport, 1940).

The cranial part of the head is large and the facial area small at birth. At this time, the relationship of the face to the cranium is 1 to 8; at five years of age, it is 1 to 5; and at maturity, 1 to 2.5. Increase in head length is due mostly to increase in facial proportions, as the cranial or upper portions grow little from birth to puberty and none afterward. The child's head is broader in relation to length than the adult's head. The increase in length is, therefore, greater than in width. By three years, the head has practically finished its growth in width but continues to increase in length until seventeen or eighteen years. Increase in size is more a function of age than of initial size. Short and narrow heads show somewhat greater increase than long and broad heads. The growth pattern in length and width is much the same for boys and girls, though boys' heads are slightly larger than girls' heads at every age (Bayley, 1936; Goldstein, 1939; Davenport, 1940; Thompson, 1954; Breckenridge and Vincent, 1955).

Proportions of the Face. Because the upper part, or cranium, completes its growth so early, the head has a disproportionate look. The top of the head appears to be too large for the face. The lower part of the head throughout babyhood and early childhood is small and undeveloped, owing primarily to the lack of teeth at first and later to the smallness of the baby teeth. The facial skeleton becomes larger in proportion to the cranium from birth to eight years, thereby eliminating the "babyish look." There is greater growth between the ages of five and eight years, especially among boys, than at any other time (Allen, 1948).

Until the second, or "permanent," teeth have replaced the "baby" teeth—and this is not until shortly before puberty—the mouth, chin, and entire lower part of the child's face are small compared with the upper part, where the brain development has progressed more rapidly. During the transition from baby to permanent teeth, there are changes in occlusion (fitting together of the upper and lower teeth) which affect the shape of the lower part of the child's face. The percentage of occlusion drops from 70 at four years to 22 at nine years and then gradually increases with age (Thompson, 1954). When the two jaws do not fit together, "malocclusion," this will not only seriously affect the shape of the lower part of the face, but it will also interfere with proper chewing and, thus, affect digestion (Krogman, 1939; Davenport, 1940; Thompson, 1954; Breckenridge and Vincent, 1955).

Malocclusion may be due to irregularities in the growth of the two jaws, variations in the size of the upper and lower teeth, thumb sucking, especially before the child is five years of age, mouth breathing, pressure on the chin, as in stomach-sleeping during the babyhood years, or tongue biting. These may cause or aggravate malocclusions (Lewis and Lehman, 1929; Lewis, 1933; Klein, 1950; Garrison, 1952; *New York Times* Report, 1954a; Breckenridge and Vincent, 1955). While malocclusions may correct themselves as development progresses, corrective work (orthodontics) is often necessary if the child is to develop a well-shaped face with teeth and chin in correct proportions and lines. The changes that occur in the shape of the face from childhood to maturity are shown in Fig. 19.

There are changes in the features of the face as well as in its shape. The *forehead* flattens, the *lips* fill out, and the *eyeballs* reach their mature size as the child approaches puberty. The *nose* is one of the most disproportion-ate of the facial features. For the first few years of life, it is small and rather flat on the face. Gradually, as the cartilage framework develops, the nose becomes larger and assumes a more definite shape. By the age of thirteen or fourteen years, it has attained its mature size. The primary *hair*, or "lanugo," of the fetus may persist for several months after birth. This is followed by "vellus," or secondary hair, which is the fine hair of babyhood. This becomes coarser in the early years of childhood and shows the charac-

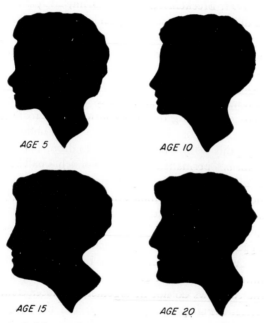

Fig. 19. Changes in facial proportions. Profiles of the same child at five, ten, fifteen, and twenty years. (*From L. Cole, Psychology of adolescence, 4th ed., Rinehart, 1954. Used by permission.*)

teristics of "terminal" hair (Trotter and Duggins, 1948). There are marked changes taking place in the quality, shape, and pigmentation of the hair as the child grows older (Duggins and Trotter, 1950).

Proportions of the Trunk. The "top-heavy" development of the baby mili-tates against good balance, and this must be corrected before the baby can sit, stand, or walk. The change in proportions which is essential to good balance comes from a gradual lengthening of the *trunk* and *legs*. The shape of the trunk undergoes rapid changes during the early years of life. During the first year, the baby becomes more thickset as a result of a greater in-crease in the girths and transverse diameters than in the lengths. This change is reflected in the proportionally greater increase in weight than in height at this age (Bayley and Davis, 1935). From four to eight years, there is a gradual decrease in the stockiness of the stem and the over-all stockiness of the body (Meredith and Culp, 1951; Meredith and Sherbina, 1951; Meredith and Meredith, 1953).

Up to the age of six years, the trunk is twice as long and wide as it was at birth. The child becomes gradually slimmer until prepuberty, when the body widens out again. From the age of six years until adolescence, the increase in body length is approximately 50 per cent. By maturity, the birth dimensions are trebled. The thickness of the trunk at maturity is not quite 2½ times that at birth. The protruding abdomen so characteristic of the small baby flattens out from about the third year, and the shoulders become broader, resulting in a more rectilinear and flat-bodied child (Thompson, 1954).

Changes in the shape of the trunk come mainly from changes in the chest and pelvic bones. At birth, the chest is rounder, the neck short, and the shoulders high. From three to ten years, the chest broadens and flattens. The ribs change from a more horizontal to a more oblique position. The neck lengthens, and this permits the shoulders to drop. The pelvis, consisting of the hip and sacral bones, is proportionally much smaller in a baby than in an adult. As children grow, the pelvis increases in size, broadens, and is less vertical. In childhood, there is little difference in the size of the pelvis in boys and girls. At puberty, however, the pelvic arch of the girl broadens much more than the boy's, and this results in an enlargement of the body circumference in the area of the hips (Breckenridge and Vincent, 1955).

Proportions of Arms and Legs. Changes in body proportions cause the body to become less apelike and more characteristically human. This is due to the relative increase in leg length. At birth, the *legs* of the infant are proportionately too short, the *arms* too long, and the hands and feet too small. Growth at different rates must, therefore, occur before mature proportions are attained. The length of the *arms* and *hands* increases between 60 and 75 per cent from birth to two years. At the age of eight years, the arms are nearly 50 per cent longer than at two years. At this time, they are very thin, with no marked development apparent in the musculature. This is responsible for giving the child the spindly, "all-arms" look so characteristic of that age (Meredith and Culp, 1951; Meredith and Sherbina, 1951). With increasing age, there is a tendency for the right arm to be longer than the left, especially in right-handed children (Van Dusen, 1939). From eight until sixteen or eighteen years, growth in the length of the arms is slow, while development in shape, owing to increased musculature, is taking place.

The *legs* of a newborn infant are short and flexed so that the soles of the feet point toward each other. As the legs grow in length, they straighten. By the time the child is six years old, his legs and knees should be straight

(Breckenridge and Vincent, 1955). During the first two years of life, the legs grow 40 per cent and, at eight years they are 50 per cent longer than at two years. Thus the legs grow at a slower rate at first than do the arms. By adolescence, the legs are four times as long as at birth; at maturity, five times as long. As is true of the legs, the arms of a child are thin and spindly until puberty (Meredith and Culp, 1951; Meredith and Sherbina, 1951). Then, as the increase in length slows down, there is a growth in the muscular development which results in a marked change in the shape of the legs. It is difficult to predict adult leg length until the time of puberty is known. In the case of girls, for example, leg length varies according to whether the menarche comes early or late (Worcester and Lombard, 1948).

The *hands* and *feet* of the newborn infant are very tiny. Before they can be used, they must increase in size as well as in muscular development. The child's hands differ from those of an adult not only in size but also in shape. The fingers are short and stubby, because of the slow growth of the bones of the fingers. They grow rapidly early in puberty and attain their mature size by the fourteenth or fifteenth year. The palm of the right hand is usually larger than that of the left, if the child is right-handed (Van Dusen, 1939). As is true of the hands, the feet grow slowly during childhood and then spurt early in puberty, reaching their adult size at approximately the same time as the hands. The pubescent growth spurt of the feet precedes the spurt in leg length (Davenport, 1932).

Before the child is five years old, the arches of his feet are well developed. The height of the arch varies markedly from child to child and is determined more by genetic factors than by exercise and use, though a heavy child frequently has flatter arches than a child of the same age who is lighter in weight (Robinow et al., 1943). There are marked individual variations in the size and shape of the feet in childhood. Boys, at every age, have larger feet than girls, and their feet reach mature size later than do girls' feet. There is some correlation between the size of the foot and the height of the individual (Meredith, 1944).

BONES

The bones of a child are not only smaller than the bones of an adult, but they differ also in proportions, shape, and composition. Development, then, consists of growth in the size of the bones, change in the number of bones, and change in their composition. Bone development has been found to follow the same general trend as growth in size; that is, development is most rapid during the first year of life, followed by a period of relatively slow development, which is followed by a period of more rapid development at the time of puberty (Bayley, 1940; Harding, 1952).

At birth, the infant has approximately 270 bones. By puberty, the number has increased to about 350. Then the number begins to decrease, as different bones fuse, so that in the mature skeleton, there are only 206 bones (Thompson, 1954). In the case of the wrist, for example, there are two or three bones at two years of age; at six years, there are six or seven bones; while between the twelfth and fifteenth year, there are eight bones. Figure 20 shows the development of hand and wrist bones in children at different ages.

In the early months of postnatal life, the bone tissue is soft and spongy. Cartilage or membrane occurs in some places where there will later be bone. The child's bones contain more water and proteinlike substances and

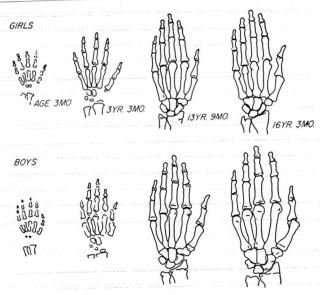

Fig. 20. Ages and sex differences in ossification of the hand and wrist. (*Based on unpublished material of N. Bayley from illustrations in T. W. Todd, Atlas of skeletal maturation, St. Louis: Mosby, 1937. From F. K. Shuttleworth, The adolescent period: a graphic atlas, Monogr. Soc. Res. Child Develpm., 1949, 14, No. 1. Used by permission.*)

less minerals than adult bones. They are more vascular, and more blood flows through them to supply materials for growth, than is true of the bones of an adult. The outcovering, or "periosteum," is thicker, and this prevents complicated fractures. The child's bones are not firmly knit together. Instead, there is much space between the ends of the bones, and the ligaments at the joints are longer and less firmly attached, than is true of adult bones.

Because the bones are soft at first, the baby's body is pliable and he can get into strange positions without difficulty, such as sucking his toes when lying on his back. In addition to this, the bones are liable to be deformed, because of pressure, unless care is taken. The shape of the head can be flattened if the baby is allowed to sleep for too long a time on his back, or the chest will be flattened if he spends most of his sleep time on his stomach. Even in the elementary-school years, bone deformities result from too short shoes or from sitting in a cramped posture at a school desk.

Growth of Bones. Bones grow in length at the ends where a strip of cartilage remains throughout the growth years. The original cartilage at the ends of the long bones is converted into bone, and thus the bone is lengthened. The bone shaft, or *diaphysis,* is separated from other bony masses at the ends, the *epiphyses,* by a strip of cartilage. So long as the two do not fuse, the bone will continue to grow in length. When the epiphysis and the diaphysis unite, the bone is no longer able to grow. Stimulation by the sex hormone, at puberty, is responsible for the fusion of the two portions of the bone. Thus the sex hormone is the factor that limits the growth of the bone (Margolese, 1948). Bones grow in width by adding new bone at their outer edges.

Ossification. Ossification, or hardening of the bones, is entirely postnatal, beginning at the early part of the first year and ending during puberty. Ossification takes place gradually, owing to calcium, phosphorus, and other mineral salts which are introduced into the bone structure. There is a gain of 60 per cent or more of mineral matter in the bones during the process of ossification. The process of ossification begins at the "ossification center" in the cartilage and gradually spreads throughout the bone. A bone may have more than one ossification center. It is estimated that there are over 800 such centers in the human body, half of which do not appear until after birth. New centers continue to appear until skeletal maturity has been attained (Thompson, 1954). When the process of ossification is finished, each bone has its characteristic shape.

Ossification is dependent largely upon the secretion of a hormone from the thyroid glands. Should this be deficient, the process of ossification will be delayed (Margolese, 1948). There is also a close relationship between ossification and nutrition. Children from the superior socioeconomic groups have been found to be accelerated in their anatomical development as compared with those from inferior socioeconomic environments. If ossification is retarded because of inadequate mineralization resulting from a thyroid deficiency or a dietary deficiency, the child will have bowed legs and other skeletal deformities, because the bones are not sufficiently hard to withstand the pressure from the weight of his body.

Ossification proceeds at different rates for different parts of the body. The fontenelles, for example, are closed in over 50 per cent of all babies by the age of eighteen months and in nearly all by two years. Ossification of the long bones of the legs, on the other hand, does not occur until puberty. There are likewise marked sex differences in rates of ossification, with girls ahead of boys at every age level (Flory, 1936; Todd, 1937; Bayley, 1946).

By using X rays of the hand and wrist, it is possible to tell at what rate a child is progressing in his osseous development and to predict the approximate ages at which he will reach puberty and the maturity of his skeletal development (Todd, 1937; Bayley, 1946; Harding, 1952a).

MUSCLES AND FAT

Increase in weight at all periods of growth is due to the development of two types of tissue, in addition to the weight of the bones, *adipose* and *muscle tissue.* In the early years of childhood, the development of adipose tissue is more rapid than that of muscle tissue, but from the ages of twelve to fifteen in girls and from fifteen to sixteen years in boys, there is a marked increase in muscle tissue. What proportion of the child's body weight will come from muscle and what from adipose tissue will depend largely upon his "body type." Children who tend toward *endomorphy* have more soft adipose tissue than muscular tissue. The tendency toward *mesomorphy,* on the other hand, means a predominance of muscle and connective tissue. In the *ectomorph,* there is not a predominance of either type of tissue (Sheldon et al., 1940).

The *muscles* play a role of major importance in regulating the vital organs of the body, such as the heart, digestive system, and glands. They are also responsible for strength and coordination of activity. At birth, muscle fibers are present in an undeveloped state. That is why the newborn infant is so helpless and his activities so weak and uncoordinated. While no new muscle fibers develop after birth, the ones that are present change in size, shape, and composition. Muscles increase in size by growth in the length, breadth, and thickness of the fibers. With growth comes an increase in weight. For the average person, the increase from birth to maturity is forty times the original weight. Up to five years of age, the muscles grow in proportion to the increase in body weight. Then, from five to six years, there is a rapid spurt in muscle growth, at which time the child's weight gain is approximately 75 per cent muscle weight. After this time, the growth of the muscles is relatively slow but is followed by a marked spurt at the time of puberty.

In early childhood, the muscles contain more water and less solids and proteins than adult muscles. In addition, they are more delicate and less firmly attached to the bones than are adult muscles. With growth, there is a change in the composition and attachment to the bones. At maturity, the muscles are five or more times as thick as at birth. Their composition changes from 72 per cent water and 28 per cent solid matter to 66 per cent water and 34 per cent solid matter. Consequently, the muscles become firmer and stronger. As the muscles become stronger, there is a strong drive for muscular activity. The child is constantly on the go, is restless when he is forced to be inactive, and frequently overtaxes his strength in his desire to be active (Damann, 1941).

As is true of other physical features, there are marked individual differences in the muscular equipment of children. Children who have broad, thick muscles have superior physical strength; those with smaller muscles are usually more agile and show better coordination in skilled activities. Some children have muscles that fatigue easily; others have muscles that show marked endurance. The condition of the muscles depends partly upon the hereditary endowment of the child and partly upon his general health condition and the use he makes of his muscles. Even within the same child, there are variations in the condition of his muscles from time to time. After an illness, for example, the child's muscle tone is lowered and he is able to do less before becoming fatigued than he can do when he is in a good physical condition. While sex differences in the muscular development of the child are not marked in childhood, these differences become pronounced at puberty when boys' muscles grow larger and stronger than girls' muscles.

There are even more marked differences in *adipose tissue* among children than there is in the case of muscle tissue. How much adipose tissue the child has depends not only upon his heredity and his body build but also upon his eating habits. There are, however, certain age changes which are generally found in all children regardless of how much or how little adipose tissue they have. From birth to nine months, there is a rapid increase, followed by an abrupt and rapid decrease up to 2½ years. The decrease slows down until approximately 5½ years, remains practically unchanged to eleven years, and then decreases rapidly between eleven and thirteen years, which is frequently called the "puberty fat period" (Stuart and Sobel, 1946; Stolz and Stolz, 1951).

Studies of the distribution of different tissues in the leg have shown that the relation of breadth of fat to breadth of bone tends to decrease with age in males and increase in females. After thirteen years of age, sex differences become increasingly great (Reynolds, 1949). In the male leg, there is more muscle, and in the female, more fat (Reynolds and Grote, 1948). Children from the superior socioeconomic classes are heavier from eight through eleven years of age than are children from inferior socioeconomic groups. This difference is due primarily to differences in amount of muscle mass and subcutaneous fat. Among girls, this is especially pronounced between the ages of six and eight years (Greenberg and Bryan, 1951).

THE TEETH

The child has two sets of teeth—the "baby," or temporary, teeth and the permanent teeth. These two sets differ in several important respects: (1)

There are 20 temporary teeth and 32 permanent ones. (2) The temporary teeth are smaller than the permanent ones. (3) The permanent teeth are of better quality and therefore more durable. The growth of teeth is a continuous process from the third prenatal month, when the teeth begin to form in the jaw, until the wisdom teeth reach their full size, between the ages of twenty-one and twenty-five years. The eruption of the temporary teeth is accompanied by discomfort or actual pain, often causing the baby to lose his appetite and become irritable and nervous. Permanent teeth, for the most part, cut through the gums without any appreciable discomfort.

Temporary Teeth. The first of the temporary teeth makes its appearance between the third and sixteenth months, with the average age of appearance between the sixth and eighth months. Approximately once in every 2,000 births, an infant is born with one or more teeth. Usually natal teeth are lower central incisors (Massler and Savara, 1950). It has been estimated that only 1 per cent of white infants erupt their first tooth before they are four months old, and approximately 1 per cent not until after the first birthday. By six months, one baby out of three has at least one tooth and, by nine months, the average baby has three teeth (Meredith, 1946a).

The lower teeth, as a rule, erupt before the upper teeth (Doering and Allen, 1942). However, the time of eruption is variable and depends upon such factors as health, hereditary trends, nutrition before and after birth, race, sex, and other factors (Meredith, 1946a; Hurme, 1948; Thompson, 1954; Breckenridge and Vincent, 1955). Girls, as a rule, erupt their first tooth slightly before boys, but between the ages of nine months and two years, boys are generally ahead of girls (Meredith, 1946a). The *sequence* of eruption of the temporary teeth, however, is more important than the age of eruption. When there is irregularity in the sequence of eruption, it is likely to throw the jaws out of position and result in poor alignment of the teeth. This may affect permanently the shape of the lower part of the face and cause even the permanent teeth to be out of line (Breckenridge and Vincent, 1955). There are certain times, especially in the fetal period, at ten months, 2½ years, and five years of age, when the temporary teeth are especially susceptible to metabolic and cellular disturbances (Massler et al., 1941).

Permanent Teeth. Even after the temporary teeth have erupted, much activity goes on inside of the gums as the permanent teeth, except the four wisdom teeth, begin to calcify. The order of calcifying is the same as the later order of eruption. On the average, the child at six years of age has 1 or 2 permanent teeth; at eight years, 10 or 11 teeth; at ten years, 14 or 16 teeth; at twelve years, 24 or 26; and at thirteen, 27 or 28. The last four of the permanent teeth, the "wisdom teeth," erupt between the ages of seventeen and twenty-five years, if they appear at all. There are two active periods of dentition for the permanent teeth, separated by a period of rest.

For girls, the rest period comes between the ages of seven years nine months and ten years, and for boys, between eight years four months and eleven years (Hellman, 1943).

Girls are more precocious in shedding their temporary teeth than are boys. They are also more precocious in getting their permanent teeth than are boys, except in the case of the "wisdom teeth" when boys are usually ahead of the girls (Klein et al., 1937; Meredith, 1946a; Thompson, 1954; Breckenridge and Vincent, 1955). Children of subnormal intelligence get their permanent teeth more slowly than do those of normal intelligence, while those of superior intelligence are slightly precocious in this area of development (Terman, 1926; Cohen and Anderson, 1931). Even before all of the permanent teeth have erupted, most children begin to suffer from dental caries. Between the ages of six and fifteen years, the average child acquires one or two caries a year (Klein et al., 1938; Breckenridge and Vincent, 1955).

DEVELOPMENT OF THE NERVOUS SYSTEM

The growth of the nervous system is very rapid before birth and the first three to four years after birth. Growth during the prenatal period, as was pointed out in the chapter on prenatal development, consists primarily of increase in the number and size of nerve cells. During the postnatal years, on the other hand, growth consists primarily of the development of immature cells present at birth, rather than the formation of new cells. After the age of three or four years, growth of the nervous system proceeds at a relatively slow rate.

Brain growth cannot be studied directly, but must be estimated from studying the brains of the dead or from external measurements of the cranial development of living children. These measurements show that brain growth is very rapid from birth to four years, slowing down between the ages of four and eight years, and then progressing very slowly until approximately the age of sixteen years, when the mature size of the brain has been attained. Since the bones of the skull are loosely connected by membranes during the first few months of life, ample space is left between the edges to allow for growth.

At birth, brain weight averages 350 grams as contrasted with adult weight, which ranges from 1,260 to 1,400 grams. One-fourth of the adult brain weight is attained by birth, one-half by the age of nine months, three-fourths by the end of the second year, four-fifths by the fourth year, and 90 per cent by the age of six years. To show how rapidly the brain grows in early childhood as compared with the latter part of childhood, it is interesting to note that at birth, brain weight is one-eighth of body weight; at ten years, one-eighteenth; at fifteen years, one-thirtieth; and at maturity, one-fortieth.

Even though the increase in the size of the brain is very slight during adolescence, owing to the fact that at the beginning of that period it has nearly attained adult weight, there is nevertheless continuation of development in the cortical tissues. By the eighth year, the brain is nearly its mature size, but the development of intercerebral association tracts and the building up of gray matter are far from complete. Development is thus internal and cannot be measured in terms of size or weight.

CHANGES IN INTERNAL ORGANS

The increase in the size and weight of the child, during the growth years, is not due to the development of bones, muscles, or fatty tissue alone. The different internal organs, connected with respiration, circulation, and digestion, are growing rapidly at this time, and this growth is partially responsible for the child's increased weight. A brief description of the development of the *respiratory, circulatory,* and *digestive systems* will show when these different types of development occur.

Respiratory System. The *lungs* at birth are small, as may be seen by the fact that the chest circumference at that age is smaller than the head circumference. By the age of two years, the circumference of the head and chest are the same; at fifteen years, the ratio of head and chest is 2:3, and at maturity, 3:5. The final shape of the chest is reached between the twelfth and thirteenth years. After that, the change is in size alone. Throughout the adolescent years, the lungs increase in volume and weight. While the growth is especially pronounced right after puberty, during the early adolescent years, it nevertheless continues until the close of adolescence.

Accompanying the growth of the lungs is an increase in breathing capacity. This is especially apparent just before and during puberty. Respiration becomes slower, deeper, and more regular (Breckenridge and Vincent, 1955). While there is a gradual decrease in respiratory rate from birth through puberty, the greatest decrease occurs during the first two years of life. At all ages in childhood, the respiratory rate is approximately the same for boys and girls (Iliff and Lee, 1952). By the seventeenth year, girls usually reach their adult vital capacity, while in the case of boys, this does not occur until several years later.

Circulatory System. The *heart,* at birth, is higher in the chest, more horizontal in position, heavier, and larger in relation to body weight than at any other time in life. Just before puberty, its relationship to body weight is less than at any other time, while during adolescence there is an increase in relation to body weight. The muscle fibers of the heart increase in size and in number of contractile fibers during adolescence. In early childhood, the heart is small, while the *veins* and *arteries* are large; in adolescence the reverse is true. The veins are smaller in relation to the arteries in childhood than later. The blood vessels grow in length and area of cross section during adolescence, and the walls become thicker and of stronger texture.

Changes in the heart and blood vessels throughout the years of growth result in changes in blood pressure, pulse rate, and body temperature. While *blood pressure* in childhood is low, there is a gradual increase which becomes more marked at puberty (Shock, 1944). This change is due to the increase in ratio of heart volume to size of the aorta. Blood pressure for boys and girls is much the same throughout childhood. Between the ages of ten and thirteen years, however, girls' blood pressure is higher than that of boys, but after this age the reverse is true (Shock, 1944; Merry and Merry, 1950). The *pulse rate* ranges between 120 and 140 in the early years of life as contrasted with the normal of 72 in adults. There is a gradual decrease in rate as children grow older, but variations are marked. The increase continues up to about fifteen years, after which it becomes almost constant. The greatest decrease comes during the first two years of life (Iliff and Lee, 1952).

At birth, the pulse rate of girls is higher than for boys. At two, they are approximately equal, and this continues to ten years of age. Between ten and fifteen years, the pulse rate decreases more rapidly for boys than it does for girls, and this difference continues up to eighteen years. At maturity, the female rate is slightly faster and more regular than that of the male (Scheinfeld, 1943; Iliff and Lee, 1952). Among young children, *body temperature* is variable. It is usually lower in the early morning than in the late afternoon or early evening. There are decreases in body temperature for both boys and girls up to thirteen years. After thirteen, the temperature of boys continues to decrease while that of girls remains nearly constant. By seventeen years of age, there is an approximate difference of 0.7°F. between the body temperature of boys and girls (Merry and Merry, 1950; Iliff and Lee, 1952).

Digestive System. In the baby, the *stomach* is tubular in shape, lies transversely in the body, and has a very small capacity. At birth, the capacity is about 1 ounce; at two weeks, it has increased to 2½ ounces; and, by the end of the first month, to 3 ounces. This contrasts with the baglike shape of the adult stomach, which not only holds a larger amount of food but which also empties more slowly. Because of the transverse position of the baby's stomach, it empties quickly, especially when the baby lies on his right side or is held semierect. Throughout childhood, the stomach empties more quickly than in adult life. The young child has a smaller stomach and intestines, the digestive juices are less in amount, and the lining of the digestive tract is more delicate than is true of adults. The school child's stomach capacity is less than two-thirds that of the adolescent or adult. The digestive tract becomes mature at puberty.

Metabolism is more rapid in children than in adults. Their energy output is also greater. As a result, they need more food, in proportion to the size of their bodies, than adults do. This is especially true in the case of boys, who, as childhood progresses, are more active than girls. The food consumption of the child is thus influenced not only by the size and shape of his digestive tract but also by his metabolic rate. For the first year of life, the baby needs more feedings than he will later. Most children require between-meal snacks to avoid fatigue and loss of energy. In addition to the greater quantity of food, they need food with energy value, such as proteins, starches, and sweets. For growth of the bones and muscles, they require minerals, such as calcium and phosphorus. The daily calorie requirements for a baby range from 900 to 1,200, and for children of eight to ten years of age, from 1,700 to 2,000 calories (Rose, 1940; McKay and Fowler, 1941; Jeans, 1950; Merry and Merry, 1950; Breckenridge and Vincent, 1955). When children are permitted to select their own food, they generally select adequate amounts for their needs and of a well-balanced type (Davis, 1939).

HEALTH CONDITIONS

Good health in childhood is essential not only to normal growth but also to normal activity. The child whose health is poor, even though he may not be actually ill, is handicapped in his mental and physical growth. Illness in childhood influences the behavior and attitudes of the child. There is evidence to show that serious or prolonged illness influences the child's attitude toward self, and this, in turn, affects the quality of his behavior in all areas of his life. Illness that leaves a damaging effect on the child's body likewise leaves scars on his personality.

Health conditions in childhood are closely associated with the socio-economic status of the family. Poor general health conditions are more frequent than good general health in children from the lower-income classes (Hardy et al., 1941). Socioeconomic status influences the diet of the child during the growth years, and this is largely responsible for the condition of his health. Income, size of family, and management are largely responsible for the quality of the child's diet (Stiebling, 1943). A comparison of elementary-school children whose diets were rated as good and poor showed that the group with the good diets was superior to that of the poor diet in physical status, dental status, in days absent because of illness, in educational ratings, and definitely superior in social adjustments (Potgieter and Everitt, 1950).

Good Health. The child whose health is good shows this not only in his appearance but also in the quality and quantity of his behavior. Children in poor health, by contrast, reveal the status of their health by their appearance and by lack of energy, decreased activity, and by emotional tensions. Some of the characteristics of a healthy child are: the mucous membranes (especially of the lips) are definitely pink; the facial expression is happy, often radiant; smiling is frequent; the eyes are bright and responsive; the skin is smooth and elastic; the limbs are rounded, because of a sufficient layer of subcutaneous fat; the muscles are well formed and their tonus is good; the stance is well balanced, erect, and graceful; the limb muscles are almost straight; the spine is straight; the shoulder girdles do not droop; the arches of the feet are well formed; and the movements of the limbs and body in walking or running are characterized by elasticity, vigor, and poise (Capon, 1945).

Periods of Susceptibility. There are certain times, during the growing-up years, that are characteristically healthy, just as there are others that are characteristically unhealthy. During babyhood, diseases are frequent and often fatal. Susceptibility to disease is very marked from three to six or eight years of age. Unless carefully segregated from other children, most boys and girls at this age are subject to a series of quarantines for different childhood diseases, as mumps, measles, or chickenpox. Normally, the period from six or eight years to the onset of puberty is a very healthy age, when physical strength and endurance are adequate to permit the boy or girl to engage in active play for hours at a time without any noticeable fatigue.

According to Bayer and Snyder (1950), "Every period of childhood has its special health hazards, none of them . . . too serious when ordinary care is given. Only a small percentage of children become afflicted with permanent ill health." In spite of the fact that modern medical methods, immunization, and new drugs have resulted in a marked decrease in infant and child mortality, the mortality rates are still high, especially during the first year of life (Cooke, 1948). The frequency of deaths increases as the baby approaches his first birthday. Respiratory illnesses cause most deaths during the first year of life, though there are seasonal fluctuations in the incidence of these illnesses. The next most common causes of death in the first year of life are gastrointestinal disturbances (Norval and Kennedy, 1949). Among children of school age, cardiovascular diseases and cancer cause more deaths than all the infectious and parasitic diseases, as whooping cough, measles, influenza, diphtheria, or poliomyelitis, (Kahn, 1951).

Common Childhood Illnesses. While children may and do contract almost every kind of illness, there are certain illnesses which may be regarded as "typical" because they are so commonly found among children of given ages. In Fig. 21 are shown graphically the most common illnesses at different times during the growth years. Colds and upper respiratory infections are most common at all ages. Communicable diseases, such as measles and chickenpox, are most common in the elementary-school years, while gastrointestinal disturbances and allergies are especially frequent in babyhood and adolescence (Bayer and Snyder, 1950). Allergic reactions, such as milk rash, hives, and asthma, are found at every age, and few children escape them (Bayley, 1940). Tuberculosis, heart diseases, rheumatic fever, and cancer are less common though more prevalent than is popularly realized (Garrison, 1952).

Diseased tonsils and adenoids are less frequent in adolescence than in childhood owing to the fact that these conditions are generally cared for in childhood (Lund et al., 1946). Girls show a higher average incidence of most diseases than do boys. This is especially true as girls approach adolescence when they have less interest in and participate less in various body-building activities than do boys (Lund et al., 1946). Girls suffer more from gastro-intestinal disturbances and endocrine symptoms than do boys (Bayer and Snyder, 1950). While first-born children do not have more illnesses than do later-born children, they do suffer more from gastrointestinal upsets, feeding disorders, constipation, stomach disorders, allergies, and asthma. It has been

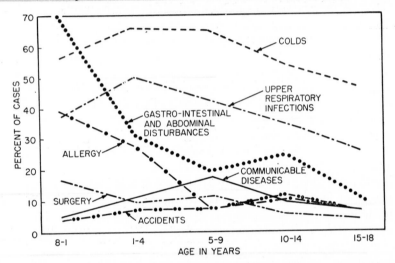

Fig. 21. Relative incidence of various categories of illness. (*From L. M. Bayer and M. M. Snyder, Illness experience of a group of normal children, Child Develpm.,* 1950, **21**, 93–120. *Used by permission.*)

suggested that this may be due to the tensions of overanxious parents in the case of the first-born (Kingsley and Reynolds, 1949).

Imaginary Illness. There is no question that all children at some time or other complain of "not feeling well" as an escape from some unpleasant duty or to avoid punishment they justly deserve. How well developed imaginary invalidism is in childhood has not yet been determined. It unquestionably occurs more frequently during the adolescent years than during childhood. In an analysis of physical complaints without organic basis, it was found that rarely were pains simulated for gaining attention. In most cases, distressing or intolerable situations were found which impaired the children's health. Complaints of illness were used to ameliorate these conditions (Preston, 1940). A wide range of physical disturbances, such as anorexia nervosa, enuresis, diabetes, asthma, allergy reactions, and ulcerative colitis, are a reflection of the relationship between the child and his parents or of the child's interpretation of this relationship (Mohr, 1948).

Effects of Illness. How great an effect childhood illnesses have on physical growth depends upon the severity, the length, and the nature of the illness. Loss in weight is almost inevitable in any case of illness, no matter how slight it may be. A long and severe illness may result in a decline in growth in height. Ordinary illnesses have no permanent measurable effect upon the body growth of school-age children (Palmer, 1936; Hardy, 1938; Evans, 1944). Temporary effects may occur, but on the whole, children with frequent illnesses in childhood show no significant difference in their growth as compared with children who are relatively free from illness.

Modification in the growth of bones occurs in severe illness. Scars appear on the bones, and the rates of growth both in size and maturity of the skeleton may be affected (Harris, 1933; Todd, 1938; Francis, 1939; Bayley, 1943; Sontag and Lipford, 1943). Deformities of the bones usually follow rickets and poliomyelitis (Dunham and Thoms, 1945). The muscles lose some of their tone, become flabby, and are easily fatigued. Anemia generally follows illnesses, especially when they have been severe. Certain illnesses have permanent effects, such as a damaged heart following rheumatic fever or damage to the brain from encephalitis (Breckenridge and Vincent, 1955).

There is no doubt that prolonged illness will affect the child's status in *school work.* The longer he remains ill and the more severe the illness is, the greater its effect is likely to be. Diseased tonsils and malnutrition have been found to have the most pronounced effect (Woofter, 1940). Illness may be the starting point for *behavior difficulties,* especially eating problems. Many children, accustomed to special attention during their illness, become aggressive and demanding when they have recovered from their illnesses (Breckenridge and Vincent, 1955). Young children who have not been accustomed to being separated from their parents may show effects differing from those following illness when their illnesses have necessitated hospitalization (Prugh et al., 1953).

Illness during the childhood years frequently leads to *personality disturbances.* It is usually not the illness itself that is responsible for the disturbances but the fact that during illness the child is pampered and the routine of his life and responsibilities is temporarily abandoned. Should the illness last for several months, the child will not only be thoroughly "spoiled," unless marked precautions are taken to avoid it, but he will also find it difficult to readjust himself to his former playmates who have learned much about social adjustment during the time he was ill. The result is likely to be an unfavorable social attitude and the establishment of solitary play habits.

Personality changes follow certain diseases in which there may be a secondary involvement of the central nervous system, as pneumonia, malaria, pernicious anemia, diabetes, or poliomyelitis (Shock, 1947). In the case of poliomyelitis, the effect on personality is directly related to the severity and lasting effects of the illness (Harris, 1950). Children suffering from asthma show fears of separation from their mothers (Harris et al., 1950). Allergic children frequently block outgoing hostilities and turn their hostilities toward themselves (Miller and Baruch, 1950). Children who are fretful, irritable, and quarrelsome show marked personality improvements when the allergies from which they had suffered are controlled. This is due to the removal of the nervous tension caused by asthma and changes in parental attitudes (Clarke, 1952).

PHYSICAL DEFECTS

Physical defects, even when slight, place limitations on what the child can do. Because of this, as Podolsky (1953a) has pointed out, "any kind of physical defect is a definite mental hazard." How much influence such defects will have will depend upon such factors as the nature and severity of the defect, the age at which this defect was acquired, how much the defect limits the normal activities of the child, and the attitude of parents, teachers, and the child's peers to this defect. A child who has rheumatic fever which leaves him with a heart condition that requires a long convalescence and militates against his taking part in the activities other children of his age engage in will be affected psychologically more than a child whose only defect is poor eyesight that can be corrected by wearing glasses (Mohr, 1948).

Types of Defects. As is true of illness, children suffer from every possible kind of physical defect. Among the most common are dental caries; speech defects; visual and auditory impairments; orthopedic disabilities; central-nervous-system disorders; heart disturbances; harelip, cleft palate; facial birthmarks; abnormalities of physique, such as webbed fingers, cross-eyes, or hunchbacks; and contractures resulting from burns (Lund et al., 1946; Maxwell and Brown, 1948; Barker et al., 1952; Garrison, 1952; Podolsky, 1953a; Breckenridge and Vincent, 1955). Some of these defects the child is born with; other defects are acquired at different times in childhood as a result of certain illnesses or accidents (Podolsky, 1953a).

The number and severity of physical defects varies. Boys, for example, are more often disabled than girls (Lund et al., 1946; Barker et al., 1952). Crippling conditions are more common among children of the poorer socioeconomic groups than among those of more favored groups (Mackie, 1948; Hurley, 1949; Garrison, 1952). Physical defects likewise vary according to the age of the child. More children are crippled before six or seven years of age than later (Hurley, 1949). Defects that show a decline in appearance with age are teeth defects, diseased tonsils and adenoids, speech and hearing defects, and defects resulting from malnutrition. On the other hand, visual defects, heart conditions, hormone defects, orthopedic defects including defects of the feet and posture, and diabetes increase with age (Lund et al., 1946; Maxwell and Brown, 1948; Garrison, 1952).

Effects of Physical Defects. The *developmental status* of the child suffering from some physical defect is usually below that of a child who is not handicapped. Blind children, for example, are slower in walking, feeding themselves, etc., than are children with normal vision because they must substitute ear-hand for eye-hand coordinations. Furthermore, they are hindered by parental desires to do things for them and to shield them from possible injury (Mikell, 1953). A defect often interferes with the child's *school achievement* (Maxfield and Fjeld, 1942; Breckenridge and Vincent, 1955). This becomes more serious as children grow older and is greatest for those with multiple handicaps, especially when there is a speech handicap (Zintz, 1951). Because physical defects often interfere with a child's activities and prevent him from acquiring the *skills* his peers have, he usually makes poorer *social adjustments* (Cruickshank, 1951). He behaves in a less socially acceptable way than a child who lacks such handicaps (Zintz, 1951).

Frequently children who are handicapped develop undesirable *personality* patterns. They are withdrawn, have more feelings of guilt and fears than children with more normal physical characteristics, and frequently feel unloved, unwanted, and insecure (Cruickshank, 1951; Zintz, 1951; Breckenridge and Vincent, 1955). Even at the preschool age, handicapped children are less docile, less active, and have less initiative than older children of the same ages (Maxfield and Fjeld, 1942). The most common effects of physical handicaps on the personality pattern of children result from the development of shame and feelings of inferiority. These, in turn, usually have one of three effects; the child may succumb to his obstacles and accept nonexpression as his lot; he may develop a compensatory abundance of overexpression to satisfy his injured ego; or he may replace suppressed modes of self-expression with alternative modes of equal merit. The last of the three is the most satisfactory (Podolsky, 1953a).

When a group of adults was asked to recall their school experiences, some who suffered from physical handicaps during their school days felt that the school work and social relationships in school compensated for many of the things they missed which their classmates enjoyed, such as sports and parties. Others reported that they suffered from the contempt of stronger children and from feeling excluded and lonely (Bühler, 1952). Whatever effect the handicap had, it is unquestionably true that the personalities of the children were influenced by the fact that the children were different from their contemporaries.

ACCIDENTS

There is no time in the life span when the individual is completely free from accidents of one type or another. However, some people have more accidents than others. This is true of children, just as it is of adults. Recently, a number of studies have been made of accidents in childhood to determine why it is that some children have more accidents than others. These studies have revealed facts about children's accidents which suggest that many of them could be avoided and thus the possibility of permanent damage to the child, either physically or psychologically, could be removed.

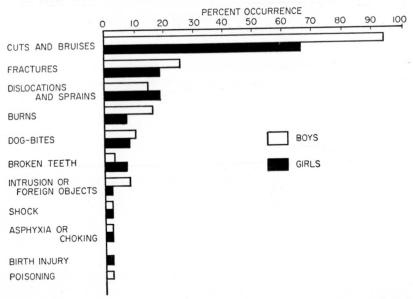

Fig. 22. Sex differences in the incidence of accidents. (*From L. M. Bayer and M. M Snyder, Illness experience of a group of normal children, Child Develpm., 1950, 21, 93–120. Used by permission.*)

Age Changes. While there are many different types of accidents that injure the child, falls have been reported to be the most frequent mechanism of injury (Hanlon et al., 1949). Of the many injuries these accidents result in, cuts, bruises, fractures, dislocations, sprains, burns, and dog bites are the most common (Bayer and Snyder, 1950). The frequency of these injuries at different ages is shown in Fig. 22. Boys have more accidents than girls (Hanlon et al., 1949; Bayer and Snyder, 1950). Approximately two-thirds of all accidents to children occur before the child is nine years old, with ages two and three years the most vulnerable and five and six the next most vulnerable. While most accidents occur in the home among younger children, in older children there are more accidents outside the home, on the playgrounds or in the streets. Most accidents occur in the afternoon and evening, with the peak between 7 and 8 o'clock (Hanlon et al., 1949; Bayer and Synder, 1950).

Variations. How the accident-prone child differs from children who suffer no more than the usual number of accidents is interesting to examine because it will throw light on the causes of differences between children in this area of their lives. The *home atmosphere* of accident-prone children is more authoritarian in that there are more commands, threats, and prohibitions than in the homes of children with fewer accidents. Such children come from larger families and are often later in birth order. Many come from broken homes. Their *school history* is likewise less favorable. Many have transferred from school to school and are known to the counselors because of their adjustment problems (Krall, 1953). In their *personality patterns,* they differ from children who have fewer accidents in that they are more aggressive, have fewer inhibitions, show less delay in expressing aggression, and reveal more verbal than action aggression (Krall, 1953). The conclusion of a study of accident-prone children who were compared with children less subject to accident was that "There is some indication that the traits which seem most likely to appear in the injury-prone are those usually considered desirable in children but which operate against them in combinations under certain circumstances to produce the injury-prone child" (Fuller, 1948).

Chapter 5

MOTOR DEVELOPMENT

One of the most rapid forms of development taking place during the early years of life is that of control over the different muscles of the body. From the helpless infant who cannot move his body from the place where he has been laid, or who cannot reach for and grasp an object held out to him, the young child emerges, in the period of a few short years, to a phase in which he is relatively independent of others.

Motor development consists of control of the movements of the muscles which, at birth and shortly afterward, are random and meaningless. But gradually, as the baby develops control over his muscular mechanism, specific pattern responses replace the earlier type of random movements. Instead of movements by the entire body, which occur in mass activity, only certain muscles or teams of muscles respond, and thus the energy expended is greatly reduced. Every child must develop effective coordination of his muscular mechanism if he is to emerge from the state of helplessness that is characteristic of the first months of life.

During the first four or five years of life, the most important development along motor lines consists of the development of *gross movements* which involve large areas of the body, as in the case of walking, running, swimming, and bicycling. After five years of age, the major development consists of the development of the *finer coordinations* which involve smaller muscle groups, as in the case of grasping, throwing and catching balls, writing, or using tools. Native reactions are elaborated into motor skills which will prove to be useful throughout life. After the foundation skills, such as self-feeding, dressing, walking, and running, have been established, the more complicated skills, as writing, playing the piano, skating, and dancing, are built up. Refinement of skills comes late (Havighurst, 1953).

CHARACTERISTICS OF MOTOR DEVELOPMENT

Development of control over the body parallels the development of the motor areas in the brain. The cerebellum, or lower brain, which controls balance develops rapidly during the early years of life and reaches practically its mature size by the time the child is five years old. The period of most rapid growth comes during the last half of the first year and the first half of the second year of life, the time when the baby is learning to walk (Gesell et al., 1940). Development also takes place in the upper brain, or cerebrum, in the early years of childhood, and this is paralleled by development of skilled movements.

Maturation and Learning. Development of muscle control comes partly as a result of maturation and partly from learning. It depends upon the maturation of neural structures, bones, and muscles, and a change in body proportions, as well as upon an opportunity to learn how to use the different muscle teams in a coordinated fashion. Before skilled movements can be learned, a state of maturity in the muscular mechanism in the child must exist. It is impossible to teach the child skilled movements until his nervous system is developed enough for him to profit from it. If teaching precedes maturation, time and energy will be wasted and interest on the child's part lost. The relative importance of maturation and learning has been discussed in detail in the chapter on Principles of Development. Training is important, however, in the development of motor skills. But there must be adequate maturation of the neuromuscular system if the child is to derive full benefit from the training (Dennis, 1941).

Pattern of Motor Sequence. Motor development does not occur in a haphazard fashion but rather in an orderly, predictable manner, as was pointed out in Chap. 1. It follows a definite sequence, in which control occurs first in the head, then in the arms, hands, and upper part of the trunk; later, in the lower part of the trunk; and finally, in the legs and feet. This head-to-foot, or *cephalocaudal,* sequence is referred to as the "law of developmental direction." It is interesting to note that the sequence of muscle control is similar to that of prenatal development of structure in which the head is more developed than the legs. Development also proceeds in the *proximodistal* direction, which means that motor development occurs earlier in the structures lying nearest to the main axis than in those in a more remote area. Muscle control, for example, appears sooner in the arms than in the fingers (Gesell, 1954).

The way in which babies are held illustrates this developmental pattern very well. At birth and shortly afterward, the baby rests his head upon the shoulder or bosom of the person holding him, and, if held away from the body, the whole head must be supported. Shortly, with control over the neck and head muscles, support is needed only at the nape of the neck, then at the shoulders, then in the back, and finally under the buttocks. The pattern of motor development is well illustrated in Fig. 23, showing the phases leading up to the assumption of an erect posture.

Even though motor development follows a pattern of sequence that is inflexible in its broader aspects, individual differences in the detail of the pattern occur. Owing to lack of opportunity for practice, the child may be behind schedule in developing control over his hands and, as a result of encouragement or aid, ahead of schedule in walking. The whole pattern of

Fig. 23. Developmental phases in the assumption of an erect posture. (*From M. B. Mc-Graw, Growth: a study of Johnny and Jimmy, Appleton-Century-Crofts, 1935. Used by permission.*)

development may be completed earlier or later than the standard times, because of individual differences in intelligence, health, and other factors.

IMPORTANCE OF MOTOR DEVELOPMENT

The earlier in the child's life that motor control is brought about, and the earlier the necessary skills are established, the better. Because the young child is more plastic than the older one, and because he has fewer skills to interfere with his learning, he can develop skills more quickly and easily than will be possible as he grows older. Likewise, his desire to learn motivates him to practice an activity until it is mastered, while an older child or adolescent is apt to become impatient if learning does not take place quickly.

Being able to control his body as well as, if not better than, his peers is important to a child for five reasons. First, it provides the child with a source of *amusement* and a means of entertaining himself. By playing with his toys and other play equipment, he can occupy his time in a pleasurable manner. Most of the play of young as well as of older children requires the use of the muscles and the ability to control his environment without help from others. Second, through his motor development, the child goes from the helplessness characteristic of the first few months of life to *independence*. The more he can do for himself, the less he is forced to rely upon others to do these things for him. This adds greatly to his self-confidence and his happiness.

Because motor abilities play a crucial role in many of the intellectual pursuits of childhood, motor development is important to the child's *school adjustments* (Jersild, 1954). In preschool and in the early grades of elementary school, much emphasis is placed on drawing, painting, crayoning, shopwork, writing, and forming numbers. The child whose motor development is such that he can compete on equal terms with his classmates will be more successful and happier in school than will the child whose motor development lags behind and who, as a result, is slow, awkward, and unsure of himself. Third-grade children who were superior in motor-performance tests were found to make more satisfactory school adjustments than those whose performance on these tests was inferior (Rarick and McKee, 1949). The majority of the child's *social contacts* are made through his play, and his play, in turn, is largely in the form of motor activities. If the child wants to have friends and playmates, he must be able to play the games they play. The child who cannot throw a ball, roller-skate, or ride a bicycle with skill becomes a group liability and is likely to have a lonely time (Breckenridge and Vincent, 1955).

The child who does not develop skills appropriate to his age level usually becomes a "wallflower," or "fringer," and this tendency to withdraw may persist into adult years (Merry and Merry, 1950). In our culture, boys are expected to learn more play skills than girls and to be more proficient in them. Girls can do poorly and still maintain their status in social relationships. Boys, on the other hand, who do poorly in games are considered "sissies" by their peers and lose status. This is true of boys of all social classes (Havighurst, 1953). Boys who rank high in athletic achievement make better personal and social adjustments than do boys who rank low in this category of their development (Biddulph, 1954).

Finally, motor development is important to a child's *concept of self*, and thus to his personality development. The child judges himself in relation to other children. It is damaging to his self-concept to realize that he consistently falls below their standards and that he is left out of things because he cannot compete on equal terms with them. As Havighurst (1953) has emphasized, "To an increasing extent, a child's conception of himself is tied up with the skills he has. It is as though his acceptance of himself comes in part from his ability to master different forms of the world outside himself. . . . As a child becomes part of an activity group, . . . he contributes cer-

Acquiring skills is essential to social contacts in childhood. (*From Child Development, a McGraw-Hill Text-Film.*)

tain skills, certain knowledge. He has an opportunity to test his skills against those of his peers. He adds to his conception of himself as his peers react to his skills." Third-grade children who showed proficiency in motor tests were found to be more active, popular, calm, resourceful, attentive, and cooperative than children who lacked such proficiency (Rarick and McKee, 1949).

While motor skills are important to a child, especially when they lead to independence, they are sometimes also handicaps to a child. The child who is able to walk, to explore his environment, and to manipulate different mechanical devices may be harmed because he has not yet developed enough caution to keep his desire to try out his newly acquired skills under control. Added to this are the anxiety his parents experience and their attempts to curb his actions (Jersild et al., 1949). In addition, with motor skills comes a desire for independence which may and frequently does lead to friction with his parents, who are unwilling to give him as much freedom and independence as he desires. He resents their interference in his activities, and this leads to many clashes between parent and child and many temper outbursts on the child's part (Jersild, 1954).

SEQUENCE OF DEVELOPMENT

Experimental studies of the development of muscle coordination have been numerous and have given ages at which the average child is able to control different parts of his body. This material will be presented according to the "law of developmental direction" rather than according to chronological age. The material has thus been divided into the following topics: (1) motor development in the head region, (2) motor development of the arms and hands, (3) motor development of the trunk, and (4) motor development of the legs.

1. MOTOR DEVELOPMENT IN THE HEAD REGION

Control of the muscles involved in eye movements, smiling, laughing, and holding up the head develops very quickly when one considers the complexity of the behavior involved. *Eye coordination,* which is very poor during the first few hours after birth, improves so rapidly that, by the end of the fourth month, even the most difficult type of eye movements should be present in every normal baby. By the end of the second month, the baby can focus his eyes on a stationary object, and by the third month, can follow a moving object (Gesell and Ilg, 1943; Gesell, 1949). At first, the focus on a stationary object is for only 4 or 5 seconds (Halverson, 1931).

In following a *moving object,* three types of eye coordination are used, horizontal, vertical, and circular. The horizontal movement is the first to appear and is present in most babies by the second month. Before the third month, the baby can follow an object that moves vertically and circularly and a moving person (Morgan and Morgan, 1944). Optic *nystagmus,* the response of the eyes to a succession of moving objects, as when one looks from the window of a fast-moving train, occurs within a few hours after birth. Ocular *pursuit* movements appear first during the third or fourth week after birth (McGinnis, 1930). Following an object, whether stationary or moving, for any length of time is difficult for children up to the age of six years, after which eye control develops rapidly (Breckenridge and Vincent, 1955). Eye coordination is not developed enough for reading before the child is six years old (Havighurst, 1953).

The *blinking* reflex, present at birth, can be called forth by touching the face near the eyes, the eyelashes, and the corner of the eye, or by allowing a current of air to strike the eyes. Later, this same response becomes voluntary and can be called forth in anticipation of the touch of an object as it approaches the eye. Voluntary blinking is present in most babies by the end of the fourth month (Jones, 1926). *Reflex smiles,* in response to some tactual, organic, or kinesthetic stimulus, appear as early as the first week of life. "Social" smiling, or smiling in response to a smile from another person, does not occur until the third month (Jones, 1926). This response has been used by many writers as a criterion for the beginning of social behavior.

Most newborn infants have the ability to *hold up their heads* momentarily (Bryan, 1930). If a baby of one month of age is supported in a prone position at chest and abdomen, he can hold his head erect in a horizontal plane, and at the age of two months, he can hold his head above the horizontal plane at an angle of as much as 30 degrees. Holding the head erect at first is for only a few seconds at a time, and because of the weakness of the neck muscles, the head often wobbles and falls forward with some force. A month or two later, the baby can hold up his head and chest by pushing with his hands and arms. When held, he can look over the person's shoulder and turn his head to survey his surroundings. Because holding up the head when lying on the back is more difficult, this ability does not appear until the fifth or sixth month, and then for only a few seconds at a time (Shirley, 1931a; Merry and Merry, 1950; Breckenridge and Vincent, 1955).

When seated with suitable support on a person's lap, most babies can hold up their heads at the age of four months. The head maintains a midposition, when the body is supine, and actively rotates, turning from side to side, at the age of four months. A month or two later, the baby is able to turn his head when seated by turning the shoulders and using the muscles in the upper part of the trunk. The ability to maintain the head in an upright position while sitting without support does not occur much before the baby is 6 months old, and then for only a few seconds. Several months later, with the strengthening of the neck and trunk muscles, he can hold up his head for periods of time varying from a few minutes to half an hour. Frequently babies become fretful and cry from fatigue when the time is extended (Gesell et al., 1940; Merry and Merry, 1950).

2. MOTOR DEVELOPMENT OF THE ARMS AND HANDS

From birth, the baby's arms and hands are in constant motion. At first, the movements consist of awkward jerks, random hittings, and opening and closing of the fingers. These movements occur even during sleep, though they are less frequent than when the baby is awake. The most common hand movement is toward the head, owing to the habit of position established during the fetal period. One of the earliest forms of coordinated movements of the arms consists of defensive movements which appear during the first few days of life. At first these are poorly coordinated, but by the end of the second week of life, there is marked improvement in coordination (Sherman and Sherman, 1929).

Eye-hand Coordination. Reaching and grasping, except in cases where the hand accidentally touches the stimulus, require eye-hand coordination, or the working together of the eyes and hands so that the former directs the movements of the latter. This is not present in the random reaching and grasping that appear shortly after birth. Not until eye coordination has occurred, between the third and fourth months, can there be any voluntary, purposeful reaching and grasping (Halverson, 1931; Gesell and Ilg, 1943; Gesell, 1949). In the early period of eye coordination, the baby looks at an object but does not grasp for it. As his eye coordination improves, he begins to reach for the object. During the fourth month, the grasping is slow and awkward. By the sixth month, a well-coordinated movement is generally developed, and several months later, the baby can touch the object he is reaching for without random movements of the arm and hand (Watson and Watson, 1921; Halverson, 1931; Spitz, 1951). By the age of six months, the baby can reach for an object, grasp it, and then carry the object to his mouth (Kuhlmann, 1922; Jones, 1926; Gesell, 1928; 1954; Halverson, 1931).

Methods of Reaching and Grasping. Studies of reaching for a cube have shown that the approach to the cube took three different forms, the *backhand sweep,* the *circuitous sweep,* and the *direct approach.* From sixteen to twenty-eight weeks, either the backhand or circuitous approach was used; from thirty-two to thirty-six weeks, a less circuitous form of approach predominated; and by the ages of forty to fifty-two weeks, the direct approach was the usual one. Up to the age of twenty-eight weeks, the hands are lifted high in reaching for the cube, but from then until the fifty-second week, the height of the approach gradually decreased (Halverson, 1931; Gesell and Halverson, 1936). By the age of one year, most babies have acquired a fairly mature pattern of reaching, but adult performance may not be achieved until the child is four or five years old (McGraw, 1941).

In the grasping reflex, which appears at birth or shortly afterward, the thumb and fingers act together as a hook, by which the baby supports his weight when the stick he grasps is raised. Before the hand can become useful for purposes other than grasping, the thumb must work in opposition to the fingers and thus function as a separate unit. *Thumb opposition* in grasping occurs, normally, between the third and fourth months and in picking up objects, between the eighth and ninth months. When the "pincer" technique has been acquired, the baby can pick up objects with a dainty grasp, using his thumb and fingers instead of his whole hand (Gesell and Halverson, 1936). The ability to grasp and hold more than one object is more difficult and appears somewhat later. The average baby of five months should be able to accept one object when handed to him, while the average baby of seven months should be able to accept two objects, and the average age for acceptance of three objects is ten months (Lippman, 1927).

3. Motor Development in the Trunk

The ability to *turn the body* from side to side, or from back to stomach, is not present at birth. By the second month, the baby should be able to turn from side to back; by the fourth month, from back to side; and, by the age of six months, to make a complete turn from stomach to stomach. This complete turn is not necessarily made at one time at first, but rather several partial turns, with rest periods between each, finally result in a complete turn of the body. In turning, the body moves first in the head region and last in the legs. The baby turns his head, then his shoulders, then his pelvis, and finally, with a pushing, kicking movement of his legs, he manages to turn his entire body (Schaltenbrand, 1928).

Sitting. The ability to sit alone, without any support, depends upon the development of the heavy muscles of the back. Before he can sit alone, the baby must have his whole trunk under control. At the age of sixteen weeks, a baby can pull himself to a sitting position. At twenty weeks, he can sit alone, when supported, with his body erect. If unsupported, he will lean forward passively, though his head is kept erect. Between the ninth and tenth months, the average baby should be able to sit alone, without support, for 10 or more minutes (Gesell and Thompson, 1938; Gesell et al., 1940; McGraw, 1941). Girls usually sit alone slightly earlier than boys, and those who have had a good home and pediatric care, sooner than those whose care has been inferior (Peatman and Higgons, 1942).

In attaining a sitting position, the baby goes from a dorsal to sitting position by turning his whole body to a ventral position, then squats on all fours, and finally pushes himself into a sitting position. By the second or third year, the young child no longer turns the whole body axis, but leaves the pelvis in contact with the floor on one side, supporting himself with his arm on that side. By the fourth or fifth year, the adult method of sitting develops, in which the body is rolled up symmetrically, with the aid of the arms on both sides. At first, when the baby sits down, he falls or topples over by giving way in the lower part of his trunk. Gradually, he learns by trial and error, combined with demonstrations, how to bend his knees and slide down instead of keeping his knees stiff and falling over. This ability is achieved by the time the average baby is a year old (Schaltenbrand, 1928; McGraw, 1935, 1941).

When the baby first sits alone, he often leans forward to keep his balance. His arms are generally outstretched at the side of his body, to help him to maintain his balance, and his legs are bowed, with the soles of his feet turned toward each other, to give him a wider base for balance. When seated in this way, the baby cannot raise himself to a standing position. If he tries to move, he generally topples over. After acquiring the ability to sit alone, many babies rock back and forth as a playful stunt.

4. Motor Development in the Legs

Most people believe that the baby learns to walk quickly. This, however, is not true. Walking really traces its origin to birth or even to early fetal life, when the infant makes kicking movements of an alternate type that closely resemble stepping. As a result of stretching and kicking, the baby learns to coordinate the muscles of his legs and trunk. Later, he develops balance and equilibrium. All of this is essential to walking and cannot be accomplished in a brief space of time. Most babies are biologically ready to walk between the ages of nine and fifteen months. The bones, muscles, and nerves of the legs and trunk have developed to the point where they are equal to the task. Then the baby is ready to walk, though he needs varying amounts of stimulation and assistance from others before he masters this ability (Havighurst, 1953).

Records obtained from carefully controlled experiments have given specific information about the normal cause of locomotor development. Creeping movements, which are "wormlike" and "lizardlike" in character, can be observed in full-term babies during the first four months of life. When prone on his stomach, or lying on his back, the young baby kicks and squirms, often moving his body a few inches. By the end of the second week of life, he can push against a hard surface, such as the end of the crib, with enough force to be able to move himself forward slightly. When held in an upright position, he at first prances and dances; later, as his muscles strengthen, he plants his feet firmly and makes definite stepping movements.

Rolling and Hitching. The earliest forms of locomotion, to be found in all babies, is *rolling*. In this, the baby moves his body by means of a very crude sort of leg and arm movements. This is usually followed by *hitching,* or locomotion in a sitting position. The baby uses one leg to push himself along and the other is doubled under him or extended, thus helping to maintain his balance. In hitching, movement of the body is aided by the arms and hands, which accompany pushing or slight kicking movements of the legs. The movement in hitching is always backward rather than forward, which is characteristic of crawling, the next stage in the pattern of locomotion. Hitching is generally present by the sixth month. In Fig. 24 are given the characteristic positions of the baby's body in hitching.

Crawling and Creeping. *Crawling* follows hitching in the normal sequence of development. It appears as early as the fourth month and reaches its peak between the seventh and ninth months. In crawling, the body is prone on the ground with the abdomen in contact with the ground. The head and shoulders are raised by supporting the weight in the upper part of the body on the elbows. The body is pulled along by the use of the arms, while the legs drag or make kicking movements. If only one leg is used to push the body forward, the other is used in an extended position to propel the body. Generally, the leg movements approximate swimming, in that the legs are drawn up to the body and then kicked out suddenly in a froglike manner.

By the age of nine months, the normal baby can *creep*. In this form of locomotion, the trunk is carried free from the floor but parallel to it, and movement comes from the use of the hands and knees. At first, the movements are arhythmic, and cross coordination is poor. With practice, rhythm appears and cross coordination is perfected to the point where only one limb moves at a time. As the baby acquires greater strength, he raises his knees from the floor, stiffens his legs, and walks "on all fours." There are marked individual differences in crawling and creeping. Some babies crawl

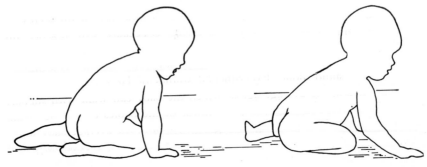

Fig. 24. Hitching. (*From L. H. Burnside, Coordination in the locomotion of infants, Genet. Psychol. Monogr.,* 1927, No. 2. *Used by permission.*)

mostly in a prone position, and others crawl while sitting or hitch. Some babies may skip either creeping or crawling, or remain in one stage for a very short time and then pass on to the next stage (Ames, 1937).

In the early stages of locomotion preceding walking, there is a marked overproduction of movement in the entire body. With practice, coordination results and spreads from the head to the leg region. While the action of the legs remains arhythmic, the arms are flexed and used in alternate fashion. Coordination is imperfect during the crawling stages, especially in the lower part of the body. By the time the baby is creeping, nearly perfect coordination appears, and a gradual increase in speed of movement is apparent.

Standing. Standing is the next step in the developmental sequence leading up to walking. Normally, standing with support overlaps creeping and crawling and is a necessary preliminary to walking. Standing with the support of furniture is an easier task for a baby than pulling himself to a standing position because, in the latter, the baby's legs have a tendency to slide under him. The median age for standing with support for one minute has been reported to be forty-two weeks and for pulling to a standing position, forty-seven weeks (Shirley, 1931a). Girls, as a rule, stand slightly earlier than boys (Peatman and Higgons, 1942).

To maintain his balance, the baby stands at first with his feet far apart, the toes turned out, the knees locked, and the head, as well as the upper part of the trunk, carried forward. This is true whether the baby stands alone or whether he supports himself by holding on to some object or person. When he falls, he generally falls backward. Gradually, the baby lessens the amount of pressure placed upon the object supporting him and finally stands completely without support. Maintaining an upright posture is possible only after a long series of preparatory coordinations (Gesell and Ames, 1940; Gesell, 1954).

Walking. After the baby has gained enough confidence in his ability to stand with support, he cautiously takes a step. Gradually, with practice, his skill increases, and he actually walks while holding on to something for support. This early *walking with support* comes when the baby is acquiring the ability to stand alone. Experimental studies of large groups of babies have shown that the average age at which the baby can walk with support is one year. By fourteen months, two-thirds of the babies of that age walk without support, and by the age of eighteen months, the average baby walks like an adult (Bayley, 1935; Gesell et al., 1940; Gesell, 1954; Breckenridge and Vincent, 1955).

There are, however, marked individual differences in the ages at which babies first walk. Some walk as early as seven or eight months, and others begin as late as eighteen months. The age at which the baby will first walk is usually compatible with the rate of his total development (Breckenridge and Vincent, 1955). To predict the age of first *walking alone*, it is a fairly safe rule to apply to double the age of sitting alone. Or, if the baby creeps, the age of walking will be approximately 1½ times the age of creeping. If the baby is precocious in sitting alone, it is safe to predict that he will be precocious in walking. If, on the other hand, he is slow in sitting alone or creeping, he will, other things being equal, be slow in walking alone.

What is characteristic of all forms of locomotion, in all babies, is that the head is held erect to enable the baby to see where he is going. In walking, the body is erect and motion comes from the use of the legs alone. At first, balance is poor. As an aid to maintaining equilibrium, the baby's arms are held outright, much like those of a tightrope walker, or are pulled up to the body. The feet are turned outward, and the legs are stiff. A rhythmic alternation of the two legs occurs. The head is held slightly forward, and the baby looks straight ahead of him, instead of at the floor. This is necessary if balance is to be maintained, though it usually results in many falls. Falls are caused also by poor general coordination and the fact that the baby raises his feet far from the floor and consequently loses his balance. Figure 25 illustrates the characteristic body posture of the baby in the early stages of walking.

Foot Positions in Walking. In early walking with support, the length of the step is short and very erratic. The length of the step increases with age up to eighteen months, when it ceases to increase and becomes very regular.

Noticeable changes are also apparent in the width of step. In early stepping, there are approximately 5 centimeters between the toes of the two feet, and the heels do not touch the floor. When the baby walks with support, there is a sudden increase in the width of the step, and this continues into the stage of walking alone. The width of the step increases until the end of the second year. In early walking with support, the toes turn outward. With improvements in walking, the feet become parallel. Outtoeing is characteristic of the early stages of stepping and walking with or without support (Shirley, 1931a).

Analysis of cinema records of baby footprints has indicated that the type of stepping movement is a more important index of progress than the number of steps taken. At first, the baby places one foot before he starts to move the other. Later, as his skill in walking improves, he will start to raise the second foot before he has completely placed the first. At six months, the baby contacts the floor only with his

Fig. 25. Walking. (*From L. H. Burnside, Coordination in the locomotion of infants, Genet. Psychol. Monogr.,* 1927, *No.* 2. *Used by permission.*)

toes and the ball of his foot. When he begins to walk, on the other hand, the whole sole of his foot is placed in contact with the floor. With improvement in walking, the contact is heel to toe (McGraw and Weinbach, 1936).

Two major changes take place in walking with advancing age. The height of the center of gravity of the legs decreases, and the path becomes smoother. In terms of energy output, the baby just learning to walk puts forth more effort for the distance covered than he will later. This greater expenditure of energy comes partly from lifting the leg higher and partly from waste motion in the irregular path the leg takes through space. "Efficiency of locomotion," as determined by the ratio between the horizontal distance covered and the length of the path of the center of gravity of the lower leg, is achieved at two or three years of age. After the gait has become established, the amounts of time each foot spends on the floor and in the air are essentially the same. In faulty or unstable gaits, this does not happen and the gait becomes asymmetrical. In a well-developed child's gait, about 70 per cent of the time in stepping is consumed in the ground stroke of the foot, and during approximately 30 per cent of the time, the leg is moving through space. Stability of gait is usually attained toward the end of the second or the early part of the third year (McGraw and Breeze, 1941).

Improved Coordination in Walking. When the baby first walks, there is an excess of movement, not in his legs alone, but in his whole body. Gradually this decreases. Coordination of the arms comes before that of the legs, and this helps to maintain a better body balance. With practice, the length of the step increases; the width and variability of the step decrease; the motion of the legs is more rapid and harmonious, resulting in a gradual increase in speed of walking; and the steps become straight rather than with toes pointing outward, which is characteristic of early walking. Likewise, the tendency to trot or walk on the toes gives way to a flatter type of stepping movement. Marked individual variations appear in the style of walking of different children. It requires several years before a characteristic gait is established. Anything, such as too tight or too stiff shoes, an overweight condition of the body, or fear of taking a long, striding step because of repeated falls in the past, will have a marked influence on the permanent style of the individual's gait.

SKILLS

After the gross motor activities, concerned principally with the larger movements of the body in reaching, sitting, standing, and walking, are developed, the young child begins to learn *skills* or the finer coordinations in which the smaller muscles play a major role. These skills will not develop through maturation, though the foundations for them come through the maturation of the nerves and muscles. Skills must be learned, but *when* they are learned is as important as *how* they are learned. There is ample evidence from studies in which control groups have received no training and were later compared with trained groups that learning is essential to the development of skills, but that the learning must be correctly timed. In running, jumping, throwing, and catching, for example, children who receive training are definitely superior to those who receive no training, but the training must be correlated with their maturational readiness to learn (Hilgard, 1933; Gutteridge, 1939; Gesell et al., 1940; Seils, 1951; Dusenberry, 1952).

Importance of Practice. Because skills are learned activities, practice is essential. But to be effective, practice must be directed. True, the child can learn skills through trial and error, but this is inefficient not only in terms of time and energy but also in terms of the end result achieved. By pointing out to the child more efficient procedures and by giving him a good model to copy, practice will produce better results than if it is carried out undirected. With training in methods of throwing a ball, children have been found to improve their skill as shown by the increased distance of the throw (Dusenberry, 1952). Furthermore, directed practice gives the child more satisfaction because the end results are better, and this satisfaction is a source of motivation to continue the practice until the skill is mastered (Breckenridge and Vincent, 1955). Older children generally profit more from training than do younger children (Dusenberry, 1952).

In the early stages of learning skills, the child's movements are not only uncoordinated and awkward, but he has a tendency to make unusual facial expressions. (*From Child Development, a McGraw-Hill Text-Film.*)

In the early stages of development of skills, the movements are clumsy, awkward, and uncoordinated. There is waste motion because the different bodily movements needed are not integrated and because many unnecessary movements are made. When a child is learning to throw a ball, for example, he literally throws it with his whole body (Dusenberry, 1952). He makes unusual facial expressions, his trunk and legs play too prominent a part in the activity, and his arms and hands do not work together, but piecemeal. Similarly, in the early stages of learning to roller-skate or ride tricycles, the child's awkward, uncoordinated movements lead to many falls, too much energy is used for the results achieved, and many of the muscles which should play an important role in the skill are tense (Garrison, 1952; Breckenridge and Vincent, 1955).

With continued practice, skills improve to the point where they are graceful, rhythmic, coordinated movements. The individual movements no longer appear piecemeal as they did in the early stages of learning, but they become fused into a pattern of action (Jones, 1939; Gesell et al., 1940; Kingsbury, 1946; Seils, 1951; Dusenberry, 1952). As Breckenridge and Vincent (1955) have pointed out, "The clumsiness of the eighteen-month-old child in walking passes into the awkward, flat-footed run of the two-year-old: and this passes into the increasing skill and balance of the three- and four-year-old; but one seldom sees the flow and ease of movement which are referred to as grace in walking or running until the child is five. So it is with roller skating or bicycle riding."

As skills develop through practice, waste movements are gradually eliminated, errors become fewer, and the fatigue accompanying the activity is reduced to a minimum. On the other hand, speed and accuracy of movement are increased, and this results in greater satisfaction for the child. Accompanying this satisfaction is greater self-assurance and a strong motivation to make further improvements through continued practice. However, practice must be *timed* to fit into the child's developmental level if improvements are to occur. Ames (1940) has reported that the babies she studied did not improve their characteristic tempo of movement to any marked extent as a result of practice. Those who crept slowly, for example, were found to climb and prehend slowly. The greatest improvements in the skill of throwing and catching balls come after 2½ years, rather than before, even when practice is given at the earlier ages (Hicks, 1930; Gutteridge, 1939; Gesell et al., 1940; Dusenberry, 1952).

Once the foundations for skills have been laid through maturation of the nerves and muscles, increased speed, accuracy, and steadiness appear with practice in the skills. *Speed* has been found to increase at a fairly uniform rate throughout childhood and up to the sixteenth or eighteenth year, but at a slower rate after the thirteenth or fourteenth year (Johnson, 1928; Goodenough and Tinker, 1930; Gates and Scott, 1931; Moore, 1937; Gutteridge, 1939; Gesell et al., 1940; Seils, 1951; Dusenberry, 1952). However, the greatest increase in speed comes early in the childhood years, and then slows down as the child approaches puberty (Merry and Merry, 1950).

Accuracy, as measured by laboratory tests of tracing and aiming at a target, improves up to thirteen or fourteen years and then comes to a standstill (Johnson, 1928; Rice, 1931; Seils, 1951). As is true of speech, the greatest increase in accuracy comes early in childhood. The six-year-old child, for example, is nearly twice as accurate in his movements as the three-year-old (Merry and Merry, 1950). *Steadiness,* as measured by how little movement occurs when the finger, hand, arm, or whole body is held as nearly motionless as possible, improves with age. When the greatest improvement occurs has not yet been determined. *Strength* increases with physical development, but not markedly until puberty, when there is a rapid growth in the size of the muscles (Espenschade, 1940; Bayley and Espenschade, 1944; Jones, 1946).

Importance of Encouragement. In the development of skills, the child needs not only opportunities for practice but also encouragement to do so. He must be provided with equipment he can use, and then he must be motivated to practice by being shown how, by being helped to meet any obstacle that arises in his practice and by being praised for his efforts so that he will derive satisfaction from the practice. In young children this is especially important because they frequently are frustrated and exhausted by their efforts to achieve finer control (Ilg et al., 1949).

Once a skill is well enough learned for the child to be able to enjoy the activity, he usually begins to "stunt." The young child, after mastering the ability to walk, starts to walk on low fences, or to walk backwards or sidewise. No sooner has he learned to ride a tricycle than he tries riding while standing up or sitting backward on the seat. The older child engages in stunts also, but for him, more so than for the younger child, the pleasure of the activity itself is not so important as the attention value this activity has. Older children constantly dare each other to try this or that stunt, and successful accomplishment of it has prestige value for the child (Gutteridge, 1939; Gesell et al., 1940; Breckenridge and Vincent, 1955).

This ability to stunt shows that the child has motor abilities far greater than is usually recognized. It further indicates that the child could use his energy and practice time to perfect skills which would be of greater use to him if he were only given the encouragement and necessary equipment. In a study of nursery-school and kindergarten children, it was found that after the children had mastered the skills related to the equipment provided for them, they either repeated the old performances or attempted to elaborate on them for lack of anything else to do (Gutteridge, 1939). Much the same is true of older children. Without equipment and encouragement to master new skills, the child is likely to use his old skills in modified ways in "stunting" (Jersild, 1954; Breckenridge and Vincent, 1955).

Sex Differences. Throughout childhood, there are relatively few sex differences in skills when boys and girls are given the same training, the same encouragement to learn, and the same equipment for developing the skills. There are, however, certain cultural factors which play a role of importance in determining what skills members of the two sexes will learn. In play, for example, girls are not encouraged to play as many neighborhood games which require speed and strength as boys are. Girls, on the other hand, are encouraged to concentrate on play activities which will develop the smaller muscles, as in doll play, crayoning, and sewing. The result is that girls usually surpass boys in skills which emphasize precision, while boys surpass girls in skills that emphasize speed and strength (Jenkins, 1930; Gutteridge, 1939; Jones, 1939; Anderson, 1949; Jersild, 1954). Sex differences become especially marked in adolescence (Espenschade, 1940; Anderson, 1949; Bayley, 1954).

TYPES OF SKILL

The repertoire of skills acquired after the basic motor coordinations have been attained varies from one child to another. What skills the child will acquire depends to a large extent upon his environment and his opportunity to learn. Children in the rural districts, for example, acquire more skills in climbing than do children in urban communities, where opportunities for climbing are distinctly limited.

Norms for Hand Skills. Tests of intelligence and motor development have shown what hand skills one can expect to find in a normal child at different ages. At *twelve months,* the baby can hold a pencil or crayon and can remove a paper cap from his head. At the age of *two years,* he can open boxes; unscrew lids from bottles or jars; turn the leaves of a book; build a tower of four or five blocks; insert a circle, square, or triangle in a form board; scribble with pencil or crayon; string beads; smear paint; roll clay; drive a nail into soap or soft wood; and cut a gash in paper with scissors. By the *third year,* the child can take care of many of his bodily needs, such as undressing himself, feeding himself, going to the toilet, and washing himself; he can dry dishes, dust, carry a tray, string four beads in 2 minutes, build a bridge of three blocks in imitation of a model, copy a circle in imitation of a model, and cover a picture with paint.

At the age of *five years,* the child should be able to fold a triangle from a paper 6 inches square in imitation of a model; copy a square when given a model to imitate; trace around a diamond drawn on paper; draw a triangle, a diagonal, and a recognizable picture of a man; cut with scissors; put toys away neatly in a box; wash himself without getting his clothes very wet; and tie a single knot around a pencil with a shoelace after looking at a model of a knot. The *six-year-old* can use his skills in carpentry to make a table, wagon, or boat; he can model with clay, make cookies and sew, copy a diamond, and help with simple household tasks such as carrying glasses and pitchers of milk without spilling (Bayley, 1935; Terman and Merrill, 1937; Cattell, 1940; Gesell et al., 1940; Strang, 1951; Townsend, 1951; Breckenridge and Vincent, 1955).

After six years of age, skilled movements with the hands may be acquired quickly and easily if the child is given an opportunity to learn and guidance as to the most effective methods to use. Control of the muscles of the

arms, shoulders, and wrists improves rapidly and reaches almost the adult
level of perfection by the time the child is twelve years old. Control of the
fine muscles of the fingers, by contrast, develops at a slower rate, as shown
by the fact that the control necessary for speedy writing or the playing of
musical instruments is not attained by most children until they are twelve
years old or older (Breckenridge and Vincent, 1955). In copying geometric
figures, which requires fine coordinations of the finger muscles, children

Position of the hand in early spoon-feeding. (*From Child Development, a McGraw-Hill
Text-Film.*)

show rapid improvement up to the age of seven years. After that age, the
improvement is slow and irregular, with the greatest improvement shown by
children with high IQ's (Townsend, 1951).

   Development of Skills. There have been a number of studies of the pattern of development of different skills. These studies have revealed that
most children pass through similar stages in their mastery of these skills.
Of the skills that have received the greatest attention, the following are
the most important.

   1. *Self-feeding.* The baby shows his interest in self-feeding first during

the latter part of the first year of life, when he tries to hold his bottle or cup and reaches for the spoon with which he is being fed. By the age of eight months, the baby can hold his bottle after it has been placed in his mouth, and one month later, he can put it in and take it out as well. By the end of the first year, he can hold his cup momentarily and he tries to feed himself with a spoon, though he usually spills most of the food as he carries the spoon to his mouth. With practice, this skill improves, and he spills less and less. While mastering the skill of using his spoon, he is also learning to hold his cup. At first, he holds on with both hands, but gradually, with practice, this skill improves and he can hold the cup with only one hand (Gesell et al., 1940).

Even though the baby is learning to feed himself with his spoon during the second year, he often prefers finger-feeding to spoon-feeding (Merry and Merry, 1950). By the end of the second year, the young child spills less food and he uses his fork in addition to his spoon. He is still unable to cut his food or prepare it for eating. During the third year, the child can spread butter or jam on his bread with a knife, and a year later, will use his knife to pull his meat apart. Real cutting, however, is too complicated a skill to be learned much before the fifth year.

Throughout the entire period of mastering skills in self-feeding, the child's attention must be concentrated on the task at hand if successful results are to be obtained. Because self-feeding requires close attention, the young child becomes fatigued, and this leads to dawdling. The peak of dawdling comes usually between the third and fourth years (Merry and Merry, 1950). As the skills improve, less attention is needed and the child can then eat and talk simultaneously. By ten years of age, the child should have good control of his eating utensils, his table manners should be more mature, and he should require only occasional help (Gesell and Ilg, 1946).

2. *Self-dressing.* Control of the hands to enable the child to put on his clothes comes later than the ability to remove his clothing. It is easier, for example, for a little child to pull off his socks and shoes than it is to put them on, and the motor skill involved in the former is much less than in the latter. The period of most rapid improvement in dressing is between 1½ and 3½ years (Key et al., 1936). Different garments present different degrees of difficulty. Stockings are easier to put on than shoes, and the putting on of a garment is easier than adjusting and fastening it. Girls as a rule dress themselves earlier and more efficiently than boys, owing partly to more flexible rotation at the wrist, partly to better general motor coordination, and partly to the greater simplicity of their clothing. By the time the child is five years old, he should be able to dress himself completely, with the exception of tying the bowknot on his shoes. This he generally learns to do by the time he is six years old (Breckenridge and Vincent, 1955).

In dressing, eye-hand coordination is necessary until the child learns to dress himself so automatically that he can do so by "feel" alone. While learning to dress himself, the child must see the button, hook, or fastener before he can manipulate it. If he cannot see the fastener, as is the case when it is located at the neck, shoulders, or back of the costume, he cannot fasten it. By three or four years of age, most children can deal with fasteners in the difficult positions just referred to if they look in the mirror. Only after the skilled movements involved in dressing are well developed, around the sixth year, can the child's hands manipulate fasteners without the aid of the eyes to guide the hands (Wagoner and Armstrong, 1928).

Self-dressing is difficult for a young child. (*From Child Development, a McGraw-Hill Text-Film.*)

3. *Writing*. Studies of writing have revealed that the development of this skill follows a fairly definite pattern in which there is a clear-cut gradient in the age changes in writing behavior (Hildreth, 1936; Ames, 1948; Ames and Ilg, 1951). Up to one year, the baby bangs and scribbles with his pencil. By eighteen months, he will scribble in the middle of the page, and by three years, he will attempt to make simple symbol units, though these are scarcely recognizable as letters (Hildreth, 1936). The body is not biologically ready for handwriting before the child is six years old. Up until that age, the nerves and muscles of the fingers, hand, wrist, and arm are not

developed enough to make the fine coordinations needed in writing (Havighurst, 1953). In his early attempts at writing, the child's hand moves from the lower right-hand corner of the paper to the center, then to the top center, and finally, to the top left. This final position comes between the seventh and eighth years (Ames, 1948).

The pattern of development in the forming of letters has been found to be as follows (condensed from Ames and Ilg, 1951):

3½ years . . . . Prints a few capital letters, large, single letters, anywhere on the page.

4 years . . . . Prints a few capitals, large and irregular, usually the initial capital of his first name.

5 years . . . . Prints first name in large and irregular letters, getting larger toward the middle or end of the name. Frequently reverses letters, especially S. Prints numbers 1 to 5, uneven and medium-sized.

6 years . . . . Prints entire alphabet in large, irregular letters with many reversals. Copies words, using all capitals with some reversal of letters and in the wrong order. Prints numbers 1 to 20, with frequent reversals in the numbers 3, 7, and 9.

7 years . . . . Most children can write, though some still print in capitals. Writing is large, straight, labored, and irregular in size and shape. Numbers are smaller, but there are many errors.

8 years . . . . Most children write by now, in large, square, and quite black letters. Capitals and looped letters are disproportionately tall. Numbers are smaller, and there are fewer errors.

9 years . . . . Children no longer print. The writing is smaller, neater, more even, slanted, and shows the beginning of an individual style. Letters are in good proportions. Beginnings of an individual style are shown in the writing of the child's name. Girls' writing is smaller, neater, and more evenly slanted than boys'.

4. *Ball Throwing and Catching.* The ability to throw and catch balls requires well-coordinated movements, not only of the arms and hands but of the entire body. As Gesell et al. (1940) have pointed out, "Skill in throwing a ball requires a fine sense of static and dynamic balance, accurate timing of delivery and release, good eye-hand coordination, and appropriate functioning of the fingers, as well as the arms, trunk, head, and legs, in controlling the trajectory of the ball." While some babies roll and may even attempt to throw balls before they are two years old, none are able to do so well. Even at four years, few can throw or catch well. By six years, most children are proficient, though there are marked variations in the skill at every age (Gutteridge, 1939).

The size of the ball influences the method of throwing and the distance thrown. At first, both hands are used and there is mass movement of the body. Gradually, the movements become more specialized and only one hand is used (Gutteridge, 1939). The norm for throwing a 9½-inch ball 12 to 13 feet is fifty-seven months, and for a 16½-inch ball, above 72 months (Wellman, 1937).

Ball catching is likewise difficult. At four years, few children are proficient, while at six years, approximately two-thirds of the children have mastered this skill. Girls on the whole are more proficient than boys in catching. The method of catching shows definite stages. At first, the child uses his whole body to clasp the ball, then two arms, with less movement. Later, the child perfects a coordinated movement of the hand, or hands, to catch the ball between the palms. A ball 5 inches in diameter is caught best by five-year-olds. A six-year-old catches well with a ball of 12 inches, only half as successfully with a ball of 8 inches, and few of that age can catch a ball of 5 inches (Gutteridge, 1939).

5. *Block Building.* In the pattern of block building, the baby first carries blocks from place to place and manipulates them in irregular masses. By three years, he places blocks in regular piles or rows to build simple structures like enclosures. Gradually, his constructions become more complex and are often used as part of dramatic play (Johnson, 1933). The more difficult structures tend to be built obliquely at the edge of a table, while the more familiar structures are symmetrically centered. The child is more likely to sit obliquely when building difficult structures than when building easy and familiar structures (Ames, 1948).

Skills Following Walking. From the age of eighteen months to the beginning of the school age, between the fifth and sixth years, the motor development in the legs consists primarily of the perfection of walking and the acquisition of related skills. *Running, hopping, skipping, jumping, climbing,* and other skills soon follow walking. Before a child is *two years* old, he can walk sideways and backward, up- and downstairs with help, and can stand on one foot and then the other with help. By the time he is *three years* old, he can walk upstairs and down alone, stand on one foot without help, and walk on tiptoe.

By his *fourth birthday,* the child can jump from a height of 30 centimeters and make a standing jump of 60 to 85 centimeters. Between the *fifth* and *sixth years,* the child can jump rope; can balance on rails, on top of a wall, on a narrow plank elevated at one end, or on a chalk mark on the floor; and can roller-skate on four wheels, but cannot ice-skate if the skates have a single runner. By the time he is *six years* old, he can ride a bicycle and keep time to music by walking and skipping. During the first three years of school, the child can dance imaginative rhythms to music, can skip to music, skate on a single runner, and participate in a wide number of games requiring skills related to walking (Jenkins, 1930; Bayley, 1935; Merry and Merry, 1950; Strang, 1951; Jersild, 1954; Breckenridge and Vincent, 1955).

Patterns of Development. As is true of hand skills, a number of studies have been made of the patterns of development of leg skills. The most important of these are as follows.

1. *Running.* Running at first is little more than fast walking with crude, uneven steps and a general clumsiness of the entire body that leads to many falls. By the age of five or six years, the young child can not only run with relatively few falls, but he can play games at the same time. When the young child first starts to run, he does so, not because he wants to get to a given place quickly, but because he derives satisfaction from the activity itself. Later, as the ability to run is well developed, he reserves this activity for occasions requiring speed.

2. *Jumping.* Jumping is at first an exaggerated stepping with one foot and then the other. Or the child may drop himself from the place of support, lifting both feet simultaneously and stepping with both feet at once. The body is not propelled forward, and as a result, the child generally lands in a sprawl and has trouble in getting up. This is the characteristic method of jumping of the two-year-old. By the age of four, the child can jump well. He now propels his body upward and forward, bends his knees, swings from a higher to lower level, and lands in a standing position. Jumping over an obstacle is difficult even for a four-year-old, and few children attempt long jumps much before they are five years old (Gutteridge, 1939).

3. *Skipping and hopping.* Skipping and hopping are modifications of jumping. While children attempt to hop before they are three years old, they are not skillful until they are six or seven years old. Hopping on two feet precedes hopping on one foot. After achieving skillful hopping, the child adds variations by hopping backward or by turning around while hopping. Because skipping is more difficult for children than hopping, few are proficient by the time they are six years old. In learning to skip, the child first introduces a hop or jump into his running. Then he skips with one foot, using a running step with the other. Later he skips with both feet, and as he becomes proficient, he introduces variations, such as crossing his feet, twirling, or skipping sideways (Gutteridge, 1939).

4. *Galloping.* Galloping, which is another modification of jumping, develops later than skipping. Not until the child is six-and-a-half or seven years old can he gallop well. The child first introduces a galloping step into his running or pounds on the strong beat of music. Later, he learns the basic movement of galloping, which is to throw the weight on the forward foot. After skill in galloping is achieved, many variations are introduced, such as galloping sideways or backward (Gutteridge, 1939).

5. *Climbing.* Climbing steps is accomplished by crawling and creeping. This occurs before the baby can walk alone. In going down steps, the baby generally goes backward. After he can walk alone, the baby goes up- and downstairs in an upright position, holding on to the railing of the stairs or the hand of a person. At first, one foot is placed on the step and the other drawn up to it. The same foot is used each time to make the advance. A similar method is used for going downstairs. Gradually, with practice, the

child lets go of the railing and uses his legs alternately, as if walking. This adult manner of step climbing is attained by four years of age, provided the child has had ample opportunity to learn (Gesell and Thompson, 1934). Girls are generally slower in acquiring skill in climbing than are boys (Gutteridge, 1939). After gaining sufficient skill to climb well, children start to do stunts, such as racing, competing, and climbing in dramatic projects.

Stair climbing is a patterned form of behavior, almost identical with that observed in creeping. Typically, the left foot moves first, then the left hand and the right foot almost simultaneously; then, after a pause, right hand and left foot. In stair climbing, the pattern is closely similar to that used for progression on level surfaces. A child who creeps on hands and knees, for example, climbs stairs on hands and knees; the child who creeps on hands, knee, and one foot climbs stairs in that fashion (Ames, 1939). Much the same pattern of behavior is found in ladder climbing as in step climbing (McCaskill and Wellman, 1938).

6. *Swimming.* How soon a child will acquire swimming skills will depend to a large extent upon the opportunities he has to learn. Few children acquire these skills much before the age of four years, and many not until several years later. Because swimming is such a highly coordinated type of skill, it requires more practice than many of the other skills of childhood. When submerged in water in a prone position, a baby a few weeks old will make rhythmical, coordinated reflex movements of the upper and lower extremities which resemble swimming. At the age of several months, disorganized, struggling movements appear, and there is a tendency to rotate the body from a prone to a supine position. This is accompanied by difficulties in respiration. Toward the end of the second year, the baby makes deliberate swimming movements, especially in the lower extremities, and shows a tendency to remain in a prone position (McGraw, 1939a).

7. *Tricycling.* By the age of two years, a few children can ride tricycles. Between three and four years, any child who has an opportunity to learn can do so. After skilled performance has been achieved, children use their tricycles for stunting, such as riding backward, turning corners, riding while standing up, and avoiding obstacles (Gutteridge, 1939; Jones, 1939).

HANDEDNESS

Whether an individual is naturally right- or left-handed or whether the predominant use of one hand is the result of training and social conditioning has been a question of dispute for generations. The popular belief is that handedness is a hereditary trait and that any attempt to interfere with it will lead to serious nervous disorders, apparent most often in speech defects. It has even been suggested that left-handedness is a sex-linked characteristic transmitted usually from the male through the female, and then back to the male (Bryngelson and Clark, 1933).

Several explanations have been given for preferential use of the right hand. One is that the left side of the cerebrum is functionally superior to the right and thus determines right-hand preference. Another is that the right hand is structurally superior to the left, owing to the position of the fetus in the uterus. Still another is that handedness is a product of "sideness," or lateral dominance, with one side functioning spontaneously in preference to the other in involuntary acts, such as focusing one eye (Giesecke, 1936).

However, experimental evidence has not borne out the theories that handedness is hereditary or that it is closely related to eyedness. In fact, evidence points to the fact that there is a greater relationship between handedness and footedness than between handedness and eyedness. When dominance occurs, it is general and affects the entire side of the body. How long this persists after birth has not yet been determined (Gesell, 1941; Dorcus and Shaffer, 1945; Gesell and Ames, 1947a). Commenting on these beliefs, Hildreth (1949b) remarks, "Hand dominance is commonly believed to be hereditary because it is difficult to explain in any other way."

In opposition to the belief that handedness is a function of some hereditary condition is the belief that it is due to learning or social conditioning (Watson, 1925). Hildreth (1949a) stresses that there is no such thing as "natural handedness." Evidence from genetic studies of children and from studies of cultural differences in child-rearing practices point to the fact that "acquiring handedness follows the laws of learning and habit formation just as any other behavior that results from practice and exercise." Furthermore, experience has proved that both children and older people can acquire new skills with either hand, regardless of the accustomed hand usage, without experiencing any emotional upset (Hildreth, 1949).

Commenting on the effects of training in the case of nursery-school children Hildreth (1948) noted that

those acts that are most strongly influenced by the child's parents or teachers tended to show high right-handed indices. Those acts were eating with spoon and fork, writing or crayoning, and to some extent, throwing. Young children tend to be right-handed in the trained things, either-handed in the untrained. Right-handedness appears to be learned behavior, initiated largely through the use of eating implements. Children who get an early start in right-handed eating tend to become right-handed. There tends to be more right-handedness in acts that are subject to social censure when performed with the left hand (p. 43).

Hildreth (1950a) further emphasizes that "Handedness should be trained, not left to chance, since manual dexterity can affect an individual's educational and vocational success."

Prevalence of Right-handedness. As civilization has advanced and machines and tools have been employed by man, there has been a need for one hand to play the dominant role and the other serves as an auxiliary. Then there are many skills which require only one hand and the auxiliary hand is unnecessary. For reasons unknown to modern man, the right hand has been considered the preferred hand, and each successive generation has accepted this as a tradition. The result is that in most cultures, there are more right-handed people than left-handed. At the present time, it is estimated that approximately 95 per cent of our people are predominantly right-handed, with a tendency for more males than females to be left-handed (Hildreth, 1948, 1949, 1949a).

What percentage of the population of a country or a community will be right-handed will depend to a certain extent upon the social attitudes toward left-handedness. At the present time, there is an increase in left-handedness due, primarily, to the prevailing popular belief that handedness is hereditary and that any attempt to interfere with left-handedness will invariably result in stuttering and other indications of nervous tension (Carrothers, 1947; Hildreth, 1949). This is in contrast to China where left-handedness is far less common than here. This is due to the fact that Chinese parents are far stricter in correcting left-handed traits than are American parents. To them, left-handedness is a departure from convention, which is strictly frowned upon. If not corrected, it is likely to be interpreted as an indication of laxity on the part of the parents (Hildreth, 1949).

However, few individuals are dominantly right- or left-handed or ambidextrous in the sense that they use both hands equally and equally well (Gesell and Ames, 1947). Most individuals use either the right or the left hand predominantly, though they use the alternate hand for certain activities other than those in which they were taught skills with emphasis on the use of one hand in preference to the other. There are numerous shifts in handedness at all ages, but the individual who uses one hand in preference to the other most of the time is generally regarded as "right-handed" or "left-handed," according to which hand is used for skills where training has been given (Jenkins, 1930; Hicks, 1931; Hildreth, 1949a; Merry and Merry, 1950; Martin, 1952; Jersild, 1954; Breckenridge and Vincent, 1955). Even among adults, left-handed individuals are less consistent in the use of their left hands than are right-handed individuals. Left-handers who were trained to write with the right hand are inclined to be ambidextrous. They favor the left hand in certain spontaneous acts, as throwing a ball, but in situations where training and social influences dominate, they use the right hand. On the whole, they are inclined to be more ambidextrous than right-handers (Humphrey, 1951).

Development of Handedness. The human infant is neither right- nor left-handed. However, early in life, he begins to show a preference for the use of one hand rather than the other (Hildreth, 1949). By the middle of the first year, most babies demonstrate an unequal use of the two hands, both in preferential use and in greater strength. This is seen first in the activity of the small-muscle groups, as in the fingers and wrists (Giesecke, 1936). However, there is no clear-cut evidence of preference for one hand throughout the first year, and babies shift from the use of the right to the use of the left hand very frequently, often showing more preference for the left than for the right hand. Shifting from one hand to the other occurs likewise during the second year, but not as frequently as during the first year (Halverson, 1933; Updegraff, 1933; Giesecke, 1936; Dennis, 1939; Lederer, 1939; Gesell et al., 1940; Gesell and Ames, 1947; Ames, 1949a; Hildreth, 1949, 1950; Gesell, 1952, 1954).

During the third year, shifting continues but is less frequent. After that, the amount of shifting decreases, so that after six years of age, there is relatively little shifting taking place. What shifting does occur will depend largely upon the activity the child is engaged in. Activities which have been trained, such as eating and crayoning, will be carried out with the right hand, though the child may shift to the use of the left hand for activities spontaneously carried out (Johnson and Bissell, 1940; Johnson and Duke, 1940; Gesell and Ames, 1947; Gesell, 1949, 1954; Hildreth, 1949, 1949a, 1950a). Nearly all children follow a comparable pattern, though at different rates and with varying emphasis on successive stages (Gesell and Ames, 1947). Shifts occur whether the child is in a sitting or a supine position (Ames, 1949a). Hand dominance is generally established earlier in children who show a preference for the right hand than in those who are left-handed or show no definite hand preference (Hildreth, 1949a).

Establishment of Hand Dominance. During the first two years of life, the child is neither dominantly right- or left-handed. He shifts from one hand to the other, though he usually shows a tendency to steer more to one hand than to the other. From the age of three to five years is the "critical period" in establishing handedness, because at that time, the child shows more and more preference for the use of one hand rather than the other. Left to chance, the child may develop habits of right-hand domination. He may, however, develop habits of using his left hand. Therefore it is essential that guidance and encouragement be given at this time, so that the child will develop more habits which require the use of his right than of his left hand. Many parents of today protest against such guidance on the grounds that by doing so, "they interfere with nature" and may cause nervous tension of varying degrees of severity in the child (Hildreth, 1950a).

Dominant handedness is advantageous to a child, not only because it eliminates the confusion that is inevitable when there is a shifting from the use of one hand to another, but also because the child can become more expert if he learns the majority of skills with one hand. The other hand, the auxiliary hand, then is trained to work as a team with the dominant hand, and this results in greater efficiency. As Hildreth (1949) has emphasized, "Only a genius would have the ability to attain equal mastery of the two hands in a lifetime so as to be able to use them alternately in the same role."

Delay in establishing hand dominance is unfortunate because it leads to confusion, uncertainty, and awkwardness in motor performance. It is likely to make the child resistant, stubborn, negativistic, nervously unstable, and tense. This in turn may lead to stuttering, reading disabilities, defects in writing, especially mirror writing and reversal of figures, spelling difficulties, and feelings of inferiority resulting from general awkwardness and poor motor coordinations (Bryngelson and Rutherford, 1937; Hildreth, 1949, 1950; Bakwin, 1950). Most children who lack hand dominance or who are slow in acquiring it are somewhat deficient in the use of both hands (Hildreth, 1949). Furthermore, they find it a great social handicap to use both hands, especially during the adolescent years (Hildreth, 1949, 1950). The child who lacks hand dominance has less strength, speed, and accuracy in his movements than does the child who is either right- or left-handed (Burge, 1952).

Right- versus Left-handedness. Whether or not the child becomes left- or right-handed is more important than that he be neither or that he shift from one to another. With the establishment of hand dominance come not only feelings of stability and security, but also opportunities to develop levels of skill that would be impossible if attempts were made to use both hands with equal or near-equal frequency for activities where only one hand is necessary. The next important question is, which hand should be the dominant one, the right or the left? The only answer in our culture is that a child should become right-handed unless it is difficult or impossible for him to do so.

There is no reason to believe that the right hand is superior to the left or that a nation of right-handed people is superior to a nation of left-handers. However, it has become traditional to regard the right hand as the preferred hand, and our culture has been built up on this traditional preference. As Hildreth (1949) has pointed out, "Probably the preference for the right in the dawn of civilization was arbitrary. At all events, right-handedness has continued to be the prevailing fashion down the ages." Evidence for this comes from archeological studies of the tools used in the Stone Age and prehistoric times, as well as the records of civilized man.

Thus, as Hildreth (1949) further explains, "Right-handedness is a cultural and social convention to which most people are trained and find it expedient to conform. . . . In an unbiased world, left-handedness would be as common as right-handedness, for the play of chance factors would be equal for the two sides." But this is not an unbiased world. Instead, as Dayhaw

(1953) has emphasized, "Our modern world is dextral-minded." Machines, home appliances, sporting equipment, methods of teaching, desk chairs, desk drawers, illumination, and the tools of our modern machine age are all designed and made for the right-handers.

Living in a right-handed world, it is certainly easier and less confusing for an individual to be right-handed than left-handed. There are many practical difficulties associated with left-handedness, especially those related to learning (Hildreth, 1949). It is confusing and frustrating to a left-handed child to have to adjust to models meant for right-handers and to learn to play games and sports when the equipment is planned for use with the right hand (Jersild, 1954). With increasing age, right-handed children show greater speed, accuracy, and strength than do left-handed children (Burge, 1952). How difficult it is for a left-handed child to learn from a model planned for right-handed children is illustrated in Fig. 26.

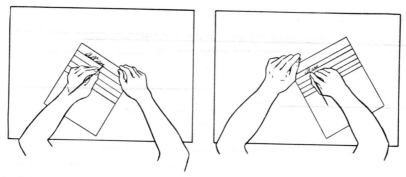

Fig. 26. Positions of right and left hands in writing. (*From G. Hildreth, The development and training of hand dominance. I. Characteristics of handedness, J. genet. Psychol., 1949, 75, 197–220. Used by permission.*)

In addition to the practical difficulties associated with left-handedness is the effect it has on the child's personality, upon his attitudes toward self, and upon his social adjustments. Because the prejudice against left-handedness has persisted since earliest times, many children are made to feel inadequate and ashamed, especially when they are constantly reminded of their left-handedness by being told to use their right hands (Hildreth, 1949; Bakwin, 1950). Because left-handedness leads to many frustrations, the effect on the child's personality is to cause disinterest, discouragement, or to lead to jealousy and antisocial tendencies (Dayhaw, 1953). Commenting on the problems of the left-handed child, Jersild (1954) maintains, "The hardship a child must bear because of being left-handed may be very light, yet there is bound to be at least some hardship connected with being a left-hander. A person cannot differ from most other people without having to pay at least a small price for such a difference."

Changing Left-handedness. As all evidence today seems to point to the fact that, in most cases, left-handedness results from learning rather than from some hereditary condition, it is obvious that a child should learn to use his right hand from the time he is capable of doing things with one hand alone. Should he have been permitted to learn to do things with his left hand, can he change and become right-handed? Experience has shown that he can (Hildreth, 1949, 1950). However, the longer he waits to shift from the use of his left to his right hand, the more difficult it will be. Whenever changes must be made and new adjustments learned, there will be nervous tension which may lead to resistance when the child is forced to change. This causes further confusion and tension for the child (Hildreth, 1949).

The tension aroused when there is interference with partially established habits and the need to make new adjustments may lead to stuttering and other forms of nervous behavior, such as nail biting and thumb sucking. These are more likely to be symptoms of the tension that prevails than the result of change of handedness. Normally, the tension will subside when the change has been made, unless there is too long a delay in making the change and the stuttering or other nervous mannerisms have become fixed habits (Hildreth, 1950; Garrison, 1952; Jersild, 1954). Resistance may be so great on the child's part that left-handedness persists in spite of attempts made to change it. A strongly left-handed child, owing either to some physical cause or to well-established habits of left-handedness, may resist conversion so strongly that attempts to break down this resistance may do permanent damage to his personality and establish habits of stuttering or other nervous forms of behavior that will persist throughout life (Hildreth, 1949b; Bakwin, 1950; Garrison, 1952).

The training methods used to change from left- to right-handed usage, the attitude of parent or teacher toward the importance of the child's making the change, and the general atmosphere which prevails in the home or school while the change is being made are responsible for the nervous disturbances that occur rather than the change itself. When the change is accompanied by constant reminders, nagging, scolding, or even punishments, the child will become confused, resentful, and tense. In the case of a high-strung, nervous child, such methods will be even more damaging than in one who is less nervous (Hildreth, 1949, 1950, 1950a; Garrison, 1952; Jersild, 1954). While being left-handed in a right-handed world may be inconvenient and may lead to personality problems resulting from feeling that he is different, it is sometimes questionable whether this is not preferable to the effects of changing handedness after habits of using the left hand have been permitted to become established. Jersild (1954) has emphasized this point of view when he says, "But right-handedness is not so important in itself that parents should interfere if the child himself shows a strong inclination to lead with his left hand as he squares off for the battle of life."

DELAYED MOTOR DEVELOPMENT

Not all children progress through the stages of motor development recorded above at the average or normal ages. There are many instances of accelerated development and even more of retarded development. In most cases, where motor development is retarded to an appreciable extent, the delay becomes apparent early. Should remedial treatment be given as soon as the delay is recognized, it could, in most instances, be eliminated or certainly minimized to a marked extent. Because skills are built upon the foundations laid by the maturation of the basic motor coordinations, delay in maturation of muscle control will result in delay in the development of skills.

Delayed motor development is serious, not only because it keeps the child from reaching the stage of independent action when he normally should, but primarily because it interferes with the social development of the child. The little child who is slow in developing control over his body finds himself unable, as he reaches the second or third year, to keep up with other children of that age. His movements are clumsy, awkward, and uncoordinated, with the result that he cannot join in the play activities of the group. If he is backward in feeding himself, dressing himself, or taking care of his own needs, he feels self-conscious and shy when in the presence of other children whose independent action enables them to take care of themselves without the aid of parent, nurse, or teacher. As a result of this early backwardness in the development of motor control, many young children develop feelings of inferiority which cause them to withdraw from the social group, and this lays the foundation for unsocial attitudes and behavior.

Causes of Delayed Motor Development. A few of the most common causes of delayed motor development are the following.

1. Poor Physical Condition. Popular opinion holds that the relationship between the physical condition of the child and his motor development is a close one. This would mean that, at a given age, the children who are in the best physical condition would be more precocious in their motor development than children of the same age who are in poor physical condition owing to illness, malnutrition, or other causes. While this is not necessarily true, because it fails to take into consideration factors other than health which contribute to the child's motor development, there is evidence that, other factors being equal, the child of superior health is more precocious in his motor development than is the child whose physical condition is poor.

Even a healthy condition before birth, as expressed in greater fetal activity, is reflected in advanced motor development during the first year of life (Sontag, 1941). Illnesses of a severe nature, operations, malnutrition, glandular deficiencies, or chemical deficiencies, as in the case of rickets, have been found to delay the ages at which babies sit, stand, and walk (Variot and Gotcu, 1927; Gesell, 1928; Smith, 1931; Dennis, 1941a, 1943; Peatman and Higgons, 1942; Merry and Merry, 1950; Garrison, 1952; Breckenridge and Vincent, 1955). In the development of motor coordinations, it has been found that a "severe illness preceding the development of any trait reduces the apparent rate of development of that trait to about 88 per cent of what it would otherwise have been" (Smith, 1931). Sensory defects, especially blindness if it occurs early, is likely to retard the motor development of the child, owing mainly to timidity on the child's part and lack of stimulation on the part of his parents (Maxfield and Fjeld, 1942).

2. *Size of the Body.* The size and body proportions of the baby exert some influence on his motor development, especially in the case of sitting, standing, walking, and later skills. The center of gravity of the baby's body must shift downward if the baby's balance is to be maintained. There must be an increase in the ratio of leg to trunk length and a decrease in the ratio of weight to height if proper balance is to be achieved. Small-boned, thin, and muscular babies have been found, in general, to walk sooner than short, rotund, or exceedingly heavy babies, though other factors than body build may be responsible for these differences (Shirley, 1931a; Strang, 1951). When weight is held constant, on the other hand, an increase of 1 inch in length at birth has been found to be associated with a mean decrease of 22 days in mean walking age. When, on the other hand, length at birth is held constant, an increase of 1 pound in weight is associated with a mean increase of 8 days in age of walking alone (Norval, 1947).

Once the muscular and skeletal equipment for sitting, standing, and walking has been developed, the future course of the child's motor development will be influenced by such factors as temperament, motor alertness, and responsiveness to the relationship of internal needs and external circumstances. Excessive weight alone is not enough to seriously delay motor development (Peatman and Higgons, 1942; Dennis, 1943a). Among older children, a child's body build has been found to be of little importance in determining his motor coordinations. However, extremely thin or stocky children show less agility than those more nearly average in build (Bayley, 1940). Obese children tend to be inactive, and this militates against their willingness to put forth the effort needed to enter into games with other children or to take care of their own needs (Bruch, 1940).

3. *Intelligence.* The relationship between intelligence and motor development, especially during the first years of life, is so marked that motor items figure largely in tests of general intelligence for children under two years of age. Babies who are slow in sitting up, standing up, or walking generally prove, as time goes on, to be backward in intellectual development. On the other hand, those who are precocious in motor development prove to be, for the most part, intellectually precocious. In the case of walking, there has been found to be a mean difference in age of an appreciable amount

between babies of high- and low-grade intelligence (Terman, 1925; Abt et al., 1929; Dennis, 1943a; Garrison, 1952). Unusually high intelligence, however, is not always accompanied by precocious walking. Other factors may be responsible for delaying the walking (Dennis, 1943a).

The relationship between intelligence and motor development is most marked during the preschool years. However, after the first fifteen months of life, the relationship becomes increasingly smaller (Shirley, 1931a; Bayley, 1933). Among older children and adolescents, on the other hand, there has been found to be practically a zero relationship between intelligence and motor performance (Abernethy, 1936; Jones, 1949). When, however, the child is mentally deficient, he is likely to be below the norm for his age in motor development also (Jersild, 1954).

4. *Lack of Opportunity to Develop Muscle Control.* In many instances, motor development is delayed because of lack of opportunity for practice. The little child whose environment is restricted to crib, coach, or play pen, or who, if given a wider environment, finds the floors so slippery that he falls and everything he leans on for support slides under his weight, is hampered in developing muscle control. The environment of an adult is, in almost every respect, unsuited to the needs of a young baby and thus offers little opportunity for him to get the practice needed for the acquisition of motor control.

Cradling practices of Hopi Indians, it has been found, do not appreciably delay the onset of walking (Dennis and Dennis, 1940, 1940a). However, lack of opportunity to practice and of materials to encourage the practice do interfere with the development of skills (Gutteridge, 1939; Jones, 1949; Garrison, 1952). This may affect the child's interests and activities as he grows older, because skills learned in childhood persist into adult years (Nestrick, 1939).

5. *Lack of Incentive to Develop Muscle Control.* Even if the young child is given an environment suited to his needs, he may be slow in developing muscle control because of lack of incentive to do so. If he is pampered and waited on and if his every wish is satisfied, it is not surprising that he becomes lazy. This, in turn, interferes with the development of muscle control, because of the lack of effort put forth by the child to acquire it. In walking, dressing, and self-feeding, this is especially true (Dennis, 1934a).

A comparison of young children from homes of high and low economic status revealed that while those from the more favored environments ranked above those from the poorer environments in verbal, practical, and emotional abilities, they were inferior to them in skills involved in self-care, such as washing the face and hands and combing the hair. The difference in this area was due largely to the greater motivation on the part of the children from the poorer environments (Gesell and Lord, 1927). Within the first two years of life, the motor development of babies from the lower socioeconomic groups is superior to that of babies from the higher groups. Permissive methods of child rearing are likewise associated with better motor development than when the baby is "pushed" by his parents, as is frequently true of those of the higher socioeconomic groups (Williams and Scott, 1953).

6. *Emphasis on Specific Movements.* Teaching specific movements before the gross movements are perfected very often delays the acquisition of skilled movements. For example, in dancing or writing, the child is expected to coordinate the smaller muscle teams before coordinating the larger ones. Because this is too complicated a task for him, it will not only discourage him but also delay the acquisition of the desired skills. The young child should, for example, be given plenty of opportunity for scribbling freely and without restraint before he is expected to perform the more complicated movements involved in drawing or writing. Similarly, a chance to practice stringing beads or buttons should precede any attempt to teach the little girl to sew.

7. *Fear.* Forcing a child to carry out a skilled movement before his muscles and nervous system are ready for it invariably results in delayed motor control. Fear which comes from falling often causes an inhibition that makes the child hesitant to repeat the act associated with failure. When the little child is forced to walk before he is ready to do so, to climb stairs when he is not sure of himself walking on a straight floor, or to dive before he can swim with ease and confidence, fear is the usual outcome, and this militates against further attempts to develop the skill. The result is a delayed development of the activity. Parental concern about the child's safety or fear that he will not come up to other children of his age often serves to intimidate the child (Breckenridge and Vincent, 1955). Parents of obese children are often apprehensive about the dangers of physical exercise, and this causes them to discourage their children from exercising. This is frequently paralleled by inactivity on the child's part (Bruch, 1940). As the child grows older, parental fear is reflected in the type of activity the child engages in (Fauquier, 1940).

Nagging, scolding, and ridicule lead to fear and resentment on the child's part. This, in turn, makes him tense and awkward. By contrast, praise and approval lead to relaxation, better coordination, and a stronger incentive on the child's part to engage in the practice necessary to improve his motor coordinations (Merry and Merry, 1950). How far-reaching the effects of fear, resulting from scoldings and ridicule, may be has been emphasized thus by Breckenridge and Vincent (1955): "Ridicule, sarcasm, scolding, or laughing at children's clumsiness in the early learning stages, or at the inevitable slips which cause dropping of objects, stumbling, or falling, may cause an emotional blocking which can result in tense movement and awkwardness throughout the child's life."

Chapter 6

DEVELOPMENT OF SPEECH

Language is the ability to communicate with others. It includes *every* means of communication in which thoughts and feelings are symbolized so as to convey meaning, including such widely differing forms of communication as the written, spoken, sign, facial, gesture, pantomime, and art. It is one of the main things that differentiates human beings from the lower forms of animals (Brownfield, 1953). *Speech,* on the other hand, is merely one form of language in which articulate sounds or words are used to convey meanings. Speech development is "sound-shaping development, a growth process proceeding from the vague, indistinct, and fortuitously shaped to the clear, distinct, and controlled" (Lynip, 1951).

All sounds made by the human being may not justifiably be classed as "speech." Vocalization, in the form of cries or explosive sounds, does not become speech until meaning is associated with the sounds made. Every form of vocalization, which occurs up to the time that the young child associates meaning with the sounds he uses, belongs to the prespeech level of development. When true speech begins is an individual matter and varies from one child to another. It is often difficult to determine whether the child is really speaking or if the words he utters are merely "parrot talk," in that he does not know their significations but imitates blindly the sounds heard.

Speech serves many purposes other than as a means of communicating thoughts, feelings, and emotions. It is used to secure information, to express the results of the individual's reasoning, to give vent to feelings and emotions, to bring about action in others, to satisfy the human need for sociability, to help the individual develop and maintain a feeling of importance of self, and to serve as a bond that holds people together (Bayley, 1940; Brownfield, 1953; McCarthy, 1954; Breckenridge and Vincent, 1955). Speech "is a kind of behavior which helps to form the world of the child; to transform him from an egocentric to a social being; to make assumptions for him; to set up conventions to guide and control him; to inform him; to instill in him thoughts, feelings, and attitudes; to make him feel secure and insecure—all these effects and many more may be brought about in the child through the use of words" (Baldridge, 1949). The child's adjustment is influenced by his speech, and his speech, in turn, is influenced by his adjustment (Baldridge, 1949).

Criteria of Speech. Two criteria should be applied to determine whether the young child has emerged from the use of prespeech forms of communication. These two criteria are: (1) The child must pronounce his words so that they are readily understandable to others rather than comprehensible only to those who, because of constant contact with him, have learned to understand him. (2) The child must know the meaning of the words he uses and must associate them with the objects they represent. "Da-da," for example, must be used only to refer to one person, or "ball," to refer only to balls and not to toys in general. "Baby talk" may satisfy the second criterion of real speech, since words are identified with objects, but it does not satisfy the first criterion of comprehensibility.

PRELIMINARIES TO SPEECH

Learning to speak is a long and complicated process. Most reports indicate that a baby does not say his first word until sometime between the ages of twelve and fifteen months. This means that for the first twelve or fifteen months of a child's life, his communications must be in forms preliminary to speech. The communication needs of the baby are expressed by gestures and expressive vocalizations. Vocalization, in the form of cries, explosive sounds, or "babbling," does not become a form of language until meaning is associated with the sounds made. When that occurs, the baby can communicate with those who know him well enough to understand what he is attempting to say, even though his vocalization may be meaningless to strangers.

Prespeech Forms. There are three preliminary forms of communication commonly used by babies during the first months of life, which serve them temporarily as satisfactory forms of communication. These are (1) *crying,* (2) "explosive sounds" which soon develop into *babbling,* and (3) *gestures.* Of the three, the second is the most important from the long-range point of view because it becomes the basis for real speech. During the early months of life, however, crying is the most frequently used of the three.

1. CRYING

In the early days of life, most of the vocalization of the newborn infant is in the form of crying (Irwin and Chen, 1946; McCarthy, 1952, 1954). This early crying is, in effect, "emergency respiration" (Ribble, 1943). It is irregular and uncontrolled (Lynip, 1951). During the first two weeks, crying appears at irregular intervals, often from a state of sleep. The infant, without any apparent reason, begins to cry intensely. This is accompanied by reddening or mottling of the skin, clenching of the fists, alternate extension and flexion of the extremities, increased activity of the entire body, irregular breathing, prolonged expiration, and increased pulse rate. Some infants hold their breath at such times, but no tearing is present.

Then, quite suddenly, the crying ends, either spontaneously or in response to maternal care (Stewart et al., 1954).

While all infants cry in this way during the early days of life, differences in amounts of such crying appear at the end of the second week of life (Stewart et al., 1954). Beginning with the third week, there is normally less crying, and by the third or fourth month, night waking, accompanied by crying, decreases (Stewart et al., 1954). Crying likewise becomes differentiated, so that it is possible for those who are familiar with babies to know what the tones and intensities of the cries signify.

Causes of Crying. Crying in young babies is a means of discharging tension from an internal or environmental source. As it is a response to distress, the cause of the distress should be investigated (Stewart et al., 1954). Among babies less than seven weeks of age, hunger has been found to be the most common cause of crying, and noise and light the least likely causes. Other causes are shown in Fig. 16. Unknown causes, it may be noted, are next in frequency to hunger (Aldrich et al., 1945). Colic is a common cause of crying during the first three months of life (Stewart et al., 1954). Older babies cry from pain, bright lights, sharp noises, uncomfortable positions, strong disturbances during sleep, fatigue, hunger, inability to move due to restrictive clothes or covers, loss or removal of a plaything, fear, and when contact with others is withdrawn (Bühler, 1930). Crying is most frequent before feeding and before the baby goes to sleep for the night (Kelting, 1934).

Before he is three months old, the normal baby has learned that crying is a sure method of getting attention. He learns also that when he does not cry, no one pays much attention to him. If, therefore, he wants attention, he calls for it by loud cries. It is not long before he has learned to use crying as a means to an end. At four months, a baby will cry when an adult ceases to play with him; at five months, he will increase his crying if an adult enters the room but pays no attention to him; and at nine months, he cries if an adult approaches another child (Bühler, 1930; Lynip, 1951). Crying is also caused in the latter part of the first year of life by fear of strange situations and unusual handling (Bayley, 1932).

The young child cries when he is hungry, tired, frightened, or when some activity he is engaging in is interrupted (Watson, 1925). Among nursery-school children, crying is predominantly social, thus indicating a more mature type of adjustment. It occurs mostly in free-play situations, especially when some older child tries to take away some possession, or when the younger child is hurt or afraid of being hurt by the older child. There is relatively little crying in routine situations, such as dressing, eating, or toileting (Brackett, 1933, 1934; Caille, 1933; Young, 1942). A comparison of crying in the home and in the nursery school revealed that young children cry at home mostly because of conflicts with adults, with siblings, at meals, or when they are injured. In the nursery school, the most common causes of crying were found to be attacks on the child's person, attacks on his property, frustrations by another child, and accidental injury (Landreth, 1941). See Fig. 27.

Variations in Crying. From the second month of life, the baby's cry is no longer a monotone, but varies in intensity, tonal quality, and rhythm.

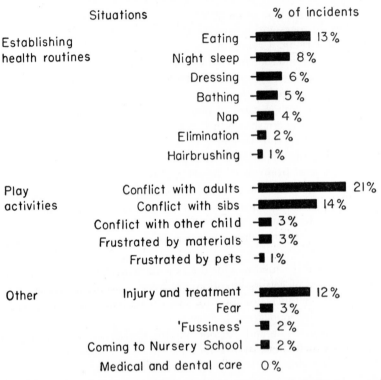

Situations		% of incidents
Establishing health routines	Eating	13%
	Night sleep	8%
	Dressing	6%
	Bathing	5%
	Nap	4%
	Elimination	2%
	Hairbrushing	1%
Play activities	Conflict with adults	21%
	Conflict with sibs	14%
	Conflict with other child	3%
	Frustrated by materials	3%
	Frustrated by pets	1%
Other	Injury and treatment	12%
	Fear	3%
	'Fussiness'	2%
	Coming to Nursery School	2%
	Medical and dental care	0%

Fig. 27. Situations causing crying in the home. (*From C. Landreth, Factors associated with crying in young children in the nursery school and the home, Child Develpm., 1941, 12, 81–97. Used by permission.*)

Pain cries are, for example, shrill, loud, and interrupted by whimpering and groaning, or short, sharp, and piercing. The cry of discomfort is low and whimpering, while that of hunger is loud and interrupted by sucking movements. Variations of crying, such as groaning, "fussing," whimpering, and sighing, appear by the end of the second month, while by the age of five months each baby makes sounds of displeasure characteristically his own. Every baby has a fairly large number of qualities of crying, and each differs greatly from every other baby in these qualities (Kelting, 1934).

Crying of colic is common during the first three months of life and is accompanied by a peculiar, high-pitched scream, alternate and forceful flexion and extension of the legs, and excessive flatus (Stewart et al., 1954). During the first five months of life, there is a rapid and consistent rise in pitch of the hunger wail, covering a range of more than an octave. This change is due to the rapid growth of the larynx at that time (Fairbanks, 1942). Cries are differentiated more by intensity than by meaning. The stress of excitement causes greater tension of the muscles, flattens the sound, and makes it more shrill. This is true especially of the cries of hunger and pain. There is, therefore, no "vocabulary" of crying. Crying is not differentiated according to changing wants, but rather by the *intensity* of wants (Lynip, 1951).

Analyses of the elements of crying have revealed that an overwhelming majority of the sounds in the cries of newborn infants are front vowels, with the *ae* sound predominating. Consonant sounds during the first ten days of life are very infrequent. Of these, the glottal sound *h* is the most frequent. *K* is heard occasionally, while *b, p,* and *m* are not heard at all (Irwin, 1941a). As babies grow older, front vowels are heard less frequently, and middle and back vowels more often. During the second quarter of the first year, more of the consonant sounds are heard, especially *h, g, m, n, b, d, k, w, l, j,* and *e* (Irwin, 1941a).

Motor Accompaniment of Crying. Crying in young babies is always accompanied by bodily action. The entire body is active, and fatigue sets in if the crying is allowed to continue over a prolonged period of time. Crying caused by fatigue is often accompanied by yawning, drooping, and rubbing the eyes, while crying caused by strange places or people is accompanied by clinging to the mother and turning away from the frightening situation (Bayley, 1932). Each baby has its own individual type of hand reaction in crying (Kelting, 1934). There is a marked difference in general body activity in crying and in noncrying. In general, crying is accompanied by vigorous limb activity, strong flexor tendencies, and the disorganizing of postures prevailing at the onset of crying. Noncrying behavior, on the other hand, is characterized by limb extension, bilateral postures, greater arm than leg activity, and the holding of set postures (Ames, 1941). These differences are illustrated in Fig. 15, page 90. As the baby grows older, less and less activity accompanies crying. By the time the child is two or three years old, crying is accompanied by no more activity than one finds with other emotional outbursts.

Reactions to Crying. How children and adults react to a baby's or child's crying will depend partly upon the age of the child and partly upon their own beliefs regarding the function of crying. Crying in young babies is a primitive reaction to situations of distress and, therefore, is an unconditioned response. Later, however, it is employed generally by a baby because his other signals are unheeded. It is a commonly accepted belief that the only means of communication a young baby has is crying, and parents, therefore, *expect* that the baby will cry and believe that one can do nothing about it. This belief, in turn, affects the baby's behavior, and he then learns that he must cry if his wants and needs are to receive any attention. He is thus *conditioned* to cry because his other modes of expression have failed to bring him what he wants. Later, it becomes a generalized response used even in mild states of want to prevent distress. The baby thus learns to cry instead of learning to use noncrying modes of communication (Rosenzweig, 1954).

Crying is often a bid for attention. (*From Child Development, a McGraw Hill Text-Film.*)

A small baby can communicate his simple wants by noncrying methods, such as smacking the lips or ejecting the tongue when hungry, squirming and trembling when cold, or sneezing when wet. If these signals are understood, the baby will then cry only in pain and genuine distress. However, as few parents understand these signals as the baby's "language," and as they believe that his only language is crying, they actually encourage him to learn to use crying as a *general* form of communication rather than as a specific form to be used only in situations of distress when no alternative has been learned (Rosenzweig, 1954).

While all infants cry in situations of distress as well as when they need attention for some wants during the first two weeks of life, before they are capable of communicating their needs through noncrying forms of communication, there is usually a difference in amount of crying babies do after the age of two weeks. Babies who continue to cry excessively have been found to be those whose mothers allowed a long time to elapse before heeding their cries, who were inconsistent about responding to the babies' cries, or who showed their own insecurity about taking care of their babies by being anxious, tense, and unable to gain satisfaction from their contacts with their babies. By the age of six weeks, babies whose needs are met promptly cry relatively little as compared with those whose needs are not met promptly or are met inconsistently. Lacking a feeling of security in their interpersonal relationships thus leads to excessive crying (Stewart et al., 1954). As Gesell and Ilg (1943) have stressed, "punctual attention to crying in the early weeks reduces the total amount of crying." In hospital nurseries where the infant's needs cannot be met as promptly as at home, because of shortages of personnel to take care of the nurseries, there are many more periods of prolonged crying during the day than are experienced when the infant is at home (Aldrich et al., 1945).

The reactions to the crying of a young child who has learned to talk are very different from the reactions to a baby. Instead of coming to his rescue, even if somewhat belatedly, parents regard the child's crying not as a request for what he wants, but as a signal that he is being "spoiled." They therefore may scold or punish him for crying. Later, the child discovers that other children look upon crying as "babyish" and scorn him for it. In a study of crying at home and in the nursery school, it was found that adults responded very differently to crying in these two situations. In the nursery school, crying was most frequently met by consoling the child, by censuring the child who caused the crying, by suggesting arbitration in property disputes, and by distracting the crying child. At home, crying was most often responded to by ignoring, reasoning, spanking, or by removing the child from the social group (Landreth, 1941). Among older children, crying is scorned to the point where the child is likely to become a social isolate. This will be discussed further in the chapter on Social Adjustments.

Effects of Crying. While crying in cases of distress is normal, too much crying, especially in cases when it is unnecessary, has many harmful effects, not only on the baby or young child, but also on the home climate. Excessive crying results in variability in gastrointestinal functions, regurgitation, night waking, and general nervous tension (Stewart et al., 1954). It affects the baby's total growth pattern; it is harmful to healthful social adjustments; it leads to feelings of insecurity when the baby feels his needs are not understood; and it affects the baby's relationships with his parents unfavorably. A quieter atmosphere in the nursery is pleasanter for all members of the family, and this affects their attitudes toward the baby (Rosenzweig, 1954).

2. Explosive Sounds and Babbling

In addition to cries, many simple sounds are heard during the first months of life. In the newborn infant, 50 per cent of all sounds uttered are the aspirate *h,* associated with the infant's gasping for breath (Irwin, 1947, 1947a; McCarthy, 1952, 1954). Later, there are grunts of pain or disgust, squeals of delight, yawns, sneezes, sighs, belching, coughing, guttural barking sounds, growls, and simulated animal cries, as the whine of a young pig or the bleat of a goat. By the fourth month, audible cries are heard, but there are no nasal sounds during the first four months of life (Blanton, 1917; Shirley, 1933; Lynip, 1951; McCarthy, 1952, 1954; Havighurst, 1953; Jersild, 1954).

Analyses of these early sounds have revealed that vowels predominate in the first year of life. The first vowels to be uttered are formed by the front of the oral cavity, and then by the back part of the oral cavity. The development of consonants is in the opposite direction, from back to front of the oral cavity. Only after the front teeth have cut through the gums can front consonants be produced by using the tip of the tongue, the lips, and the teeth (Chen and Irwin, 1946; Irwin and Chen, 1946; Irwin, 1947, 1947a, 1948; Lewis, 1951; McCarthy, 1952, 1954). By the middle of the first year of life, babies produce most of the vowel elements and about half of the consonants. This is in contrast to the first month of life when only about half of the vowels are produced and very few consonants (Irwin and Chen, 1943; McCarthy, 1953). In summary, McCarthy (1952) has pointed out, "It appears, then, that in the field of linguistic development there is some evidence that gross motor development precedes finer motor coordination in the speech musculature. . . . Vowel sounds may, therefore, be thought of as the raw material of language, somewhat analogous to the mass activity of the infant in the motor realm, and consonants may be considered to involve the specific movements which become individuated in order to produce true speech."

These early sounds are explosive in character and are caused by chance movements of the vocal mechanism. What sounds are uttered depend largely on the shape of the oral cavity which modifies the stream of air expelled from the lungs and passing over the vocal cords (McCarthy, 1952). They are unlearned and are universally found in all nationalities and races. They are found even among the deaf. There is no deliberate attempt on the baby's part to produce these sounds. They are called forth as responses to physical needs and as accompaniments of general bodily activity (Merry and Merry, 1950). Some of these sounds are accompaniments of states of comfort, while others accompany states of discomfort (Lewis, 1951). Because they have no significance for the baby and are not used as a form of communication, they may be regarded as a playful activity which gives enjoyment to the baby. This type of vocalization is usually referred to as "cooing."

Many of these early sounds will disappear as the baby's vocal mechanism develops and he is capable of making other sounds. Some will be retained and develop later into babbling, and still later, into words (Jersild, 1954). As Lynip (1951) has emphasized, "The infant's vocalizations have no more relation to an adult's words than his leg kickings have to a grown-up's genuflections. It therefore follows that the beginnings and changes of vocalization must be considered as a gradually unfolding process from the simple to the complex shrouded in the mysterious veils that conceal the miracle of growth of all organisms—not to be crudely analyzed in measurements applicable only to a restricted variety of adult sound productions."

Babbling. Gradually, the number of sounds the baby can produce not only increases, but there is an increasing definiteness of utterance of various sounds. At first, vowels are combined with consonants, as "da," "ma," "ugh," or "na." Later, with practice, vocal control makes it possible to repeat these sounds by stringing them together, as "ma-ma-ma-ma" or "ugh-ugh-ugh." This is real "babbling," or "lalling" (Shirley, 1933; Merry and Merry, 1950; Lynip, 1951; Garrison, 1952; Jersild, 1954; McCarthy, 1954). Owing to his ability to control the flow of air over the vocal cords, the baby can pronounce sounds at will. Babbling is, therefore, a form of vocal gymnastics, voluntarily produced, but with no real meaning or association value for the baby.

The age of babbling is between the third and twelfth months, with a peak around the eighth month. How soon the baby will begin to babble and when he will abandon babbling in favor of more mature communication in the form of speech will depend largely upon the development of his vocal mechanism and his incentive to use his vocal mechanism for speaking instead of babbling. Some babies babble into the second year, at which time other babies have abandoned babbling in favor of speech (Shirley, 1933; Gesell and Thompson, 1934; Merry and Merry, 1950; Lewis, 1951; Lynip, 1951; Garrison, 1952; McCarthy, 1954).

Babbling is a form of "play speech" in that sounds are "uttered for the mere delight of uttering them" (McCarthy, 1954). It occurs mostly in periods of contentment, more frequently when the baby is alone than when he is with others who can amuse him (Lewis, 1951). That the baby derives enjoyment from listening to his own voice may be seen by the fact that he often smiles and laughs at the sounds he is making and, further, by the fact that deaf babies babble less than normal babies. They begin to babble at the usual age, but soon lose interest when they cannot hear their voices (Latif, 1934; McCarthy, 1954).

At no time is babbling linked with specific objects, people, or situations. Therefore it is not real speech. It is engaged in only so long as the baby enjoys it or until an opportunity arises for another form of play of a more enjoyable type to the baby. It is seldom related to adult sounds, though the sounds made with the mouth open more closely resemble adult sounds than those made with the mouth partially closed (Lynip, 1951). However, with practice, the baby increases the number and variety of sound combinations, and he acquires variations in pitch and inflection so that his babbling takes on a conversational tone. In a social situation, he may try to join in the conversation by babbling, and parents, who become accustomed to the babbling, may fail to distinguish it from real speech (Merry and Merry, 1950). Thus, while babbling at first serves no immediate purpose other than the pleasure it gives the baby, if continued, it soon proves to be a splendid opportunity to learn to control the different muscles connected with the vocal mechanism.

3. GESTURES

The third preliminary to speaking consists of the use of gestures. At first, gestures often accompany unintelligible vocalizations, suggesting that the baby is trying to make others understand him (Jersild, 1954; McCarthy, 1954). This has been called "whole-body language" (Latif, 1934, 1934a). Gradually, this is abbreviated as the baby discovers that he can make himself understood by gestures alone, and he therefore substitutes gestures for speech. If, however, his gestures are not understood, or if they do not bring forth the desired results, he will then use crying as a means of communicating his needs or wants (Rosenzweig, 1954). Thus gestures like crying are substitutes for speech, not a form of play, as is true of babbling.

Commonly observed gestures during early babyhood are pushing the nipple from the mouth with the tongue, turning the head away from the nipple, or allowing food to run out of the mouth, which shows that the baby is not hungry; smiling and holding out the arms, which indicate that the baby wants to be picked up; squirming, wriggling, and crying during dressing and bathing, which show that the baby resents the restrictions to his activities; pouting when displeased; and reaching movements, which indicate efforts to accept, reject, or avert (Merry and Merry, 1950; Jersild, 1954). Most gestures made by babies are easy to understand if parents will take the time and make the effort to do so (Rosenzweig, 1954).

The difference in the baby's use of gestures and that of the adult is primarily due to difference in purpose. The baby uses gestures as a *substitute* for speech, to enable him to express wants, feelings, and emotions for which he has no other means of expression (Jersild, 1954). In the case of the adult, on the other hand, gestures are used as a *supplement* to speech, to emphasize the meaning of words and to make them more forceful and effective. As the baby learns to speak, he has less and less need for gestures. Intelligent children who are encouraged by their parents in the use of speech have little need for gestures (Valentine, 1942). In communities where the frequent use of gestures is regarded as bad form, the young child gradually abandons the use of gestures and substitutes words for them. In our culture, members of the lower socioeconomic groups often use gestures more than words. In the upper classes, gestures are used much less frequently (Bossard, 1954).

LEARNING TO SPEAK

Speech is a skill. Like all skills, it must be learned. Because it involves so many complicated activities, speech is a skill that develops more slowly than the motor skills described in the preceding chapter. As is true of all skills, speech development is built upon the foundations established by the maturation of the various parts of the speech mechanism. There is no single speech organ ready for use at birth or even shortly afterward. Speech is produced by the coordinated activity of the lip, tongue, and throat muscles as well as by the larynx and tongue. It takes time for these to mature adequately for the complicated patterns of speech, and it takes time and practice on the part of the young child to perfect the coordinated actions of these organs.

At birth, the oral cavity is small with a short anterior to posterior measurement. The palate is flat and lacks the arch characteristically found in older persons. The infant's tongue is proportionally too large, filling much of the oral cavity and even protruding much of the time. As the baby grows older, changes in size and shape of the different parts of the vocal mechanism occur. Throughout the early months of life, the infant lies down most of the time. The uvula and soft palate are pulled downward by the force of gravity, with the result that the nasal passage, which is very small, is virtually blocked off, making the pronunciation of nasal sounds impossible. Many of the consonant sounds are produced through the coordination of the lips and teeth. As the baby has no teeth until the fourth to sixth month, the production of these sounds must wait upon the development of his front teeth (McCarthy, 1952). At birth, the nerves and muscles of the vocal apparatus are fairly well developed (Havighurst, 1953). Their use, however, must wait upon the development of the other parts of the vocal mechanism.

Many babies are biologically ready to learn to talk before they do so. There is evidence that there is a period of "speech readiness" when speech is more easily acquired by the young child than at other times. This period has been found to occur between the ages of twelve and eighteen months in most babies. If the baby does not make use of this period of readiness, he is likely to become emotionally disturbed. This results when the child is unable to express his feelings because of delayed or inadequate speech (Havighurst, 1953). Delayed speech, except in cases of marked mental deficiency, generally results from lack of opportunity to learn or from lack of motivation to learn, even when the opportunity is present. Only rarely is delay traceable to delay in the development of the speech mechanism.

Imitation. The ability to reproduce sounds heard is too complicated for a young baby. During the first six months of life, babies make many meaningless sounds in their cooing and babbling. In the presence of other people, the baby will sometimes imitate them by "talking back," but he does not imitate the sounds they are making. He is merely imitating *soundmaking in general* (Valentine, 1942). This is called the "echo-reaction stage" of imitation (Stengel, 1947; McCarthy, 1953). Even before he can imitate specific sounds, the baby acquires the ability to imitate the intonations and inflections of the voices of others (Shirley, 1933). By the age of six months, there will be some elemental imitation of sounds, such as "re-re-re," and of simple syllables, as "mama" and "dada," by eleven months (Bühler, 1930).

"Readiness to imitate" occurs toward the end of the first year of life. At that time, the baby attempts to imitate the specific sounds he has heard, many of which had not previously appeared in his babbling (Valentine, 1942). From the many babbling sounds he has used, people around him select certain ones to repeat, and these he eventually learns to associate with certain objects, people, and situations (Havighurst, 1953). Vowel sounds are imitated first. However, babies make no real success in imitation of either vowel or consonant sounds until they are nearly a year old. Their imitations are only approximations of the sounds they have heard (Lynip, 1951). Some of the intelligence tests and developmental norms for babies place imitation of simple words tests at the ten-, eleven-, and twelve-month levels (Gesell, 1928; Bayley, 1940; Cattell, 1940).

Beginning with the fortieth week of life, the baby tries to imitate the words his mother uses (Lynip, 1951). His attempts to imitate standard words increases with age, and there is also an increase in the number of words attempted. However, increase in correctness of imitation proceeds slowly (McCurry and Irwin, 1953). Specific training in pronunciation leads to better results than when pronunciation is left to chance (Strayer, 1930). Since the child imitates the speech of those about him, whether it be good or bad, it is essential that he have a good model to copy. The child imitates defective speech, such as poor pronunciation, and grammatical errors, as readily as he imitates correct speech. Even stuttering is sometimes traceable to imitation.

Association of Meanings. Association of meaning with different sounds follows the technique of the conditioned reflex. Certain sounds are selected from those the baby uses by the people around him and are repeated in certain situations until he learns to associate them with those situations (Havighurst, 1953). If, for example, a word is said by another when an object is given to the baby, the baby learns, after several repetitions, that that particular combination of sounds stands for the object presented. The more often he sees an object when the name of that object is given, the more quickly he will emerge from the "parrot" stage in which he merely imitates words he has heard and progress into a phase of speech development that may justifiably be called "true speech." Figure 28 shows the way a child learns to associate meanings with words.

There are two ways in which a child associates meanings with words. The first is the *direct,* or explicit, way, in which the adult names a thing or defines a word for the child; the second is the *indirect,* or implicit, way when, through experience with concrete and/or verbal context, the child associates meanings (Werner and Kaplan, 1950). What meaning is associated with different words depends largely upon the environment in which the child lives, especially the environment of the home (Brownfield, 1953). As is true of learning to pronounce words by imitation, training in association of meaning with words results in the child's learning more words and with

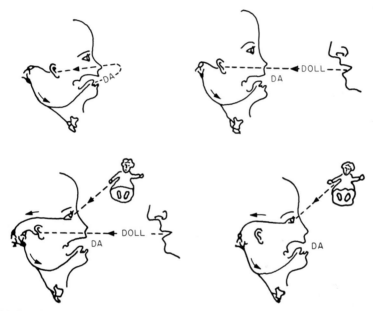

Fig. 28. Development of language habits in the young child. (*From F. H. Allport, Social psychology, Houghton, Mifflin, 1924. Used by permission.*)

more correct meanings than when the matter is left to chance (Strayer, 1930). The ability to associate meaning with words develops slightly later than the ability to imitate sounds heard. By the time a baby is a year old, he first indicates that he recognizes the sounds that he has heard an adult use in association with a specific object (Lynip, 1951).

All meanings are first learned in connection with a specific object, person, or situation. Young children do not generalize. Instead, they emphasize the particular or isolated aspect of the word, not the categorical, or "class," feature of the word. For example, when a young child learns to call his father "Daddy," he is likely to call all men he comes in contact with "Daddy" also. Only gradually does he learn to generalize and to apply general meanings to general categories and specific words to specific objects or situations. Older children, by contrast, are able to stress the abstract, or "class," features of certain words (Baldridge, 1949; Feifel and Lorge, 1950; Merry and Merry, 1950).

Motivation. The young child learns to speak according to his needs. If he can get what he wants without bothering to ask for it, he does not put forth the effort needed to learn so complicated and difficult a task as speaking. When substitutes for speech, such as crying or gestures, serve his purpose adequately, and when he discovers that he can get what he wants by using them, his incentive to learn to speak is weakened. This leads to delayed speech in babyhood and to a limited vocabulary in the childhood or adolescent years. When "baby talk" is understood by parents, the young child is likely to continue to talk in this manner until he starts to play with other children, who, he discovers, do not understand him as his parents do. This supplies him with the motivation to speak in an understandable manner. Studies of multiple births have revealed that twins and triplets are generally delayed in speech development because they associate mainly with one another and learn to understand their own jargons, thus eliminating the motivation to speak so they can be understood by others (McCarthy, 1954).

The child learns to use the words he needs. In the section of the chapter relating to the building up of a vocabulary, it will become apparent that the child not only learns first the words for which he has the greatest need, but also that he uses substitutes, such as slang terms, when he wishes to express an idea but lacks adequate words to convey his meaning. The prime "needs" of the young child which act as incentives to his learning to talk are (1) the desire to secure information regarding his environment, and later about himself or his friends, the need for which is readily apparent by the age of 2½ to three years; (2) to give commands or express wants, like "want to go 'bye-bye'" or "give baby ball"; (3) to bring the child into social relationships with others; and (4) to express his thoughts and ideas.

Pattern of Development. Speech development follows a pattern much the same for all children. While it is true that some children learn to talk more quickly than others, this acceleration is an accompaniment of rapid development along other lines, notably muscle coordination. What deviations from a characteristic pattern exist are, for the most part, trivial and the product of different environmental conditions than those commonly found (Lynip, 1951). Regardless of the language learned, all children learn in much the same manner the world over. The rates of learning vary with the native endowment of the children, the samplings observed, and the environmental stimulation they receive (McCarthy, 1954). As Goldstein (1948) has emphasized, "Whatever language we consider, we observe, in the acquisition of sounds, the same sequence in time." The age of learning to talk is approximately the same in all cultures, though it may be slightly later in primitive than in civilized cultures. In our culture, children from the lower classes learn slightly later than those from the higher classes, but according to the same pattern (Havighurst, 1953).

The pattern of learning to speak, McCarthy (1952, 1954) has found, closely parallels the pattern of development of postural control. Cooing and vocalizing in response to social stimulation come just about the time the baby is able to hold his head erect, between the second and third month. Babbling begins between the sixth and seventh months, just after the baby has mastered the skill of sitting alone. The baby says his first words at the end of the first year, at approximately the time when he is standing alone. Between the fifteenth and eighteenth months, when the baby is walking alone, his breathing is more thoracic and he becomes increasingly more independent. His independence at this time is "also revealed in the realm of language, for it is at this same period that he begins to enlarge his vocabulary and to combine two and three words into rudimentary sentences" (McCarthy, 1952).

The pattern of speech development is marked by spurts and resting periods, or *plateaus*. As is true of adults, a baby or young child is incapable of giving conscious attention to two things simultaneously. Whenever a new motor act is being established, whether it be reaching and grasping, sitting alone, standing, or walking, there will be a temporary plateau in the pattern of speech development (Shirley, 1933). Between the ages of nine and eighteen months, when the baby is mastering the skill of walking, the urge to walk seems to be more powerful than the urge to talk. After walking becomes habitual, the baby's attention is again directed toward talking, and a spurt in learning to talk follows.

MAJOR TASKS IN SPEECH DEVELOPMENT

The child, in learning to speak, has four major tasks that must be mastered. These are interrelated, and successful achievement in one is essential to successful mastery of the others. The four tasks, each of which will be discussed in detail, are (1) *comprehension of the speech of others*, (2) *building a vocabulary*, (3) *combining words into sentences*, and (4) *pronunciation*.

1. COMPREHENSION

Comprehension of the meaning of the speech of others precedes the use of words, and at every age, the passive, or "comprehension," vocabulary is larger than the active, or "speech," vocabulary (Garrison, 1952; McCarthy, 1954). This is much the same as occurs when an adult learns a foreign language. The adult understands words spoken by others and can follow a conversation in that language before he can talk intelligibly to others or take part in a general conversation. The baby's understanding of the behavior of others does not begin with his understanding of words but with his understanding of the actions and gestures of others (Latif, 1934). This is shown by the fact that a baby is quieted by being talked to, he distinguishes between friendly and angry talking, and he is, in general, responsive to affective intonations of the voice even before he gives evidence of understanding gestures or of showing differential responses to words (Lewis, 1951).

In the development of comprehension, the baby responds affectively to both the intonational pattern of what he hears and to the situation in which he hears it. Later, when he hears the word alone, he is able to respond to it without the situation in which its meaning was learned (Lewis, 1951). A baby can understand his mother through "emotional contagion" because he understands nonverbal signs, such as her smile or the tone of her voice (Brownfield, 1953). According to Bossard (1954), there are three distinct forms of communication between the mother and her baby: her speech, her facial expressions, and her actions.

It is often difficult to tell how much of a little child's comprehension is due to an understanding of the words themselves and how much to facial expressions and gestures. Very young children learn to comprehend the meaning of commands, such as "No-no," "Stop," "Come here," or "Lie down," partly because of an association with the act, as lifting the hand when the words "No-no" are spoken, and partly through an interpretation of the tone of voice used by the individual who gives the commands. Up to the age of eighteen months, words must be reinforced with gestures if the speaker wants to be sure that the child will comprehend what he hears. Even simple directions, such as "Put the cup on the table," need to be supplemented by a gesture of pointing to the table and to the cup.

From standard tests of intelligence and from normative summaries, we know approximately what level of comprehension can be expected of a child of a given age. At sixteen weeks, a baby will turn his head to the sound of a human voice and will show that he recognizes his mother by smiling. Between six and eight months, he adjusts to words, and at twelve months, to simple commands. Before he enters school, he has a large enough passive vocabulary so that he can understand instructions given even by unfamiliar people, can understand the meaning of stories read to him, and can distinguish the similarities and differences in simple words. Listening to the radio and watching television are proving to be assets to the development of young children's comprehension vocabularies (Holmes, 1932; Gesell and Thompson, 1934; Terman and Merrill, 1937; Cattell, 1940; Garrison, 1952; McCarthy, 1954; Breckenridge and Vincent, 1955).

2. BUILDING A VOCABULARY

In the development of vocabulary, two distinct forms may be recognized: (1) The *general vocabulary,* consisting of words with a general meaning that can be used in a variety of different situations. Such words as "man," "beautiful," and "go" belong to this class. (2) The *special vocabulary*, consisting of words with specific meanings, which can be used only for certain situations. Because words of the general vocabulary are more useful than those with specialized meanings, they are learned first. At every age, the general vocabulary is larger than the special vocabularies.

1. General Vocabulary. In the development of a general vocabulary, the young child does not learn all parts of speech simultaneously. Rather, he learns first the words that will be most useful to him and which are easiest to learn, like the names of objects or persons. He learns last the parts of speech which are least useful and most difficult to use, the pronouns, for instance, because he can readily substitute nouns or gestures for them.

The first words used by the child are *nouns*, generally consisting of monosyllables, taken from favorite sounds the child has babbled. Later, these are doubled or trebled. These words are used to designate persons or objects in the child's environment, such as "mamma," "dada," "choo-choo," or "babe." After the child has learned enough nouns to apply names to the people and objects in his environment, he begins to learn *verbs*, especially those which designate action, "give," "take," "hold," and so on. *Adjectives* and *adverbs* appear in a baby's vocabulary from the age of 1½ years, while *prepositions* and *pronouns* appear last. The adjectives most commonly used at first are "good," "bad," "nice," "naughty," "hot," and "cold," which are applied principally to people, food, and toys. The earliest adverbs to appear in the child's vocabulary are generally "here" and "where." The difficulty the young child experiences in trying to discover when to use "me," "my," "mine," or "I" to refer to himself causes no small amount of confusion and thus results in his avoiding their use as long as possible.

Analyses of the different parts of speech used in early speech have revealed that, up to eighteen months, nouns predominate. By the time the child is two years old, there are proportionally fewer nouns in his speech and more verbs, articles, conjunctions, prepositions, and pronouns, especially "I" and "me." Later, "we," "us," and "you" are used proportionally more. Descriptive adjectives are used with increasing frequency between the ages of 2½ and 4½ years. Among nursery-school children, nouns and interjections decrease in usage with age, while articles, verbs, conjunctions, prepositions, adverbs, and pronouns increase in varying degrees. The greatest change in proportions of the different parts of speech used by the young child comes before he is three years old. By the time the child is using complete sentences with a fair degree of grammatical accuracy, the percentages of the various parts of speech he uses are determined by the conventions of the language he speaks (Carroll, 1939; Young, 1941, 1942, 1942a; Garrison, 1952; McCarthy, 1954).

Size of Vocabulary. How many words will appear in the child's vocabulary at different ages depends to a large extent upon the intelligence of the child, what chance he has had to learn new words, and whether there has been an incentive to learn words. Not only does the child learn new words, but he also increases his vocabulary by learning new meanings for old words (Werner and Kaplan, 1950, 1950a). For example, the word "orange" may be known only as a type of fruit at first. Later, the child discovers that this word also refers to a color, and still later, that it is a complex color, made up of a combination of red and yellow. In estimating the increase in vocabulary with age, one must take into consideration not only the number of different words the child knows, but also the number of different meanings he knows for different words (Thevaos, 1951; Jersild, 1954).

Vocabulary growth starts slowly during the first two years of life, increases more rapidly in the preschool years, and then increases at an accelerated pace after the child enters school. This rapid increase after entering school comes partly from the direct teaching of words and their usages by teachers, partly from interesting associations with objects and experiences, and partly from the child's reading for pleasure, listening to the radio, and watching television. Estimates of size of vocabulary at different ages have revealed that the size of the child's vocabulary is larger than usually estimated. The average first-grader knows between 20,000 and 24,000 words, or 5 to 6 per cent of the words in a standard dictionary. By the sixth grade, he knows approximately 50,000 words, and when he enters high school, about 80,000 words, or 22 per cent of the words in a standard dictionary (Carroll, 1938; Seashore and Eckerson, 1940; Smith, 1940, 1941; Rinsland, 1945; Schulman and Havighurst, 1947; Gewirtz, 1948, 1948a; Baldridge, 1949; Seegers and Seashore, 1949; Strickland, 1951; Bryan, 1953; Havighurst, 1953; Jersild, 1954; McCarthy, 1954).

There are, of course, marked individual differences in size of vocabulary at every age. These differences are not due alone to reported differences resulting from studies made of different-sized groups and different techniques employed in these studies, but they are real differences. These differences appear as early as eighteen months of age and become increasingly greater as children grow older (Shirley, 1931a; Gesell et al., 1940; Breckenridge and Vincent, 1955). While differences in intelligence are partially responsible for differences in size of vocabulary at every age, environmental influences, opportunities to learn, and motivation to learn are also factors that play roles of major importance.

Size of vocabulary influences not only the child's speech but also his writing. The number and variety of words utilized in his writing has been found to be directly related to the size of the child's oral vocabulary. Success in writing thus depends upon the child's achievement in oral language (Fea, 1953). The serious significance of vocabulary size has been emphasized thus by Garrison (1952): "The number of words a child knows determines in large measure his school progress, and failure to progress normally has far-reaching significance. Words are the means by which the child learns about his world. If his knowledge of words is grossly inadequate, the interpretation of his environment will be correspondingly so. In an age of radio, television, films, rapid transportation, and world relationships, the child needs to know many words and to be able to use them. Failure tends to result in impaired social adjustment" (pp. 228–229).

2. Special Vocabularies. Early in childhood, when attention is concentrated on the development of a usable vocabulary, the child has little time to build up special vocabularies, which, on the whole, are more superfluous than essential. From the age of three years, however, special vocabularies are built up at the same time that words of general usage are being learned.

The most important of the special vocabularies, and the ages at which they are developed, are as follows:

a. The "Trick" Vocabulary. This consists of words pronounced correctly by the child in response to the request of another. The little child is asked to say long and complicated words, like "Mississippi" and "esophagus," for the delight of the adults encouraging him. As the child rarely knows the meaning of the words he speaks, their use is therefore merely a form of "showing-off." The age at which the "trick" vocabulary is most used is between one and two years.

b. The "Etiquette" Vocabulary. This type of special vocabulary consists of such words as "please," "thank you," or "I'm sorry." The child should learn to use these words as soon as he can speak coherently. How large this vocabulary will be is entirely dependent upon the training the child has received.

c. Color Vocabulary. Because of the young child's interest in color, names of different colors are learned at an early age. Most children know the names of the primary colors by the time they are four years old (Cook, 1931). How soon they will learn other color names will depend partly upon their interest in colors and partly upon their opportunities to learn color names.

d. Number Vocabulary. While many young children of 2½ or 3 years of age can count up to 10 or more, it is questionable whether they understand the meaning of the words they use. Their number vocabularies therefore fall into the category of "parrot speech." However, through play or direct teaching, the child gradually learns the meaning of many numbers. In the 1937 Revision of the Stanford-Binet Test, the child is expected to be able to count three objects, blocks, beads, or pennies, at the age of five years, and at the age of six years, know the meaning of the words "three," "nine," "five," "ten," and "seven" well enough to count out the number of blocks requested from the twelve that are placed before him.

e. The Time Vocabulary. Because of the diversity of activities characteristic of the different parts of the day, the child comes to know the meaning of words related to them. By the age of six or seven years, the child should know the meaning of such simple words as "morning," "afternoon," "night," "summer," and "winter." When he enters school, he soon learns the names of the different days of the week and months of the year.

f. The Money Vocabulary. While to the very young child, all coins are "money" or "pennies," to the child of four or five years, the different coins begin to have specific names, according to their size and color. How large the child's money vocabulary is depends upon the child's environment. Children of poorer environments have, as a rule, larger money vocabularies than children from the better neighborhoods because they are often entrusted with money when sent on errands by their parents. Before childhood is over, the child should know the names of all forms of currency in common use in his country and may even know the names of some foreign coins.

g. The Slang Vocabulary. "Slang" is a form of unauthorized speech. This means that slang words are not to be found in a dictionary, or their use is not sanctioned by authorities on correct speech. Should these words prove to be offensive to those who hear them, they are generally referred to as "swearing." The dividing line between "slang" and "swearing" thus depends primarily upon the personal reaction to the words heard.

During early childhood, the use of slang or swear vocabularies is purely imitative and without any real significance so far as the user is concerned. The child uses words of this sort to identify himself with the older children or to show off by shocking the adults of his environment. In the poorer neighborhoods, the slang vocabularies of young children are, on the whole, larger than those of children of better neighborhoods, where, as a rule, children hear fewer words of this type. Likewise, sex differences are negligible.

From the age of seven or eight years, the use of slang is no longer imitative or "show-off" in its purpose but rather serves as a means of expressing feelings and emotions for which the child has no adequate form of vocal expression. While the child may invent some of the swear or slang words he uses, this vocabulary is, for the most part, an imitation of the words used by high-school students. He thus not only has the satisfaction of a readily usable vocabulary for emotional expression, but he also has the added satisfaction of self-importance which comes from identifying himself with high-school or college students. Girls, as a rule, use less slang and less objectionable slang than do boys, who favor words that more closely resemble swearing (Melville, 1912; Kasser, 1945). Both boys and girls of school age use slang freely, and the words they use are the ones in vogue at the time.

Children from four to eight years of age characteristically "go tough." They use many bombastic phrases, "dirty words" referring to sex and elimination, and many tabooed words, especially those relating to religion. They have not invented these words but have heard them from older children or adults. Objectionable as they may be to adults, they serve to inflate the child's developing ego, to create the impression that he is a good sport and not tied to parental apron strings, and to identify him with the group with which he wishes to be associated. Profanity is often used by little boys to compensate for their feelings of inferiority and inadequacy. It makes them seem big and important. It thus adds to their feelings of masculinity and superiority over the younger boys and over the girls whom they now regard as the "weaker sex" (Merry and Merry, 1950; Breckenridge and Vincent, 1955).

h. Secret Language. A very common accompaniment of the preadolescent gang behavior is the development of a secret language in the form of "pig Latin," written symbols, or signs made with the fingers. The purpose of such language is to enable the child to communicate with the other members of the gang without having the gang secrets made known to those outside the gang. The beginning of the secret-language age comes around the eighth year and extends to approximately the fifteenth year, with a peak between the tenth and thirteenth years. While both boys and girls use secret language in its different forms, it is, however, more popular among girls than among boys. Girls delight in spending hours trying to develop words, signs, or symbols that cannot be understood by the uninitiated. Figure 29 illustrates three forms of secret language.

The main purpose of secret language is to outwit others. Children resent the watchful eyes of their elders and the tendency of these elders to "pry" into their private affairs. In school and at home, they want to communicate with their friends without having teachers or parents know what they are saying. Then, too, secret codes are means of welding together the "gangs" of childhood and keeping outsiders from discovering the gang's secrets. Most children's gangs, as will be pointed out later, have their own forms of secret language. From the child's point of view, knowing a code and being able to communicate with others by this medium of expression is a source of satisfaction, and it adds greatly to his feelings of security and belonging. Furthermore, secret language encourages mental alertness and ingenuity on the child's part. To outwit others, he must be more ingenious and more alert than would be necessary if he used more conventional forms of communication (Brownstone, 1940; Bender, 1944; Merry and Merry, 1950; Breckenridge and Vincent, 1955).

3. Forming Sentences

"Single-word" Sentences. Combining words to form sentences generally begins before the child's second birthday. In the earliest sentences, one word alone is used, a noun or verb that, when combined with a gesture, expresses a complete thought. For example, "give," when accompanied by pointing to a toy, means "give me the toy." The word "ball," when accompanied by the holding out of the arms in the direction of the ball, means the same

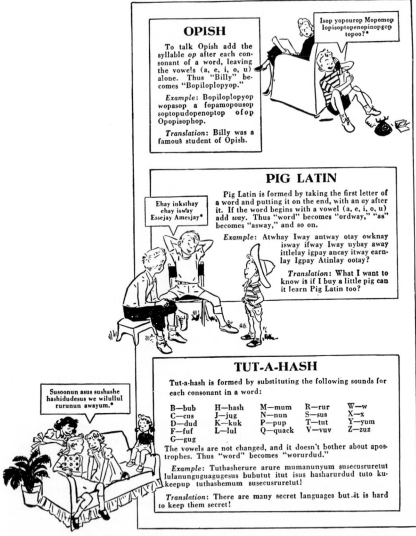

OPISH

To talk Opish add the syllable *op* after each consonant of a word, leaving the vowels (a, e, i, o, u) alone. Thus "Billy" becomes "Bopiloplopyop."

Example: Bopiloplopyop wopasop a fopamopousop soptopudopenoptop ofop Opopisophop.

Translation: Billy was a famous student of Opish.

Isop yopourop Mopomop lopisoptopenopinopgop topoo?*

PIG LATIN

Ehay inksthay chay isway Essejay Amesjay*

Pig Latin is formed by taking the first letter of a word and putting it on the end, with an *ay* after it. If the word begins with a vowel (a, e, i, o, u) add *way*. Thus "word" becomes "ordway," "as" becomes "asway," and so on.

Example: Atwhay Iway antway otay owknay isway ifway Iway uybay away ittlelay igpay ancay itway earn-lay Igpay Atinlay ootay?

Translation: What I want to know is if I buy a little pig can it learn Pig Latin too?

TUT-A-HASH

Susoonun asus sushashe hashidudesus we wilullul rurunun awayum.*

Tut-a-hash is formed by substituting the following sounds for each consonant in a word:

B—bub	H—hash	M—mum	R—rur	W—w
C—cus	J—jug	N—nun	S—sus	X—x
D—dud	K—kuk	P—pup	T—tut	Y—yum
F—fuf	L—lul	Q—quack	V—vuv	Z—zuz
G—gug				

The vowels are not changed, and it doesn't bother about apostrophes. Thus "word" becomes "worurdud."

Example: Tuthasherure arure mumanunyum susecusruretut lulanunguguagugesus bububut itut isus hasharurdud tuto kukeepup tuthashemum susecusruretut!

Translation: There are many secret languages but it is hard to keep them secret!

Fig. 29. Secret language. (*From C. Brownstone, Why children's secret language? Parents' Magazine, May, 1940. Illustrations by Dorothea Warren. Used by permission.*)

thing. This "single-word" type of sentence is used first from approximately twelve to eighteen months of age, after which the child begins to put two or more words together and supplements these with gestures and vocal inflections.

By the time the child is two years old, he combines words into short sentences, most of which are incomplete, but which nevertheless express, with the aid of gestures, a complete thought. These sentences contain one or more nouns, a verb, and occasionally adjectives and adverbs. The less essential words, such as prepositions, pronouns, and conjunctions, are omitted. Typical sentences of this type are "Hold doll." "Go bed." "Go bye-bye." "Want drink." By the time the child is four years old, his sentences are nearly complete, and by a year later, they are complete in that all parts of speech are used. The six-year-old uses nearly every form of sentence, a noteworthy achievement when one considers the difficulties involved in combining words into sentences (Shirley, 1931a; Davis, 1937a; Anderson, 1939; Gesell et al., 1940; Young, 1941, 1942; Maddock, 1947; Merry and Merry, 1950; Garrison, 1952; Havighurst, 1953; Jersild, 1954; McCarthy, 1954; Breckenridge and Vincent, 1955).

The early sentences used by a child are simple in structure. Up to the age of four or five years, compound and complex sentences with their dependent or coordinate clauses are rarely used. After that, however, they are used with greater frequency with each successive year (Fisher, 1934; Gesell et al., 1940; Garrison, 1952; Jersild, 1954; McCarthy, 1954; Breckenridge and Vincent, 1955). Sentence length increases up to the age of 9½ years, after which there is a tendency for the length to remain static or decrease slightly. Young children are apt to increase the length by combining two or more simple sentences with the conjunction "and." Older children, by contrast, increase the length by adding to the complexity of the sentence through the use of clauses.

At every age, there are marked individual differences in both the length and the pattern of the sentence. Bright children and those from the higher socioeconomic groups usually use longer and more complex sentences at every age than do those who are not so bright or who come from poorer class homes. Girls, likewise, are superior to boys in their sentence usage at every age (Davis, 1937a; Garrison, 1952; McCarthy, 1954). There are variations in sentence length and structure among white and Negro children, but this is likely to come more from socioeconomic status differences than from racial differences per se (Anastasi and D'Angelo, 1952). Perhaps the greatest variations at different ages come from differences in the situation in which the child is when he speaks. When playing with their contemporaries, children are likely to converse more in phrases than in complete sentences (Maddock, 1947). When with adults, on the other hand, they converse in longer sentences. In a classroom situation where there are both children and a teacher, the child's sentences are longer even than when conversing with an adult alone (Fisher, 1934; Smith, 1935, 1939; Young, 1941; Hahn, 1948; McCarthy, 1954).

Grammatical Errors. Grammatical errors are common up to the age of three years. This is due to the difficulties the young child has in putting words together. His major problems are in the use of pronouns and verb tenses. At the age of two years, few children use pronouns correctly, while at the age of three years, about 75 per cent do. The confusion of single and plural tenses is likewise great. Typical examples of errors made by young children are, in *verbs*, use of "can" and "may," "lay" and "lie"; in *nouns*, "mans" instead of "men" and "tooths" instead of "teeth"; in *articles*, use of "a" and "an"; in *agreement of subject and verb*, "it don't"; and in *confused parts of speech*, "I am going to the low (bottom of page)" and "Give me the rub (eraser)" (Smith, 1933).

From the age of three years, the child tightens his hold on grammar but at a slower rate than he expands his vocabulary (Havighurst, 1953). Each year there is improvement in the child's grammatical structures, though children still make grammatical mistakes throughout the elementary school years and into high school and college (Davis, 1937a, 1939; Jersild, 1954; Mc-Carthy, 1954; Breckenridge and Vincent, 1955). Errors occur likewise in their written compositions, in approximately the same forms and proportions as occur in their speech (Symonds and Daringer, 1930). Children from the lower socioeconomic groups, where they hear patterns of incorrect speech more than do children from the more privileged homes, generally make more grammatical errors at every age than do those from the more privileged homes (Davis, 1937, 1939).

In an attempt to explain the continued use of grammatical mistakes in spite of the efforts made in school to correct these mistakes, Havighurst (1953) has given the following reasons. According to him, the child shows remarkable reasoning ability, but the English language has "little reason to its structure." Even though the child reasons, he still makes mistakes. For example, to show an act is past, he is told to add "ed" to the verb. He then says, "I rided the street car." He is corrected and told he should say, "I rode the street car." Reasoning on this basis, he later says, "I gode to the store," but is told this is incorrect and he should say, "I went to the store." Then he tries logic once more and says, "I wented to the store."

4. Pronunciation

The pronunciation of words is learned by imitation in the case of young children. The child copies the sounds he hears and thus pronounces words as he heard others pronounce them. He pronounces words incorrectly as easily as correctly. In early childhood his ability to imitate sounds is so flexible that his entire pronunciation can readily change in a short period of time, should he be placed in a new environment where those with whom he associates pronounce words differently from those with whom he formerly associated. By adolescence, on the other hand, pronunciation has settled into a habit and is hard to change.

Between the ages of twelve and eighteen months, much of the baby's speech is incomprehensible. His pronunciations are so poor that only members of the family who are accustomed to interpreting his speech can understand much of what he is trying to say. After eighteen months, an improvement begins, and this increases gradually until the child is three years old, after which his pronunciations begin to show marked improvements. Up to then, in spite of the fact that the baby attempts to say many words, little improvement is noted in the correctness of his pronunciations (Shirley, 1933; Fisher, 1934; Davis, 1937a; McCurry and Irwin, 1953; McCarthy, 1954). The inability to understand the incomprehensible speech of the baby leads to many misunderstandings of what he wants, and this, in turn, proves to be frustrating to him (Jersild, 1954). This, unfortunately, encourages the baby to revert to the only kind of language he has found to be satisfactory, crying (Rosenzweig, 1954).

After the third year, marked improvements in pronunciation appear. While most children continue to mispronounce some words, even after they enter school, the improvements in pronunciation are marked enough so that only traces of infantile pronunciations appear (McCarthy, 1930, 1954; Wellman et al., 1931; Fisher, 1934; Davis, 1937a; Templin and Steer, 1939; Jersild, 1954; Breckenridge and Vincent, 1955). Typical infantile pronunciations are "wain" for "rain" and "dat" for "that." Most infantile forms are gone by the time the child is five or six years old, after which his pronunciations gradually approximate the adult level.

As is true of all other aspects of speech development, there are marked individual differences in pronunciation. Some young children speak so distinctly that they may readily be understood by others. On the other hand, equally as many children pronounce their words so poorly that it is impossible to do more than guess what they are trying to say, or a member of the family must act as their interpreter. These variations depend partly upon the rate of development of the vocal mechanism, but mostly upon the guidance and help the young child receives in mastering the difficult skill of combining sounds into meaningful words. The ability to pronounce words so they can be understood by others than members of the family frequently lags behind the development of a rather large vocabulary. It is more usual than unusual for a young child to know the meanings of more words than he is able to pronounce in a comprehensible manner (Jersild, 1954).

Studies of the sounds and the sound combinations the young child has the greatest difficulty in pronouncing correctly revealed that consonants and consonant blends are more difficult for children to pronounce than are vowels and diphthongs. Some of the easiest consonants for a child to pronounce are *t, p, b, m,* and *n.* Easy vowels are *i, a, e,* and *u.* Among the consonants difficult to pronounce are *z, w, d, s,* and *g.* Difficult consonant blends consist of *st, str, sk, dr,* and *fl* (Wellman et al., 1931; Templin and Steer, 1939; Roe and Milisen, 1942; Métraux, 1950; Spriestersbach and Curtis, 1951). Little consistency has been found in the misarticulations of young children (Spriestersbach and Curtis, 1951). Articulatory defects are due more often to auditory confusions than to muscular incoordination (Sheridan, 1945).

Tonal Qualities. Typically, the tone of the baby's voice is high-pitched. At first, there are no nasal sounds, but these appear as changes take place in the development of the vocal mechanism (McCarthy, 1952). Gradually, the tone of voice changes, so that, by the time the child is three years old, it is less high-pitched than it previously was and the child's pronunciations are stronger as well as clearer. At this time, there are often voice tremors, and the voice becomes stronger and louder (Ilg et al., 1949). Many young children develop a nasal quality in their voices, if their adenoids become enlarged. By the time the child is four years old, his normal speech tone frequently has a strained, raucous quality. Frequently, he expresses himself in "high, full-volumed" yells (Métraux, 1950).

One of the most characteristic and, at the same time, unfortunate aspects of speech during the school years is the coarsening of the tonal qualities of the voice. This is not the result of maturation, but comes from screaming and shouting, which so invariably accompany play at that age. This strain on the vocal mechanism, at an age when it is not strong enough to withstand such strain, generally results in a coarsening of the tonal qualities to such an extent that it can never be overcome completely. To the child, this is of little importance, especially in the case of boys who assume the attitude that talking in a pleasant voice is a sign of a "sissy."

SPEECH DISORDERS

At the time when the young child is learning to speak, speech disorders are most apt to develop. Because of the difficulty the young child has in controlling his speech mechanism, disorders of one sort or another can develop just as readily as correct speech unless control is exercised by those who are responsible for the care of the child. The seriousness of speech disorders is not limited to the fact that each year they are allowed to continue makes it increasingly difficult to correct them. Speech disorders, even in mild forms like "baby talk," are serious handicaps to social adjustments. If continued to school age, the disorder increases the child's anxiety and interferes with his social adaptation (Missildine and Glasner, 1947). It is not uncommon for boys and girls to laugh at classmates whose speech is defective or to mimic them. This ridicule soon develops a shyness and feeling of inferiority on the part of the afflicted child, resulting in withdrawal from the group.

Even before his school days are over, the child who suffers from speech disorders has generally become silent and morose or openly rebellious. He lives in a daydream world of his own making or asserts himself in some anti-social manner (Despert, 1946a). Being subjected to constant humiliation and frustration adds to the child's nervous tension and thus intensifies his speech difficulties. The effects of such experiences can and often do leave a permanent mark on the individual's personality (Merry and Merry, 1950). Boys and girls with speech defects rarely become leaders in school or college activities, nor do they rise to the top of their classes in scholastic work. Almost every child with a speech disorder shows some sign of maladjustment (Moncur, 1951).

There are many problems that are connected, either directly or indirectly, with speech disorders and which tend to intensify the disorders already present. Among young children, problems of food finickiness, constipation, enuresis, sleeplessness, exaggerated fears, and nightmares are common (Beckey, 1942; Glasner, 1949). Other problems, especially among older children, that stem from speech disorders are failure to take advantage of scholastic opportunities; impaired relationships with parents, resulting in feelings of insecurity in the home; effects on the home atmosphere and on the different members of the family; effects on later earning power; and the effects on the individual's self-evaluation and personal adjustment (ASHA Committee Report, 1952).

Causes of Disorders. Few speech disorders are hereditary. Occasionally a defect in speech can be traced to a tongue-tied condition, or to deformed teeth, palate, lips, or jaws. But the majority of speech disorders are due to environmental causes, faulty learning, caused by imitation of a poor model such as a foreign accent, or attempts to speak quickly because of excitement. Imperfect hearing and muscular weakness of the tongue and lips, owing to lack of full use and excessive nervousness, may also be the causes of speech disorders. Errors in pronunciation, for example, are more often due to crude perceptions than to inability to pronounce the elemental sounds (Bean, 1932). Unfavorable environmental conditions are generally responsible for the more serious speech disorders (Karlin et al., 1940).

TYPES OF SPEECH DISORDERS

Speech disorders may be divided, roughly, into two classes: (1) *errors* and (2) *defects*. The difference between the two is largely arbitrary and one in which the severity of the disorder is the outstanding characteristic. In the case of speech errors, the cause is primarily faulty learning, while in speech defects, emotionality and malformation of the mouth may also be responsible for the trouble.

1. Speech Errors. Speech errors, which are so common in babyhood, but which usually disappear by the time the child enters school, generally arise from faulty learning that has not been corrected by those in charge of the child. "Baby talk," often regarded as cute, is in reality speech in which simple errors, easily corrected, are allowed to persist. From eighteen months to four or five years is the period of "baby talk." At this time, the young child tries to say everything he hears. But he makes only a sketchy effort, omitting the harder details. For example, he omits the "r" from "cream" because it takes considerable effort to pronounce two consecutive consonants and calls it "keam." Young children cling to the consonants or vowels which they learn first and which, as a result, have developed into stronger habits. For example, a young child may be able to pronounce "r," but having learned to pronounce "w" first, he calls a roll a "woll." Baby talk varies from child to child because children vary in the order in which they learn to pronounce the different letters or combinations of letters (Havighurst, 1953).

2. Speech Defects. Speech defects are more serious than speech errors, not only in their causes but also in their effects on the attitude and social adjustment of the individual in later life. Because of their seriousness, they have been more carefully studied than speech errors, and attention from both the physician and educator has been given to them. There are a number of speech defects, the most common of which are the following.

a. Lisping. This consists of letter-sound substitutions, the most common form of which is the substitution of "th" for "s" or "z," as in "Thimple Thimon" for "Simple Simon." Other common forms of letter-sound substitutions are "s" for "th" or "sh"; "sh" for voiceless "l"; "r" for "u"; or "u" or "y" for "r." Among preschool children, lisping is one of the most common speech defects. But because lisping is the source of much ridicule, most children whose lisp is not due to a physical cause learn to overcome it early in their school careers. The result is that there are few lispers to be found among high-school or college students.

Two of the most usual causes of lisping are deformation of the jaw, teeth, or lips and a tendency to cling to infantile speech. In the case of the former, when the lower jaw protrudes beyond the upper, there is apt to be a slight lisp. During the transitional stage from first to second teeth, or the "toothless" age, there is often a lisp which, if not checked, may become a habit. Most lisping, however, is a type of infantilism. The child continues to talk in this babyish way because he discovers that others think it "cute" and laugh at him. In many cases, adults talk to him in lisping tones, in imitation of his lisp, giving him an incorrect model to copy.

b. Slurring, or Indistinctness of Speech. Slurring is due to inactivity of the lips, tongue, or jaw. It is sometimes caused by paralysis of the vocal organs or lack of development of the tongue, especially of the musculature of the tongue, which often is an accompaniment of rickets. In other cases, an emotional attitude of timidity may be responsible for inactivity of the lips and tongue. The child frightened by the presence of other people keeps his lips partially closed and mumbles his words. Finally, it may be due to rapid speech, caused by excitement in which the child, in his haste to say all that he wants to say, rushes through the words without pronouncing each carefully and distinctly. This last cause is responsible for the cases of slurring that occur for the first time during the school years.

c. Stuttering. Stuttering is hesitant, repetitious speech accompanied by spasms of the muscles of the throat and diaphragm. This results in inability to produce sounds. It comes from a disturbance of the normal rhythm of breathing due to partial or total failure of the speech muscles to coordinate. The result is that the speech pattern is jerky, labored, hesitant, and repetitious (Missildine and Glasner, 1947; Hildreth, 1950). It resembles a case of stage fright (Garrison, 1952). Stuttering is often accompanied by a deadlocking of speech in which the individual is temporarily unable to produce any sound. As the muscular tension is released, this is followed by a flood of words which will soon be checked by another spasm.

The spasms of stuttering differ in different individuals and also differ, from time to time, in the same individual. People who stutter in oral reading or conversations may not do so in singing, talking over the telephone, or speaking in public (Blanton, 1929; Merry and Merry, 1950). Stuttering is often accompanied by certain facial spasms, such as facial grimaces, blowing of the cheeks, blinking of the eyes, wrinkling of the forehead, and protruding of the mouth (Johnson, 1942; Despert, 1946a). This calls attention to the stuttering and, in children, is often responsible for the ridicule of other children.

Prevalence of stuttering. Almost all children stutter at some time or other during the preschool years. Studies of the onset of stuttering have revealed that approximately 85 per cent of American children today begin to stutter between the ages of 2½ and 3½ years. Frequently, stuttering then decreases, only to flare up again at the time of entering school, at the age of six years. Usually this early stuttering is only temporary and clears up as the child grows older. During the first three grades of elementary school, stuttering is more frequently found than in the upper grades or in high school. While some stuttering occurs for the first time during adolescence, the onset of stuttering after the child is nine years old is unusual. By adult years, only 1 or 2 per cent of the population stutters (Blanton, 1929; Davis, 1939; Bender, 1944; Kastein, 1947; McCarthy, 1947, 1954; Glasner, 1949; Ilg et al., 1949; Hildreth, 1950; Métraux, 1950; Breckenridge and Vincent, 1955).

Stuttering in the preschool years is due mainly to the discrepancy between thought and speech tempos. The young child whose vocabulary is still limited and who is just mastering the skill of combining words into sentences is trying to say more than he is equal to saying. This is the age when he is anxious to communicate with others and to make new social contacts. It is also the age when he is trying to be independent and, as a result, has a negativistic attitude toward adult authority. Stuttering at the beginning of school comes mainly from the adjustment problems connected with the change from the narrow environment of the home to the broader environment of the school. Going to school is one of the serious steps in the emotional weaning of the child. That nervous tension is strong at this age may be seen by the fact that many children revert to thumb and finger sucking and other nervous mannerisms (McCarthy, 1947, 1954; Missildine and Glasner, 1947; Hildreth, 1950; Breckenridge and Vincent, 1955).

Causes of stuttering. All children experience a period in their speech development when there is a discrepancy between the tempo of their thoughts and the tempo of their speech. Likewise, all children must make adjustments to the environment of school. Why, therefore, do some children stutter while others do not? And why do some continue to stutter while others stutter only for a short time, during periods of difficult adjustment? Studies of primitive peoples have revealed that stuttering does not occur among them (Missildine and Glasner, 1947). This leads to the question of whether there are factors in civilized life that are responsible for this form of defective speech.

Studies of stuttering have revealed a number of causes. Some emphasize the importance of heredity and claim that stuttering "runs in families." Others stress the association of stuttering with handedness and emphasize that stuttering is caused by changes from left- to right-handedness (Bryngelson, 1935; Hahn, 1943; Merry and Merry, 1950; Garrison, 1952; Breckenridge and Vincent, 1955). Most, however, emphasize that stuttering is a learned reaction and is psychological in origin, resulting from environmental pressures. Three types of stutterers have been identified: the relatively healthy child whose environment is confused; the severely disturbed child with stuttering as only one symptom; and the dependent, confused, fearful, shy, anxious, and restless child. The third type is by far the most numerous (Glasner, 1949). A comparison of a group of stutterers with a group of nonstutterers revealed that stutterers showed more and more severe symptoms of maladjustment than did the nonstutterers. This difference is shown in Fig. 30. The most common symptoms of maladjustment found in the group of stutterers were nervousness, tendency to experience enuresis, nightmares and night terrors, "fussy" eating habits, and the need for frequent discipline (Moncur, 1955).

Environmental conditions that are commonly found in the homes of stuttering children are parents who are perfectionistic, overprotective, dominating, overanxious about the child's welfare, especially his speech, and pressure on the child to learn two languages simultaneously. Prematurely born children or children whose birth has been difficult are often the victims of overprotective parents. The type of environment just described causes children to be nervous, easily upset, overanxious, and tortured by feelings of lack of love and understanding in the home and by feelings of guilt when they do not come up to parental expectations. These are the psychological conditions that lead to stuttering and which prolong it beyond the age when children normally stutter (Davis, 1939, 1940; Cooper, 1942; Johnson, 1942; Bender, 1944; Despert, 1946a; Kastein, 1947; McCarthy, 1947, 1954; Missildine and Glasner, 1947; Johnson et al., 1948; Duncan, 1949; Glasner, 1949; Hildreth, 1950; Boland, 1951; Moncur, 1951, 1952; Christensen, 1952).

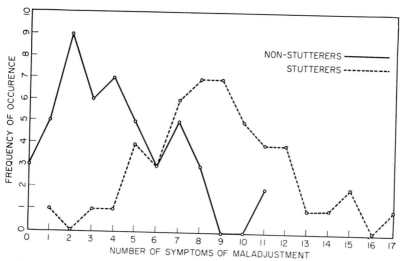

Fig. 30. Symptoms of maladjustment among stutterers and non-stutterers. (*From J. F. Moncur, Symptoms of maladjustment differentiating young stutterers from non-stutterers, Child Develpm., 1935, 26, 91-96. Used by permission.*)

d. Cluttering. Cluttering is a rapid, confused, and jumbled type of speech which is often mistaken for stuttering. It is usually accompanied by motor awkwardness and is found mainly in children whose speech development has been delayed. It represents an exaggeration of the errors of speech made by normal people. Unlike the stutterer, the clutterer can improve his speech when he is careful and pays attention to what he wants to say. The more the stutterer pays attention to his speech, the worse it is (Bakwin and Bakwin, 1952).

THE CONTENT OF SPEECH

What children talk about at different ages is important, not only because it gives evidence as to the size of the child's vocabulary and ability to combine words into sentences, but also because it gives a clue as to the personality and the dominant interests of the child. It tells us how he feels about himself, his relationships with others, and how he compares himself with his peers. In early childhood, "the pattern of personality is clearly woven in the fabric of speech" (Shirley, 1933a). Like the adult, the child talks about the things that are most important to him, and thus we know what his dominant interests are.

Furthermore, the child's speech tells us something about his emotional states, whether he is happy, frightened, jealous, or curious. As Bayley (1940) has pointed out, the child's speech is a "thermometer of emotional reactions." There are individual differences in the child's need for speech as

Whispering to one's friends is a way of outwitting others. (*From Child Development, a McGraw-Hill Text-Film.*)

a form of expression. There are also differences in the uses children make of speech. What each child talks about, therefore, and what manner of expressing himself he uses are, in general, compatible with his personality traits (Shirley, 1933a).

At first, the young child's speech generally accompanies *motor activity*. Running, playing, eating, and bathing, all have some vocal accompaniment, whether shouts, grunts, squeaks, or words. All of these have a definite relationship to what the child is doing and are in reality a form of "thinking out loud" (Métraux, 1950). The little girl playing with her doll will say, "I cover dolly," as she puts a cover over the doll, even though there is no one in the room to listen to what she is saying. Very little of the young child's speech is conversational, but rather approaches monologue in the form of a running commentary on his own actions (Smith, 1926; Métraux, 1950).

As children grow older, they not only talk more, but there is also an improvement in the quality of their speech. Increase in amount of talking is generally greater than increase in the vocabulary they use while talking. Among four-year-olds, for example, there is four or five times as much talking when children are with others as occurs when they are two or three years old, but they use only slightly more than three times as many different words as do the younger children (Jersild and Ritzman, 1938). With age, there are likewise shifts in conversational topics and in the form of expression of these topics. In early childhood, conversations relate for the most part to the child and his interests, and relatively few are devoted to topics in which the child is not involved.

Types of Speech. The speech of children has been classified in two major categories: *egocentric speech* and *socialized speech*. In the former, the child either talks for himself or for the pleasure of associating with anyone who happens to be present. There is no attempt to exchange ideas or to consider the other person's point of view. Egocentric speech is thus "pseudo conversation," or a form of "collective monologue." It is seen in monologues accompanying actions and in soliloquies occurring when the child is alone or with others who are paying no particular attention to him. This egocentricity springs from the child's intellectual limitations. It is shown also in the child's inability to analyze his own thought processes and check on the conclusions he draws (Piaget, 1926, 1932; Jersild, 1954).

The second type, *socialized speech*, occurs when social contacts are established between the child and his social environment. Socialized speech is subdivided into five forms: (1) *adapted information*, in which thoughts or ideas are exchanged or a common aim may be pursued; (2) *criticism*, involving the child's remarks about the work or behavior of others, and specified in relation to an audience; (3) *commands, requests*, and *threats;* (4) *questions;* and (5) *answers* made to real questions. In this form of speech, the child may be talking to someone else, but frequently his own interests play a dominant role in what he says and how he says it. While egocentric speech may be an aid to the development of the child's thinking, socialized speech is an aid to his social adjustments (Piaget, 1926, 1932; Merry and Merry, 1950; McCarthy, 1954).

During the first two or three years of life, most of the young child's speech is egocentric. Gradually, as his contacts with others increase and as his desire to be one of a social group grows stronger, he uses speech as a social tool (Métraux, 1950). Just when there will be a marked shift from egocentric to socialized speech is difficult to tell. Various experimenters have reported different ages, ranging from two to seven or eight years (Piaget,

1926, 1932; McCarthy, 1929, 1930, 1954; Adams, 1932; Fisher, 1934; McConnon, 1935; Huang and Chen, 1936; Arrington, 1939; Sanford, 1942; Young, 1942; James, 1943; Maddock, 1947; Métraux, 1950; Ames, 1952; Jersild, 1954). However, as Arrington (1939) has stressed, "Clearly the tendency is for children to talk more to other people and less to themselves as they grow older." This is illustrated in Fig. 31.

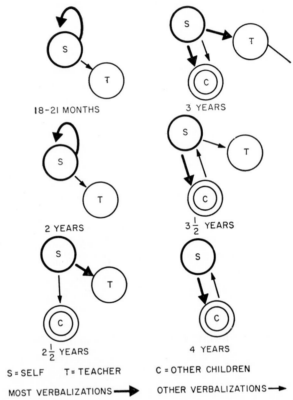

Fig. 31. Early forms of interpersonal verbalization. (*From L. B. Ames, The sense of self of nursery school children as manifested by their verbal behavior, J. genet. Psychol., 1952, 81, 193–232. Used by permission.*)

Just when there will be a shift from egocentric to socialized speech will depend not so much upon chronological age as upon other factors. The child's personality is an important determinant. Children whose self-concept is egocentric will continue to talk about themselves and show little interest in talking to others for a longer time than will children who are able to assess themselves more realistically. Experiences with others enable the child to acquire a degree of social maturity which will be reflected in the extent to which the child can understand and share the points of view of others. As the group with which the child finds himself grows larger, the child's speech becomes more socialized and less egocentric. When with children of their own age, socialized speech is more pronounced than when children are with adults (Arrington, 1939; Williams and Mattson, 1942; Young, 1942; McCarthy, 1954).

Conversational Topics. What children talk about when they are together or with an adult will be influenced by their ages, the breadth of their experiences, and their personality patterns. For the most part, young children talk about the most commonplace, simple subjects in a homely situation. They concentrate mainly on themselves and their activities, bringing into their conversations their families and their relationships with different members of the family (Sprague, 1929; Shirley, 1938; Maddock, 1947). Many topics of conversation, characteristic of adults in our society, appear in a rudimentary form in the conversations of preschool children. Topics such as clothes, likes and dislikes, where one lives, and matters of everyday routine predominate (Murphy, 1937).

Among older children, there is a wider variety of topics in their conversations, owing to the broadening of their experiences. Much of their conversations centers around school, its activities, the teachers, their lessons; their own accomplishments; their families, including their siblings, their relatives, and the family pet; games and sports; trips and excursions; clothes; shows and other forms of entertainment they have engaged in; and personal experiences (Zyve, 1927; Dawson, 1937). There is a shift, with age, not only in the number of different topics discussed, but also from general to specific emphasis on these topics (Dawson, 1937).

How important the child's opportunity for broad experiences is in determining what he will talk about has been shown in a comparison of orphanage and nonorphanage children. Orphanage children were found to talk more about the parts of the body, play materials, activities and routines, buildings and furnishings, than the nonorphanage children. Nonorphanage children, on the other hand, talked more about other children, activities, clothing, and nature than the orphanage children did. They also mentioned a greater variety of topics (Moore, 1948). Children, like adults, talk about their interests. The more experiences they have, the broader their interests, and as a result, the more varied their conversational topics.

Boasting. Every child likes to boast. What he boasts about, however, changes with age. Young children boast about material possessions, such as clothes, toys, family cars, or servants. The older child boasts more about the strength and skill in games than about his material possessions. The greatest amount of boasting generally comes between the ages of eight and twelve years, the time when both boys and girls are especially anxious to win favor from their contemporaries and ensure their status in the group (Dawson, 1937). What they boast about at that age depends largely upon the values of the group. Boys, for example, boast especially about their strength because strength and skill are highly valued among boys of this age (Hetzer, 1930). Much of the name calling of the older child is a form of boasting. If he calls another a "dumbbell," an "idiot," or "skinny," he is indirectly inflating his own ego by the implication that the child he is ridiculing is inferior to him (Breckenridge and Vincent, 1955).

Criticism. Criticism is generally associated with the later childhood years and early adolescence. Few people think of younger children as being critical of others in their speech. This, however, is not true. While some children make favorable criticisms about others, most of their criticisms are unfavorable. These are generally made behind the other child's back. Young children use criticism to gain the assistance of some other person in a situation that is beyond their control, as when their activities or possessions are being interfered with. Their criticisms then take the form of *tattling,* in which they complain about the other person behind his back. Typically, the young child will go to a parent or teacher with such complaints as "He took my ball," or "He broke my skate and now I can't skate."

Older children address their criticisms to the person criticized more than do younger children. They use criticism mainly to comment on the conduct and personalities of others, whether it be the other's lack of knowledge, his clumsiness, his failure to do what he was expected to do, or his clothing and personal appearance. Sometimes these criticisms are made in the hopes of correcting the shortcomings of the other child, but usually they are for the satisfaction of demonstrating the speaker's superiority (Smith, 1932; Dawson, 1937). Most children, especially boys, are brutally frank in their criticisms of even their best friends. With those whom they dislike or to whom they feel superior, they do not hesitate to add ridicule to their criticism.

A very common form of criticism in childhood is *name calling.* Beginning around the age of three years, children use name calling partly to relieve injured feelings and partly to let other children see how they feel about them. Typical examples of this childish name calling are, "You're a crazy cat," "You're a lazybones," or "You're silly." Name calling not only increases in usage with age, but it contains a wider range of adjectives in the criticism of friends and companions (Smith, 1932). Elementary-school children, even those from good home environments where such language is rarely heard, "go tough" in their dealings with other children. They seem to feel that they must use fairly obvious means to make their point. As a result, they do not hesitate to call other children by such names as "dumbbell," "sissy," or "fat potato." As is true of all forms of criticism, name calling is a method of expressing their developing egos (Breckenridge and Vincent, 1955).

FACTORS INFLUENCING SPEECH DEVELOPMENT

While the pattern of speech development is much the same for all children, there are marked variations in the rate of development, the size and quality of vocabulary, and the correctness of pronunciation at every age level. A number of factors are responsible for these variations, most important of which are the following.

1. Health. Severe and prolonged illness during the first two years of life has been found to delay the beginning of speech and the use of sentences by one to two months (Smith, 1931). Should severe or prolonged illness occur in childhood, the child will be cut off from contacts with other children, and as a result, his speech development suffers. Added to this is the fact that he has little incentive to talk because he is not feeling well or because his every need or desire is anticipated for him. A young child who is deaf or hard-of-hearing is certain to be slow in learning to talk and to have a poor pronunciation compared with other children of the same age and intellectual development. Likewise, the deaf child will, at every age, have a smaller vocabulary than other children. The reason for this is obvious. Because the child learns to talk through imitation, he is greatly handicapped if he cannot hear what others say, and as a result, he lacks an adequate model to imitate (Gesell et al., 1940; Garrison, 1952; Breckenridge and Vincent, 1955).

2. Intelligence. The relationship between intelligence and speech has been found to be so marked that it is frequently claimed that the child's speech is the best single indicator of his intellectual level. This holds true not only for the onset of speech and intelligibility at early ages but also for the size of vocabulary at different ages throughout childhood (Terman, 1926; Shirley, 1933; Williams, 1937; Gewirtz, 1948; Merry and Merry, 1950; Garrison, 1952; McCarthy, 1954; Breckenridge and Vincent, 1955). Among babies, there is an increase in correlation between speech sounds and level of intelligence up to two years, after which there is a strong relationship between speech development and IQ (Spiker and Irwin, 1949). It has been suggested from studies of early speech sounds that consonant types and consonant-vowel frequency ratio in a baby's babbling is a better predictor of later intelligence than any of the present measures of infant intelligence (Catalano and McCarthy, 1954). While early language development is a predictor of intellectual development, it should be used with caution. A child who is precocious in his early speech development is usually normal or above normal in intelligence. On the other hand, a delay of several or many months in beginning to talk is not at all a sure sign that he is dull (Jersild, 1954).

Studies of mentally deficient children have shown that only about one-third of them speak normally. The lower the intellectual rating, the poorer the speech (Sirkin and Lyons, 1941; Garrison, 1952). A low-grade feeble-minded child of five years has been found to be comparable in speech-sound status to babies a year and a half old (Irwin, 1942). Children of intellectual superiority, on the other hand, have been found to show marked linguistic superiority, both in size of vocabulary and in length and correctness of sentence structure (Terman, 1926; Fisher, 1934; Young, 1941; McCarthy, 1954). In addition to their maturity of expression, they show marked maturity in the content of their speech. Before their elementary-school days are over, they can learn several languages with little or no confusion, they are able to speak before groups, and they enjoy dramatization (Holling-worth, 1942; Merry and Merry, 1950). Among elementary-school children, there is a high correlation between knowledge of word meanings and over-all school achievement (Traxler, 1945). On the other hand, children with articulation defects often have reading disabilities and do poor school work (Yedinack, 1949).

3. Socioeconomic Status. Studies of the relationship between speech and the socioeconomic status of the family have shown that children of the poorer social environments are delayed in speech development as compared with children of the better environments. This may be due to differences in intelligence or to opportunities to learn, or both. In forms of vocalization which are purely "instinctive," as in the case of crying, no differences are found between babies of high and low classes (Hetzer and Reindorf, 1928). Comparisons of the mastery of speech sounds of babies of business, clerical, and professional families with those of laboring-class families revealed no significant difference between the two groups during the first year and a half of the babies' lives. After that, more speech sounds appeared in the vocalizations of the babies from the higher groups (Irwin, 1948, 1948a).

From then on, differences in speech development, in size of vocabulary, sentence forms and correctness, and in pronunciation become increasingly great as children grow older. Children of the upper socioeconomic groups talk sooner, talk better, and talk more than do those of the lower groups. At every age, the articulation of children of the upper groups is superior to that of children of the lower groups (Gesell and Lord, 1927; Hetzer and Reindorf, 1928; Day, 1932; Davis, 1937b; Bühler, 1939; Young, 1941; Hughes, 1945; Davis and Havighurst, 1947; Schulman and Havighurst, 1947; Merry and Merry, 1950; Havighurst, 1953; Jersild, 1954; McCarthy, 1954). Children from the higher socioeconomic groups talk more, and more spon-taneously, than do those from the lower groups (Gesell and Lord, 1927).

While intelligence may play some role in determining these variations, differences in environmental influences cannot be overlooked. Environ-mental factors that have been found to be closely correlated with the young child's speech development are number of children's books the child sees, opportunities for constructive play, the number of hours the child is read to or told stories, the number of adults in daily contact with the child, and the number of playmates the child has (Van Alstyne, 1929). Children who associate primarily with adults have been found to be more precocious in their speech development than are children whose associations are mainly with children. The child from the higher socioeconomic groups is likely to have more associations with his parents, especially with the mother, than is the child from poorer groups whose mother may work away from home or who has too many home duties to be able to devote much time to him (Jersild, 1954). Then, too, parents from the upper groups feel that speech is very important, not only as a reflection on the home status and training the child receives, but also as a means of success in life. As a result, the child from the upper socioeconomic groups is encouraged, if not actually forced, to learn to speak early and correctly (Merry and Merry, 1950).

4. Sex. During the first year of life, no sex difference in vocalization has been found. But beginning with the second year, sex differences in favor of girls appear. Girls show a greater mastery of speech sounds, even before they begin to talk, than do boys (Irwin and Chen, 1946). In childhood, boys are slower in learning to talk, their sentences are shorter and less grammatically correct, their use and comprehension vocabularies are smaller, and their pronunciation of words is less accurate at every age than is true of girls. These differences become more pronounced with every passing year and are greater among children of the lower socioeconomic groups than among those of the higher groups (McCarthy, 1930, 1954; Young, 1941; Merry and Merry, 1950; Anastasi and D'Angelo, 1952; Havighurst, 1953; Jersild, 1954).

According to Havighurst (1953), no one knows just why girls are ahead of boys in their speech development or if this is characteristic of our culture alone. McCarthy (1953), however, has tried to explain this sex difference in terms of family relationships. According to her, during the first year of life, when no real sex differences in quantity or quality of vocalization have been found (Irwin and Chen, 1946), the baby babbles back to the mother approximations of the sounds made by her. This is the "echo-reaction" stage of babbling (Stengel, 1947). At this time, babies of both sexes show similar feelings toward the mother.

However, very soon after babyhood is over, girls identify themselves more with their mothers than do boys, who try to identify themselves with their fathers. Because, in our culture, the father is away from home more than the mother, boys have fewer and less intimate contacts with the father than girls have with the mother. The closeness of the mother-daughter relationship throughout childhood helps the girl to learn to speak sooner and better than the boy. Furthermore, because there is a greater difference in tonal quality between the boy's voice and the adult male voice than between the girl's voice and the adult female voice, learning in boys is less satisfactory because the echo reaction of the boy is less favorable than that of the girl (McCarthy, 1953).

Speech defects are much more common in boys than in girls. Estimates of the prevalence of different defects range from 2:1 to 8:1, in favor of the boys. With the exception of lisping, which is more often found in girls than boys, all other defects are more common among the boys. There is evidence that the ratio becomes larger as children grow older. By adult years, for example, it has been estimated that there are eight male stutterers for every one female stutterer (Gesell et al., 1940; Hahn, 1943; Despert, 1946; Hildreth, 1950a; Merry and Merry, 1950; Garrison, 1952; Morley, 1952; McCarthy, 1954; Breckenridge and Vincent, 1955). The explanation for this sex difference given by McCarthy (1953) is that boys are more emotionally insecure than girls, they have more troubles and are punished more harshly than girls are. Furthermore, with the father away from home so much of the time, the boy cannot identify himself with the father as the girl can with the mother and thus derive a feeling of security. This is essential to the emotional stability needed as the basis of good speech.

5. Family Relationships. Studies of institutional children and of babies reared in orphanages have shown how important family relationships are to speech development. Babies in institutions cry more than those at home (Aldrich et al., 1946), but they babble less and make fewer different sounds than do family babies, even than those from families in the lowest socioeconomic groups. This is due to their lack of close personal relationship with the mother or the mother substitute, which results in a general retardation in their development, the most serious and permanent of which is in the area of speech development. They are slow in learning to talk and are retarded in language development throughout their lives (Skeels et al., 1938; Goldfarb, 1943, 1945; Ribble, 1943; Freud and Burlingham, 1944; Gesell and Amatruda, 1945; Brodbeck and Irwin, 1946; Spitz, 1946; Buxbaum, 1949; Lewis, 1951; McCarthy, 1952a, 1954; Thompson, 1952).

Not only is the amount of time spent with the mother during the early years of life important to the child's speech development, but also the kind of relationship that exists is of tremendous importance. A healthy parent-child relationship facilitates speech development, while an unhealthy relationship, in which the young child is babied and pampered, may not only result in speech retardation but may also lead to such speech defects as lisping, stuttering, and slurring. Many of the most serious cases of stuttering have been found in children whose family relationships are marked by emotional tensions (Allen, 1947; Milner, 1951; McCarthy, 1952a, 1954; Thompson, 1952). These unfavorable relationships affect the child's speech even after he goes to school and his social horizons broaden.

Size of family has been found to be important in the child's speech development. In early babyhood, the presence or absence of older siblings has been found to have no relationship to the amount or type of vocalization the young baby does. Speech-sound development progresses in the same pattern for only children and for those with older siblings (Irwin, 1948b). However, as the child grows older, marked differences appear. The only child has been found to be definitely superior to children with siblings in every phase of linguistic skill (Davis, 1937b). The reason for this is that the only child has longer periods of being the center of the mother's attention than do children with siblings (McCarthy, 1954). Furthermore, only children are spared sibling rivalry, which sometimes manifests itself in speech disorders, especially stuttering (Missildine, 1946; McCarthy, 1954).

Twins and triplets have been found to be retarded in their speech development as compared with ordinary siblings. This is especially true during the early years of life, when their environment is mainly in the home and their social contacts are almost exclusively with one another. They are slower in beginning to speak, and the size of their vocabularies, the length and correctness of their sentences, and their articulation are inferior to those of singletons of the same ages. Retardation increases between two and five years, as compared with singletons, but by the time they are nine years old, their speech retardation is partially overcome. This is more true of multiple births from the higher socioeconomic groups than from the lower (Day, 1932, 1932a; Davis, 1937b; Howard, 1946).

The explanations given for speech retardation of children of multiple births is that they have their own jargon, or "secret language," which they imitate instead of imitating an adult model. Furthermore, from the moment of birth, they have no time when they have the same close personal relationship with the mother that a singleton has, and they are thus deprived of the affectional relationship with the mother which provides the groundwork for the development of normal speech (McCarthy, 1954). Then, too, because they are able to communicate with one another through their own secret jargons, combined with gestures, grunts, and facial expressions, they have little incentive to learn to speak so that they can be understood by others (Howard, 1946). When they receive special care, as was true of the Dionne quintuplets, every need was anticipated and met without their asking for it (Blatz et al., 1937). Most cases of multiple births are similarly deprived of the necessary motivation to learn to speak.

6. Bilingualism. Because of the commonly accepted belief that it is easier to learn to "talk like a native" in a foreign language before one is five years old rather than later, many parents have their children taught some preferred foreign language while they are learning their native tongue. This is very apt to delay the child's learning to speak, because of the confusion that results when the child tries to say one thing to one person in his native tongue and the very same thing to another person in a foreign language. His thinking, likewise, is apt to be confused, and he is therefore self-conscious about talking, because he is not quite certain about the correct word to use on that particular occasion.

Learning two languages simultaneously necessitates the learning of two words for every object the child wishes to name or every thought he wishes to express. It also requires the learning of two sets of grammatical forms, one generally in direct conflict with the other. This is no easy task for a high-school student, so it is readily understandable that it is an extremely difficult task for a young child. The young child, when learning two languages simultaneously, is likely to combine the two languages into one and not be able, until he is older, to separate them into two separate language systems (Leopold, 1949).

Studies of the effects of bilingualism in the preschool years have revealed that while bilingualism does not seem to delay the first use of words, it becomes increasingly more handicapping with each passing year (Smith, 1935a). In either language, the mother tongue or English, bilingual children have been found to be retarded in speech development, as shown in size of vocabulary, sentence length and construction, and articulation, as compared with monolingual children. By the time of school entrance, there is such a marked retardation in speech development that the child is not advanced enough in either language to be ready for school instruction. Even if his inferiority is not as marked in the mother tongue of the family as in English, he is still poorly equipped for adjustments to our schools (Smith, 1935a, 1939, 1949; Merry and Merry, 1950; Anastasi and DeJésus, 1953; McCarthy, 1953, 1954; Jersild, 1954; Breckenridge and Vincent, 1955).

Two conclusions regarding the problem of bilingualism in the preschool years are important because they express the rapidly growing opinion of psychologists and educators regarding this matter. According to Thompson (1952), "There can be no doubt that the child reared in a bilingual environment is handicapped in his language growth. One can debate the issue as to whether speech facility in two languages is worth the consequent retardation in the common language of the realm." Much the same point of view is expressed by Smith (1949), who says, "It would seem unwise to start any but children of superior linguistic ability at a second language unnecessarily during the preschool years."

Because the bilingual child is not ready, linguistically, for school, his adjustment to school is even more difficult than the monolingual child experiences. Not being able to communicate satisfactorily in the language used in the classroom adds to the feeling of insecurity most children normally experience when they first enter school (McCarthy, 1953). The result is that the bilingual child is handicapped in his school adjustment from the very start (Anastasi and Cordova, 1953). This is shown in his poor academic achievements throughout elementary school, even when his intelligence is adequate for him to do academic work of a higher caliber (McCarthy, 1954).

Achievement on intelligence tests likewise reflects the handicap of bilingualism. This is especially true of tests which make use of language (Seidl, 1937; Arsenian, 1945; Darcy, 1952; Altus, 1953; Anastasi and Cordova, 1953; Jersild, 1954; McCarthy, 1954). Extreme lack of test sophistication and poor emotional adjustment to the school situation further increases the child's poor adjustment to tests (Anastasi and Cordova, 1953).

The effects of bilingualism on social and emotional adjustments are even more serious than the effects on academic achievement. When the bilingual child tries to express his thoughts in words, he senses or is aware of the tittering, laughter, annoyance, or boredom of other children. He is often embarrassed enough to refuse oral communication and thus becomes a "quiet child." This leaves a serious scar on his developing personality (Koenig, 1953). Even as late as the college years students with a bilingual background have been found to make poorer emotional and social adjustments than do those with a monolingual background (Spoerl, 1944). The least harm to the bilingual child comes when he is in a school and neighborhood environment where there are a number of other children of the same national origin as his and who, likewise, have to meet the problem of bilingualism (Fishman, 1952; Jersild, 1954). How successfully the child can overcome his foreign accent will have a marked influence on how lasting will be the effects of bilingualism (McCarthy, 1953).

Chapter 7

EMOTIONAL DEVELOPMENT

The emotions play a role of major importance in the child's life. Not only do they add pleasure to his everyday experiences and serve as a motivation to action, but they also prove to be a handicap to him. The effects of the emotions on the physical well-being of the child may be very harmful, especially when the emotions are strong and frequent. Interference to digestion and sleep and digestive upsets resulting from emotional tension prove to be damaging to the pattern of physical development. The child's school work suffers when emotional tension is present because his ability to concentrate suffers. This is especially apparent in reading problems, which are more common among children predisposed to emotional tension than among those predisposed to emotional calm.

Too frequent and too intense emotional outbursts are detriments to the child's social adjustments. And the child who makes poor social adjustments is likely to experience unhappiness and feelings of inadequacy and of inferiority, all of which serve to intensify the already existing emotional tension. These feelings, likewise, prove to be damaging to the child's concept of self and thus leave a lasting scar on his developing personality. How successfully or unsuccessfully the child adjusts to life is, as a result, greatly influenced by his emotional experiences in childhood (Breckenridge and Vincent, 1955; Jersild, 1954, 1954a). Adult memories of happy and unhappy childhood experiences have revealed how intense these emotionally toned experiences were and how lasting their effects on the child (Dudycha and Dudycha, 1933, 1941; Child, 1940; Thompson and Witryol, 1948; Wall, 1948; Barschak, 1951; Bühler, 1952; Jersild, 1954a).

Whether the emotions will prove to be helpful or harmful to a child depends not so much upon the frequency and intensity of emotional experiences as upon the *kind* of emotional experiences. Certain emotions, especially fear, anger, and jealousy—often called the "unpleasant emotions" —are harmful to the child's development. Other emotions—especially the "pleasant emotions"—as affection, happiness, joy, and curiosity, are not only helpful but essential to normal development in the childhood years. A child who is deprived of stimuli that will call forth curiosity or who is frustrated in his every attempt to satisfy his curiosity by direct exploration or by asking questions will not attain the level of mental development he is

214

capable of. Similarly, lack of opportunities to experience reasonable amounts of happiness and joy are likely to warp the pattern of the child's personality.

The most serious and most damaging effects, however, will come when the child is deprived of opportunities to experience affection. As Jersild (1954a) has commented, "There is something emotionally satisfying about being loved, and there also is something very practical about it." Deprivation of opportunities to love and be loved, as is true in the case of babies and young children reared in orphanages, results in a delay in their normal physical and mental development, it retards the pattern of their speech development, and it seriously affects the pattern of their personalities (Skeels et al., 1938; Goldfarb, 1943, 1945; Bakwin, 1949; Spitz, 1949; McCarthy, 1953; Jersild, 1954a). The general effects of emotional deprivation are illustrated in Fig. 32. Children who are deprived of love over a period of time may contemplate suicide. When suicide does occur in childhood, it is usually of an impulsive character motivated by a desire to punish parents or others they think are responsible for their lack of love, or it may be motivated by feelings of guilt and a desire for self-punishment (Despert, 1952).

The effect on the emotional development of deprivation of opportunities for normal expressions of love is especially pronounced. The baby, brought up in such an environment, becomes emotionally un-

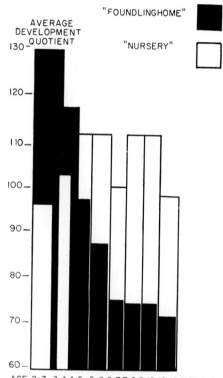

Fig. 32. Comparison of development of foundling-home and nursery (raised by own mothers) children. Bar chart shows the average of the developmental quotients of all children tested within the 30 days reaching from the beginning of the month to the end of the month. (*From R. A. Spitz, The role of ecological factors in emotional development in infancy, Child Develpm., 1949,* **20,** *145–155. Used by permission.*)

responsive (Goldfarb, 1943). He is listless, quiet, and unresponsive to the smiles and coos of others; he shows patterns of temper tantrums, with violent kicks and screams as if seeking attention; and he gives a general appearance of unhappiness (Bakwin, 1949). Should the deprivation of emotional interchange start late in the first year, a condition may develop which resembles depression in the adult. Manifestations of emotional displeasure greatly increase, and anxiety, in the nature of panic, appears. Babies sometimes scream by the hour. Should there be a reestablishment of emotional interchange, there is a rapid resumption of normal development. This is true, however, if the separation from the person or persons who supply the baby with stimuli to love does not last for more than three months. Should it, however, be a separation for five or more months, reestablishment of close personal contacts with the loved one will not produce an improvement, but the developmental decline continues at a slower rate (Spitz, 1949).

PATTERN OF EMOTIONAL DEVELOPMENT

At birth and shortly afterward, the first sign of emotional behavior is general excitement to strong stimulation. This diffuse excitement is part of the mass activity present at birth. There are no indications of clear-cut, definite emotional patterns that can be recognized and identified as specific emotional states. Often before the period of the newborn is over, the general excitement becomes differentiated into simple reactions that suggest pleasure and displeasure. The *unpleasant responses* are elicited by changing the baby's position abruptly, sudden loud noises, hampering the baby's movements, wet diapers, and cold objects applied to the baby's skin. Such stimuli result in crying and mass activity. *Pleasant responses,* on the other hand, can be elicited by rocking, patting, warmth, snug holding, and sucking. The baby shows his pleasure by a general relaxation of the entire body (Bakwin, 1947; Spitz, 1949; Banham, 1951; Bousfield and Orbison, 1952; Jersild, 1954, 1954a).

Beginning with this simple differentiation that appears shortly after birth, the baby develops certain emotional patterns which may readily be recognized in his behavior. Even before the end of the first year of life, emotional expressions are definite enough so that they may be recognized as similar to emotional states in adults. As the child becomes older, he displays an increasing repertoire of emotional responses, recognizable to adults as *joy, anger, fear, jealousy, happiness, curiosity, envy,* and *hate.* These forms of emotional behavior can be aroused by a wide range of stimuli, including people, objects, and situations which were originally ineffective.

Genetic Sequence in Emotions. A number of attempts have been made to determine just what is the pattern of development of emotions from the simple, undifferentiated state of excitement present at birth. This has been done by observing babies and young children over a period of time to see at what time a particular emotional response usually appears and what form it takes then and later. Spitz (1949) has traced the pattern of emotional development from the state of diffuse excitement present at birth to the changes that are apparent in the emotional behavior at the age of one year. According to him, there are no pleasurable emotions present at birth, only a state of quiescence. The state of excitement present at that time is in the nature of displeasure. During the first two months, pleasure and displeasure come in response to *physical* stimulation. By the third month, pleasure is aroused by *psychological* stimulation, as shown in the baby's smile in response to the human face. Slightly later, displeasure can be aroused by psychological as well as physical stimuli, as may be seen in the baby's reaction to being left alone.

After the sixth month, the negative emotions take the lead. First, there is anxiety; two months later, possessive emotions toward toys appear; between the ninth and tenth months, jealousy can be aroused; and between the tenth and twelfth months, disappointment, anger, love, sympathy, friendliness, enjoyment, and a possessive sense of property are all distinguishable. "These," according to Spitz, "are the main stations of emotional development in the course of the first year of life." Even though they may vary widely in ages for different babies, the general pattern remains the same for all.

Banham (1951) has traced the pattern of emotional development throughout the life span. See Fig. 33. She, too, starts with the undifferentiated reactions present at birth and shows how they become more differentiated and specific in nature and related to certain definite events as threatening events, interfering restrictions, and refreshing movements. The state of excitement, as may be seen in this figure, is first differentiated into *distress* and *delight*. Distress later develops into anxiety, fear, shame, anger, jealousy, disgust, disappointment, and restlessness. Delight, on the other hand, is differentiated into joy, elation, hopeful anticipation, affection, and sex love.

Not only does the general state of excitement present at birth develop into specific emotional patterns, but the emotional responses become less diffuse, random, and undifferentiated also. At first, the baby shows displeasure merely by screaming and crying. Later, his reactions include resisting, throwing things, stiffening his body, throwing back his body, running away, hiding, and verbalizing his displeasure (Blatz et al., 1935). With increasing age, there is an increase in linguistic responses and a decrease in motor responses (Bridges, 1931). This is especially apparent in responses to fear- and anger-provoking stimuli.

HOW THE EMOTIONS DEVELOP

As Spitz (1949) has observed, "Emotions are not present ready-made from birth. Like any other sector of the human personality they have to develop." Emotional development is due to *maturation* and *learning,* not to either one alone. The fact that a certain emotional reaction does not appear early in life is no proof that it is not innate. It may develop later with the maturing of the intelligence of the child or with the development of the endocrine system. Through learning, objects and situations which at first

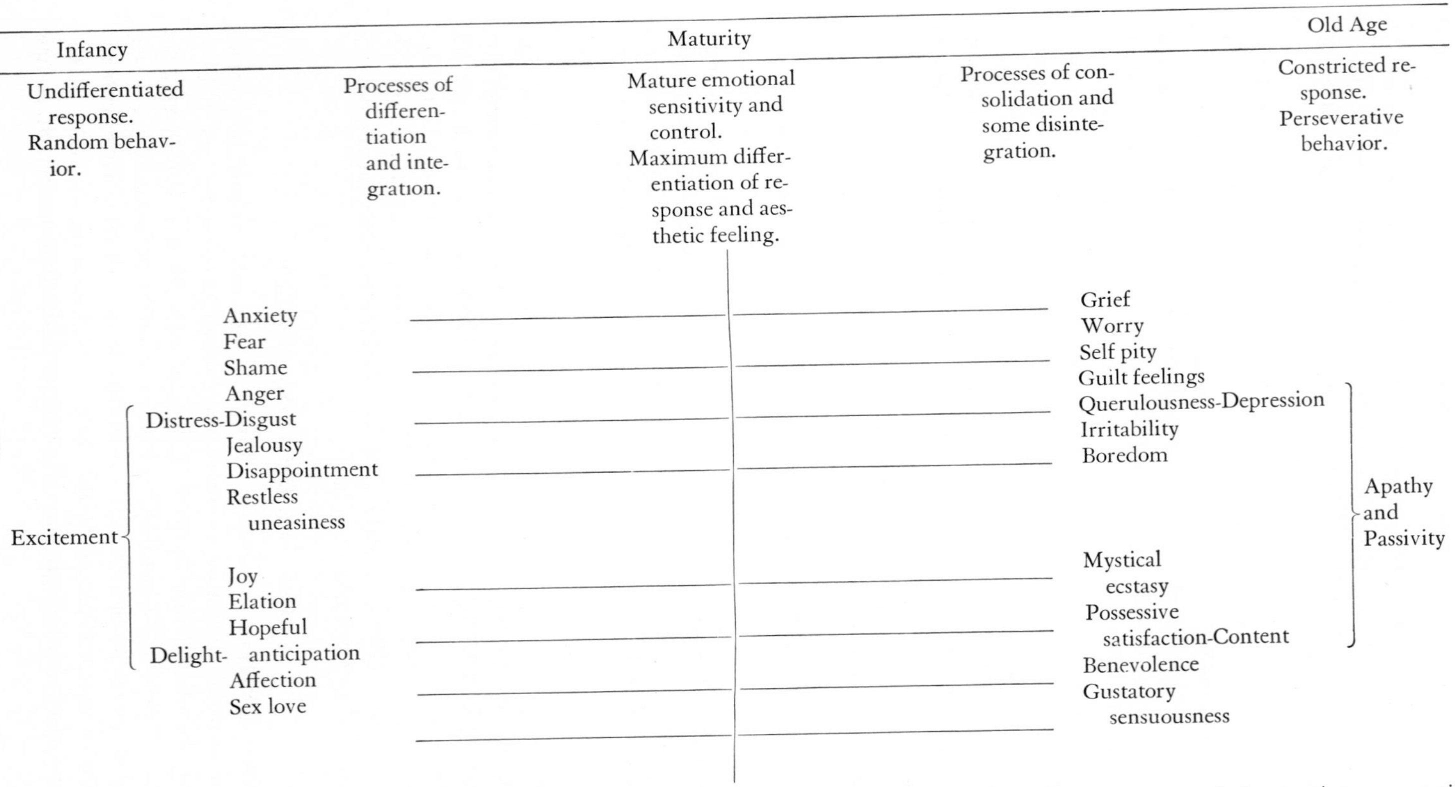

Infancy

Undifferentiated response. Random behavior.

Processes of differentiation and integration.

Maturity

Mature emotional sensitivity and control. Maximum differentiation of response and aesthetic feeling.

Processes of consolidation and some disintegration.

Old Age

Constricted response. Perseverative behavior.

Excitement

Delight — Joy, Elation, Hopeful anticipation, Affection, Sex love

Distress — Anxiety, Fear, Shame, Anger, Disgust, Jealousy, Disappointment, Restless uneasiness

Grief, Worry, Self pity, Guilt feelings, Querulousness-Depression, Irritability, Boredom

Mystical ecstasy, Possessive satisfaction-Content, Benevolence, Gustatory sensuousness

Apathy and Passivity

Fig. 33. Schematic presentation of a genetic theory of life-span emotional changes. (*From K. M. Banham, Senescence and the emotions: a genetic theory, J. genet. Psychol.,* 1951, **78**, 175–183. *Used by permission.*)

failed to call forth emotional responses may later come to do so. The rapid growth of experience in childhood and the broadening of social contacts give rise to many complicated emotional situations (Bayley, 1944).

With growth and development, a child responds differently to different specific situations. What may frighten him at one age may arouse his curiosity at another, and still later, may produce no emotional reaction at all. Similarly, other stimuli which formerly produced no emotional response later produce responses of varying degrees of intensity (Garrison, 1952). Learning and maturation are so closely interwoven in the development of emotions that it is at times difficult to determine the relative effects of the two.

1. Maturation. While the ability to respond emotionally is present at birth, even in prematurely born infants, maturing emotions require gratification if optimum health is to be attained (Bakwin, 1947). This is dependent upon neural and endocrine development. The infant is essentially a precorticate organism. Establishment of cortical control, especially in the frontal lobes, is not achieved until adulthood. How this affects the pattern of emotional development has been demonstrated by studies of animals in which removal of the cortex caused them to be extremely placid. When the frontal lobes are removed in humans, their emotional behavior is lacking in depth, they are inhibited, and transition from one emotional state to another occurs rapidly. This explains the typical emotional behavior of children and shows that mature emotional reactions must wait upon the development of the cortical centers, especially of the frontal lobes (Bousfield and Orbison, 1952).

Intellectual development in children results in an ability to perceive meanings not previously perceived, to attend for a longer time to one stimulus, and to concentrate their emotional tension on one object instead of dissipating it, as is true of all mass activity in the early months of life. With growth of imagination and understanding, things affect the child emotionally in a manner that is different from his earlier experiences when these mental abilities were less well developed. Increase in ability to remember and anticipate likewise affects his emotional reactions. Thus he becomes responsive to stimuli to which he was impervious at an earlier age (Shirley, 1933; Jersild and Holmes, 1935; Bousfield and Orbison, 1952; Jersild, 1954, 1954a; Breckenridge and Vincent, 1955).

How children's emotional reactions are influenced by their ability to understand the meaning of the situation has been demonstrated by studies of children's reactions to war. The younger child reacts to an air raid as an immediate threat, while the older child sees in it a possibility of a policy of destruction which the enemy might carry out at a future time (Jersild and Meigs, 1943; Jersild, 1954a). As Lund (1940) has emphasized, with added maturity there is an increase in objects and situations that have emotional value for the individual.

Not only is intellectual development, dependent upon cortical maturation, important in the development of the emotions, but development of the endocrine glands, especially of the adrenals, is likewise essential to the development of a mature level of emotional behavior. The baby is relatively lacking in the endocrine products that sustain some of the physiological response to stress. In the case of the adrenal glands which play a dominant role in the emotions, it has been found that there is a rapid decrease in size after birth. By the age of two years, the adrenals are approximately 120 per cent below their birth weight. Then they gain rapidly up to five years, slowly from five to eleven years, and more rapidly up to sixteen years, at which time they have regained their birth weight. Until the growth in size has increased, there will be less adrenin produced and secreted. This has a marked influence on the emotional states in childhood (Scammon, 1930; Bousfield and Orbison, 1952).

Studies of changes in fear responses and stimuli that give rise to fear at different ages during early childhood have shown the close relationship of fear to intellectual and endocrine maturation. At first, fear is general, more like a state of panic than specific in form. As the child grows older, his fear responses become more and more specific. Instead of crying, he avoids situations which frighten him, he holds himself aloof, or he withdraws partially or totally from the situation. There is likewise a change in situations causing the fear. Not until the child is four years old, for example, does he appreciate the potential dangers of snakes and, as a result, show fear of snakes (Jones and Jones, 1928). Fear of strange people and strange situations comes only when the baby or young child appreciates the fact that they are strange (Bridges, 1931; Bayley, 1932). A child who is precocious in his mental development will be afraid of things which other children of his age will not fear until a year or two later (Holmes, 1935). In describing the way in which fear "waxes and alters with growth," Gesell (1929) contends that "this pattern is as much the product of organic growth as the various stages in the elaboration and perfection of prehension."

2. Role of Learning. The child is not born with innate emotional responses to any specific stimulus, but learns to respond emotionally as a result of his experiences. The child, for example, has no innate fears of the dark or of high places. The maturation of his sensorimotor and intellectual abilities and of his endocrine system, which underlie his emotional behavior, result in an increased receptivity to the environment. Thus, in turn, the child becomes increasingly more susceptible to emotional stimulation by particular objects and situations. His actual experiences in life determine largely the pattern of his emotions and the form of their expression which each individual develops (Banham, 1951).

Conditioning. Through learning, objects and situations, which at first failed to call forth emotional responses, later come to do so as a result of *conditioning,* or learning by association. The famous experiment on "Albert" by Watson and Raynor (1920) demonstrates how a baby learns to be afraid. Albert, at nine months of age, was shown a large number of objects, a rabbit, dog, monkey, white rat, and cotton wool. In no instance did he display fear. Later, he was conditioned to fear the white rat in the following manner. When the rat was first presented to Albert, he reached for it. At that moment, a loud noise was produced by striking a steel bar with a hammer behind the child's head. This resulted in a startled response on Albert's part and he fell forward on his face. The next time, when the loud noise accompanied the presentation of the white rat, he whimpered. After five more presentations of the rat and the noise, the rat was presented alone. Albert cried, withdrew, and showed a typical fear response.

Carrying the experiment further, Watson and Raynor found that Albert's fear of the rat had spread to similar objects, such as a rabbit, dog, sealskin coat, and cotton wool, all of which had been shown to Albert before the conditioning experiment started, and for which he showed no fear whatsoever. The spreading of emotional reactions to other stimuli may be quite direct, specific, and related. Or it may involve indirect or intermediate steps, as when the child dreams about the thing that frightened him and thus becomes afraid of the dark. As Jersild (1954) has emphasized, "The most essential element when such a 'spread' takes place is the fact that something frightened the child or left him in a state of apprehension or fear. The conditioning process does not in itself create a new fear but provides an object, condition, or circumstance other than the one that frightened him in the first instance and with which his fright becomes associated" (p. 345).

After a particularly frightening experience, the child is likely to show a heightened tendency to be afraid of the thing that frightened him and of other things as well (John, 1941). Thus, the spread of conditioned emotional reactions is facilitated. The aftereffects of frightening experiences will be greater when the child has had a past history of being anxious and easily disturbed than if he had formerly been more stable. Experiences in the home or in the school which threaten the child's self-esteem, and thus his self-confidence, tend to increase his predisposition to be anxious and easily frightened. Such states make the spread of conditioned emotions broader and result in more intense conditioned reactions (Jersild, 1954a). The child who has a satisfactory affectional relationship with his parents is better able to develop affection for others than is the child whose family relationships are less satisfactory and who, as a result, finds it difficult to "spread" his affection to others (Jersild, 1954).

Imitation. Emotional reactions to certain specific situations can be learned by observing them in others, as well as by conditioning. The child imitates the emotional behavior he observes in adults or children and responds in an emotional manner to situations that at one time were incapable of producing emotional responses. A correlation of .667 has been reported between the fears of preschool children and their mothers, suggesting that the child had learned to fear certain situations by observing the mother's fear in those situations (Hagman, 1932). The effect of the mother's emotional attitude on the child comes from the mother's "emotional tension" (Dunbar, 1944). Babies less than four weeks old have been found to refuse the breast if the mother was tense. Older babies sometimes violently resisted food when the mother was tense but ate well when fed by a relaxed person. Thus babies who are brought in close contact with a tense person perceive the emotional state of that person and "respond to it in a consistent manner" (Escalona, 1945).

Emotions are "contagious" in that they spread from person to person. This is true of older children as well as of babies. One child may be angry at a teacher or parent because of some imagined mistreatment from that person. Soon all of his friends are likewise angry at that person. A cross teacher is likely to have a room full of cross children, most of whom will go home cross and disagreeable. A child, on the other hand, who is anxious and fearful may learn to be calm from being associated with a teacher or a friend who is calm. The degree of "contagion" of an emotion depends not so much upon the age of the child as upon the emotion itself. As Breckenridge and Vincent (1955) have pointed out, "The strength or valence of the emotion determines whether it will dominate another emotion or be dominated by it. Adults of normal emotional strength in dealings with children are, on the whole, stronger in emotional valence than are children, and can, therefore, set the tone of the group."

CHARACTERISTICS OF CHILDHOOD EMOTIONALITY

The emotions of the young child differ markedly from those of the adult. An analysis of characteristic features of the child's emotions, contrasted with those of the adult, will make these differences apparent. These characteristics are the following.

1. Children's Emotions Are Brief. Typically the young child's emotions last only a few minutes and then end abruptly. Because the child expresses his emotions in overt actions, he "clears his system," and as a result, the emotion lasts for a relatively short time as contrasted with the long-drawn-out emotional reactions of the adult. As the child grows older, social restraints on the overt responses which formerly characterized his emotional reactions lead to "moods," or emotional states drawn out over a period of time, and expressed slowly rather than in short, abrupt outbursts.

When the child is with playmates of his own age, free from parental or other adult restraints, he expresses his emotions freely and quickly. In the presence of adults, however, the child begins to display moodiness around the fourth year, and this tendency reaches its peak during adolescence. The typical moods of childhood are "sulkiness" from restrained anger; "scariness," "jumpiness," and "timidity" from repressed fear; and happiness or "good humor" from controlled joy.

2. Children's Emotions Are Intense. The young child's emotional outbursts are characterized by an intensity which is seldom observed in the emotional reactions of an adult. His emotional responses lack gradations or degrees of intensity, with the result that his response to a trivial situation will call forth an emotional reaction of as great intensity as a situation of a more serious type (Hollingworth, 1928; Isaacs, 1940; Bousfield and Orbison, 1952). To adults, unfamiliar with childish behavior, the intense emotional reactions of a little child to a petty annoyance are the source of great surprise and wonder. This is especially true in the case of fear, anger, and joy, all of which are expressed in pronounced overt responses (Isaacs, 1940). The disturbed child has the same emotional development as a normal, well-adjusted child, but in the disturbed child the negative emotions are more frequent and more intense than in the well-adjusted child (Moustakas, 1955).

3. Children's Emotions Are Transitory. The transitory character of the young child's emotions, which results in a rapid shift from laughter to tears, from anger to smiles, or from jealousy to affection, is incomprehensible to many adults because it is so different from the way in which the typical adult expresses his feelings. The child's behavior, which at one minute is characterized by an intense outburst of one emotion, suddenly shifts to an equally intense outburst of a totally different emotional reaction. Reactions from extreme shyness to extreme exuberance and boisterousness are characteristic of preschool children (Ilg et al., 1949).

This transitory characteristic of the child's emotional behavior leads many adults to question whether the child feels as deeply as an adult does. The rapid shift from one emotional response to another would suggest that he does not. But this may be due to other causes than shallowness of feeling. Because he expresses his emotions in an unreserved manner, thereby clearing his system of pent-up emotions; because of lack of complete understanding of the situation, owing to his immature intellectual development and limited experiences; and because of a shorter attention span which makes it possible for him to be diverted easily, the little child's emotions swing quickly from one emotional extreme to another. The child's emotional states are similar to those of a person whose frontal lobes have been removed and whose emotional behavior is described as "childish" because it is lacking in depth, because it is uninhibited, and because transitions from one emotional state to another occur rapidly. This is in marked contrast to "mature" emotional behavior which is characterized by greater stability (Bousfield and Orbison, 1952).

4. Children's Emotions Appear Frequently. Children's emotions occur more frequently, on the average, than do those of the typical adult. The reason for this is that as the child grows older, he has greater ability to make adjustments to situations that justifiably call forth emotional reactions than he had when he was younger and less experienced. Because he has learned that social disapproval or punishment often follows an emotional outburst, he tries to meet situations by reactions other than emotional ones. The result is a gradual decrease in the frequency of emotional responses.

5. Children's Emotional Responses Are Different. Observations of children of different ages show wide variability in their emotional responses. Among newborn infants, the patterns of response are similar. Gradually, however, as the influences of learning and environment are felt, the behavior accompanying the different emotions is individualized. One child in fear will run out of the room, another will hide behind his mother's skirt, while still another will stand his ground and cry. The same is true for all other emotional patterns.

Johnson (1936) presented nursery-school children with three carefully controlled laboratory situations designed to be annoying or fear provoking. Marked differences in emotional responses, ranging from caution and timidity to soliciting help from others, were observed. Differences in emotional responses of children to health examinations have been reported by Shirley and Poyntz (1945). Some children cried, some actively resisted, and some tried to withdraw. Similar results have been reported when children receive dental treatment. Some cry, some smile or laugh, and others display no emotional reaction at all (Bell, 1943).

6. Emotions Can Be Detected by Symptoms of Behavior. An adult is generally able to hide his feelings and emotions well enough so that it is difficult for others to know just how he feels. Not so with children. Even though they may not show their emotional reactions directly in behavior related to the way they feel, their emotionality can be detected by tension, restlessness, fidgeting, daydreaming, frequency of micturition, nervous mannerisms as nail biting, thumb sucking, eye blinking, and rubbing the genitals, speech difficulties, lack of appetite, babyish behavior, frequent crying, obstinacy, and hysterical outbursts. Boys generally show more symptoms of emotionality than do girls (Coleman and McCalley, 1948; Ilg et al., 1949; Malone and Massler, 1952; McCarthy, 1954).

7. Changes in Strength of Emotions. At certain ages, certain emotions are strong and then wane. Other emotions, formerly weak, later become strong. For example, little children show marked timidity in the presence of strangers or in strange places. Later, when they realize there is nothing to be afraid of, their timidity wanes. Similarly, temper tantrums have been found to reach their peak before the child enters school, after which time they decrease not only in frequency but also in intensity (Goodenough, 1931; Merry and Merry, 1950). Figure 34 shows changes in four emotional patterns. This apparent instability in emotional strength is due partly to changes in the strength of drives, partly to the development of the child's

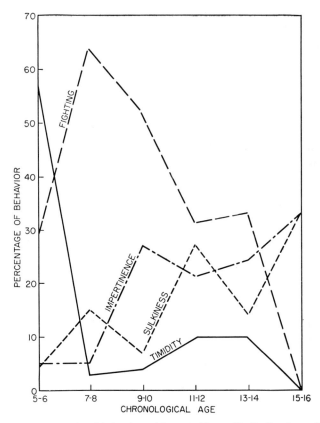

Fig. 34. Changes in emotional behavior with age. (*From K. C. Garrison, Growth and development, Longmans, 1952. Used by permission.*)

intellectual capacities, and partly to his changes in interests. As Cole (1954) has pointed out, "It may suddenly strike a third-grade child that school-work is competitive, and this new idea may generate in him a feeling of shame because he has thus far puttered happily about at the bottom of the class."

8. Changes in Emotional Expressions. The little child wants what he wants when he wants it. He does not stop to consider whether this will be harmful to him or to others, nor does he consider whether the price he will have to pay is worthwhile. Unless he gets what he wants, he will become angry and fly into a fit of temper. Similarly, when frightened, he does not hesitate to run away and hide or to show his fear by crying. Even when happy, he does not wait to express it at a convenient time or place. He smiles or laughs, even though this may appear to others to be a case of "gloating" (Mahler, 1945; Breckenridge and Vincent, 1955).

At a very early age, parents try to teach their children to control their emotional expressions by punishment, criticism, reasoning, or approval, depending on the child's age and the parents' concepts of the best methods of child training. Later the child is confronted with pressures from the social group outside the home to restrain his emotional expressions. He discovers that the emotional outbursts that had proved to be effective means to an end are now regarded as "babyish." At home and in school, his desire for conformity to group approval in this area of his behavior may become so strong that it becomes a form of "adaptive anxiety" (Davis and Havighurst, 1947). By the time his childhood days are over, the child knows that social approval is dependent upon the degree of control he is able to exert over the expressions of his emotions.

Some children are fortunate in learning how to control their emotional behavior to conform to socially approved patterns, while at the same time deriving satisfaction for their own needs. This they learn mainly from guidance on the part of parents and teachers (Bankston, 1954). In most cases, however, emotions are "driven underground." As Jersild (1954) has emphasized, "The child learns to disguise his feelings, or to hide them, or to express them in devious ways. Many children also learn to disapprove of themselves for having intense feelings. But they cannot rid themselves of their inborn (and essential) tendencies to be frightened, angry, grief-stricken, and ashamed. . . . They are under pressure to play false with their feelings, and a child does this when he is seething with resentment against his elders, but, instead of showing this directly, he breaks bottles on a public highway as though it were 'just for fun.' . . . Children are under pressure also to conceal their emotions from themselves, to play false with themselves. . . . This appears noticeably in connection with feelings springing from grief, sorrow, pain, or anxiety so acute that the individual feels helpless and feels like breaking into tears" (pp. 303–304).

COMMON EMOTIONAL PATTERNS OF CHILDHOOD

After the early months of babyhood have passed, a number of differentiated emotional patterns, each with its own specific form of behavior, may be observed. The most common of the emotional patterns characteristically found in childhood, the stimuli which arouse them, and the form of response made, are the following.

1. FEAR

A baby is protected as much as possible from fear-provoking stimuli, such as strange people and places, loud noises, and people or things coming upon him suddenly and unexpectedly. However, these days of protection are limited. Before the end of the first year of life, fear-provoking stimuli begin to affect the baby. With each passing year, as the child's horizons broaden and as his independence from parental protection increases, there are more and more things that are likely to frighten him. Furthermore, as his intellectual development progresses, he recognizes threats in objects, situations, or even people, which formerly he was incapable of perceiving. As a result, his fears are not only more numerous, but they are likely to be more intense. That fears of children are not the product of the culture may be seen by the fact that Dakota Indian children have been found to have fears similar to American children (Wallis, 1954).

Fear is valuable to a child only so long as it is kept from becoming too intense and thus serves as a warning of danger. Unfortunately, most children learn to fear things which are not dangerous, and this fear acts as a block to action that might prove to be useful or enjoyable to them. Of even greater seriousness, many children develop so many and such intense fears that their physical and mental well-being is affected. Unless satisfactory outlets are provided for this emotional tension, the child's health will be adversely affected, his outlook on life will be warped, and his adjustments to people will be unfavorable. Fear, thus, becomes a handicap to a child instead of a warning of potential dangers (Merry and Merry, 1950). This is especially true of needless fears, many of which are irrational (Jersild, 1948).

Origin of Fears. Whether fears are rational or irrational, they both have their foundations in the child's experiences (Jersild, 1948). Sometimes children are unaware of their fears and merely experience states of *anxiety,* or a generalized form of fear, which makes them unduly apprehensive in situations where there is nothing to fear or causes them to take a defensive reaction, thus avoiding possibilities of experiencing a situation which might lead to fear (Kestenberg, 1946). While it is true that most fears are learned, they are nevertheless not all learned in the same way. Some fears come from direct association of experiences with stimuli that naturally arouse fear, such as loud, harsh noises. Others are acquired through imitation of those who are afraid, such as fear of thunderstorms which has been learned by imitating the fear behavior of a parent, sibling, or playmate. The third type of fear comes as an aftermath of some unpleasant experience, as fears of doctors, dentists, hospitals, large animals, and certain people. Unpleasant dreams may give rise to such fears (Watson, 1925; Jersild and Holmes, 1935; Lawton, 1938; Kestenberg, 1946; Jersild, 1948, 1954).

What Children Fear. What frightens a child depends upon many factors, especially the child's age, his past experiences, and the level of his intellectual development. Thus, no two children can be expected to have exactly the same fears, though there is evidence, from studies of large groups of children of different ages, that there are certain fears characteristically found at different ages. These might be called the *typical fears* of children of those ages. Not all children will experience all fears characteristic of their age levels, and some will have fears infrequently found, because of their own individual experiences, which may differ markedly from the experiences of other children of their age level.

In spite of the restricted environment of *babyhood,* even young babies have some fears. Before babyhood is over, the number of fears has increased. Most babies learn to fear certain things, especially those associated with loud noises or falling. In general, the most common fears of babyhood are loud noises, animals, strange persons, places, or objects, dark rooms, high places, sudden displacement, being alone, and pain (Watson, 1925; Hagman, 1932; Jersild and Holmes, 1935; Holmes, 1936; Jersild, 1936, 1954, 1954a; Lawton, 1938; Merry and Merry, 1950; Garrison, 1952; Breckenridge and Vincent, 1955).

Young children are afraid of more things than either the baby or the older child. This is the peak period of fear in the normal pattern of development. The young child is capable of recognizing dangers which formerly he was unable to recognize, but his lack of experience is not adequate to enable him to realize that those dangers may not be personal threats. For example, fear of snakes usually appears between the ages of 3½ and 4 years, and then wanes when the child is capable of realizing how remote a threat a snake in a zoo is to him (Jones and Jones, 1928). Likewise, growth of memory makes it possible for the young child to remember many unpleasant or terrifying past experiences, such as visits to a doctor or dentist. Then, too, development of imagination, without accompanying increase in reasoning ability, encourages the young child to develop many fears related to imaginary experiences, animals, or people he has heard or read about. In a physical threat situation, such as walking a plank, young children have been found to be frightened at first by the novelty of the situation and to ask for help. Those who were most dependent were found to be those who had been accustomed to depending most on their mothers at home (Heathers, 1953).

Fear among young children is general rather than specific at first. It is more like panic or emotional tension than a fear of a specific thing. Later it becomes more specific and is associated with specific objects, people, or situations. For example, a very young child is frightened by any unusual experience, such as an illness or a new method of handling, as toilet training or feeding with a different eating utensil, or by the possibility of being separated from a loved one, especially the mother. Later, such general fears wane and are replaced by more specific fears associated with past experiences.

Many fears of young children are carried over from babyhood, especially fears of being left alone, of dark places, of strange people and places, of animals, of high places, and of loud noises. Many of the new fears they acquire are *imaginary* in nature, as their fears of ghosts, robbers, skeletons, boogies, of characters and places they have heard about in the stories read to them or have seen in movies and on television. Their fears of animals are more related to strange and unusual animals than to those they come in contact with in daily life, such as dogs, cats, and horses (Hagman, 1932; Holmes, 1935; Jersild and Holmes, 1935; Jersild, 1936, 1954, 1954a; Lawton, 1938; Isaacs et al., 1941; Edelston, 1943; Gesell and Ilg, 1946; Ilg et al., 1949; Merry and Merry, 1950; Garrison, 1952; Prugh et al., 1953; Breckenridge and Vincent, 1955).

In the preschool period, marked changes have been found, not only in the type of object or situation which arouses fear, but also in the number and severity of fears as the child grows older. Fear of animals is progressively more frequent up to four years and declines afterward, as is true also of fears of strange people, objects, and situations, of noises, and of strange events. Fears of the dark and being alone, of the imaginary, fanciful and supernatural increase with age. This is especially true of fears associated with death and of characters recalled from stories and pictures. Before the child enters school, there is a beginning of fears of possible accidents, ill-health, dying, and of ridicule (Jersild and Holmes, 1935; Pratt, 1945). There is a definite and consistent decrease in number and severity of fears as the child grows older. For three-year-olds, for example, the average number of fears has been reported to be 5.5 as contrasted with an average of 3.2 fears for six-year-olds (Jersild and Holmes, 1935b).

After children enter school, there is a marked change in the type of fears they experience. While they still show some fears of tangible objects and concrete situations, their fears are concentrated on imaginary, fanciful, supernatural, or remote dangers; on the dark and imaginary creatures associated with the dark; on death or being injured; on the elements, especially thunder, lightning, and storms; and on characters recalled from stories, movies, comics, and television. There is a marked increase in fears related to self or status. Not only do older children show greater fears of bodily injury and illness than do younger children, but they also are afraid of being ridiculed, of being "different," and of failures (Holmes, 1935; Jersild and Holmes, 1935; Pratt, 1945; England, 1946; Gesell and Ilg, 1946; Winker, 1949; Jersild, 1954, 1954a). At this age, sex differences in things feared are marked. Girls not only show more fears than do boys, but they also are afraid of different things. In the case of animals, for example, boys are more afraid of wild animals, while girls are more afraid of insects and spiders. School work troubles boys more, while girls are more troubled about illness, disease, darkness, and night (Pratt, 1945).

Characteristics of Fear Stimuli. In spite of the large number of stimuli that have been observed to arouse fear in children, several characteristics stand out as all-important. This suggests that it is not the stimulus itself, but rather *the way that it is presented,* that determines whether or not a fear response will be aroused. An important characteristic of all fear stimuli is that they occur *suddenly and unexpectedly,* which gives the child little opportunity to adjust himself to the changed condition (Jones and Jones, 1928; Kestenberg, 1946). Fear of strangers, which most babies show, is due in part to the fact that the baby is adjusted to see a familiar face and is unable to adjust himself at first to the sudden appearance of a stranger (Watson, 1925). As the child grows older and becomes more mature intellectually, he can adjust himself more quickly to sudden and unexpected circumstances.

Closely related to the qualities of suddenness and unexpectedness is that of *novelty* or *strangeness.* Stimuli that embody the element of novelty are apt to arouse fear, while the same stimuli, after the element of novelty has disappeared, will not arouse fear. Many instances of fear in the presence of familiar people can be traced to the fact that they are dressed in an unfamiliar way, as when the child's nurse wears her street clothes in place of the accustomed uniform. As soon as the child recognizes the nurse and the element of novelty in her appearance disappears, the fear itself disappears.

Effect of Child's Condition. The child's condition, physical and psychological, at the time the fear stimulus is presented, will determine to a large extent how he will respond. If he is tired, hungry, or emotionally disturbed, he will respond with greater fear than if his condition were more favorable. Likewise, if he is alone, his reaction will be different from what it would be if he were with his mother, his nurse, or others in whom he has confidence. Should he remember similar experiences which, in the past, were unpleasant or even terrifying, he will react with fear to the new situation, which, in and of itself, would normally not arouse fear but which reminds him of the old, terrifying experience.

A number of studies have revealed how fear varies according to the condition of the child. Bright children are aware of the possibilities of danger in situations in which their less bright contemporaries see no danger, and as a result, the bright child is likely to show more fears (Boston, 1939). Children from better homes have more fears than do those from poorer homes. Likewise, their fears are more related to their personal safety, as fears of accidents and illness, while the fears of children from poorer homes are concentrated more on the supernatural and things remote from their experience (Jersild and Holmes, 1935; Jersild, 1936; Merry and Merry, 1950). Children who have been subjected to punishments where fear and threats of fear are used have more fears than do children subjected to different types of punishment (Jersild, 1954a).

The personality pattern of the child plays an important role in determining his susceptibility to fear. Children who are insecure show a greater tendency to be easily frightened than do children who are emotionally more secure (Pritchard and O'jemann, 1941). Likewise, anything that lowers the child's self-confidence will increase his susceptibility to fear (Jersild, 1954). Memories of past terrifying experiences not only make the child afraid of similar experiences but increase his susceptibility to all fear stimuli (John, 1941). Being with others who are frightened makes a child more susceptible to fear, while being with those who are calm decreases this susceptibility (Hagman, 1932; John, 1941). As the number of individuals in a group increases, fears are shared, and this increases the total number of different fears for each child (Pratt, 1945).

Thus it becomes apparent that it is difficult to predict when a child will be frightened and what will give rise to his fear. Fear is not dependent on a given stimulus alone, such as a loud noise, strange face, or animal, but on the surrounding circumstances, the manner in which the stimulus is presented, the child's past experiences, the child's present physiological and psychological condition, and many related circumstances. One child will show fear and another will show no fear in identical situations. The only way one can predict whether or not a child will be frightened in a particular situation and how intense his fear will be is by acquiring a knowledge of the child's past history of fear reactions and his present physiological and psychological condition.

Fear Response Patterns. Fear displays itself in an *attempt to withdraw* from the object that aroused it. Accompanying this is whimpering, crying, a sudden and temporary holding of the breath, and a checking of the activity the child is engaged in. Under three years of age, the response occurring in fear is typically one of helplessness and the cry is the baby's call for help. He hides his face and gets as far away from the feared object as he can, by creeping or walking. He hides behind a person or a piece of furniture and remains there until the fear subsides, or until he feels that it is safe to emerge.

As the child grows older, the overt responses in fear are checked as a result of social pressure. The crying reactions cease, though the characteristic facial expressions remain and the child withdraws from the feared object. The 3½-year-old, for example, protects himself from fear stimuli by saying, "No," or "I can't do it," or by isolation from the things that aroused his fear (Ilg et al., 1949).

Older children not only inhibit the impulse to show fear when confronted with a fear situation, but they try to keep away from any situation if they have any reason to believe it might prove to be frightening. If confronted with a fear stimulus, they may express their fear indirectly in a general motor discharge, more like a temper outburst than a fear reaction (Kestenberg, 1946). Shyness, which is a type of fear reaction, consists of nervous mannerisms such as pulling at the ears or clothing, bending the head to one side, and then coyly raising it to look at others (Shirley, 1931a).

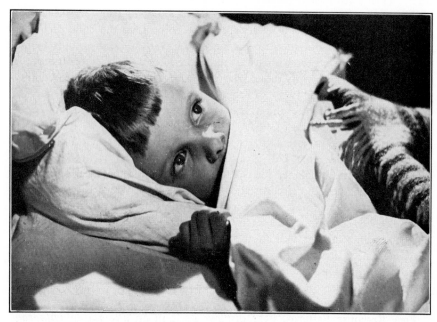

Changes in emotional expression occur with age. The older child does not run away and hide when frightened but covers his head so he will not see the frightening object. (*From Child Development, a McGraw-Hill Text-Film.*)

How marked is the effect of social pressure on the child's fear reaction has been explained thus by Jersild (1954):

By virtue of the premium that is placed on not being afraid, of not revealing that he is afraid, the child may be driven to the point that one of his fears is the fear of showing fear. Many children, at quite an early age, get the idea that it is shameful to be afraid. In many persons, by the time they are adult, this goes to the extent that they are so afraid at the thought of revealing fear that they do not dare to appeal for help. By a tragic twist of logic, some such people see themselves not as frightened persons but as brave people who have the courage to go it alone (pp. 346–347).

Controlling Fear. Because fear, except as a restraint on action in the presence of danger, is more harmful than helpful to a child, it is desirable to prevent its appearance as much as possible. Merely diverting a child's attention from something he might fear or that he is beginning to show signs of fearing is only a temporary measure but fails to be of any value when the child must meet a situation alone (Morgan, 1942). To avoid the fear that is almost inevitable when a child is suddenly and unexpectedly confronted with a new and different stimulus, forewarnings in preparation for this may prove to ward off later fear (Burlingham and Freud, 1949). However, parents and teachers cannot always anticipate what a child will fear and, as a result, cannot always forewarn him of it. Then, too, as Jersild (1954) has pointed out, "The very fact that his elders go out of

Social imitation, in which the child is given an adult model of fearlessness, is one of the best ways of overcoming fear. (*From Child Development, a McGraw-Hill Text-Film.*)

their way to forewarn him may, under some conditions, endow an event with terrifying qualities and thus aggravate rather than forestall a child's fear."

Once a fear has been learned, it is difficult to eliminate or to control it. This is especially true of fears in which the child is conscious of only certain aspects of the past experiences that have conditioned him to respond with fear to this new situation (English and Pearson, 1945). Of the many techniques tried in the elimination of fears, the ones that have been found to produce the best results are giving the child an opportunity to become acquainted with the feared stimulus of his own accord; leading him gradually into contact with the thing he fears; encouraging him to acquire skills that will be of specific aid to him in dealing with the feared situation; building up pleasant associations with the feared object; verbal explanations and reassurance, combined with a practical demonstration of the harmlessness of the feared object; social imitation in which the child is given an adult model of fearlessness; and an opportunity for self-expression which will lead to self-scrutiny and personal reorientation, thus resulting in a changed concept of self (Jones, 1924a; Hagman, 1932; Jersild and Holmes, 1935a; Holmes, 1936; Slater et al., 1939; Conn, 1941; Taylor, 1942; Updegraff, 1942; Merry and Merry, 1950; Garrison, 1952; Jersild, 1954, 1954a).

Ineffective techniques, on the other hand, consist of ignoring the child's fears; coercing the child to come in contact with the feared situation by physical force, scoldings, ridicule, or invidious comparisons; completely removing the cause of the fear for the time; verbal appeal to the child to be brave; and offering palliatives for the child's symptoms of fear (Jones, 1924a; Jersild and Holmes, 1935a; Jersild, 1954). That many of the methods used to eliminate children's fears are not effective has been shown by studies of adult recalls of childhood experiences. Many of these recalls are of experiences which were intense in childhood, such as fears of animals; of dangers through falling, drowning, illness, and operations; of the supernatural; of the dark; of being alone; of failure; and of being ridiculed (Jersild and Holmes, 1935; Bühler, 1952; Jersild, 1954).

2. WORRY

Worry is an imaginary form of fear. It is a fear not aroused directly by a stimulus from the child's environment. It may come from imagining situations which could arise and which might, in turn, affect the child. It may also come from books, movies, comics, the radio, or other popular recreations. Because worries are caused by imaginary rather than real stimuli, they are not found among very young children. The child must reach a stage of intellectual development in which it is possible for him to imagine things not immediately present before he is capable of worrying.

That many of the so-called "fears" of older children are, in reality not actual fears but "worries," in the sense that they are the product of the child's imagination rather than the direct response to a stimulus from the child's environment, has been shown by studies of what children say they are afraid of and what they say are the "worst happenings" they have experienced. For example, 14 per cent of a group of children questioned said they were afraid of animals, but only 2 per cent of the group had ever been attacked by animals. Nineteen per cent claimed to be afraid of ghosts, but none had, of course, ever seen a ghost (Jersild et al., 1933). Worries about school work and not being promoted are very common. In one group of elementary-school children, 53 per cent said they worried about not being promoted, while the promotion policy of the school was to promote all but about 1 per cent of each class (Jersild et al., 1941).

Thus it is apparent that worries are usually illogical and exaggerations of what is likely to happen. However, they are normal in childhood and are found in even the best-adjusted children (Jersild, 1954a). When children get together and talk about their fears, there is a tendency for each child in the group to imagine that such experiences could happen to him. As a result, he develops new worries, many of which have no relationship to his own experiences (Pratt, 1945).

Common Worries. As is true of fears, there are marked individual differences in what children of different ages worry about. There are, however, certain trends that are commonly found among American children at different ages. The most common worries center around home and family relationships and school problems, with the latter becoming more common as children grow older and progress further in school. Typical family worries relate to the health and safety of members of the family and being scolded or punished by the father or the mother. School worries center around being late for school, failing tests, being scolded or punished by the teacher, school reports, and being left behind in school. In addition to home and school worries, children are concerned about their health, about dying or being killed, about their personal and social adequacy, about economic problems, and about their clothes. School worries, on the whole, are more common than out-of-school worries. Girls worry more than boys, especially about school and safety (Zeligs, 1939, 1945; Pintner and Lev, 1940; Jersild et al., 1941; Jersild, 1954, 1954a).

How much worries of children are influenced by social pressures, especially those from the home environment, has been demonstrated in a study in which worries of children in 1923 were compared with worries in 1943. Worries about storms showed a marked decrease, as illustrated in Fig. 35. The explanation given for this decrease is the change in attitudes toward natural phenomena in the past several decades. No longer is there the old-fashioned fearful gathering of the family during a thunderstorm at night, so prevalent in past generations. Thus the child of today is not shown a pattern of worry, as was true in the past. Similarly, declines in worries about sickness, accidents, diseases, germs, tuberculosis, and death may be traced to modern medical methods, which have made illness less terrifying to adults and, hence, less of a source of worry to children. Changes in social attitudes toward sin and morals have likewise been reflected in a decline in children's worries about these matters (Pressey, 1946).

Anxiety. Worries, especially when frequent and intense, may lead to *anxiety*, a "painful uneasiness of mind concerning impending or anticipated ill." Many worries, like fears, are irrational. They come not from the object or situation feared but represent a projection of uneasiness or distress within the individual (Jersild, 1954, 1954a). There has been found to be a strong relationship between the number and severity of children's worries and psychoneurotic traits (Zeligs, 1939). Thus, children who are prone to worry more than one normally finds at their age level are likely to develop a state of anxiety which interferes with their adjustments.

The child, like the adult, is often unaware of the cause of his anxiety. He does not realize that it comes from feelings of insecurity within himself and not from the external situation to which he projects his fear. In fear, the child can perceive the threat situation, while in anxiety, there is merely

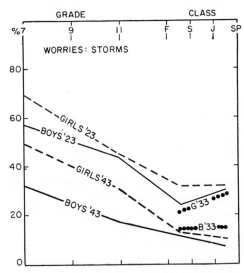

Fig. 35. Decline in worry about storms resulting from changes in social pressures. (*From S. L. Pressey, Changes from* 1923 *to* 1943 *in the attitudes of public school and university students, J. Psychol.,* 1946, **21**, 173–188. *Used by permission.*)

a general state of uneasiness he cannot perceive (Jersild, 1954). Anxiety tends to increase with age. It is more commonly associated with child-child relationships than with child-adult relationships or with routine activities, such as going to bed alone (Dorkey and Amen, 1947). Girls, on the whole, tend to experience greater anxiety than do boys. Generalized anxiety is more common among older children than any one specific fear (Cummings, 1944).

3. ANGER

Anger is a more frequent emotional response in childhood than fear (1) because there are more anger-provoking than fear-provoking stimuli in the child's environment and (2) because many children discover at an early age that anger is a good way to get attention or to satisfy their desires. Each year, as the child grows older, there is an increase in the number of situations that arouse his anger. The result is that the child *displays more angry reactions,* of one form or another, with increased age, *while the fear reactions decrease,* owing to his increased ability to realize that in most instances there is no real need for fear.

There is, however, a close relationship between fear and anger. Sometimes the child vacillates between the two, while at other times, both fear and anger are aroused at the same time and by the same stimulus (Kepler, 1934; Anastasi et al., 1948; Jersild, 1954a). In a well-protected environment, where a child can be shielded from fears more than from anger-producing stimuli, anger is likely to be more common than fear (Felder, 1932). However, as Jersild (1954a) has pointed out, this difference may be more apparent than real. There are greater social pressures on the child to conceal his fears than his angers, and, furthermore, the child frequently finds means of avoiding situations he dreads, thus eliminating what might otherwise have been a display of fear.

Stimuli to Anger. In general, the *situations that give rise to angry responses* consist of those involving body restraint; interference with movements the child wishes to make either by others or by his own inabilities; blocking of activities already in progress; thwarting of wishes, plans, and purposes the child wants to carry out; or a number of cumulative irritations. As Jersild (1954a) has pointed out, "The occasions that elicit anger parallel the course of development. A child's susceptibility to anger at any given maturity level is influenced by the *limitations* and by the *urges, strivings,* and *activity tendencies* that are characteristic of that level."

Babies respond with angry outbursts to minor physical discomforts, interference with physical activities, and activities connected with physical care, as bathing and dressing. His growing independence makes him want to do some of these things for himself. Then, when he is given an opportunity to do more for himself, he often becomes angry at his own ineptitude. If he cannot put a garment on or get food to his mouth with a spoon or fork, he is angry. His inability to make himself understood through his babblings or his early attempts at speech likewise irritates him. Then, too, he becomes angry if people do not give him as much attention as he craves or if his possessions are interfered with.

Preschool children are angered by many of the same conditions that anger babies. They especially resent interference with their possessions, they object to having to do what they are told to do, and they fight continuously with other children who grab their toys or interfere with their play activities. Their feelings are easily hurt by comments from others or by punishments. And they are angry when the toys or objects they try to handle do not work out as they want them to or if they make mistakes in what they are attempting to do (Watson, 1925; Goodenough, 1931; Felder, 1932; Ricketts, 1934; Gesell and Ilg, 1946; Ilg et al., 1949; Merry and Merry, 1950; Garrison, 1952; Jersild, 1954, 1954a; Breckenridge and Vincent, 1955). There is one common element in the temper tantrums of young children, a response to *compulsion.* The tantrum occurs when the child is told to do something he does not want to do, when he is denied something he wishes to have, when there is some change in the routine of his daily life, or when he fails to achieve something he is trying to do (Isaacs, 1940).

In an *older child,* any thwarting of desires, interruption of activities in progress, constant faultfinding, teasing, "lecturing," or making unfavorable comparisons with other children will lead to anger. He likewise becomes angry at his own mistakes and ineptitude, when he feels that he or his friends are unjustly reprimanded or punished, or when he is slighted, neglected, or ridiculed by other children. As his interests outside the home increase, there are more sources of annoyance and anger outside the home than in the home (Jersild and Tasch, 1949; Jersild, 1954a). Boys have been found to be easily irritated by such inconveniences and annoyances as a flat tire on their bicycles, doing things they don't like, disappointments and not getting what was promised them, while for girls, the chief irritations proved to be not being permitted to play outside, having their hair pulled, or being punched (Zeligs, 1941).

Social annoyances most commonly reported by older children consisted of being blamed for something they had not done, or by other persons' cheating, doing unfair things, or bullying. At home they were annoyed when whipped or scolded, especially for something they had not done. School annoyances included getting low marks, being with teachers who have pets, having the mother come to school, or having certain teachers. Personal-conduct annoyances most frequently reported included cursing, telling lies, biting fingernails, having bad habits, and being accused of lying (Zeligs, 1945). The older child frequently sets goals beyond his abilities, and when he fails to reach these goals, he becomes angry at himself or tries to find a scapegoat to blame for his failures.

The older child experiences more emotional tension from frustrations than does the young child. *Frustration* is the feeling of helplessness, disappointment, inadequacy, or anxiety that comes whenever any drive is blocked (Cole, 1954). In his desire to be independent, the older child constantly finds blocks in his path. His parents, his teachers, or society do not permit him to do what he wants to do. Sometimes the blocks are of his own making. He wants to do certain things for which he has neither the training, skill, or experience. He then becomes angry when this desire is thwarted.

Anger Responses. The *form of expression* of anger *varies* from one child to another, owing partly to environmental restraint and partly to learning.

In babies and very young children, individual differences are much less pronounced than they are later in childhood and adolescence. In spite of the fact that children express their anger in different ways, most expressions can be classed in two major categories, *impulsive* and *inhibited*. Impulsive expressions consist of responses directed outward against a person or object that has angered the child. Inhibited responses, on the other hand, are kept under control or "bottled up" within the child. Impulsive responses, especially among older children who are able to keep their responses under better control than do young children, are found mostly among children whose parents are inconsistent and immature and who do not, as a result, give their children the necessary motivation to control aggression (Beeler, 1953).

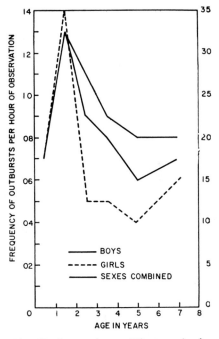

While there are marked variations in the anger response among different children of different ages, and even in the same child in different situations, there are certain responses which are *typical* of different age levels. In *babies,* anger responses are, at first, random and diffuse. The baby cries, screams, kicks, arches his back, struggles, and twists his whole body. Later, he directs his actions toward the person or object that has angered him. He throws himself down on the floor, kicks, screams, hits, bites, holds his breath, and does

Fig. 36. Age and sex differences in frequency of anger outbursts. (*Based on material from F. L. Goodenough, Anger in young children, University of Minnesota Press, 1931. From K. C. Garrison, Growth and development, Longmans, 1952. Used by permission.*)

anything he can to harm anyone or anything in his reach. He throws things; he breaks whatever he can lay his hands on; he "gets rough" with other children, animals, and his parents; he slaps, pokes, pushes, and spits (Goodenough, 1931; Gesell and Ilg, 1946; Merry and Merry, 1950; Garrison, 1952; Jersild, 1954, 1954a; Breckenridge and Vincent, 1955).

During the preschool years, temper tantrums reach their peak, generally between the ages of two and four years, after which there is a decline in the frequency and intensity of the child's angry outbursts. See Fig. 36. The violence of the tantrum is usually out of all proportion to the stimulus that gave rise to it. However, as temper tantrums seem to occur among all children of all circumstances at approximately the same ages, there is reason to believe that they are a normal phenomenon of growth (Goodenough, 1931; Isaacs, 1940; Ilg et al., 1949). Most children, owing partly to social pressure and partly to increased ability to do the things they want to do, combined with an understanding of why they are not permitted to do certain things, have fewer and fewer tantrums as they grow older (Goodenough, 1931; Felder, 1932; Ricketts, 1934; Isaacs, 1940; Merry, 1943; Geleerd, 1945; Gesell and Ilg, 1946, 1949; Merry and Merry, 1950; Jersild, 1954, 1954a).

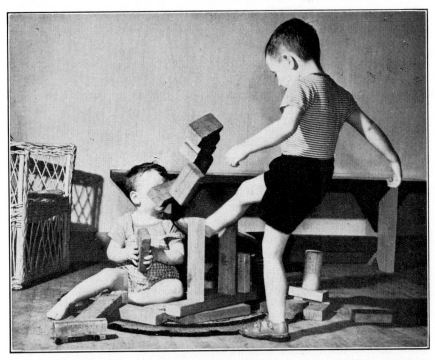

Kicking is a common expression of anger in young children. (*From Child Development, a McGraw-Hill Text-Film.*)

A temper tantrum may last only a few minutes, rarely more than five minutes, but it is violent and directed against a person or thing that the child believes was responsible for thwarting some desire on his part. The child is more destructive than the baby in his attacks, and he does not hesitate to hurt others by any method he can, whether it be hitting, kicking, biting, spitting, punching, poking, pulling, etc. If he is thwarted in his efforts to reach the person or thing that angered him, he is likely to throw himself on the floor, kick, scream, hold his breath, sob, or do anything he has discovered from past experience will give him attention and perhaps remove the obstacle that stood in the way of his doing what he wanted to do.

Little children soon add new responses to the typical temper-tantrum pattern. At the age of four years, language is added to the repertoire of responses, and this gradually replaces much of the typical temper-tantrum behavior. The child uses name calling, boasting, tattling, threats of running away and of killing the offender, or sarcasm and mimicry. In addition to verbal fighting, other expressions of anger, less commonly found, consist of doing forbidden things, such as overturning furniture or opening things he has been forbidden to touch; trying to hurt himself, especially by biting and head banging; finding a scapegoat, especially a younger child or animal, and venting anger on him; or they have their outlet in aggressive fantasy play (Goodenough, 1931; Felder, 1932; Caille, 1933; Ricketts, 1934; Jersild and Markey, 1935; Isaacs, 1940; Merry, 1943; Gesell and Ilg, 1946; Merry and Merry, 1950; Garrison, 1952; Jersild, 1954, 1954a; Breckenridge and Vincent, 1955).

The *older child* is forced to learn new ways to express his anger if he wants to avoid social disapproval. As Jersild (1954a) has commented, "No sooner has a child acquired the ability to direct his anger at the object of his wrath than he comes under pressure to inhibit his expression of anger. For a child to give vent to his anger is uncomfortable and annoying to others and it may even be dangerous to others or to the child himself. . . . So in the process of development human beings learn a great variety of ways of giving vent to anger and hostility other than in open and direct attack" (p. 886). Angry outbursts decrease, thus, from social pressures, from the child's increase in skills which overcome some of his ineptitude, and from strenuous play which helps to act as a "safety valve" for pent-up emotional energy (Updegraff and Keister, 1937; Fite, 1940; Baruch, 1941; Korner, 1947).

Temper outbursts become increasingly less violent with each passing year. While older children continue to fight, kick, push, tease, poke, throw stones, and bully, they gradually substitute other responses which meet with less social disapproval than overt aggression does. Verbal attacks in the form of name calling, ridicule, sarcastic comments, swearing, boasting, threats, rudeness, and sauciness gradually replace bodily attacks. When an older child is angry at a classmate, he excludes him from the group activities and often refuses to speak to him. He may take out his anger on animals, smaller children, children against whom there is some prejudice, or even on his parents and relatives. Or he may refuse to do what he is expected to do, or if forced to do so, does as badly as possible, out of spite. Some children show their anger by hurt feelings, sullenness, feeling abused, feeling sorry for themselves, threatening to run away, or even inflicting physical pain on themselves in a fit of anger. Thus, as it becomes apparent, the form of expression of anger among older children is much more varied than the anger expressions of babies or even of younger children (Osborne, 1937; Gesell and Ilg, 1946, 1949; Frenkel-Brunswik, 1948; Merry and Merry, 1950; Horney, 1951; Garrison, 1952; Jersild, 1954, 1954a; Breckenridge and Vincent, 1955).

As anger soon *settles into a habit,* if called forth frequently, it is obviously wise to avoid anger-arousing situations whenever possible. The child must learn when to become angry and when not. Thus, control consists of directing the use of anger into socially acceptable channels rather than restraining it. Too much frustration without adequate outlet for anger may result in temporary or permanent harm to the child's developing personality. How a child will respond to frustration will depend largely upon his age and past experiences in meeting anger-provoking situations. Some children are aggressive and assertive; others are withdrawn and insecure; others feel sorry for themselves; while others respond by negativistic actions, crying and doing just the opposite of what they are supposed to do (Frederiksen, 1942; Seashore and Bavelas, 1942; Sargent, 1945; Symonds, 1949; Merry and Merry, 1950; Jersild, 1954, 1954a).

4. Jealousy

Jealousy is a normal response to actual, supposed, or threatened loss of affection (Vollmer, 1946). It is an outgrowth of anger, giving rise to an attitude of resentment directed toward people, while anger may be directed toward people, toward oneself, or toward things. Jealousy may take the form of an outburst closely resembling a temper tantrum, or it may take forms in which the resentment the individual feels is barely recognizable. Often there is some fear combined with anger in the jealousy pattern. The jealous person feels insecure in his relationship with a loved one and is afraid of losing status in that person's affection (Jersild, 1954). What causes jealousy, and what form it takes, is greatly influenced by training and the treatment the individual receives from others. Whatever form it takes, it leads to unhappiness on the part of the individual who experiences it, and it often leads to maladjustments of a minor or major degree of seriousness (Garrison, 1952). Attitudes of jealousy in childhood may affect the individual's attitudes toward people and toward the world, not only in childhood but throughout his entire life (Jersild, 1954a).

Stimuli to Jealousy. The *situation* that calls forth jealousy is always *a social one,* involving people, especially those for whom the child has a feeling of affection. In the young child, it is the parents or other adults who have taken care of him who call forth jealousy. Because of the child's craving for attention and affection, he often finds himself in competition with another child. Clinical studies of jealousy in young children have shown that jealousy is a very common emotional experience, originating, generally, with the birth of a younger sibling, when the child is from two to five years old. This does not necessarily occur (Watson, 1925). However, it is more usual than unusual, especially when the older child is the firstborn and has been accustomed to having the full attention of his parents until the arrival of the new baby.

Preparation for the arrival of a new baby in the household does not always eliminate jealousy. Children prepared ahead of time for the arrival show little less jealousy than those who receive no preparation at all (Sewall, 1930). A young child is usually not mature enough to comprehend all the implications of this event (Merry and Merry, 1950). Jealousy sometimes occurs as a result of age differences among siblings. The younger child resents the privileges given to the older child, while the older child, in turn, resents the affection and attention the younger child is receiving. Then, too, there is the matter of parental favoritism. Without realizing it, many parents show greater interest in the children who are attractive, affectionate, or gifted than in those who lack these qualities or show them to a less marked degree.

In the parent's desire to have his children come up to certain standards or to surpass other children, he may set goals too high for his child to attain. The child is made to feel inadequate or guilty because he falls short of parental expectations, or he may be compared unfavorably with a sibling who has attained the parental expectations. As Jersild (1954) has pointed out, such competitive attitudes on the part of parents "probably contribute more to the development of jealous attitudes in children than the more spontaneous expressions of affection, enthusiasm, admiration, or sympathy which a parent now displays toward one child, now toward another."

Many children show jealousy toward one parent, especially the father. Because of the child's constant association with the mother, he develops a proprietary attitude toward her and, as a result, resents her display of affection for the father. When there is friction between parents, the child who resembles one parent in appearance, temperament, or interests, may be used as a scapegoat in the hostile struggle between the parents. Because it is impossible for the child to gain satisfaction from his resentments against the parent who rejects him, he is likely to project his resentment to the sibling who is favored by the parent and thus show jealousy toward him (Jersild, 1954a).

As children begin to develop interests outside of the home, around the fifth and sixth years, jealousy toward a member of the family becomes less pronounced. It may, however, show itself in the child's reactions toward schoolmates or classmates, especially toward those who excel in school work or athletics or those who rank as the unquestioned leaders of the group. In the school, when a teacher has "pets," or makes unfavorable comparisons between children, jealousy is likely to occur and to be as intense as sibling jealousy (Merry and Merry, 1950). Many children are jealous of their schoolmates who are more successful in school work and sports or who have more friends than they (Jersild, 1954a).

Most children, even young children, are jealous of others who have more or bigger material possessions than they. The child whose playmates have toys he does not have wants similar toys and feels abused if he cannot have them. Among siblings, "two of everything" does not necessarily solve the problem (Sewall, 1930; Macfarlane, 1938). The older child feels that he should have more than the younger by virtue of the fact that he is the older. As the child grows older, he is jealous of other children who live in a larger house than his, whose families have more cars than his, who have television sets when he doesn't, who have more clothes than he has, or who go away on trips oftener and to more "exciting" places than he does.

Jealous Responses. Jealousy is charged with tension and usually is discharged in a variety of reactions, the most common of which have been found to be:

1. Aggression or hostility against the rival, or, in extreme cases, against everyone
2. Identification with the rival, as seen in regression to infantile ways
3. Withdrawal from the beloved person
4. Repression, especially by an "I don't care" attitude
5. Masochism, especially around the age of puberty, as seen in the self-pity of a martyr
6. Sublimation and creative competition (Vollmer, 1946)

The child who is jealous will show different forms of behavior at different times and in different situations. His behavior toward the same person will likewise vary from time to time, ranging from attacks to attempts to win favor. Most of his behavior, however, shows an underlying feeling of uncertainty and insecurity and suggests that he is trying to vindicate or prove himself even when he has no visible rival. The repertoire of jealous responses used by any given child is that of a troubled person who tries out many techniques in the hopes of meeting his problem (Jersild, 1954a). Observations of the reactions of a four-year-old child to the arrival of a sibling showed a variety of adaptive behavior patterns the child was trying out in her adjustment to this important change in her life. These included actively seeking attention, finger sucking, frank verbal aggression toward the baby, and aggression toward the parents (Anonymous, 1949). Sometimes the jealous responses assume the form of an obsession that takes complete possession of the child's thoughts; sometimes the responses are sporadic and appear only when the child is directly confronted by the conditions that produce jealousy (Jersild, 1954).

Among young children, jealous reactions may be direct or indirect. *Direct* reactions are aggressive in form and consist of attacks by hitting, kicking, biting, pushing, punching, or scratching the person the child regards as a rival or against the person whose attention he craves. Sometimes these attacks are so intense as to constitute a real danger. Or he may use *indirect* and more subtle techniques, such as reverting to infantile forms of behavior, as bed wetting and thumbsucking; bids for attention in the form of fears never before experienced or food idiosyncrasies; general naughtiness; destructiveness; verbal expressions, as tattling and name calling; unwonted display of affection helpfulness; venting his feelings on toys or animals; or he may be subdued as if grieving (Foster, 1927; Sewall, 1930; Markey, 1935; Levy, 1937; Merry and Merry, 1950; Neisser, 1951; Garrison, 1952; Jersild, 1954, 1954a; Breckenridge and Vincent, 1955).

Among older children, jealous responses are more varied and more indirect than among younger children. Some aggressiveness does occur, more often at school and on the playground than at home. Older children, however, concentrate more on *indirect* expressions of jealousy, such as teasing and bullying younger children and animals; instigating quarrels; destructiveness; being sulky, surly, and disagreeable; assuming a martyr's role and brooding or complaining about their plight; daydreaming, especially of the martyr type; swaggering, strutting, and assuming an attitude of nonchalance; conspicuously ignoring others; varying degrees of competitiveness in school or in play; tattling; making disparaging comments; lying and cheating, and using "dirty words" or gossiping about others (Levy, 1937; Neisser, 1951; Garrison, 1952; Jersild, 1954, 1954a). As Garrison (1952) has commented, the jealous child "may become a loud-mouthed show-off or a very 'good' child." Each child has his own method of showing jealousy, which, he has discovered through trial and error, gives him satisfaction.

Individual Variations. The amount and intensity of jealousy in children vary markedly. Definite *sex differences* in jealousy exist. Two out of three jealous children are girls. The *peak of jealousy* comes between three and four years of age, with another peak during adolescence. Jealousy is associated with *age differences* of eighteen to forty-two months. Sixty-seven per cent of the children of that age difference showed jealousy as compared with 33 per cent whose age differences are greater or less than eighteen to forty-two months. There is more jealousy in children of the higher *intellectual* levels than in the lower.

The *oldest child* in the family is more often the jealous one than later-born children. This may be explained by the fact that the oldest child, having been the center of attention before the new baby arrived, hates to share the parents' love with the younger children. A larger number of jealousy cases occurs in girl-girl combinations than in boy-boy or boy-girl combinations. In small families of two or three children, jealousy is a more common experience than in larger families or in families where there is an only child.

Jealousy is often a product of the home situation, especially of the attitude of the mother and the method of discipline used. The less attention the mother pays to her children, the less likely they are to be jealous. Over-solicitous mothers, on the other hand, have a high percentage of jealous children. Likewise, those who are inconsistent in discipline produce jealousy in their children more often than those whose discipline is more consistent. Jealousy is often intensified by parental attitudes, especially those of nagging or unfavorable comparisons with other children in the household. The jealousy of the child is in direct proportion to the strength of the maternal bond. This means that the closer a child is to his mother, the more he has to lose when she turns away from him (Foster, 1927; Ross, 1930; Sewall, 1930; Smalley, 1930; Macfarlane, 1938; Bossard, 1953, 1954; Jersild, 1954, 1954a).

5. Joy, Pleasure, Delight

Joy, which in its milder forms is known as pleasure, delight, or happiness, is a positive emotion, because the individual experiencing it makes no attempt to remove the situation giving rise to it. He accepts the situation or attempts to continue it because of its pleasant effects. There are definite age trends in the amount as well as in the stimuli that elicit smiling and laughter (Ames, 1949).

Stimuli to Joy. The situations which give rise to joy differ from one age to another. The health and general bodily conditions of the child also influence his emotional responses. As the child grows older, more situations and also more complex situations call forth the joyful emotions. They are always accompanied by smiling or laughing and can readily be detected because of these overt responses. Unlike the emotions already discussed, joy is generalized and undifferentiated rather than specific in form.

Among *babies,* the pleasant emotions of joy, happiness, and delight come from physical well-being. They are also associated with the baby's activities, such as cooing, babbling, creeping, standing up, walking, and running. As Jersild (1954) has commented, "Like the healthy puppy who frisks playfully even though no fleas are biting him, the child draws satisfaction from being active on his own accord." His pleasure is greatly increased when the activity is difficult for him or when there is some obstacle he must overcome to carry out this activity. Babies derive keen enjoyment from being played with by others, whether it be tickling or simple little games as "peek-a-boo," clapping hands in unison, or the sudden appearance of the other person from behind a door. A gay approach by another is enough to give rise to a smile or a laugh (Watson, 1925; Jones, 1926; Washburn, 1929; Bridges, 1930; Bühler, 1930, 1932; Leuba, 1941; Gesell and Ilg, 1946; Ames, 1949; Jersild, 1954, 1954a; Breckenridge and Vincent, 1955).

While many of the same stimuli that gave rise to joyful reactions in babies call forth similar responses in *preschool children,* the preschool-child responds to more different stimuli than does the baby, and he is more influenced by situations in which other children are present. His pleasure comes mainly in activities in which others are involved, primarily children, and is especially strong when his achievements surpass those of other children. He is pleased by new discoveries, especially when obstacles have been in his way to these discoveries. He likes to initiate games and take the lead in introducing humorous elements into these games. Teasing others, playing pranks, and putting animals or other children in a predicament give him a feeling of superiority which leads to pleasurable emotions. He can see incongruities in real situations as well as in comics, on the television screen, or in the movies. Because he can understand slapstick comedy better that more subtle forms of humor, he enjoys humor of that type best of all (Watson, 1925; Kenderdine, 1931; Ding and Jersild, 1932; Justin, 1932; Brackett, 1934; Blatz et al., 1937; Laing, 1939; Gesell and Ilg, 1946; Jersild, 1954, 1954a; Breckenridge and Vincent, 1955).

As *children grow older,* similar stimuli arouse the pleasant emotions as in the younger ages. Physical well-being, incongruous situations, play on words, slight calamities, and sudden or unexpected noises never fail to call forth a smile or a laugh. In addition to these, the older child responds with laughter to situations in which he feels superior, especially those which offer an opportunity for him to achieve success. Release from the strain of pent-up emotions, such as anger or fear, and general physical well-being serve to call forth the pleasant emotions. These emotions are, for the most part, more pronounced when the individual is with the group than when he is alone.

The older child derives keen pleasure from mild dangers, especially when he is successful in doing something he has been told not to do because it is dangerous. The pleasure comes mainly from the feeling of superiority this gives him. Similarly, while he enjoys all jokes relating to people in predicaments or incongruities, he gets special satisfaction from jokes and comics relating to such forbidden subjects as sex and elimination. Practical jokes, especially when older children or adults are the victims, please him because they give him a feeling of superiority. The satisfaction from eating foods, especially those that are usually forbidden, or from taking a taste of liquor or a puff of a cigarette comes mainly from the feeling of superiority he has when he is not caught in the act (Gregg, 1928; Wilson, 1931; Brackett, 1933, 1934; Blatz et al., 1937; Brumbaugh, 1939; Laing, 1939; Gesell and Ilg, 1946; Garrison, 1952; Jersild, 1954, 1954a; Breckenridge and Vincent, 1955). A comparison of what children regard as happy or joyful occasions showed that older children more often than younger emphasize pleasures connected with self-discovery and achievements, successes, benefits befalling them, and happy, successful relationships with people (Jersild and Tasch, 1949).

Responses in Joy. The joyful emotions are always accompanied by smiling or laughing and a generally relaxed state of the entire body. This contrasts markedly with the tenseness that occurs in the unpleasant emotions of fear, anger, and jealousy. Children smile and laugh more as they grow older (Ding and Jersild, 1932). They also smile and laugh more in the presence of others, especially other children, than when they are alone (Kenderdine, 1931). There has been found to be an increase from one smile every six minutes at eighteen months to one smile every $1\frac{1}{3}$ minutes at four years. The ratio of laughs to smiles increased from 1 laugh to 10 smiles at eighteen months to 1 laugh to 3 smiles at four years (Ames, 1949).

A detailed study of the characteristic expressions of smiling and laughing in little children showed that smiling changed greatly as the baby grew older. At the age of twelve weeks, smiling was expressed by a round, open mouth, twitching of the lips and other facial muscles, together with a protrusion of the chin and the sounds "ah-ah." At the age of thirty-two weeks, the mouth opened, thus raising the cheeks; the tongue protruded; the gums were exposed; the eyes were half-closed, causing wrinkles at the outer corners; the arms, hands, and legs were waved around; and jargonlike sounds, together with babbles, formed the vocalization. At one year, a great individualization in the smile of different babies appeared.

Laughing proved to be much more stereotyped in its form than was smiling and did not vary to any appreciable extent during the first year of life. The mouth in laughter was found generally to be widely opened and round in shape; the tongue rarely protruded from the mouth, but was generally flat on the bottom of the mouth cavity. Even though the mouth was wide open, the gums were little exposed, and lower and upper teeth displayed by only one of the babies studied. The eyes displayed increased brightness and were generally almost closed, especially in the last quarter of the first year of life. The cheeks were drawn down by the lower jaw and thus gave a leveled appearance to the face.

Only twice was flushing of the cheeks recorded. Little activity in the nose was recorded, with only an occasional wrinkling at the bridge apparent. The chin protruded slightly, and the head was tilted backward, especially from the ages of sixteen to thirty-two weeks. After laughter, the hands and arms were usually active. During laughter, however, the arms were most often relaxed at the side of the body or held straight outward. The same was true of the legs. The trunk, instead of bending forward as in the case of adults, remained relatively stationary. Respiratory changes were more marked than in smiling and were observed by pulsations of the abdomen (Washburn, 1929).

6. Affection

Affection is an emotional reaction directed toward a person or thing. A young child's affection for others appears spontaneously, and it will be aroused by a minimum of social stimulation (Dennis, 1938a). However, learning plays a role of importance in determining the particular persons or objects to which the child's affection becomes attached (Jersild, 1954a). Affection is conditioned or built up as a result of pleasant experiences with a particular person. The little child learns to have affection for those who take care of his bodily needs, who play with him, and who, in general, are responsible for giving him pleasure and satisfaction (Jersild, 1954). Because a child's affections are learned, not innate, his affection for members of the family as well as for those who have no blood tie with him depends upon the way they treat him and whether or not his association with them is of a pleasurable sort. Children who show little affection for others generally display such characteristics as devaluation of the self, dependency, anxiety, and conflict. These consume his energy, make him "self-bound," and interfere with emotional exchange with others (Alexander, 1951).

As early as six months, a baby shows affection for a particular person or persons within the family circle (Goldfarb, 1945). From then on, his affectionate behavior develops along with his social contacts. The more people he comes in contact with and the more pleasurable these contacts are, the more people he has affection for. His affections develop primarily in relation to people and only secondarily in relation to things. The things the child has an affection for are the "love objects" which are substitutes for a human object of affection (Banham, 1950). Later, he shows affection for those people outside the home who recognize him as an individual and who help him to break his early bonds with his home. These people he regards as his "friends" (Cole, 1954).

How much affection the child has for others depends largely upon how much affection has been shown him. As Garrison (1952) has emphasized, "Love seems to be a two-way affair and grows best when it is both given and received. A constant rejection in the home may leave the child's capacity for giving forth affection undeveloped, or may cause him to seek affection from individuals outside the home. Overaffection and indulgence may have as undesirable effects as lack of affection or rejection. . . . There is, therefore, the danger that overaffection for one or both parents will tend to exclude affection for children of the child's own age level" (pp. 169–170). Normally, a child transfers a part of his affection from one or both parents to others, especially to his playmates (Merry and Merry, 1950). Even before puberty, a child may become infatuated with or romantically attached to a member of the opposite sex (Jersild, 1954a).

Stimuli to Affection. Babies develop affection for people in their own environment, men and women, adults and children alike (Banham, 1950). Not only human beings, but animals and inanimate objects, especially toys, are the objects of their affection. After the first year of life, the child discriminates little between inanimate and animate stimuli in the demonstration of affection. In fact, the young child's affection for a toy or a family pet is often as pronounced as it is for a member of the family.

Studies of babies and young children have revealed that there is a pattern in the types of stimuli that call forth affection. A baby under five months of age expresses affection indiscriminately for all who approach him in a friendly manner. During the second half of the first year, he behaves affectionately toward familiar people, though strangers may win his affection quickly. During the second year, he includes himself, his toys, and other possessions in his affection. Then, during the next year, his affection is extended to children (Banham, 1950). At this time, his affection may be concentrated on a toy, a pet, or even some inanimate object, as a blanket, a spoon, or an old sweater (Jersild, 1954).

Until the child goes to school, most of his affection is concentrated on members of the family. Within the family group, the child's affection for different members of the family occurs in varying degrees, depending largely upon the child's association with them. Most young children have greater affection for their mothers than for their fathers, and this difference becomes greater as children grow older. This is explained by the fact that the mother is a more constant companion to the child than is the father and that the father, as a rule, becomes a stricter disciplinarian as the child grows older. After the child is six, the father usually plays with the child less, punishes him more, and gives him fewer gifts. Children claim that they like best the parent who caters to their material wants, who expresses affection for them, who plays most with them, and who punishes them least (Simpson, 1935).

In the case of siblings, the affection the child has for them depends largely upon the way they have treated the child. In a large family, there are likely to be varying degrees of affection for different siblings (Bossard, 1953). If, for example, an older child should "adopt" one of the younger children as his special pet, a stronger affection will exist than when an older child treats a younger as a nuisance or ignores him. Similarly, two children in a family who are close enough together in age to be companionable, to share common interests, to be loyal to one another and not tattle will have stronger affection for each other than exists when there is little in common (Jersild, 1954). Girls frequently look up to and admire an older brother, if the brother pays any attention to them or treats them in a kindly fashion.

Affectionate Responses. Childish affection expresses itself by hugging, patting, and kissing the loved object or person. The toys of which the child is fond are hugged and patted until they are literally hugged to pieces. Kissing is a less frequent expression of affection in young children than hugging and patting, but as the child approaches the adolescent years, his affection is more and more expressed by wanting to kiss or be kissed by a person for whom he has a feeling of deep affection. While changes occur in the form in which affection expresses itself at different ages, the degree of expressiveness of this emotion depends largely upon the amount of affection the child has received from others, especially during the early years of life.

The baby whose behavior indicates a desire for affection will express affection for others in proportion to the affection shown him. Should he be rebuffed, ignored, and neglected, he will turn his affection inward and become preoccupied with self. Later he may seek outside companionship as a compensation for the lack of affection he receives at home. Babies who, at the other extreme, are smothered with affection, are likewise encouraged to turn their affections inward. Parents who are oversolicitous and over-demonstrative do not encourage the baby to express his affections, but rather encourage him to focus his affection on himself (Banham, 1950).

During the first two years of life, there has been found to be a pattern in the forms of affectionate response. Affectionate behavior is first shown in an outgoing, striving, and approaching form. Babies under five months of age fix their gaze on a person's face, kick, hold out and wave their arms, try to raise their bodies, smile, and turn their trunks. These movements at first are so uncoordinated that the baby is unable to reach the loved object. He expresses his affection indiscriminately in this manner to all who approach him in a friendly manner. By the sixth month, the baby has enough control over his arm movements to reach the loved one. By this time, he is able to distinguish familiar persons from strangers, and he responds differently to them. To strangers, he shows a fear reaction, while to familiar people, he shows affection. At this age he begins to respond reciprocally to cuddling by reaching for the loved ones's face and by mouth fondling.

There is no evidence that self-love comes before affection for others. Instead, throughout the first year, love for others predominates with no concern for self. During the second year, however, whether the baby will turn his love outward or toward himself will depend largely upon how he is treated. At this time, he shows anticipation at the sight of the mother or some familiar person, while at the same time showing withdrawal and shyness at the sight of strangers. Should the mother or other familiar person neglect him, or should he interpret her preoccupation with a new baby in the family to mean neglect of him, he will respond much as he does in the presence of a stranger, by withdrawal behavior and by turning the affection he was prepared to give to the familiar person on himself. Should this type of experience be repeated frequently, it is likely to result in a withdrawn form of behavior, suggesting that the young child lacks affection for anyone and that his primary concern is with himself (Banham, 1950).

Throughout the childhood years, affection shows itself not only by wanting to kiss, hug, fondle, and touch the loved one or object, but also by a strong desire on the child's part to be with the loved person and to assist him in whatever he is doing. Typically, the little child takes with him, wherever he goes, a toy for which he has a deep affection, and he wants to play constantly with a pet animal. Young children likewise show marked affection for their siblings. Affectionate responses in sisters have been found to include patting, hugging, and kissing; verbal expressions, as love names and endearing statements; and attempts on the part of older sisters to protect and help the younger sisters (McFarland, 1938).

Until the latter part of childhood, when a certain degree of antagonism develops between boys and girls, there is a display of affection for siblings of the opposite sex as well as for playmates of the same or of the opposite sex. After the child enters school, he is likely to begin to feel that demonstrations of affection are "childish" and to be embarrassed by them. He then shows his affection for members of the family and friends by wanting to be with them and by exchanging confidences with them. So long as his parents show a genuine interest in him and in his interests and activities, he is satisfied that they love him. He, in turn, shows his affection for them by wanting to be with them, to do things with them, and to come to them with his problems. Spontaneous expressions of affection, however, do occur even in older children, at home or with their playmates. The freest and most frequent expressions of affection, especially among younger children, occur in children of the lower socioeconomic groups (Murphy, 1937).

7. CURIOSITY

Interest in the environment is limited during the first two or three months of life unless a strong stimulus is directed toward the baby. After that, anything *new* or *unusual*, which is recognized as such by the child, is certain to arouse the curiosity of the child. This in turn motivates him to explore until his curiosity has been satisfied. His interest is not limited to material objects in his environment. He is interested in people, why they dress and behave as they do, why old people differ in looks and behavior from younger people, and why boys and men are different from girls and women in looks, in manner of behavior, in voice, and in countless other ways. Long before he enters school, the child's curiosity has been aroused by such mechanical devices as electric-light switches, gas burners, vacuum sweepers, radios, television sets, and automobiles.

Responses in Curiosity. Curiosity is, in the case of young babies, expressed by tensing the face muscles, opening the mouth, stretching out the tongue, and wrinkling the forehead. At first, a slight startle may accompany curiosity, suggesting that the baby is frightened by new and unfamiliar objects. Soon, however, as he explores the object, the startled expression gives way to pleasure and laughter. By the second half of the first year, bodily expressions of interest occur in the form of stretching the body, leaning toward the object, and grasping for it. As soon as the baby gets hold of the object, he begins a more thorough exploration by handling, pulling, sucking, shaking, and rattling it. Thus, the different sense organs are stimulated, and the baby discovers meanings through the use of these channels. This sensory-exploration-motor-manipulation period extends from the middle of the first year to the third or fourth year. During that time, the little child breaks and harms many objects, not intentionally, but because his relatively poor muscle coordination makes him clumsy and awkward.

Social pressure, in the form of admonitions and punishment, acts as a check on the satisfaction of curiosity through direct exploration. Therefore, as soon as the child is old enough to put words together in sentences, he asks *questions* about the things that arouse his curiosity. The "questioning age" begins around the third year and reaches its peak at approximately the sixth year, when the child enters school and begins his formal education. How important a role questioning plays in the satisfaction of the child's curiosity depends to a large extent upon the satisfaction the child receives from those whom he questions. When the child is old enough to read without giving too much attention to the mechanics of reading, he discovers that he can satisfy his curiosity through *reading* about things for which he has not been able to find an adequate solution in direct exploration or questioning. Motivated by the desire to explore, the child of eight or nine years of age devotes much of his leisure time to reading.

FACTORS INFLUENCING EMOTIONALITY

In every child, as in every adult, the state of emotionality varies from time to time, depending on such factors as health, time of day, and environmental influences. Any attempt to control the emotionality of the child must take into consideration these factors, because emotional control can be brought about best by eliminating the factors which act as predisposing causes. The most important of the factors predisposing the child to emotionality are the following.

1. Fatigue. When the child becomes tired, owing to too little rest, too much excitement, inadequate food for his needs, or other less common causes, he is predisposed to irritability and temper tantrums. This holds true for every age during the childhood years, but is especially serious in the early years of life when the child does not recognize fatigue as such and continues to play actively instead of resting at the time when he really needs to rest. Time out to rest, accompanied by a drink of fruit juice to give extra effort and ward off fatigue, has been demonstrated to result in less negative behavior among nursery-school children than when no break in midmorning was given or when water was substituted for fruit juice (Keister, 1950). The hungrier the child, the more prone he is to angry outbursts (Dollard et al., 1939).

2. Poor Health. When the child is in poor health due to malnutrition, digestive disturbances, diseased tonsils and adenoids, defective eyes, poor teeth, or colds, he is predisposed to emotionality, just as in the case of fatigue. Any temporary condition of poor health, such as fatigue from a restless night or irregular bowel movements, tends to make children irascible and predisposes them to temper outbursts (Goodenough, 1931). Children

who have a history of frequent illness are more emotionally upset and unstable than are children whose health is better (Garrison, 1952). Among
healthy children, ages seven to eleven years, there have been found to be
fewer emotional disturbances and less emotionality than at other periods
of childhood and than among less healthy children (Dingwall, 1949).

3. Time of Day. Because the child becomes more fatigued at certain times
of the day than at others, it is not surprising to find that these times are
accompanied by pronounced emotional disturbances. In babies and young
children, the periods preceding the scheduled eating and nap times are the
ones when emotionality is apt to be at its height. If the child's schedule is
interfered with and eating or nap time is delayed, the period preceding it
is generally one of pronounced fussiness and irritability. This holds true
for older children as well as for younger (Goodenough, 1931).

4. Intelligence. Studies of mentally deficient children of different ages
have shown that there is less emotional control, on the average, among those
of the lower intellectual levels than among children of the same ages who
are bright (Meltzer, 1937). However, children with greater intellect have
greater emotional scope. They are more able to perceive the tragic and
comic, to sense and to fear omens of future calamity, to anticipate in their
feelings and thoughts the future consummation of their hopes, and to acquire a wider range of interests which may be blocked or fulfilled by their
experiences (Jersild, 1954a). Even among young children, those who are
bright are more sensitive to things that might endanger them than are less
bright children of the same age levels (Holmes, 1935; Boston, 1939; Despert,
1942; Jersild and Meigs, 1943; Jersild, 1954, 1954a).

5. Social Environment. A too exciting environment, in which there is
too much tension from bickering and quarreling, from too crowded a
schedule, or from too many exciting experiences for which the child is not
well prepared, such as radio programs, movies, entertaining, or trips, all
tend to heighten the child's emotionality. More frequent temper outbursts,
for example, have been found in homes where there are visitors or more
than two adults (Goodenough, 1931). As Jersild (1954) has commented,
"The more adults in the home, the more occasion for everyone to get in
everybody else's hair." A calm, secure, happy home life, on the other hand,
results in less emotionality among children (Garrison, 1952).

How the child is handled by adults, the number of restraints placed on
his activities, the type of discipline used to control his behavior, and the
ease with which he can get what he wants from others, all contribute to his
emotionality. Furthermore, the child can develop habits of emotionality
from being with others, whether adults or children, who are themselves
highly emotional. Children from poor general social level, for example,
have been found to be more emotionally unstable than those who come
from good, middle-class homes where the home environment is generally

more stable and there is less emotional tension among the members of the home environment (Springer, 1938).

The social environment of the school influences the child's emotionality just as does the social environment of the home. Nursery-school children who are urged by adults to do such things as take off their coats or wash their hands showed more mood shifts, less stability, and less happiness than did those who were given more freedom to plan their own activities (Lee, 1932). Grade placement of elementary-school children affects their emotional

When parents are unafraid of the dark, this will have a profound influence on the child's reaction. (*From Child Development, a McGraw-Hill Text-Film.*)

stability. When a child is overaged for his grade, he tends to be emotionally unstable. This is true also of bright children who are usually younger than their classmates. Such children become the target of other children's teasing, and this leads to feelings of insecurity and anger, with their accompaniments of emotional tension (Turner and Eyre, 1940).

6. Family Relationships. Parental attitudes are often responsible for a child's emotionality. Emotional symptoms are most commonly found among children whose parents neglect them, who are away at work for a large part of the day, who are overanxious about their children, who constantly talk about their children's ailments or behavior, who make babies out of them by helping them too much, who "spoil" them by giving way to them too much, or who make them the center of home life. Overprotected children show more nervous symptoms, while neglected children are more often antisocial and aggressive in their emotional behavior (Cummings, 1944). "Planned-for children," many of whom have perfectionistic mothers or parents who have too great ambitions for their children, are especially subject to emotional problems (Sloman, 1948).

First-born children are, proverbially at least, "spoiled." It is therefore not surprising if the oldest child of a family is more emotional than the later-born children. The first-born has learned from experience that the use of the emotions is a quick and easy way to get what he wants, and as a result, the child develops the habit of giving way to emotional outbursts. Similarly, the youngest child of a family, if he has been "babied" by parents and older brothers and sisters, develops habits of emotional reactions as the easiest method of dominating the social situation. How great emotional stability or instability the only child will show depends largely upon parental attitudes toward him.

7. Level of Aspiration. While many emotional problems arise because parental expectations are beyond the child's potentialities and the child is made to feel inadequate by parental criticism or disappointment, some emotional instability is directly traceable to the child's own level of aspiration. Children, owing to lack of experience and lack of knowledge of their own capacities, often aspire to the impossible. If they lack the abilities and the skills to achieve the goals they have set for themselves, they feel inadequate. Too many and too repeated failures result in emotional tension, an accompaniment of all feelings of inadequacy (Garrison, 1952). As Jersild (1954a) has pointed out, "Anything that lowers a child's confidence in himself, anything that threatens his self-regard or threatens to disturb the role he wishes or pretends to play or threatens to block goals which he regards as important, may increase his tendency to be anxious or afraid."

What threatens the child's level of aspiration will vary from age to age and may even vary from time to time in the child's life. While his aspirations are of his own making, they are, nevertheless, influenced by what he knows or thinks others expect of him. To illustrate how aspirations vary, Jersild (1954) has pointed out, "When he is able, or thinks he is able, to walk by himself on rough ground, he may be angry if someone tries to take his hand, whereas earlier, when this feat was beyond what he expected of himself, he was glad to take a hand or be carried, and even later, when the rough terrain is no longer a challenge, he again may be quite glad to hold a hand or to get a lift." Thus, only when an aspiration of the moment is threatened will there be any effect on the child's emotional stability.

Chapter 8

SOCIAL DEVELOPMENT

Social development means the attaining of maturity in social relationships. It is the "process of learning to conform to group standards, mores, and traditions, and becoming imbued with a sense of oneness, intercommunication, and cooperation" (Freeman and Showel, 1953). This involves the development of new types of behavior, a change in interests, and the choice of new types of friends. The *social* individual is one who not only wants to be with others but who wants to do things with them. In contrast to the social individual is the *gregarious* one who craves the presence of others, is lonely when away from them, but whose desire for companionship is satisfied when he is in the presence of those of his own kind, regardless of contacts of any sort. Gregarious behavior is characteristic of most animals of the lower levels, while social behavior is characteristic of higher animals and of human beings.

No child is born social, in the sense that he can get along well with others. He must learn to make adjustments to others, and this ability can be acquired only as a result of opportunities to be with all types of individuals, especially during the years when socialization is an important phase of the child's development. Like all development, this requires planning and guidance on the part of those who are in charge of the child if the most desirable results are to be achieved. Because the social group exerts so marked an influence on the personality of the child, it is obvious that the members of the social groups should be selected because of the desirable influence they can exert over the child. This guidance must come from adults, because the child is too young and inexperienced to be able to guide his own development in the most advantageous way.

That becoming socialized and learning to live successfully in the social world is difficult has been shown by studies in which adults were asked to recall happy and unhappy experiences at different periods of childhood. In one study, unpleasant experiences were found to predominate in late childhood, between the ages of six and twelve years. Of the memories of these unhappy experiences, the majority were related to problems of living in a social world, as being forced to do unpleasant things, being verbally disciplined, harboring feelings of guilt, being teased and ridiculed, and fighting with friends (Thompson and Witryol, 1948). Very young children find their first social experiences outside the home emotionally disturbing. The younger they are, the more disturbing these experiences are (Heathers, 1954).

Opportunities for Social Contacts. As Harris (1946) has pointed out, "Socialization does not proceed in a vacuum." If the child is to learn to live socially with others, he must have ample opportunities to learn. The sooner he is given these opportunities, the easier it will be for him to learn patterns of behavior that will faciliate his adjustments to social groups. Even before he enters school, it is helpful to a child to have opportunities to supplement the social contacts with members of the family in his home and other children in the neighborhood with contacts in a nursery school or kindergarten where there will be direction and guidance in making social contacts successfully (Jersild, 1954). Each year, as the child grows older, he is given more opportunities in the school, Sunday school, and different community organizations for contacts with other people, especially children of his own age and level of ability. As a result, there is a gradual increase in social participation throughout the childhood years (Mayo, 1950). See Fig. 37.

How much advantage a child will take of opportunities offered outside the home for social participation will be influenced by the pattern set by his parents. It has been found that the extent and intensity of social participation on the part of a child is closely related to the extent and intensity of his parents' social participation (Anderson, 1943). Children brought up in institutions where there are restrictions on social participation are less mature socially than those who are given normal opportunities for participation. This immaturity is shown in fewer contacts with others, less interest in social life, less initiative, and less planning for the future (Bodman et al., 1950).

While social participation is essential to social development, too much participation may prove to be as harmful as too little. The child who is dissatisfied if he is away from others fails to develop resources within himself to be happy when circumstances force him to be away from others. Indiscriminate sociability, which consists of being with others just for the sake of companionship without taking into consideration congeniality of interests or other factors, does little to develop healthy social attitudes on the part of the child. The *kind* of social contacts the child has is more important than the number of contacts (Lehman and Anderson, 1927; Witty, 1931; Breckenridge and Vincent, 1955).

Influence of Social Group. Every child, like every adult, is dependent upon other people for his existence. This dependence is complete at birth and during the early years of babyhood. As the child becomes older, he becomes less dependent upon the social group. Nevertheless, he still needs the group and cannot live without contacts with others. During each succeeding year his relations with others become more complex, and he must come in contact with more people, as well as with people of different types. Most of these people do not have the personal interest in him that his parents have, and consequently they do not try to make his adjustments to them easy, as is usually done at home.

Not only is the child dependent upon the social group, but of even more importance, the social group upon which he depends determines to a large extent what type of individual he will be. Because he is plastic, both physically and mentally, his development can be influenced and molded into a pattern determined by the members of the group with whom he is most

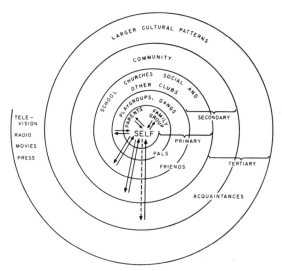

Fig. 37. The widening of the child's social contacts and resultant interaction. The thickness of the arrow represents the probable relative degree of interaction between the self and the various individuals and groups. (*From F. J. Brown, Educational sociology, 2d ed., Prentice-Hall, 1954. Used by permission.*)

often associated. At no age is he free from the influence exerted by his associates. This influence is especially pronounced during the early years of life, because this is the time of greatest plasticity. At that time, the child's family is the most influential socializing agency in his life. When he goes to school, his teachers and his peers begin to exert an influence over his socialization. Peer influence is usually greater than teacher influence (Berenda, 1950).

One of the most important ways in which the child's peer group influences him is by helping him to achieve independence from his parents and become an individual in his own right. Through his associations with his peers, he learns to think independently, to make his own decisions, to accept points of view and values not shared with his family, and to learn forms of behavior approved by the group to which he belongs. This is a part of the weaning process "through which he changes from complete dependence on others into a person who can hold his own with his own age group and move with his age group into youth and adulthood as an equal" (Jersild, 1954).

The influence of the group and the adjustment the child makes to it depend to a certain extent upon how acceptable the child is to the group. The popular child will be influenced by the group more than the child who finds himself an outcast from the group, and in a different manner. When a child masters the skills that put him in a position of superiority over the group, he will have greater self-confidence and show more ascendant behavior than will the child who is socially unacceptable to the group because he cannot do what the group does (Jack, 1934). The child who finds himself unacceptable to the group will go to any length to win the attention and approval of the group. Should his efforts fail, he may become angry and vindictive or he may revert to earlier forms of social contact, mainly in the home, where he can find the security of status he craves (Jersild, 1954). Whichever path he follows, it will influence his attitudes and behavior to a marked degree.

The influence of the group likewise depends upon the degree of social distance that exists between the child and the group members (Bogardus, 1948). Roughly, three types of social groups have been recognized: the *primary* group, which has the strongest bonds of intergroup relations, such as the family group or the child's peer group; the *secondary* group, which is characterized by more casual relationships, as social clubs, religious bodies, and play groups organized for a specific play activity; and the *tertiary* group, which is marginal and transient in character, as groups of people the child comes in contact with on buses, trains, or in the movies (Brown, 1954). Of these three types of social groups, the primary unquestionably has the greatest influence on the child. The degree of influence exerted by the different types of social groups is illustrated in Fig. 37.

Pattern of Development. Social development follows a pattern, in an orderly sequence, not only in the type of social behavior displayed at each age but also in the type of companions selected. This means that normally every child should pass through certain phases of becoming socialized at approximately the same age as other children pass through the same phases. As is true of other types of development, bright children are accelerated in this development, while dull children are retarded in their progress toward social maturity. Knowing what the pattern of social development is, one can readily predict that at a certain age the child will be timid in the presence of strangers; at another age, he will crave the companionship of individuals of his own age and sex; while at still another age, his interests will be centered on members of the opposite sex.

Studies of groups of children have revealed that there are age levels in social development. While the two-year-old is solitary in his play, he is nevertheless influenced by older children to the extent that he imitates their behavior both in play and in his conduct. The 2½-year-old refuses to share toys with others and grabs toys from them, ignores requests, and refuses to comply. The three-year-old shows the rudiments of team play and the four-year-old shows the beginnings of group influences by being conscious of others' opinions and trying to gain attention by "showing-off" (Blatz and Bott, 1927; Gesell and Thompson, 1934; Hattwick and Sanders, 1938; Gesell and Ilg, 1946, 1949).

At first, young children lack group feeling. Then a phase of partial adjustment occurs during which the child begins to establish his role and to play in a somewhat coordinated fashion with others. In the third phase of the pattern of social development, group relationships are established and the child enjoys group life. At this time, the group invents and organizes its own group names and becomes an independent unit, free from adult supervision and interference (Friedman, 1951). Throughout the latter part of childhood, there is an increase in social contacts. The size of the group and the frequency of participation likewise increase (Hartley, 1946).

IMPORTANCE OF EARLY SOCIAL EXPERIENCES

Because the first social group for the child is his family, that group plays an important role in establishing his attitudes and habits. Furthermore, it will influence his approach to other groups with which he will come in contact as he grows older. The family group contributes to the child a readiness to belong or to feel that he is an accepted part of the subsequent groups which he enters. If he is accepted at home, the feeling of belonging will carry over to other groups. Furthermore, the child learns to appreciate and understand people of all kinds through his associations with the members of his immediate family, his relatives, and the neighbors (Hattwick, 1940). The child's social behavior and attitudes are not determined by any one particular aspect of the home or other early environmental influences, but rather by the total character of the environment in which he grows up (Portenier, 1943).

Studies of the social adjustments of children have revealed some of the early influences which determine the quality of their social behavior. Children who come from more favorable socioeconomic homes, where opportunities exist for healthy physical and psychological development, make better social adjustments than do children from poorer socioeconomic groups (Bonney, 1944; Neugarten, 1946; McDonald et al., 1949; Garrison, 1952). The type of relationship that exists between the child's parents, sibling relationships, parent-child relationships, and the position of the child within the family group, whether first-born, middle, last-born, or only child, are all contributing factors to his social adjustments (Baruch, 1937; Garrison, 1952; Bossard, 1953, 1954).

Of all the environmental factors in the early years of life which influence the child's social behavior and attitudes, perhaps the most important is the type of child-rearing methods used by his parents. Young children who are raised *democratically* show behavior of an active, socially outgoing type, both hostile and dominating as well as friendly. Their aggression and bossing is, on the whole, successful, and they are not likely to have inferior status in the group. Later they learn to control their nonconforming and aggressive behavior, thus maintaining a favorable status in the group. In the democratic home, there is not only freedom but also a high level of interaction between parent and child through the parents' spontaneous expression of warmth. The child is encouraged to engage in activities demanding intellectual curiosity, originality, and constructiveness.

Children who are *indulged*, on the other hand, show physical apprehension and lack of skill in muscular activities. They are nonaggressive, experience many frustrations, and have a tendency to be resentful. This makes them inactive and withdrawn in their social relationships. While such children do not face the problems of learning to control their aggressiveness and bossiness, as do children brought up more democratically, their major problem is to achieve a satisfactory degree of social interaction. The child from a well-controlled home who has been subjected to *authoritarian* child-rearing methods is quiet, nonresistant, well-behaved, and unaggressive. His curiosity, originality, and fancifulness are restricted by pressures from his parents. Thus, authoritarian control produces conformity but limits freedom to grow creatively, while democratic control frees the child to explore and experiment but does little to help him conform to cultural demands. Of the three types of child rearing, the child from the democratic home usually makes the best social adjustments (Baldwin, 1948, 1949).

Behavior and Attitudes. The social behavior and attitudes of a child, even as he grows older and comes in contact with more and more people outside the home, are reflections of patterns prevalent in the child's home. The foundations are laid in early childhood, when the social environment is restricted to the home, and only slight changes and modifications occur in these behavior patterns and attitudes as the child grows older (Freeman and Showel, 1953). Each year, as the child grows older, he becomes increasingly aware that he is expected to conform to certain patterns of behavior and to overcome his aggressiveness and antisocial behavior. Children from middle-class families are under greater pressure to conform than are those from lower-class families or even than those from families of the upper classes (Griffiths, 1952).

As is true of behavior patterns, childhood is the period when the child's basic social attitudes, such as his attitudes toward certain people, certain social groups, and social life as an experience that is pleasant or unpleasant, are learned. These attitudes are acquired as a result of the process of social adjustment. The child accepts the attitudes of others in his desire for status in the group (Brown, 1954). True, these basic social attitudes may change with later experiences, but attitudes do not change easily. This will be illustrated in the section of this chapter that deals with prejudice (see pages 289–291). By the end of childhood, there are many social attitudes the child has absorbed from his parents, teachers, and peer group, or from his contacts with the world through his personal experiences or through radio, television, books, and other media of mass communication. Unless he discovers that his social attitudes are responsible for making him unpopular, he is not likely to change them (Havighurst, 1953). Social attitudes that lead to poor social adjustments are most subject to modification and change as the child grows older (Finley, 1946).

Consistency of Behavior and Attitudes. To determine how consistent the social behavior and attitudes established in childhood are as the child grows older, attempts have been made to discover whether the child's adjustments improve with age and whether he becomes more or less acceptable to his peers. A follow-up study of a group of kindergarten children 10 years later to see if there was a significant correlation between the adjustments they made in kindergarten and later revealed that of 21 children, 10 improved, 10 remained the same, and only one declined slightly in his adjustments. While good attitudes on the part of teachers may prove to be helpful in improving the social adjustments of a child, parental attitudes are more important in determining the social adjustments a child makes. Even if children are "subjected to great strain, illness, suffering, and very poor guidance techniques, they can still adjust well if they are loved" (Ryan, 1949).

Because the child's social behavior is consistent as he grows older, it is important that good foundations be laid during the early years of life (Hartley, 1946). As Bain (1954) has pointed out, "When the child enters school, he begins to reap the rewards or suffer the ills which flow from the first six years of life." If his home has done a good job, the child can adjust to others and to social patterns easily and adequately. He is not forced to learn the hard way. He knows what to expect, and he is prepared to evaluate the new social realities he will meet. The child, on the other hand, who gets off to a bad start, acquires a reputation that follows him from class to class (Jersild, 1954). The result is that he is likely to continue to make poor social adjustments unless he receives some help in improving the poor foundations of social behavior and attitudes established in his early childhood days in the home environment.

PATTERN OF SOCIAL DEVELOPMENT

Social behavior begins when the baby first distinguishes between *persons and objects.* Just when this occurs is difficult to determine exactly and must be judged in terms of the overt responses of the baby. Because the environment of little babies is, on the whole, somewhat similar in major features, the beginnings of social behavior vary less from one baby to another than later on, when individual differences in environment are of a more pronounced type. For that reason, the pattern of social behavior for the first two years of the child's life is similar, in most respects, to that of other children of the same age and intellectual level.

1. PRESOCIAL BEHAVIOR

At birth, the baby is nongregarious, as may be seen in his complete lack of interest in people. So long as his bodily needs are taken care of, he does not crave or even miss the companionship of others. He does not distinguish between people and inanimate objects. He merely responds to stimuli in his environment. Much of what is popularly regarded as social behavior is, in reality, uninfluenced by social contacts. The crying baby can, for example, be quieted by lifting up the bed on which he is lying without disturbing him or without making any sound whatever. Likewise, change in position may lead to crying without any interaction with a person (K. Bühler, 1930).

During the first two months of life, the baby's reactions to external stimuli come only when the stimuli are intense, as in the case of loud noises, bright lights, or strong touch stimuli. He does not even distinguish between the human voice and other noises. In fact, he responds more often to noises than to the human voice because of the greater intensity of the former. He, likewise, gives similar responses when touched by a person or an object. Soon, however, he learns to distinguish between people and inanimate objects because of the prominent role people play in his life. From the beginning of the third month, gregarious behavior supplants nongregarious. The baby shows contentment when in the presence of others, but is discontented, unhappy, and "fussy" when by himself. At this time, also, there is a beginning of true social behavior.

2. BEGINNINGS OF SOCIAL BEHAVIOR

The first social responses of a baby are to *adults.* This is due to the fact that normally the baby's first social contacts are with an adult. Positive social responses predominate at first, as may be seen in the following pattern of responses and the ages at which they normally appear. By the end of the second month, the baby turns his head when he hears a human voice, and *social smiles,* or smiles in response to a smile of an adult or a clucking sound, appear. At this time, the baby expresses pleasure in the presence of others by kicking, smiling, and waving his arms in a random, uncoordinated fashion. During the third month, babies stop crying when talked to, but they can also be quieted when their attention is diverted by a rattle or some other mechanical device. At this age, they show a beginning of interest in people by crying when a person leaves them. Most babies, at this time, show by their behavior that they recognize their mothers (Jones, 1926; Bühler, 1930; Bridges, 1931; Washburn, 1932; Shirley, 1933; Dennis, 1935c, 1941; Gesell et al., 1940; Spitz, 1946; Gesell and Ilg, 1949; Merry and Merry, 1950; Garrison, 1952; Jersild, 1954).

In the fourth month, the baby makes anticipatory adjustments to being lifted, shows selective attention to the human face, looks in the direction of the person who leaves him, smiles in response to the person who speaks to him, shows delight in personal attention, and laughs when being played with. From the fifth or sixth month, the baby reacts differently to smiling and scolding and distinguishes between friendly and angry voices. To attract the attention of persons near or to entertain them, babies display the following types of behavior: bouncing up and down, breathing hard, making a "funny mouth," wrinkling up their noses, waving their arms, kicking, coughing, and blowing. At this age, babies recognize familiar persons with a smile, laugh in peekaboo play, imitate simple acts, such as the clapping of hands and waving of arms, resent opposition or interference, and show for the first time definite expressions of fear of strangers (Bühler and Hetzer, 1928; Bühler, 1930; Shirley, 1933; Kelting, 1934; Gesell et al., 1940; Spitz, 1946, 1949; Gesell and Ilg, 1949; Merry and Merry, 1950; Jersild, 1954).

During the sixth month, the baby's advances to adults are more aggressive. He pulls the adult's hair, grabs his nose, his eyeglasses, or his clothes, and explores his different facial features. By the eighth or ninth month, the baby attempts to imitate the speech of others by repeating syllables heard and likewise imitates simple acts and gestures observed in others. Between the tenth and twelfth months, he plays with his image in the mirror and even kisses it as if it were another person. At twelve months, he can refrain from doing things in response to "no-no" or some other form of request, and at the same age, he shows definite fear and dislike of strangers by drawing away and crying when a stranger approaches. From the fifteenth month on, there is an increasing interest in adults and a strong desire to be with them and to imitate them. At two years, the child can cooperate with adults in a number of routine activities. Thus, in a relatively short period of time, the baby has changed from a passive member of the family who receives much attention but gives little in return to an active member who initiates social contacts and who is a part of the same social group that constitutes the family (Shirley, 1933; Gesell and Ames,

1947; Gesell and Ilg, 1949; Merry and Merry, 1950; Garrison, 1952; Jersild, 1954).

Reactions to Other Babies. Social reactions to individuals of the same age as the baby lag behind the social reactions to adults. The first indication that a baby perceives another occurs between the ages of four and five months, when the baby smiles at another child or shows attentive interest in the cry of another. From six to eight months, lack of interest in other children leads to few contacts with them. Friendly contacts consist of looking at, smiling at, and reaching out and grasping another child, while unfriendly contacts consist of blind attempts to get hold of material from another child, often resulting in impersonal fights. Between nine and thirteen months, the baby explores other babies by pulling their hair or clothes, imitates the behavior and vocalization of others, and shows for the first time cooperation and social use of material. Fighting becomes intense and personal. When a toy is taken away by another, the baby becomes angry, fights, and cries (Bühler, 1930; Bridges, 1931, 1933; Beaver, 1932; Maudry and Nekula, 1939; Merry and Merry, 1950; Jersild, 1954).

Social reactions toward other children during the second year develop rapidly. From the thirteenth to the eighteenth month, the young child's interest shifts from play materials to the playmate. There is a decrease in fighting for toys and an increase in cooperative use of them. When a toy is taken away, the child is apt to fight by pulling hair or biting. He smiles and laughs in imitation of another child. During the last half of the second year, the child is definitely interested in play with children, and play materials are now regarded as a means of establishing social relationships. The child cooperates with his playmate, modifies his behavior to adjust to his playmate's activity, and engages more frequently in games with other children. Even at this early age, young children are united as a group in their behavior on certain occasions, as when waiting for a nurse's signal before handling their spoons (Bridges, 1931, 1933; Merry and Merry, 1950; Garrison, 1952).

Early Forms of Social Behavior. As a result of contacts with others, certain forms of social behavior begin to develop at this age. In order to become a part of the social group, the baby *imitates* those about him, both adults and other babies. He first imitates facial expressions, such as laughing and crying, around the third month, then gestures and movements, as waving bye-bye, shaking the head, or throwing a kiss, from the age of six months, and still later, around the twelfth month, he imitates the sounds heard in his environment, like "choo-choo," "tick-tock," "ding-dong," or the simple sounds in the speech of others. From this as a foundation, speech is built up. During the second year, when the baby learns to feed himself, dress himself, manipulate his toys, and, in general, act like those around him, it is through imitation that this behavior is possible.

By the fifth month, the baby begins to distinguish familiar people from strangers. This results in *timidity* and *shyness* in the presence of strangers, appearing first around the sixth month and generally pronounced from the ninth to twelfth months, the period commonly known as the "strange age." At this time, the baby reacts to strangers with a solemn stare, puckered lips, whimpering, and crying. He hides his head and clings to the person holding him. At the same time, he continues to be friendly with those whom he knows. Toward the end of the second year, there is another "strange age." How pronounced it will be depends largely upon the opportunities the baby has had to come in contact with different people and new environments. At this time, there is an ostrichlike desire to hide from strangers, shown by the common reaction of burying the head in the mother's lap, hiding behind a piece of furniture, shyness about accepting things from strangers, and refusal to speak, even to say "good morning." This self-conscious, shy behavior is especially pronounced between sixty-six and eighty-six weeks of age (Bühler, 1930; Shirley, 1933; Gesell et al., 1940; Gesell and Ilg, 1949; Breckenridge and Vincent, 1955).

Rivalry, especially in play with other children, appears during the second year. The baby tries to take the toys of others, not because he wants them, but because it gives him pleasure to assert his superiority in this manner. This generally leads to crying on the part of the child who has been deprived of his toy. Rivalry also may be seen in the bid for attention and affection of an adult, which, if not satisfied, leads to jealousy on the child's part.

Social cooperation, which, like rivalry, is essential in social contacts, appears first in the baby's play with adults in peekaboo and similar games. Because the adult is willing to do the lion's share of giving and taking, cooperation is successful. But with others of approximately the same age, the baby cannot cooperate for more than a few minutes at a time, with resulting inability to play with other little children successfully at this age (Bühler, 1930; Shirley, 1933; Gesell and Ilg, 1949). *Resistant behavior,* as expressed by tensing the body, crying, and refusing to do what he is asked to do, becomes pronounced after the baby is eighteen months old and continues to be a common form of reaction to adults, even after the baby has achieved a certain degree of independence (Jersild, 1954).

3. Social Behavior in Early Childhood

In the preschool years, from ages two to six years, children progress from being relatively unsocial to distinctly socialized individuals. During this short period of time, the child learns to adapt himself to others and to cooperate in play activities in which several children are involved. He consequently is prepared for active participation in the group when his school days begin. Most of the important types of social behavior necessary to adjustment to others begin to develop at this time. Even though they are not well enough developed to enable the child to get along successfully with others at all times, there is, nevertheless, an important beginning which will serve as the foundation for further development as the child's social horizons broaden.

The number of contacts the child has with other children at this time is an important factor in determining how far this development will progress. Among nursery-school children, four-year-olds are more successful than two-year-olds in establishing social contacts (Mallay, 1935). Children who have had nursery-school experience enter into a decidedly larger number of social contacts in kindergarten than do those who have never had nursery-school experience (Jersild and Fite, 1939). By the spring term, however, even the "new" children make marked progress, as shown by the number and success of their social contacts (Jersild and Fite, 1939; White and Williams, 1939).

During the preschool years, there is a great change in the child's social world, from a small world centered in the family to an expanding world centered in the peer group. As he enters into this new social world, the young child has more independence to come and go than he formerly had and greater freedom to make his own social contacts. He must now find a place for himself in this expanding world where the peer group will gradually replace the role played by the family during the earlier years of his life. To be ready for this new social life, the child should have learned what is expected of him by his family and others, be ready to accept responsibility, and have a concept of self in relation to others of a realistic enough sort to enable him to adjust successfully to them (Havighurst, 1953).

Relations with Adults. The young child not only spends less time with adults than he did when he was younger, but he also derives less enjoyment from them. With each succeeding year, his interest in playmates of his own age increases, and with this comes a decrease in interest in adult associations. While the two-year-old is passive, dependent, and relies on adults for attention and assistance, a year later he resists adult influence and wants to be independent. He then becomes self-assertive and difficult to handle. After he is four or five years old, however, he gradually becomes more friendly and cooperative, seeking the approval and trying to avoid the disapproval of adults (Bridges, 1931; Gesell and Ilg, 1949; Ilg et al., 1949; Merry and Merry, 1950; Garrison, 1952; Jersild, 1954; Breckenridge and Vincent, 1955).

Even though the young child spends less time with adults with each succeeding year and becomes more resistant to adult authority, he is, nevertheless, greatly influenced by them not only in the pattern of his behavior but also in the establishment of social attitudes. His parents and teachers are primarily responsible for setting the pattern for the social attitudes the child will have, whether these attitudes be of good will and friendly cooperation to all or intolerance and prejudice against others who are different from the child, even though this difference may not mean inferiority (Garrison, 1952).

Relations with Other Children. Before the age of two years, young children engage in solitary play. This is true even though they may play in the same room and with toys similar to those used by other children playing there. This is *parallel play,* in that there is no interaction taking place even though the activity is similar for all. The only contact with others consists

Social play begins when children are three or four years old. (*From Child Development, a McGraw-Hill Text-Film.*)

of imitating them, watching them, or attempting to take away from them a toy which has attracted the child's attention. Two or three children may engage in parallel play, but rarely more than that. At this age, children relatively more often resist the social advances of other children than is true of the older ages.

From the age of three or four years, owing to increased ability to control the body, to handle objects, and to talk, there is an increase in social play. Little children now begin to play together, to talk to one another while they play, and to select from the children present those with whom they prefer to play. The size of the play group increases with age, from two members at three years to three or four members at six years. Even then, the group splits, and the children play in twos. Approximately two-thirds of the two-child groups are unisexual. The most common behavior of these groups consists of watching each other, holding conversations, and making verbal suggestions (Beaver, 1932; Parten, 1932, 1933; Green, 1933; Updegraff and Herbst, 1933; Murphy, 1937; Gesell et al., 1940; Gesell and Ilg, 1949; Merry and Merry, 1950; Garrison, 1952; Jersild, 1954; Breckenridge and Vincent, 1955).

Throughout the years of early childhood, the child is self-centered in his social behavior. He likes to boast of his achievements and even of his family. When he cooperates, he does so when it is convenient to him and he does not permit his own interests or activities to be interfered with. While this shows a shift away from the egocentric behavior of the baby, the shift is far from complete. Even after the young child has apparently abandoned solitary or parallel play in favor of cooperative play with one or more children, he may from time to time revert to the simpler forms of social behavior. This is especially likely to happen when he is thrown with a group of strange children. Under such circumstances, he may approach them in a sequence of behavior patterns that follow closely the general pattern of early social development, from solitary to parallel to cooperative play, until he feels at home with them (Jersild, 1954).

Even in the simplest forms of social groupings, the child begins to show the influences of other children on his behavior and attitudes. In parallel play, for example, one child who is a "snatcher" may cause conflicts and quarrels among the other children that would not appear had it not been for this aggressive child. Similarly, a child whose behavior is slightly more mature than the behavior of the rest of the group exerts an influence over others to the extent of encouraging them to take part in cooperative play. In the same way, the young child's attitudes toward other children and toward adults is influenced by the attitudes of the children he is associated with. A child who has no personal grievance against a nursery-school teacher may, for example, come to think of her as "mean" because he has heard some of his playmates label her as such.

Forms of Social Behavior. As a result of early social contacts with children and with adults, the child begins to develop types of social behavior which will prove to be invaluable to him in late childhood, as well as in mature life. Because, as a baby, he was helpless and required constant care, every young child is self-centered. Play with other children soon teaches him to adjust himself to group life, to give and take, and to share his possessions with his playmates. Through imitation of the actions, words, and emotions of others, the child tries to make himself like his playmates and to conform to a pattern approved by the group to which he belongs.

Many of the forms of behavior that appear in early childhood appear, on the surface, to be unsocial or even antisocial, rather than social in their outstanding characteristics. In reality, each is important in the socializing process. Each plays a role in the transition of the child from an unsocial, egocentric individual to a social one. Some of the most unpleasant behavior of this age level and the most difficult to handle is, nevertheless, most important in the developmental pattern. Because of pressures placed on the child from his environment and obstacles in the path of his normal methods of behaving, the child must learn, through trial and error, combined with guidance from his parents and teachers, how to satisfy his own needs and

Cooperative play begins early in childhood but is short-lived at first and leads to many quarrels. (*From Child Development, a McGraw-Hill Text-Film.*)

wants, while, at the same time, behaving in conformity with the pattern approved by the group. Early childhood, when other children are mastering the same developmental tasks, is the time when foundations are laid which will determine how well or how unsuccessfully he can adjust as his environment becomes broader and when he will not have the protection and guidance of his parents.

Of the characteristic forms of behavior that appear when the young child is in a situation involving either adults or children, the following are the most common.

Negativism. Negativism is a form of exaggerated resistive behavior, "re-

plete with all of the emotional concomitants of infantile self-assertion"
(Ausubel, 1950). When the child has a particularly difficult time fitting his
wants into those of other people, it causes him to be "cranky," stubborn, and
downright rebellious at times (Banham, 1952). This makes the child hard
to manage and difficult to live with. It is often aggravated by the fact that
adults do not take into consideration that a child may have wants that are
important to him, that he is incapable of doing things as well or as quickly
as an older child or adults can, and that he has been so accustomed to having
things done for him that it is hard for him to adjust to doing things for
others, how and when they wish them to be done.

Negativism is a product of social situations. It occurs as a result of the
aggressive use of discipline or an intolerant attitude toward normal childish
behavior on the part of adults. It generally appears in connection with the
established home routine, when the child refuses to comply with the adult's
requests that he carry out a certain activity at a scheduled time, such as
coming to the table for supper when his plate is placed on the table. It also
appears in situations involving strangers, whether the situation be a social
call or an intelligence test (Rust, 1931). The more the child is frustrated by
adult interference, the more negativistic his behavior will be (Frederiksen,
1942).

Resistant behavior is first noticeable at about eighteen months of age and
reaches a peak around the third year. It is so common at this age that it is
regarded as normal and almost inevitable (Ilg et al., 1949; Ausubel, 1950;
Banham, 1952). If a child does not show negativism at any time, there is
reason to believe that he is either physically below par and lethargic or that
his environment is so artificially controlled to avoid all friction that he will
be "headed for difficulty later on" (Jersild, 1954). After the fourth year,
there is usually a decline in negativism, owing partly to social influences,
partly to the fact that the child learns that it is to his advantage to comply,
and partly to the fact that the adults in his environment have learned to
respect the child's desires (Gesell and Ilg, 1949; Allen, 1951).

The *form* that negativism takes varies with age. Among young children,
there are many forms ranging from simple opposition to active execution
of the opposite of what is expected. It may take the form of "physical tenseness," which is the opposite of "cuddliness"; of failure to carry out a request,
even though he apparently understands; of pretending not to hear or
understand; of stubbornness in connection with all routine activities, such
as eating and toileting; and of many little acts of self-assertiveness, such as
commanding, demanding, walking away, or hiding when he is called. Some
young children carry negativism to extreme forms of refusing to urinate,
holding their breath until they are literally blue in the face, refusing to
swallow food, or forced vomiting (Reynolds, 1928; Rust, 1931; Caille, 1933;
Plaut, 1941; Ilg et al., 1949; Banham, 1952; Jersild, 1954).

Between the ages of four and six years, there is a decline in physical resistance and an increase in verbal forms. The child uses "no" as an answer to all sorts of suggestions, questions, and amiable approaches, and there is a growing use of protective lying. He uses such subtle methods as pretending not to hear or to understand, refusal to see the point, insistence upon referring to a subject that has been closed, carelessness in carrying out requests or duties, annoying others, and repeated complaints. Around the eighth year, the child develops a blasé protection against outsiders and a sort of "water off the duck's back" attitude. His parents find he will never listen to reason (Caille, 1933; Plaut, 1941; Ilg et al., 1949; Jersild, 1954).

Variations in negativism at different ages have been found to exist. There is no significant relationship between intelligence and negativism. Children of all intellectual levels seem to be subject to this form of behavior at approximately the same ages. Likewise, there are no marked sex differences in negativism. However, in the higher socioeconomic groups, boys show slightly less negativism than do girls. This difference has been explained by the fact that boys of the higher socioeconomic groups are more likely to be spoiled than are girls. On the whole, children show more resistance to other children than to adults (Levy and Tulchin, 1925; Reynolds, 1928; Goodenough, 1931; Caille, 1933; Dawe, 1934; Jersild and Markey, 1935; Ausubel, 1950, 1952; Jersild, 1954; Breckenridge and Vincent, 1955).

The socializing influence of negativism may not be recognized by parents and teachers who regard such behavior as unreasonable and a nuisance. However, as Banham (1952) has pointed out, it plays a role of importance in the social development of the child. According to her,

Contra-suggestibility, negativism, and obstinacy in children may be taken as signs of potentiality for good social adjustment. They are forms of behavior that are unsatisfactory in themselves, but that at least show vitality, motivation, and the beginnings of selective sensitivity to a complex social situation. They indicate that the child is capable of developing social and emotional attachments and antagonisms. . . . Children become excessively obstinate when demands are made that are impossible for them to execute, when the demands are humiliating, unfair, or exceedingly disagreeable or painful. Obstinate contrariness is a compensatory adaptive reaction, only partially successful, in the interest of self-preservation, growth, and development. It is likely to change to cooperative behavior when the child finds something he can do that will bring satisfaction to him while complying with the wishes of those for whom he cares (condensed from pp. 84–85).

Aggression. Aggression is a common reaction to frustration. The more frustrated the individual, the more aggressive he becomes. Should a child be punished for his aggressiveness, it will cause more frustration and, thus, more aggression. Hence the attempts to reduce aggression have failed. A child may restrain his aggressiveness while his parents are around because of fear of punishment, but this only serves to produce more frustrations, which will lead to even greater aggressiveness when the parents are not around (R. R. Sears, 1951). The child is not aggressive just for the sake of being aggressive, but rather because something has happened to keep him from achieving some goal that is important to him (Breckenridge and Vincent, 1955).

There are many causes of aggressiveness. Which will dominate at any given age will depend largely upon the individual child. Aggressiveness

Bodily attacks are characteristic of young children's quarrels. (*From Child Development, a McGraw-Hill Text-Film.*)

may come from the child's desire to have attention and to demonstrate his superiority. It may be a form of self-protection arising from the fact that the child feels insecure and is on the defensive. Or it may be an expression of jealousy on the child's part. Among younger children, aggressiveness often comes because a child bumps into others, interferes with what others are doing, enters a group where he is not wanted, or takes something belonging to another child without asking permission (Appel, 1942; Gardner, 1952; Jersild, 1954; Breckenridge and Vincent, 1955). Sometimes it comes from poor social relationships, while at other times, it indicates an improved sociability on the child's part (Jersild and Fite, 1939). Among younger children, there is usually less aggressiveness than among older, primarily because they have fewer and briefer contacts with other children than do older children, and as a result, they have fewer opportunities for aggressiveness (Muste and Sharpe, 1947). By the third year, however, there is a definite increase in aggressiveness as children's contacts with other children become more frequent (Ilg et al., 1949).

The aggressive child does a lot of attacking. These range from mild physical attacks with the hands, feet, and some bothersome or painful gadget to more serious attacks in which the child who is attacked may be badly hurt. Other *expressions* of aggressiveness are moroseness, uncommunicativeness, or sharp, cutting remarks. When repeated over and over again, they become a pattern, and the child is then labeled an "aggressive child" (Gardner, 1952). During the early years of childhood, aggressiveness is more completely expressed than it is as the child grows older. From the four- to five-year level, there is a gradual decrease in the direct expressions of aggressiveness and a progressive increase in indirect or deflected expressions of hostility, especially in the form of verbal attacks and blaming others. This is indicative of growing self-control (Gesell and Ilg, 1946; Ferguson, 1954).

What type of aggression the child will use will depend upon many factors, as the type of environment in which he is, the attitude of parents or teachers to the child, and the type of children with whom he is associated (Body, 1955). How intense his aggression will be will depend largely upon the degree of frustration of his needs (Ferguson, 1954). Maladjusted children at each age level are distinctly less able to control aggressive responses than are well-adjusted children. They either have not acquired the patterns of socially acceptable reaction to frustration, or they find it more difficult to participate in such learning (Rosenzweig and Mirmow, 1950; Rosenzweig and Rosenzweig, 1952). To be well adjusted and socially acceptable, the child must, as he grows older, either modify the aim of his aggression or must gradually impersonalize the object of his aggression (Gardner, 1952).

Quarreling occurs whenever one child attacks another child's person or property. It takes many different forms: the most usual are destroying the other child's work, taking away the toys the other child is playing with, screaming, crying, and actual bodily attacks, such as biting and pushing. Quarrels and friendships go hand-in-hand. Even the best of friends quarrel. In fact, there are more quarrels among friends than among children who have little in common (Green, 1933, 1933a). Among young children, conflicts over property are more numerous than conflicts in which an attack on the child's person is the starting point (Murphy, 1937).

Quarrels among young children last, on the average, about 30 seconds and occur approximately every 5 minutes while the children are together (Green, 1933a). Most children settle their own quarrels by one child's yielding to the force of the other child. Most often, the younger or weaker child is the one who yields. At other times, a parent or teacher interferes and puts an end to the quarrel. Only rarely is a quarrel ended by the interference of another child, by a compromise, or by one child yielding voluntarily (Dawe, 1934). Quarrels are rarely accompanied by severe or prolonged aftereffects among young children. After a quarrel, children are cheerful and friendly more often than they are resentful (Dawe, 1934; Jersild and Markey, 1935). However, the child's attitude toward quarreling is a direct reflection of parental attitudes and of rules imposed by parents at home (Fite, 1940).

Many factors influence the frequency, severity, and form of quarreling. Quarreling generally reaches its peak at the age of three years, then declines in frequency but lasts longer, and the fighting is harder as children grow older (Forest et al., 1934; Jersild and Markey, 1935; Jersild and Fite, 1939; Appel, 1942). The type of activity engaged in influences the frequency and type of quarreling. Constructive play of any type and meddlesome, destructive activities lead to most quarreling because they all involve comparisons. Least quarreling occurs when the play is individual or takes the form of quiet, intellectual pursuits (Green, 1933a). Boys at every age quarrel more than do girls, they start more quarrels, they retaliate more, and their aggressions are more dynamic and outgoing. Girls are more aggressive when playing with boys than when playing with girls (Greene, 1933a; Muste and Sharpe, 1947; P. S. Sears, 1951; R. R. Sears et al., 1953). Children of the lower socioeconomic groups are usually more aggressive and quarrel more than do those of the higher socioeconomic groups (McKee and Leader, 1955).

Sibling status influences the amount and severity of aggression. Older siblings are less aggressive than younger siblings or only children (P. S. Sears, 1951). This is illustrated in Fig. 38. The mother's attitude has been found to be an important factor in facilitating aggression in children. The mother who blames the child for his aggressions, who feels that punishment is a good device for teaching the child and that it is, therefore, her duty to punish, or who blames herself because she is tired and cross is likely to facilitate aggression in children (Nowlis, 1952). The number of quarrels a child engages in is closely related to the child's general activity. The more the child "gets around" and the more contacts he has with children, the more quarreling he is likely to do (Jersild, 1954). And, finally, quarreling is influenced by the amount of adult guidance there is in getting along amicably with other children (Jersild and Markey, 1935; Fite, 1940; Appel, 1942; Chittenden, 1942; Bailey, 1946; Jersild, 1954; Breckenridge and Vincent, 1955).

Teasing and *bullying* are aggressive forms of behavior closely related to quarreling. Teasing consists of a mental attack on another in an attempt to "get his goat" and thus arouse an angry response on the part of the individual attacked. This may consist of calling others nicknames that arouse their anger or putting emphasis on their physical or mental weaknesses. In bullying, on the other hand, the attacker attempts to inflict physical pain on others because of the pleasure he derives from watching their discomfort and their attempts to retaliate. Typical forms of bullying consist of pulling hair or clothes of others, pinching, poking, pushing, sticking pins into others, or putting thumbtacks on chairs just as others are ready to sit down.

Older or larger children more often engage in these aggressive forms of behavior than do small or physically weak children. The younger children in the home or in the school class are generally made the "butts" of the older children. Not all children, however, engage in these forms of aggressiveness. Boys tease and bully more, on the average, than do girls, and children who show feelings of inferiority or insecurity engage more in these activities than do the socially better-adjusted children. Within a family, the older children are more apt to tease and bully than are the younger ones.

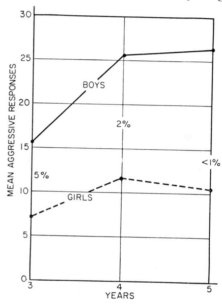

Fig. 38. Frequency of aggression of boys and girls in the early years of childhood. (*From P. S. Sears, Doll play aggression in normal young children: influence of sex, age, sibling status, father's absence, Psychol. Monogr., 1951, 65, No. 6. Used by permission.*)

Rivalry. Rivalry is characterized by a desire to excel, or to outdo others, and is always stimulated by another person. It is therefore a form of social behavior. Competition for prestige is apparent at the age of four years. Before then, the idea of competition is not grasped by children (Hirota, 1951). When children of two years of age are placed in test situations in which competition usually appears in older children, they show no signs of the competitive spirit. Instead, they merely look occasionally at the other child. A year later, some competition appears, but it is eclipsed by other social attitudes, especially imitation. By four years of age, however, the child has a better idea of excelling and is then interested in excelling. By the age of six years, most children have a well-developed competitive spirit (Greenberg, 1932; Leuba, 1933). Children from the lower socioeconomic groups are more competitive at every age than are those of the higher socioeconomic groups. This is especially true of boys (McKee and Leader, 1955).

When competing with strangers, children are quieter than when competing with their friends. When in competition with their friends, on the other hand, they become noisy and excited (Philp, 1940). Young children, as a rule, will persist in a task longer when competing with others than when working alone (Wolf, 1938). Rivalry, followed by quarreling, is more common in the presence of a third person, especially an adult, for whose attention the children compete, than when competition is between two children alone (Gottemoller, 1943). One of the most common forms of competition among young children takes the form of bragging about being first in some activity or about material possessions they claim are superior to the material possessions of the other child (Jersild, 1954).

Competition is very common in the home, especially when jealousy exists between siblings. It is often intensified by the attitude of the mother who, as a child, experienced rivalry in her relationships with her siblings and which was never fully resolved. This "will in all probability set the stage for the reliving of the old drama, once she becomes a mother " (Hilgard, 1951). In spite of the fact that sisters show rivalry in many different situations in the home, this does not seem to affect their relationships with one another. Sisters who show rivalry most often have been found to be as companionable as sisters who show little rivalry (McFarland, 1938).

Cooperation. The young child, at two or three years of age, is self-centered and quarrelsome. It is therefore difficult to get him to play in a cooperative manner with other children. Should his activity be with adults, it is the adult who does the major part of giving, while the child takes what he wants with little attempt to reciprocate. Most of the play with other children is parallel play, with only occasional interchanges. By the end of the third or fourth year, there is an increase in cooperative play, and group activities are longer in duration. The more opportunity the little child has to be with other children, the sooner he will learn to cooperate with them. Cooperative group work is not understood much before the child is six or seven years old. It is greater when the groups are friendly than when non-friendly (Hirota, 1951). The stronger the friendships, the more cooperative the behavior will be (Wright, 1943).

Ascendant Behavior. Ascendant behavior is "any kind of behavior by which an individual attains or maintains mastery of a social situation, or attempts to do so, so he is in control of his own act and can carry out his purposes" (Mummery, 1950). It is the tendency to dominate others, or "bossiness." This tendency is nearly universal among young children and usually shows itself first in the child's relationships with adults. The 3½-year-old, for example, accepts adults as contemporaries and insists upon having the full attention of the adult whom he is with. He calls on the adult for help, especially when he is with other children, and is very demanding in his attitudes (Ilg. et al., 1949).

With other children, the young child will use commands, threats, or force to gain his objective (Anderson, 1939). He will attempt to secure the materials he wants from his playmates, to direct or influence their behavior, and will attempt to resist mastery by others (Mummery, 1947). Among nursery-school children, girls have been found to be significantly more dominating than boys in play situations. In the case of kindergarten children, the reverse is true. Boys are more dominating than girls. When children are paired with those of the opposite sex, the girls are bossier than the boys (Anderson, 1937, 1939).

Children who are especially assertive toward their contemporaries have been found to derive this pattern of behavior from their home environments. Such children come from homes where there is friction over disciplinary policies, many restrictions on their behavior, general home discord, and many coercive suggestions from their parents. Furthermore, if the parent's attitude toward the child is one of dissatisfaction with the way in which the child meets his requirements, if there is little rapport between parent and child, and if the parent shows little understanding and is unready or unwilling to give the desired explanations to natural questions from the child, assertiveness toward others is likely to be shown (Meyer, 1947).

It is a common belief that Northern children are more assertive than Southern children. The usual explanation for this is that Southern children are encouraged to be quiet and relatively inactive by their Negro nurses in accordance with the pattern of the "little lady" or "little gentleman." It is believed that they have fewer quarrels with their playmates, have more socially acceptable techniques for getting along with others, and are more amenable to suggestions from adults. However, a study of nursery-school children in the North and in the South has revealed no evidence of differences in ascendancy between Northern and Southern children (Mummery, 1950).

Selfishness. The young child is egocentric in his interests. This is the result of the attention to his needs and wants during the babyhood days of helplessness. He demands what he wants, and if this is denied, he will protest by crying or displaying his anger in a temper tantrum (Goodenough, 1931; Ilg et al., 1949). Only after the child begins to play with others does he learn to submerge self-interest in the interests of the group. To discover at what age the child's selfishness begins to decrease, children were asked to divide an unequal number of nuts between themselves and another child. The selfish tendency was found to reach its zenith between the ages of four and six years, to diminish after that, and to have disappeared completely by the age of twelve years.

Generosity, on the other hand, was found to increase after the age of five or six years, to reach a high point between the ages of seven and eight years, and to fluctuate after this. This trend is illustrated in Fig. 39. It is apparent that there is a decline in selfishness coinciding with a decline in egocentrism. Poor children have been found to be less selfish than children from rich families. Children from large families are more often generous than children from small families, while only children are the most selfish. Thus, selfishness or unselfishness is determined by the age of the child, the socioeconomic condition of the family, and the number of children in the family (Ugurel-Semin, 1952). Children do not become altruistic simply because they grow older. Only a deliberate effort on the part of parents, teachers, and others to foster this will bring about its development (Turner, 1948).

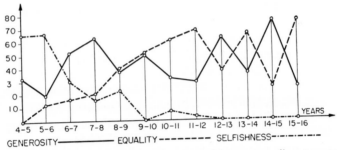

Fig. 39. Frequency of generosity, equality, and selfishness, according to ages. (*From R. Ugurel-Semin, Moral behavior and moral judgments of children, J. abnorm. soc. Psychol., 1952, 47, 463–477. Used by permission.*)

Social Approval. Even a young baby likes to be noticed and to hold the center of attention. From the fourth or fifth month, consciousness of self reaches a point in the development of the child where it requires an outlet. Long before the baby can talk, he "senses" that he is the center of admiration and attention. He enjoys being noticed by others and is unhappy when no one pays attention to him. With each succeeding year, the child becomes increasingly anxious to win the approval of others, first that of adults and later that of individuals of his own age. The desire to impress his companions, as well as the adults of his environment, often brings the child into conflict with adult regulations and the codes of the social group. Absence of social approval not only causes the child to be unhappy, but often drives him to behave in a socially unacceptable way which, he has discovered from experience, invariably brings forth the attention of others, even though it is usually not accompanied by their approval.

The child is highly sensitive to social praise and blame, whether it comes from adults or from other children. He therefore tries to regulate his conduct to win praise and avoid disapproval. At first he is influenced more by adults than by children. A frown or a nod of approval means more to him when it comes from an adult than would any similar expression of approval or disapproval which came from his contemporaries. However, after the third year, approval and disapproval from his contemporaries begin to mean more to him than when they come from adults. This is well illustrated by a study which showed how the young child's food preferences are influenced by his desire to win the approval of the group, especially of the leader. The example set by the leader was found to cause not only immediate but lasting modifications in the child's original taste preferences (Marinho, 1942).

Sympathy. Sympathy is a form of social behavior in which a child is affected by the emotional states that another individual, whether it be adult or child, experiences. An extensive study of sympathetic behavior in nursery-school children has revealed some important facts about this form of social behavior in young children. Children of two and three years of age did not as a rule respond sympathetically to black-and-blue wounds, swellings, lumps, and minor flesh distortions which might, to an adult, suggest discomfort or illness, Red Ridinghood being eaten up by the wolf, pictures of accidents, funerals, being crippled, or carrying crutches. The three-year-olds generally, though not universally, responded to people whose distress involved bandages, blindness, injuries colored with mercurochrome or iodine, red swellings, scars or scratches; to deprivation of toys, food, or mother; to physical dilemma, such as being caught in a play pen or bicycle; to an interference with activity of child having to stay in bed; to frustration in activity; to attack by another child; to incompetence to do a job undertaken; to an accident, such as a fall; or to crying.

Sympathetic responses on the part of young children consist of helping others; removing or attempting to remove the cause of distress; comforting others by pets, pats, hugs, and kisses; punishing the cause of distress; protecting and defending the person in distress; warning, or telling an adult or other child about an individual in distress; asking questions to find the cause of distress; and suggesting or effecting solutions. Occasionally unsympathetic responses are observed, and these consist of laughing at the person in distress, using the situation to play his own role, usually a dominating one, attacking a child in distress, or merely staring instead of sympathizing (Murphy, 1937). Some young children show sympathy to the extent of being kind to a newcomer in a group or of defending the rights of younger children or those who are unable to defend themselves (Berne, 1930; Bridges, 1933; Breckenridge and Vincent, 1955).

Marked individual differences in sympathetic behavior are apparent at every age. At two or three years of age, no sex differences occur, though at later ages, girls are more sympathetic than boys. While sympathy increases with both mental age and chronological age, it is more dependent upon the personality pattern of the child than upon either mental or chronological age. The child who is self-centered and absorbed in his own difficulties, who feels insecure as a result of unpleasant experiences in the past, or whose past experiences have been such that he cannot understand the suffering of another will show unsympathetic behavior. Furthermore, children will vary from time to time in the amount of sympathy they show. As the child gains more self-confidence, he is likely to be less sympathetic than when he was somewhat unsure of himself. When a child is responsible, either directly or indirectly, for the distress of another, he will be less sympathetic than if the distress were caused by another child. Sympathy, likewise, is dependent to a large extent upon the child's ability to comprehend the situation. This depends partly upon his mental and chronological age and partly upon his previous experiences (Murphy, 1937; Macfarlane, 1938; Jersild, 1954, 1954a).

4. SOCIAL BEHAVIOR IN LATE CHILDHOOD

After the child has entered school and has come into contact with other children, he loses interest in playing around the house, alone, or with one or two companions. He likewise now considers it a bore and not a treat to accompany his parents on picnics, parties, or family gatherings. At the same time, interest in individual games gives way to group games, and play without companions loses its charm. The child has entered what is often called the "gang age," an age when social consciousness develops very rapidly.

As the child moves out from the family circle into the world of his contemporaries, he must learn to get more and more satisfaction from them. He must learn ways of approaching strangers, whether shy or bold, friendly or standoffish. He must also learn how to treat his friends. He becomes a member of a "peer group," and this group will gradually replace the family group in its influence over his behavior and attitudes. The peer group has been described as an "aggregation of people of approximately the same age who *feel* and *act together*" (Havighurst, 1953).

That adjustment to this new social group is difficult for a child may be seen in the fact that most six-year-olds are explosive, rebellious, rude, stubborn, brash, and boisterous. They are "out of focus" or in a *period of disequilibrium,* more because of the adjustments they must make to school than because of any physical changes taking place at that time (Gesell and Ilg, 1946). However, once the child has made adjustments to the new environment of school, his behavior improves. He shows greater responsibility, helpfulness, independence, and good humor. While he may find it difficult to take aggressiveness directed toward himself or to understand behavior that differs from his standards of good and bad, he gradually learns to adjust to these changes too (Stendler and Young, 1950).

Even before the end of the first grade, there is a marked growth in general maturity as shown in helpfulness, self-confidence, independence, self-control, and willingness to assume responsibilities. How mature the child is will depend upon the type of home training he has had in his preschool days (Harris, 1954; Harris et al., 1954, 1954a). Most children show improvement in their ability to get along with other children, and many children who were considered to be "problem children" show improvement after experiencing the socializing influence of being in school (Stendler and Young, 1951). However, there is no abrupt shift in the type of social relationships just because the child is suddenly thrown with a large group of children in school. Instead, there is a gradual increase in group play, from the sixth to the eighth year.

During this transition from the "pregang age" of early childhood to the "gang age" of late childhood, which extends from approximately eight years until puberty, the child goes from one group to another or from group to individual activities. The "shifting-group" stage bridges the gap between the pregang and the gang ages (Furfey, 1931; Gesell and Ilg, 1949; Garrison, 1952; Breckenridge and Vincent, 1955). The informal play group of the early school days is small in number, two or three children. It is formed to carry out a specific play activity of the moment and, thus, is transitory in character. The activity itself is the basis for the organization of the group, not liking for a specific child as is true later. Within the group, the leadership shifts from one child to another, depending on which child takes the initiative in the specific activity the group is carrying out at the moment. There are many quarrels, but these are generally short in duration and have no permanent effect on the make-up of the group (Brown, 1954).

"Gangs." The "gang" is a spontaneous local group, without any authorization from outside and without a socially approved aim. It is formed by the children themselves, without any support from parents, teachers, or youth leaders. It is the result of a spontaneous effort on the part of children to create a society adequate to meet their needs. As such, it is a substitute for what adult society fails to give, and at the same time, it offers relief from adult supervision. The gang may not be hostile to the adults in authority or organized without their knowledge. But gangs do not need adult consent, nor are they subjected to any control from outside. They supply their own authority. The gang is not necessarily the product of a subnormal environment. It often develops where the environment is good (Furfey, 1926, 1930; Thrasher, 1927; Crane, 1951, 1952; Wolman, 1951). There is a more definite pattern in the gang make-up than in the informal groupings of earlier days. The members are selected because they are able to do things the others enjoy doing, not because they live near each other or because they can do what one or two members want to do at the moment. The gang exists independently of activities and then selects the various activities it will engage in (Brown, 1954).

From the time they are six or seven years old, boys and girls normally find increasing pleasure in being with small groups of their own sex. They find being alone unpleasant, and if restrained from being with their friends, for even a day, they become fretful, restless, and unhappy. Thus the gang begins to dominate the child's life. It sets the styles in the clothing the child wants to wear, the type of play activities he engages in, and his ideals of right and wrong. Gangs develop their own systems of mores which give them cohesiveness and protect their identity as in-groups (Crane, 1951). Belonging to a gang gives the child not only companionship and an opportunity to have fun, but it also gives him a feeling of pride to have achieved this status, and as a result, he develops a strong loyalty to his gang.

There are certain devices used by gangs to increase the feeling of group belongingness on the part of the members. Of these, the four most common are (1) *gang names*, many of which are taken from the street or neighborhood where the members of the gang live or from some popular book, movie, or comic; (2) *secret signals*, passwords, communication codes, or secret languages, as "pig Latin"; (3) some *insignia* worn by all the members of the gang, as a cap or arm band; and (4) *initiation ceremonies* in which the skills or physical endurance of a child is tested before he is admitted to membership in the gang. Boys, more often than girls, use one or more of these devices to create loyalty within the gang and to make each member feel that he is important because he is an accepted member of the gang (Crane, 1952).

Sex Differences. Boys, as a rule, start to form gangs earlier than do girls. Both lose interest in gang life early in adolescence. Because girls mature sexually sooner than boys, this means that the girl's gang experience is shorter than that of the boy. Girls' gangs are usually smaller than boys', they are much more closely organized and surrounded with more secrecy, their leaders are more autocratic, and they are less likely to welcome new members than are boys (Crane, 1952). To nongang members, girls sometimes are very unsocial in their behavior, even going to the extremes of refusing to speak to girls in their classes who do not belong to any gang or who belong to a rival gang. Boys are more likely than girls to include in their gangs boys of slightly different ages, thus making a hierarchic social system possible. Their leaders are chosen from the older, stronger, or more ambitious boys who are more adventuresome and who, as a result, have won the admiration of the younger or less adventuresome members. Because of the prestige they have, they exert marked control as well as marked influence over the other members (Wolman, 1951).

Meeting Place of Gangs. The meeting place of the group differs according to the community. In the case of boys, it may be a street corner, garage, barn, shed, space in a cellar, vacant lot, deserted house, school playground, or the corner drugstore. Girls, whose activities are generally more closely supervised than are those of their brothers, usually meet at the home of one of the members, at the school playground, or at the corner drug or candy store. Whatever meeting place may be selected, it is always one where there will be a minimum of adult interference and supervision, so that the activities of the group may be carried out more or less secretly, and where, at the same time, there will be opportunities for the sort of activities favored by the gang (Furfey, 1926; Crane, 1951, 1952; Wolman, 1951).

Gangs like to meet where they will be away from the watchful eyes of adults. (*From Child Development, a McGraw-Hill Text-Film.*)

Gang Activities. The activities of the group are numerous and vary with the community. The most important ones include play of all types, such as sports, card games, going to the movies or theater; mechanical and constructive activities, such as making their own rendezvous; social activities in the form of hikes, picnics, parties, and dramatic productions; reading; annoying other people, especially members of the other groups, members of the opposite sex, and old people; fighting, stealing, gambling, drinking, and smoking, which are forbidden activities at this age; or exploring, which sometimes leads to wandering off for several days or which may be satisfied by camping trips under the supervision of an adult.

Gang activities often border on rowdyism. Boys are apt to be noisy, happy-go-lucky, careless, trick-playing. In many of the boys' groups, the activities are characterized by a mob spirit, which leads the individual members of the group to do things they have learned are forbidden and which they would never consider doing alone. The tendency toward hoodlumism, vandalism, or general annoyance to the community originates within the group, and each member feels obligated, because of loyalty to the group, to do what the group does, no matter whether he knows it to be right or wrong. The excitement and reassurance that come from doing what others do tend to break down even the most rigidly established codes of behavior (Furfey, 1926; Crane, 1951, 1952; Wolman, 1951).

Forms of Social Behavior. There are a number of different types of social behavior developed as a result of gang life in late childhood. Some facilitate social adjustments, some interfere with them. On the whole, however, these are the types of social behavior which will, with modifications and changes as the child grows older, result in improved social adjustments. They are the foundations of social behavior normally found in the adults in our culture today.

One of the most important types of social behavior in the gang age is *susceptibility to social approval and disapproval*. As soon as the child begins to crave the companionship of others, he begins to crave their approval; at the same time, he tries to avoid their disapproval. In dress, speech, and behavior, he strives to win the approval of those with whom he plays. Should a conflict arise between the standards of the home and those of his playmates, the child will invariably side with the latter, because, at this age, their approval means more to him than does that of adults. Experimental studies of children's reactions to praise and reproof have revealed that they are strong motivating forces in the child's life, whether in work or play, and that the most effective use is in the presence of other children. Older children respond to these incentives more than do younger children, though praise is more effective for the younger children and reproof for the older children (Hurlock, 1924, 1925; Warden and Cohen, 1931).

Suggestibility. Perhaps at no other age in life is the normal individual as suggestible to those about him as he is during this period. The desire to be an accepted member of the group leads the child to comply with the wishes of the group as a whole and accept without question whatever form of activity the leader may suggest. Studies of misdemeanors of school children have shown that the peak of misdemeanors usually comes between the ages of seven and eight years, the age at which the child passes from individual play to group play, when there is the development of marked loyalty to the group. This loyalty, in turn, renders the child highly suggestible to the members of the group, especially to the leader (Blatz and Bott, 1927). Joy in the wanton destruction of property reaches its peak during the gang age. While boys are more vigorous, bold, and less inhibited in their destructive escapades than are girls, they are both motivated by a desire to do what their friends are doing, as is revealed by the fact that destructiveness almost always occurs when children are with their companions, in a group (Clark, 1952).

Contrasuggestibility. While accepting in a more or less unquestioning manner the suggestions of the group, the child begins to revolt against adults and to act in direct contradiction to them. This contrasuggestibility, which leads to many misdemeanors, is usually strongest in those whose suggestibility to the group is very pronounced. In the presence of adults, they rebel against suggestions which, had they come from their own playmates, they would doubtless have accepted without hesitation. They stubbornly do what they are warned not to do, as stepping in deep snow when told not to or leaving their umbrellas at home when their mother tells them to be sure to take them to school.

Rivalry and Competition. Interest in the social incentives of rivalry and competition becomes very pronounced at this time, as is readily apparent in the interest shown in games and sports. Competition with other individuals, or rivalry between groups, are equally stimulating to the child and may be used as incentives in situations where the activity in and of itself may not prove to be interesting, as is sometimes true in the case of school work. Of the three types of competition that are usually found during the gang age, rivalry among group members for recognition within the group itself, conflicts between the gang as a unit and rival gangs, or conflicts between the gang and organized agencies of society have different effects on the socialization of the child. The first is likely to lead to hostility and quarreling within the gang, thus serving to weaken the solidity of the group and the loyalty of each member of the gang. The second, on the other hand, serves to build up solidity and feelings of loyalty, while the third, if kept from leading to destructiveness and defiance of adult authority, serves to develop independence on the part of the gang members (Anderson, 1936; Brown, 1954; Breckenridge and Vincent, 1955).

Competition among older children, even more so than among younger, is likely to lead to much quarreling. It may take the form of aggressive fighting, not unlike that found among younger children, or it may take more subtle forms, such as criticisms of others, "ganging up" on a single child who may be disliked for his annoying behavior or because he belongs to a minority group, teasing and bullying others, ignoring a child or a group of children, or arguing without any real provocation and with the apparent desire to make the other person uncomfortable or annoyed (Garrison, 1952; Jersild, 1954; Breckenridge and Vincent, 1955). Quarreling among older children is often intensified by an authoritarian attitude on the part of the adult who supervises them, whether it be a parent, teacher, or recreational leader (Lewin et al., 1939; Lippitt and White, 1947).

How rivalry affects the child's behavior will vary according to the age of the child and his personality pattern. In some cases, group rivalry, which involves cooperation within the group, is more powerful than individual rivalry, while in other instances, the opposite is true (Hurlock, 1927; Maller, 1929). When the winner of a competition is rewarded with a prize, there is a tendency for the losers to suffer a "let-down" later. This is more marked in individual than in group competition (Stendler et al., 1951). Competition is keenest and the aftereffects less pronounced when competition is between individuals or groups that are evenly matched (Jersild, 1954). The larger the group, the more agreement there will be among the individual members, the less likelihood of competition, and the greater the possibility of each child's being influenced to comply with the suggestions of the leader (Murphy, 1937; Hare, 1952). While most children are interested in competing because success in competition brings social approval and prestige, excessive competition or competition on an unequal basis, where the child's chances of success are slight, may eliminate these satisfactions (Garrison, 1952).

Good Sportsmanship. Good sportsmanship, or ability to cooperate with the group to the extent of submerging individual personalities into the group patterns, is an outgrowth of group life. The child soon learns that he must "play the rules of the game," and any infringement upon these, such as cheating, tattling, lying, or the use of underhanded methods, will not be tolerated. When working together for a common reward, children show more positive interactions, such as helping each other and sharing materials, while competing against one another results in more negative interactions, as appropriating materials, making unfriendly remarks, and efforts to obstruct or dominate others (Stendler et al., 1951). A too lively interest in one's friends may, however, prove to be a stumbling block in the way of doing fruitful work together (Blos, 1941).

Sympathy. Sympathy in its true form, involving an understanding of the situation, appears for the first time during these years. However, it is only in its crudest form and lacks the fine sensitivity to situations which appears later. This makes the behavior of the child seem to be somewhat "hard-boiled," or "tough." Bullying and teasing younger children, animals, and servants are quite common at this age. Children are likely to be more altruistic in their dealings with strangers than with friends, though this varies from child to child (Wright, 1942). Only with training will altruism increase appreciably (Turner, 1948).

Social Insight. Social insight is the ability to put oneself in the psychological shoes of another and to perceive a situation from his perspective. It is the ability to feel imaginatively and to think oneself in the total mental-emotional attitude of another person (Brownfield, 1953). To make good social adjustments, one must be able to perceive and predict the behavior, thoughts, and feelings of others. In common social situations, this is not too difficult. Prediction is based first on the individual's behavior, then on the meaning of the behavior, and lastly on the deeper attitudes or feelings (Bender and Hastorf, 1950). The ability to discriminate emotional reactions from facial expressions is one of the earliest forms of social insight (Gates, 1923, 1925; Fields, 1953).

Social insight normally increases with age, owing partly to mental maturation and partly to learning from social experiences. Girls, as a rule, have slightly more social insight at every age level than do boys. However, it is not much before the end of the childhood years that social insight is well enough developed for the child to be able to understand the behavior and feelings of other children (Dymond, 1949; 1950; Witryol, 1950; Ausubel et al., 1952; Dymond et al., 1952; Tarwater, 1953; Taft, 1955). Children whose social perception is superior to that of their peers usually make better social adjustments and receive more social acceptance than do those of inferior ability in this area (Buck, 1952; Dymond et al., 1952; Tarwater, 1953; Taft, 1955). With increase in social perception there is a tendency for children to begin to like or dislike others, and this leads to social acceptance or rejection (Jersild et al., 1933).

In the latter years of childhood, children not only have a better understanding of the behavior, motives, and feelings of others, but they begin to be aware of class distinctions, socioeconomic status, and the prestige values associated with such status (Stendler, 1949; Hollingshead, 1949; Centers, 1950). This is, in part, responsible for the prejudice and social discrimination which appear at this age. There is also an increase in self-perception, or *self-discovery*. The child is able to see himself as others see him later than he can perceive the meaning of the behavior of others. However, for successful social adjustments, self-insight is as important as social insight (Rogers, 1948; Jersild, 1951, 1952, 1954; Ausubel et al., 1952; Dymond et al., 1952; Tarwater, 1953; Taft, 1955).

Snobbishness. Social discrimination, or snobbishness, is an unsocial form of behavior which makes its appearance during late childhood. Members of a play group soon develop the attitude that any member of the group is all right, while anyone who is not a member of the group is inferior to them. This sort of snobbishness, based on whether one belongs or does not belong to the group, is the starting point for adolescent snobbishness, which is based on wealth, social status, and similar criteria characteristic of adult snobbishness.

Discrimination. Discrimination is a form of unsocial behavior closely allied to snobbishness. It is based on the belief of superiority due to belonging to a majority group, rather than to any efforts on the individual's part or to the socioeconomic status of his family. Back of all discrimination is *prejudice*, an attitude on the individual's part that tends to classify anyone of a minority religious, racial, or ethnic group as inferior. No child, of course, is born with prejudices. As Zeligs (1951) has aptly put it, "Children catch their prejudices from their social environment." While some prejudices develop because of unpleasant personal experiences with individuals of certain groups, most prejudices develop as if by contagion, from imitating the attitudes and behavior of those with whom the child is most closely associated. Frequently, the older child's attitude is influenced by his desire to gain status in the group (Brown, 1954).

Prejudices are generally acquired slowly and over a period of time. The child acquires his ethnic values and racial attitudes as he learns other social lessons, from adults, from his peers, and from his life experiences. Groups that are segregated in schools or in the community he assumes are inferior because society treats them as inferiors (Vosk, 1953). Few parents actually teach their children to be prejudiced. However, their own attitudes and behavior, their restrictions on the playmates of their children, and the tendency to stereotype all individuals of a given racial or religious group with certain physical, behavioral, and mental characteristics result in a pattern of prejudice which their children imitate. It is not the parents' attitudes alone, but the whole home influence, that is responsible for the development of prejudice (Allport and Kramer, 1946; Radke and Sutherland, 1949; Ammons, 1950; Clark and Clark, 1950; Harris et al., 1950; Zeligs, 1950, 1950a, 1950b, 1950c, 1951, 1952, 1953, 1954, 1955; Bird et al., 1952; Goodman, 1952; Radke-Yarrow et al., 1952; Clark, 1953; Frenkel-Brunswik and Havel, 1953; Springer, 1953; Vosk, 1953).

How prejudiced the child becomes depends partly upon his home environment, partly upon the neighborhood and community in which he lives, and partly upon the degree of prejudice his playmates have. Boys have been found to be more prejudiced than girls, Southern children more than Northern children, children from professional families less than those from the lower socioeconomic groups, and those with fewer opportunities for contact with groups against which there is prejudice are more prejudiced than those with more contacts. Children brought up in homes where authoritarian child-training methods are used are generally more rigid and intolerant in their attitudes than are children from homes of a more democratic type. The most important of all the factors that have been found to influence the degree of prejudice the child has is his own personality pattern. Children who show a high degree of prejudice have been found to be rigid, illiberal, intolerant, and punitive in their attitudes. They usually suffer from marked feelings of inadequacy, inferiority, and insecurity. Frequently, they come from broken or unhappy homes or from homes where they feel unloved and unwanted (Frenkel-Brunswik, 1948, 1951; MacKenzie, 1948; Ackerman and Jahoda, 1950; Goff, 1950; Gough et al., 1950; Gruesser, 1950; Lindzey and Rogolsky, 1950; Mussen, 1950; Pearl, 1950; Razran, 1950;

Zeligs, 1950a; Chyatte and Schaeffer, 1951; Mead, 1951; Vosk, 1953; Wieder, 1954).

Prejudice affects the child who is prejudiced just as it does the victim of his prejudice. It makes him rigid, intolerant, cruel, and vindictive in his behavior, a pattern which may and often does extend to his relationships with people against whom he has no prejudice. Children against whom there is a prejudice come to believe that the social environment is hostile (Vander Werf, 1951). They are subjected to ridicule, teasing, bullying, physical aggressions, and are ignored and left out of things. Some react to this treatment by withdrawal from the social group; others react by excessive aggressions in the form of defensive reactions; still others turn their hostility against society in general and become potential delinquents. Relatively few children react to discrimination by accepting it as a challenge to show others their worth (Goff, 1949, 1950; Bird et al., 1952; Mussen, 1953).

Sex Cleavages. In the early years of childhood, boys play with girls much as they did during babyhood. No antagonism exists between the sexes at that time. As late as the first, and sometimes the second, grades in elementary-school years, boys are willing to play with girls, provided the girls can keep up the pace they set in their play. Little boys may even show a marked interest in some girl in their class and prefer to associate with her rather than with a boy. However, during the third grade, when children are approximately eight years old, an antagonism develops between the sexes which leads to a marked cleavage between them. They belittle each other's interests, skills, and activities; they refuse to associate with one another, even at parties; and they are constantly bickering, name calling, and quarreling when thrown together in the home. For the most part, the boys are the aggressors in this battle of the sexes. The girls, in turn, retaliate by refusing to associate with the boys and return in kind the treatment they receive from the boys. Should a boy show any interest in a girl at this age, he is regarded as a "sissy" by his contemporaries. This antagonism usually persists until puberty, when it becomes intensified for a short time and expresses itself in active antagonism toward all members of the opposite sex. Little boys may, even before the age of eight years, show the typical sex antagonism of an older boy if they are associated with older boys and imitate their attitudes as they do their behavior (Furfey, 1926, 1930; Campbell, 1939; Koch, 1944; Moreno, 1947; Gesell and Ilg, 1949; Garrison, 1952; Brown, 1954).

There is no evidence that sex antagonism comes from physical causes or from the maturation of any mental ability. Rather, all evidence points to cultural influences. There are cultural pressures on both boys and girls to develop interests appropriate to their sex, to engage in activities that are culturally sex-linked, and to regard one sex as superior and the other inferior, instead of *different*. This makes it difficult for boys and girls to become friends, even if they should want to. Any attempt on the part of either boys or girls is likely to be met with amusement on the part of parents and scorn on the part of their contemporaries. Furthermore, boys and girls acquire as part of their social learning values which are different. For boys, even mothers seem less important than they did when the child was younger because they have no recognized status assigned to them as men do from their occupations. Thus, it becomes apparent that the cleavage between the sexes is a product of cultural forces, not of any factor inherent in the children themselves (Bonney, 1944a, 1954; Koch, 1944; Merry and Merry, 1950; Zeleny, 1951; Garrison, 1952; Stoodley, 1952; Jersild, 1954; Breckenridge and Vincent, 1955). Children with low social status, who suffer from feelings of inadequacy and insecurity as a result, generally show greater antagonism toward members of the opposite sex than do children whose social status is more secure (Zeleny, 1951). Boys, as a result of their feelings of masculine superiority, are generally less antagonistic toward girls than girls are toward boys, in spite of the fact that they were primarily responsible for arousing the antagonism (Tschechtelin, 1945; Bonney, 1954). As Bonney (1954) has pointed out:

Accepting inter-personal attitudes which exist between and within sex groups in any classroom is much more likely to be due to such factors as level of socio-economic home background, the extent to which boys and girls have enjoyed pleasant associations in groups, the extent to which they have been separated in seating and eating situations, and the extent to which teachers and other adults have encouraged or minimized sex differences by direct and indirect teachings, rather than to constitutional differences or to so-called natural stages of sex development.

One of the far-reaching effects of sex antagonism in the latter part of childhood is the bearing it has on the development of social skills, such as the ability to talk to people, to be at ease in social situations, to have good manners, and to know the socially correct things to say and do. These social skills are important to good social adjustments not only in childhood but throughout life (Breckenridge and Vincent, 1955). Because boys regard all social skills as "sissified" and scorn all opportunities for social contacts where such skills may be learned, they are markedly inferior to girls in this area of their development. Even as early as the fourth grade, boys have indicated, on a self-rating scale, that they feel inadequate in social relations as compared with girls. This agreed with teachers' estimates and is in close agreement with general observations of the social behavior of members of the two sexes (Bonney, 1944a).

Evaluation of Gang Influences. The gang plays a role of major importance in the socialization of the child (Crane, 1951; Wolman, 1951). It is a time of profound change, when the child starts as an individual and ends as a member of a social whole. As Furfey (1926) has pointed out, the child "learns civics from his teacher, but democracy from his gang." He "finds himself" because others find him (Murphy et al., 1937). Through group influences, the child receives important training in social behavior that could not be obtained with comparable success under conditions imposed by adult society. There is an awakening of social consciousness at this time which is fundamental to all social behavior. The child liberates himself from adult dependency and domination by allying himself with the peer group and getting its support. As Crane (1952) has emphasized, the gang tests the barriers placed upon the child by adults. The child then establishes a new system of barriers, accepted by the members of the gang, and these restraints play an important role in his socialization.

Havighurst (1953) has shown that the gang can help the child in four ways: to get along with his agemates and to know how to behave in a way that is socially acceptable to his peers; to develop a rational conscience and a scale of values to replace the moral values of his parents which he accepted as an "authoritarian conscience"; to learn appropriate social attitudes, as how to like people, enjoy social life, and group activities; and to achieve personal independence by gaining emotional satisfaction from friendships with his peers instead of relying on his parents for this satisfaction as he did when he was younger.

Gang life favors the development of both good and bad qualities in the child. For the most part, the good far outweigh the bad. On the good side, it teaches the child to be democratic, to fit his desires and actions into those of the group, to cooperate with the group, to develop skills which will enable him to do what his peers do, and to eliminate selfishness and individualism. At the same time, it develops self-control, fair play, courage, justice, forbearance, loyalty, fidelity, devotion to a cause, loyalty to a leader, insight into the nature of the social process, and sensitiveness to the motives and feelings of others. In his competition for status, the child tries to improve himself and to change his egocentric interests into group interests. As Brown (1954) has pointed out, "Such learning matures children."

On the other hand, there are undesirable qualities developed as a result of gang life, such as the use of slang and swearing, the telling of salacious stories and jokes, truancy, mischievousness, attitudes of contempt for rules and those in authority, the breaking of home ties and the shifting of loyalties from home to group activities, snobbishness, discrimination against those of minority groups, and the breaking down of ideals established in the home after years of teaching. However, most of these undesirable effects of gang life are transitory in nature. As the child grows older, they are eliminated, and the socializing influence of the gang results in a better-adjusted individual than is true of the child who has not had the experience of being a member of a gang during his childhood years.

Chapter 9

SOCIAL ADJUSTMENTS

How successfully the child will adjust to the social group will depend largely upon how closely he conforms to the approved patterns of behavior of the group. No child can hope to fit into a social group and be accepted by the members of that group unless he is willing to learn to conform to patterns the group approves of. In our modern society, there is no place for the "rugged individualist" who defies conventions and who disregards the mores of the group. He may, and unquestionably will, attract attention, but the attention will be of an unfavorable sort. The child who learns to conform to socially approved patterns of behavior, by contrast, is accepted by the group and achieves status in the group. Through group interaction he then learns to adjust to other people and, thus, becomes a socially well-adjusted individual.

Cultural Patterns. Culture is the regulator of behavior, excluding that which is clearly hereditary, among the members of a single society (Bagby, 1953). It includes "all behavior which the human being exhibits in conformity with his family, his playgroup, his school group, his social class, his church, and all his other human groups" (Davis, 1949). Within any society, the cultural units are the different social classes. In America, there are no external or recognized ranks but great differences in wealth and sharply drawn distinctions in status. Each social class is a subculture with its own social expectations of the behavior of each of its members. To fit into that social group, the child must be trained to conform to the expectations of the group (Davis, 1949; Goldschmidt, 1950).

In a typical American community, there are usually four or five social classes: the upper, upper-middle, lower-middle, upper-lower, and lower-lower. The status of the individual is determined by the occupation of the male head of the family, the source of family income, the type of house the family lives in, and the type of dwelling area in which the house is located. As communities grow larger, social differentiation and stratification become more pronounced (Hill and McCall, 1950). In most communities, approximately one-half of the population belongs to the middle class. In small communities, there may not be an upper class, or the "elite," who are markedly differentiated from the rest of the community groups by possession of power and wealth. Under such circumstances, the upper-middle class is the dominant class of the community (Goldschmidt, 1950). As

Centers (1949) has pointed out, social class "permeates the fabric of daily living and determines the associations, attitudes, interests, politics, and outlook of the members."

Class Values. Every social group has its own social values which are strong influences on the behavior of the members of that group (Witryol, 1950). The upper class, for example, stresses family background and leisure pursuits. The upper-middle class has values oriented toward the upper class, thus putting stress on the importance of money and position in the community. The working, or lower-middle class, by contrast, rejects the ideal of advancement through individual achievement in favor of the ideal of collective action for social gains. The lowest class does not expect to advance either through individual or collective efforts and thus places stress on the importance of enjoying what one has (Goldschmidt, 1950).

The family is the main mediator of culturally defined values. These values for the social class to which the parents belong are interpreted for the child by his parents (Seward, 1946; Davis and Havighurst, 1947; Havighurst, 1953). Membership in a social-class group affects the child by restricting his learning to a particular social pattern of behaving and believing. This pattern is, in many respects, different from the pattern a child of a different social group would be expected to learn (Davis and Havighurst, 1947; Warner, 1949). The pattern of values must be accepted by the child and must be conformed to if he is to be accepted by the members of the group (Pope, 1953a). Pressures brought to bear on the child, first by the family and later by the peer group, the school, and the people in the community he comes in contact with, produce a personality constellation typical for children of that social class (Milner, 1949).

To be accepted by members of another social class, the child must take over the ideas, beliefs, values, and behavior patterns of individuals of the social class with which he wishes to identify himself. When the individual wants to be accepted by members of a social class higher than that of his family, he is known as a "climber" if he has accepted the patterns of behavior and values of that class to the point where he is able to operate easily among his peers. If, on the other hand, he is only tentatively accepted by them, he is known as a "strainer," a status which gives him little satisfaction and security and which indicates that his adjustments are poor. The "static" individual is one whose family background and peer status have the same relative values, whether high-, middle-, or low-class values. "Clingers" are individuals who are peripheral to or isolated from their peers. They have not adopted the behavior patterns of the group to which they belong to make good enough adjustments to be well accepted by their peers. If, on the other hand, they make no effort to adopt the values of the group, they are potential "decliners" whose acceptance will be by a lower social-class group (McGuire and Clark, 1952).

How markedly social values differ from different social classes may be illustrated by a study in which the prestige values for boys and girls of low and high socioeconomic groups were contrasted. Among twelve-year-olds, in the higher group, both boys and girls are expected to show a tendency to conform to adult standards of behavior and to admire certain conventional rules of decorum, especially when at parties. This is not stressed by members of the lower group. Among boys of the lower group, prestige values are associated with restless behavior, untidiness, attention getting loquacity, fighting, and nonconformity in classroom behavior. Boys of the higher group, by contrast, are expected to fight only when necessary, to be friendly, conforming, and personable with girls, to be good students, and to conform to classroom standards of behavior.

Girls of the lower social group are admired if they are assertive, pugnacious, attention-getting, bossy, and tomboys. By contrast, girls of the higher social groups are expected to be submissive, well groomed, to avoid tomboy behavior, and to behave in a grown-up manner (Pope, 1953, 1953a). There are marked social-class differences in what a child learns in school, how he feels about his teachers, his peers, and the school experience in general (Davis and Havighurst, 1947). Prestige values in leadership likewise vary from one social group to another. Among boys of the lower classes, the admired leader is aggressive, belligerent, and domineering, the typical "bully." By contrast, the admired leaders among boys of the higher social classes are active and skilled in competitive games, and they demonstrate daring, but domineering behavior, or "bossiness," makes them unpopular (Pope, 1953, 1953a).

Sex-role Values. Every social group has an approved pattern of behavior for members of the two sexes. From earliest childhood, the girl learns to conform to this pattern by identification with her mother, just as the boy learns to be "masculine" by identifying himself with his father or with older boys. Through differential training in the home and social pressures from their peers, teachers, and other adults, children learn their approved sex roles. Boys are allowed greater freedom, their emancipation is speeded up, and they are held to less exacting codes of behavior than are girls. Once a stereotype of appropriate "masculine" or "feminine" behavior is learned, the child can be assured of social acceptance. Lack of conformity to the socially approved sex role, on the other hand, leads to criticism and social ostracism (Benedict, 1938; Davis, 1941; Parsons, 1942, 1947; Seward, 1944, 1946; Komarovsky, 1946, 1950; Gorer, 1948; Mead, 1949; Rabban, 1950; Wallin, 1950; Gough, 1952; Sherriffs and Jarrett, 1953; Jersild, 1954).

Social-class values for boys and girls are important factors in determining the approved social behavior. From the earliest years of life, boys and girls of the lower-class families are provided with models and enforcements to bring about sex-appropriate behavior. Children of middle-class families, by contrast, receive no clear-cut training in sex-appropriate behavior in the early years of life. Later, however, pressures from parents and peers make them aware of behavior patterns considered appropriate for their sex groups (Benedict, 1938; Rabban, 1950; Havighurst, 1953). While what constitutes "proper" changes from group to group, certain factors are constant, such as being a good sport and being friendly. For boys, there is a socially approved pattern which constitutes being a "real boy," in that he is good at games, willing to take a chance, and friendly. By the fifth grade, boys differentiate between being reserved and being submissively docile. For girls, the socially approved pattern is less clearly defined, and it changes more than does the approved pattern for boys. By the fifth grade, there is a change from the concept of the "little lady" to that of the "tomboy." Both boys and girls must conform to the socially approved pattern for their age, sex, and social-class group if they are to secure group approval and acceptance (Tuddenham, 1951).

CHOICE OF COMPANIONS

Even before the baby is a year old, he shows stronger attachments for one person than for another. The attachments are for the person or persons who take care of the baby and thus further his needs and desires. Adults, during the first year or two of a baby's life, prove to be the most desirable companions because they satisfy his desire for playmates while at the same time satisfying his needs. In addition to that, they play with him when a child of his own age or slightly older engages in play with his own toys.

In Early Childhood. In the preschool days, the child's companions are usually adults of the family, brothers and sisters, or a few children from the immediate neighborhood. The social environment is that of his home or immediate neighborhood. When he enters school, however, his group of companions widens, and he has an opportunity to select playmates from a larger group than was possible during the days when his environment was limited to the home and the neighborhood. By 3½ years, friends are very important to a child. He selects one or two from a group whom he wants to sit beside or play with. They may be of the same sex as he or of the opposite sex (Ilg et al., 1949). With each passing year, the child spends more time with his friends and he develops more friendships with different children (Garrison, 1952). These are a part of a small clique with which the young child identifies himself, and they are congenial because of similar interests and similar abilities (Biehler, 1954).

In the choice of companions, the older child differs greatly from the baby who willingly accepts as his companions anyone regardless of age or sex who will do things for him. The child becomes more selective in

choosing his friends. Such factors as age, intelligence, and good sportsmanship become very important, though the sex of the child is of less importance
in determining whether or not he will be chosen as a playmate than it is
later (Hagman, 1933; Parten, 1933; Fite, 1940; Lippitt, 1941; Koch, 1944;
Laughlin, 1953). By the age of four years, children show a definite preference for playmates of their own sex, and unisexual friendships increase as
the child grows older (Chevaleva-Janovskaja, 1927; Challman, 1932; Hagman, 1933; Koch, 1933, 1944; Dahlke, 1953; Jersild, 1954). Race cleavages
also appear at this time when children begin to show a decided preference
for friends from their own racial groups (Koch, 1944; Springer, 1950).

Because of the limited environment of the typical child, companions are
almost always selected from the immediate neighborhood. This means that
the child must choose from the neighborhood children those boys and girls
whom he finds to be the most satisfactory companions for him. Should none
prove to be of his liking, one of four courses of action is open: he must
modify his behavior to fit into that of the children available as companions;
he may develop "imaginary companions" who will play with him as he
wishes; he may fall back on the companionship of his parents and siblings;
or he may develop solitary interests and play alone. None of these courses
of action proves to be satisfactory to the child except the first.

In Late Childhood. When the child enters school and begins to be interested in group play, new criteria, combined with old ones, are used in the
selection of his playmates. Propinquity in the school or neighborhood is
responsible for throwing together individuals from whom companions are
selected. Unlike the adolescent or the adult, who may select his friends from
a distance, the child must select his friends from the immediate neighborhood in which he lives. Within this neighborhood, he selects as companions
those of the same size, sex, chronological age, mental age, social maturity,
and interests. To be able to make satisfactory choices of friends, the child
should be placed in a school or neighborhood which furnishes the maximum
number of associates who are close to the child in the qualities essential to
congenial friendship. As children grow older, personality traits play an important role in the selection of their friends (Seagoe, 1933; Pintner et al.,
1937; Bonney, 1946; Koch, 1946; Potashin, 1946; Austin and Thompson,
1948; Faunce and Beegle, 1948; Grossmann and Wrighter, 1948).

Unless home pressures are applied to the child's choice of friends, the
young child does not discriminate against those of different races, religions,
or socioeconomic status. However, the older child shows a definite preference for playmates of his own racial group (Koch, 1944; Radke et al., 1950).
By the fifth grade, children also take into consideration socioeconomic
status in the selection of their friends (Neugarten, 1946). While children
of the lower social classes have more freedom of choice in the selection

of their friends than do children of the middle classes whose parents put pressure on them to choose the "right" type of friends, nevertheless the lower-class child often finds himself barred from participation in social activities with children of the middle class. He is thus forced to select his friends mainly from his own social class (Havighurst, 1953). During the gang age, children discriminate against those of another school, neighborhood, or gang, not because they are inferior to them, but because they belong to another group against which there is a feeling of rivalry.

The older child's companions are those whose interests are similar to his. (*From Child Development, a McGraw-Hill Text-Film.*)

Imaginary Playmates. The young child who has, for one reason or another, no real playmates often imagines that he is playing with another child. These imaginary companions are lifelike to the child, possessing names, physical characteristics, and abilities to do things which one normally associates with real children. The child derives keen pleasure from playing with his imaginary playmates, and this fills a gap in his social life. Girls more often have imaginary playmates than do boys, and to girls the playmates are more realistic than they are to boys. Imaginary playmates are more prevalent among children of superior intelligence than those of average intelligence, and among only children or among siblings where there is a large age difference (Terman, 1925; Hurlock and Burstein, 1932; Jersild et al., 1933; Svendsen, 1934; Bender and Vogel, 1941; Bender, 1944; Ames and Learned, 1946).

Imaginary companions in most instances are little boys or girls and only rarely take the form of an adult, a fairy, or an animal. Sometimes they are of the child's own sex and sometimes of the opposite sex. They always have a name. The name may be a commonplace one, or it may be an unusual one, taken from real people, from stories, or created by the child himself. The child plays with his imaginary playmate as if he were a real individual. He even talks to his playmate, and in many instances the child takes his playmate with him wherever he goes. No matter what the activity may be, the real child is the boss, and the imaginary playmate is a submissive follower.

The usual age for imaginary companions is between three and four years, with 3½ years the high point. By the time the child enters school and has playmates of his own, he usually abandons the imaginary companion, though he may occasionally play with him when he is lonely (Ames and Learned, 1946; Ilg et al., 1949; Merry and Merry, 1950). As so many children during the preschool years have imaginary companions, if only for brief times, this may be regarded as "normal." In the case of children whose relationships with their parents are emotionally unsatisfactory, or who are lonely because they find little congeniality in the companionship with their siblings or other children, because of their superior intelligence, imaginary companions are not only more frequently found, but they are likely to persist for a longer time (Bender and Vogel, 1941; Bender, 1944; Ames and Learned, 1946). There is not one type of personality that predisposes children to have imaginary companions. Children who are happy and well adjusted to other children and adults have imaginary companions during the preschool years just as do children who are timid, lonely, or who exhibit personality difficulties (Ames and Learned, 1946).

In one study of children who had imaginary playmates, 34 of the 40 children studied had such personality difficulties as timidity in the presence of other children, a domineering manner with other children, fear in physical activities, sensitivity, an undemonstrative manner, evasiveness and irresponsibility, eagerness for being in the limelight, and fear of being outdone by others (Svendsen, 1934). To determine the long-term effects of imaginary companions, a group of college freshmen who had had imaginary companions as young children was compared with a group who had never had such playmates, with the use of the Bernreuter Personality Inventory. The results showed that the girls who had had imaginary companions were less neurotic, lacked self-sufficiency, disliked solitude, and more often sought advice and encouragement than did the girls who had never had imaginary companions. In addition, they were less introverted, were more dominating in face-to-face situations, were wholesomely self-confident and well adjusted to their environment, and were sociable and gregarious (Wingfield, 1948).

Pets. All children like to play with pets. Even little toddlers enjoy romping with a tame kitten or puppy. As the child grows old enough to want playmates to share his play time, he finds a pet, especially if the pet is a dog or cat, a satisfactory substitute when no human playmates are available. Interest in dogs and cats has been found to increase rapidly from seven to fourteen years, with a peak around the twelfth year. Both boys and girls prefer dogs to cats, and their interest in playing with cats culminates sooner than their interest in dogs. This is especially true in the case of boys (Lehman, 1928).

There are many things a child gains from having a pet, other than the fact that it is a substitute for human companionship. In the case of a dog, the child finds an outlet for his affection. It serves as a source of ego satisfaction and gratification; it satisfies the child's desire for power; and, most important of all, it serves as an effective social aid. The child makes many contacts in the neighborhood, not only with children but with adults as well, when he has his dog with him. For a child who is timid and shy, this often proves to be an effective method of making contacts he would hesitate to initiate if he were alone (Bossard, 1953). Thus, a pet may prove to be more than just a substitute playmate for a child. Furthermore, the pet does not develop in the child the unsocial traits so often found among children who have substituted imaginary playmates for real playmates.

Persistence of Friendships. When children are young, their major interests are centered in the home. Playmates are relatively unimportant to them until they are mature enough to be able to engage in cooperative play. In the early stages of cooperative play, quarreling is frequent but is short in duration. It does not seem to affect the child's willingness to play with the child with whom he has just quarreled. Among preschool children, friendships, thus, remain relatively stable over a period of time. In one study, for example, it was reported that 73 per cent of a group of three-year-olds had the same friends for a period of six months (Jersild and Fite, 1939). Up to the age of five years, there is a high consistency of choice of the same playmates over a period of time (Hagman, 1933).

Among older children, by contrast, fluctuations in friendships begin to appear (Seagoe, 1933). From five years of age up to puberty, there are fluctuations in friendships, though these fluctuations become less pronounced with each passing year. Stability in friendships appears somewhat earlier for girls than for boys. There is little relationship between social acceptance and friendship fluctuation, as may be seen by the fact that children who are well accepted change their friends almost as much as those who are less well accepted (Horrocks and Thompson, 1946; Thompson and Horrocks, 1947; Horrocks and Buker, 1951). Increase in stability of friendships is shown in Fig. 40. When elementary-school children were asked their reasons for changing their friends, the most common reasons given were lack of recent contact, a recent quarrel, replaced by another child, incompatibility, conceited, bossy, disloyal, and underhanded. The reasons least frequently given were that the friend was selfish, rude, discourteous, unkind, dull, noisy, or silly (Austin and Thompson, 1948).

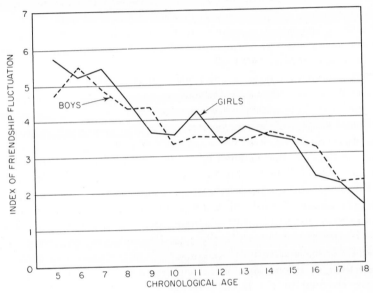

Fig. 40. Friendship fluctuations of boys and girls at different age levels. (*From J. E. Horrocks and M. E. Buker, A study of friendship fluctuations of preadolescents, J. genet. Psychol., 1951, 78, 131–144. Used by permission.*)

LEADERSHIP

In any group of children, no matter how young the children may be, the relationship is seldom one of equality. One individual usually stands out as a recognized leader. Popularity and leadership are not synonymous, though they are usually found together. A leader is always popular, though a popular individual is not necessarily a leader. Many popular individuals at every age are liked because they are easygoing and readily adapt themselves to social situations, but they lack other qualities that a leader must necessarily have. To be a leader, the child must be able to adapt his behavior to the needs of the group, must elicit positive reactions from the group, and must demonstrate his willingness and ability to carry cooperative tasks through to their completion (Gibb, 1947; Stogdill, 1948; Sanford, 1949; Zeleny, 1949).

Studies of leadership have revealed that leadership is not an inborn trait, but that it develops over a relatively long period of time (Link, 1944). It requires considerable exertion on the individual's part. If it comes by chance, to fill a void left by another, it is not likely to persist (Jennings, 1937, 1944). The roots of leadership are found in childhood experiences (Allen, 1952). Of these experiences, the most important are closely related to parental attitudes regarding child-rearing methods. Parents of children who show leadership ability are less protective, less restrictive, and permit the child greater freedom than do parents of children who become followers (Miles, 1946). Once the child has acquired the prestige of being a leader, this prestige carries over from one situation to another, and thus leadership becomes a persistent characteristic of the individual (Gibb, 1947). Leadership status is usually concentrated in a few children (Bogen, 1954). They are the ones who are popular with their peers, though friendship and leadership are not highly related. A child may have many friends and not be selected as a leader, though fellowship is one functional component of leadership (Hollander and Webb, 1955).

First Appearance of Leadership. Leadership ability shows itself as soon as two children are placed together. The dominant child takes the toys that appeal to him. Should the toy be in the possession of another child, he will push, pull, kick, and do everything within his power to get it. By the age of ten months, the baby is usually conscious of his triumphs, and a smile of self-satisfaction lights up his face. The baby who has been forced into a position of submission looks sorrowful, whimpers, or cries. The older, stronger, and more skillful baby takes the lead and dominates the smaller, weaker, and less skilled baby (Bühler, 1930; Shirley, 1933).

Leadership in Early Childhood. The child leader is characteristically superior to the other members of the group in size, intelligence, and generally in age. Because of his superior age and intelligence, he has more suggestions to offer for play, and thus the other children are willing to follow his lead. Sex is an unimportant factor in leadership at this age. Girls often assume the role of leadership over boys as well as over other girls. Likewise, social status, nationality, or physical attractiveness are not as important qualities now as they will be later. Fairness and social responsibility to the group, on the other hand, are important characteristics of the child leader. The child leader is usually characterized by ascendant behavior which is accompanied by social responsiveness, a tendency to resist adult control, and expressions of a rivalrous, competitive attitude. The child leader shows marked self-confidence (Jack, 1934).

At first, the child tries to dominate other children by the same technique that he used for adult domination, namely, crying, hitting, and temper outbursts. He soon discovers that this does not prove to be as effective as when used on adults, and he then modifies it. There is, however, during the early childhood years, a marked tendency for the leader to be the tyrannical boss of the group. Little consideration for others appears in the leader's behavior. He expects them to follow his wishes in an unquestioning manner and becomes angry or sullen if they rebel. Should his technique become too tyrannical, the leader finds himself displaced and another child is recognized as the new leader by the group. In contrast to the "bully," who tries to lead by brute force, is the "diplomat," whose technique is to lead by artful and indirect suggestions, bargains, or even bribes and threats. Such leaders generally gain and hold a following longer than do the leaders whose major technique is brute force and a bossy attitude (Parten, 1932a; Jack, 1934).

Leadership in Late Childhood. During late childhood, the leader represents the group's ideal. He must be a good athlete and an all-round good sport. As boys of this age are subject to hero worship, it is natural for them to follow the person who possesses the traits they most admire. Should the leader fall short of the group's expectations and should he display traits which they dislike, he soon loses prestige and is replaced as leader by another who, at the moment, more closely approximates the group's standards.

As childhood progresses, leaders are needed for different activities, as school and class offices, sports, gangs, and community groups, like the Boy and Girl Scouts. The same child will not necessarily have the qualifications needed for all such groups. Thus, as is true of adolescents and adults, there is a tendency among older children to select leaders for specific group activities (Caldwell and Wellman, 1926; Stogdill, 1948). However, there is no question about the fact that prestige and experience gained from serving as a leader in one group activity will carry over to other activities and give the child who has been a leader an advantage over the child who may be equally suited for leadership in this particular activity but who has never been a leader.

Numerous studies of the characteristics of leaders in late childhood have revealed some of the most important characteristics of such leaders. They include slightly above average chronological age, intelligence, scholastic achievement; good looks; some outstanding physical feature that is admired by the group; adventuresomeness; desire to lead and ambition to be a leader; and such personality traits as dependability, sociability, responsibility, good-naturedness, generosity, fairness, good work habits or efficiency, and good social and self-adjustments. Leaders show above-average refinement and generally belong to families of slightly superior socioeconomic status as compared with the rest of the group. They are generally the oldest or other than the youngest member of the family. Rarely do they rate high in ascendancy or bossiness. They are keenly alive to the social situation, and are able to evaluate the wishes of the group, and to assess their own abilities realistically. They show, thus, good social insight as well as self-insight (Partridge, 1934; Pigors, 1935; Lippitt, 1941; Alexandria, 1946; Lasswell, 1948; Stogdill, 1948; Brody, 1950; Maas, 1951; Wolman, 1951; Gordon, 1952; Bell and Hall, 1954).

An interesting comparison of a group of fourth-grade children revealed the differences in characteristics of leaders and nonleaders at this age. Personality dimensions most often found in adult leaders, as dependability, ability to finish an assigned task, resourcefulness, and self-confidence, were found among the leaders. Instead of aggressiveness, the leaders showed themselves to be quiet, fair, and capable children. Intelligence was not found to be as important as classroom habits. The leaders listened carefully, followed instructions, were resourceful and dependable in class, and got their work done. They were self-confident, cooperative, showed emotional stability, kindness, humor, and marked insight or awareness of the wishes of the group. The better the child was adjusted, the greater his chances of being selected as a leader.

By contrast, the children who were not selected as leaders were found to be emotionally immature in that they pouted when their wishes were blocked or reverted to the babyish habit of crying; their work habits were poor, even if their IQ's were as high as those of the children chosen to be leaders; they tried to win recognition for themselves and had more anti-social tendencies, more nervous mannerisms, were more aggressive and less cooperative in group situations; they showed less mental energy and initiative; and were less well adjusted socially than the leaders (Mason, 1952). Even as a child, the leader must perceive the needs of the group members and act in a way to satisfy the greatest number and the most important of these needs (Bell and Hall, 1954). As Stogdill (1948) has summed up the whole matter, "The average person who occupies a position of leadership exceeds the average member of his group to some degree in the following respects: sociability, initiative, persistence, knowing how to get things done, self-confidence, alertness to and insight into situations, cooperativeness, popularity, adaptability, and verbal facility."

The *technique of leadership* among older children differs from that which proved to be successful among younger children. The leader can be authoritarian and despotic in his methods only when the group is very large and when he has won the admiration and respect of every member (Wolman, 1951). For the most part, however, the leader must give the rest of the group some choice, and they must agree to his suggestions and be willing to follow them (Hirota, 1951). In a small group, there is likely to be less agreement among the members than in larger groups. The leader influences greatly the amount of agreement there will be. The larger the group, then, the more leadership skill the leader will need to retain his position of leadership (Hare, 1952). The child who has had little or no previous experience as a leader is likely not to possess this skill as he grows older and the size of the group the leader must be able to control becomes larger.

SOCIAL ACCEPTANCE

Social acceptance—or "popularity," as it is generally called—is an index of the success with which an individual has taken his place in a social group and the extent to which his associates like to work and play with him. More specifically, *popularity* means general admiration of an individual, even though one may not associate with him. *Acceptance,* by contrast, means being chosen as an associate for a realistic activity in a group of

The social isolate may lack social acceptance because he has little interest in the group and its activities and prefers to do things he considers interesting. (*From Child Development, a McGraw-Hill Text-Film.*)

which one is a member (Northway, 1946). An active member of a group is not necessarily popular or accepted. Sometimes a child who is literally in everything and pushes himself into the different groups in his school class is thoroughly disliked by his classmates. *Rejection* may result when a child is actively disliked because of his behavior, or it may come because the child is so shy, withdrawn, and nondescript that no one wants to associate with him (Northway, 1946). A *social isolate* may occupy a position of lack of acceptance in the group because of his behavior or because he has little interest in the group and prefers isolation or the companionship of adults to the companionship of his peers.

There is no direct relationship between social acceptance and the desire for social contacts. Furthermore, there is no indication that any child is completely lacking in the desire to relate himself to his peers (Hartley, 1946). Whether or not a child will be accepted in a given group depends not upon the child himself, but also upon the tastes and interests of the group or groups available for him to associate with (Jersild, 1954). As Dymond et al. (1952) have pointed out, "One's place in a group seems to depend not so much on one's role-taking ability per se but also on social techniques which vary with the structure and function of the particular group." However, if the social climate of a school class or any other group is to be good, there must be proportionately more children who are accepted than those who are rejected by their classmates (Forlano and Wrightstone, 1955).

Degrees of Acceptance. How much social acceptance a child will enjoy will vary according to the child and the groups available for him to associate with. And how intimate his relationship is with the group or with different individuals within the group will likewise vary (Bogardus, 1948; Wittenberg and Berg, 1952). There is no evidence that the degree to which a child accepts others will be closely related to the degree to which others accept him. He may accept many and be accepted by many or few. Similarly, he may be accepted by many and show an accepting attitude toward many or few (Cunningham, 1951). It is very rare, however, for any one child to be accepted by every child with whom he comes in contact. As Jersild (1954) has put it, "No one, in other words, has a corner on the market of social acceptability."

Social acceptance ranges from the *star* to the *social isolate*. The star is the child who is at the center of an admiring group of persons who claim him as their most intimate friend, even though he does not reciprocate many of these friendship choices, either because of indifference or because he does not want to show favoritism and thus alienate friends (Chapin, 1950). At the other extreme is the isolate, who either voluntarily withdraws from the social group because of lack of interest in the children with whom circumstances place him or because they reject him. Between these extremes are levels of acceptance which serve to place the individual in the pattern of status relationships (McGuire and Clark, 1952). This is illustrated in Fig. 41.

Awareness of Acceptance. By the time the child reaches the fifth grade, he is well aware of the level of acceptance he has achieved in the group (Northway, 1946). Each year, as he grows older, he is better able to tell how others feel about him (Ausubel et al., 1952). His awareness of the degree of acceptance he has comes from many sources, the three most important of which are the way others *treat* him, whether they want to play with him or shun him, whether they accept him on a par or not with other children; the *nickname* that originates for him among his friends, whether pleasant or unpleasant, whether complimentary or derogatory (Dexter, 1949); and the name of the *category* in which he is grouped. Levels of acceptance are designated by such names as "wheels" (the top crowd, or the ones who run everything); "brains" (students, or those who take little interest in anything but studies); "mice" (the quiet ones who are inoffensive and ineffectual); "drips" (would-be wheels who make others uncomfortable); and "dopes" (would-be brains who arouse antagonism) (McGuire and Clark, 1952).

Effects on Attitudes and Behavior. The importance of social acceptability lies in the fact that much of a child's social adjustment depends upon the degree to which his contemporaries find him acceptable. The child who is

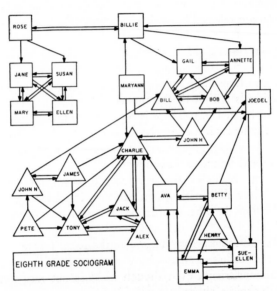

Fig. 41. A sociogram showing how the popularity of different members of a group is determined. (*From R. A. Clark and C. McGuire, Sociographic analysis of sociometric valuations, Child Develpm., 1952, 23, 129–140. Used by permission.*)

popular is happy and secure. He learns to get along with others and develops socially acceptable behavior because he is one of the group. He is mentally free to turn his attention outward and hence becomes interested in people and things outside himself (Vicery, 1946). If he is too popular, however, he is likely to become indifferent toward others (Chapin, 1950). The unpopular child, on the other hand, finds himself an outsider, and this makes him unhappy and insecure. He feels that he is "different," and as a result, becomes timid or resentful (Hartley, 1946). As Frank and Frank (1954) have pointed out, "The results of being left out of a group, or the price paid for staying 'in' with a small few, involves self-doubt, mean, harmful tactics toward others and, in most cases, a personal philosophy of life that may be self-destructive."

When rejected by others, the child often develops problem behavior (Northway, 1946). In an attempt to force himself into the group that has excluded him, he develops many socially unacceptable forms of behavior which add to his unpopularity and push him further out of the group. In addition, he becomes "self-bound," thinking more about himself than about others. This sets up barriers to interaction and makes later acceptance difficult, if not impossible (Kidd, 1951). Children with low peer acceptance have been found to be considerate toward those with high peer acceptance

A child is well aware of his status in the group. If he is asked to play with others, he knows that he is accepted. (*From Adolescent Development: a McGraw-Hill Text-Film.*)

and those who are new in the classroom. They are inconsiderate toward those who, like themselves, enjoy low peer acceptance. Children with high peer acceptance are considerate toward others with high peer acceptance, but inconsiderate toward those whose peer acceptance is low, or only slightly lower than theirs, or who are new in the classroom. Commenting on these findings, it was suggested that there is "a kind of 'peck order' in the social hierarchy" (Forshay, 1951).

Popularity Traits. Traits that make a child popular and accepted vary from *age* to age and from *group* to group (Tuddenham, 1951; Garrison, 1952). Among first-grade children, the quiet, inconspicuous children are more popular than the active, talkative, and aggressive ones (Tyler, 1951). By the third grade, on the other hand, the quiet children are likely to be overlooked, while those often mentioned by their teachers for undesirable behavior are the ones most often mentioned by their peers for desirable behavior (Bonney, 1947; Brieland, 1952). Acceptance values differ according to the *socioeconomic* status of the group. Boys of the lower socioeconomic groups are more admired by their peers if they do not conform too closely to adult standards of behavior, while those of the upper socioeconomic groups are admired when they conform more closely to adult standards (Pope, 1953). There are likewise *sex differences* in admired traits. Boys admire "real boys," those who are adventuresome, assertive, and competent in sports. Girls, up to the fifth grade, admire the "little lady" who is quiet and reserved, after which they change and show a preference for the "tomboy" type of girl (Tuddenham, 1951).

There are, however, certain characteristics which distinguish socially acceptable children of different ages and in different groups. For the most part, these characteristics remain fairly constant through the childhood years, and then change, to a certain extent, as the individual emerges into adolescence. No one single trait distinguishes the popular from the unpopular child. Instead, the distinguishing quality is the *degree and direction of outgoing energy*. The child is popular because of what he is and what he does that wins the admiration of others. He makes himself felt in the group by doing things that make him stand out from the rest of the group and that win the admiration of others, rather than because he refrains from doing things that they would dislike. In other words, a child is popular far more because of what he does than because of what he refrains from doing (Bonney, 1943; Northway, 1943a, 1946; Grossmann and Wrighter, 1948). Social acceptance is, thus, closely related to the child's ability to distinguish himself from his associates (Hardy, 1937).

Children who turn their energies outward are friendly, cooperative, adjust without making a disturbance, comply with requests, accept gracefully what happens, and make good adjustments to adults as well as to children. They are kind to others, share what they have, are willing to take turns in any game the group plays, and show impartiality in the dealings with the members of the group. They assume responsibilities, participate in and enjoy social activities, feel secure in their status, and compare themselves favorably with their peers. The personality pattern of the highly accepted child is that of the expansive, dynamic, objective individual, free from fears and anxieties (Koch, 1933; Hardy, 1937; Lippitt, 1941; Bonney, 1943, 1947; Kuhlen and Lee, 1943; Northway, 1946; Grossmann and Wrighter, 1948; Brody, 1950; Smith, 1950; Baron, 1951). The popular child is usually a good student, not because of greater intelligence, but because he is conscientious in his studies (Brown and Morris, 1954).

Unpopularity Traits. Whether or not a child will be popular in a given group depends partly upon his own qualities and partly upon the group. A child who is too different from the other members of the group in appearance, intelligence, personality, family background, interests, or any one of a number of different traits is likely to be regarded by the group as "queer" or "different." As such, the child will not be an acceptable member of that group. Should he, however, be placed in a group with other children whose interests and abilities are more nearly like his, his chances of social acceptance will be greatly increased (Hollingworth, 1926). The behavior deviations of an unpopular child may be the result of lack of acceptance, not the cause of it (Brown and Morris, 1954).

Children who are unpopular may be shy, retiring, lacking in energy, socially disinterested, listless, and reserved. As a result of their behavior, they are likely to be overlooked by other children or to be rejected by them because they do not fit into the pattern of activities of the group. Other children who are unpopular may be energetic, but they turn their energies into channels that make other children dislike them. They try to win attention and acceptance by annoying others through different forms of aggressive behavior, as shouting, bullying, showing off, insisting on having their own way, and refusing to comply with the rules and regulations that other children accept. In a less aggressive manner, they annoy others by dawdling, doing things in their own way, failing to carry out assigned tasks, and being silly, and thus keeping other children from concentrating on what they are trying to do. They often complain, bid for sympathy and help from adults, or run away at a time when it is inconvenient for adults to go after them. In general, they make nuisances of themselves (Koch, 1933; Lippitt, 1941; Loeb, 1941; Kuhlen and Lee, 1943; Northway, 1943a, 1944, 1946; Frenkel-Brunswik, 1946; Bonney, 1947; Moreno, 1947; Smith, 1950; Tyler, 1951; Laughlin, 1953; Denhoff, 1954).

The personality pattern of an unpopular child is that of the ingrown, self-bound, self-centered person. He is restless, suffers from feelings of insecurity and inferiority, and lacks a feeling of belonging. He is more likely to have personality disturbances of greater or lesser severity than is the popular child. Frequently, he feels so frustrated that he becomes aggressively antagonistic to others, especially to adults in authority or to other children who assume leadership roles. No matter how hard he tries, he invariably feels that he has made a failure of what he has undertaken. Such unfavorable self-concepts lead to poor adjustments, and these, in turn, result in greater unpopularity as the child grows older (Northway, 1946; Bonney, 1947; Grossmann and Wrighter, 1948; Brody, 1950; Baron, 1951). As a result of these unfavorable self-concepts, unpopular children are less effective in working with others on a skillful social level, and this tends to increase their unpopularity (Rosen, 1952).

Factors Influencing Popularity. Certain factors, it has been found from analyses of popular children, contribute to a child's popularity, while other factors actually militate against it. The different factors which influence the degree of popularity enjoyed by children throughout the preschool and elementary-school years are as follows.

1. *Sex.* While it is true that there are popular boys just as there are popular girls in any age group, there are indications that girls, as a group, enjoy greater popularity than do boys. Among nursery-school children, girls have been found to be more popular than boys (Koch, 1933). Among older children, girls at every age are generally more highly socialized than boys of that age and, as a result, make better social adjustments (Bonney, 1942, 1944a). Girls with brothers generally make better social adjustments and are more popular than girls who have only sisters (Hardy, 1937).

2. *Intelligence.* Bright children and those who are successful in their school work are better liked than those who are less bright. Very bright children, on the other hand, tend to be inconsiderate of the rights of others or so indifferent to them that they make no real attempt to adjust to them. Younger children in a group are generally more popular than overage children who are less bright and who, as a result, are likely to feel inferior and thus make poor adjustments. The relationship between mental age and social acceptance is greater than between chronological age and social acceptance (Koch, 1933; Hardy, 1937; Bonney, 1942a; Grossmann and Wrighter, 1948; Taylor, 1952). Children who are academically competent, especially those who read well, are more popular than those whose academic work is of a lower caliber. Children who enjoy reading as a leisure-time activity are as socially acceptable as those who read little (Bonney, 1942a; Morgan, 1946; Grossmann and Wrighter, 1948; Mitchell, 1949). Children who are not promoted with their classmates are usually not popular with children who are regularly promoted. Their friends are in the higher grades, but because of lack of promotion, they lose contact with them and, as a result, have few friends among the children in their classes (Sandin, 1944; Laughlin, 1953).

3. *Physical Condition.* A healthy child is more likely to be a happy child than is the one whose health is poor. The most popular children are generally vigorously healthy and in a better all-around condition than their classmates. Furthermore, they are usually superior to other children in tests of physical achievement (Hardy, 1937). Children whose health is generally poor, owing to poor diets or illness, are likely to be socially maladjusted, thus causing them to be unpopular (Everitt and Potgieter, 1952). Physically handicapped children are usually shy and withdrawn or overly active, thus causing them to be unpopular (Denhoff, 1954).

4. *Looks.* While younger children are not so "looks-conscious" as they will be when they reach the age of adolescence, they are not unaware of the attitude of others toward physical attractiveness and unattractiveness. Looks are taken into consideration in the selection of friends and leaders, even though this factor may play a minor role, as compared with the role

it plays during the adolescent years. (Kuhlen and Lee, 1943; Tyler, 1951; Cannon et al., 1952). Size has not been found to be a significant factor in popularity, as is shown by the fact that short boys and tall girls are among those best liked (Hardy, 1937).

Among elementary-school children, looks are rated high in choice of friends (Tryon, 1939; Kuhlen and Lee, 1943; Austin and Thompson, 1948; Cannon et al., 1952). In one study, two-thirds of the popular children were rated as having an attractive appearance, while less than one-fifth of the unpopular children were so described. No child who was called "ugly" was among the popular, and no child who was described as "very attractive" was among the unpopular (Hardy, 1937). Girls at all ages rate personal attractiveness as more important in the choice of friends than do boys (Cannon et al., 1952). By the fifth grade, tidiness has a fairly high value in popularity (Tuddenham, 1951). This, however, is more true of girls than of boys (Tryon, 1939). The most popular children at all ages are those who are in complete accord with the group norms in dress, grooming, and manners (Bonney, 1947).

5. *"Halo" Effect of Popularity*. According to popular belief, "nothing succeeds like success." It is generally conceded that the successful individual has an advantage over those who are less successful or who are unable to create the impression of being as successful as he. This "halo" effect of success plays no small role in determining who will be popular and who will not (Kuhlen and Lee, 1943). The child's reputation and status in the group are determined partly by his actual behavior and partly by the picture other children carry in their mind of him and about the social group to which he belongs (Morgan, 1946). This means that once a child has received a reputation, based on the impressions others have of him, it is hard to change. The accepted remain accepted, and the rejected remain as outcasts of the group. Even when the outcasts receive help, they make little headway in becoming more popular (Singer, 1951). Older children give more consideration to the reputations among group members of individuals in choosing their friends than do younger children (Staker, 1948).

Popularity among children is quite highly concentrated in a few, with a tendency for most of the children to choose a few who stand at the top. Those who are most popular in the classroom are generally most popular on the playground as well (Bonney, 1942a). While children are not accepted on the basis of their play skills alone, if they are already accepted, superiority in skills helps to increase their acceptance (Northway, 1946). The child who has a close personal relationship with another child is generally well accepted by other children. The child without a close personal friend, on the other hand, may not be rejected by other children, but he is not generally sought out as a companion by other children. To remedy this situation, he may choose the "stars" with whom he has little, if any, contact. He is thus protected from rebuff and can rationalize about his contact with the stars in his sphere as one might about a motion-picture celebrity (Potashin, 1946).

6. *Proximity to Group.* The more contacts a child can have with other children, the greater will be the chances for him to form friendships and become an accepted member of the group. If, however, his personality pattern is such that others dislike him, close proximity can just as readily increase social rejection. Studies of children who are transported to school by bus have revealed that they have fewer friends and are less popular than those who live within the neighborhood of the school (Bonney, 1951). Among adolescents who can use the family car for transportation to school activities, this factor is far less important than it is in the case of younger children (Blanchard, 1947; Becker and Loomis, 1948).

Length of residence in a community is not as important a factor in popularity as is often believed (Morgan, 1946). Among elementary-school children, those who have moved once or twice or have been in a school system for a period of one to three years have been found to have greater acceptance among their classmates than those who have been in one school throughout their entire academic life, or who have moved around a lot, or have been in one school system for less than one year (Downie, 1953).

7. *Family Background.* The type of adjustments parents make to each other is reflected in the child's social adjustments. This holds true more for the type of adjustments made by the mother than by the father, and for younger children as compared with older children (Baruch, 1937). The relationships the child has with his siblings likewise is reflected in the type of adjustments he makes outside the home. On the whole, the child from a happy home, where there is little friction and tension, will be more popular than the child who comes from a home marked by friction among the different family members (Bossard, 1953, 1954).

While some investigations report that children from smaller-sized families are more popular than those from larger families (Hardy, 1937; Bonney, 1944), others report that the child from a large family is more popular (Dexter, 1949; Loomis et al., 1949). In-between children are generally more popular than the oldest or youngest of the family, while only children, if they come from a superior socioeconomic group, may make good social adjustments (Bonney, 1942a, 1944), but generally they are less popular than children with siblings (Dexter, 1949). The explanation given for the popularity of children from larger families is that they have learned to make social adjustments in the home, and this gives them a pattern of behavior which helps them to be popular outside the home (Dexter, 1949; Bossard, 1953, 1954). A home that requires the child to assume some responsibility prepares the child for better social adjustments than the home that does not require such responsibilities (Brody, 1950). Overprotective parents or parents who set up blocks against the child's participation in activities with his peers are likely to deprive the child of the social learning necessary for popularity then and as the child grows older (McGuire, 1953).

8. *Socioeconomic Status.* Most popular children at all ages come from homes that are superior in cultural, social, and economic conditions. The least popular children, on the other hand, come from homes which are inferior in social and economic status (Hardy, 1937; Bonney, 1944, 1947; Grossmann and Wrighter, 1948; MacDonald et al., 1949). There is a close correlation between the social acceptance of a child and the level of occupation of the father (Morgan, 1946; Bossard, 1954). By the fifth or sixth grades, socioeconomic status plays an even more important role in social acceptability than it did in the younger grades, and it becomes increasingly more important as the child grows older (Neugarten, 1946). A child from a low socioeconomic status can enjoy high peer acceptance only when he takes over the values and behavior patterns of his higher-status classmates. If he does this successfully, he is known as a "climber" and will enjoy more peer acceptance than the child from a low socioeconomic status who does not attempt to accept the patterns of the higher group or does so unsuccessfully (McGuire and Clark, 1952).

9. *Social Insight.* The personality pattern of the child and the degree of adjustment he makes to the social group are important in social acceptance (Bonney, 1942a; Greenblatt, 1950). These, however, are largely dependent upon the social insight and self-insight of the child. How well accepted the child will be depends upon his success or failure in sizing up others in the group as well as himself (Bogardus, 1948; Davitz, 1955). Children who are unpopular or who are "fringe" members of a group may not be lacking in insight, but rather in the social skills necessary to capitalize their ability (Dymond et al., 1952). Because children under eight or nine years of age are rarely able to perceive the attitudes of others toward them, good social adjustments to a group are not possible much before that age. With each passing year, the child's social insight and self-insight increase, with the result that those who are superior in these personality characteristics are usually more acceptable than those who lag behind in this development (Ausubel et al., 1952). Growth of social insight is illustrated in Fig. 42.

10. *Degree of Adjustment.* The well-adjusted child is much more acceptable to both his peers and adults than is the poorly adjusted child (Dahlke, 1953). This, in turn, is influenced by the degree to which he accepts himself and is willing to suit his level of aspiration to his abilities (Jersild, 1954). This will be discussed in more detail on pages 568–570. In self-acceptance, one of the most important areas is that of psychosexual development. The well-adjusted child must accept his sex role as prescribed by the social group to which he belongs (Cassel and Saugstad, 1952).

Persistence of Popularity. Marked shifts in sociometric status are comparatively rare. Instead, children tend to maintain the same general social status, and this tendency becomes more pronounced as the child grows older (Bronfenbrenner, 1944). In a newly organized group of unacquainted individuals, there is considerable trial and error before the preference patterns crystallize. During this period, friendships change frequently (Hunt and Solomon, 1942). However, once the group becomes acquainted and friendships are established among the different members of the group, there are marked individual differences among the members in regard to the popularity each member enjoys. Once established in a certain sociometric

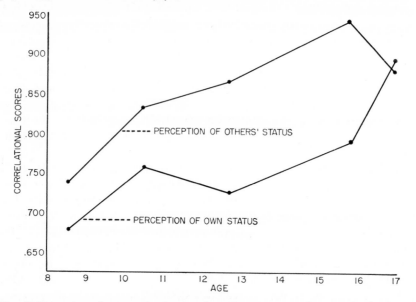

Fig. 42. Perception of own and others' sociometric status at various age levels. (*From D. P. Ausubel, H. M. Schiff, and E. B. Gasser, A preliminary study of developmental trends in sociopathy: accuracy of perception of own and others sociometric status. Child Develpm., 1952, 23, 111–128. Used by permission.*)

status within the group, the child retains this status month after month (Northway, 1943, 1946; Jennings, 1944; Bronfenbrenner, 1944; Witryol and Thompson, 1953). Even when there is a large turnover in the class, as shifts occur in the population or children go from elementary to junior high school, constancy of social status within the group remains (Tryon, 1939; Kuhlen and Lee, 1943; Kernstetter, 1944; Laughlin, 1953). Social-acceptance scores are almost as constant as intelligence and achievement-test scores (Bonney, 1943, 1943b; Taylor, 1952).

Once the group receives a total impression of an individual, it is hard to change that impression. This means that the socially accepted remain accepted and the outcasts remain outcasts (Singer, 1951). The individual's acceptance score in one group is a reliably accurate index of what his acceptance score will be in a reasonably similar (culture-age) group (North-way, 1946). What fluctuations there will be in status within a group will occur mainly in the middle group of socially accepted children, those who are only partially accepted. Furthermore, it can be predicted that "chance events . . . windfall successes and failures, have little influence on the acceptance scores" (Northway et al., 1947). How stable a child's social acceptance will remain over a period of time will depend partly upon the stability of the group and the extent to which there is a turnover of children who are able to attain a high degree of social acceptance (Bonney, 1942; Witryol and Thompson, 1953).

Improving Social Acceptance. It is not so easy to improve the child's social acceptance as many believe. This is because it is difficult to change the impression the child makes on his group. If he antagonizes other children or if he loses favor with them, it will be a long, hard process to reinstate himself in their favor. Even with help, the child who is a social isolate and has been rejected by the group makes little headway in winning their acceptance (Bonney, 1943, 1943b; Singer, 1951). One complicating factor is that the child's lack of acceptance is not fully recognized by his parents who have a tendency to overestimate his adjustment in social relationships (Langford and Alm, 1954). Teachers who do recognize the child's poor adjustments among his peers frequently judge him favorably because of the good impression he makes on them (Bonney, 1947). By the third grade, there is considerable difference between teachers' and pupils' evaluations of desirable behavior (Brieland, 1952).

Furthermore, when adults withdraw completely and let children make and run their own groups, "devastating things can happen," such as teasing, bullying, extreme and harmful competition both socially and academically (Frank and Frank, 1954). On the other hand, with guidance and help, many children who are not picked out and accepted by their peers at first may become acceptable members of the group (Buswell, 1953). This makes it possible to weld the class into a democratic group where the talents and skills of the isolates can be utilized (Brown and Morris, 1954). Unless this is done, the child who is not picked out by the group at first will feel insecure, and this makes later acceptance increasingly difficult to achieve. Once isolation is started, it becomes a circular reaction (Buswell, 1953).

To improve the child's social acceptance with his peers, the child's concept of himself, of the group, and of social activities and the group's concept of the child must be changed. These concepts are closely interrelated, with the former dependent upon the latter. Many attempts have been made to increase the child's social acceptance by his peers, and these have met with considerable success. These attempts consist of giving the group a chance to get to know a child who is shy and withdrawn by giving him an opportunity to work and play with other children in the group through seating arrangements in the classroom, through group projects, and by rotating leadership for different group projects. The child who is lacking in skills needed to keep pace with the activities of his peers is given help in acquiring these skills. Class discussions of popularity and the effect of lack of popularity on a child help to make children more understanding and tolerant of others they have treated as outcasts (Osborne, 1937; Fite, 1940; Elliott, 1942; Nedelsky, 1952; Rosenthal, 1952; Sandman, 1952; Wilkins, 1952; Hayes and Conklin, 1953; Kinney, 1953; Spector, 1953; Brown, 1954). When the child is an isolate because of his minority-group status, the group can learn to be more tolerant of him either through direct or vicarious experiences with individuals of minority groups (Hayes and Conklin, 1953).

Equally as important as changing the group's attitude toward the child is changing the child's attitude toward himself, toward the group, and social activity with his peers. The unpopular child compares himself unfavorably with others, and this makes him feel inadequate, and he wants to avoid the group and the activities of the group. Often he turns to the parent or teacher and depends upon them for his social contacts (Baron, 1951). Only by helping the child to understand himself and to accept himself can he learn to make satisfactory adjustments to others. This should be a planned feature of the child's education (Jersild, 1951). Children who have been helped to acquire competence in certain performances gain greater self-confidence, are more willing to enter into situations where there are other children, and as a result, they make better social adjustments (Jack, 1934; Jersild, 1954).

The child who does not know how to go about making friends can be shown how to do so, while the child who has annoying mannerisms can be helped to correct these and can be encouraged to display any talent or skill he may have which will place him in the limelight and thus win the favorable attention of other children (Nedelsky, 1952). Figure 43 shows the changes which occurred in one group from October to January, during which time attempts were made to increase the social acceptance of the isolates. While the stars still remained the stars, the number of isolates was reduced from seven to three in this short period of time.

Limitations. No adult, whether parent or teacher, can dictate to children whom they will like or be willing to accept as a member of their play group. This is the prerogative of the group. All the adult can do is to create situations which will enable the group to see the child in a more favorable role (Nedelsky, 1952). While marked gains in social acceptance are often made by children who have been helped to improve their social behavior, the chances of making such gains are greater when the group is small than when it is large (Kinney, 1953; Spector, 1953). The important thing is to help the child gain enough self-confidence so that he will make an effort to become a member of the group before he becomes resigned to playing the role of an isolate and develops forms of compensation which will militate against later acceptance. This should be done before the group gets so into the habit of thinking of him as a "fringer" that they may overlook any potential abilities he may have (Jersild, 1954).

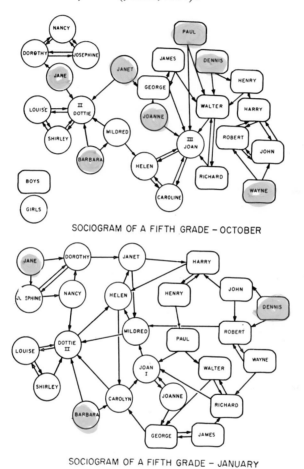

SOCIOGRAM OF A FIFTH GRADE – OCTOBER

SOCIOGRAM OF A FIFTH GRADE – JANUARY

Fig. 43. Improvement in social acceptance from October to January. Note that "Dottie" and "Joan" are still the "stars," while the number of social isolates has been reduced from seven to three. (*From F. J. Brown, Educational sociology, 2d ed., Prentice-Hall, 1954. Used by permission.*)

Gaining the reputation of being an isolate or a fringer may result in a persistence of that status, just as the reputation of being a star will persist as the child passes from one school grade to another. As Jersild (1954) has pointed out, "A youngster who, for one reason or another, has received a bad reputation in the elementary grades may still be plagued by it in junior high school, for even though many of the children there are new to him, one first-class gossip from the former grade may be able to stir up doubts and suspicions against him."

While every child wants to be socially accepted and while being well accepted is not only beneficial to the development of a healthy concept of self and of social skills which will enable the child to adjust successfully in any group in which he finds himself, persistent social acceptance from year to year does not necessarily guarantee a wholesome adjustment on the child's part, nor does it necessarily mean that the child's social development is progressing in a manner that will guarantee wholesome adjustments in adult life. If the child is accepted by his peers because they admire and respect him, well and good. If, on the other hand, he is accepted because he is willing to do as he is told by the group, is willing to sacrifice personal values and standards of behavior to buy his popularity, and to play a role imposed upon him by the group, even if that role is contrary to his own standards of behavior, then the price of acceptance is too high to pay and the temporary satisfaction the child derives from this acceptance will be outweighed by the permanent damage it may do to his personality and to his moral values (Wittenberg and Berg, 1952). Only when social acceptance and wholesome social and personality development go hand in hand is social acceptance an ideal to be striven for by every child.

Chapter 10

PLAY

Play is a term so loosely used that its real significance is apt to be lost. It relates to any activity engaged in for the enjoyment it gives, without consideration of the end result. It is entered into voluntarily by the individual and is lacking in external force or compulsion. The individual plays for the fun of playing and for no ulterior motive. It differs from *work,* which is an activity toward an end, in which the individual carries out the activity, not because he enjoys it, but because he wants the end result. Children distinguish between work and play on the basis of exterior conditions; i.e., work is class activity or helping around the house, while play is everything else. Bright children emphasize that work is a useful activity, while play is useless; work is a serious activity requiring application and attention, while play is a restful and easy activity (Cousinet, 1951).

Many people attempt to make a distinction between work and play activities, but there are no activities which may be classed as either one exclusively. Whether they belong to one category or the other depends upon the individual's attitude toward them. Collecting may be a form of play for a child or an adult who makes it a hobby, but it may also be work for the person who collects articles to sell at a profit. Drawing may be a pleasant pastime, engaged in by child or adult, but if the motive is to enter one's drawings in contests to compete for prizes, or to earn a living as an artist, drawing becomes a form of work rather than play. Any time that a play activity is directed toward an end other than enjoyment, as in the case of competitive games and sports, it assumes the aspect of work.

Many play activities of young children are imitations of adult activities. The child, in his play life, reproduces the activities he has observed among the adults of his environment. Because the activities in any community are more or less stereotyped in form, especially the activities of the home, the play of little children is very similar, regardless of the neighborhood environment in which they have been brought up. As children grow older and begin to associate with other children, their play is in imitation of the play of older children of the community. One generation passes down to the next generation the forms of play which it has found most satisfactory.

VALUE OF PLAY

Play is such an accepted part of child life that few people stop to consider how important its role is in the development of the child. *Physically,* play is essential if the child is to develop his muscles properly and exercise all parts of his body. Active play also serves as an outlet for surplus energy, which, if pent up, makes the child tense, nervous, and irritable. Play helps the child to *comprehend* and *control* the world in which he lives (Millichamp, 1953). It enables him to *experiment* and test out his abilities without taking the full responsibility for his actions (Jersild, 1954). Through it, he learns to distinguish between reality and fantasy (Barker et al., 1943).

Without play, especially play with other children instead of with adults, the child becomes selfish, self-centered, and domineering. From his play with others, he learns to share, to give and take, to cooperate, and to submerge his personality into that of the group. It is true that he might learn to *behave in a social manner* through his contacts with other children in school, but the typical school class or school-supervised play offers little opportunity for social behavior, as compared with free play outside of school. It likewise gives the child an outlet for the desire for *social contacts* which is rarely satisfied in the home, unless there are many children of approximately the same age, or in school, where too many restraints are placed on free social intercourse.

Within the family, make-believe play helps to reduce fraternal hostilities between older and younger siblings (Cahn, 1949). By playing with other children, the child learns how to establish social relationships with strangers and to meet and solve problems such relationships bring (Axline, 1951). This helps the child to develop as a person (Millichamp, 1953). Through cooperative games, the child learns to give and take and to cooperate with others (Cornelius, 1949). He learns to be a good loser as well as a gracious winner (DuBois, 1952). In play, the child assumes many different roles, thus teaching him which roles give him the greatest satisfaction and at the same time enabling him to establish the most satisfying relationships with others (Jersild, 1954).

Play is *educational.* The young child, through his play with toys of all types, learns to know the shapes, colors, sizes, and textures of objects, and their significance. Later, as he grows older, he develops many skills from playing games and sports. Exploring, collecting, and other favored forms of play in late childhood furnish the child with much information about the world he lives in that could not be obtained from school books. Reading, plays, concerts, and well-selected movies broaden the child's information while at the same time giving him much enjoyment. From his play, the child learns about himself and his abilities, thus helping him to establish a clearer concept of self (Axline, 1951).

Play is *therapeutic.* In everyday life, the child needs some release from the tensions that the restrictions imposed on him by his environment give rise to. Play serves this purpose by helping him to express his emotions (Millichamp, 1953). Fantasy play serves as an outlet for anxieties and the tensions anxiety brings (Symonds, 1946; Amen and Renison, 1954). Many of the needs and desires which cannot be met in daily life are met in play, and thus the frustrations of daily life are lessened for the child. Through his play, the child is often able to formulate and carry out plans which help him to solve problems that are of great importance to him in his private life (Axline, 1947; Mitchell and Mason, 1948; Frank and Hartley, 1951; Hartley, 1952; Hartley et al., 1952; Jersild, 1954).

From the child's play, *adults discover* many things about the child that they could learn in no other way. Among young children, doll play gives information about the environment and attitudes the child has been subjected to and the effects of these early experiences, especially maternal attitudes, on him (Winstet, 1951). The adult learns how the child establishes relations with other children and what the child's concept of himself is from observing his play with other children (Axline, 1947, 1951). Spontaneous drawings or drawings of the human form prove to be excellent revelations of the child's adjustments to people and his concept of himself in his relation to others (Bach, 1945; Machover, 1949; Merry and Merry, 1950; Reichenberg-Hackett, 1950; Jersild, 1954).

Finally, play is one of the most important forces in the *moral training* of the child. True, he learns what the group considers right and wrong in the home or in the school, but the enforcement of the acceptance of moral standards is never so rigid there as in the play group. The child knows that he must be fair, honest, truthful, a good sport, a good loser, and self-controlled if he is to be an acceptable member of the play group. He also knows that his playmates are far less tolerant of his lapses from the accepted codes of behavior than are the adults of his home and school environments. He therefore learns to toe the mark more quickly and more completely in play than at any other time.

CHARACTERISTICS OF CHILDREN'S PLAY

The play of children is in many ways different from that of adults. There are also certain characteristics of child play which may be found in whatever group of children one studies. These characteristics serve to show how different child play is from adult play. The outstanding characteristics of child play are as follows.

1. Play Follows a Pattern of Development. From early babyhood to maturity, certain definite play activities are popular at one age or another, no matter what the environment, the nationality, or the economic status of the child. Even though the popularity of a given type of play may rise and fall and the form of activity change with increase in maturity, there is no definite beginning or end to a given play activity. The time when the play is especially popular, however, is much the same from one group of children to another.

Play, at first, is very simple, consisting primarily of random movements and stimulation of the sense organs. Later, with development of intelligence, play becomes increasingly complex. Toy play is engaged in during early childhood and reaches its peak during the seventh or eighth year. This is known as the "toy age." However, after the child enters school, his play interests begin to change. During the first year or two of school, there is an overlapping of play activities characteristic of early childhood and those characteristic of late childhood. The favored play activities of early childhood persist for a few years while, at the same time, new play interests are developing. At first, the child is interested in running games, and after that, sports with strict rules and regulations become the favorite pastimes. Likewise, reading interests and interest in movies, collecting, television, radio, singing, and construction all occur in a more or less regular order and at times which conform to a pattern of development. Late childhood is often called the "play age" because there is a wider range of play activities than at any other time.

Block building passes through four distinct stages in development. At first, the child merely handles, carries, and piles blocks in irregular masses; in the second stage, construction of rows and towers begins; in the third, patterns and techniques develop; in the fourth, the child dramatizes and reproduces actual structures (Johnson, 1933). Definite patterns likewise appear in drawing, starting with scratching and dotting with a crayon at one year and developing into pictures against backgrounds by the time the child is eight years old (Bell, 1952). There are seasonal patterns in children's play with certain favorite activities for different seasons, such as roller-skating in the spring and football in the fall (Sullenger et al., 1953).

2. Play Activities Decrease in Number with Age. Late childhood is often described as the "play age," not because more time is devoted to play, as the name would suggest, but because a greater variety of play activities is engaged in than at any other time. There is an overlapping of the play activities characteristic of childhood and those of the adolescent years. Consequently, it is not at all unusual to find the nine-year-old playing with dolls, trains, or other childhood toys while at the same time taking an active interest in sports of the high-school or college ages, such as baseball, basketball, or football. For both boys and girls, the smallest number of games are played between four and six years, most between seven and nine years, while between ten and thirteen years, there is a falling off of interest in games (Conn, 1951).

Between the ages of two and six years, play activities include dramatic play, block play, water play, use of graphic materials, finger painting, music, and rhythms (Hartley et al., 1952). At this time, the child's play is creative, dramatic, repetitive, imaginative, and inventive (Reece, 1954). During the first three grades of school, there is an emphasis on play involving bodily activity, doing something or going somewhere, rather than on activities of a more intellectual or aesthetic type. At this time, only a small minority of children emphasize reading or music in their play (Jersild and Tasch, 1949). Among eight-year-olds, an average of 40.11 different play activities has been reported as engaged in during one week as compared with an average of 17.71 per week in the case of those twenty-two years old or older (Lehman and Witty, 1927a). Social play activities, involving play with other children, likewise decrease with age. At 7½ years, an average of 27 are engaged in as compared with 21 at 11½ years and 13 at 16½ years (Witty, 1931).

Decrease in the number of play activities is due partly to less time available for play, partly to a greater understanding of their interests and abilities on the part of the members of the older group, and partly to a longer attention span which enables older children to enjoy one play activity for a longer time than is possible with a younger child.

3. Time Spent in Play Decreases with Age. Babies and young children spend most of their waking time in play. Except for bathing, dressing, eating, and toileting, the young child's waking hours are free to spend as he wishes. As he grows older, however, his leisure time decreases because of new duties imposed on him and because of the time spent in school. The result is that the child must select from the different play activities those which please him most and concentrate on them. This becomes increasingly true as the child reaches adolescence and his leisure time is more and more limited.

4. Time Spent in Specific Activities Increases with Age. Because of poor concentration, little children go from one toy to another or from one play activity to another. The result is that they must have a large number of playthings if their interest is to be sustained. A two-year-old, for example, can attend to a play activity for 6.9 minutes, on the average, as compared with 12.6 minutes at five years (Van Alstyne, 1932). There is also an increase in the time spent in one activity as the child grows older (Bridges, 1929). When play materials are interesting to them, nursery-school children will persevere in a play situation even when the activity is difficult for them (Wilson, 1955).

5. Childhood Play Is Informal. The play of little children is spontaneous and informal. The child plays when and with what toys he wishes, regardless of time or place. He does not need special play equipment. As a matter of fact, he often derives more pleasure from playing with objects belonging to adults than from his toys. Likewise, he does not need special play clothes. He plays just as often when dressed in his best clothes as when he is wearing play clothes. A special place reserved for play is not necessary at this age; and he does not make appointments to play at a certain time, as adults do.

Gradually, play becomes more and more formal and much of the spontaneity of the child's play disappears during adolescence. Even during the gang age, the child feels that special clothing, as a baseball suit; special equipment, as a tennis ball instead of a rubber ball; and a special place for play, as a baseball diamond or tennis court, are essential. Appointments

Because of poor concentration, it is difficult for young children to remain interested in any play activity for any length of time. (*From Child Development, a McGraw-Hill Text-Film.*)

to meet and play at a definite time are made, and each player is expected to appear promptly so as not to inconvenience the other players. This trend toward formality in play increases every year, with the result that, in adolescence, play is a serious thing, and not the informal, casual activity that is so enjoyable to the young child.

6. Play Is Less Physically Active as the Child Grows Older. The adolescent's play involves little energy. This contrasts markedly with the play of little children, which is very active. Likewise, it is very different from the play of older children, who prefer games and sports of the most active type and who care little for the sedentary play activities so popular during the adolescent years. During the first three grades in school, children prefer play that is active (Jersild and Tasch, 1949). From grades 4 through 8, on the other hand, the most popular forms of play consist of listening to the radio, going to the movies, reading, listening to music, roller-skating, and playing different games (Sullenger et al., 1953).

TYPES OF PLAY

How the child plays will depend largely upon his age. At different ages, different forms of play predominate. Likewise, the form a given type of play takes will depend upon the child's age and level of development. The following are the favorite types of play of the childhood years.

1. FREE, SPONTANEOUS PLAY

The earliest play to make its appearance is free, spontaneous play. This type of play is characterized by lack of rules and regulations and is, for the most part, solitary rather than social. The child plays as he wishes to play and stops playing when he is no longer interested in it. This is especially pleasurable in the case of young children who find it difficult to play in a definite way or to conform to rules and regulations. Informal play of this type loses popularity late in childhood, when competitive games are more favored.

Play of this type is mostly exploratory. The baby derives keen enjoyment from stimulating the sense organs and thus experiencing different sensations. At first, most of his play is with his limbs, because lack of motor coordination makes play with toys very difficult. By the time the baby is three months old, control of his hands is well enough developed to enable him to play with toys or any objects within his reach. He explores his toys by sucking, banging, and pulling at them and investigates objects such as cloth, fur and wool, eyeglasses, or watch chains.

Free, spontaneous play involves the use of toys, though toys are not essential. After the child has explored his toys extensively enough to find out how they work, he uses them for make-believe play or construction. Owing to poor motor coordination, the little child, during this exploratory period, is apt to be very destructive. He pulls to pieces or breaks his toys, not willfully, but unintentionally, because they are not strong enough to withstand the strain that the child's exploratory behavior places on them. By the end of the second year, the child turns his attention to more advanced and complicated forms that tax his developing mentality to a greater extent than the simple, free play of babyhood. At times, he reverts to this play for a year or two, but with each year, it becomes less and less satisfying to him. As a result, he abandons it in favor of play of a more advanced, more highly organized type.

2. Make-believe Play

Make-believe play is play in which the child, through language or overt behavior, deals with materials or situations as if they had attributes other than those they actually have. It is a "game of illusion" in which the child acts with "every fiber of his being" (K. Bühler, 1930). Dramatic impersonation begins as early as ten months to one year of age, though the usual time is between the ages of 1½ and 2 years (Jersild, 1954). Children learn much of their make-believe play from older children, especially siblings. In a group of children of wide age range, there is more imaginative behavior than in a group of the same age and sex, because the younger children learn imitatively from the older children in the group (Markey, 1935).

Dramatic play serves many functions in the child's life. Among these are ability to transcend his actual limitations and go beyond the restrictions imposed by reality; ability to realize his wishes vicariously; and ability to rid himself of irritations, to remove or overcome conditions which annoy or thwart him in real life (Jersild, 1954). The more strongly the child is frustrated, the more make-believe play he will engage in. The poorly adjusted child engages in more make-believe play than does the well-adjusted child (Symonds, 1946). Observations of nursery-school children at play revealed that those who spent the most time in manipulative play had the lowest anxiety scores, while those with higher anxiety scores devoted more time to make-believe play. Highly intelligent children at this age play on a constructive, creative level (Amen and Renison, 1954). The child pretends to be someone he loves and admires and whom he would like to resemble. By assigning a role to a doll, toy animal, or some other toy, he changes his own status (Peller, 1952).

Pattern of Make-believe Play. Studies of make-believe play in children have shown that it follows a definite pattern in its development. Markey (1935) noted that children under three years of age showed a predominant interest in *personification*, such as talking to dolls or inanimate objects, or games involving imagined creatures, as a "bogey man"; in *make-believe use of materials*, including the imaginative naming of objects, as calling a slide a train, or simple, overt, imaginative behavior, as drinking from an empty cup; and in *make-believe situations*, involving a complicated use of materials, such as playing house. In most instances, their play is related to the materials before them. After three years of age, *make-believe use of materials* proved to be the most typical imaginative activity. As children grew older, the materials were used in increasingly more complicated ways, such as using sand to build a tunnel instead of merely digging into it with a shovel. In addition to this, children after three years of age engage in play involving *make-believe situations, constructive activities* with raw materials, and *dramatic play* of a more or less complicated type.

Forms of Make-believe Play. The make-believe play of children is a mirror of the culture which surrounds them, in that it dramatizes events of their everyday lives. Everything the child hears or sees is repeated in imitative form in his play (K. Bühler, 1930). Not only does imitative play mirror the culture of the community in which the child lives, but it also reflects the spirit of the particular period in which the child is growing up. For example, during the Second World War, both boys and girls played in imaginary settings involving soldiers, tanks, guns, airplanes, and different activities related to war (Garrison, 1952).

The pattern of dramatic play may come from movies, television, or the comics. (*From Child Development, a McGraw-Hill Text-Film.*)

The usual patterns of imaginative play of young children are (1) *domestic patterns,* including playing house, furnishing a house, cooking, eating, having tea parties, taking care of babies and being fathers and mothers; (2) *selling* and *buying;* (3) activities connected with *transportation,* as riding in automobiles or trains, being engineers, putting in gas or air, and sailing boats; (4) *punishing,* playing policeman, and gun play in general; (5) *burning* and playing fireman; (6) *killing* and *dying;* and (7) playing the part of *legendary persons,* as Santa Claus, Cinderella, and the Big Bad Wolf (Murphy, 1937). "Playing house" is a universal favorite with children of the preschool years. The younger children play the role of passive participants who allow themselves to be led around by the older ones who assume the roles of "mama" or "daddy." Frequently, playing house involves such complex activities as setting the table, having the doctor for a sick baby, or putting the doll to bed (Parten, 1933). Older children dramatize the stories they have heard or read and the movies or television shows they have seen. Instead of playing that they are people of everyday life, they play that they are fairies, Indians, "G" men, or bandits.

Dramatizations are reproduced with astonishing fidelity, and even the tone of voice of the person imitated is copied so well that one could almost believe the real person was speaking. Few stage properties as such are needed. A hat, cane, long skirt, or some articles of clothing usually associated with the person imitated is all the child needs to imagine that he is that person. A rug placed across two overturned chairs or the carpet pulled up at one end for the child to crawl under serves as a tent, a den, or a cave. The basement becomes an ogre's den, the hallways of the house are secret passages in a castle, and the lawns are the battlefields where important contests are fought. Each year, as the child grows older, he pays more and more attention to details, with the result that stage properties are increasingly important to his dramatizations.

3. Constructive Play

Interest in construction is an important element in the play of children. Up to the age of five or six years, construction is more or less a matter of chance. The child puts together objects without a preconceived plan or pattern, and if, by chance, they should resemble a familiar object, he is delighted with his achievements. From the age of six years, materials are used specifically and appropriately for building and construction. The child who is too realistic or too much of a dreamer does not play creatively. With age comes the ability to distinguish between reality and fantasy. Then play becomes less make-believe and more constructive (Barker et al., 1943). Children differ markedly in their constructive ability (Vernon, 1948).

Forms of Construction. Early forms of constructive play consist of making mud pies, constructing mountains or tunnels from sand, and playing with blocks, beads, scissors, clay, paint, crayons, and paste. The child uses these to make things that have a definite meaning and can be recognized as such, though their practical use is of secondary importance. In block building, for example, children give names to their structures, such as "house" or "boat," shortly after the second year. After the third year, block construction is coordinated with dramatic play (Guanella, 1934).

Constructive play is popular in late childhood and manifests itself in the building of tents, playhouses, huts, snowmen, and dams. It generally takes the form of large, crude work in the case of boys and is carried out in connection with their outdoor play. Among girls, on the other hand, construction is of a finer and more delicate sort, as is seen in making doll clothes, paper dolls, and drawings; in painting or clay modeling. In block building, girls tend to build quieter scenes of everyday life, especially those centering around the home or school. Boys, on the other hand, build in more varied ways and put more emphasis on the outdoor scenes (Erikson, 1951). Because of the popularity of construction at this age, it is one of the important phases of the routine life at summer camps for boys and girls.

At first, the child is pleased with whatever he makes and proudly displays it to anyone who happens to be present. Later, however, he becomes more critical of his workmanship and not only ceases to boast about it but often covers it up or even demolishes it if others come to look at it. This is especially true of drawing and painting. Between the fourth and eighth grades interest in all handicraft wanes, except in the case of cooking (Sullenger et al., 1953). This is true of both boys and girls unless they have a definite talent for some specific form of creative work, such as painting, drawing, or clay modeling. Under such conditions, it becomes a hobby which is engaged in as the child's favorite form of solitary play, then and into maturity.

Drawing. One of the most frequently used outlets for the creative fervor is drawing. Owing to poor muscle coordination, the young child cannot actually draw, but he takes keen delight in scribbling in which he makes crude and often totally aimless movements with pencil or crayon. To him, drawing is a means of expression rather than a means of creating beauty. The finished product is far less important than the creation of it. As the child's perception becomes more discriminating, his confidence in his ability to draw decreases (Gesell and Thompson, 1934).

Drawing is an expression of what is uppermost in the child's mind at the moment. His first drawings are symbolic and are not direct copies of objects. The child draws things as he remembers them, but he is not interested in perspective, proportions, or relationships. He puts in details that interest him, such as buttons on a coat, while at the same time omitting essentials, such as a man's body or the engine of an automobile. Later, as the child becomes more mature, he outlines or sketches objects partly from memory and partly from direct observation of them. From about the sixth year, the child tries to reproduce in his drawings what he sees and begins to show regard for size, perspective, and correctness of detail. By the time the child is eight years old, perspective in drawing is well developed (Leroy, 1951). Transparency, or drawing a person or object as it would be viewed in an X-ray picture, decreases with age and is quite rare after eight years of age (Leroy, 1950). Except when a child is truly gifted, originality in his drawings disappears very soon (Cappe, 1947). Young children show more interest in color than do older children whose major interest is in form. The young child draws mainly with a crayon, while the older child draws with a pencil.

From the time the child is six years old, the major change in the pattern of development of his drawing consists of elaboration of ground against which the objects are drawn (Bell, 1952). There is no variation in the pattern of sequence of the stages of drawing ability when children complete incomplete drawings or draw the entire object. A partial figure of a man, for example, can hasten the addition of parts of the drawing, but it does not distort the order in which the parts emerge. In free drawings, eyes appear first on the head. They tend to appear first in completion drawings, even though the arms and legs, not the eyes, are suggested by the forms given (Ames, 1945).

A pattern of development is likewise found in the drawings of simpler forms, such as circles, squares, and triangles. Changes in the order, direction, and orientation of the lines have been noted, as follows:

Vertical line. Moves gradually from directly on the model, across the paper to the right and then back to near the left-hand margin. The line gradually lengthens.

Horizontal line. Moves gradually down the page, finally returning to one-fourth down from the top. It gradually lengthens.

Circle. Is first copied counterclockwise, then clockwise, and then again counterclockwise. At the earliest ages drawing starts at the top of the circle, then later at the bottom, then still later again at the top.

Square. The trend is from four separate lines which overlap to the corners to a one-line figure with square corners. The order of drawing the four sides varies considerably, but at 54 months and after many draw the continuous line starting by drawing the left side downward and continuing counterclockwise (Gesell and Ames, 1946).

When a design is too difficult for a young child to reproduce, he tends to simplify the drawing according to certain principles. The tendencies are to substitute something meaningful for a meaningless design; to unify and "close" the design; and to introduce rhythm, symmetry, or conventional proportions when these are lacking. There is a tendency to shorten a rectangle, to "square" anything with angles, to substitute a circle for any design that suggests roundness, to widen angles, and to simplify designs all over by omitting details. "The tendency is," she noted, "toward more primitive and habituated response, resulting in mental economy and least effort" (Hildreth, 1944). At no time is there any indication that the child is attempting to build up a whole from isolated parts. His drawings are always wholes, even when many parts are missing (Hildreth, 1944). In young children, drawings are scattered at random over the paper, and later, as the child grows older, he combines the separate drawings into a unit (Barnhart, 1942).

Because the child draws mainly from memory, his drawings are usually inaccurate and incomplete. There is a marked lack of proportions, as may be seen in pictures of people whose heads are often larger than the trunk. The faces are rigid and expressionless, and there is a tendency to follow a stereotyped pattern with all people, all houses, or all animals similar in design. Ornamentation appeals to the child, and he therefore concentrates more attention on it than on other parts of the drawings. Animals are frequently drawn with heads that look like human heads, but with bodies and four legs like animals. Among young children, transparency is common in their drawings. When drawing a house, for example, the rooms are shown through the walls. By the time the child is six or seven years old, his drawings become compositions, with a relationship between the different parts (Barnhart, 1942; Goodenough and Harris, 1950; Merry and Merry, 1950). When children draw spontaneously, it is unusual for them to draw anything bizarre or eccentric, even though many of their drawings may, to an adult, appear to be caricatures (Gesell, 1928).

Subjects of Children's Drawings. What a child draws will change as he grows older. As early as two years of age, there is a great difference in children's ability to draw what they want to draw (Knauber, 1931). Among young children, drawings usually represent familiar objects, people, houses, and animals. There are few drawings of designs. The human form is most popular, with the adult form slightly more popular than the child's form (see Fig. 44). Houses and trees are likewise popular subjects of the drawings of young children, while animals are less frequently drawn. Young children like color in their drawings, though this is not always appropriately used. Most of the drawings are stereotyped in pattern, and the ornamentation is proportionally too large for the rest of the drawings. As children grow older, more emphasis is placed on the drawing of machines and designs, and fewer drawings are of the human form. There is also an increase in interest in drawing animals, houses, flowers, and trees (McCarty, 1924; Knauber, 1931; Hurlock and Thomson, 1934; Meier, 1939; Hughes and Stockdale, 1940; Baumgarten and Tramer, 1943; Goodenough and Harris, 1950; Merry and Merry, 1950; Elkish, 1952). Older children frequently draw comic strips with a variety of subject matter (Witty, 1941, 1941a).

Sex differences in the subjects of children's drawings appear early. Boys draw the human figure less than girls do, but they are better than girls at representing the bodily proportions correctly. Girls are more interested in ornamenting their drawings of the human figure than are boys. Between the ages of five and eleven years, children draw people of their own sex more than of the opposite sex. By eleven or twelve years, however, girls begin to draw more figures of the opposite sex than of their own sex. Sex awareness is apparent in such characteristics as hair, clothes, and facial features by the time the child is six years old. Girls draw full-faced figures more often than do boys, who draw profiles as often as the full face. Boys often draw airplanes, tanks, and battle scenes, while girls rarely do. Boys, likewise, draw machines more often than girls do (Goodenough, 1926; Baumgarten and Tramer, 1943; Weider and Noller, 1950; Jolles, 1952). Children of the higher *socioeconomic groups* draw more details than do those of the same

Fig. 44. Typical drawings of a man by first-grade children. (*From M. M. Hughes and L. Stockdale, The young child and graphic expression, Childhood Educ.,* 1940, **16,** 307–314. *Used by permission.*)

ages but of lower socioeconomic status (Weider and Noller, 1950). The *intellectual level* of the child influences the quality as well as the subject of his drawings (Goodenough, 1926; Ames, 1945).

Crayoning and Painting. Creative activities involving the use of crayons and paint are popular during childhood and follow much the same pattern of development as drawing. At two years of age, the child begins to experiment with crayons; by three, he can control the use of his crayon; at four, imagination enters into his activities; by five, he begins to be self-conscious about his work (Gesell et al., 1940). The use of water-color paints follows shortly after the child uses crayons and is an equally popular form of self-expression. The young child derives keen enjoyment from covering pages of paper with bright colors, selected and combined by him without adult supervision or interference. Finger painting, a glorified form of mud-pie play, in which the paints are the consistency of mud and are put on the paper with the finger or the hand, has recently become popular in childhood. While regression is the usual reaction to frustration, this has not been found to be true in the case of children's paintings. Frustrated children have not been found to regress to lower levels in color, line, and form painting (Thomas, 1951).

Young children like to listen to their favorite music on a record player. (*From Child Development, a McGraw-Hill Text-Film.*)

Music. Regardless of whether or not they have musical talent, little children like to sing. The baby first engages in this form of self-expression when he introduces rhythm into his babbling. It gives him keen enjoyment to listen to the singing of his babbling, and he laughs heartily at himself. According to Jersild (1939), children give a bodily response to music while they are yet in the cradle. Later, they spontaneously walk, hop, and clap to the accompaniment of music. The child's first attempt at singing may even precede his ability to talk. By the age of four or five years, most children can sing simple melodies, can beat good rhythm, and can recognize simple tunes. Even though the child does not know all the words of a song, he will supplement with words of his own.

Producing music, whether by striking keys of a musical instrument, winding a music box, or turning on a victrola or radio, is very popular with young children. While they enjoy listening to music produced by others, the enjoyment that they derive from their own music, even though it be of a vastly inferior caliber, is far greater. They enjoy rhythms and dancing, which is often little more than walking to music. Because music in all forms in which the child may take part is such a pleasing, as well as wholesome, form of self-expression, it is strongly encouraged by parents, nursery schools, and kindergartens.

The child's interest in music has been found to follow a pattern in its development. At two years, the child dances to radio or phonograph music; at three, he likes to watch and listen to a phonograph, he can recognize several melodies, and he may have his favorites; a year later, he can run the phonograph himself, he likes to experiment with the piano, he can sing songs correctly and likes to dramatize these songs, and he can identify simple melodies; at five years, the child may pick out tunes on the piano and learn to play a few familiar, simple melodies, and he likes to sing or dance to music on the radio or phonograph; at six years, he enjoys his own phonograph records; at seven, the child has a craving for piano or dancing lessons, and he likes to use various percussion instruments; at eight, he shows less desire to practice, but he likes to have an audience when he plays, to play duets, and he may even change a passage in a piece of music to one of his own invention; at nine years, the child really applies himself to practicing music, he is beginning to be interested in composers, and he enjoys executing staccato or legato notes (Gesell and Ilg, 1946).

Singing is the most frequently used form of musical expression, because to use it does not require technical training, as is true of the playing of all forms of musical instruments. The types of songs children like best vary according to their major interests at the time. During the first four grades in elementary school, school songs are the most popular. Interest in this type of song begins to decline in the fourth grade and drops consistently after that. As the child grows older, there is an increased interest in classical, folk, and patriotic songs. There is less interest also in religious and holiday songs with age, and increased interest in popular and dance music.

Study of specific songs preferred in these classifications showed that children prefer songs of easily perceived tonal values and slow cadence. This is because such songs are "singable" and can thus be enjoyed by all, whether or not they have musical ability. Also, these songs can be learned without too much effort and thus are not regarded as part of a singing lesson. Slow singing was found to be popular because it is relaxing and restful (Boynton and Boynton, 1938). Differences in socioeconomic status have been found to have no influence on children's reactions to classical music. Their reactions are influenced mainly by their familiarity with the music (Fisher, 1951). If properly directed, the child's interest in music may lead to one of his most popular leisure-time activities as he grows older (O'Brien, 1953).

Writing. Creative play in the form of writing stories or poetry is commonly found in adolescence. But among children in general, writing is looked upon more as a school lesson than as a form of play. Only after having mastered writing and spelling to such a degree that both can be carried out without too much effort and aid from others, does the child use them in creating stories or poems. Writing poetry is one form of creative writing which children enjoy. Negro children have been found to write poetry much more frequently than white children. However, with increase in age, interest in writing poetry decreases for children of both the white and Negro races (Lehman and Witty, 1928b).

4. COLLECTING

From the age of three years, there is a desire on the part of every normal child to collect things which interest him temporarily. In *early childhood*, the things collected are usually valueless and trivial. Once they are collected, they are generally forgotten or little attention is given to them. They are put in the child's pockets, or in some special place in the playroom, and then forgotten. From six years to adolescence, there is a strong tendency on the part of children to make collections. In fact, this is one of the most popular forms of play among boys at that age, though girls, as a rule, collect more things than do boys. The peak age for collecting comes at ten years for boys and a year later for girls (Durost, 1932). Among older children, collections are kept in some place where they will not be disturbed, as attics, cellars, desks, old trunks, jars, boxes, or baskets. At first, children collect anything that attracts their attention. Later, they become more selective in their choice of objects and collect only a few things which, at the moment, interest them especially. At every age, boys collect different things than do girls (Whitley, 1929).

5. GAMES AND SPORTS

Simple games, generally referred to as "mother games" because they are more often played with the mother than with any other person, begin to make their appeal during the second half of the first year. Finger play, pat-a-cake, peekaboo, hide-and-seek (behind furniture, a piece of cloth, or merely a hand), pigs-to-market, mirror play, and similar games, passed down from one generation of babies to another, seem to have a universal appeal. By the time the baby can walk, he gets keen enjoyment from hiding from others to see if they can find him.

In early childhood, around the fourth or fifth year, the child becomes interested in the *neighborhood games*, played with other children in the neighborhood. These are of the *undefined-group* type, in which any number of children can take part. One child may organize the game and get the others to play with him, or the game may be organized by an older child or an adult. In these games, the children copy one another and follow definite orders from the leader. Games at this age are simple, brief, with few rules, and are often invented on the spot. Frequently, they are modified as play goes on (Reece, 1954). Typical games of this sort are tag, hide-and-seek, puss-in-the-corner, dodging, run-sheep-run, advancing statues, and cops-and-robbers.

Among older children, games become largely competitive in spirit. (*From Child Development, a McGraw-Hill Text-Film.*)

By the age of five, the child plays games to test his skills, such as walking on street curbs, walking on a crack in the pavement, jumping down steps, hopping on one foot, skipping, jumping rope, bouncing balls, or playing jacks. These are of a lower social organization than *neighborhood games* because they are individual rather than group and because their competitive element is of relatively little importance. What games of this type the child will play will depend largely upon his motor and intellectual development (Jersild, 1954). By the age of ten or eleven years, games become largely competitive in spirit. Solitary play is abandoned, and the typical neighborhood games which reigned in favor earlier give way to *team, pair,* or *double-pair games.* Interest is now concentrated on skill and excellence. At first, the play is largely individual, with little cooperation with the other players. The child is not a good team player at first because he wants to dominate the play instead of limiting his efforts to his own role. Gradually, however, he learns to cooperate with the other players and, as a result, has more enjoyment. By the time he reaches adolescence, the typical child is a good team player in that he can cooperate with the other players and adhere strictly to rules.

Values of Games and Sports. Games and sports are not only pleasant forms of play for the child, but they also have great value as socializing agents. From them the child learns how to get along with other children, to cooperate in different activities, to play the role of a leader as well as a follower, and to evaluate himself and his abilities realistically by comparing himself with his playmates. DuBois (1952) has pointed out that while adults are inclined to allow a child advantages in playing games, his contemporaries will yield no point. What he wins from them must be in fair play. According to DuBois,

this challenges the child to develop skill, and in due course he is stimulated by victory and makes even greater effort. . . . When young people do not participate in sports, the scales are heavily weighted against their successful social and emotional adjustment; they frequently are headed for trouble, because they have not had the opportunity to learn to win humbly, to lose gracefully, and to endure physical discomfort to attain a goal. In short, they have not had the privilege of learning the discipline of good sportsmanship, so necessary for a happy adult life (pp. 370–371).

6. READING

From early in the first year, little babies like to be sung to. They enjoy the rhythmic sounds of lullabies and nursery rhymes, sung or recited in a singsong voice. Around the age of two, they like to look at picture books containing large pictures of people, animals, and familiar household objects printed in bright colors. While looking at the pictures, they enjoy being told simple stories about them. Even if the young child cannot understand the words, he enjoys the flow of sounds, the vocal inflections of the reader, and his facial expressions. In addition, being read to is a pleasant experience for a young child, especially if he is sitting on the lap of his mother or someone who is near and dear to him (Jersild, 1954). Early reading experiences have a marked influence on the child's later reading interest. They influence not only how much he will read but also what he will read (Almy, 1949; Gates, 1949; Hildreth, 1949; McKee, 1949; Russell, 1949, 1949a; Ephron, 1953).

Early Reading Interests. Storybooks which have been read to the child so often that he knows them almost by heart and picture books appeal mostly during the early childhood years. The young child likes his books to be small so that he can handle them easily, with attractive pictures and short stories. Because he does not always understand the meaning of the words he hears when the stories are read to him, he enjoys listening to stories in jingles and rhymes (Garrison, 1952; Jersild, 1954). For the most part, young children like stories that are factual. The more facts of life the young child has, the more antagonistic he is toward fantasy in stories. The mother's

Before they can read, children like to look at pictures while being read to. (*From Child Development, a McGraw-Hill Text-Film.*)

attitude toward fantasy has an important influence on the young child's attitude. The mother who feels that fantasy is superfluous or that it encourages flight from reality influences the child to prefer realism in his stories. Most young children, however, enjoy fantasy in stories, and they like to identify themselves with the characters of the stories they hear (Wolfenstein, 1946).

The young child is not free to select what he wants to have read to him. The adults in his life, whether teacher in nursery school or kindergarten or parent, supply him with books from which he must select the stories he likes to hear. Within these limitations, most young children prefer stories about familiar people and animals in their everyday lives. They like the children's classics, such as *The Three Bears, Mother Goose,* and *Cinderella,* and modern books, such as *Little Black Sambo* and *Mary Poppins*. By the kindergarten age, they like humorous stories, dramas about Western life, and the comics. Their favorite characters are animals, boys, and girls, with only slight interest in adults, fairies, and babies. They like these characters for their personal qualities or because they are funny. Because of the child's belief in animism, stories that deal with animals that behave like human beings are very popular (Wilson, 1943, 1943a; Witty et al., 1946; Garrison, 1952; Freidson, 1953; Jersild, 1954).

Reading Interests of Late Childhood. Like the young child, the older child is somewhat limited in what he can read by what is available to him. At first, he is limited by books provided for him by his parents. As he grows older, he may borrow books from his friends or from the school or public library. However, there are certain cultural pressures that influence his reading interests. He learns to read what he is supposed to read and what is considered appropriate for his sex (Child et al., 1946; Seward and Harris, 1951; Jersild, 1954). How much and what he reads is greatly influenced by class values (Warner and Lunt, 1941; Brown, 1954).

Furthermore, as the child grows older, his reading tastes change. He calls what he does not like "babyish." In reality, it is because what formerly excited him no longer does so. With intellectual growth and school experiences, he becomes more realistic and regards everything related to fantasy as "phony" (Freidson, 1953). Of the three major interest patterns in reading, adventure and violence, love and glamour, and educational content, there are marked changes in preference as the child grows older. For example, third-grade children are mostly interested in comics, fairy tales, humor, and mystery, but show little interest in informative content and none in love (Lyness, 1951, 1952). Changes in these interest patterns with age are illustrated in Fig. 45.

What children like in books cannot always be predicted by adults. Whether they will prefer realism or fantasy will depend largely upon whether they have learned to like fantasy during their early childhood years, and this, in turn, will depend largely upon their mothers' attitudes toward fantasy (Wolfenstein, 1946). The format and illustrations appeal more to some children than to others, and the appeal is usually different from what appeals to adults. Furthermore, the reading ability of the child will determine what he will like. Children with reading difficulties will, it is obvious, like books of a lower level than those whose reading ability is superior. Too much emphasis on description, whimsy, and scenes and customs that are foreign to the child's experience will make the book unpopular with him, even though it may be rated high by adults (Williams, 1939; Rankin, 1944; Jersild, 1954).

Studies of the reading interests of school-age children have revealed that there is a preference for certain types of books at different ages. The enjoyment the older child derives from reading is for the most part due to the satisfaction of the spirit of adventure, so strong at that age. As the child is carried into an imaginary world created for him by the book, he imagines himself doing the things he would like to do but which, in everyday life, he may not be able to do. At the age of six and seven years, the main interest in reading lies in stories about nature, the wind, birds, trees, and flowers. There is a beginning of interest in fairy tales, but these must be short, simple, and for the most part in dialogue form. Any book for this age must contain more pictures than reading matter.

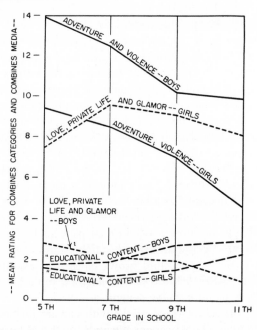

Fig. 45. Patterns of interest in different types of mass communication. (*From P. I. Lyness, Patterns in the mass communications tastes of the young audience, J. educ. Psychol.,* 1951, **42,** 449–467. *Used by permission.*)

The most favored reading for the eight-year-old child is fairy tales. The fantastic, imaginative element of these stories appeals to the child at this age. Rather closely related to the interest in fairy stories is the interest in stories of other lands, especially when they center around children. By the age of nine, interest in fairy tales begins to lag, owing to the fact that training in schools makes it increasingly difficult for the child to believe in fairy-tale elements. This is especially true of boys, whose reading interests at nine shift to stories of boy life, mainly of the Boy Scout type. They also like stories of adventure, comedies, and horror, or "spooky," stories. Toward the end of childhood, there is generally a rage for reading, which places reading high among the most favored play activities. This is especially true of girls. It is quite usual for boys and girls to read one or two books for pleasure every month.

As children reach puberty, their reading interests become more "sophisticated." They are more mature in their outlook, and this is reflected in their reading interests. The eleven-year-old is interested mainly in tales of adventure and mystery. Science and invention are popular reading topics for boys, while home and school life and topics more popular with girls. Girls retain an interest in fairy and animal stories, but boys at this age have entirely outgrown their interest in this type of book. At the age of twelve years, the climax of the "reading craze" is reached, an age which coincides with the beginning of preadolescence, when boys and girls are beginning to show a desire for isolation.

Because of the beginning of a hero-worship tendency, books of legendary or historical heroes, as well as biographies of great men and women, thrill the twelve-year-old. Books about invention, athletics, and adventure are very popular with boys, while girls show a preference for books relating to home, boarding-school or college life, adventure, stories written for boys, nature stories, and Bible stories. At the age of thirteen, these reading interests become intensified, but few new reading interests develop (Terman and Lima, 1927; Witty et al., 1946; Lyness, 1951; Garrison, 1952; Freidson, 1953; Jersild, 1954).

While young children like rhythmic sounds in their reading, older children show little interest in reading poetry. By the third or fourth grade in school, there is little interest in poetry, especially among boys. Very few girls and even fewer boys claim that they prefer poetry to other types of reading (Terman and Lima, 1927; Lazar, 1937; Witty et al., 1946). It has been suggested that lack of interest in poetry on the part of the older child may be due to the way in which poetry is usually presented to the child and that his interest could be increased if he were encouraged to write poetry (Garrison, 1952).

Individual Differences. While there are fairly well-marked age differences in reading preferences, within each age group are differences even greater than one finds from one age to another. These differences depend more upon the sex and intelligence of the readers than upon any other factors. Boys like reading matter that concentrates on adventure, violence, mystery, sports, travel, science, and war, subjects which have little appeal for girls, who prefer stories dealing with real life with everyday characters and a flavor of romance. They also like biographical material relating to women and stories about self-improvement. These sex differences become more pronounced as children grow older (Thorndike and Henry, 1940; Thorndike, 1941a). While children of different levels of intelligence have similar reading interests at the same ages, bright children read more and they select books of a higher caliber than do dull children (Thorndike and Henry, 1940; Thorndike, 1941a).

Magazines and Newspapers. From the fifth grade on, interest in reading newspapers and magazines increases to the point where the older child spends more time reading them than he does reading books. Boys show a greater interest in newspapers, while girls show a greater interest in magazines. Among bright children, the "better" type of newspaper and magazine appeals, while among those who are not so bright or those who come from poorer homes, there is a preference for the tabloids and for children's magazines or, as they grow older, for the more sensational type of magazine (Johnson, 1932; Lazar, 1937; Lyness, 1951; Brown, 1954; Breckenridge and Vincent, 1955). When children first begin to read newspapers, their main interest is in the comic strips. Gradually, as a result of their school studies and concentration on current events in school, they read the news of the day, foreign news, political news, and editorials (Brown, 1954).

Comics. Comics are cartoon stories in which the story element is less important than the pictures. Relatively few of the comics published today are humorous. Most of them relate to adventure rather than to comedy. Their appeal is principally emotional rather than intellectual. Comics are "skewed toward reality." When the situation is real, the people are unreal; if the situation is unreal, the people are real (Spiegelman et al., 1952). The characters of comics are occasionally humorous, but for the most part, they are "serious fellows, intent on dangerous adventure and noble deeds." To accomplish these ends, they use methods ranging from magic to "just plain violent means." Regardless of the method used or the motive which inspired the character's act, good always triumphs in the end (Frank, 1942). Not all characters in the comics are people. In fact, about 50 per cent of the comics today have animal characters, and they are particularly important in humor (Spiegelman et al., 1952).

The comics present a vivid and realistic picture of contemporary American life with characters from every walk of life. They reflect the cultural patterns of acceptance and rejection regarding ethnic groups (Merry and Merry, 1950; Spiegelman et al., 1952). There is every type of comic to appeal to all ages and all tastes. They may appear in newspapers in the form of "comic strips" or in magazine form as "comic books." Comics include all types of adventure, humor, romance and sex, animal antics, detective stories, literary classics, and even stories from the Bible. Approximately equal space is devoted to humor and crime (Malter, 1952). The newspapers of today usually carry a number of comic strips of different types, and the stores offer every type of comic book available. The child of today is, thus, literally surrounded with comics. Most children buy some of the comics they read, and others are obtained by "swapping" with their classmates and friends. There is great prestige associated with the ownership of a large number of comics for swapping purposes (Butterworth and Thompson, 1951).

As early as three or four years of age, before the child can read or understand many of the words read to him, he asks to have the comics read to him (Jersild, 1954). From then on, interest in the comics increases rapidly, reaching a peak during the sixth or seventh grade, and then declining. However, even among high-school students, approximately two-thirds claim that they read the comics regularly. While individual differences exist in degree of interest in reading the comics at different ages, studies of elementary-school children have revealed that the mean number of comics read in the fourth through the sixth grades, the time when comic-book reading reaches its peak, ranges from 12 to 14 comic books a week (Wilson, 1941;

Interest in the comics increases as children grow older, and this often becomes their favorite "reading." (*From Child Development, a McGraw-Hill Text-Film.*)

Witty, 1941, 1941a, 1952, 1955; Witty and Coomer, 1943; Butterworth and Thompson, 1951; Shalter, 1951; Brown, 1954). Among children six to eleven years of age, 96 per cent of the boys and 91 per cent of the girls read the comics regularly (Zorbaugh, 1944).

The child's first interest in reading the newspaper is centered around his interest in the comic strips. Long before he is interested in the news of the world, he has become a daily reader of the comic strips of the newspaper (Lehman and Witty, 1927a; Wilson, 1941; Brown, 1954). Boys at every age read comics more than do girls (Witty, 1941, 1941a, 1955; Butterworth and Thompson, 1951). The slow learner reads comics much more than does the rapid learner, and he concentrates on a different type of comic (Thorndike and Henry, 1940; Thorndike, 1941). Negro children, as a group, read the comics more than do white children of the same ages (Witty and Moore, 1945).

Favorite comics. As in the case of books, so among the comics, too, children have their favorites. What appeals to them will, however, differ according to age and sex (Witty et al., 1942; Strang, 1943). Their interest at every age follows the general pattern of interest in stories in books and magazines (Lyness, 1951). Among preschool children, the favorite comics are those in which animals dress and talk like humans, such as Bugs Bunny and Mickey Mouse (Frank, 1944). In the early grades of elementary school, sex differences in interest begin to be apparent. Boys like excitement and adventure, with little concern for realism. By identifying himself with such comic-book characters as Superman or Dick Tracy, the child likes to imagine that he, too, can do all sorts of wonders and have all kinds of exciting experiences. The greatest appeal comes from comics with fast action, plenty of danger, a hero who wins by the narrowest margin, and plenty of conversation. The boy who is beginning to be interested in science likes comics which are centered around all kinds of impossible scientific devices, and these rarely seem incredible to him (Witty et al., 1942; Strang, 1943; Bender, 1944; Frank, 1944).

Girls in the early grades of school like comics featuring women, children, and animals. However, they prefer women who can perform marvellous feats or who have athletic superiority. They are less interested in adventure, mystery, and thrills than are boys and show a greater interest in animal comics than do boys of the same ages (Strang, 1943; Bender, 1944; Frank, 1944). By the fifth grade, marked sex differences appear in the type of comics liked by children, and there are also changes in interest among the children of both sexes as they grow older. Boys continue to prefer action, adventure, and plenty of thrills. This is the age when hero worshipping begins, and boys like comic-book heroes they can identify themselves with. They also like humor, but the comics must be "masculine" in tone and content to appeal to the older boy (Hill and Trent, 1940; Strang, 1943; Bender, 1944; Frank, 1944; Butterworth and Thompson, 1951).

As Butterworth and Thompson (1951) have pointed out, boys from the sixth grade on are "attracted to those magazines whose contents, action, and stories are predominantly masculine and are written from a masculine standpoint, whose central characters find adventure through the mastery of danger, whose stories feature a good deal of crime and violence, whose main theme is sports and athletics, and whose chief appeal is humor." The older girl begins to like comics which have actions related to the opposite sex, especially the type in which a handsome hero rescues a damsel in distress in just the nick of time.

The older girl, like the boy of that age, prefers humor in comics, but she prefers romance to adventure. She wants her comics to be "feminine" in characters and actions, but there is some tendency for girls at this age to like the typically "masculine" comic also (Hill and Trent, 1940; Strang, 1943; Bender, 1944; Frank, 1944; Butterworth and Thompson, 1951). Commenting on the favorite comics of girls from the fifth grade on, Butter-

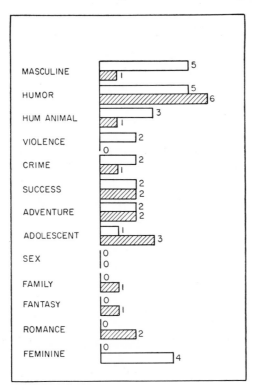

Fig. 46. Frequency with which characteristic "appeals" appear among most popular 10 comic books for boys and girls. (Girls' values are cross-hatched.) (*From R. F. Butterworth and G. G. Thompson, Factors related to age-grade trends and sex differences in children's preferences for comic books, J. genet. Psychol., 1951, **78**, 71–96. Used by permission.*)

worth and Thompson (1951) state, "Girls show a preference for comic books that feature feminine characters and pursuits, typical adolescents, a certain element of romance, dating, etc., and all varieties of humor." In Fig. 46 are shown the types of comics that appeal to boys and girls at different ages.

Reasons for interest. Not all children read the comics for the same reasons. There are, however, certain reasons for the widespread interest that children show in comics, and these interests are pretty universally found among children of the same age levels. The value of the comics, according to Bender (1944), like that of the folklore of other times, is that they "serve as a means to stimulate the child's fantasy life and so help him solve the individual and sociological problems inherent in his living." Should comics be reduced to the real, Bender further commented, this would tend to make them "more threatening and productive of anxiety, because they offer no solution to the problem of aggression in the world."

Comic-book material and comic-book characters frequently fit the needs of the individual child. Through identification with characters in the comics, the child has an excellent opportunity for the solution of many of his emotional and personal problems (Bender and Lourie, 1941). As Podolsky (1952) has stressed, "The current crop of comics appeals to the child's love for the supernatural and the imaginative. They deal with mystery, blood-shed, crime, and murder. They pass the bounds of the physical, leave the intellectual, and play heavily in the emotional field."

These are by no means the only reasons given for the appeal of the comics to children. Other reasons for appeal are that they offer the child escape from the humdrum reality of the daily routine; they are easy to read, especially for poor readers; they are cheap, exciting, mysterious, thrilling, and humorous both in characters and actions; the characters do things the child himself would like to do; they present characters that have bravery, strength, beauty, and unfailing ability to master difficulties; they are often in serial form and thus give the reader something to look forward to; the art of the comics is easy to understand and colorful; and they often give good moral lessons (Hill and Trent, 1940; Frank, 1942, 1944; Reynolds, 1942; Strang, 1943; Bakwin, 1953). Few reasons for lack of interest in the comics have been given. These are, for the most part, given by good readers and are preference for books; comics aren't real; pictures aren't as pretty as those in books; and comics are "kid stuff" (Strang, 1943).

Vocabulary of comics. One of the most common objections raised by educators and parents to the child's reading of comics is that the reader learns many undesirable words through this medium. To find out just how much slang actually is used in the comics that children prefer, Hill (1943) analyzed the 16 comics ranked highest in popularity by a group of children. In these comics, only 1 per cent of all words used were slang. There was, however, a slight tendency for the children to prefer those comics employing the greater amount of slang and other distortions.

R. L. Thorndike (1941), in a vocabulary analysis of four complete comic books (*Superman, Batman, Action Comics,* and *Detective Comics*), found that the bulk of the vocabulary was standard English. Twelve per cent of the words were "respectable" slang ("brainstorm," "buddy," "adios") and 10 per cent "vulgar" slang ("awk," "betcha," "conk"). Furthermore, Thorn-dike reported, most of the standard words were at about the level of difficulty appropriate for the upper elementary-school or even junior-high-school child.

Evaluation of comics. There is no question about the fact that the widespread popularity of the comics will guarantee that they will be an important part of the child's reading for many years to come. It is impossible to keep a child from reading comics, once he goes to school and associates with other children. Nor should any attempt be made to prevent it. Like everything else, comics have their good and their bad features.

Most adults who are concerned about the effect of comics reading on children emphasize the harmful effects of the comic books, not the comic strips in the newspapers. They emphasize mainly the danger of comic books to the child's character and mental health, rather than the cultural undesirability of the comics. They believe there are certain comics which are suitable for children and which are drawn specifically for children, such as comics about animals, children, and families, and these they believe children can read without any harm. On the other hand, they center their disapproval on comics which stress adventure, horror, and sex. Men, as a whole, disapprove of children's reading of the comics less than do women; younger parents disapprove less than do older parents; and comics readers among adults are less concerned about the harmful effects of comics than are nonreaders (Zorbaugh, 1949).

There are many arguments given *in favor of* the comics. Some of these are:

1. The comics constitute a kind of modern folklore, corresponding to the Greek and Norse myths (Strang, 1943).

2. The comics supply to children of limited reading ability a form of reading experience which is thoroughly enjoyable to them (Strang, 1943). They may, however, be used to motivate the child in the development of his reading skill (Garrison, 1952). They stimulate the child to read further and break down his resistance to reading if the material is presented as entertainment (Bakwin, 1953).

3. The educational attainment of children who read comics frequently is almost identical with that of children who read infrequently (Witty, 1955).

4. If children actually read the text of the comics, they will profit by extensive supplementary reading and will be introduced to a wide range of vocabulary, including many words which they repeatedly encounter in other reading (Strang, 1943).

5. The comics offer an excellent technique for propaganda, especially antiprejudice (Bakwin, 1953).

6. They serve as effective methods of simplified teaching (Bakwin, 1953).

7. They meet children's needs for overcoming, in imagination, some of the limitations of their age and ability and for obtaining a sense of adventure denied them in real life (Strang, 1943).

8. To normal children, the comics offer the mental catharsis which Aristotle claimed for the drama. Thus the readers are released from feelings of inadequacy and insecurity and from fear of aggression toward or from others (Strang, 1943).

9. They are cheap, and therefore the child can buy them and have freedom of choice (Bakwin, 1953).

10. They give the child pleasure by offering him a chance for identification (Bakwin, 1953).

11. There are no more behavior problems among children who read comics frequently than among those who do not (Witty, 1955). Those with the best critical understanding are best adjusted, even when they read comics frequently and have the greatest interest in them (Lewin, 1953).

12. Normal aggressive reactions find release in fantasies stimulated by comic books (Cavanaugh, 1949). Through identification with the characters in the comics, the child is able to adjust himself better to life (Bender, 1944).

The arguments *against* reading the comics are:

1. The comics tend to crowd out reading of a more desirable sort (Strang, 1943). They distract the child from more worthwhile literature (Bakwin, 1953).

2. Many poor readers merely get the story from the pictures without making an effort to read the text (Strang, 1943).

3. The adventures portrayed in the comics are so far removed from reality that children do not acquire an understanding of the world as it is, such as they can obtain from their reading of material that is closer to real life (Strang, 1943).

4. There is little or no progression of reading experience within the area of the comics (Strang, 1943).

5. The art of most comic strips is of inferior quality (Strang, 1943; Gruenberg, 1944). This holds true also for the stories and language used in them. (Bender, 1944; Bakwin, 1953).

6. They tend to overstimulate the child with material relating to sex, frightening experiences, and violence (Bakwin, 1953).

7. They keep children from other activities and interests (Bakwin, 1953).

8. Opposition of parents to comic reading may lead to disagreements, arguments, secretiveness, and feelings of guilt on the child's part (Bakwin, 1953).

9. They lead to juvenile delinquency. However, there is no evidence that comics entice youth into crime. Rather, those responsive to crime portrayals on occasion used the ideas and techniques seen in the comics. Comics are thus often used as "scapegoats" (Thrasher, 1949). While delinquents read many more "harmful" and "questionable" comics than do nondelinquents, this may not be a cause-and-effect relationship. However, it may keep the spiral of delinquency alive among the delinquents (Hoult, 1949).

10. The child who finds it necessary to bury himself in the comics usually does so because his real world is uninteresting or intolerable (Merry and Merry, 1950).

11. Comics have an unfavorable effect on the child's attitudes. According to Podolsky (1952), "The attitude fostered by the comic books pervades the child's daily life both in school and at home. At school he becomes a daydreamer or an idler in the belief that some miracle will intervene to save him from his just deserts; he acquires the idea that no academic preparation for life is necessary, that just a bit of brawn and foxiness will see him through. At home the child is prone to become a 'dead weight.' The household is managed to care for him, yet he is interested neither in how things are managed nor in any participation therein. He is making a very poor preparation for the democratic life which predicates and necessitates the cooperative effort of all citizens."

7. Movies

Attending moving pictures, theaters, and concerts is a popular form of play during childhood. In communities where amusements of this type are limited to moving pictures, nearly every child attends moving-picture shows occasionally, some as often as once a week. Five-year-old children attend movies only occasionally, and these are usually movies meant for children. By six years, children become restless and often close their eyes or cry. A year later, some children are attending movies weekly, others only occasionally. From eight years of age on, weekly movie attendance is common, and the usual time is on Saturday afternoons, when many neighborhood theaters have special programs for children (Lehman and Witty, 1927a; Gesell and Ilg, 1946; Lyness, 1951; Garrison, 1952). As children reach adolescence, movie attendance is less frequent (Witty, 1952).

Movie Preferences. Movie interests parallel reading interests, except that comedy plays a greater role in movies than in reading (Lyness, 1952). The major motive for attending movies is "thrill." Anything that involves adventure or mystery offers a thrill which children do not get from everyday life (Miller, 1930). Many children, as they grow older, prefer going to movies to reading books or playing games because the former offers more thrills than do the latter (Seagoe, 1931). Sex differences in movie preferences are not apparent before the age of six years. Little children, whether boys or girls, like comics and animated films, especially those with animals as the main characters (Miller, 1930; Gesell and Ilg, 1946; Garrison, 1952). Sex differences in movie preferences begin around the age of six years and become more pronounced as children reach adolescence. These differences parallel the differences shown in reading interests. Boys are especially interested in movies with adventure, war, cowboys, and Indians. Girls, on the other hand, prefer movies with dancing, singing, and animals. Both boys and girls like comedies and cartoons; they want the heroes to be active and the heroines pretty. Throughout childhood, both boys and girls dislike love stories, though girls begin to be interested in such films slightly earlier than do boys (Miller, 1930; Seagoe, 1931; Gesell and Ilg, 1946; Garrison, 1952). Children who are unhappy, because of unfavorable conditions in the home or elsewhere, are quite likely to become addicted to crime programs. They use this type of escape from their unhappy surroundings in much the same way as an adult uses alcohol. They "drown their unhappiness in artificial excitement, thus obtaining a slight measure of relief" (Podolsky, 1952).

Influence of Movies. The influence of movies on children is great. How great this influence is will depend upon two major factors: what they already know and what they are able to remember from the movies they see. As Fearing (1947) has pointed out, what an individual "gets" from movies is determined by his background and his needs. He takes from it what is usable by him or what will function in his life. Younger children remember less of what they see in movies than do older children. Children retain about 70 per cent as much as do adults, and these memories persist over a period of three or four months (Charters, 1933; Holaday and Stoddard, 1933; Merry and Merry, 1950).

There is no question about the fact that movies give the child pleasure and provide him with the excitement he does not get from his everyday life. For young children, the movies provide ideas which they use in play, such as games of cowboys or Indians. The older child gets ideas about how to behave, about the world in which he lives, and about people of different types. This may lead to tolerance or intolerance, depending on how the characters are shown and the situations in which they are placed. The less knowledge they have, the more influenced they will be by the movies they see (Thurstone, 1931; Peterson and Thurstone, 1932; Blumer, 1933; Wiese and Cole, 1946; Garrison, 1952).

On the other hand, movies often have a pronounced emotional effect on children in that they frighten the child, causing nightmares or daytime fears that are difficult for the adult to understand unless he knows the circumstances that have given rise to them. Eating disturbances, due to emotional tension, cause the child to lose weight or to be in poor health. Nail biting and other nervous mannerisms are likewise frequent aftermaths of too much movie attendance on the part of children. Many children suffer from eyestrain and general fatigue as a result of attending movies in the late afternoon or evening following a busy day in school or at play. All of these effects are intensified if the movies contain horror elements (Podolsky, 1952).

8. Radio

Radio listening is one of the most popular forms of amusement among American children today (Lyness, 1951; McKellar and Harris, 1952). It is preferred to the movies because it is cheaper, more readily available, and can be used at any hour of the day when the child is indoors. It is especially popular on rainy days or when the child is at home in the late afternoons and evenings. Interest in listening to the radio begins during babyhood when the baby enjoys hearing music or simple jingles over the air. However, it is not much before the child is three years old before he shows any real interest in radio listening. By five, the child listens to scattered radio programs; at six, he listens several hours a week; and at seven, radio listening becomes a part of his regular routine. He has certain programs he likes to hear daily and is annoyed when he misses one of them. With each passing year, into adolescence, interest in listening to the radio increases (Eisenberg, 1936; Gesell and Ilg, 1946; Lyness, 1951).

The school child spends from one to three hours daily in listening to the radio. This, for the average child, is more than the time devoted to leisure reading or attendance at the movies. In many cases, it is more than the time spent in play with other children, in games and sports. While boys usually listen to the radio more than do girls, there is no marked sex difference at any age. Children with high IQ's listen less than do those with lower IQ's, and those who are the better students in school listen less than do the poorer students. Rural children, who have fewer opportunities for a variety of play activities than have urban children, spend more time listening to the radio than do urban children. As is true of reading the comics, the better-adjusted children listen to the radio less than do the poorly adjusted, and their program preferences are different (Eisenberg, 1936; Clark, 1940).

Program Preferences. Until 1929, the only radio programs for children were bedtime stories. Since that time, however, programs designed primarily for children have become so numerous that, at almost every hour of the day when children are free to listen to the radio, there are several programs for children of different ages, from which they may choose those that appeal to them. However, what the child listens to at a given time is determined largely by what is available at that time. He may be forced to listen to certain types of program in which he has little interest and be deprived of hearing other programs in which he would have a real interest if it were possible for him to listen to them at the time they were available.

In general, the child's program preferences at different ages follow his preferences for reading and movies (Lyness, 1952). The preschool child listens to children's programs which deal mainly with animals and familiar people doing familiar things. He also likes simple music, whether songs or instrumental. By the age of six years, children's programs begin to lose their appeal. Now he wants programs that are entertaining rather than educational. He likes plays dealing with adventure, mystery, crime, comedy, and music of the popular-dance type. Quiz shows appeal to the older child as do dramas of domestic life, slapstick comedies, sports reports, and occasionally, the news of the day. For the most part, the older child dislikes programs of a serious nature, such as classical music, educational, religious or historical talks. Boys have a narrower range of program preferences than do girls. They prefer programs emphasizing adventure, mystery, comedy, and crime, while girls like popular music and plays dealing more with comedy than with adventure and crime (Eisenberg, 1936; DeBoer, 1939; Clark, 1940; Lazarsfeld and Stanton, 1944; Gesell and Ilg, 1946; Ricciuti, 1951; McKellar and Harris, 1952; Podolsky, 1952). In Fig. 47 are shown the program preferences for boys and girls at different ages.

Effects of Radio. There is a tendency to overestimate the undesirable effects of radio listening and to underemphasize the educational and other advantages of listening to the radio (McKellar and Harris, 1952). Some hold that radio listening gives the child an outlet for his aggressive tendencies, while others maintain that by catering to it, the child's appetite for violence is cultivated. The fact that a high percentage of children listen to radio programs in which violence and crime are stressed would suggest that children need the tension-releasing experience such programs offer (Ricciuti,

1951). However, there is no question about the fact that the effect of radio listening will be influenced by the amount of time spent in listening and the type of program habitually listened to.

The favorable influences of radio listening have been noted to be as follows: it offers the child a form of entertainment within the home and thus acts as an incentive to keep the child at home and with the family more

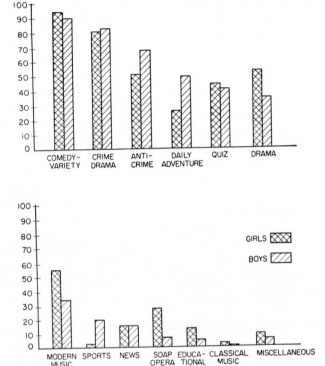

Fig. 47. Percentages of habitual listeners among boys and girls to different radio programs. (*From E. A. Ricciuti, Children and radio: a study of listeners and non-listeners to various types of radio programs in terms of selected ability, attitudes, and behavior measure, Genet. Psychol. Monogr., 1951,* **44**, *69–143. Used by permission.*)

than he would be if there were fewer things for him to do at home; it increases the child's knowledge about history, current events, geography, literature, and many other subjects, and it supplements what he learns in school; it improves his speech by increasing his vocabulary, improving his grammar, and giving him a good model of diction; it encourages him to read to supplement his knowledge of subjects he has heard about over the air; and it offers him models with whom he can identify, thus acting as an incentive to self-improvement (Eisenberg, 1936; Clark, 1940; Breckenridge and Vincent, 1955).

On the other hand, criticisms of radio listening emphasize the harmful effects to the child. These are most pronounced when the child concentrates his listening on programs of violence, crime, and mystery. Terrifying programs affect the general physical condition of the child by producing nervous tension, which causes sleep and eating disturbances. Nightmares, loss of sleep, poor appetite, and loss of weight are the results. Then, too, children rebel against going to bed at suitable times if there are programs they are anxious to hear. This means that they get less sleep than they need or they go to bed angry and emotionally upset because they are missing their favorite programs (Eisenberg, 1936; Clark, 1939; Preston, 1941; Ricciuti, 1951; Podolsky, 1952; Breckenridge and Vincent, 1955).

The child who spends much of his time listening to the radio has too little exercise for his normal development and for a healthy condition. His school work suffers partly because he does not give enough time to his studies and partly because he does not concentrate when he is studying. As Podolsky (1952) has pointed out, "Children cannot be expected to pay attention or concentrate on dull school subjects when their nervous systems are overwrought, their minds still weary from lack of sleep, their digestion disturbed." Many children claim that they can study better when listening to the radio than when studying in a quiet room. In a test of the reading of sixth-graders during the playing of the radio, it was found that reading was adversely affected by variety but not by musical programs. There was less effect on those with high IQ's than on those whose IQ's were lower (Mitchell, 1949). The avid radio listener often picks up a vocabulary of slang and other forms of speech which are undesirable (Eisenberg, 1936). Children who are habitual listeners to the radio are more adversely affected in every way than are those who listen only occasionally. Furthermore, the age of the child likewise influences the degree of effect listening will have on him (Ricciuti, 1951).

9. TELEVISION

Television is one of the newest and most popular forms of entertainment of today's children. While television sets are not owned as widely as are radios, there are few neighborhoods where there is not at least one television set where children will be able to watch certain programs with a certain amount of regularity. Because television is new and different and because it combines the features that appeal to a child in both the movies and radio, the time spent on television watching is out of all proportion to other forms of play for far too many children. Reports indicate that television watching is more time-consuming among children of the lower socioeconomic groups than it is among those of the higher groups (Riley et al., 1949; Seagoe, 1952; Witty, 1955).

The appeal of television, like that of other forms of amusement, varies markedly from individual to individual and from age to age. For the preschool child whose time for play is far greater than it is for the school child, television watching is an added activity, not a substitute activity. It is another form of play he engages in and from which he derives enjoyment (Riley et al., 1949; Battin, 1953). The peak of interest in television watching comes around the sixth year and then begins to decline gradually as children have more school work and as their interests in games and sports with their friends increase (Witty, 1951a). In one study, 90 per cent of first- and second-grade children said they preferred television to radio as compared to 50 per cent of the seventh- and eighth-grade children (Witty, 1952). As they reach adolescence, radio is preferred to television (Lyness, 1952). There has been found to be no relationship between interest in television watching and IQ, but poor students enjoy television more than do good students. Excessive television watching is usually found among poor students. Whether this is a cause-and-effect relationship or whether television watching is a form of compensation has not yet been determined (Witty, 1951, 1952, 1955). Television appeals more to poorly adjusted children than to those who are better adjusted (Podolsky, 1952; Duvall, 1954; Witty, 1955).

Time Spent on Television. How much time the child spends on television is dependent upon many factors. The peak usually comes between the ages of five and six years, when the average amount of time reported is four hours daily (Witty, 1951a; Brown, 1954). After the child enters school, the time declines to an average of two to three hours during the school week, and more time over the week ends. As children grow older and are permitted to stay up later at night, the amount of time spent in television watching tends to increase slightly up to twelve years, and then declines (Witty, 1951, 1955; Seagoe, 1952a; Battin, 1953). Time spent in television watching is affected by whether or not the child's family owns a television set. Children whose parents own sets watch much more than do those who must rely upon invitations from friends and neighbors to share theirs (Maccoby, 1951; Witty, 1952, 1955; Battin, 1953; Wells and Lynch, 1954). Children watch television more in winter than in summer (Fogler, 1953; Witty, 1955).

How long the family has owned a television set likewise influences the amount of time spent in watching programs. For the first six months of ownership, it is like a "new toy" for the child in that it dominates his playtime. After that, he may become bored or indifferent, thus spending relatively little time in watching programs (Witty, 1951; Fogler, 1953; Wells and Lynch, 1954). Usually, however, after the novelty of television watching has worn off somewhat, children set up well-defined patterns of televiewing (Battin, 1953). In one study, it was reported that sixth-graders spent nearly one-third of their waking time on Saturdays and Sundays in front of the television screen and an average of 2 hours daily during the week (*New York Times,* 1954b). The usual times are in the later afternoon and after the evening meal, though many children manage to watch television before they go to school and during or after their noon meal, in addition to the other times (Weathers, 1954).

Program Preferences. Program preferences follow much the same pattern as do preferences for reading, movies, and radio (Lyness, 1952; Seagoe, 1952). However, the child's favorite types of programs are not always the ones he most frequently sees. He must see what is available at the times of day when he is free to watch what appears on the screen (Seagoe, 1952a). Preschool children like simple stories about animals and familiar people, music, cartoons, and simple comedy. First- and second-grade children like puppet shows, cowboy presentations, harmless mysteries, humor, family-life situations, and prize-presenting programs. By the third and fourth grades, interest in imaginative programs increases, such as those about rockets and spaceships, and in variety shows, mystery and detective stories, dramatic plays, and music. Fifth- and sixth-grade children like much the same type of program as do those in the grade below, but they also like presentations dealing with science and feats of skill. However, at every age, there is a wide range of interests reflected in a wide range of preferences (Fogler, 1953). Stories, comedy, cartoons, and music are always popular at every age (Scott, 1953).

When children first start to watch television, they will watch any program available. After six months of television watching, however, they learn to be more discriminating in their choice of programs. They develop well-balanced program preferences and want variety in their programs as well as well-written programs (Battin, 1953). In this, they are helped by television guidance at school to select programs which will tie up with their school work (Fogler, 1953). In one study, 61 per cent of the children reported that they had no help from their parents in selecting programs, although 82 per cent of the group reported that they watched television with their parents (Scott, 1953). Children of today are selecting programs of a better type than they did several years ago. On the whole, the kinds of programs they are now selecting or would like to have are close to what their parents and teachers would choose for them (Witty, 1954).

Effects of Television. Ever since television watching became a popular form of amusement for children, there has been great concern about it among parents and educators because of its competition with reading and other leisure-time activities. Some maintain that television has more harmful effects than good; others take the opposite point of view (NABRAT Report, 1954). However, as Witty (1951a) has pointed out, "It has been shown that children and youth are taking television in stride and are making adjustments which, in many cases, result in a successful assimilation of television in their total patterns of interest and activity."

Among young children, many dream about the television programs they have seen, and these dreams are often of the nightmare type (Evry, 1952; Podolsky, 1952). Parents often have difficulty in getting their children to bed on time because the children do not want to miss a program that appears after their usual bed hour. As a result, they get too little sleep (Maccoby, 1951; Weathers, 1954). Many children who watch television frequently are nervous, especially if they have watched terror programs (Evry, 1952; Podolsky, 1952). As Podolsky (1952) has shown,

There is a natural tendency of the child's mind to continue turning over throughout the night what he has seen or heard before going to sleep. There is a deepening of impressions the next day by retelling and re-enacting these things during play-time. There is a potent tendency in children to vicarious participation in plots seen or heard, so that, in recollection or dreams, the child substitutes himself and family for the victim or victims, thus intensifying unwholesome emotional reactions, often to a state of fearful struggle against a terrifying threat to the safety or existence of himself as well as members of his family.

Because there are only a limited number of leisure hours in the day, the time the child spends on television watching is bound to cut into other activities. The result is that the child spends less time on other forms of play, especially out-of-doors play and play with other children (Maccoby, 1951, Evry, 1952; Weathers, 1954). He attends movies less (Coffin, 1948; Swanson and Jones, 1951; Witty, 1951a, 1952, 1955; Seagoe, 1952), and he listens to the radio less (McDonagh, 1950; Swanson and Jones, 1951; Witty, 1951a, 1952; Seagoe, 1952). He usually reads less, even devoting less time to comics than he formerly did. Reading of books is usually more affected than is reading of magazines and newspapers (Coffin, 1948; Swanson and Jones, 1951; Witty, 1951a, 1952, 1955). What he does read, however, is likely to be of a better caliber and is motivated by what he has seen in different television programs (Dempsey, 1954 Greenaway, 1954; Wells and Lynch, 1954; Morgan, 1955).

How television watching affects the child's school work depends partly upon how good a student he is and partly upon how long he has been watching television. Some children are influenced favorably by television watching in that they are motivated to "follow up" what they have seen on the screen and thus fill in gaps in their school curriculum (Gamble, 1951; Greenstein, 1954). This stimulates them to read material they might not otherwise have read (Battin, 1953; Greenstein, 1954). The better student, after the novelty of television has worn off, does not allow it to interfere with his school work (Battin, 1953). The poorer student, by contrast, continues to be unfavorably affected by television watching even after the novelty should have worn off (Witty, 1955). Among older children, 30 per cent claim that television helps them with their school work, while 70 per cent say that it hinders them by taking time from their homework (Witty,

1951a, 1952). The teacher's attitude toward the effects of television on children's school work is influenced largely by whether the teacher owns a set or not. Nonowners have been found to be less tolerant than owners (Witty, 1951a, 1952).

Television watching affects the pattern of family leisure-time activity. It produces closer physical proximity but restricts social interaction (Coffin, 1948; Swanson and Jones, 1951). It prevents the family members from reading, conversing, and playing (Maccoby, 1951). Less time is spent outside the home and more within the home (Coffin, 1948; Swanson and Jones, 1951). It stimulates new family interests and widens the circle of family friends (Riley et al., 1949). There are more visitors in the home, less visiting outside the home, less driving for pleasure, and less attendance at movies (McDonagh, 1950). Many parents use television as a "pacifier" for their children in place of discipline (Maccoby, 1951).

To a child, what he sees on a television screen is so real that attitudes established after viewing different programs are likely to be transferred to real-life situations. In a study of the effects of television programs on children's concepts and attitudes toward law enforcement, it was found that children tended to believe that sheriffs were dishonest, that criminals today are treated "mean," that it is all right to "beat up" criminals, that it is all right for police to be dishonest to trick criminals, and that criminals of today are "smart." Greater influence on children's attitudes toward law enforcement was found among the children of the lower than children of the higher socioeconomic groups (Scott, 1954).

Children who view crime programs are likely to become callous and unsympathetic. As Podolsky (1952) has stressed,

Seeing constant brutality, viciousness, and unsocial acts results in hardness, intense selfishness, even in mercilessness, proportionate to the amount of exposure and its play on the native temperament of the child. Some cease to show resentment to insults, to indignities, and even cruelty toward helpless old people, to women, and to other children. Altruistic impulses not followed by appropriate actions soon become sterile and non-existent. . . . The effects of habituation in the form of callousness to the suffering of others, begins as early as the seventh year and it mounts year by year, leading to an ever-increasing amount of over-exciting horrors. Crime and horror are found to be uppermost in the minds of the addicts much of the time, day and night.

FACTORS INFLUENCING PLAY

Not all children play alike. While it is true that the play interests of the child conform more or less closely to a pattern, there are, however, variations which may be traced to one or more of the following factors.

1. Health. It is a well-known fact that healthy children play more than sickly ones. The healthier the child, the more surplus energy he has, over and above the requirements for living, and hence the greater his energy for play. Reports from public-health nurses, charity workers, and teachers show that underfed and undernourished children are much less playful and that they care less about the toys given to them than do healthy children.

2. Motor Development. The degree of motor development attained at a given age plays an important role in determining what the child's play will be. When, for example, the child is incapable of throwing and catching balls, he cannot take part in the many ball games that his classmates do, even though he may be of the same age as they. Similarly, poor motor coordination makes it impossible for a child to cut, crayon, paint, or make many of the things from which young children derive such keen enjoyment. In a study of wheel play materials, such as wagons and tricycles, it was found that the child's play was markedly dependent upon the degree of neuromuscular coordination he had attained. At the age of twenty-one months, for example, the child pulled and pushed the toys; at twenty-four months, he pulled and pushed with control and directions; at twenty-nine months, he propelled for at least 7½ feet; and at thirty-six months, he propelled skillfully (Jones, 1939).

3. Intelligence. As early as the first year, the child's play is greatly influenced by intelligence. Bright babies are more active and playful than dull ones, and their play shows greater ingenuity. As the baby passes into the second year, marked differences are apparent in the play of bright and dull babies. The bright child rapidly advances from sensory to imitative play, and soon the element of imagination is apparent. This is not true of the play of dull children. Month after month, their play shows little change, and it is soon obvious that they are lagging behind other children of the same age. The older they become, the more apparent is this gap. When a child's play is conspicuously different from that of other children of the same age, the child's intelligence diverges far from the average (Hollingworth, 1926).

In the choice of play materials, children with normal or above-normal intelligence show a markedly greater preference for play materials which lead to constructive activity than do those who are mentally defective. Children of normal intelligence also show a greater stability in the duration of their interest in each play material chosen than do the defectives (Horne and Philles, 1942). Children of high IQ's during the preschool years show an interest in equipment for dramatic play and creative activities, such as clay, scissors, and paint. Their interest in books is for information, enjoyment, and withdrawal from the group (Maybury, 1952).

Among older children, differences in play among those with high and low IQ's becomes even more marked than among younger children. Bright children show an interest in a greater variety of play activities, and they spend more time in play than do the dull (Lehman and Witty, 1927, 1927a,

1928; Boynton and Ford, 1933). Bright children are more solitary and less social in their play interests; they spend more time in reading; and they participate in fewer activities that involve vigorous physical play than do children of average intelligence. Bright children show far less interest in games and sports than do those of average intelligence, but more interest in intellectual games, such as card and guessing games (Terman, 1925; Lehman and Witty, 1928; Boynton and Ford, 1933). Bright children enjoy collecting and have more hobbies than do other children (Boynton, 1941).

The role of intelligence in the play of the child is especially noticeable in reading. Early interest in reading and ability to read are found in children with high intelligence-quotient scores. Very bright children at every age spend more time in reading than do children of average intelligence, and they have a wider range of reading interests. The type of reading they prefer also differs from that of the average child. Gifted children enjoy reading dictionaries, atlases, encyclopedias, science, history, biography, travel, folk tales, informational fiction, poetry, and drama. Fairy tales are disliked and detective stories preferred above crude adventure and mystery. Emotional fiction appeals less to gifted than to average children, and an interest in romance occurs even before the child is ten years old (Terman, 1925; Hollingworth, 1926; Terman and Lima, 1927; Lehman and Witty, 1927a; Maybury, 1952).

4. Sex. During the early years of life, there is no real difference in the play activities of boys and girls. Given the same environment and the same toys, no really significant difference would be apparent until the "gang" age. But inasmuch as there are, in most homes, different environments and different toys for the two sexes, differences in play begin to appear at an early age. Children become aware at an early age that there are certain types of play appropriate for boys and others for girls. Parental attitude, toy selection, examples of their playmates and older children all help to enforce the cultural pattern (Conn, 1951).

In play with toys, girls favor dolls, doll furniture, beads, and blocks, while boys prefer trains, cars, horses, autos, airplanes, and tools. Boys play more strenuously than girls and prefer such games as baseball, football, and marbles, while girls like jumping rope, hide-and-go-seek, and playing house or school (Benjamin, 1932; Conn, 1951; Honzik, 1951; Maybury, 1952). Even when playing with the same materials, as blocks, the constructions made by boys differ from those made by girls (Honzik, 1951). Sex differences in reading, in type of radio and television programs preferred, and in movie preferences have already been discussed in earlier sections of this chapter. At all ages, boys show a greater range of play interests than do girls (Honzik, 1951). The most pronounced differences in the play of boys and girls appear late in childhood, during the "gang age" (Lehman and Witty, 1927).

5. Tradition. Play, like many other aspects of daily life, is influenced by tradition. It is traditional for girls to play with dolls and household toys, regardless of whether or not they interest the girl. Likewise, there are certain play activities that are traditionally attributed to boys, such as playing soldiers or playing with trains. Traditional forms of play are much the same the world over. For example, blindman's buff, in different forms, is played in many countries of Europe. Tag, in different forms, is played by the children of Burma, Iraq, and in the Sahara Desert, as well as in most European countries (United Nations Report, 1953).

Traditional games which children for generations have enjoyed are taught to each new generation of children as soon as they are able to learn them. Hide-and-go-seek, tag, blindman's buff, and cops and robbers are just a few of the games that are passed along from one generation to another. Among the lower-income groups, tradition plays a more important role in influencing a child's play than it does in the higher-income groups, where more money can be spent for new and different toys.

6. Season. What the child plays depends to a certain extent upon the season of the year (Sullenger et al., 1953). Roller skates, jumping ropes, jacks, and bicycles come out with the first warm days of spring. Summer brings a shift of interest to wading, swimming, and boating; then the cool days of fall renew the child's interest in the more active play enjoyed during the spring months. With the approach of winter, the child looks forward to snow for sledding, snowball fights, ice-skating, and in rural districts, sleigh riding. Games and sports are likewise influenced by the seasonal factor. As a general rule, the more active games are reserved for the cooler months of the year, and those that require less exertion for the warmer months. Baseball, for example, because it is less strenuous than football or hockey, is regarded as a spring and summer sport, while football and hockey are reserved for the cooler months of fall and early winter.

7. Environment. Children play mostly in their own neighborhoods or in their own yards. As they grow older, they play on the streets or in vacant lots near home. Only about one-fourth of them play in the parks or in park playgrounds in the vicinity of their homes (Sullenger et al., 1953). Thus, the environment in which they live has a marked influence on how much they will play and what types of play they will engage in. If there is no suitable place for play near their homes or little equipment available for them to use, they will spend much of their free time just "hanging around," perhaps playing games or merely watching other children and adults, or getting into mischief (Reeves, 1931).

Children from poor environments play less than do children from better environments. This is due, in part, to a difference in health. But, to a large extent, it may be traced to the fact that children from poor environments have fewer toys, less time, and less space in which to play than do those who come from economically better environments. While it is true that there are often more play companions available in the poorer environments, this factor alone is inadequate to compensate for the other factors mentioned. Rural children, because of their geographic isolation, play few games because of the difficulty of organizing groups of children. They have less equipment for play and usually less free time because they are expected to help with the work on the farm or in the home. Urban children can count on more playmates, unless they live in neighborhoods where there are few children of their age levels, and they usually have more play equipment (Lehman, 1926; Merry and Merry, 1950).

8. Socioeconomic Status. Children of different social-class backgrounds engage in play activities that are both quantitatively and qualitatively different (MacDonald et al., 1949). While these differences are not great during the early years of childhood, they become increasingly so as children grow older (Merry and Merry, 1950). Among children of the higher socioeconomic groups, there is an increasing preference for play activities which cost money, such as tennis, swimming, or watching athletic contests, while children of the lower socioeconomic classes engage in play activities requiring little expenditure of money, such as jacks, ball games, or tag (Boynton and Wang, 1944). The social class to which the child belongs influences the kind of books he reads, the movies he sees, and what type of organized recreational clubs he belongs to (Volberding, 1948). Children of economically privileged families engage in more cultural activities, as dancing, music, and art lessons, dramatics, choir, and organized activities, as Girl and Boy Scouts, than do children from less economically privileged homes (Cramer, 1950).

A detailed comparison of the play activities of children from different socioeconomic backgrounds revealed that children from the upper-middle class (Group A) and lower-middle class (Group B) were especially active in such clubs as Boy and Girl Scouts; they spent more time with their families and in activities connected with the church; they spent more time in reading and listening to the radio, and took music lessons more often than did the children from the lower classes. By comparison, children from the lower class (Group D) and from the upper-lower class (Group C) spent more of their time at the movies, played out of doors in the evenings more, and belonged more often to neighborhood clubs than did the children from the upper- and lower-middle classes (MacDonald et al., 1949). These differences are illustrated in Fig. 48.

9. Amount of Leisure Time. The amount of leisure time the child has determines not only the amount of time he plays daily, but also the type of play engaged in. With limited time, the child engages in play that can be completed in the time available, and when limited free time is the result of duties imposed upon him, he is apt to be tired when playtime comes. He consequently engages in play activities that require only a small expenditure of energy. The amount of leisure time the child has for play depends primarily upon the economic status of the family. In the case of children living in a residential suburban community, it was found that those of the higher economic level had few home duties and little or no work outside the home. The children from the poorer homes, on the contrary, had less time for leisure activities because of the duties imposed upon them (Fox, 1934).

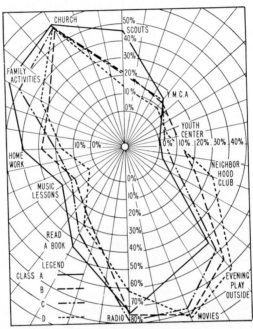

Fig. 48. Percentages of children of different social classes who engage in certain leisure activities. (*From M. MacDonald, C. McGuire, and R. J. Havighurst, Leisure activities and the socioeconomic status of children, Amer. J. Sociol., 1949, 54, 505–519. Used by permission.*)

10. Play Equipment. The amount and type of play equipment available have a marked influence on the play life of the child. Given certain types of toys, the child will use them, and his play activities will thus be influenced by them. Should the play equipment, for example, favor constructive play, as in the case of blocks, sand, or hammer and nails, the play will, of course, be primarily constructive. Predominance of dolls, household equipment, or soldiers puts emphasis on imaginative, make-believe play. Because the child's play is creative, dramatic, imitative, imaginative, and inventive, he needs equipment for all types of play, both for indoor and outdoor play (Merry and Merry, 1950; Maybury, 1951; Reece, 1954).

Except in poor homes, the young child's play needs are well met, for the most part. But as children grow older, they need equipment for team games and sports of all types. Lack of such equipment necessitates finding other outlets for their play interests. Often the play needs of the older child are not met as they are for the preschooler or the adolescent (Reece, 1954). Because children spend relatively short periods of time in any one type of play, they need a wide variety of equipment in the form of toys and materials for different forms of play. Too much equipment is just as bad as too little. A limited amount of well-selected equipment, on the other hand, encourages the child to be more resourceful in his play and to be more social than when there is too much equipment (Johnson, 1935). Some of the most popular toys for children are those made at home and which offer the child an opportunity to do things with the toys which are impossible in many of the ready-made toys (Leonard, 1952).

At first, the baby uses toys for exploration. He shakes, rattles, pulls, pushes, sucks, and uses whatever other methods he can to discover what the toys are, how they work, and all about them. Several years later, toys are used for play in imitation of adult activities and, still later, for dramatic, make-believe play. As the child approaches adolescence, his play interests shift from toy play to games and sports, with the result that his need for toys passes. He may, however, cling to a favorite toy because of some sentimental attachment for it and use it as a "keepsake" rather than as a plaything (Bridges, 1929; Hulson, 1930; Parten, 1933; Vance and McCall, 1934; Maybury, 1951).

Chapter 11

DEVELOPMENT OF UNDERSTANDING

At birth, as James (1890) pointed out many years ago, the child's consciousness is a "big, blooming, buzzing confusion." He has no understanding of his environment or of what he observes around him. Gradually, as a result of maturation and learning, the child begins to understand what he observes, and consequently his environment begins to be meaningful to him. But, as no two children have the same intellectual abilities or the same experiences, no two individuals can be expected to have the same understanding of an object or situation. As a result, each child interprets his experiences in terms of memories of previous experiences.

Discrimination begins early in life. At two weeks, the baby gives momentary heed to a dangling ring. By the time he is a month old, he regards it for a prolonged time, and by three months, he combines this with manipulation. At the same age, he vocalizes to sound stimuli, is aware of strange situations, and makes anticipatory adjustments to lifting (Bayley, 1933). All of these forms of behavior show the baby's ability to discriminate and to react adaptively to more and more things in his environment (Jersild, 1954). By the time the child enters school, he has a store of several hundred concepts. These, for the most part, are simple, such as roundness, redness, animal, dog, food, and love. From then on, concepts develop rapidly, with the result that, when he reaches adolescence, he has several thousand concepts (Havighurst, 1953).

CHILDREN'S CONCEPTS

Concepts are not direct sensory data but something resulting from the elaboration and combination of such data. They depend upon the individual's previous experience. They are experiences which tie together or link discrete sensory experiences (Vinacke, 1951, 1954). They are symbolic in that they depend upon properties of absent situations and objects as well as upon the properties of situations and objects present at the time the response is made. The common elements in diverse objects or situations serve to unite these objects or situations in a common concept (Hull, 1920). Frequently concepts have an "emotional weighting." They are complex affairs which are continuously changing with experience and with new knowledge on the child's part (Brownell and Hendrickson, 1950).

366

The child's concepts of the world in which he lives increase as his ability to perceive relationships between new and old situations increases. New meanings and new implications become a part of a system of interrelated ideas (Brownell and Hendrickson, 1950). The more readily the child can associate new meanings with old experiences, the more meaningful these old experiences become. Development of the concept of *orange,* for example, comes from the association of new meanings with the original meaning of an orange as a fruit. When the child learns that a specific color is called *orange,* that a type of tree is called *orange,* that a drink is called *orange* juice, and that a certain kind of flower is called *orange* blossom, he gradually understands *orange* to mean more than a fruit, as he had originally thought of it. His concept of *orange* is broadened and developed through new experiences associated with old experiences.

Concepts are not always conscious, nor are they always verbalized (Munn, 1955). Many of the child's concepts exist in different degrees of perfection and are not well enough formulated for the child to be able to express them in terms understandable to an adult. Many concepts exist in the child's mind, but he is unable to express them in verbalized form because of his limited vocabulary. Furthermore, many of the child's concepts are so different from those of an adult that the adult is apt to overlook them completely. The result is that it is impossible for the adult to know just what these concepts are or to be able to study them in an objective way.

Importance of Concepts. And yet it is important to know what the child's concepts are. Concepts determine what the child knows, what he believes, and, therefore, to a large extent, what he does (Russell, 1953). The child's concept of self, for example, determines how he behaves in relationship to others. Similarly, his concepts of others, especially of those who are different from him in color, religion, or socioeconomic status, will determine how he reacts to them, whether with tolerance or intolerance. The child's thinking as well as his actions is markedly influenced by the quality and quantity of his concepts.

HOW CONCEPTS DEVELOP

Because of their limited knowledge and experience, children cannot perceive an object or situation in the same way as an older or more experienced person can, though their sense organs are equally well developed. Like an adult, they interpret new experiences in relation to knowledge formerly acquired. Children at first perceive things on their face value. They are unable to interpret what they observe except as it appears to them at the time. Any subtle meaning, not apparent at first glance, escapes them. Young children interpret pictures first in terms of static form and later in terms of activity. Not until they are more mature do they interpret the picture in terms of their thoughts and feelings (Amen, 1941). By adolescence, the individual can interpret cartoons in terms of abstract meanings. Until then, the interpretations are made on face value and are concrete in form (Shaffer, 1930).

It is difficult to tell whether children, especially young children, get more meaning from a total impression than from an analytical approach to a situation. Observations of children show that they perceive meaning, no matter in what position they view the object, as when they look at pictures in a book sideways or upside down. This would suggest that they perceive more meaning from an impression of the total object or situation than from an analytical approach to it (Newhall, 1937). Girls, at every age throughout childhood, are inclined to perceive an object as a whole, while boys tend to abstract details from the whole (Rose and Stavrianos, 1943).

Methods of Development. Development of meaning progresses rapidly during the early years of life. At first, the baby discovers the meaning of the objects in his immediate environment through *sensory exploration* (Russell, 1953). He looks, listens, and smells, tastes, and touches everything within his grasp. As a result, he observes meanings which, when fused with meanings previously observed, cause strange and unfamiliar objects to become familiar and no longer the source of mystery that they previously were. The more often he can observe an object, with short time intervals between the observations, the more quickly will it become meaningful to him. The baby comes to know the mother, for instance, more quickly than he does the grandmother, because of the more frequent opportunities to observe the former as contrasted with the latter.

When motor coordination has reached a point in its development which enables the child to handle things at will, *motor manipulation* supplements the information formerly gained through sensory exploration alone (Russell, 1953). The child is an explorer and his curiosity takes many turns (Jersild, 1954). Through touching and handling objects, the child discovers qualities such as smoothness, softness, or warmth, which could not be observed by looking at them alone. Too often, the hands-off policy, which so many adults enforce, results in depriving the child of one of the most valuable sources of information that he has. Lack of well-developed motor control may lead to destructiveness, but this destructiveness is usually accidental rather than intentional. Given an opportunity to explore with adult supervision and aid, the young child will satisfy his curiosity with minimum destructiveness and, at the same time, will discover many meanings he would not discover if left to his own devices. Without this exploration, his concepts would be meager in content (Gesell and Ilg, 1949).

As soon as the child is old enough to put together words in a sentence, he begins to *ask questions* about things which arouse his curiosity. The "questioning age" begins around the third year and reaches its peak at the time the child enters school, at approximately six years of age. How important a role questioning will play in the development of understanding after that time depends to a large extent upon what success the child has in satisfying his curiosity in this way. He will unquestionably continue to use this method of gaining information throughout the rest of his life, but how useful it is to him will depend upon the satisfaction he derives from it during the early years of childhood.

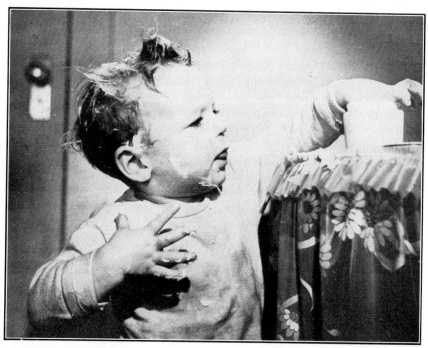

Through sensory exploration, the child discovers new meanings. (*From Child Development, a McGraw-Hill Text-Film.*)

While it is true that the young child is motivated to use questioning primarily because of genuine curiosity, he also asks questions to check upon or to supplement the information he has gained through his own experimentation. In many instances, he is not satisfied with what he has been able to discover through his own experimenting, and he then tries to supplement what he has learned by questioning those whom he believes to be better informed than he. Questioning is also motivated at times by a desire to attract and hold the attention of others, rather than by genuine curiosity. If such be the case, the child shows little interest in the answers given to his questions, and more often than not he asks the same question several times. Girls ask more questions than boys; children from the upper socio-economic groups more than those from the lower groups; and only children, more than those who have siblings (McCarthy, 1930; Davis, 1932; Smith, 1933a; Fisher, 1934; Russell, 1953; Jersild, 1954).

Before the child is capable of *reading,* he learns many meanings from looking at pictures, from being read to, or from having stories told to him. Even the simplest story books introduce new meanings into the child's life, and his careful observation of pictures shows him details of objects and persons which he formerly had not noticed. Because children enjoy looking at the same books, time after time, and hearing the same stories so often that they can repeat them word for word, they acquire more specific factual material than if their interest were of a more casual, superficial sort. Added to this is the fact that they will ask innumerable questions about anything that arouses their curiosity in what they see or hear and, in that way, supplement their information.

To perceive meanings, the child must be able to see *relationships.* With each succeeding year, new experiences are interpreted in terms of previous experiences, and the child associates meanings with the new ones, as a result of his realization of how they are related to what he has already learned. The greater the similarity between the new and the old, the more meanings the child can associate with it, provided he is able to perceive the relationships that exist. As a result of this, new experiences become increasingly more interesting to the child and stimulate his curiosity to explore them further.

Before the baby is a year old, observation of his behavior shows that he is interpreting new happenings in terms of what he has already learned. This ability is very pronounced from the time he is three years old and accounts, to a large extent, for the marked increase in knowledge that is apparent at that age (Piaget, 1930; Deutsche, 1937; Huang, 1943; McAndrew, 1943; McHugh, 1944; Jersild, 1954; Munn, 1955). By the time a child is two years old, he is capable of making simple generalizations (Welch, 1939). There is a steady increase with age in the child's ability to group together things that belong together and to give abstract, conceptual explanations of the groupings (Reichard et al., 1944). The ability to see relationships is easier and more accurate when the material is in line with his experiences (Oakes, 1947).

In the development of perception, *training* plays an important role. While it is true that anything new or interesting arouses the child's curiosity, there are nevertheless many things that he would not notice unless his attention were directed specifically toward them. The more he is encouraged to observe details, the more meaningful the objects in his environment become. Toys, if properly selected, help to develop the child's perception of space and color, just as well-selected books and pictures help him to develop an ability to perceive the beautiful or the comic. Likewise, strict adherence to a definite time schedule enables the child to judge time better than a haphazard schedule would. Music in the home, as a part of the play life of the child, builds up not only an appreciation of music but also a genuine fondness for it.

Factors Influencing Concept Development. What types of concepts the child will develop and how many will depend upon many factors. *Sense organ deficiency* will result in concepts different from those of a child whose sense organs function normally. The child who is color-blind, for example, will perceive objects in his environment differently than will the child with normal vision. Similarly, total or partial deafness will cause the child to build up concepts in which sound will play little or no role.

Intelligence plays a role of importance in the development of children's concepts. With maturation of intelligence, especially in the areas of memory and reasoning, the child's ability to develop concepts increases. However, chronological age seems to be as important as mental age in determining the conceptual ability of the child (Deutsche, 1937; Long and Welch, 1942; Vinacke, 1951). Of greater importance than intelligence in the development of concepts is the child's *opportunity for learning*. While learning ability depends upon intelligence, lack of opportunity to learn will influence markedly both the quantity and quality of concepts the child develops. The correlation between concept development and experience is greater than between intelligence and concept development (Vinacke, 1951).

Early concept formation is based on *concrete experiences.* Later, many of the child's concepts are based on *vicarious experiences* afforded by reading, movies, lectures, etc. For example, after seeing camels, the child can form a concept of a llama from pictures and descriptions, such as "South American animal something like a camel" (Havighurst, 1953). The concepts most familiar in a given locality are acquired earliest, while the less frequent ones are acquired later. Likewise, those related to the child's experiences, such as concepts of clouds, the flying of airplanes, or the rising of bubbles in water, are acquired earlier than concepts relating to objects or situations of a less familiar type, such as the functions of the heart and muscles, the meaning of gravitation, or the geological origin of hills and lakes (Oakes, 1947).

In a study of the child's concepts of different internal organs, as the lungs and stomach, and their functions, it was found that there was no positive correlation between the child's mental and chronological age and the concepts he had. On the other hand, there was a marked correlation between the child's concepts and the degree of knowledge his parents had. There was also a high correlation with what the child had learned in school about bodily functions (Nagy, 1953a). Similarly, the child's concepts of birth were found to be closely correlated with the amount and type of sex instruction he had received at home and in school. For example, Hungarian children, who are taught less in sex matters than American or British children, tend to have more fantasy than real concepts of birth. Children who attended schools high in sex prejudice were found to have fewer and less accurate concepts of birth than those who attended schools low in sex prejudice (Nagy, 1953).

The influence of opportunity to learn on the development of the child's concepts is shown also in *social-class* differences in concepts. Some concepts are general in a culture, such as concepts of time, space, and numbers. Others, by contrast, are specific to a social class, as in the case of concepts of "nurse," "maid," or "travel." In the case of the latter type, the child's concepts will be determined to a large extent upon the socioeconomic group to which his family belongs (Havighurst, 1953). What concepts a child will develop and what meanings he will associate with these concepts will depend to a marked degree upon his opportunities for learning. Variations in experience, thus, are mainly responsible for differences in concepts among children (Deutsche, 1937; Ordan, 1945; Oakes, 1947; Havighurst, 1953; Nagy, 1953, 1953a).

CHARACTERISTICS OF CHILDREN'S CONCEPTS

Children's concepts differ from those of adults more in degree than in kind (Vinacke, 1951). This is due to the fact that children have less experience and knowledge than adults (Hazlitt, 1930). If, therefore, the child's concepts are to be understood, they must be viewed from the child's point of view, not from the adult's. Concepts which may, to an adult, seem "illogical" are not so from the point of view of a child whose experiences are different from those of an adult and whose knowledge is, as a result, more limited (Wolff, 1947).

Studies of children's concepts have revealed that there is a *pattern of development* similar for all children, though the time needed to develop concepts and the level of development attained will depend partly upon the child's intelligence and partly upon his opportunities for learning. Children's concepts change with increasing age, but the change is more in the nature of a gradual progress than in definite stages (Brownell and Hendrickson, 1950; Vinacke, 1951). In developing, concepts go from concrete to abstract, from vague to clear, and from inexact to definite as new meanings are associated with old to become part of a system of ideas (Brownell and Hendrickson, 1950). Some concepts are more highly developed than others, and some never reach the higher levels of development, as may be seen by the fact that adults sometimes have concepts similar to those of children (Vinacke, 1951).

Developmental trends have been noted in many areas of concept development. In concepts of time, space, size, number, living, death, causal relationships, religion, and of morals, patterns of change from one age to another have been found to occur in large groups of children. These changes will be discussed in later sections of this chapter. The important thing to note is that, in a given culture where values and knowledge of a similar kind exist, children acquire, in the process of growing up, concepts which are similar to those of other children in that culture (Havighurst, 1953). This makes it possible for individuals to understand each other and to predict, with reasonable accuracy, what different individuals will do in different situations.

Concepts develop *from the simpler to the more complex levels.* From the preabstract period, children enter a period of development, about the twenty-sixth month, when they are able to grasp *first-hierarchy concepts,* such as that "men" and "women" are "people." About the middle of the fourth year, they enter the *second-hierarchy* period, when they are able to grasp such concepts as "potatoes" are "vegetables," "apples" are "fruit," and both "vegetables" and "fruit" are "food." With advancing age, the child is able to grasp concepts of still higher hierarchies, when concepts become increasingly complex (Welch, 1940; Welch and Long, 1940, 1940a, 1943; Colby and Robertson, 1942; Long and Welch, 1942; Reichard et al., 1944; Vinacke, 1951, 1954).

Concepts progress from *general to specific* in the pattern of their development. The young child first responds to the *total situation* rather than to any one part of it. He does not notice details as quickly as he observes the object as a whole. The result is that objects or situations which have elements in common are responded to as if they were the same, and the young child develops concepts of a general type in which meanings are vague and unformulated. With experience, the child distinguishes partial elements of objects and groups together those that have features in common. In this early type of classification, the object's function and structure play a dominant role in the child's understanding of its meaning.

With increase in maturity, there is a tendency for the child's concepts to become more specific. No longer is the concept of *toys,* for instance, vague and indefinite to the point that it is applied to any object with which the child plays. Rather, it becomes specific and is applied only to playthings as such, objects which have no other function and are used for no other purpose. In a qualitative analysis of children's responses to words in the Stanford-Binet vocabulary test, it was found that the responses given by younger children differed markedly from those given by older children. The younger child usually employs description and inferior explanation, while the older child stresses the class features of word meanings. In defining "gown," for example, the younger child says "you wear it," while the older child defines it as "an evening dress" (Feifel and Lorge, 1950).

Children's drawings have revealed that the child first perceives wholes rather than parts unrelated to wholes (Hildreth, 1944). With increase in age, there is a tendency to perceive the specific rather than the general. The older child perceives more details and related objects than he did when he was younger, and there is a decided increase in the accuracy of these perceptions. In most instances, the child puts some background in his drawings. This indicates that the child has a tendency to perceive things as a unit, even though certain things stand out in a more clearly defined manner than do others (Hurlock and Thomson, 1934). What a child perceives is stressed in the details of his drawings. This is illustrated in Fig. 49.

Concepts are *cumulative.* In the development of concepts, the child builds new meanings on old. Only when old concepts have been found to be erroneous does the child discard them and build a completely new concept from its beginning. Furthermore, in the building of concepts, the child

Fig. 49. What a child perceives is shown by the details he stresses in drawings. Drawing of a car by a child of six years one month, with an IQ of 115. (*From J. L. Thomson, Children's drawings: an experimental study of perception, unpublished master's essay, Columbia University Library, 1933. Used by permission.*)

may, at a later date, associate meanings previously acquired in some related area, but whose relationship to the present concept was not perceived before (Strauss, 1952). This is seen in some school studies, such as social studies, when the child does not always see, at the time he is studying them, the relationship to material learned in some other course of study in school (Eaton, 1944).

Children's concepts are often *erroneous.* The child often misinterprets what he hears or what he observes (Brownell and Hendrickson, 1950; Russell, 1953). He may see, hear, smell, taste, or feel correctly, but the error in observation results from the association of wrong meanings with what he has observed. Unless the errors are corrected soon after they occur, the association, through repetition, becomes firmly established, and as a result, faulty concepts are developed. Misconceptions formed early in childhood are especially serious because they are often not detected by adults until they have become so firmly established that it is difficult or, in some cases, impossible to eradicate them later.

One of the earliest and, at the same time, one of the most important investigations of the accuracy of children's concepts of objects or experiences in their everyday lives was made by G. Stanley Hall in 1891. According to his findings, children have more faulty information when they enter school than one would expect. Children from the better neighborhoods were found to have fewer faulty concepts than children from the poorer neighborhoods. Likewise, there were fewer misconceptions regarding objects or experiences common in a neighborhood than there were for less common ones.

Studies following along the lines of Hall's pioneer study have revealed similar findings (Huff, 1927; Probst, 1931; Jersild, 1954). Misconceptions, it has been found, are closely related to the characteristic concepts held by the child at that age. In the case of numbers, for example, errors are related to the concepts of addition, subtraction, or multiplication which the child is learning at that time (Ilg and Ames, 1951). Errors are systematic, not accidental or uniquely individual. They are found at each level of development and are fairly uniform among children of that level of development (Strauss, 1952). It should not be overlooked, however, as Jersild (1954) pointed out, that a "child may possess vast stores of information that are meaningful and useful to him in his everyday life, even though he may be lacking in information on many items of knowledge that adults take more or less for granted."

Seriousness of Misconceptions. Misconceptions are serious, not only because it is difficult to revise them if they are permitted to persist, but also because of their effects on the child's adjustments. In his school work, the child is handicapped by misconceptions regarding words used by the teacher or in his textbooks (Russell, 1953). If his concepts are limited or faulty, it is difficult for him to understand the teacher's explanations or to grasp the meaning of these explanations (Jensen, 1939; Jersild, 1954). Likewise, when reading for pleasure or watching movies or television, he will misinterpret what he hears or sees if his concepts of certain words are faulty.

The major source of difficulty arising from misconceptions is to be found in the area of social relationships (Russell, 1953). The child who misinterprets what others say or do will not be able to make very satisfactory adjustments to them. Children who do not perceive their own status in the group accurately will be more handicapped in their social adjustments than they would be if their errors were limited to the perception of the status of others. However, to make good social adjustments, the child must be able to perceive accurately not only his status in the group but the status of different children within the group as well (Ausubel et al., 1952). Boys show a tendency to underrate themselves more than girls do. The explanation given for this is not that girls are better adjusted than boys, but rather that girls tend to overrate themselves as a form of compensation for feeling inferior to boys (Tschechtelin, 1945).

Causes for Misconceptions. Errors in perception, resulting from the association of faulty meanings with what has been observed, may be traced to a number of causes, the most important of which are the following:

1. *Faulty information,* resulting from what the child has been told or what he has read. When parents, for example, are not certain about the correct answer to the child's question, they may "make up" an answer, so as to satisfy his curiosity; they may give him information which they sincerely believe is correct but which is erroneous in one respect or another; or owing to preoccupation with other interests, the individual questioned may misunderstand the child's question and answer it as he thought the child had asked it. Or the child's information may be faulty because he has read material from unauthoritative sources or from books which are out of date so that the material given in them has been disproved by recent discoveries.

2. *Superstitious beliefs,* handed down from generation to generation and accepted in an unquestioning manner by the child, frequently give rise to misconceptions. Children from homes of inferior socioeconomic status are likely to be influenced more by superstitious beliefs than are children from homes of a higher status (Peatman and Greenspan, 1935, 1936; Ter Keurst, 1939; Vinacke, 1951).

3. *Misunderstanding of words* used in explanation to the child. Since the young child's comprehension is limited, because of his limited vocabulary, he may misinterpret the meaning of the words used by others in explanation of material about which he is seeking information.

4. *Faulty reasoning* may cause misconceptions. When two objects or two words are alike in one or more aspects, the child concludes that they are alike in every way. As a result, he establishes misconceptions based on conclusions drawn from too limited data.

5. *Vivid imagination* in the form of dreams or daydreams may lead to conclusions not justified by the data available. In developing his concepts, the dreamer supplements data obtained from actual experiences with data of a purely imaginary sort. Many of the "white lies" of early childhood can be traced to misconceptions from this source.

6. *Limited experience* makes it impossible for the child to judge things with as great accuracy as he could if his experience had been broader. This is apparent in laboratory studies of illusions. Because of limited experience and lack of critical attitude, children may readily associate completely wrong meanings with what they observe, without realizing how incongruous the association is (Garrison, 1952; Russell, 1953; Jersild, 1954).

Variations in Errors. While it is true that all perception is subject to error and that the extent of the errors is closely related to the age of the individual, there are nevertheless errors within each age group, depending more upon what is observed than upon the abilities of the subject to observe or the opportunities he has had to acquire information. As a general rule, it may be said that the more subjective the perception, the more influenced it is by personal bias or prejudice, which, in turn, results in faulty concepts. Objective facts, on the other hand, may be observed incorrectly because of insufficient knowledge on the subject's part to enable him to perceive them correctly. Such common misconceptions as "telephone wires are hollow," "flowers have no function for the plant," "the heart beats only when we are sick or frightened," and "water is lighter than air" are caused by faulty or inadequate information which the child has acquired from his contact with others or by misinterpreting what he has read (Oakes, 1947).

Faulty concepts about self, on the other hand, are not caused by faulty information but rather by personal bias. The child, like the adult, prefers to think of himself as *he would like to be,* with traits and characteristics that are approved by the social group with which he associates. If asked, then, to judge himself, he will do so in terms of the ideal self rather than in terms of the real self. In an experiment in which children were asked to check one word in a pair that more nearly described them, it was found that children tended to overestimate the presence of socially desirable traits and to underestimate the presence of socially undesirable ones. This tendency was stronger in older children who are more aware of the opinions of others than are younger children (Hurlock, 1927a). Boys, at every age, tend to underrate themselves, and this becomes stronger as boys grow older (Hurlock, 1927a; Tschechtelin, 1945). The ability to perceive one's own status in the group is consistently inferior to the perception of the status of others at every age (Ausubel et al., 1952).

SOME COMMON CONCEPTS OF CHILDREN

What concepts the child has is purely an individual matter, depending on his age, his intellectual level, and the opportunities he has had to learn meanings related to the objects and experiences of his daily life. However, there are some concepts which are so commonly found among children in a given culture that one can assume that they are "typical" of the children of that culture. Of these, the following types are most common.

1. CONCEPTS OF LIFE

Because of the young child's limited experiences and knowledge, he does not distinguish between living and inanimate objects. On the contrary, he believes, as do primitive peoples, that all objects have the same life qualities that one finds in the human being and are, therefore, *animate. Animism,* or the tendency to ascribe consciousness to inert objects, is one of the outstanding characteristics of the young child's perception. As a result, his concepts are realistic, and consequently they are often faulty.

Piaget (1929) recognizes four successive stages in the animistic concepts of young children. In the first stage, when children are four to six years old, everything that is in any way active is regarded as conscious, even though it be stationary. In the second stage, which occurs between the ages of six and seven years, consciousness is attributed only to things that can move. The sun and a bicycle, for example, are regarded as conscious, while a table or a stone, both of which are inert, are not. Between the ages of eight and ten, the third stage, an essential distinction is made between movement that is due to the object itself and movement that is introduced by an outside agent. Bodies that can move of their own accord, as the sun or the wind, are looked upon as conscious, while objects that receive their movement from without, such as bicycles, are regarded as devoid of consciousness. In the fourth and final stage, which begins at the age of eleven years, consciousness is restricted to plants and animals, or to animals alone.

More recent studies of children's concepts of living have revealed that children do not actually pass through definite stages in the development of their concepts of living, but rather there is a gradual transition in the development of these concepts. Furthermore, it is impossible to assign any specific age to any phase in the development of these concepts. Children differ markedly in their concepts of living at different ages, and even by adolescence, some individuals may have concepts similar to those of children. Children distinguish between "living" and "having life." "Living" is more often applied to inanimate objects than "having life." When they say an object is "alive," they usually do not attribute sensory or functional attributes to the object. Thus, the child does not mean what an adult means by "alive." To a child, this usually means "active," and this is not animism in the correct meaning of the term. From kindergarten on, there is a progressive decrease in the number of children who attribute life to inanimate objects (Grigsby, 1932; Mead, 1932; Dennis, 1938, 1942, 1943b, 1953; Russell and Dennis, 1939; Russell, 1940, 1940a; Russell et al., 1940; Bruce, 1941; Huang and Lee, 1943, 1945; Strauss, 1951; Garrison, 1952; Klingensmith, 1953; Munn, 1955). Even young children, when asked "What makes the engine go?" recognize that the presence of a human being is necessary for the guidance of the engine (McAndrew, 1943).

Closely related to the child's concepts of living are his concepts of *death*. What these concepts are will depend largely upon the religious instruction he has received. Children's concepts of death have been found to range from brutal destruction to liberation (Bernarda, 1949). In one study of large groups of children, it was found that changes occurred in their concepts as the children grew older. Children between the ages of three and five years look upon death as a departure or change of abode. They deny that death is a regular and final process, because at this level of development, they look upon everything, including the dead and lifeless, to be alive.

Between the ages of five and nine years, death is personified and is considered a person. They do not try to explain why death occurs, because they do not recognize death as a process which occurs as the result of certain conditions and in certain circumstances. They do, however, regard death as an eventuality. Children nine years of age and older regard death as a process which is inevitable. This concept is closely related to the child's concepts of cause and effect which make the child regard death in a more realistic manner than he did when he was younger (Nagy, 1948). It is unusual for children to wonder what happens after death much before they reach the adolescent years (Kuhlen and Arnold, 1944). Only when their religious instruction has emphasized life after death in terms of Heaven or Hell does the child have any definite concept of life after death.

2. Concepts of Causality

The ability to see cause-and-effect relationships develops gradually, not in stages, as Piaget (1930) contended. This ability is more closely related to the child's experiences and opportunities for learning than with either his chronological or mental age (Deutsche, 1937; Oakes, 1947; Vinacke, 1951; Nagy, 1953, 1953a). At every age, there is a wide range of concepts among the children of that age. Even in the same child, some of his concepts of causality will be immature, while others will be mature. The degree of development attained will depend largely upon his experiences. Concepts that are related to the child's experiences will be better developed and more accurate than those relating to less familiar experiences (Oakes, 1947).

As a rule, children under seven or eight years of age have inaccurate and incomplete concepts of causality. By the time the child is eight or nine years old, he can understand cause-and-effect relationships regardless of special instruction (Lacey and Dallenbach, 1939). There seems to be no difference in the difficulty of learning concepts of causality relating to the child's body and those relating to natural phenomena. Both are dependent upon the development of the child's reasoning ability and the experiences he has had. The young child's concepts are usually illogical, inaccurate, and magical in content. There is little indication that they understand cause and effect (Deutsche, 1937; Oakes, 1947; Vinacke, 1951).

A study of the child's concepts of *birth* revealed that the child first explains the origin of the baby from the baby himself, then from the mother, and finally, from the father also. After the age of eight years, it is unusual for a child to explain birth without taking into consideration the role played by the mother. Only after eight years of age, on the other hand, does the child comprehend the role played by the father. Even then, many children have concepts which include only the role played by the mother. Many young children think of the origin of babies as coming from God, the stork, or from a store. What concept the child will have at any age will depend largely upon what he has learned about birth from his home or school environment (Nagy, 1953).

The child's concepts of *bodily functions* are likewise dependent largely upon the opportunities he has had to learn about these functions. Up to the age of seven years, most children have a concept of the *brain* as being in the head, round in shape, and composed of bone, blood, and skin. Only after the fifth or sixth grades does their concept include flesh and cells. For the most part, children think of the brain as made up mostly of bone, indicating a confusion between the skull and the brain. Until children are eight years old, they attribute to the brain mainly intellectual activities, especially thinking. Even after eight years of age, there is little indication that they understand the functions of the brain. *Nerves* are thought of as threads covering all or part of the head, and with the major function of "feeling." Many confuse "nerves" with "nervousness." Like the brain, children think of the nerves as composed mainly of bone, blood, and flesh (Nagy, 1953a).

Concepts of *breathing* are as erroneous as those of the brain and nerves. The child sees little relationship between breathing and life. To him, breathing takes place mostly in the nose, mouth, and throat, and the air circulates somewhere in the head region. It is not until children are nine years old that they recognize breathing as a process of taking in and expelling air. They do not think of it in terms of interchange of oxygen or of having any effects on the body, though they recognize the necessity of breathing. It is only toward the end of childhood that the lungs are recognized as the organs of breathing. To older children, lungs are represented as round bags, made of bone, skin, blood, and flesh. Some children locate the lungs in the head or neck, while few locate them in the chest (Nagy, 1953a).

To a child, the *digestive process* takes place in the mouth and stomach. He does not recognize the digestive tract as a system composed of different organs. The stomach is usually located in the upper part of the trunk and is believed to be composed of skin, bone, flesh, and blood. The child believes that the stomach is meant for storing or eating food. The purpose of eating is vague to children. Likewise, they have little understanding of the relationship between eating, digestion, and elimination. As is true of other bodily processes, they fail to see the cause-and-effect relationship between eating and living (Nagy, 1953a).

Children are inclined to attribute all diseases to *germs*. If any germ gets into the body, they believe this necessarily makes them ill (Nagy, 1951, 1953b). A young child draws a germ as a dot or as some abstract figure. Children eight years of age and older think of germs as abstract figures or animals, such as a fly or worm. The child's concept of germ is shown in Fig. 50. They believe that germs enter the body through the mouth, nose, or skin. When there, they make the person ill, damage the body, or live in the body. Germs can leave the body, they believe, through the mouth, nose, skin, or anus, by coughing, sneezing, or anal evacuation. When the doctor gives medicine, that pushes the germ out of the body. The body is thought to react automatically; any germ or medicine is believed to provoke instantaneous change. Children do not take into consideration the condition of the body (Nagy, 1953b).

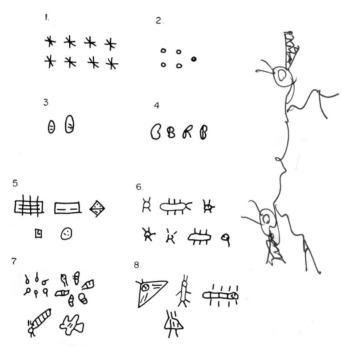

Fig. 50. Children's concepts of "germs." (*From M. H. Nagy, The representation of "germs" by children, J. genet. Psychol., 1953, 83, 227–240. Used by permission.*)

3. Concepts of Space

Judgments of direction and distance are difficult for young children and can be learned only through experience. In judging space accurately, the child must learn to compare the space to be perceived with familiar objects whose size or distance from him are known. He must learn to regard the degree of clearness of outline and color and the amount of detail visible as clues, and he must learn that different sensations in the eyes, resulting from convergence or strain, help him to interpret what he observes.

Little babies rarely reach for objects more than 20 inches away from them, which shows that they have some estimate of distance even before they are a year old. Gradually, with practice in reaching for objects, the child learns not only how far away the objects are from him but also in what direction they are. He learns early to judge small distances because he has plenty of opportunity to do so. As soon as the baby begins to creep and crawl, and later to walk and run, he has more opportunity to evaluate distance and size. Because he is exceedingly active, he can build up many associations with his activities which will enable him to perceive size, distance, and shapes both indoors and outdoors (Gesell and Ilg, 1949).

From his play with blocks, carts, tricycles, and other favored play equipment, the child soon learns the common cues which enable him to perceive short distances accurately, provided they are studied in relation to his own body. Longer distances, because they are unrelated to his own body—for example, the distance between two trees or the length of a street block—are extremely difficult for him to perceive. It is generally not until adolescence that the child has the ability to perceive long distances correctly, and even then his judgments are often erroneous.

Perceptions of distance, direction, and size are all improved by training. Toys and kindergarten equipment, as beads for stringing, blocks, cylinders, form boards, puzzles, nests of cubes, tricycles, sleds, and coasters, all give the child an opportunity to measure in terms of "long" and "short." In connection with kindergarten and school work, he learns the meaning of inches, feet, yards, pounds, and the different standard measures of space and weight, even though the concepts may be formalized to the point that they are difficult for him to apply to his everyday experiences.

Varieties of Concepts. The baby can discriminate between *simple geometric forms* (circle, square, cross, triangle, and oval) as early as six months of age and can use this discrimination as a learning cue (Ling, 1941). Terman and Merrill (1937) find that a child of average intelligence should be able to insert a circle, square, and a triangle into a three-hole form board at the age of two years. There is a gradual improvement in ability to perceive differences in form from two to six years of age (Baldwin and Wellman, 1928). Between fifteen months and two years of age, concepts of triangularity and other forms are established (Munn and Steining, 1931; Gellermann, 1933; Vinacke, 1951, 1954). As early as three years, concepts of roundness are well enough developed for the child to be able to distinguish cylindrical and two-dimensional roundness (Long, 1940).

To determine which plays a more important role, form or color, in the apprehension of an object, objects were presented in such a way that the child had to match on the basis of form or color, but never both simultaneously. Children under three years of age were found to match on the basis of form rather than color; children from three to six matched on the basis of color; while those over six matched on the basis of form (Brian and Goodenough, 1929). Baley (1948) has formulated the principle that "with the progress of the child's development, formal elements in his perception take more and more predominance over the material elements, such as color." In figure-ground discrimination, the preschool child's perception of ground is nearer the adult level than is his perception of figures (Meister, 1949).

The ability to distinguish between right and left is difficult for a child and is somewhat late in developing. The ability begins at about five years of age and develops fairly rapidly between the ages of six and seven years. From then until nine years, the development is at a slower rate (Swanson and Benton, 1955). Elementary-school children do not have a well-generalized notion of the cardinal *directions*. While they may identify south and east they are likely to fail to identify southeast. Furthermore, they have difficulties in using directions correctly in describing locations of places, though they can fairly accurately locate cities, especially nearby cities. Girls, as a group, were found to be inferior to boys in space orientation (Lord, 1941).

The ability to judge *distance* develops more rapidly than ability to judge direction. By the time a child is four years old, his perception of distance is similar to that of adults (Updegraff, 1930). On the other hand, perception of *depth* is slow in developing. Even at five or six years of age, children's ability to see three dimensions in objects is poor (Garrison, 1952). By the time the child is five years old, he can compare the *speed* of two moving objects with a fair degree of accuracy (Fraisse and Vautrey, 1952).

Concepts of *relative size* appear first between the ages of three and four years, when the child becomes aware of the fact that he must consider himself as one object among other objects in space. He is then able to understand the relativity of the position of objects (Meyer, 1940). At this time, children can select the largest and smallest objects from a group placed before them, and by the time they are five years old, they can select middle-sized objects. However, the extent of the difference in size influences slightly the response made. If the difference in size is very small, the perception of relative difference becomes increasingly inaccurate (Hicks and Stewart, 1930; Thrum, 1935). In judging body sizes, nursery-school children can perceive realistically the body sizes of their parents and of themselves. For example, they perceive the father as the larger parent, and themselves as smaller than their parents. Children at this age have a tendency to perceive members of the opposite sex as larger than members of their own sex (Katcher and Levin, 1955).

Between the ages of three and four years, children are more influenced by the effect of illusion in different geometric figures when they attempt to judge relative size than they are when they are younger (Dixon, 1949). So long as the shape of two geometric figures is the same, children have little difficulty in determining which is the larger. When, however, different shapes are used, there are more errors in their judgments (Long, 1941). Concepts of "big" and "little" develop earlier than the concept of "middleness" (Hicks and Stewart, 1930; Thrum, 1935; Welch, 1938, 1939, 1939a,

1939b, 1940). Not much before the child is nine years old does he show as much accuracy in judging "middleness" as he does in judging "big" and "little" (Graham et al., 1944; Vinacke, 1951). From his experience with standard objects in the distance, he learns that objects appear to be smaller when they are far away (Garrison, 1952).

4. CONCEPTS OF WEIGHT

Accurate judgments of weight depend partly upon judgments of size and partly upon knowledge of the weight of different materials. This is often confusing to a little child who has not yet learned from experience that different materials have different weights. A ball of cotton, for example, is judged to be heavier than a block of wood of smaller size, or a lead weight, because the cotton is larger in size than either the wood or the lead. The child's judgments are more in terms of size than of weight, and as a result many accidents with toys and household objects occur. This is due to the fact that the child does not make the necessary muscular adjustments to handle them without breakage. A small *objet d'art,* for instance, picked up by the child in his curiosity to examine it, may slip through his fingers and break because he did not expect it to be as heavy as it was and did not make the necessary motor adjustments to handle it safely.

Gradually the child learns, from experience with toys and articles with which he comes in constant contact, that certain things are "heavy," while others are "light." Of even greater importance, he learns that he must consider what the object is made of and not judge it in terms of size alone. He discovers from experience that if he wants to determine just what the weight of an object is, he must pick it up, not merely look at it. If he holds it with his fingers, or places it in the palm of his hand, and then moves his hand up and down, as if lifting the object, its true weight becomes more evident than if he merely holds his arms stationary. These cues, as aids in the perception of weight, are learned gradually and depend to a certain extent upon the variety of experiences the child has had.

5. NUMBER CONCEPTS

Words relating to numbers are used soon after the child starts to speak, but rarely is their meaning known. The use of number words, between the ages of two and three years, is thus merely a form of "parrot" speech. What a number really means to a child and when he can use it in a meaningful way is difficult to determine. Like other concepts, the development of number concepts appears to be a function of age and of the educational development of the child (Douglass, 1925; Long and Welch, 1941). Terman and Merrill (1937) found that the average child of four can count two objects; the average child of five can count four; and the average child of six can count twelve objects.

The developmental pattern of number concepts has revealed no distinct stages but gradual improvement in the understanding of the meaning of numbers as the child grows older and as his experiences broaden. The developmental pattern of number concepts has been found to be as follows (Ilg and Ames, 1951):

1 year .... "One-by-one" pattern of manipulating objects (rudiment of counting).
18 months .... Can build a tower of three to four cubes.
               Uses the word "more."
2 years .... Distinguishes between one and many.
               Says "two balls" when handed a second ball.
2½ years ..... Counts by rote, 1, 2, "lots."
               Can give "just one" cube on request.
3 years .... Can count two objects.
               Can give "just two" cubes on request.
4 years .... Counts with correct pointing to three objects.
               Verbal counting without pointing exceeds counting of objects.
5 years .... Most children can count 13 pennies.
               One-third can count to 30 or more.
               Most mistakes come after the number 9.
6 years .... Can count to 100.
               Can count by tens to 100.
               Can count by fives to 50.
               Can add correctly within 10.
               Can subtract correctly within 5.
7 years .... Can count by fives and tens to 100.
               Can add within 20.
               Can subtract within 10.
8 years .... Can count by twos to 20.
               Can count by threes to 30.
               Can count by fours to 50.
               Can add within 25.
               Can subtract within 25.
               Can deal with simple fractions, multiplication, and division.
9 years .... Number concepts to 1,000 or beyond.

From grades 2 to 11, there is a gradual increase in understanding of indeterminate number concepts, such as "few," "several," and "some" (Brotherton et al., 1948). At every age, there is a sex difference in favor of girls in number concepts. Children of the higher socioeconomic groups have more and more accurate number concepts than do those of the lower groups (Martin, 1951). The development of number concepts for boys and girls is shown in Fig. 51.

6. Money Concepts

Money becomes meaningful to a child only when he has an opportunity to use it. Until his experiences include the use of money, his concepts will be of a vague, indefinite type. True, he will be able to identify the different coins in common usage, but the names attached to these coins will be relatively meaningless to him because he does not know what value they have or what they can buy. Because few children in our culture have much opportunity to use money for anything but saving until they reach the school years, the development of their money concepts during the preschool years will be slow and will lag behind the development of many other types of concepts.

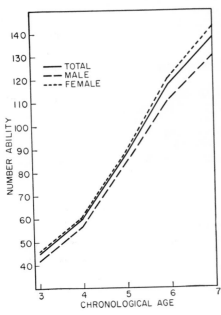

Fig. 51. Development of number concepts in young children. (*From W. E. Martin, Quantitative expression in young children, Genet. Psychol. Monogr., 1951, 44, 147–219. Used by permission.*)

At five years of age, a child can name pennies only. A year later, he can name pennies, nickles, and dimes, and some children know how many pennies there are in a nickel or dime. The seven-year-old knows what a quarter is, and many children can tell how many pennies there are in a quarter (Ilg and Ames, 1951). At that time, the child can ask for correct change in a store. The child at 8½ years can match equivalent amounts with different coins, even when the money combinations are complex (Schuessler and Strauss, 1950). Young children do not realize that money is connected with buying. By five years of age, however, they begin to understand that money has to do with buying, though they do not understand that specific coins must be used for buying different things. A nickel buys a 5-cent candy bar as well as a larger bar, according to their concepts. By the age of 6½ years, the child realizes that a nickel will buy more than a penny but less than a dime. He also realizes at this time that money can buy services as well as objects, and that change is sometimes, though not always, given when money is used to make a purchase. By the age of seven years, the average child knows exactly how much more or less each coin is worth than every other coin (Strauss and Schuessler, 1951; Strauss, 1952).

7. Time Concepts

Time perception in adults is none too accurate, but it is even worse in the case of children. This explains the apparent disobedience of young children when they fail to come home at the appointed time. They are unable to judge time correctly, and because of their interest in play or some other activity, time passes more quickly than they realize. The restlessness of a child during a social call or when riding on trains or in automobiles may be traced to the fact that time passes slowly for the child who is bored because he is idle.

Time concepts are slow in developing. At the age of five years, the child has the merest rudiments of conventional time knowledge (Bradley, 1947). Concepts of time are abstract and involve subjective appreciation. The child, for example, understands numbers on a clock or the time of some daily occurrence because they are specific. But anything as remote from the child's daily experiences as historical time is difficult for him to comprehend. Furthermore, because time has varying meanings and is not connected with the present alone, it is very confusing to a child. For example, "now" will be "yesterday" when tomorrow comes (Bromberg, 1938).

It is difficult for a child to have an understanding about time in the past or time in the future. He can understand "short-time age" better than "long-time age," but it is harder for him to imagine "tomorrow" than to understand "yesterday" (Friedman, 1944). Many time concepts, especially those relating to conventional time, are dependent upon the growth of number concepts. A child cannot, for example, understand completely the meaning of "month" until he has a correct concept of 30 or 31 and their relationship to 7 days (Harrison, 1934). Understanding of dates in historical time, of the word "generation," and of chronological order is especially difficult for children (Friedman, 1944).

Learning of Time Concepts. In learning time concepts, the child first learns those that have a personal reference, and later, those that are more remote from his experience. By the age of six years, for example, he has a good comprehension of conventional time, but it is not until he is nine or ten years old that he can comprehend long periods of time in the past (Bradley, 1947). Direct training is of less value than impressions that accumulate in the process of growing older. The child must build up a foundation of related concepts, mainly those relating to numbers, before training can be of much value (Pistor, 1939, 1940; Jersild, 1954).

Understanding the meaning of time depends upon the use of cues, such as the time of such regular activities as meals or going to school (Springer, 1952). If these cues are to be of value in understanding time, however, they must be within the framework of the child's own experience (Garrison, 1952). Errors occur mainly when indefinite cues are used (Farrell, 1953). The young child, for example, has no idea of the length of time nor means by which to judge it. In order to estimate time units successfully, one must take into consideration the activity engaged in. One hour spent in play seems much shorter than an hour spent in school. Until the child learns that he must consider his activity when he estimates time, he cannot judge it correctly. Much of the dallying over eating and dressing, which occurs between the ages of three and five years, may be traced to faulty time perception.

Perception of the time of day, day of week, or season of the year is more accurate because the child can associate specific activities with the time, and this acts as a cue to enable him to interpret them correctly. Day is distinguished from night because the former is light and the latter dark and because day is the time when he can be up and night is the time when he must sleep. Morning is perceived as different from afternoon because of the difference in activities. Morning is playtime for the young child, and afternoon is nap time and the time for clean clothes. The days of the week are likewise known through the activities associated with them. Sundays are usually known first, because the father is at home, and the routine of the day is often interrupted for family trips.

Genetic Sequence. In spite of the fact that marked individual differences appear in the child's orientation in time, Ames (1946) noted that time concepts come into use in a relatively uniform sequence and at about the same relative time in the life of every child. The pattern of development she found to be as follows.

Words indicating the present come first, then words relating to the future, and finally, words indicating the past. The use of "today," for example, appears at twenty-four months; "tomorrow," at thirty months; and "yesterday," at thirty-six months. This suggests that time in relation to ends of things is understood before time in relation to beginnings can be grasped.

The ability to tell at what time a thing happens in terms of some activity appears before the ability to give an actual clock time. Children know morning or afternoon at four years; what day it is, at five years; the names of the days of the week, at five; and what time it is, at seven years. At that age they also know what month it is and what season. When they are eight years old, they know what year and what day of the month it is, and they can name the month correctly.

By the time they are five years old, children can first tell correctly when they go to bed; by six, when they have supper, when they get up, when they go to school, and when afternoon begins. Most children can tell their ages when they are three years old; when their next birthday will be, at four; and how old they will be on the next birthday, by the time they are five years old.

In learning to tell time by the clock, there is a genetic sequence which is much the same for all children. At first, the child can tell time by the hour, then the half hour, and later, by the quarter hour. He can set the clock first by the hour, then by the half hour, and last, by the quarter hour. At first, children do not understand the meaning of the difference in length of the hands. When this is learned, they can set the hands correctly to indicate the time of day (Springer, 1951, 1952). Most children can learn to tell time by the clock when they are six years old (Friedman, 1944, 1944a; Ames, 1946; Bradley, 1947; Vinacke, 1951).

Concepts of Duration of Time. Understanding time intervals and being able to estimate them correctly is difficult for children, and this ability develops later than the ability to understand the meaning of time as it is related to different activities. Longer intervals are usually underestimated, while shorter ones are exaggerated (Friedman, 1944). The best evaluation has been found in intervals from 30 seconds to 1 minute in duration (Elkine, 1928). A comparison of the ability of fifth-grade children and college students to estimate intervals of time revealed that the college students were only 15 to 18 per cent superior to the children. The fact that children were as successful as they were suggested that they had already developed certain clues for estimating time (Gilliland and Humphreys, 1943).

Concepts of Historical Time. Concepts of time in the past are hazy until the child is well along in school. By the time he is 9 years old, he can comprehend a long period of time, but he is unable to associate specific events with it (Bradley, 1947). The ability to think of the past as different from the present passes through two stages in development. The first, or "negative," stage is one in which the past differs from the present, as, for example, the wearing of skins or the worship of idols. In the second stage, the child not only distinguishes historical periods, but he also forms a picture of successive epochs not unlike that formed by the adult (Oakden and Sturt, 1922). Concepts of historical time are often vague and confused because they have been taught in terms that are abstract and remote from the child's experiences (Jersild, 1954).

8. Concepts of Self

Sometime during the first year of life, the baby discovers himself (Ames, 1952). However, he does not distinguish between himself and his environment as early as he distinguishes other people from the environment. He is, for example, aware of his mother's hand before he is aware of his own hand, and he identifies his mother's voice before he identifies his own vocalizations (Gesell and Ilg, 1949). He is able to recognize others in a mirror or in pictures before he recognizes himself (Zazzo, 1948). However, because the baby is primarily egocentric, he forms concepts about himself before he forms concepts about other people (Ames, 1952). These concepts are then used as a standard by which he interprets others.

The child's concepts of self develop first in relationships with the mother, then with the teacher, and last with his contemporaries (Ames, 1952). In the development of his concept of himself as an individual, the development of awareness of self is not a unitary process, nor does it take place all at one time. Instead, the child perceives different aspects of himself at different times (Sarbin, 1952). He distinguishes between himself and others before he forms concepts of his appearance and of his abilities. Each year, as the child grows older, as his experiences broaden, and as his intellectual capacities mature, his concepts of himself grow through the discovery of new qualities and new potentialities. In the development of a healthy personality pattern, it is essential that there be a change in the concepts of self as new self-discoveries are made (Jersild, 1954).

In the development of concepts of self, children often build up two distinct concepts. (1) Self-concept comes from external experiences and contacts with others. The child has specific concepts relating to his body, his appearances, and how he compares in abilities of different types with the children with whom he associates. This type of concept is developed first, because the child's earliest experiences are objective. As the child reaches the school age, subjective experiences become more meaningful to him. (2) As a result, he establishes another type of concept of self based on his thoughts, feelings, and emotional experiences. It is often difficult for him to coordinate the subjective and objective concepts, and consequently he is apt to think of himself as a dual personality, with a specific appearance and with a specific personality make-up. Gradually, as the child reaches adolescence, the subjective and objective concepts of self fuse, and the adolescent perceives himself as a unified individual.

Pattern of Development. The baby discovers meanings about his body through handling the different parts and by looking into a mirror. This begins as early as the fourth or fifth month. He watches his fingers; pulls at his hair, ears, nose, and toes; and watches his movements in a mirror whenever he has an opportunity to do so. When a baby or young child tries to localize himself, as he looks at himself in a mirror, his first reactions are largely limited to his eyes. This is true around the age of sixteen weeks. Later, he observes his arms, hands, feet, fingers, toes, and tongue. With advancing age, the area of regard expands to include the whole body image and surroundings (Gesell and Ames, 1947a). The spatial localization of the self in young children, as indicated by pointing, is usually in the abdomen and lower thorax. This is the area formed by the boundaries of the visual field (Horowitz, 1935).

By the second or third year, the child can distinguish between a thing belonging to his own person and himself (Lewin, 1935). The child's concept of himself as an independent person comes mainly from his ability to distinguish himself from other people (Allport, 1937). Self-consciousness, as shown in shyness in the presence of others, appears around the sixth month. Later, the baby cries when someone frowns or speaks harshly to him, and between the ages of two and three years, the development of negativism (pages 271–273) indicates that he is well aware of the difference between himself and other people (Allport, 1937; Ames, 1952; Banham, 1952; Jersild, 1954). Typically, the four-year-old engages in excessive boasting about himself, his abilities, his relatives, and his possessions. This shows his need for strengthening his sense of self (Ames, 1952).

By imitating other people's behavior, the child discovers his own psychical qualities (Piaget, 1932). By the time a child reaches school age he can understand the meaning of competition and appreciate in some fields of his activity how he compares with others. Many children at this age are capable of a certain amount of self-criticism, and many are sensitive to the possibility of ridicule, failure, and the loss of prestige. This is likely to make the child shy and self-conscious in such performances as singing and drawing, which formerly had been quite spontaneous (Jersild, 1954).

When asked to evaluate themselves on a reputation test, children tend to put emphasis on favorable traits and those correlated with popularity for that sex, such as amiability and docility for girls and daring and sportsmanship for boys. However, favorable self-judgments decline as children grow older, and favorable judgments of others increase, showing the effects of social learning (Hurlock, 1927a; Tuddenham, 1952). At every age, the child is able to judge the degree of acceptance others have better than his own social acceptance (Ausubel et al., 1952). From the way he is treated by others, the child can tell what concepts they have of him, and this affects his concept of self. He tends to exaggerate the bad qualities he becomes aware that he possesses, and this leads to feelings of inadequacy which are shown in shyness and self-consciousness. An accurate perception of his own status does not come until the child reaches the eleventh or twelfth grade (Ausubel et al., 1952).

The child comes to discover himself through a progressive comparison of his own body with other people's bodies (Piaget, 1932). This leads to an awareness of sex differences (Horowitz, 1943). Among young children, this is one of their greatest concerns, as has been shown by the type of questions children ask (Hattendorf, 1932). Not only do children become aware at an early age of physical sex differences, but they notice differences in urination posture of the two sexes (Conn, 1940). For the most part, they accept their recognition of sex differences without shock. Only when the attitudes of adults are unfavorable or when words naming them carry shame or embarrassment are the children themselves embarrassed (Conn, 1939).

To determine the child's awareness of sex differences, children were given toys representing boys and girls. At the age of three years, both boys and girls showed an incomplete recognition of sex differences in the dolls and in themselves. By the time they were four years old, however, their recognition was practically perfect. Thus, by the time a child is four years old, he is aware of his own sex, of clothing and hair styles as marks of sex differences, and is beginning to be aware of the appropriate sex role for his sex (Rabban, 1950). When drawing pictures, children from eight to eleven years of age draw such appropriate sex differences as hair, clothing, physical differences, and facial differences. There is a tendency to draw figures of their own sex larger than those of the opposite sex. Children of the higher socioeconomic groups include more sex characteristics in their drawings than do children of the lower groups (Weider and Noller, 1950). By the age of eight years, there are striking differences in children's drawings of male and female figures (Knopf and Richards, 1952). These differences are illustrated in Fig. 52.

Fig. 52. Differentiation in male and female figures appears in children's drawings by the age of eight years. (*From I. J. Knopf and T. W. Richards, The child's differentiation of sex as reflected in drawings of the human figure, J. genet. Psychol., 1952, 81, 99–112. Used by permission.*)

Shortly after children become aware of sex differences in appearance, they become aware of differences in appropriate sex roles. They are aware of what is expected of them as members of one sex. This they learn from identifying themselves with parents of the same sex as they and from parental training and pressures. The boy learns that he must be aggressive, extroverted, not easily scared, and a good sport if he is to be considered a "regular boy." The girl, on the other hand, discovers that the approved role for her is that of the docile, quiet, and easily managed "little lady" (Hattwick, 1937; Tryon, 1939; Ferguson, 1941; Frank, 1944; Koch, 1944; Seward, 1946; Rabban, 1950). At four years of age, boys begin to take on a tough masculine role (Ames, 1952). Boys are more clearly aware of sex-appropriate behavior than are girls, while both boys and girls of the working class are earlier and more clearly aware of their sex-role pattern than are children of the higher classes. For children of the working class, this awareness comes between the ages of four and five years, while for children of the higher class, it does not come until they are six years old. Girls of the middle class do not fully acquiesce to the appropriate sex role even by the time they are eight years old (Rabban, 1950).

The explanation given for the later awareness of sex-appropriate behavior among girls of the middle and upper classes is that in these classes girls and boys are treated alike and even dress alike in shorts and overalls for play; there is less demand for girls to do housework; and there is greater tolerance of the "tomboy" pattern than is true of girls of the working classes (Rabban, 1950). Furthermore, mothers of the upper and middle classes are more dissatisfied with their sex role than mothers of the working classes, and hence do not train their daughters for the "little lady" role as early as do mothers of the working classes (Seward, 1946; Komarovsky, 1950).

The child's concept of self includes not only an awareness of his sex but also an awareness of his racial background. When asked to identify themselves with pictures of white and Negro children, preschool children of the Negro group were found to have more definite concepts of their difference from the white group and their similarity with the Negro group than did

Shortly after children become aware of sex differences in appearance, they are aware of differences in appropriate sex roles. (*From Child Development, a McGraw-Hill Text-Film.*)

the white children. By the age of three or four years, children are able to identify themselves as belonging to one group as distinct from the other (Clark and Clark, 1939; Horowitz, 1939). Because children identify themselves with members of a certain race on the basis of physical characteristics, such as hair and eyes, they have difficulties in making such identifications when pictures represent individuals of mixed races. This has been found to be true of children of Oriental groups (Springer, 1950).

Children of the fifth grade and older not only are aware of their racial-group membership, but they show a definite preference for children of the same racial group as they (Moreno, 1934). Between the ages of four and five years, children begin to use ethnic designations rather than personal ones in answer to the question, "What are you?" and after five years, their concept of self and of others is expressed mainly in ethnic terms, such as "American," "colored," "Jewish," or "Italian" (Hartley et al., 1948).

In the preschool years, the child becomes aware that there are differences in social status and that each individual is identified with a given social class (Hollingshead, 1949; Stendler, 1949; Centers, 1950). The child learns that certain parental occupations are identified with certain social-class status. On this basis, he is then able to identify himself with a given social class. By the time he reaches adolescence, he includes in his concept of himself as an individual his social-class status as determined by the occupation of his father. Girls tend to identify themselves consistently higher than do boys (Centers, 1950).

Influence of Concepts of Self. Of all concepts, perhaps the type that has the greatest influence on the child is that relating to himself as an individual. In fact, his concept of himself has been found to be a prime determinant of his behavior. The child often shows a lack of self-acceptance and a desire to appear different from what he is (Strang, 1954). The child whose self-concept includes unfavorable comparisons with others behaves in a manner that leads to poor social adjustments, just as does the child whose self-concept includes comparisons of a too favorable sort with those of other children. Only when the self-concept is in harmony with the concept held by others can the child make good social adjustments (Ausubel et al., 1952; Jersild, 1952, 1954).

9. Social Concepts

Social concepts, or concepts relating to people and social situations, are developed from social perceptions. *Social perception* means the ability to understand, from observing facial expressions and behavior of others, what their thoughts and emotional reactions are. It includes the ability to "size up" the personality of others quickly, accurately, and on the basis of the cues available. If the individual is to make satisfactory social adjustments and get along with reasonable success with all types of people, he must develop social perception. As a result of his ability to size up others, the child then modifies his own behavior to fit into the accepted social pattern. He thus becomes socialized to the extent that he is a welcome member of the social group to which he belongs.

Social perception results from observing the behavior, emotional expressions, and voices of others. The baby differentiates the voice from other sounds by the time he is one month old, and at the age of two months he shows an interest in people by smiling and laughing when he comes in contact with them. By the third month, he can differentiate between strangers and familiar persons, while at the age of six months he is greatly influenced by facial expressions. It is not until he is eight months old that he responds to the emotional behavior of others in a way which signifies that he has an understanding of the facial expressions. An angry face causes the baby to turn away, while a smiling face leads to aggressive movements, such as coming toward the stranger, holding out his arms, or handing him a toy (Hetzer and Tudor-Hart, 1927; Bühler and Hetzer, 1928; K. Bühler, 1930; Spitz, 1946).

Social concepts include, as the child grows older, not only an understanding of the feelings and emotions of others as expressed in their overt reactions and facial expressions (Gates, 1923; Kellogg and Eagleson, 1931; Bruner and Tagiuri, 1954), but also an understanding of their meanings (Gesell and Thompson, 1934; Gesell and Ilg, 1949). In addition to what he observes, the child interprets the behavior of others on the basis of his "underlying perceptual-cognitive organizing process" (Golein, 1954). Thus, the child's social perceptions are colored by his past experiences, by what he has heard others say or what he has observed in their behavior, and by social pressures from the group. As MacLeod (1951) has pointed out, "We do not always perceive things as they really are. . . . We perceive them as we want them to be, as we expect them to be, or in terms of an unconscious bias . . . and these are in large measure socially determined."

The child, for example, judges individuals of other races not by what he himself observes in these individuals but by what he has heard adults say about them or how they behave toward them. His social concepts are thus influenced by adult values (Radke et al., 1949). When Negro and white children were asked to predict teachers' attitudes toward Negro children, it was found that Negro children estimated the teachers' attitudes to be more prejudiced than did white children, showing the influence of ego involvement. Children of the lower socioeconomic groups were more influenced by the factor of ego involvement than were children of higher socioeconomic groups (Ames, 1952).

When a teacher shows a preference for certain pupils, there is a tendency to estimate the sociometric status of those pupils to be higher than it is, while the popularity of the pupils she least prefers is likely to be underestimated (Gronlund, 1950, 1950a). The child's concepts of individuals of different races are markedly influenced not only by parental attitudes but also by the child-training methods the parents have used (Harris et al., 1950). With discussion and study of the causes of human behavior, children's social concepts can be modified and changed, and this influences their behavior in relation to the people or social situations that were discussed (Stiles, 1950). It is thus apparent that the child's social concepts include socially conditioned elements which are subject to change when new values are substituted for old values.

Development of Social Concepts. The child's social concepts are influenced by his own past experiences with certain types of people and certain types of situations as well as by his awareness of the different cultural values of the people with whom he is associated. As children grow older, they perceive differences in people not only in appearances but in their actions, and they like or dislike what they perceive. This determines how they will respond to others (Harris, 1946). They are able to discriminate in social-behavior values better as they grow older and to evaluate what adults will approve or disapprove of. Girls are slightly more discriminating in this respect than are boys (Witryol, 1950). They are able to size up both adults and their contemporaries more accurately than they could when they were younger and to develop more specific concepts of them in terms of socially approved behavior (Amatora, 1952; Ausubel et al., 1952). Even within the family, they develop specific concepts of the role played by the mother, the father, and other family members (Hartley and Krugman, 1948).

Prejudice against certain racial groups plays an important role in the development of the child's concepts of individuals of these groups. As early as the preschool years, the child can distinguish individuals of different races on the basis of skin and hair color and other physical features (Clark and Clark, 1939, 1940, 1950; Horowitz, 1939; Allport and Kramer, 1946; Koch, 1946; Radke et al., 1949; Ammons, 1950; Radke and Trager, 1950; Goodman, 1952; Landreth and Johnson, 1953). The degree of difference between the child's physical appearance and that of individuals of other groups influences the age at which he becomes aware of the difference. In the Negro, for example, dark pigmentation of the skin leads to earlier race awareness on the part of the white child than when the skin coloring is lighter (Goodman, 1951). Children of mixed Oriental races cannot be identified as early as those of one specific Oriental group (Springer, 1950). Children of minority groups are sensitized at an earlier age to racial differences than are those of majority groups (Goodman, 1951).

Racial awareness is increased with social learning. The child learns from his parents, his playmates, and others with whom he comes in contact certain things about people of different races. What he learns may be favorable or unfavorable, depending upon the cultural values of the people with whom he associates. As a result of these experiences, he develops stereotypes of different racial groups, and these become a part of his concepts of individuals of these groups (Meltzer, 1941; Radke and Sutherland, 1949; Radke et al., 1949; Zeligs, 1950, 1950d; Goodman, 1951; Landreth and Johnson, 1953). For example, children's concepts of Norwegians include such information as Norwegians are good fishermen and sailors, their ancestors were the Vikings, they are strong and brave, they make fine toys and wood carvings, they are good dancers, they ride on skis, and they enjoy the northern lights (Zeligs, 1952).

The child's concepts of race include not only the appearance of people of different racial groups but their occupations, their clothing, their living quarters and their personalities and abilities. These concepts become increasingly linked with racial concepts as children grow older (Radke and Trager, 1950). For example, the American child's concept of a Scotsman is that he is jolly, thrifty, a good bagpipe player, and was brave in early times (Zeligs, 1952). In a doll-play interview, white children assigned inferior social roles to Negroes; they gave poor houses to the Negro dolls and good houses to the white dolls; and when describing what the Negro dolls might be doing, they mentioned work activities instead of leisure activities, which they assigned mainly to the white dolls (Radke and Trager, 1950).

Racial concepts have a marked influence on the child's behavior in social situations. To individuals of certain groups he will be hostile, while to others he will be friendly. As a rule, children prefer individuals of their own racial groups to individuals of other racial groups. Furthermore, in assessing individuals of other races, the child is more and more influenced, as he grows older, by the stereotypes he has of different racial groups. He judges all individuals of a specific group in terms of the stereotype he has learned, through experiences and through his social contacts, in relation to that group (Radke and Sutherland, 1949; Ammons, 1950; Radke and Trager, 1950; Springer, 1950). In recent years, there has been a trend toward greater interest in and appreciation for all people. This has decreased wrong and grotesque ideas about people of different races and, in turn, has influenced the behavior of children toward individuals from these groups (Zeligs, 1948).

The child's social concepts include identifications with different *social classes.* Children become aware of social-class distinctions at an early age, and this increases to the adolescent years when it reaches the adult level. The child identifies others with different social classes, mainly on the basis of the fathers' occupations (Hollingshead, 1949; Stendler, 1949; Centers, 1950). Class consciousness at different ages is illustrated in Fig. 42, page 316. Children are also conscious of social problems, as shown in their conversations, though there is little indication of personal concern (Dawson, 1937; Zeligs, 1942). Children of the upper social classes are more conscious of the qualitative aspects of certain problems, while children of the lower classes are more conscious of the quantitative aspects.

In the case of poverty, for example, children of the lower classes are more conscious of the personal and social disorganizations wrought by poverty than are children of the upper classes. Children of the upper classes, on the other hand, think of poverty as existing generally in the country, but it is of little personal concern to them. Children who are bright recognize a wider range of problems associated with poverty, while those who are less bright think mainly in terms of personal problems associated with poverty. Boys tend to be more realistic and girls more sympathetic in their attitudes toward poverty. Likewise, boys are aware of more problems associated with poverty than are girls (Estvan, 1952).

10. Concepts of Beauty

Nothing is beautiful or ugly in and of itself. How it is perceived is thus a matter of individual association. What the young child perceives as beautiful is what he likes. People whom he likes are regarded as beautiful, no matter how they may be judged by others. Children's concepts of beauty are generally confused and contain many nonaesthetic elements, such as health, moral values, and comfort. When judging beauty in people, for example, ten-year-olds mentioned mainly the clothes, hair, and eyes, but very infrequently referred to features, coloring, or shape of body (Spiegel, 1950).

Cultural pressures play an important role in influencing the child's perception of beauty in the human body. In the case of facial features, it has been found that there are developmental trends in aesthetic preferences for thickness of lips, width of mouth, distance between eyes, and length of nose. With increasing age, there is an increasing similarity to adult standards (Taylor and Thompson, 1955). Cultural pressures are likewise important in influencing the child's preferences for certain geometric figures. In the case of rectangles, there is a trend toward the adult preference for the "golden-section" ratio with increasing age among children (Thompson, 1946; Shipley et al., 1947). This has been found to be true also for children's preferences for isosceles triangles (Austin and Sleight, 1951).

Studies of what children of different ages consider beautiful have revealed that they like pictures of *familiar* people and animals doing familiar things. They like commonplace things, such as houses, boats, trees, and airplanes (Barnes, 1902; Olney and Cushing, 1935; Lucio and Mead, 1939). Oriental children were found to prefer pictures of Orientals, while non-Orientals prefer Caucasians. Boys prefer pictures of boys, while girls prefer pictures of girls (Springer, 1950). Children like *action* in pictures, but it must be the type of action that is familiar to them. If the picture has a definite center of interest, this makes the interpretation easier for the child. He likes any action theme with human interest or that deals with exciting events (Whipple, 1953). Landscapes without people or animals have little appeal for the young child, though the older child likes landscapes if they contain familiar objects, as houses, trees, rivers, or flowers (Blonsky, 1932; Olney and Cushing, 1935).

Pictures that are *realistic* (true to life) appeal to children much more than do those which are highly stylized (curves and certain realistic details are omitted). The drawing or painting must have a realistic approach to the theme to appeal to children (Mellinger, 1932; Bon and Lopez, 1953). Even when not colored, they prefer a picture that is realistic to one that is not (Whipple, 1953). Only when color is realistic do they prefer it to an uncolored picture (Rudisill, 1952). And they like *simplicity* in pictures because they can comprehend the meaning better. As children grow older and can understand better what they see, they like more complexity (French, 1952). The popularity of the comics is due partly to their simplicity (see pages 344–350 for a discussion of why children like the comics).

At all ages, children like *color.* What colors they like and how saturated they like them to be will depend mainly upon the child's age. The younger the child, the better he likes colors which are bright and gaudy. No color is too bright to please him, whether it be used in clothing or toys or merely as a sample in a test. Pastel shades and subdued hues are perceived as ugly by young children. With increasing age, however, this attitude changes. By adolescence, both boys and girls show a marked tendency to prefer the duller shades and less saturated hues, and they regard the saturated colors as "loud" or "hideous." Most children prefer blue, red, and green to all other colors, with black, white, yellow, and orange least liked. Boys show a preference for red, while girls prefer blue and violet (Dashiell, 1917; Katz and Breed, 1922; Cook, 1931; Garth and Porter, 1934; Olney and Cushing, 1935; Lark-Horovitz, 1937, 1939; Lucio and Mead, 1939; Alschuler and Hattwick, 1947a; Blum and Dragositz, 1947; Staples and Conley, 1949; Bon and Lopez, 1953).

In pictures, children do not like too much color because it gives the impression of artificiality. They want the colors used to create the impression of realism (Rudisill, 1952). Preferences for certain *color combinations* are very indefinite in young children. As they grow older, red-blue and red-green are the favorite combinations, while orange-green is the least favored combination. At every age, more pronounced individual differences occur for color combinations than for preferences for individual colors. This is due, to a large extent, to the different associations various individuals have with color combinations (Dashiell, 1917; Bon and Lopez, 1953).

Liking for *music* on the part of young babies is apparent from the fact that they like to be sung to or to hear music, even before they are a year old. Many emotional outbursts or painful experiences are quieted by means of music. From their early association with music, they learn to like certain types rather than others. Because the songs and music which a young child first hears have a definite "tune" or rhythm, the child learns to like music of that type and prefers it to music which lacks a definite tune. By the time he is three, the young child has definite preferences for certain types of music and has his "favorites" within each type. The more often he hears his favorites, the more beautiful they are to him. With each succeeding year, his affection for the old and familiar increases, and this is an important factor in determining his standard of what is beautiful in music.

In addition to the role played by association in aesthetic perception in music, understanding of meaning is also important. By kindergarten age, the child can discriminate pitch and intensity with a fair degree of accuracy, can pitch his voice when a model pitch is given, and can march in time to the rhythm of music. From then on, he shows preferences for certain tone intervals or harmonies and for certain types of music. There are marked individual differences in children's preferences, depending partly upon training and partly upon their musical aptitude (Dashiell, 1917; Jersild, 1954). Even in classical music, differences in preference are dependent largely upon musical knowledge and familiarity of the music to the listener (Fisher, 1951; Keston and Pinto, 1955).

Factors Influencing Concepts of Beauty. Individual differences in perception of the beautiful result from many different factors. Children prefer the *familiar* to the unfamiliar, and what is familiar or unfamiliar to a child will depend largely upon his past experiences. The child, for example, prefers traditional to "modern" art because it is familiar to him, and he prefers familiar classical music to that which is unfamiliar (Terman, 1922; Olney and Cushing, 1935; Todd, 1943; Katz, 1944; Springer, 1950; Fisher, 1951). How well he can *understand* what he hears or sees plays an important role in his attitude toward it. Pictures which are simple and realistic in production and music which lacks complexity are easy for children to understand, with the result that they like them (Fisher, 1951; French, 1952; Jersild, 1954).

The ability to understand is closely related to the level of the child's *intelligence.* Children of average intelligence emphasize the subject, while those of superior intelligence emphasize the meaning of what they observe. They want a picture to tell them a story. Very bright children are influenced also by technique and originality, while children of average intelligence are more influenced by personal or associative qualities (Lark-Horovitz, 1937, 1938, 1939; Lucio and Mead, 1939). Children like to *identify* themselves with the hero of a picture and what he is doing. If the picture affords an opportunity for this, the child's appreciation of it is increased (Walton, 1936; Lark-Horovitz, 1938).

Training in the principles of art and general knowledge of what is considered beautiful play an important role in the child's aesthetic appreciation. Gradually, as the child grows older, he acquires adult standards of taste (Drought, 1929; Voss, 1936). The *cultural patterns* of the social group are a factor of importance in determining what the child will perceive as beautiful. Through association with adults, little children come to accept the adults' criterion of beauty, often without questioning whether or not it fits into the pattern of their own likes or dislikes. A thing is pretty because "Mommy says so" or ugly because the teacher has told them it was.

The important role the cultural patterns of the group play in the child's aesthetic perception is well illustrated by responses to the aesthetic-comparison test in an intelligence-test series. At the age of 4½ years, for example, one of the tests in the Terman and Merrill (1937) series consists of showing the child three cards with pictures for comparison. In each case, the child is asked, "Which one is the prettiest?" Few children, unless they are definitely below average in intelligence, fail to select the one which, according to adult standards, is considered to be the prettiest. In spontaneous drawings, half of a group of children produced rectangles approximating the proportions of the "golden section," recognized by adults as the most beautiful proportions (Cordeau, 1953).

11. CONCEPTS OF THE COMIC

Nothing is comic of its own accord. Whether we perceive something to be comic or not depends to a large extent upon the meanings we associate with it. Like all other types of perception, perception of the comic is dependent to a large extent upon past experiences and upon how the memories of these experiences are associated with new experiences. In addition, reactions to comic situations depend upon the mood and emotional reactions of the individual at the time when the comic situation appears. A child, during a temper tantrum, can see nothing funny in a situation which, under normal conditions, would seem to be very funny. Similarly, the health of the child influences his ability to perceive the comic element of a situation.

The development of concepts of the comic depends upon the development of other concepts. Until a child is able to understand the meaning of size, for example, he is unable to see incongruities. Similarly, until he has developed concepts of different social roles, he is unable to see the humor in a situation in which a person in a position of authority finds himself in a predicament. Because much humor is based on language, the child must know the meaning of words before he can appreciate jokes or even simple puns (Laing, 1939; Omwake, 1939; Britt, 1949; Wolfenstein, 1951, 1954; Jersild, 1954).

Pattern of Development. Concepts of the comic follow a pattern in their development which is influenced to a certain extent by the age, intelligence, and interests of the child. Many similar elements are found in the concepts of comic of young children, older children, and adolescents. However, there is a change from the more concrete and obvious to the more subtle and abstract as the child grows older. In the case of jokes, they must be simple in content and technique while the child is still young, if he is to understand them. As he grows older and his comprehension increases, he is better able to understand more complex and abstract jokes (Merry and Merry, 1950; Wolfenstein, 1951, 1954).

There are three stages of "juvenile humor" which appear before it reaches its mature form. These are:

1. *Humor as pleasure,* which is characteristic of the first three years of

a child's life and is expressed in direct response to any pleasing approach, such as tickling.

2. *Humor as funniness or curiosity,* which appears at the third year and expresses itself in laughter when anything appears funny to the child—as anything strange or unusual, whether it be the feeble walk of an old person or the abnormal size of a nose.

3. *Humor as comic and caricature,* beginning at the school age. By that time, the situation that gives rise to humor is no longer that of the unusual or the strange, but one that is comical in which they may be involved, or which they may witness—for example, a fat woman trying to pass through a small gate or a boy in farm clothes walking barefoot down Fifth Avenue in New York City. Incongruous situations produce the humor at this age (Harms, 1943).

A pattern has also been observed in the interpersonal relationships in the child's comic reactions. Up to the age of 2½ years, most humor activities are related to the child himself, though some are self-initiated with a teacher. At three, humor is self-initiated with the teacher, but the child makes few responses to the teacher's humor or to that of other children. There are, however, frequent humorous approaches to other children. From 3½ years on, there are more humorous relations with other children and fewer with a teacher (Ames, 1952).

Comic Concepts in Young Children. Vocal play is one of the earliest forms of humor in babies. The baby also perceives comedy in annoying people, dropping things handed to him, and blowing bubbles in water. After the first year, making faces, hiding from people, and then laughing when they look for him, and doing stunts are considered by him to be amusing (Fenton, 1925). Among preschool children, humor is called forth mainly by slapstick situations involving physical incongruities, by noises and grimaces made by the child himself or others, by word play, by the funny antics of animals, by comic drawings, and by simple jokes. Surprise and suspense are fundamental elements in the perception of the comic at this age (Kimmins, 1928; Kenderdine, 1931; Justin, 1932; Murphy et al., 1937; Omwake, 1939, 1942; Piret, 1940; Merry and Merry, 1950; Jersild, 1954). Development of humor runs parallel with general intelligence and emotional development. Before the child can recognize incongruities in the situation, he must be able to understand them, just as he must comprehend the meaning of words in puns and jokes (Kenderdine, 1931; Laing, 1939).

Comic Concepts in Older Children. The school child will laugh at anything when others do, whether he thinks it funny or not. As is true of the younger child, the older child sees humor mainly in incongruities or in the unusual; in the abasement of dignity; in people who defy authority as they would like to do but fear doing because of punishment; and in the misfortunes and predicaments of others, as someone stumbling or falling, especially when it is a person who is looked up to and respected. Clowns in the circus or comedy situations in the movies or on the television screen appeal to the older child because they contain one or more of these elements of humor.

Comic pictures that appeal contain much of the same elements as found on the screen. Because of his greater understanding of words, the older child enjoys puns, riddles, and jokes, especially those relating to forbidden subjects, as sex. At this time, practical jokes have a strong appeal. These are usually aimed at people in authority or people against whom the child has some prejudice. They are enjoyed by the child because he is able to "get even" with that person by making him appear ridiculous, by putting him in a predicament, or by embarrassing him (Kimmins, 1928; Murphy et al., 1937; Brumbaugh, 1939; Omwake, 1939, 1942; Brumbaugh and Wilson, 1940; Britt, 1949; Merry and Merry, 1950; Jersild, 1954).

Chapter 12

MORAL DEVELOPMENT

Morality is conformity to the moral code of the social group. The term comes from the Latin word *mores,* meaning manners, customs, or folkways. To act in a moral way means, thus, to act in conformity to group standards of conduct. Immorality is failure to conform or behavior directed against the interests and welfare of the group. Unmoral or nonmoral behavior, on the other hand, is behavior which, even when unfavorable to the group, is so, not because of intended harm on the part of the individual, but rather owing to ignorance and lack of knowledge of what is socially approved.

Moral standards may vary from group to group, depending upon what has been accepted by the group as socially approved behavior. Even within a community, different social classes and different religious groups often have their own individual codes of behavior. Moral behavior, thus, is based partly on moral standards set by the social or religious group to which the individual belongs and partly on standards of behavior set by the child-training methods which are used by the child's parents. There have been found to be differences in standards of sex behavior for individuals of different social classes (Kinsey et al., 1943, 1953) and for members of the two sexes (Seward, 1946).

True Morality. True morality is behavior which conforms to social standards and which is also carried out voluntarily by the individual. It comes with the transition *from external to internal authority* and consists of conduct regulated from within. It is accompanied by a feeling of personal responsibility for the act. Added to this, it involves giving primary consideration to the welfare of the group, while personal desires or gains are relegated to a position of secondary importance. Because true morality is so highly developed and so complex, it is rarely found in children. It should appear during the adolescent years, but whether it does so or not will depend to a large extent upon the type of moral education the child has been given (Piaget, 1932; Havighurst and Taba, 1949; Wrenn, 1949; Havighurst, 1953; Breckenridge and Vincent, 1955).

Moral development of the highest type involves two aspects, the *intellectual* and the *impulsive.* The child must learn what is right and what is wrong, and as soon as he is old enough he must understand why it is so. In addition to this, he must develop the desire to do what is right, to act for the common good, and to avoid wrong. This can be accomplished most successfully by associating pleasant reactions with what is right and unpleasant reactions with what is wrong. To ensure his willingness to act in a socially desirable way, the child must receive the approval of the group. In addition to that, he must have plenty of opportunities to take part in group activities, so that he can learn what the group expects. When a conflict occurs between social codes and the individual's impulses, a morally mature person knows how to handle this conflict to his satisfaction and to the satisfaction of the group (Aldrich, 1948).

MORALITY IS LEARNED

According to tradition, children are born with a "conscience," or the ability to *know* what is right or wrong. In keeping with this belief is the belief that misbehavior is the result of some inherited weakness, the origin of which is ascribed to either the mother's or the father's side of the family. Those who hold to such beliefs maintain that the child cannot be reformed, and as a result, little time or effort is given to his moral training. The justification for corporal punishment, in the form of spanking, slapping, or whipping the child, was founded on the belief that such punishment would "drive out the devil" and thus make the "naturally bad" child into a good child (Merry and Merry, 1950).

Studies of concept development and of patterns of behavior have revealed that, at birth, the child has no conscience and no scale of values (Havighurst, 1953). Thus, he is neither moral nor immoral. Instead, he is *nonmoral,* in the sense that his behavior is not guided by moral standards. Before he can behave in a moral way, he must learn what the group to which he belongs believes to be right or wrong. This he will learn gradually through the childhood years, partly from the teachings of parents, teachers, or others in authority, and partly from imitating the behavior of those with whom he most often comes in contact (Justin, 1950; Havighurst, 1953; V. Jones, 1954). The parent-child relationship is more important in the moral development of the child than any other factor, even than that of peer pressure (Cooper, 1950; Ausubel, 1951).

No child can be expected to build up a moral code of his own. He must be taught the standards of right and wrong as they are handed down from one generation to another. He must learn the moral concepts which the social group has found to be useful through successive years. It must not be left to his discretion to decide what is right or wrong, nor should he be permitted to act as he pleases, without considering the group. Through contacts with others, he has an opportunity to see how they evaluate his behavior. It is especially important that he have plenty of contacts with both adults and children who are not members of his family and who will not make allowances for his behavior as members of his family are apt to do. Learning to judge one's own conduct and that of others comes through actual personal experiences and not through moral teaching or "preaching" of right and wrong.

The lawmakers set the pattern for the moral behavior of the child. Parents and others who are responsible for the guidance of the child's development must then help the child to learn to conform to this pattern. If the socially acceptable pattern of behavior is accompanied by satisfaction, it will be repeated and in time become habitual. Eventually, with proper guidance and training, the child should conform to moral standards of right without external force. It is desirable that the child's behavior be voluntary rather than dominated by force. This can be accomplished only after the child has learned to distinguish between right and wrong and has built up a desire to do what the group considers right, because of anticipated social approval or reward (Havighurst and Taba, 1949).

Learning to behave in a socially approved manner does not come overnight. Instead, it is a long, slow process which extends through the childhood years and into adolescence. By the time the child is twelve years old, however, his behavior should be more stable and more in accordance with the mores of the group than it was when he was younger (Havighurst, 1953). With increasing age, the child becomes increasingly aware that he is expected to conform to rules and regulations and to overcome his antisocial behavior. Middle-class children, as a rule, learn to conform earlier than do those of the lower or upper classes (Griffiths, 1952). Variations in moral codes, however, slow down his learning. If there is a conflict between the home code and that of his peers, he may accept the latter and learn to conform to their code rather than to the family code which he had previously learned (Havighurst and Taba, 1949; Colm, 1951).

PHASES OF MORAL DEVELOPMENT

Moral development has two phases, separate and distinct, but both essential if true morality is to be attained: (1) *the development of moral behavior* and (2) the *development of moral concepts*. Moral knowledge does not guarantee conduct consistent with it. The reason for this is that the child's behavior is motivated by factors other than his moral knowledge. Social pressures, how the child feels about himself and the way he is treated by his family and peers, his desires at the moment, and many other factors influence how he will behave when a choice must be made (Jersild, 1954). Studies of honesty have revealed correlations of approximately .25 between moral knowledge and conduct (Hartshorne and May, 1928a; V. Jones, 1936). Thus, one can predict with only a small degree of accuracy from a child's moral knowledge what his conduct will be.

In a study of the relationship between moral knowledge and behavior in the case of selfishness, different stages were found to exist. At first, egocentric action prevails, and judgment is subordinate to its exigency. Later, the child understands the value of a moral rule as a social constraint, but he does not necessarily obey it. When he is older, moral thought directs conduct only by way of social constraint. In the highest phase of development, the child begins to direct his actions himself, and thus moral knowledge and behavior are likely to be more closely related than they were when behavior was influenced mainly by social constraints (Ugurel-Semin, 1952).

1. DEVELOPMENT OF MORAL BEHAVIOR

It takes a young child many years to learn to act in a manner approved by the social group. This he may learn through reward and punishment, through unconscious imitation, or through reflective thinking (Havighurst and Taba, 1949). The whole purpose of discipline is to teach the child what is right and to see to it that he acts as society expects him to act. If discipline has been of the right type and if it has been used consistently, instead of in a haphazard manner, ethical conduct sooner or later becomes habitual. When pleasant associations, in the form of praise, social approval, and reward, are tied up with socially desirable behavior, ethical conduct is learned more quickly than it otherwise would be.

Teaching the child what is right and wrong is not enough. He may, as a result of teaching, have a wide fund of moral concepts, but he cannot be expected to apply his moral knowledge to meet concrete experiences in everyday life. For that reason, he must be guided in the development of habits of action. The child may know, for example, that it is wrong to cheat in school, to take money from the mother's pocketbook, or to lie in order to escape punishment for wrongdoing. But his knowledge is limited to abstract concepts, and he cannot be expected to apply it to specific situations until he is old enough to see of his own accord the relationship between concept and specific situation.

Studies of honesty have revealed that young children must learn moral behavior in *specific* situations and that they cannot be expected to apply moral concepts, learned in the abstract as "ideals" or "examples," to specific situations. Should a new situation arise, the child cannot be expected to transfer his knowledge of right or wrong conduct to that situation unless it is similar enough to situations he has experienced in the past to be able to see the relationship between the new and the old. The development of moral behavior consists, thus, of learning habits, and these will function only in similar situations (Hartshorne and May, 1927, 1928).

How Moral Behavior Is Learned. From this we may conclude that learning to behave in a socially acceptable manner follows the same laws as all other forms of learning. The child must *first learn to make correct specific responses in specific situations.* He learns, as a little child, to conform to standards of conduct in the home. Later, when he goes to school, he learns to conform to the school's standards, and when he becomes a member of a play group, he conforms to the standards of that group. Should the standards of the home, the school, and the play group all agree, it will be easy for the child to see the similarity *and thus,* in time, *develop abstract concepts* of right and wrong. If, however, they differ from one situation to another, the child is confused and wonders why he is punished for an act which in another situation was ignored or looked upon as socially acceptable.

Of even more serious consequences, a condition of this sort makes it impossible for the child to develop moral concepts that will hold for the same act in different situations. If, for example, the child is permitted to sneak cake from the cake box or candy from a box which he has been told not to touch, is it surprising that he is confused when he is punished for taking pencils from other children's desks at school or money from the mother's pocketbook? Stealing should be regarded as wrong in every situation and should be punished consistently, if the child is to learn to behave in accordance with the codes of adult society.

Transfer-of-training experiments have shown that transfer comes only when situations are similar. This is likewise true of moral training. When the objective aspects of a situation are the same, transfer can be expected to occur. When they are different, it is questionable whether or not transfer will take place. Will the child, for example, who learns not to take money from a pocketbook transfer this habit to cash registers? The objective features of the two situations are different, and consequently the child may not see the common features of the two, which are so obvious to an adult. Moral training should therefore involve teaching the child to look for *common features of apparently different situations.* This, of course, involves analysis of a too complex sort to expect in a young child. But the child of eight or ten years of age can be taught that it is wrong to take money belonging to other people, whether it comes from their pocketbooks, from their desks or bureau drawers, or from a cash register. It is in this way that moral training can lead to the development of moral concepts of a general rather than of a specific sort.

2. DEVELOPMENT OF MORAL CONCEPTS

The second phase of moral development consists of the learning of moral concepts, or the principles of right and wrong in an abstract, verbal form. This, of course, is too advanced for a young child, and it is therefore necessary to wait until the child has the mental capacity to generalize and transfer a principle of conduct from one situation to another, before he can be expected to learn moral concepts. It is true that language skills make this easier, because concepts are derived from concrete cases. Nevertheless, the child must be mentally mature enough to see the relationship between an abstract principle and concrete cases and to associate these with memory images of specific situations. The ability to relate systematically sets of rules to different situations develops gradually as the child's experiences increase (Strauss, 1954).

In the development of moral concepts, patterns related to the development of the child's intelligence, his social and emotional development, and the development of systems of values from the cultural environment in which he lives have been found to exist. In the development of unselfishness, for example, six stages in the pattern were noted. These were egocentrism, characterized by a purely selfish attitude; sociocentrism, or obedience to moral and religious rules and customs; awareness of social reactions in the form of fear of social disapproval; superficial reciprocity based on feelings of guilt if sharing is not equal; deeper and enlarged reciprocity, based on the desire to maintain good relations with one's friends; altruism in the form of desire to make sacrifices for others; and, finally, a sense of justice, based on the belief that this is the right thing to do (Ugurel-Semin, 1952).

General Moral Concepts. Concepts are at first specific and relate to the specific situations in which they were learned. As the child's capacity for comprehending relationships increases, his concepts of right and wrong in different though related situations merge. As a result, general concepts are gradually learned because the child is able to recognize a common element in a variety of situations. In order to do this, the child must have actual personal experiences with real situations. He cannot be expected to understand general moral concepts if they are taught to him as such and consequently have little meaning because of their lack of association with real experiences.

The child's comprehension of moral concepts is closely related to general maturity and intelligence. Up to the age of nine or ten years, the child's concepts are definite and concrete rather than abstract and general. They are in terms of the child's immediate personal relationships, such as disobeying mother or hurting the cat. After the age of nine years, on the other hand, concepts become more generalized, as, for example, stealing is wrong rather than it is wrong to steal a ball (Macaulay and Watkins, 1926). The preschool child is incapable of such abstract thinking, and as a result, when he defines "good behavior," he does so in terms of specific acts, such as "obeying mother" or "helping mother," while "bad behavior" consists of not doing what the mother wants or saying bad words (Radke, 1946).

One of the greatest difficulties the child meets in learning moral concepts comes from the fact that they often vary with situations, and these differences are too subtle for a child to understand. It is very difficult for him to comprehend, for instance, why it is wrong to take a cookie from a box in a store when he is permitted to help himself at the cookie jar at home. Likewise, he cannot understand why it is wrong to take money that has been put in his bank when it is all right to use money from his pocketbook. In both cases, he argues, the money is his.

Moral Values. As the child develops *generalized* standards of what is desirable, appropriate, and right and what is undesirable and wrong, he is expected to use them to think through problems of conduct and to make decisions about his behavior. However, these generalized concepts are greatly influenced by the moral values of the people with whom the child associates (Edwards, 1949). These values become a part of the child's generalized moral concepts, and they change as the child becomes more mature and as he associates with more people and with people whose values may differ from those of his parents (Havighurst and Taba, 1949; Hawkes, 1952; Havighurst, 1953; Dukes, 1955). By the time the child is twelve years old, his values should begin to show greater stability than they did when he was younger (Havighurst, 1953).

The child's concepts of goodness and of "good behavior" change, for example, from relationship with gratification to postponement of gratification leading to future rewards. As the child grows older, peer recognition is more valuable than adult recognition, and as a result, he measures "goodness" in terms of what his peers believe it to be (Wolfenstein, 1950). In spite of variations in values between adults and children, and between different individuals within the same age groups, the child gradually accepts adult values and coordinates them with his moral concepts (Edwards, 1949).

Self-judgments. The child learns to judge his own conduct as "good" or "bad" in terms of the consequences of his acts. If his training has been of a consistent sort, he soon learns to judge a certain act as "bad" because punishment of one sort or another invariably follows the act. Another act, on the other hand, is judged as "good" because invariably praise or some other forms of social approval accompanies it. As he grows older, he must learn to judge his behavior in terms of the social consequences, regardless of personal consequences. He thus thinks of how the group will judge his behavior and not how he himself will be affected by them. In the "gang" age, for example, telling tales on the gang to parents or teachers may give the child a temporary personal satisfaction because it puts him in the limelight. But he soon discovers that the members of his gang regard this with great disfavor, and it therefore becomes a "wrong" thing to do.

After the child has developed moral concepts which can be applied to specific situations and can be used to evaluate the rightness or wrongness of behavior, he may be said to have developed a "conscience." The belief that a child is born with a conscience which tells him what is right or wrong is no more valid than the belief that he is born with innate knowledge of right and wrong. Moral concepts must be learned just as he must learn to use his moral concepts to judge the moral value of different forms of behavior in situations where a choice must be made and where there is no one to tell him how he should act. The conscience has been described as "those ego values which collectively may be referred to as 'conscience' and which are incorporated from the prevailing values or norms of one's group; they are imposed by parents, school, church, play group, clique, etc. These ego values . . . are not, in many cases, conducive to the satisfaction of biogenic needs or the 'derived drives' traceable to them" (Sherif, 1948).

When the child develops the "warning and punishing voice of conscience," he carries it with him wherever he goes and uses it as a guide to his behavior. What constellation of concepts and values the child's conscience will contain and how strong or weak it will be will depend upon the type of moral training the child has had. The conscience has been found to be stronger in middle-class children than in those from the lower classes (Havighurst, 1953). When the child's conscience becomes too rigid, it is likely to lead to anxieties which will militate against the child's adjustments and lead to unhappiness (French et al., 1950; Jersild, 1954). Instead, the child should be encouraged to recognize the frailties of human nature and to develop tolerance for minor weaknesses in himself as well as in others (Justin, 1950).

Discrepancies between Moral Concepts and Behavior. Experimental studies have revealed that discrepancies between moral concepts and moral behavior are greater than is popularly believed. Abstract knowledge of what is wrong does not keep children from cheating when a particular situation arises in which they are tempted to cheat (Hartshorne and May, 1928). Children who say it is "wrong" to be aggressive with their classmates are not consistent in their behavior when playing with them (Fite, 1940). Delinquent children rarely are ignorant of the wrongs they do. Their ethical knowledge is very similar to that of nondelinquents (Bartlett and Harris, 1935; Hill, 1935; Glueck and Glueck, 1950).

The discrepancy between moral knowledge and moral behavior is generally due to emotional and motivational factors. In anger, a child may do something he knows is wrong to "get even" with the person who has angered him. Or he may find it expedient to behave in contradiction to what he knows is right. This may force a child to sacrifice some of his abstract concepts of right and wrong (Havighurst and Taba, 1949). A child may cheat, for example, because parental pressures have been used to force him to get better grades than he is capable of getting without cheating. Or he may be motivated to cheat to avoid being left behind when his friends are promoted to the next grade. Cheating may vary in degree according to the situation in which the child is placed. Children have been found to cheat more in scoring their own test papers when their errors were small than when they were large (Gross, 1946).

Frequently moral concepts conflict with one another. Truthfulness, for example, may conflict with loyalty to one's friends or with ideals of courtesy and sympathy. A child may knowingly tell a lie to spare the feelings of another just as an adult may (V. Jones, 1954). Then, too, a child may find discrepancies between what his parents say and what they do. This confuses him and leads to imitation of their behavior. If it is all right for them to preach one thing and do another, he feels that it is all right for him to do the same (Jersild, 1954). Furthermore, children are sometimes confused when abstract concepts must be applied to situations that have little in common with situations they have previously met. A child knows it is wrong to steal from a person but is sometimes confused about whether taking things from a public park falls in the same category (Stendler, 1949a). Discrepancies between concepts and behavior are especially likely to occur when moral concepts of the parents differ from those of the child's peers (Colm, 1951). Boys are more subject to such discrepancies than are girls (Ausubel, 1951).

The child who recognizes that his behavior falls short of what he knows is right is likely to feel guilty and feel ashamed of himself. In the case of selfishness, children who have a selfish attitude feel justified in their selfish behavior, even when they know selfishness is disapproved of. Children who, on the other hand, have a disapproving attitude toward selfishness have vague feelings of disapproval for their own selfishness and sometimes show it by such gestures as hesitancy before acting (Ugurel-Semin, 1952). The more often a child behaves in a way that is in contradiction to what he knows is right, the more likely he is to develop feelings of inadequacy or to try to justify his behavior by projecting the blame to someone else, thus freeing himself from any feeling of guilt for his acts.

PHASES IN MORAL DEVELOPMENT

The moral development of the child, like other phases of his development, follows a pattern in which certain types of morality may be expected to appear at different periods in the growth of the child. There is no sharp dividing line between the different phases. Rather, the development is graded, and the transition from one period to another occurs slowly and over a period of months. Many attempts have been made to divide the moral development of the child into distinct stages with specific age levels for each. However, experimental studies of large groups of children have revealed marked individual differences in the moral development of children of the same ages. They have shown that no distinct dividing line can be drawn between one type of moral behavior and another and thus justify labeling these divisions as "stages."

The characteristic moral behavior of children in the different developmental phases is briefly summarized below, and the gradual progress toward more mature moral standards has been stressed.

1. MORALITY IN BABYHOOD

The baby, as was pointed out in the beginning of the chapter, is neither moral nor immoral. He is *nonmoral.* This is in contrast to the view, held by some, that a baby is naturally immoral and needs punishment to teach him to be good, and also to the opposite opinion that the baby is born good but is corrupted by worldly influences. Neither point of view is correct. The child is not born with good or bad moral standards, or with any moral standards. He must learn to act in ways which are judged to be good by the social group and to refrain from doing what the group considers wrong.

To the baby, standards of right and wrong as accepted by the group mean nothing. His behavior is guided by impulse, and he judges right and wrong in relation to the pleasure or pain the act affords him rather than in terms of the good or harm done to others. The baby is too young, intellectually, to realize that an act is wrong unless ill-effects follow. He thinks only of how this behavior affects him personally, and he feels no obligations to modify his behavior because of others, unless his behavior is accompanied by unpleasant consequences.

A "guilty conscience" from wrongdoing is unknown at this age because it requires the development of definite standards of right and wrong. By the age of three or four years, however, the child whose discipline has been consistent knows what is acceptable, and therefore right, and what is disapproved of, and therefore wrong. Likewise, a sense of duty or obligation to others is lacking. The baby does what pleases him regardless of how it affects others. Nor does he think of doing things to please others. Even though his act may cause distress or pain to another, he has no feeling of remorse.

At this age, standards of property rights are unknown. The baby takes things which please his fancy, regardless of ownership. A toy in a shop or in another child's house may easily be carried off by the baby, should it happen to appeal to him. No thought of stealing enters into the act. Even when he is told not to touch things that belong to others, he forgets when a new and different object arouses his curiosity. The more consistently the baby is told not to touch something because it is "mother's," or not to touch another object because it is "Mrs. Smith's," the sooner he will learn to respect the property of other people.

2. MORALITY IN EARLY CHILDHOOD

From three to six years of age, the foundations of moral conduct and the basic moral attitudes of the social group should become established. At this time, the child is not told why this act is right or wrong, but he is merely told how to act, and he knows that, unless his behavior conforms to standard, he will be punished. Because of his mental immaturity and limited experience, the child cannot be expected to understand the why and wherefore of rules. He can, however, comprehend the magnitude of the various offenses because of the severity of punishment associated with the acts.

The unmoral character of the child's conduct is apparent in the fact that the child conforms to the conduct standards set by his environment, as a means of avoiding social disapproval or punishment, or to gain social approval and reward. This leads him to do what is right without actually knowing why he acts as he does. By the time the child is five or six years old, habits of obedience should be established, provided, of course, that the child has had consistent discipline. If his acts are bad, it is more often from ignorance than from willful disobedience.

Concepts of right and wrong are being established at this age through the association of such words as "good," "bad," "naughty," and "nice" with specific acts. These associations come from rules laid down in the home relating to specific acts and situations. The young child learns that certain forms of behavior are "good," while others are "naughty," and that praise or reward follows the former, while scolding or punishment follows the latter. He soon comes to regard behavior in terms of "good" or "bad," and thus specific moral concepts are established. This shows a definite awareness of the mores of the group, even though the group is limited, for the most part, to his family. The discrepancy between moral concepts and moral behavior is marked at this age. Even though right and wrong are expressed in words, they are often not followed by actions related to them.

The child may rebel against adult authority; he may try to evade the rules of conduct laid down by the adults of his environment; and he may try to test out their authority by attempting to "get away with" forbidden acts; but he does not, at this age, question the justice of the rules. He does not even suggest the possibility of alternatives of the act, as the older child does. He merely obeys or disobeys the rules, but he does not bring up the question of whether or not he will be permitted to substitute an act more pleasing to him for an act which he is expected to perform. If, for example, he has been taught that it is wrong to take home a toy belonging to another child, he either does or does not take it. He never brings up the alternative of "borrowing it for a few days and returning it later."

Before five or six years of age, the child does not feel guilty when he does what is wrong. When caught in a wrong act, the child will become embarrassed, frightened of possible punishments, or will rationalize to explain why he behaved as he did. If, on the other hand, he is not caught, he will not bother about his wrong act, nor will he feel guilty because he has acted in contradiction to what he knows is right. When he is selfish—and selfishness reaches its peak between four and six years of age—he has no feelings of shame or guilt about his behavior (Ugurel-Semin, 1952). As for lying, he does not actually appreciate the fact that what he says may be considered a "lie" and, as a result, does not show shame or guilt.

3. Morality in Late Childhood

The moral code of the older child is determined to a large extent by the moral code of his group. The boy or girl, from six years of age to adolescence, learns to behave as the group expects him or her to behave and conforms rigidly to the group's standards of right and wrong. When he must make a choice between the moral standards of his parents and those of his friends, he will generally choose the latter (Havighurst and Taba, 1949; Colm, 1951; Havighurst, 1953). By ten or twelve years of age, the child can understand the underlying principle and reason for rules. He has the ability to make moral discriminations, and he has a large fund of verbal morality, or learned concepts of right and wrong as they relate to different situations. He lacks true morality in that he is unable to judge for himself whether an act is right or wrong but must rely on what he has learned in regard to it.

The older child, provided the basis of morality has already been established, has a strong sense of justice and honor. He believes that it is wrong to lie, to carry tales, to be cowardly, to abuse the small or weak individual, to take things belonging to others, or to betray one's friends. He has well-developed moral concepts about honesty, property rights, and moral courage (Beller, 1949; Havighurst and Taba, 1949; Ausubel, 1951; Havighurst, 1953). Between the ages of seven and eight years, the child is most unselfish, but after that, selfishness begins to increase. Poor children and children from large families are generally less selfish than those who are richer or who come from smaller families (Ugurel-Semin, 1952). Changes in selfishness with age are shown in Fig. 39, page 280.

In late childhood, moral values are being established as a result of the child's experiences in the home and in his contacts with other children. Some of these values will remain relatively unchanged throughout life and will serve to influence his behavior in adulthood much as they have in childhood. Others will be modified and changed from time to time in childhood as his contacts outside the home bring him into conflict with values that differ from those of his parents (Bavelas, 1942; Turner, 1948; Beller, 1949; Hollingworth, 1949; Thompson, 1952; Ugurel-Semin, 1952; V. Jones, 1954; Dukes, 1955). How much the child is willing to accept the values of his peers, especially when they conflict with those of his parents, depends largely upon the degree of social acceptance the child has (Lewin and Grable, 1945).

Knowing what values others place on different types of behavior serves to influence the child in making moral decisions. Knowing, for example, that honesty is more valued than cheating leads the child to be honest in the hopes of winning social approval from the group (Hartshorne and May, 1928). On the other hand, when the child recognizes that honesty is more valued by his peers than generosity, he will strive harder to be honest than to be generous (Mitchell, 1943). The moral behavior that is most highly valued, such as honesty, is less likely to change with age than is moral behavior that is less highly valued by the group (V. Jones, 1946). Changes in moral concepts with age are shown in Fig. 53.

The older child is contemptuous of those who lie, cheat, or steal, if his group believes such acts to be wrong, and his standards of honor are rigid and unalterable. He will strongly condemn anyone whose behavior falls

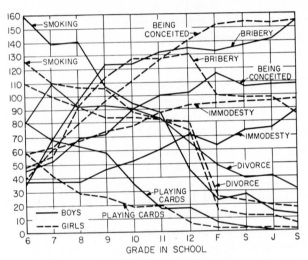

Fig. 53. Changes in age with things thought wrong. (*From S. L. Pressey and F. P. Robinson, Psychology and the new education, Harper, 1944. Used by permission.*)

below his standards of morality, and his contempt for the transgressor is expressed in no uncertain terms. His attitude toward those who do not conform is one of pronounced intolerance. While condemning others for violating rules, the older child will often question the justice of the rules. Should the gang leader take the position that a certain rule is "unfair," the gang as a whole will take sides with him, and a stormy protest will be the outcome. The gang will then champion the cause of the offender, and treat as a martyr one who has been subjected to unfair treatment.

Not only does the older child condemn others for behavior that falls short of socially approved standards; he also condemns himself if he behaves thus. The older child learns to censor his behavior by standards of conduct he has learned from the group. Before childhood is over, the child's attitude toward law closely approaches the adult attitude (Lockhart, 1930, 1930a).

However, children are likely to have different standards for behavior in different situations at this age. In the case of lying, for example, one group of children, eight to twelve years of age, felt it was worse to lie to the father than to the mother because the father can "punish harder" while the mother will "understand" better (Lerner and Murphy, 1941). In the case of stealing, the child knows by the time he enters school that stealing is wrong. He thus condemns himself when he steals just as he does others who steal (Eberhart, 1942).

DISCIPLINE

Discipline means a "process of training and learning that fosters growth and development." It comes from the same word as "disciple"—one who learns or voluntarily follows a leader. The parents and teachers are the leaders, and the child is the disciple who learns from them the ways of life that lead to usefulness and happiness (DuBois, 1952). When the child learns the ways of life approved by the social group, he is able to make selective responses to external stimuli and demands involving self-restraint and self-control. This involves a selective capacity or judgment regarding appropriate responses; appropriate inhibitory and regulatory mechanisms to hold in check impulses which may interfere with the individual's adjustments; and permissible gratifications of pleasure cravings and channels for effective and purposeful activity (Slavson, 1951).

Attitudes toward Discipline. As DuBois (1952) has pointed out, "from time immemorial, discipline has been regarded as an essential ingredient of man's life. Experience has demonstrated that objectives can be achieved and individuals can be happy only if human energies are directed in an orderly fashion. Since a person's desires often conflict with the desires of others, society has set up regulations for the common good, to which each member of the group must adhere or suffer a penalty." However, what methods of discipline are used to achieve the common good will be dependent upon the socially accepted philosophies of the nature of man. When it was believed that sinfulness was innate, society sanctioned cruel and punitive methods of disciplining a child. In recent years, however, there has been a relaxing of these methods (Dickenson and Lewin, 1951).

To determine how great the changes in disciplinary methods have been in recent years, Radke (1946) compared the discipline used by parents of a group of preschool children with that used by their grandparents, as reported by the children's parents. This comparison showed a general trend toward less autocratic, unreasonable, and emotional discipline and in the direction of standards advocated by child psychologists. In recent years, there has been a certain amount of misunderstanding and confusion about the meaning of discipline, and this has led to ineffectiveness in training children. As a result of this, children are likely to grow up in a society in which the attitude toward discipline is inconsistent and varies from person to person and from home to school (Geisel, 1951).

The result of the modern transition from discipline based on the belief of innate sinfulness to the belief that wrong behavior is the result of the type of training the child has received has been the development of two conflicting concepts of discipline, the "negative" and the "positive" concepts. According to the negative concept, discipline is control of persons by *external* authority which is usually arbitrarily applied. It is a form of restraint on impulses frequently through distasteful or painful means. This is synonymous with punishment. However, punishment does not operate in weakening the individual's tendencies to act in a socially disapproved manner, nor does it give assurance that the abandoned line of activity will be replaced by more acceptable behavior.

The positive concept of discipline is synonymous with education and counseling in that it emphasizes *inner* growth in the form of self-discipline and self-control by the individual. This, in turn, leads to motivation from within rather than force from without. Negative discipline forces immaturity on the individual, while positive discipline encourages maturity of behavior (Froe, 1953). Since the principal function of discipline is to teach the easy acceptance of needful restraint and to help direct the child's energies into useful and socially acceptable channels, the positive type of discipline will achieve this end more successfully than the negative (Bakwin and Bakwin, 1951).

Principles of Discipline. Discipline consists primarily of habit formation and thus involves four essential principles. (1) The child must act in a desirable manner and eliminate undesirable behavior; (2) he must associate satisfaction with desirable and dissatisfaction with undesirable acts; (3) he must make the desirable act so automatic that it will, in time, be repeated of its own accord without need of supervision; and (4) he must learn to substitute desirable for undesirable behavior.

Even though positive motivation, in the form of reward, brings better results than negative motivation, in the form of punishment, punishment should not be eliminated. The recognition of the possible consequences of an act is essential to all moral behavior. This involves the ability to foresee what will happen if an undesirable act is carried out—an ability which is not found in individuals of low-grade intelligence. Because the recognition of possible consequences of an act necessitates an evaluation of the act, every child must learn to weigh alternative acts with consequences associated with each. He thus learns to decide for himself whether the act is worth its "price tag."

Rules and laws serve two useful purposes in discipline: (1) they act first as an educational agency, to acquaint the child with the standards of conduct that are acceptable to the group, and (2) they are restrictive, in that they restrain undesirable behavior. By the adolescent years, provided discipline has been of the right sort, rules and laws should not be needed. But, if they were not used, many individuals would quickly lapse into unsocial behavior. They thus serve as a preventative to antisocial behavior.

Rules, to be effective, must be consistent. Otherwise, the child is at a loss to know what to do and whom to obey. In an experiment with nursery-

When discipline is wholesome, the child learns to conform willingly to social standards. (*From Child Development, a McGraw-Hill Text-Film.*)

school children, commands were given in pairs by two adults. When the commands were identical, the tendency was toward obedience. But when the two adults gave different and incompatible commands, the child some-times vacillated between the activities, obeying one or the other, or both in turn, but frequently obeying neither adult. The emotional consequences of such discipline were often severe (Meyers, 1944).

Need for Discipline. It was formerly believed that a child needed dis-cipline because society required him to behave in a certain way and would tolerate no deviations from the approved pattern. Now it is recognized that the child needs discipline if he is to be a happy, well-adjusted individual. He needs the steadying influence of discipline because his values change so often that this gives him a feeling of insecurity. When he knows what is expected of him, he has the steadying influence of values and attitudes that remain relatively unchanged. Furthermore, discipline helps him to direct his energies into approved channels, thus enabling him to behave in an approved manner (Hacker and Geleerd, 1945; Geisel, 1951; Lourie, 1951; DuBois, 1952).

As Geisel (1945) has pointed out,

The infant comes among us as a little savage, and the first fifteen years of his life are in a very real sense the disciplinary years, for his growing-up is really a process of learning to do right things at the right time, in the right place, and meaningfully. . . . Children do not characteristically yearn to become civilized. They do not wish to be ordered, trained, disciplined. . . . As a rule, they do not yearn to live orderly lives. They want to be free to make their own decisions. . . . But they are generally reluctant to make their decisions on the basis of the greatest good to the greatest number. In short, they are reluctant to discipline themselves.

There are certain needs that discipline fills for a child and thus adds to his happiness and adjustments. These are:

1. Discipline gives the child a feeling of security to know where his boundaries, limits, and freedoms are. He needs to know how far he can go and what he may or may not do.

2. He needs to live according to certain standards in order to have less feeling of guilt. From time to time, he is bound to do some wrong things and feel guilty. However, too much feeling of guilt makes him unhappy and poorly adjusted.

3. When a child does the right thing, it makes it possible for adults to praise him. Praise is equivalent to love as the child interprets it, while scolding and disapproval are interpreted as lack of love and as rejection. The child needs love to develop successfully.

4. Discipline serves as an ego-bolstering motivation to the child to accomplish what is required of him.

5. Discipline helps the child to develop a conscience—the "internalized voice" that directs him to do this or that. Pressures from adults over a period of time become the pattern for the internalized voice of conscience to guide the child in making choices of his own (Geisel, 1951).

The child who lacks discipline cannot develop into a happy, well-adjusted individual. However, no child is experienced enough to know how to discipline himself. Adults can help the child to learn to behave in a socially approved manner so that he will eventually learn to discipline himself (Lourie, 1951). This they can do (1) by setting an example of willing acceptance of discipline; (2) by proper timing of discipline to avoid trying to have the child do something before he is capable of understanding the reason for it; and (3) by helping the child to understand the purpose and benefits of self-discipline, which can be done by explaining the rules to the child and by praising him for following them (Geisel, 1945).

Types of Discipline. What type of discipline is used depends upon the child's parents, their training and education, and the type of environment in which the child lives (Bakwin and Bakwin, 1951). Many techniques are used to discipline children, some of which are good while others are likely to lead to unfavorable attitudes on the child's part, even though they bring improved behavior at the time. However, what technique is used is less important than *how* it is used (DuBois, 1952).

Geisel (1951) has given some suggestions as to how discipline can be applied most successfully. These suggestions are:

1. When pressure is applied, the child must be reassured that he is loved. He must be reassured that the pressure applies to the *act, not to him.*
2. Those in control must stand together and be consistent in their discipline to give the child a feeling of security.
3. The child must be pressed to behave in certain ways by praising him for acceptable behavior and by withholding privileges for unacceptable behavior.
4. Adults must give the child an example of well-disciplined lives.
5. Adults must help the child to understand why certain arrangements are required.
6. The right time must be chosen for introducing rules and regulations.

While the common method of disciplining children in most households is to spank the child when he misbehaves, there is a growing tendency to frown upon spanking and all other forms of corporal punishment. Today, many different disciplinary methods are in use, some proving to be more effective than others. Reasoning with the child, scolding, making the child feel ashamed of his behavior, spanking, slapping, and bribing are more frequently used than praise or reward (Long, 1941). Undesirable disciplinary techniques that are commonly used consist of threats of withdrawal of affection, invidious comparisons, ridicule, sarcasm, belittling, harping on a misdemeanor, excessive disapproval, corporal punishment, deprivation of things that might be considered a child's right, such as food or allowance, and threats of future punishment which make a child unduly apprehensive (Bakwin and Bakwin, 1951).

Punishment. Punishment serves two major functions in discipline: (1) it acts as a deterrent to prevent repetition of socially undesirable acts, and (2) it acts as a means of showing the child what the social group regards as right or wrong. If it is to achieve the desired results, punishment must not serve as an outlet for the pent-up anger of the person who has been offended or as a penalty for wrong deeds committed in the past. As the child's criterion of the seriousness of his offense is based on the severity of the punishment he receives, the necessity for consistent punishment should be apparent. Unfortunately, because most parents and other adults punish in anger, this criterion loses its value. If the child learns that inevitably a wrong act will result in a given punishment, he will think twice before carrying out the wrong deeds he may have contemplated.

In Fig. 54 are shown different types of punishments used by parents as reported by parents at the time the child entered nursery school and a year or so later. The comparison shows the permanency of the types used. It also indicates that more punishments are used as the child grows older. Only two —praise and reward, and ignoring—show a decrease in usage. Analysis of the punishments from the point of view of the influence they are presumed to have on behavior reveals that most are aimed at undermining the child's power or restricting his freedom—spanking, depriving, isolating, frighten-

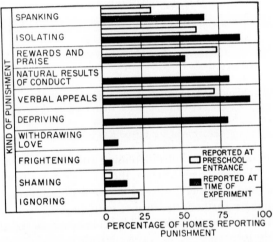

Fig. 54. Kinds of punishment reported by parents. (*From M. J. Radke, The relation of parental authority to children's behavior and attitudes, University of Minnesota Press, 1946. Used by permission.*)

ing, shaming, and withdrawing love. Less restrictive and less power-reductive forms are praise and rewards, reasoning, and verbal appeals (Radke, 1946).

Among young children, mothers do most of the punishing. When fathers punish, it is usually by deprivation or by physical methods, rarely by verbal forms (Gardner, 1943). Parents are far more favorable to the use of corporal punishment as a means of control than are persons who have a background of training in child development (Coast, 1939). Various forms of punishment have been reported for older children, the most common of which are deprivation, verbal methods, and physical methods. Disobedience is the most common single cause for punishing the older child (Gardner, 1943).

Most adults think of corporal punishment, especially slapping the hands or spanking, as the most effective form of punishment to use in dealing with the wrongdoings of the child. Contrary to popular opinion, corporal punishment is one of the least satisfactory types, because it seldom is actually associated in the child's mind with the act for which the child is being punished. Because corporal punishment is generally administered when the adult is angry, it tends to condition the child to dislike the punisher. Since the anger of the adult is a more dominant factor in the situation than the act itself, the child tends to associate the whipper with pain rather than the wrong deed with pain. For that reason, the real value of this type of punishment is lost.

If corporal punishment is used, it should be administered while the act is going on and not delayed until a later time or left for someone else to administer. When the punishment is delayed, the association in the child's mind between the act and punishment is not made, and consequently the whole value of the punishment is lost. Corporal punishment, if used at all, should be used only up to the age when the child is capable of comprehending what is said to him, which is between the second and third years. After that time, a form of punishment more definitely related to the act should take the place of corporal punishment.

Any form of punishment that has no direct relationship to the act is, like corporal punishment, less effective than a form of punishment that has a direct relationship to the act. For that reason, scolding, depriving the child of pleasure, isolating him from his playmates when the wrong act had nothing to do with them, putting him to bed without supper, or other similar punishments, are not as effective as the adults who use them expect them to be. It is far easier, it is true, to use some "stock punishment," regardless of the situation involved, and it requires far less ingenuity on the part of the user. But this does not serve its purpose as well as an individual punishment would.

Punishment is generally given to correct faults in behavior, without taking into consideration the child's motive. This obviously is unfair to the child. The adult who administers the punishment should make a definite effort to analyze the child's behavior in order to discover what motivated the wrongdoing. From the child's point of view, the fair thing is to tell him, as soon as he is able to understand, why the punishment is given. This not only emphasizes the educational value of punishment, but it eliminates the possibility of the child's interpreting it as due to personal annoyance on the part of the individual who administers the punishment.

Through punishment or fear of punishment, it is possible to get obedience from a child. But the effects on the child are often bad, especially if the parents try to modify too quickly and at too early an age the child's natural drives. Unless suited to the act, punishment is not educational. To a child, punishment means pain inflicted by an older, bigger, and stronger person than he because a rule, made arbitrarily by an adult, has been broken. Furthermore, punishment is likely to create resentment and hostility, and it inhibits thought and action. As a result, it rarely fosters learning and, thus, defeats its purpose. If used successfully, emphasis should be placed on what punishment is supposed to teach the child, and it should never be humiliating, as is true of corporal punishment (DuBois, 1952).

According to Havighurst (1952a), there are only two kinds of people who may safely allow the punishment of the child to serve as a release for their aggressions. *Parents* may do this safely within narrow limits because they are so close to the child emotionally that the child can accept occasional punishment from them without doubting their affection for him. Total strangers may likewise punish a child for inflicting damage on their property or taking their possessions. By doing so, they teach the child that he will be punished for infringing on the rights of others and to have proper respect for others. On the other hand, there are certain people who should not punish a child by aggression. They are the ones who have frequent relationships with the child but are not very closely bound to him emotionally, as teachers, club leaders, and neighbors. Instead of punishing, they usually find that reward is a more effective way to achieve their purposes.

Rewards. Too much emphasis on punishment leads the individual to lose sight of the value of using rewards in the discipline of the child. If the child is to learn to act in a socially desirable way, it must be worth his while to do so. For that reason, rewards must be used to build up pleasant associations with the desired act. But this does not mean artificial rewards or "bribes" that have no relationship to the act.

Like punishment, rewards should have a direct relationship to the act that one wishes to have repeated, and in that way the pleasant associations will motivate the child to repeat it. Perhaps the simplest and yet most effective reward is social recognition in the form of praise. This can always be tied up with the act, as "You cleaned up your room very well, Johnnie." At the same time, it satisfies the desire on the part of every normal child for social recognition.

Gifts are sometimes given as rewards for good behavior. As Jersild and Tasch (1949) have pointed out, the "child's gratitude often seems to go quite beyond the material value or even the practical usefulness of what is given." A gift as a reward may be a token of affection, it may represent a respect for the child's abilities and achievements, it may serve as a form of encouragement, or it may be a token of confidence. In any instance, it adds to the child's feeling of self-importance. Under no conditions, however, should the gift be a bribe for good behavior or a form of payment for learning to behave in a socially approved way (Jersild and Tasch, 1949). Few parents report that they reward or punish children for their report cards from school. Those who do, however, give gifts or money mainly (Stendler and Young, 1951).

It is commonly believed that praising or rewarding a child for good behavior will make him conceited and encourage him to rest on his laurels.

When positive techniques, in the form of praise, encouragement, or balanced criticism are used in school, desirable responses on the part of children have been reported to outweigh the undesirable in the ratio of 46 to 1. Consistently desirable responses were reported, regardless of what kind of positive technique was used. Even some of the children who showed undesirable responses at first later showed desirable responses (Belogianis et al., 1944).

Evaluation of Discipline. Discipline should not be evaluated in terms of the immediate results obtained when certain types of discipline are used. Children can be forced into a pattern of behavior approved by adults and can quickly be made into "perfect little ladies or gentlemen." However, the harm done to their personalities may be so great that the price will be too heavy. As DuBois (1952) has pointed out, "Parents must think in terms not only of the immediate behavior at two, six, or sixteen years . . . but also of the ultimate results of discipline at twenty, forty, and sixty, when parental control is no longer in force. Then the individual must be constructively self-directed or else suffer remorse because of violation of his personal code or be punished by society when his conduct is contrary to its laws."

There are certain wholesome and unwholesome functions of discipline which must be kept in mind when disciplinary techniques are evaluated. The major wholesome functions are:

1. To teach the child that the world responds in orderly fashion to his actions, and thus he learns that certain behavior will always be followed by punishment, while others will be followed by praise. Consistent discipline helps the child to learn that there is a moral orderliness in the world.

2. To teach the child a *reasonable* degree of conformity, but not too much conformity.

3. To help the child develop self-control and self-direction. Then he can make wise decisions on his own responsibility and develop a "conscience."

The unwholesome functions of discipline are:

1. To intimidate the child.
2. To release aggression by the disciplinarian (Havighurst, 1952a).

When discipline is wholesome, it is neither too strict nor too lenient, but it is always *consistent.* The severity of the discipline used has been found to bear no relationship to the moral character of the child. Some children who are very severely disciplined have been found to have very good characters, just as is true of some children who have been leniently disciplined. On the other hand, consistency of discipline is very closely related to moral competence. The child who is consistently disciplined is better adjusted than the child whose discipline has been inconsistent (Havighurst, 1952a). Children who are well adjusted differ from those who are poorly adjusted in greater sense of freedom, in better integration of behavior, and in a more realistic approach to life situations (Martin, 1951).

Overly strict parents literally push the child into going too far to assert his independence. Expecting absolute and immediate obedience leads to disciplinary problems (Colm, 1951). The overdisciplined child feels that the whole world is hostile, and he acts accordingly (Hacker and Geleerd, 1945). This leads either to submission or rejection of authority. As Frank (1949) has pointed out, "The stricter the parents, the stronger may be the revolt and the more outrageous the 'hell-raising' or the more submissive conformity to parents and priggish self-justification." Too much rebellion against too strict discipline may eventually lead to delinquency. The child often goes to extremes to prove himself a hero to himself (Colm, 1951).

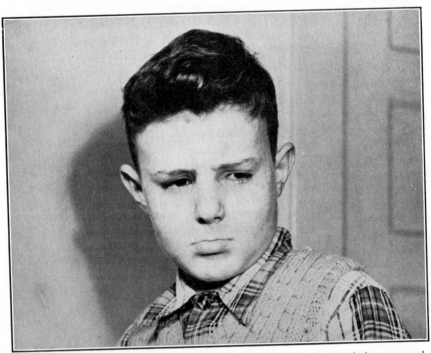

The child who feels that home discipline is too strict or unfair frequently becomes surly and rebellious. (*From Child Development, a McGraw-Hill Text-Film.*)

Too lenient discipline, on the other hand, leads to confusion on the child's part. The child feels insecure, and this leads to fear, anxiety, and excessive aggressiveness (Geisel, 1951). When parents can never make any demands on their children, the children take advantage of parental uncertainty and assert themselves. Furthermore, they feel cheated out of the pride of achievement, and they develop a feeling of contempt for their parents' "softness." This likewise leads to disciplinary problems. The child is best disciplined if parents feel secure in their role of being the "authority" to the child (Colm, 1951).

Children's Reactions. If discipline is to serve its function of teaching the child to behave in a socially acceptable manner, it is essential that the disciplinary methods used shall create a healthy attitude on the child's part toward discipline and toward those in authority. The more physical punishment is used on children, the less they tend to face reality and the more they depend on adult affection and attention. "Natural results of the child's acts" foster attractive personality and independence of adult affection or attention. Scolding or making the child afraid tends to make children unattractive and dependent. Using temper, extracting a penance from the child, or doing the first thing that pops into the parent's head tend to make children less attractive, less able to face reality, and less sociable (Ayer and Bernreuter, 1937).

Most children feel that their parents should be firm or strict, require obedience, and not spoil children. Many feel, however, that their parents should criticize constructively and reason with children instead of punishing them (Sowers, 1937). When a group of nursery-school children was asked what their mothers or fathers should do when their children were naughty, most of them recommended spankings. A few suggested isolation, and even fewer, scolding and talking cross (Radke, 1946). Most children prefer the mother to administer the punishment because they feel that she is more lenient than the father (Fuller, 1931; Gardner, 1947).

The assumption is that effective disciplinary techniques will prevent recurrence of undesirable behavior. When children were asked how they felt after they were punished, most of them reported that they felt unhappy and had memories of physical pain. Very few, on the other hand, reported feelings of penitence or resolutions for better behavior in the future (Radke, 1946). Studies of adolescents and adults have revealed that the effects of discipline persist and affect both the personality and the behavior of the individual as he grows older. Very strict discipline is often associated with personality maladjustments, unhappiness, and delinquency (Stogdill, 1937). The following characteristics have been noted among young adults whose childhood discipline had been very strict:

1. Dislike for parents, as shown in rude answering, irritation, and being ashamed of parents.

2. Combative attitudes developed in relation to parents were carried out in other relationships and took the form of feeling that teachers had been unfair to them, quarrels with friends, and grudges against some people.

3. Infantile dependence, as shown in bashfulness, being finicky about food, curious about sex matters; desire to be little again; and inability to decide on future vocation.

4. Social maladjustments, as seen in unpleasant nicknames, teaching by others, and being hurt by things said and done by associates.

5. Tendency to guilt, worry, and anxiety (Watson, 1934).

Variations in Attitudes. Children's attitudes toward discipline are influenced by a number of factors. *Boys* generally resent unfair discipline more than do girls, and they rebel more against corporal punishment than girls do (Stott, 1945; Radke, 1946). Attitudes are influenced by the *socioeconomic* and *cultural* groups to which the child belongs. Children from poorer groups more often favor an appeal to authority to meet disciplinary problems than do those of the better socioeconomic groups. Children of the poorer groups tend to hold the individual child responsible for any violation of rules of conduct, and they advocate punishment for the child more often than do children from better social backgrounds. The latter seem to comprehend better an environmental basis for misconduct and to suggest that the circumstances which produced the misbehavior be changed.

In case of truancy children of low socioeconomic status suggest that the truant officer should punish the child who plays hookey, while children of better socioeconomic status suggest that the truant might be unhappy in school. If so, they suggest that a change of school might solve the problem. As a general rule, children from the poorer groups are inclined to favor punishing the culprit and avenging his misdeeds, while those from better homes are more tolerant in their attitudes (Dolger and Ginandes, 1946). Underprivileged children tend to evaluate parental disciplinary methods as being too strict, while children of average socioeconomic status think their parents are too easy. Fathers are considered "too easy" more frequently than are mothers (Duvall, 1937).

Children who are *bright* evaluate discipline differently from those who are less bright. They react differently to rules and are likely to be bored by too many rules. Lack of definite limits on their behavior tends to make them insecure and unhappy. On the other hand, when they meet the demands of school and society, they are happy. They are very sensitive to fairness, especially on the part of teachers (Strang, 1954). The child whose intelligence is not of such a high level is likely to become resentful when disciplined because he does not always understand rules and thus feels that he is being treated unjustly.

MISDEMEANORS

A misdemeanor is mischievousness, disobedience, or willful badness of a minor sort. Most little children learn, unfortunately, that they get more attention when they are naughty than when they are good. They therefore are often intentionally naughty because they feel that they are being ignored. Even though they are punished for it, the pleasure they have derived from being in the spotlight far outweighs the temporary discomfort of the punishment. Much of the destructiveness of young children is not caused by clumsiness or lack of motor control but by a willful attempt to attract attention to themselves.

Groups of older children delight in willful misbehavior because it gives each member a sense of personal importance. If the misbehavior takes the form of annoying others, such as ringing door bells, letting air out of automobile tires, or drawing pictures on pavements, houses, or fences, the group members derive special pleasure from feeling that they are masters of the situation. Even though misbehavior in school, in the form of whispering, passing notes, or tormenting other pupils, is sure to result in some form of punishment, the youth feels that it is well worthwhile, because all eyes in the classroom are focused on him, and all pupils listen attentively while the teacher scolds or administers punishment.

Misdemeanors increase throughout late childhood and reach their peak shortly before adolescence. At this time, the child is making a transition from parental to group authority, with the result that in many cases there is a lessening of external control over his behavior. Boys are more troublesome in the home and in the school than are girls. Boys show more tendency toward serious conduct disorders than do girls, and as they grow older, there are more cases of delinquency among boys than among girls (Olson, 1930, 1949; Maller, 1937; Schwartz, 1949). This may be due partly to the fact that girls are more submissive than boys and are more influenced by what they know is expected of them than boys are and partly to the fact that boys are more ag-

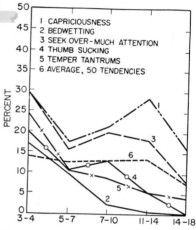

Fig. 55. Most frequent misdemeanors at three to four years. (*From A. Long, Parents' reports of undesirable behavior in children, Child Develpm., 1941, 12, 43–62. Used by permission.*)

gressive than girls (Hartshorne and May, 1928; Dollard et al., 1939; V. Jones, 1954). However, as Dickson (1932) has pointed out, "The child who does not have behavior difficulty is not normal."

Home Misdemeanors. In the process of growing up, most children pass through periods of "disequilibrium" when they are difficult to manage and when misbehavior is more common than at other times (Ilg et al., 1949). In a study of troublesome behavior in the home at different age levels, Long (1941) reported that the most common forms for children of three to four years of age were capriciousness, bed-wetting, seeking attention, thumb-sucking, temper tantrums, and dawdling, all of which are associated with immaturity. These, for the most part, wane in frequency of appearance as the child grows older (see Fig. 55).

In the seven- to ten-year-old group, there was a lessening of the behavior tendencies most frequent among younger children. In their place, however, appeared new forms of behavior indicative of the children's inadequate technique for entry into the rapidly expanding experiences of later childhood. Willfulness, for example, which occurred more frequently than at earlier ages, is indicative of a method used by individuals still inexperienced in socially acceptable ways of getting what they desire. This type of behavior drops rapidly as the child grows older. Other forms of undesirable behavior characteristic of this period are irritability, a tendency to be easily discouraged, and the state of having many fears. These, like willfulness, suggest the difficulties children of this age experience in orienting themselves to new experiences (see Fig. 56).

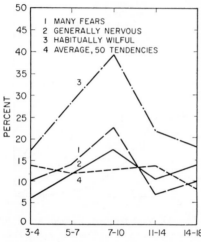

Fig. 56. Most frequent misdemeanors at seven to ten years. (*From A. Long, Parents' reports of undesirable behavior in children, Child Develpm., 1941, 12, 43–62. Used by permission.*)

Sex differences in undesirable home behavior were not found to be great, but a few that are significant are worth mentioning. More boys than girls of the three- to four-year-old group were hostile and suspicious, while more girls than boys were willful. In the seven- to ten-year-old group, more girls than boys were disobedient and overly conscientious, while more boys than girls were easily angered and had uncontrollable tempers.

An interesting aspect of Long's study was the analysis of the mother's influence on children's misdemeanors. Children whose mothers were more than 28 years older than the children, it was found, were quarrelsome and willful. There was a significantly low frequency of stealing and sneaking among children whose mothers were less than twenty-eight years of age at the birth of the child. Uncontrolled temper, antagonistic or resentful attitudes, resisting bedtime, and excessive mischief were reported more frequently among children whose mothers did not attend school beyond high school. Among those whose families were rated below the median of the group, habitual stubbornness, excessive mischief, bad table manners, and being satisfied with efforts below real ability were reported very frequently.

School Misdemeanors. In school, teachers are very sensitive to antisocial behavior and are most likely to be annoyed by childish behavior which interferes with the smooth functioning of the teacher's own affairs and activities or by behavior which interferes with the smooth functioning of the classroom, such as lying, tattling, physical aggression, destruction of property, showing off, and demanding attention. Teachers are also disturbed by children who never complete their assignments, except under compulsion, by stealing, cheating, daydreaming in the classroom, vocal aggressions such as improper language, boisterousness and talking out of turn, carelessness with work or appearance, and by children who are nonconformists in that they refuse to follow regulations or have no regard for the rights of others (Wickman, 1929; MacClenathan, 1934; Clark, 1951; Kaplan, 1952).

A comparison of the ratings of behavior problems of children by teachers and mental hygienists has revealed that teachers rate overt, objective behavior, such as disobedience, impudence, defiance, disorderliness in class, and profanity, as more serious than do mental hygienists, while mental hygienists consider a subjective type of behavior, as being unhappy, depressed, withdrawing, or overcritical of others, as more serious. Teachers consider problems related to honesty, sex, truancy, and classroom order especially serious. Most of the problems teachers consider serious relate to what the child does rather than to what he fails to do (Stouffer, 1952).

Common Forms of Misdemeanors. Dishonesty in different forms is very common in childhood. One of the most common forms is *lying*. Morgan (1942) has classified children's lies into seven types: (1) the playful lie, due to the make-believe play of imagination; (2) the lie of confusion, owing to inability to report accurately the details of some incident or to the beclouding of the issue by suggestions of another; (3) the lie of vanity, designed to draw attention to one's self; (4) the lie of malevolence or revenge, motivated by hate; (5) the excusive lie, resulting from fear that follows rigid discipline; (6) the selfish lie, which is calculated to deceive others so that one may get what he wants; and (7) the loyal or conventional lie, to safeguard a friend.

Among young children, untrue statements are generally not meant to deceive others but are due primarily to fantasy. Others are due to exaggerations, inaccuracies, and to imitation of dishonesty in adults (Ariamov, 1948). In some cases, pressure from adults to say the good and proper thing to others encourages the young child to lie. In addition, many young children learn to lie to protect themselves from punishment or threat of punishment. Under such conditions, when a child becomes dishonest, it is primarily the fault of the adults with whom he associates (Stains, 1954).

Older children will sometimes lie or blame others to avoid the punishment they know they deserve because of a wrongdoing willfully carried out. A small percentage of children, usually boys, consider it "smart" to try to "get away with" wrongdoing without being punished for it. This attitude is fostered by an environment in which adolescents or adults boast about their success in escaping punishment for wrongdoing or by an environment in which the child is actually taught to believe that it is all right to do a wrong thing provided one is clever enough to "get away with it." Most lies, however, are due to fear of punishment, disapproval, or ridicule (Leonard, 1920). Lying children, for the most part, come from unstable homes where they are frequently unwanted and suffer from inconsistent discipline (Lewis, 1931).

Dishonesty, in forms other than lies, appears in the preschool years, but it is more pronounced late in childhood. Boys and girls learn, from their own experiences or from those of their friends, ways and means of deceiving others, especially parents and teachers. They may pretend to be ill to avoid carrying out an unpleasant task; they may hide objects broken unintentionally or pretend that someone else did it; they may feign ignorance of a rule which they have broken; they may cheat in school work or athletics; or they may steal. All these forms of dishonesty are found in childhood; and few children are free from dishonesty in one form or another.

Among older children, one of the most common forms of dishonesty is *cheating* in school. While cheating varies in amount according to the situation, there is a tendency for boys to cheat more than girls and for those of low-grade intelligence to cheat more than those who are brighter. Because grades are more important to older children than to younger, it is not surprising that cheating increases as children grow older. There is less temptation for children who do good school work to cheat than there is for those whose school work is of a lower grade. Children from the better socioeconomic groups cheat less than do those from the poorer groups (Hartshorne and May, 1928; Gross, 1946; Beller, 1949; Ausubel, 1951). By adolescence, concepts of honesty are well established (Havighurst and Taba, 1949).

Attitudes toward honesty include the child's concepts of *property rights.* The child learns at a young age that it is wrong to steal or to make use of possessions of others without their knowledge and consent. However, the seriousness of stealing is interpreted differently at different ages (Havighurst and Taba, 1949). When boys in grades 1 through 12 were asked to rate 20 offenses in order of seriousness, it was found that their attitudes changed toward different offenses as they grew older. Below are listed the offenses which they regarded as more serious in the upper grades, those that became less serious, and those which did not show a significant change.

Offenses which gained in seriousness:
  To snitch fruit from a peddler's stand
  To swipe flowers from a park
  To take a wheel from a wagon you find in the alley
  To swipe your mother's wrist watch and pawn it
  To lift $1 from your father's pants' pocket when taking the pants to the tailor
  To swipe $1 from your boss's desk
  To take a wagon from a boy's back yard
  To sneak a rubber ball from a dime-store counter
Offenses which lost in seriousness:
  To keep $1 you find on the street without trying to find the owner
  To keep a candy package you find after it has fallen from a truck

To help yourself to chocolates from a box in your sister's room
To borrow your brother's baseball without asking
To ride on the streetcar for half fare when you should pay full fare
To sneak by an "L" cashier without paying
Offenses which did not change in seriousness:
To swipe $1 from your brother's bank at home
To keep $1 you see a man drop from his pocket
To keep a ball and glove you find in the school yard
To snitch three tickets from a movie cashier
To steal candy and cigarettes from a boxcar
To swipe and sell lead pipes from an old warehouse

As may be seen from the above lists, the offenses which gained in seriousness all involved actual stealing in one form or another. In the second group, the less serious offenses related to hoodwinking the utilities, keeping found property, and using the belongings of sibs in the home. When asked the reasons for their judgments, the younger boys gave as their reasons the fear of punishment more frequently than did the older boys. By contrast, the older boys gave as their most frequent reason the unwillingness to injure others (Eberhart, 1942).

Destructiveness of property is usually unintentional in young children. Their lack of muscular coordination and their curiosity about new and different things lead them to explore, and this often results in destructiveness. However, when the young child is angry, he frequently destroys his possessions and those of others as a form of retaliation. When a group of college students was asked to recall their motives for destructiveness when they were children, the men said they were influenced by the crowd situation with its accompaniment of the enjoyment of excitement and hostility toward the individual whose property they destroyed. Girls claimed that they were motivated more by the enjoyment and excitement than by hostility toward individuals. After boys and girls are ten years old, there is little destructiveness. When the urge to destroy is present, it is resisted mainly through fear of the law or of punishment. Few college students could imagine still enjoying the act of destructiveness (Clark, 1952).

Truancy becomes an increasingly common form of misdemeanor as children grow older. When the child is unhappy in school, due to poor school work or lack of social acceptance, he is likely to play hookey. Many truants come from broken homes where they have parents or siblings who are delinquent. Often they have changed schools frequently and have repeated grades. They are frequently disciplinary problems in the classroom because of their antisocial behavior, their use of attention-getting devices, their aggressive behavior, and their poor work habits. Many truants have poor health records, are sickly and pampered at home, and are only children or the only boy or girl of the family (Mullen, 1950).

FACTORS INFLUENCING MORAL DEVELOPMENT

The moral development of children is influenced to a large extent by the type of environment the child has from earliest babyhood. Of the many factors in the child's environment that influence his morality, the following are the most important.

1. The Family. The influence of parents, as well as other members of the family, takes four distinct forms. (1) The family's behavior acts as a model for the behavior of the child, who imitates what he observes in others. (2) By the use of approval or disapproval, reward, or punishment, the family teaches the child to behave in a socially desirable manner. (3) By planning the punishment to fit the misdeed, the family can teach the child to recognize the severity of his wrongdoing. (4) The family can do much to motivate the child to do right. The family is the transmitter of the culture of the group to the child. The home is the training center for ethical values of a given culture (Groves, 1940; Frank, 1948; Justin, 1950).

Children under normal conditions look up to and admire their parents, relatives, and older brothers and sisters. If the conduct of these individuals is undesirable, the child will accept it as standard and behave in a manner disapproved of by the members of his social group. If, for example, adults boast about breaking traffic laws, or if they lie about illness to get out of a social obligation, the model of conduct thus set is far from desirable for the child to copy. When discipline is reasonable and consistent, the child will develop moral competence in the form of self-control and self-direction (DuBois, 1952).

The type of relationship that exists between parent and child will determine what influence parental guidance and discipline will have on the child's moral development. When family relationships are good, the child will be more influenced by his parents than by anyone else in his moral behavior (Hartshorne et al., 1930; Liu, 1950; V. Jones, 1954). Among young children, strong emotional reactions have been observed when the children were asked to do something which was contradictory to rules laid down in the home by the parents. Even young children have a feeling of guilt when they disobey parental rules (Fite, 1940).

When, on the other hand, parent-child relationships are unfavorable or when the child's home is broken by divorce, separation, or death, there is a deterioration in the quality of the child's moral behavior and a change in his attitude toward misbehavior. Unfavorable parent-child relationships are frequently reflected in such misdemeanors as truancy, dishonesty, and destructiveness, and as the child grows older, in juvenile delinquency (Wallenstein, 1937; Berman, 1948; Symonds, 1949; Cooper, 1950; Mullen, 1950; Stott, 1950; Clark, 1952; V. Jones, 1954).

The *socioeconomic status* of the family plays an important role in the moral development of the child (see Fig. 57). While it is true that children from homes of favorable socioeconomic status do steal, lie, or become truants, this is far less likely to occur than among children of the lower socioeconomic groups (Pisula, 1937). There are different social pressures and different moral values in homes of different socioeconomic status. Middle-class children, for example, regard cheating as more serious than do those of lower classes (Harrower, 1934). Parents of the lower economic groups have a more authoritarian attitude toward punishment and use different disciplinary techniques than do parents of the middle-class groups (Dolger and Ginandes, 1946; Jersild, 1954).

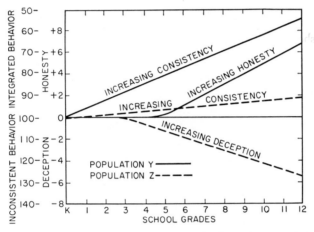

Fig. 57. Contrasting trends of honest behavior and of consistency of that behavior among children of superior (Y) and underprivileged (Z) socioeconomic groups. Children from the superior economic group become more honest and more consistently honest with age, whereas children from the underprivileged group become more deceptive and more consistently deceptive with age. (*Based on data from H. Hartshorne, M. A. May, and F. K. Shuttleworth, Studies in the organization of character, Macmillan, 1930. From F. K. Shuttleworth, The adolescent period: a graphic atlas, Monogr. Soc. Res. Child Develpm., 1949, 14, No. 1. Used by permission.*)

2. Playmates. When the child reaches the school age, a large percentage of his waking time is spent away from the home. As his contacts are more with children of his own age than with adults, it is not surprising to find that his playmates exert a tremendous influence over his behavior as well as his moral concepts. Even in the case of nursery-school children it has been found that the influence of companions is powerful enough to cause the children to deviate from parental rules in their attitudes toward aggression. With the development of "group feeling" came an increasing independence of adult rules, accompanied by an increase in the influence of group authority. Group authority consisted of (1) patterns derived from adult rules, (2) patterns from experience in dealing with other children, and (3) patterns from other child groups resulting from criticisms of other groups. If the attitude of the group deviated markedly from the home pattern, a strong conflict on the child's part resulted (Fite, 1940).

As children become older and spend more of their time with their friends, the influence of the gang becomes greater than it was during the preschool years when social groupings are loosely knit. Among gang-age children, the standards of the gang not only influence the moral outlook and behavior of all of its members, but they are especially important in influencing the newcomers (Thrasher, 1927). The conduct of individuals in a group is frequently "group-linked." The behavior of the individual under the influence of the standards of one group may not be typical of his conduct when alone or when with another group (V. Jones, 1936). The influence of the child's companions on his behavior is greatest when his companions are actually with him and in a position to influence his behavior by example, suggestion, and favorable or unfavorable reactions to his attitudes and behavior (Hartshorne and May, 1928; V. Jones, 1954).

When a group is small and made up of members who are close friends, the influence of the group on the child's behavior will be greater than when the group is large or when the membership in the group shifts frequently. This is seen in the case of morale in classrooms where the group remains intact over a period of time and where standards of behavior are established and adhered to by the children in the class (V. Jones, 1936). These standards will vary according to what socioeconomic group the majority of the children belongs to (Centers, 1949; Havighurst and Taba, 1949).

3. Schools. While it is true that children's moral knowledge increases as they pass from grade to grade in school, this alone is not enough to have a marked influence on the quality of their moral behavior. On the other hand, the type of relationship the child has with his teachers and with the children in his class does have a marked influence on his behavior (Hartshorne and May, 1928a). Inferior behavior may result from an authoritarian type of teacher, but once begun, it is not likely to change until the child is under the influence of another teacher who is more democratic in her methods. The personality of the teacher and the way she handles the classroom situation are more important than emphasis placed on character and citizenship training (Hartshorne and May, 1928a; V. Jones, 1936, 1954; Anderson et al., 1946).

When the relationship between teacher and pupils is good, the general morale of the class improves. With this comes improvement in behavior on the part of the children in the class (Anderson et al., 1946). In the case of deceitfulness and cheating, pupil-teacher relationship has been found to be more important than the formal educational philosophy of the school in determining the degree of classroom dishonesty (Ausubel, 1951). Because most teachers come from middle-class homes, there is a tendency to emphasize middle-class moral values in the school. In the case of pupils from middle-class homes, this serves to reinforce their home training. Children from the lower classes, on the other hand, sometimes find such values not entirely in accord with the values they have learned at home. While some children accept these new values, others are likely to be confused by them and to turn against the school, rejecting the moral concepts it teaches (Havighurst, 1946). If moral training in the school is to be effective, there must be not only a good pupil-teacher relationship but also opportunities for discussion of moral concepts and for putting them into practice in actual situations (V. Jones, 1936).

Competitive athletics, which are so popular in late childhood, offer splendid opportunities for moral training. Through sports, the boy or the girl learns to be fair, to be a good sport, and to subordinate selfish interests for the good of the group. Any behavior that does not measure up to the moral code of good sportsmanship will not be tolerated. Too much emphasis on winning, however, encourages the player to cheat. If he plays fairly and loses, he feels inferior and thus is tempted to cheat.

4. Sunday School and Church. From church, Sunday-school, or home instruction, the child learns that certain things are wrong because they are acts against God's laws and are therefore punishable in the life to come. Even though not caught, the child is often told that he will receive his punishment in due course of time. This differs from social enforcement in that it stresses God's disapproval and future punishment rather than present punishment of a tangible sort. Good religious instruction will help to interiorize the controls of the child's conduct (Ligon, 1939; V. Jones, 1954).

Wholesome religious experiences have a marked influence on the values of children and help them to learn to behave in a moral way (Woodruff, 1945). It is not the degree of religious knowledge which the child has that is important, but rather the attitudes and values established as a result of religious instruction (Hightower, 1930). A definite relationship has been found between the spiritual and religious health of the child and the quality of his behavior (Manwell and Fahs, 1951). Children who attend Sunday school or church have been found to cheat less and be more honest in other respects than children whose attendance is limited (Hartshorne and May, 1928, 1929; Maller, 1930). Delinquents are, as a rule, less inclined to have religious experiences than are nondelinquents (Wattenberg, 1950).

5. Recreational Activities. How the child spends his free time has been found to have an important influence on his values and on the quality of his behavior. Because it is assumed that the child's moral standards are influenced by his reading, parents and teachers encourage children to read books which will contribute to the establishment of desirable moral concepts. However, this is often counteracted by the child's reading of comics, especially those stressing crime and horror themes (see pages 349-350 for a discussion of the influence of the comics). Concentration on crime reports in newspapers can be as damaging to the child's moral concepts as too much comic-book reading (Baker, 1943; Doob, 1948). Careful control of the child's reading helps to establish healthy moral values (Child et al., 1946; Gray, 1947; V. Jones, 1954).

Because children attend movies more and more frequently as they grow older and because they tend to accept uncritically what they see on the screen, movies have a marked effect on the child's values. They help to mold his outlook on life, to create a desire for riches and luxury, and they suggest the ease of crime. Unless the movies the child sees are carefully selected and harmful elements from the movies censored before they are shown, they can have a detrimental effect on the child's moral behavior. However, this is not so likely to happen in the case of well-adjusted children as it is among those who are less well adjusted (Thurstone, 1931; Dysinger and Ruckmick, 1933; Blumer and Hauser, 1933; Cressey and Thrasher, 1934; Dale, 1935; Healy and Bronner, 1936; Shull, 1940; Fleege, 1945; V. Jones, 1954). Listening to the radio and watching television can have much the same influence on the moral behavior of the child as movie attendance does (see pages 350-359 for a discussion of these recreational activities and their effects).

6. Intelligence. The relationship between intelligence and morality is important, but it is not so important as was previously believed. It is true that the child needs intelligence of a certain degree to be able to distinguish between right and wrong and to be able to foresee the consequences of his acts, but that does not necessarily mean intelligence of a superior level. Other factors than intelligence, as has been demonstrated in the preceding section, play a role of importance in determining the moral behavior of the child. Hartshorne and May (1928), for example, found a correlation of .50 between intelligence and honesty scores in the case of school children. This would suggest that there is little more than chance relationship between intelligence and honesty in the group they studied.

Studies of very bright children have revealed that they are superior to children of average intelligence in honesty, truthfulness, and similar moral traits. In Fig. 58 are shown differences in stealing, cheating, and lying among children of different levels of intelligence. However, even very bright children have some weak moral characteristics, as may be seen by the fact that one out of every five very bright children has more faults than the average of the population (Terman, 1925). According to Wiggam (1941),

The chief reason why intelligence and right conduct tend to go together more often than not is that intelligent individuals know that right conduct is simply intelligent conduct—the conduct that gets the best results. . . . Brilliant children tend to choose the right conduct simply because they see it is the course of action that promises the best consequences. An intelligent child or adult discovers he can get what he wants in life more easily and surely by honesty than by deception, by kindness than by cruelty, by accepting social duties than by dodging them (pp. 262–263).

7. Sex. There is no evidence that boys and girls differ in morality as a result of native factors. On the other hand, as V. Jones (1954) has pointed out, "Our culture does not expect the same behavior patterns of girls that

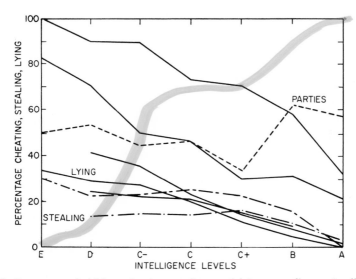

Fig. 58. Percentage of children cheating, stealing, and lying according to intelligence-test levels (E is equivalent to IQ's under 60, and A to IQ's of 140 or over). Except in a party situation, there is a marked tendency for cheating to decrease with increasing intelligence. (*Based on data from H. Hartshorne and M. A. May, Studies in deceit, Macmillan, 1928. From F. K. Shuttleworth, The adolescent period: a graphic atlas, Monogr. Soc. Res. Child Develpm., 1949, 14, No. 1. Used by permission.*)

it expects of boys, and the training that it gives them is different." Studies of honesty have revealed that girls tell more lies of a social type than do boys. There is a tendency for them to lie to win the favor of others more than boys do (Tudor-Hart, 1926). Dishonesty in social situations has also been found to be greater among girls than among boys in the case of cheating in a "party test." In other situations, cheating is no more common among members of one sex than among members of the other sex (Terman, 1925; Hartshorne and May, 1928; V. Jones, 1936, 1954). Boys, on the other hand, misbehave more in school and at home than do girls, and as they grow older, they are more likely to become delinquent than are girls (Olson, 1949; Schwartz, 1949).

Chapter 13

SOME CHILDHOOD INTERESTS

An interest is a learned motive which drives the individual to act in accordance with that interest. It is defined as preoccupation with an activity
when the individual is free to choose. When the child finds an activity
satisfying, it continues to be an interest. Because every interest satisfies some
need, the stronger the need that is being satisfied, the stronger and the
more lasting the interest. The child who has a strong need for companionship, for example, will direct his energies into activities which will bring
him into contact with others. The more frequently the child expresses
his interest in activity, the stronger it will become. On the other hand, interests are subject to extinction through disuse (Murphy, 1947; Harris,
1950a).

The development of interests closely parallels the child's physical and
mental development. A child could not, for example, have a real interest
in ball games until he had the strength and muscle coordination necessary
for ball play. Similarly, a child could not be interested in history until his
intelligence had developed to the point where he could comprehend the
meaning of historical facts. Limitations in his physical and mental capacities or in his experiences will set limits on his interests (Harris, 1950a;
Garrison, 1952). As a child develops, he changes both physically and
mentally. With these changes come changes in interests. This is especially
apparent at puberty when physical changes of a pronounced type occur
(Wilson, 1938).

Interests depend not only on the physical and mental status of the
child but also upon his opportunities for learning. This, in turn, is dependent upon his environment and upon the interests of the adults with
whom he is most closely associated. It is the environment of his childhood years that offers him the opportunity to develop certain interests and
cuts him off from the opportunities to develop other interests which might
prove to be more satisfying to him. As the environment of the child broadens to include his school, his neighborhood, his community, and finally the
whole world, new opportunities are opened up for the acquisition of other
interests. That is why many of the interests of childhood are abandoned
and are replaced by other interests as the child emerges from childhood
into adolescence, and then into maturity.

When a child fails to acquire certain interests, due to lack of opportunity to learn them, he may be penalized throughout life. Many adults report that they regret they did not acquire more interests in childhood than they did as a basis for interests in adult life. There are many indications that the range of interests a child acquires is narrower than it should be on the basis of the child's abilities. It is good for a child to cultivate interests that will enable him to realize his varied potentialities and to become acquainted with interests that might serve his needs. The child who lives in an environment that offers opportunities for many interests and who is associated with adults who can encourage him to develop interests that will be most satisfying to him has an opportunity to acquire a wholesome idea of his own worth and to become a well-adjusted individual (Jersild and Tasch, 1949; Jersild, 1954).

Interests are markedly influenced by *likes* and *dislikes*. Patterns of likes and dislikes are established early and remain relatively stable over the years. When the child enters school, he likes most things. Likes are much the same for all children, with little difference between boys and girls. However, these likes and dislikes are general rather than specific. For example, a child will like anything that falls in the category of "play" and dislike anything that might be considered "work." With each passing year, marked sex differences begin to appear in what children like and dislike.

By the time the child is ten years old, patterns of interest are present. These have developed through the acquisition of *dislikes* by children whose initial attitude toward everything was favorable, not through the emergence of likes and dislikes on a neutral ground. The child acquires broad, general attitudes about one's sex, about work, and what is appropriate for individuals of each sex. As a result of the acquisition of likes and dislikes, patterns of interest are established. The boy, for example, will dislike anything that might be classed as "sissy" or "inappropriate." Boys, more so than girls, develop dislikes for anything that is "work" and, as a result, acquire antiwork and anti-intellectual attitudes which markedly affect their interests (Tyler, 1955).

Boredom is the opposite of interest. It lacks the element of satisfaction that accompanies interest, and it is accompanied by activities which fail to interest, stimulate, or challenge the individual who is carrying out these activities. When children are bored, they are likely to get into mischief and cause trouble for others in the hope of stirring up some excitement, thus turning a boring situation into an interesting one. For the most part, children experience boredom when they are forced to do things which do not fit their needs or give them satisfaction. This is especially true of school work where the curriculum and method of teaching must be planned for the group rather than to meet the needs of each individual child in the group (Jersild, 1954).

DETERMINATION OF INTERESTS

There are many ways in which it is possible to find out what a child's interests are. Through an observation of what objects a child plays with, buys, collects, or uses when it is apparent that there is an element of spontaneity in his activity, it is possible to get a clue as to his interests. The degree of his interest may be determined by the length of time he spends with the activity in a given period of time or by what he says he enjoys doing or says he engages in frequently (Harris, 1950a). However, as Jersild (1954) has pointed out, many activities that occupy much of the child's free time, such as listening to the radio or watching television, do not seem to represent strong interests on the child's part but a lack of something better to do.

Other clues to the child's interests are the questions he asks (pages 368–370), what he talks about when he is with his contemporaries (pages 205–206), what he reads about when he is free to select his books (pages 341–349), or what he draws and paints spontaneously (pages 331–335). One of the most satisfactory ways of determining a child's interests at a given age is to study his wishes. When asked what they would like to have if they could have anything they wanted, most children state very frankly wishes for things that interest them most. A person's wishes reveal, either directly or indirectly, something concerning his outlook on life and what he wants from it (Jersild and Tasch, 1949). An analysis of the child's wishes gives a clue to the personality of the child, the state of maturity he has attained, and the values he has formed from his cultural background (Wilson, 1939, 1939a).

Among young children, most wishes emphasize material possessions, as toys, money, clothes, and material improvements in the home. By the time the child reaches the school age, there is a decline in wishes for material objects and a change in the type of object he would like to have. A little child, for example, may wish for a tricycle, while the older child will wish he had a bicycle, motorcycle, or even an automobile. The elementary-school child concentrates his wishes on personal achievement, personal improvement, skills to earn money and gain independence, and greater popularity and social acceptance. He wishes he had better living quarters, could travel and see the world, and be morally better. By the sixth grade, the child's wishes become less egocentric and more social in that he wishes for things that will help others as well as things which interest him (Jersild et al., 1933; Wilson, 1938; Witty and Kopel, 1939; Zeligs, 1942; Jersild and Tasch, 1949; Cobb, 1954; Jersild, 1954). Girls put more emphasis on personal attractiveness and popularity, while boys emphasize skills, personal achievement, and independence (Jersild and Tasch, 1949; Cobb, 1954). Negro children put more emphasis on material possessions than do white children of the same ages (Boynton, 1936a; Gray, 1944a).

SOME CHARACTERISTIC INTERESTS

Because of the many variables which influence the development of a child's interests, there are marked individual differences in the interests of children, just as there are among adults. There are, however, certain interests which are commonly found among children of our American culture and which are fostered by environmental influences that are fairly universal in this culture. These are the interests which will be discussed in the following pages.

1. RELIGION

Religion is, according to Webster's dictionary, "the outward act or form by which men indicate recognition of a god or gods to whom obedience and honor are due." It involves a desire for help, security, and consolation not given by the world, a dependence on a power outside of oneself, a feeling of confidence in the power appealed to, and an emotional reaction of a reverential sort. *Religion includes two elements, belief and practice.* Both of these are important not only in childhood but also in adolescence. At different ages, however, the relative importance of the two is not the same.

Religion is a product of the child's environment and is developed partly by the example set by his parents, as in the case of churchgoing and grace at meals, and partly by direct, formal religious instruction in the home, Sunday school, or church. Of the two elements of religion, belief and practice, major emphasis is placed on the latter. To the little child, religion is ritual. He learns to pray at home and later learns the ritual of the faith of his parents through Sunday-school and church attendance. There is evidence that religious observances play a less important role in American family life today than they did in the past (Reuss, 1954).

Interest in Religion. The young child is curious about the universe, as well as about the everyday world in which he lives. He thinks of them as being on an equal basis, and there is no metaphysical meaning associated with them. Between the ages of three and four years, the child's questions often relate to religion. "Who is God?" "Where is heaven?" "How do you get there?" (Davis, 1932). Mysteries centered around birth, death, growth, and the elements are explained in religious terms.

The child accepts almost any answers given to his questions, and these satisfy him temporarily. But, in many cases, they are not adequate later and often lead to doubt and skepticism during the adolescent years. Similarly, stories of heaven, hell, angels, devils, and miracles are accepted on faith.

What he believes depends upon what he has been taught at home or in Sunday school. However, because the child lacks the ability to think in a critical manner, his beliefs are often flatly contradictory, as shown, for instance, by the fact that a child may believe God to be a wonderful person, but also that He would strike a man dead with a stroke of lightning for profanity (MacLean, 1930).

The stories in the Bible have marked appeal for the child in much the same way as fairy stories do. They relate to people, countries, and situations so different from those of the child's everyday environment that he enjoys hearing certain of the Bible stories time after time, just as he enjoys a repetition of his favorite fairy stories. Interest in persons is always greater than interest in doctrines, though at different ages children show preferences for different parts of the Bible. Children under eight years of age have been found to prefer stories relating to the birth and childhood of Jesus and the childhood of such characters as Samuel, Moses, Joseph, and David, while older children show a greater interest in the historical books of the Old Testament (Dawson, 1900). Most children are interested primarily in persons and happenings rather than in doctrines (Garrison, 1952).

Religious Attitudes. The young child is *reverent* in his attitude toward religion. To him, the pageantry of the religious service and the beauty of the church decorations are awe-inspiring. When taught to regard these in a reverent manner, he does so and thus derives a feeling of security from them. Typically, the religion of little children is *egocentric* and self-seeking. To them, prayers and worship are means of attaining some childish desire, and their attitude is primarily one of being good because of the reward to be obtained. This attitude is in keeping with the child's personality. As he is accustomed to having things done for him by adults, just so he visualizes God as a person who will do things for him. To the young child, for example, Christmas is a time to receive toys and gifts, and not the time when giving to others means much to him.

Religion at this age is *formal*. This is due to the fact that in the early religious training of the child emphasis is generally placed on the verbal aspects of religion. The child learns to recite stereotyped phrases, as "God is Love," and to say his prayers, even though he does not know what they mean. The very words he learns to recite are different from those used in everyday speech, with the result that the meaning of the thought is lost to him. Any attempt to simplify this merely adds to the child's confusion.

The religion of the older child, like that of the young child, is *egocentric*. This is well illustrated in the study made by Freeman (1931) of first-grade pupils' concepts of Christmas. They believed Christmas to be an occasion to appease their acquisitive tendencies to a pitch of greediness. As Freeman pointed out, all were "strong on getting," with very little thought of "giving." Typical reactions were as follows: "Last Christmas I got a tricycle and the next year I got a mamma doll." "I like Christmas because Santa has brought me a wagon and a new brown suit."

Little sentiment or emotionality accompanies religion at this age, because religion is an impersonal experience. Sermons, to make their appeal to youth, must be *concrete*. The stories and illustrations must be specific in application. Religion, to the child, is a means of self-improvement, of avoiding sin and its consequences. His attitude is not affected by an emotional element, which colors the attitude of the adolescent or the adult. Even the thought of sin or punishment is impersonal and unemotional.

Religious Training. Among primitive peoples, religious training is included in the public ceremonies of the tribes. They recognize adolescence as the age for religious instruction, and they expect the adolescent to accept the religion of the tribe at that time. This implies that they regard religion as too complex for children and thus defer instruction along religious lines until the child is old enough to comprehend its meaning. The age of religious comprehension is, for them, the age of puberty.

This attitude contrasts markedly with Christian and many other religions, which start religious instruction as soon as the child can comprehend words. This is generally given as preparation for admission to the church and is so theological that it is usually far beyond the ability of the little child to understand.

Because so many adolescent boys and girls become skeptics and agnostics, many parents try to forestall this by rigid religious training in childhood, on the theory that, if religious concepts are fully established before the age of skepticism, they will eliminate the trouble that comes when doubts arise. This, however, is usually not the case. The more rigid and dogmatic the training in childhood, the more likely the adolescent is to doubt the religious concepts he had formerly accepted in an unquestioning fashion.

Because the child is not a miniature adult in mental make-up, a religion that is suited to an adult is no more suited to a child than are adult stories. If religion is to mean anything to a child, it should not only be concrete in form and presented in language that the child uses constantly, and thus can understand, but it should also be presented in a less dogmatic fashion than is usually the case. The child wants to satisfy his curiosity by asking questions. Religious instruction should provide for this if it is to fulfill its purpose.

Children who receive religious instruction have more factual information about religion than do those whose religious instruction has been slighted. However, most children get some information about religion from their friends or from reading, even if they have had no formal instruction (Wheeler and Wheeler, 1945). Most of the Sunday schools emphasize formal rote learning and dogmatic instruction rather than interpretation of the doctrines of the religion they are teaching. When emphasis is placed on authoritarian instruction, the child has no opportunity to question what he is taught. Instead, he is expected to accept what he has learned on a passive basis and to let faith supplant reason (Hartshorne and Lotz, 1932),

Wholesome religious education should be more than learning facts. Principles of the religious nature are more important for the child than facts (Van Dorn and Mayfarth, 1949). From religious training, the child should be able to establish values and to derive the feeling of security that comes from such values. This is essential if the child is to be happy and well adjusted as he grows older (Kuhlen and Arnold, 1944; Bahm, 1946; Allport et al., 1948). It is through religious training that the child will be able to develop integrity and self-realization (Jersild, 1954).

When religious training in childhood has been neglected or when it has been inadequate or of the wrong type for the child's level of development, the child is likely to become atheistic or agnostic in his beliefs as he becomes older and to take little or no part in church activities. Most adolescents or young adults who lose interest in religion or who develop an antagonistic attitude toward their family religion or toward religion in general are the product of the wrong type of religious training in their childhood days (Allport et al., 1948; Garrison, 1951; Kuhlen, 1952; Landis, 1952; Withey, 1952). The more religious training the child has, the more likely he is to feel the need for religion as he grows older. Individuals, on the other hand, who have had little religion in their lives during childhood generally feel little need for religion as they grow older (Allport et al., 1948).

Religious Beliefs. The child's religious beliefs are based on the concepts he develops as a result of his religious training. This, in turn, is dependent upon environmental influences, mainly in the home and Sunday school he attends. When, for example, the child is taught to think of God as a person who will become angry when a person does a wrong thing and that He sends storms, earthquakes, and sickness to punish people for their sins, the child will have very different beliefs about religion than he would have had God been presented in a different manner. Furthermore, with teaching of this type, it is not surprising that the child develops definite and concrete concepts (Betts, 1934).

The religious beliefs of a young child are based on realistic concepts. He thinks of God, heaven, hell, angels, and the devil in terms of the pictures he has seen of them or the stories he has been told about them (Kuhlen and Arnold, 1944). Later, as the child's comprehension increases and as his experiences with everyday life have been more varied, his concepts will change. His concept of God as a father will be influenced by his experiences with his own father and with the fathers of his friends. Likewise, his concepts of sin and forgiveness will reflect the ways he has been treated when he misbehaved (Jersild, 1954).

In spite of the fact that children have different religious instruction and different experiences in their daily lives, it has been found that the development of their religious concepts follows a pattern that is similar for all. This pattern closely parallels their intellectual development and is as follows:

1. The *fairy-tale stage*, between the ages of three and six years. In this stage, all pictures had one common characteristic. The children expressed their version of the deity as a fairy-tale conception. The child's God experiences were distinguished from his usual fairy-tale experience by a kind of awe that the child had for the high and exalted.

2. The *realistic stage*, which begins when the child enters school and continues through the elementary-school age. The child's concept of God now turns from a fairy-tale type into a definite reality. At this age, the child seems willing to adapt himself to institutionalized religion and its teaching. Symbols now most frequently represent God, such as the crucifix and the Jewish star. Next in frequency were pictures of priests or priestlike persons representing mediators of God. Angels and saints were represented as human figures.

3. The *individualistic stage*, during adolescence, in which no one specific religious concept is shown but rather manifold types of expression. The three common types are (*a*) religious imagination expressed in a conventional and conservative way according to the existing cult forms, with no original religious fantasy; (*b*) more originality shown, resulting from a strong consciousness of the basic individualistic character of religious experience; and (*c*) originality far removed from the adolescent's religious environment (Harms, 1944).

Because the child tends to regard everything in his environment as *animate*, he interprets religion in that way. He believes that everything is alive and he endows the sun, moon, stars, and all the elements with the same life qualities that human beings have. God, to him, is a man, like any man among his acquaintances. He interprets what he is taught in terms he can understand. By the age of six or seven years, he reserves his animistic beliefs for objects that move, such as the sun and moon. If children are to experience mysticism in their religious beliefs, the adults with whom they are associated must be more sensitive to the mysterious (Fahs, 1950).

How pictures of people and scenes foreign to the child's everyday experience can distort young children's religious concepts has been well illustrated by Murphy's (1937) statement that children are apt to learn of Jesus, "not as an ideal grown-up who helped people, but as a little baby whose mother put him in a straw thing in a barn instead of a crib, and to whom queer-looking men in striped gowns brought presents no baby could use. They learn, too, that there was a bad king, with a ferocious face, of whom the baby's mother was afraid, so that she had to take him a long way from home, riding on an animal that is not seen in the city, nor even in the zoo" (p. 34). Distortions of religious concepts, due to mis-understanding of the words used to describe or explain them, are common in the case of young children. Jersild (1954) gives, as an example of this, the case of a young child who told his mother about Jesus' 12 bicycles (disciples) and who was puzzled about the "consecrated cross-eyed bear" (consecrated cross, I'd bear).

Because the child builds up concepts about unknown people, places, and situations in terms of those he knows, it is not surprising that his concepts about the unknown as taught him in his religious instruction become confused with already developed concepts. Vagueness and confusion of meaning in concepts relating to spiritual experiences, as "conversion," "Savior," and "Christian," have been found to be greater than in concepts relating to special religious days or places, as "Christmas," "Sunday," and "church" (Bose, 1929).

Specific Concepts. Studies of children's religious concepts have revealed that while they are specific in nature, they vary in detail according to the pictures the child has seen and the teachings he has had from adults. Most children have a concept of *God* as a person, made of flesh and blood, not as a spirit or ghost. He is very large, has a kindly or stern face, is old, wears long white flowing garments, and has a white beard or whiskers. Some children think of God as wearing a crown and having wings. God's role is that of a creator, a provider, and a controller of natural phenomena. He can see everything everywhere and He spends his time watching people to see how they behave. If they are bad, he punishes them, though he can be supplicated through prayer. While all children think of God as all-powerful, some think of him as kind, while others regard him as terrifying and awe-inspiring. Most children think of God's abode as in the heavens or in the clouds (Hall, 1891; Leuba, 1916; Case, 1921; Mudge, 1923; MacLean, 1930; Jones, 1943; Kuhlen and Arnold, 1944).

Like his concept of God, the child's other religious concepts are influenced by the religious training he has received and the pictures he has seen. *Heaven* is a place where people have everything they want, especially the things they have not had in daily life, and where there is eternal hap-piness and peace. The people who go to Heaven become *angels* and wear long flowing white garments with wings to enable them to fly around. It is ruled over by God just as the earth is. *Hell,* by contrast, is a place where there is eternal unhappiness and punishment, ranging from fire to being deprived of all pleasures. It is ruled over by the *Devil,* who is in the form of a man with horns and tail and who carries a pitchfork. He is red all over as is Hell.

Most children believe in *miracles* and accept the fact that God could do anything. *Church* is a place where people are made good, while *Sunday* is a day of fairly strict religious observance. Good people say their *prayers* daily and can expect to have them answered. The *Bible* was written by God, every word of it is true, and it is sinful to doubt the Bible. What happens to a person *after death* depends on what sort of life he lived on the earth. These concepts, in general, are very similar for all children of the Christian faith (Hall, 1891; MacLean, 1930; Carlson, 1934; Kuhlen and Arnold, 1944; Allport et al., 1948; Remmers et al., 1951; Gilliland, 1953; Brown, 1954).

Closely related to the child's religious concepts is his concept of *Santa Claus.* Children under four years of age accept every detail of the Santa Claus myth. The five-year-old accepts the realism of Santa's clothes, his hearty laugh, and his reindeer. By the time the child is six years old, he is aware of the fact that many children doubt the existence of Santa Claus, but he tries to repel all suspicion. A year later, there are moments of skepticism, but he clings to his belief because of the enjoyment he derives from it. By the time the child is nine, the Santa Claus myth has been abandoned (Gesell and Ilg, 1946).

Religious Doubt. While most young children accept religious teachings on faith and believe implicitly whatever they are taught, whether it be in answer to their questions or merely as a part of the routine religious instruction at home or in Sunday school, there are times when almost every child expresses doubt. This is apt to occur when the children's prayers were not answered. Religious doubt is more frequently experienced by very bright children than by those whose intellectual development is of a lower order. When the young child does question his religious teaching, his reactions are unemotional and objective. When the episode that gave rise to the doubt is passed, his doubt likewise passes and is quickly forgotten.

The older child is often confused about denominational differences in religion and questions which doctrines are right. Likewise, he may become critical of some of the religious concepts he learned when he was a little child. This may be due to the inadequacies and inconsistencies in his religious teaching which leads the child to try to reconcile the conflicting information he gets (Case, 1921), but it is more likely to result from his studies in school, especially his study of science. By the time the child reaches adolescence, his greater mental maturity and his increased knowledge lead to serious religious doubts (Kuhlen and Arnold, 1944; Allport et al., 1948; Gilliland, 1953).

Very often a critical attitude is assumed by the child because he enjoys asking questions to put the Sunday-school teacher "on the spot." What thus appears to be religious doubt is, in reality, little more than a form of childish smartness. How superficial the critical attitude of the child is may be seen by the fact that he is not worried or distressed because he cannot or will not accept in an uncritical fashion what is taught him. He forgets the whole matter after Sunday school is over. This contrasts markedly with the adolescent, who ponders over the matter and becomes emotionally disturbed when religious concepts conflict with scientific or pseudoscientific ones.

Children's Prayers. Almost as soon as a little child can pronounce words, the average parent believes it is time for him to learn to say his prayers at night before going to sleep. Most children accept the idea of praying as a part of the routine of going to bed and only occasionally take an irreverent attitude toward it. If the child is taught to end his prayer with the plea, "God bless Mommy, God bless Daddy," and this is repeated for all his friends and relatives, the prayer has somewhat more of a personal meaning for him than it otherwise would have, though the meaning of the word "bless" is unknown to the child.

The prayers that appeal most to a child are those which contain action and are familiar (Welford, 1946). While most younger children say prayers in a somewhat parrotlike fashion as they have memorized them, the older child often makes up his own prayers (Jersild, 1954). Children under eight years of age feel that prayer is a way of talking to God and that God answers prayers by telling children how to be good or what to do or not do. There is also a strong emphasis on requests for material things and for help in doing things the child feels he is incapable of doing alone. The older child puts more emphasis on asking for help than for material objects, for forgiveness for wrongdoing, or he may even use prayer as a way of thanking God for His help (MacLean, 1930; Fahs, 1932; Sherrill, 1939; Kuhlen and Arnold, 1944). On the whole, however, children's prayers are a form of "begging ritual" (Manwell and Fahs, 1951) with emphasis on "pennies-from-heaven" (Jersild, 1954).

An analysis of prayers of children has revealed that they fall into three major categories, each of which relates to specific things the child seeks through prayer. These three categories are (Fahs, 1932):

1. Variety and abundance of the good things of life for which little children are encouraged to thank God. These blessings range from "the morning light" to the "clothes we wear." This idea is expressed in grace said at the table. An example of this type of prayer is

> For my big ball and kiddie car
> On which I ride so fast and far
> Thank you, Father, thank you.

2. Direct petitions for special privileges, such as protection and care, especially during the night, and for guidance. This is illustrated by the child's favorite prayer:

> Now I lay me down to sleep,
> I pray thee, Lord, my soul to keep.
> If I should die before I wake,
> I pray thee, Lord, my soul to take.
> If I should live for other days,
> I pray thee, Lord, to guide my ways.

3. Prayers for personal help in doing things which the children are led to believe they cannot achieve by themselves, such as,

Father lead me day by day
Ever in thine own sweet way.
If I'm tempted to do wrong
Make me steadfast, wise, and strong.
Show me what I ought to do,
Teach me to be pure and true.

While the child uses prayer as a means of requesting many things from God, as in the case of the awkward boy who, finding himself inferior in sports, prayed, "O God, help me to run fast" (Fahs, 1932), the child is often disappointed when his requests are not granted and, in time, is likely to become skeptical of the value of prayer. The result is that he prays voluntarily less than he formerly did. True, he may pray from force of habit or because it is expected of him, but he has little confidence that it will bring any results. Thus prayer in the older child and the adolescent is likely to degenerate into a ritual with little meaning for the individual (Beekman, 1947; Allport et al., 1948; Brown and Lowe, 1951; Remmers et al., 1951).

Religious Services. Religious services in Sunday school or church may appeal to the child because of their colorful pageantry. He usually likes to sing, and the ritual of the church service intrigues him. He enjoys looking around at people at worship, to see what they are doing. His attitude is a strange mixture of awed reverence and curiosity. Because there is a tendency for the child to be active, he should be an active participant in religious expressions, such as singing hymns and participating in religious dramas and festivals at Christmas and Easter, and in rendering social service in the name of religion (Smith, 1941).

When the novelty of the service wears off, the child begins to rebel against church attendance. He enjoys going to Sunday school only so long as his friends go, too. He likes young people's organizations, such as gymnasiums in the cities and "sociables" in small communities, picnics, holiday celebrations, and outings. His interest is thus primarily social rather than religious. At this point, a rather small percentage of boys and girls *attend* Sunday school and an even smaller percentage go to church. As a general principle, the percentage becomes smaller as the community becomes larger. That is, in large cities a smaller percentage of children attend religious services than are found to do so in small towns or country villages (Lantz, 1949).

When families attend church very infrequently, the child is less active than when the families are more active participants in church affairs. Families split by death or divorce are less active participants than families that are not split. When both parents have different religious affiliations, they are less active in church affairs than when split by divorce. If one parent has no church affiliation, there is little religious participation. These factors influence the child's church attendance. Children brought up in homes where there is little religious observance in the form of grace at meals, Bible reading, or child training in bedtime prayers are less active in their church attendance than children from homes where there are more home observances of religion, but not significantly so (Anders, 1955). By the time children reach the high-school age, there is a marked decline in Sunday-school and church attendance, especially among boys (Punke, 1936; Elias, 1949; Recreation Survey, 1954).

2. DEATH

Every child, at some time or other, becomes deeply interested in and concerned about death, funerals, and what happens to the individual after death. When this interest will appear and how strong it will be depends, to a large extent, upon environmental influences. When death comes close to a child, through the death of a pet animal, a member of the family, or a friend, the child's interest will be stronger than if the death is of a person whom the child knows only slightly.

As is true of the child's interest in religion, interest in death is of an objective, impersonal sort. The child regards it as something that happens to other people, but he does not think of it in relation to himself. Furthermore, because of his limited ability to comprehend the meaning of things not immediately present, it is difficult, if not impossible, for him to grasp the meaning of the finality of death. Children are not, as a rule interested in or concerned about their own deaths. They think of death as being in the remote future, too far away to be of any real concern to them (Schilder and Wechsler, 1934).

The child's lack of concern about his own death may be explained by the fact that he is unable to comprehend the real meaning of death while he is still young. Studies of children's concepts of death have revealed that they develop according to a pattern as follows:

1. Between the ages of three and five years, the child denies death as a regular and final process. He attributes life and consciousness to the dead and believes that a dead person or animal is only asleep. Furthermore, he wants to know where and how the person continues to live after death. He is puzzled about how the person can move in a coffin. Between the ages of five and six years, he begins to think of death as a gradual or temporary thing, but he does not comprehend the meaning of its finality.

2. Between the ages of five and nine years, death is personified, being imagined to be either a separate person or one identified with the dead.

3. Only after the age of nine years does the child recognize death as the cessation of corporeal life and as inevitable (Nagy, 1948).

How death is presented to a child will influence greatly not only his concept of death but also the degree and kind of interest he has in it. A child who has had a traumatic experience related to death will not only fear death but will also have a very different interest in death than has the child whose experience has been of a pleasanter sort (Caprio, 1950). Children think of death more as resulting from violence than from disease. It is considered not as the natural end of life but as the result of the hostility of others or as punishment for wrongdoing, with God generally thought of as the punishing agent (Schilder and Wechsler, 1934). Movies, television, and comics contribute to this concept of death.

All children are, at some time or other, afraid of being alone or of being abandoned by the death of parents and loved ones. Many worries of older children concern the possibility of death of their parents which they fear mainly because of what will happen to themselves (pages 234–235). If religious teaching emphasizes taking the child away from the loved one and punishing one or the other for wrongdoing, it is likely to establish a real fear of death, which may be so pronounced that it will become an obsession with the child.

As Jersild (1954) has pointed out, "The image of being abandoned into the hands of a wrathful and avenging God who will punish children for their sins is not one to comfort a child. The picture of hell from which there is no escape, a hell which in its description and geographic placement is definitely out of reach of his parents (who probably are going to heaven anyway, and between the two there is a vast gulf) offers about as bleak a prospect of abandonment as any child can imagine." Even as late as adolescence, the individual is still uncertain as to what happens after death (Anthony, 1940; Kuhlen and Arnold, 1944; Allport et al., 1948; Bernarda, 1949).

3. THE HUMAN BODY

One of the earliest forms of exploratory behavior of young babies is watching and investigating their own bodies. When lying flat on his back, the baby will hold his hands before his eyes, wiggle his fingers, and watch what happens. Much of the pulling of his hair, nose, or ears; the poking of his fingers into the different orifices of the body, as the mouth, ears, nose, and navel; and the scratching of his skin and hair are exploratory in nature. Later, when he discovers a mirror and how it works, he spends much time observing himself in it (Gesell and Ilg, 1946, 1949).

By the time the child is 3½ years old, there is a greater interest in the body than in younger children. Children of this age are especially interested in their own bodies, how they function, and what the different parts of the body are used for (Gesell and Ilg, 1946, 1949). This interest is shown in comments and questions about the various parts of the body; by examining the navel, eyes, hair, breast, and anus; by looking at themselves in the mirror and calling the attention of other children to different parts of their bodies, and by some tendency toward exhibitionism. Like many other interests of the child, the interest in his body is objective and impersonal. The behavior of children during elimination is just as matter-of-fact as brushing their hair (Dillon, 1934).

Children under 3½ years of age generally do not differentiate between the sexes. Even difference in the appearance of the genitals does not carry a sex significance, but is accepted like individual differences in hair or eye color. By the time the child is five years old, however, he recognizes anatomical differences between boys and girls, but only as incidental characteristics. Most emphasis is placed on differences in styles of clothing, manner of wearing the hair, customs of the two sexes, and names. This may be seen in such comments as "Boys wear ties and girls do not" and "Boys have short hair" (Dillon, 1934).

The youngest ages at which children have been found to name the various differences between the two sexes are as follows (Conn and Kanner, 1947):

Differences	Youngest age at which differences were named, years
Hair	4
Clothes	5
Eyes	5
Hands	5
Face	6 (almost 7)
Complexion	7
Legs and feet	8
Figure	8
Strength	8
Gait	9 (almost 10)

To discover how children react to the discovery of genital differences, Conn (1939, 1940, 1948) questioned children four to twelve years old. The reports given showed that a large percentage responded to the first sight of genital differences with tranquil, unperturbed acceptance. Even though they were not prepared, the unexpected did not upset them. Some referred to the genitals as "funny" (meaning "strange"), because they were surprised at not seeing the same genitals in the opposite sex as they themselves had. Only a small percentage of the children indicated that they felt that something was "wrong," that girls had once had the same genitals as boys, but they had been cut off or broken off. There were varying degrees of curiosity about the differences in the genitals, but the average child was not upset about the matter.

The child's interest in his body does not, as a rule, include interest in health. Children who are healthy have little concern about how to keep their bodies in good condition, or fear that they will suffer from illness that may damage their bodies. In spite of the emphasis placed on the importance of good health in the home and school, few children are really interested in health unless their health is so poor that it handicaps them in doing what other children do. It is not until the child reaches adolescence and appreciates the relationship between health and looks or health and the activities he wants to engage in that he becomes health-conscious (Symonds, 1937; Lantagne, 1950).

4. SEX

It was formerly believed that the child was asexual and that sex behavior was dormant until puberty. Any behavior related to sex was regarded as abnormal or as a sign of precocious sexual development. Likewise, any emotional reaction that related to sex was believed to be dormant until puberty. When sex emotions appeared, this was regarded as an indication of the end of childhood and the beginning of maturity. Freud (1920) was the first to emphasize that "from the third year on, there is no longer any doubt concerning the presence of a sexual life in the child." He further contended that childhood sexuality is responsible for the type of mature sexuality attained in adult years. In addition, Freud was the first to recognize the fact that the sex development of the individual follows a pattern as definite and predictable in form as the pattern of development of other aspects of the child's life.

It is now known not only that there is sexuality in childhood, but that it differs markedly from the sexuality that occurs after the puberty changes have taken place. As contrasted with the definite and focalized sexuality of adolescence, it is of a generalized and diffused sort. Likewise, while sexuality is a dominant factor in the life of the adolescent and has a wide influence on his behavior, in the child it is of only secondary importance and plays a relatively inconspicuous role in his life.

Sensitivity in the genital region during the early years of life has been reported as an indication of early sexuality. Erection of the penis occurs as early as the second month of life and is frequently observed in boys of the preschool age. This is usually caused by fullness of the bladder, external stimulation of the genital organs, or some external irritation rather than by sexual thoughts (Moll, 1923; Conn, 1940a; Kinsey et al., 1948). Tumescence, accompanied by restlessness, crying, stretching, and flexing the limbs stiffly, has been observed in male babies as early as the third week of life (Halverson, 1940).

Love Object. The young baby's first love is for himself. In this *autoerotic* stage, which lasts for the first five or six months of life, the baby shows no attachment for others. The first object of attachment is the *mother, nurse,* or *person who takes care of the child.* Gradually, during the babyhood years, love attachments are extended to other members of the home environment, whether members of the family or servants. The strongest attachments are for those who make the child's associations especially happy. Even household pets and toys may become the object of the young child's affection. Often, the attachment to a pet or a toy and the affection for it are stronger than the love directed toward persons.

When the child begins to play with *other children,* he singles out one or two children and develops a strong emotional attachment for them. At first, the affection is directed toward an older child who, like the adult, makes the child the center of attention. Because associations of this sort are pleasant to the child, he builds up an affectionate attitude toward his playmate. At the end of the preschool age, as children of the same age learn to play together in an amicable fashion, the child singles out one or two children of his own age for whom he shows real affection. Like his associations with adults for whom he has an affectionate attachment, his contacts with the children he loves are always pleasant.

Which sex the young child favors will depend to a large extent upon his associations. In the case of adults, the baby and the very young child most often favor the female members of the household because their most frequent associations are with them. Later, should the male members of the home prove to be more indulgent, the child may transfer his affection to father, uncles, or older brothers. Little girls very often show a preference for fathers and brothers, while little boys show a preference for their mothers and sisters. This may be explained by the treatment they receive from the different members of the home group.

In the choice of playmates of their own age, little children play with members of both sexes. Even in the preschool groups, there is a tendency toward unisexual friendships, as was stressed in the chapter on social development. This increases as the child grows older, with the result that, by the time the child reaches kindergarten or first grade, there is a marked tendency for boys to prefer boys, and girls to prefer girls. Girls will include boys in their play more readily than boys will include girls. The following characteristics of the sex development of children, five to eight years of age, have been observed:

1. Children will play with boys or girls and are not embarrassed when found with members of the opposite sex.
2. They are not embarrassed by physical affection from adults or by physical contact with members of the opposite sex.
3. They are not self-conscious about their bodies, and they show no signs of modesty.
4. Boys and girls fight one another.
5. Boys show no special courtesy toward women.
6. They do not differentiate play or work as "girl's" or "boy's" (Campbell, 1939).

During childhood, *an occasional romance* between a boy and girl grows up. There is, in this type of romance, an attitude of affection and respect on the part of the boy, accompanied by a desire to serve the beloved. This may consist merely of carrying her books to and from school and protecting her from the teasing and torments of a boys' gang. It differs markedly from adolescent romances in that there is no physical expression of affection, other than perhaps an occasional shy holding of hands. The attitude of the girl toward the boy may be likewise one of deep affection, but there is no desire on her part for physical demonstrations of this affection.

Girls are more tolerant in their attitude toward childhood romances than are boys. They may snicker at and make jokes about the girl who is engaged in such a romance, but they do not exclude her from their group, as the boy is excluded from the boys' gang. In many instances, there is definite evidence that they are envious of the girl who has a boy to accompany her to school and who receives thoughtful attentions instead of the annoyances that they have been accustomed to receive from other boys.

Expressions of Affection. The expressions of affection for the loved one consist of patting, fondling, or kissing, and a desire for close, personal contact. This may take the extreme form of following the loved one wherever she goes and raising stormy protests if this is impossible, as when the mother or the nurse leaves the house without taking the child along. Pets and favorite toys are caressed, hugged, kissed, and carried around wherever the young child goes until they literally fall to pieces. If permitted to do so, the child takes a beloved toy to bed and hugs it in his arms, even while asleep.

Shirley (1933) refers to reports by mothers of the earliest signs of affection in the behavior of babies. This is shown by patting the mother's breast while nursing and by cuddling down contentedly when held at the mother's shoulder. During the seventh and eighth months, the mothers reported that the babies showed affection by patting the mother's face, turning their cheeks to be kissed, clasping the mother around the neck, laying their cheeks on the mother's, hugging, and biting. The expressions of affection through patting and hugging, Shirley believed to be spontaneous, while the other expressions were taught the babies by their parents.

Expressions of affection in young children are of brief duration. Children may show great fondness for a person while that person is present, but as soon as the individual leaves, he or she is forgotten. It is definitely a case of "out of sight, out of mind." When a beloved member of the family leaves the home, as in the case of death or divorce, or when the nurse leaves the household, the young child never seems to miss the person. He soon transfers his affection to an individual who is present and forgets about the former individual who had dominated his affection.

Sex Antagonism. From six to twelve years of age, there is a gradual development of an attitude of antagonism between the sexes. Boys and girls who formerly played together in an amicable fashion begin, during the first or second grade of school, to play more predominantly with individuals of their own sex. And with the growth of interest in play activities of members of their own sex comes the attitude, on the part of boys, that girls' play is "silly" or "sissified," while girls regard boys' play as "rowdy" or "hoodlum." It is not surprising, then, to find that antagonisms between the two sexes that grew up in relation to play activities develop into a general attitude of antagonism toward the opposite sex (Lehman and Witty, 1927a; Furfey, 1930; Koch, 1944; Garrison, 1952). Elementary-school children have been found to rate members of their own sex higher in personality traits than members of the opposite sex. Each sex shows a decided preference for members of the same sex until the eighth grade, when the two sexes come closer together (Amatora, 1954).

Causes of Sex Antagonism. There is, in this antagonism between the two sexes, *no indication of a physiological cause.* Rather, the cause is *social,* and the blame can be placed on the early training in play activities which puts emphasis on different play for the two sexes. An increase in the antagonism comes from the fact that, instead of taking the attitude of "live and let live," boys delight in teasing, tormenting, and interfering with girls' play, while girls, in self-defense, never miss an opportunity to get their revenge by telling tales on boys at home or in school. It is not surprising, then, to discover that, even in the household, quarrels between brothers and sisters are far more common than expressions of affection (Neustadt and Myerson, 1940; Alpert, 1941; Davis, 1944; Kinsey et al., 1948, 1953; Amatora, 1954).

Effects on Behavior. As a result of this antagonistic behavior, the two sexes spontaneously draw apart. Even in school classes where both sexes are taught together, boys prefer to sit on one side of the room and girls on the other. During recess, before and after school, the boys group together, as do the girls, and avoid one another as much as possible. Any attempt to bring them together, as in parties, arouses a storm of protest on both sides. Even when brought together in family gatherings, boys and girls of this age are barely civil to one another. Sex antagonism is so extreme in boys that they do not want anything that resembles a girl. Figure 59 shows graphically the typical attitude of boys toward girls at this age.

Among girls, the antagonistic attitude toward boys is *less pronounced* than in the case of boys. As a matter of fact, it is more nearly an attitude of indifference than of active antagonism in situations in which the girls ignore the boys, instead of tormenting them. They regard boys as rough, dirty, vulgar, and ill-mannered, and their play as boresome. But, if left alone, they pay no attention to the boys. Likewise, instead of making fun of love in others, as boys do, their attitude is one of indifference (Maller, 1929; Campbell, 1939; Smith, 1939; Koch, 1944; Kinsey et al., 1948, 1953; Amatora, 1954. See pages 291–292 for more details about sex antagonism).

Curiosity about Sex. In the process of exploring his body, the baby sooner

or later touches his sex organs. He then discovers that this results in a
pleasurable sensation. By chance, he discovers his navel and derives fun
from putting his fingers in the "hole." Other than that, sex arouses no
curiosity on his part until approximately the end of the third year, when
the boy notices that his body differs from that of the little girl, that he
stands up when he goes to the toilet while she sits down, and that adults
have certain physical features, such as "bumps" and hair on the body, which

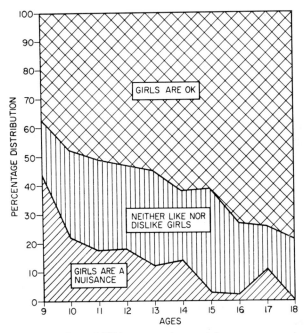

Fig. 59. Anonymous reactions of 700 boys, age nine to eighteen, to a question concerning
their attitude toward girls. (*Based on unpublished data of R. T. Sollenberger. From
F. K. Shuttleworth, The adolescent period: a graphic atlas, Monogr. Soc. Res. Child
Develpm.*, 1949, **14**, No. 1. *Used by permission.*)

little children do not have. The genitals are the focus of interest in the
young child (Conn and Kanner, 1940). The young child's attitude is
completely impersonal and objective, with none of the morbid interest
one associates with adolescent curiosity.

Six-year-olds show an active and frank curiosity about sex matters, more
far-reaching in scope than that shown by preschool children. They are
definitely aware of differences in the body structure of the two sexes and
seek an explanation for this difference. This curiosity is not purely intellectual, but has a strong emotional drive. As children grow older, sexual
curiosity becomes disguised and less outspoken. The curiosity and interest

remain aggressive, however, and are often of a sadistic nature. They may even take on an obsessional character and remain confined in scope (Alpert, 1941).

When a new baby arrives in the household or neighborhood, the young child is naturally curious to know where it came from. Any explanation that is logical he will accept, and this will satisfy his curiosity for the time at least. Preschool children generally think of babies as coming from God or as being bought from stores. About one-third refer to the hospital as the place where babies are obtained. By the time children are seven or eight years old, they know that doctors bring babies, and they are aware of the fact that the mother has some role in the coming of the baby. Children from nine to eleven years old have heard their playmates discuss various conceptions of the origin of babies, and some know about genital contact. Very intelligent children are generally precocious in their knowledge of reproduction (Conn, 1948).

In spite of the child's curiosity about sex, there is an almost universal resistance on the part of children to the acceptance of the truth regarding sex. This resistance comes from fears due to (1) the alliance of the genital and urinary tracts and the close proximity of both to the lower end of the gastrointestinal tract; (2) punishment and prohibition of pleasurable sensations that come from the stimulation of the genital areas, fear of mental dullness, insanity, or loss of strength; and (3) fear of injuring someone through sex aggression (Gardner, 1944).

Expressions of Curiosity. As Conn (1940a) has pointed out, "all children, at one time or another, ask questions concerning a variety of topics. It is therefore not surprising that they also include questions about the topic of sex." But, when the topic of sex is raised, parents frequently become embarrassed or even shocked, in spite of the fact that the parent helped the child to express himself on previous occasions. Many parents try to avoid discussions of sex on the grounds that they want to "prevent calamities." The result of this attitude is to drive the child elsewhere for information. This is shown by the fact that the average child from the ages of four through twelve years asks his parents less than two questions about sex. The more intelligent the child, the more questions he is likely to ask (Conn, 1948).

Among preschool children, the most common questions relate to the origin of babies, the coming of another baby, the sex organs and their functions, and physical sex differences. Among older children, emphasis is placed on questions about the origin of babies, the process of birth, and the relation of the father to reproduction (Hattendorf, 1932). Typical questions asked by three- to twelve-year-olds are: "Will she have baby birds some day?" "Do the baby deer come out of an egg like the chickens do?" "Does it hurt the baby deer when it comes out of the mother deer?" "Does the baby calf come out of the mother?" "Do they look like little seeds?" (Davis, 1932.)

One of the difficulties children have in obtaining information about sex through questioning is lack of an adequate sex vocabulary. However, most children acquire names for the genital organs, such as "thing" for both the male and female genital organ. They have a few they reserve for the female genital—"puss," "hole," "susie," and "pocketbook." The male genital is generally referred to as "teapot," "piece of rope," or "hose." Most children have two or three synonyms and use these interchangeably (Conn and Kanner, 1947).

Sex curiosity frequently expresses itself in *exploration* of the sex organs. At the age of six, mutual exploration is common. The search to discover what the sex organs are and how they function is often carried to dangerous extremes, such as the insertion of short, unclean, or rusty objects into body orifices. "Doctor games" are popular at this age and give the child an excuse to examine the sex organs of his playmates. Among eight-year-olds, sex behavior consists of mutual exploration of a homosexual and heterosexual sort, such as matching masculine prowess in the toilet, peeping, smutty jokes, provocative giggling, some masturbation, obscene language, and "secrets" about "boy-girl" favorites. Much the same behavior is observed in children from nine years of age until puberty, except that there is progressively more provocative heterosexual behavior. The most common forms are insertion of the penis into the girl's vagina, manual exploration associated with direct observation of the reproductive anatomy, exhibitionism, and oral contacts (Alpert, 1941; Ramsey, 1943a; Kinsey et al., 1948, 1953).

Sex play with members of the same sex, *homosexual* play, is likewise a form of sex exploration. This is more common than heterosexual play. It generally takes the form of exhibition of the genitals, manual manipulation of the genitals, mutual manipulation of the genitals, and anal or oral contacts with genitals. In the case of both heterosexual and homosexual play, the child generally engages in such play with companions close to his own age, though the initial experience is often with an older child or an adult (Alpert, 1941; Ramsey, 1943a; Kinsey et al., 1948, 1953). Children who engage in sex play are normal both physically and mentally, though they often have an inadequate family life (Bender and Paster, 1941), and it is found among children in primitive as well as in civilized cultures (Mead, 1949; Pitje, 1951). Most sex play ends with the onset of adolescence (Kinsey et al., 1948). The trend in sex play is shown in Fig. 60.

Much that is considered *masturbation* is not really so. It is a form of sex exploration and is carried out primarily to satisfy the child's curiosity about the genital organs and the sensations he receives when stroking,

fondling, or playing with them. Technically, the term "masturbation"—
though it is widely used, even in scientific literature, to describe the
behavior of young children in the stimulation of their genital organs—
should be reserved for cases of genital stimulation which is followed by
pleasurable feeling or orgasm. During the first six years, the child at some
time or other, in the process of investigating his body, discovers by chance
that touching the genitals gives more pleasurable sensations than touching
any other part of his body. It is not surprising that the little child repeats
the act, especially when he is alone and has little to engage his attention and
interest. Manipulation of the sex organs may also be aroused by local
irritations or pressure from too tight clothing (Ramsey, 1943a; Kinsey et al.,
1948, 1953).

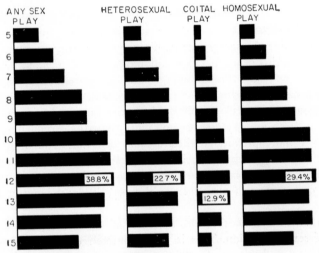

Fig. 60. Types of sex play among children. (*From A. C. Kinsey, W. B. Pomeroy, and
C. E. Martin, Sexual behavior in the human male, Saunders, 1948. Used by permission.*)

Among young children, masturbation serves to release tension. The
young child makes no attempt to conceal play with his sex organs nor does
he show shame or guilt when caught in the act (Dillon, 1934). The school
child who has learned from scoldings or punishment that playing with
his sex organs is considered naughty generally practices masturbation when
alone. If he has not discovered the pleasurable sensations that come from
playing with the sex organs through his own exploration, he generally
learns to do so from watching other children or from the suggestions
of older children. Boys are generally introduced to masturbation as a "new
sport" by older boys or by adults (Kinsey et al., 1948; Hollingshead, 1949).
Most girls learn from their own exploration or from watching other girls
(Landis et al., 1940; Kinsey et al., 1953). Almost always, these practices

are carried out in the absence of adults, when the child is in bed, or when he is studying. Masturbation has been reported to be more common among boys than among girls (Koch, 1935; Landis et al., 1940; Ramsey, 1943a; Kinsey et al., 1948, 1953).

Sex Education. Sex instruction, if it is to be complete and adequate to meet the needs of present-day life, should be of two types: *constructive* and *preventative. Constructive education* should build up healthy attitudes about sex and marriage, while *preventative education* should not terrify the child

Constructive sex education helps to build healthy attitudes about sex. (*From Adolescent Development, a McGraw-Hill Text-Film.*)

because of the morbid emphasis on the ill effects that come from sexual promiscuity, but should teach the child what to avoid in his sexual relationships, just as he is taught what to avoid because of the possible danger to him in other aspects of his life. If the preventative teaching be of this type, it will tend to establish a healthy attitude of caution, which will have a pronounced effect on the behavior of the individual, especially during the adolescent years.

There is no one best time to give sex instruction. It varies from one child to another and should be determined by the child's curiosity. As a general principle, the time for giving sex instruction and the amount given should be determined by the child's questions rather than by any set rules. Whenever the child asks questions about sex, he should be given information in a correct, matter-of-fact way, just as he would be if his questions dealt with the weather or why we live in houses instead of huts.

Most children have a considerable amount of information about sex before they are ten years old. This information relates mostly to the origin of babies and sex differences. Little information is given about puberty changes, though girls are often informed about menstruation shortly before the menarche, or first menstruation (Hattendorf, 1932; Terman et al., 1938; Ramsey, 1943; Kinsey et al., 1948, 1953). One obstacle to giving children adequate sex instruction is their limited knowledge of standard terms used to refer to sex. Most children use vernacular terms when they refer to sex matters and are, therefore, unfamiliar with technical terms and their meanings. Because of this fact, children find it difficult to read even the simplest printed matter on sex (Conn and Kanner, 1947).

Sources of Information. Most children, especially boys, get their first information about sex from their companions or from their own experiences. Much of their information comes from the grapevine and from dirty jokes and stories. Girls, by contrast, usually get their first information from their parents, though they, like boys, get much information from their companions, from dirty stories and jokes, and from books. When instruction is given in the home, the mother usually instructs the girl while the father instructs the boy (Landis et al., 1940; Ramsey, 1943a; Duvall and Motz, 1945; Rockwood and Ford, 1945; Kinsey et al., 1948, 1953; Elias, 1949; Hollingshead, 1949; Lee, 1952).

How adequate the child's sex instruction will be will depend to some extent upon the knowledge his parents have. Children from professional homes usually have more and more accurate information about sex than do children from clerical, skilled, or unskilled-laboring-class homes (Phipps, 1949). Children whose mothers are employed, especially when they are in professional or executive work, usually have more information than children whose mothers are housewives (Lee, 1952). Few children, even when they reach the adolescent years, feel that their sex instruction has been adequate (Landis et al., 1940; Ramsey, 1943a; Duvall and Motz, 1945; Brown, 1948; Kirkendall, 1948; Ellis and Fuller, 1950). Girls who have one or two foreign-born parents claim they have had a better sex education than girls whose parents are American feel that they have had (Duvall and Motz, 1945). There is a trend toward giving sex instruction earlier now than was true in the past and toward getting information more from parents and relatives than from playmates and relatives (Landis, 1951). These trends are illustrated in Figs. 61 and 62.

Attitude toward Sex. Whether the child's attitude toward sex will be favorable or unfavorable will be influenced by the attitudes of the people from whom he gets his information. The "conspiracy of silence" in the home tends to lead to unfavorable attitudes (Desenberg, 1947). Children who get their first information about sex from their parents or from school have more favorable attitudes than do those who receive most of their

Fig. 61. Proportion of rural and urban women in two generations who received first sex information before age thirteen. Note that rural women of both mother and daughter generations more often received sex information in the preadolescent period than did urban women. (*From P. H. Landis, Marriage preparation in two generations, Marriage Fam. Living,* 1951, **13**, 155-156. *Used by permission.*)

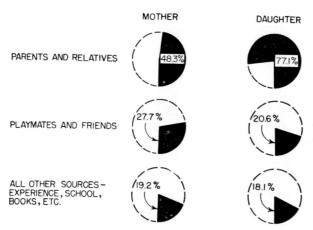

Fig. 62. Proportion of two generations receiving first sex information from specified sources. The percentages total more than 100 because several subjects mentioned more than one source. (*From P. H. Landis, Marriage preparation in two generations, Marriage Fam. Living,* 1951, **13**, 155-156. *Used by permission.*)

information from their companions or similar sources (Duvall and Motz, 1945; Drucker et al., 1952; Lee, 1952). Children whose parents are better educated and who belong to the higher socioeconomic groups have more favorable attitudes than do children whose parents are less well educated and who come from lower socioeconomic groups (Lee, 1952). Children who receive their information from parents, doctors, nurses, adult friends of the family, school, or reading have been found to have more favorable attitudes than do those who receive most of their instruction from the clergy (Drucker et al., 1952).

When the child is made to feel ashamed or guilty because of his questions about sex or because of sex play, he is likely to establish an unfavorable attitude toward sex. This is likewise true when adults are amused by the sexual manifestations of the child (Hoch and Zubin, 1949). As early as the third or fourth year of the child's life, social pressures are beginning to be felt in the child's attitude toward sex. There is also the beginning of social-level differences in attitudes at this time. The ease or embarrassment with which children discuss the genitals, the origin of babies, or other matters related to sex suggest that the child has already acquired some of the influence of the social attitudes (Kinsey et al., 1948).

5. IDEAL SELF

Because of his interest in himself as an individual, every child has an ideal that he would like to attain. This ideal self is generally a concept built up from his contacts with people, from his readings, and the movies or television shows he has seen. For the most part, it is beyond the reach of the child because it is too remote from his abilities to make its attainment possible. Very few children are satisfied with themselves as they are. As a result, they want to appear different from what they are and to behave in a manner that will make them more popular and successful (Strang, 1954). The ideal self is thus a concept built up to fill a need and to act as a guide to the attainment of what they want to be.

Sources of Ideal. Studies of children's ideals have revealed the sources from which the child derives his ideal. These studies have shown that the child's ideal changes as he grows older and that his experiences outside the home have a marked influence on the concept of ideal self he develops. For the most part, the ideal comes from the child's immediate environment and is derived from his contacts, either directly or indirectly, with people he admires and would like to resemble. Most children follow a pattern of ideals, which is as follows:

Parents
Teachers and parent-surrogates, such as club leaders
Successful agemates and those just older than the child
Glamorous adults, such as movie stars, athletes, and soldiers
Heroes read about
Attractive young adults within the individual's range of observation (Havighurst, 1950, 1953)

The young child first selects as his ideal a parent or some member of the family. By the time he reaches the second grade and his contacts have broadened, his ideal is his teacher or some acquaintance outside the home or school. From then on, there is an increasing interest in ideals from outside the home and remote sources, such as history, contemporary affairs, or the stage and screen. By the time the child reaches adolescence, his ideal is likely to be some young adult whom he knows and admires (Hill, 1930; Jersild et al., 1933; Stoughton and Ray, 1946; Havighurst et al., 1946; Winker, 1949; Havighurst, 1950, 1953). Very few children choose foreigners as their ideal. When historical or public characters are chosen, they are generally Americans (Hill, 1930). Very few ideals are taken from literature, fiction, or religion (Hill, 1930; Stoughton and Ray, 1946).

Boys choose more ideals from remote environments at every age than do girls. They idealize those who have important roles and status in our society. Girls, by contrast, generally idealize people who have made a success in social life and who are attractive in appearance (Hill, 1930; Winker, 1949). As the child grows older, association with people in positions of prestige has a marked influence on his choice of an ideal (Havighurst et al., 1946). Boys who come from the higher socioeconomic groups more often idealize their fathers than do boys from the lower groups (Carpenter and Eisenberg, 1938). It is not until adolescence that class consciousness plays an important role in the child's selection of his ideal (Havighurst et al., 1946; Abbe, 1950).

How important a role the child's environment plays in the choice of his ideal may be seen by the fact that while young children's main desire is for material possessions, the child in the elementary school begins to desire to "be someone." This desire usually reaches its peak between the ages of fifteen and sixteen years. The older child realizes better than does the younger child the importance of an established place in society, and this changes his concept of what is valuable from material possessions to social status. His ideal is then selected because the individual represents a well-recognized position in our society (Winker, 1949). Children from the lower socioeconomic groups more often name a glamorous person as their ideal than do children from the higher socioeconomic groups (Havighurst et al., 1946).

From the different people he idealizes as he grows older, the child builds up a *composite* picture of the ideal self. In this concept, he combines the qualities of his parents with those of outsiders as his ego ideal (Havighurst et al., 1946). Younger children have only very general ideas of what they would like to be and how they would like to change themselves. Older children and adolescents have very specific ideas about these matters (Winker, 1949). Very few boys would like to change to a girl, if they could, while more girls would like to be boys because of the greater advantages boys enjoy. Among elementary-school children, only about one in five would like to change from what they are. Those who would like to change want to change for the better, either physically or morally (Jersild et al., 1933; Jersild, 1954).

Effects of Ideals. The ideal the child selects represents the values stressed in the culture in which the child lives and the values within that culture that appeal most to him. In his attempt to imitate his ideal, the child accepts these values as his own, and they serve as models for his behavior (Jersild, 1954; Martin, 1954). While values within any social group in a culture change as children grow older, there are certain values that remain unchanged from age to age (Hawkes, 1952). In Fig. 63 are shown changes in values from the fourth through the sixth grades. The child's sex role likewise plays an important part in determining what values he will accept from his ideal and what ideal he will select. Boys almost always select male ideals, while girls select female ideals (Mead, 1949; Estvan, 1952).

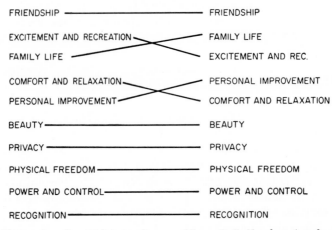

Fig. 63. Changes in values with increasing age. (*From G. R. Hawkes, A study of personal values of elementary-school children, Educ. psychol. Measmt, 1952, **12**, 654–663. Used by permission.*)

Few children are capable of attaining their ideal self. Because of inexperience, the child tends to overestimate his capacities, and he is often encouraged by his parents to believe that he can do anything he wishes, so long as he tries hard enough. For the most part, the child's ideal is more of an index of his "wishful estimate of his ability than of his real ability" (Hirsch, 1939). As Jersild (1954) has pointed out, "the idealized image of the self clashes with reality for there is something false about it—it is out of gear with the 'real self' that might have developed; it is burdensome for a person to live up to this assumed role, to keep the pose, to live as if he were or had to be something he is not cut out to be."

If a child clings to a glamorized ideal for too long, he is in for trouble. Not only will he fall short of his ideal to the point where he will feel frustrated and inadequate, but he may find himself out of step with his contemporaries.

As ideals change frequently during the childhood years, a child who keeps an ideal self based on a parent or teacher may find that his friends regard this as a case of "apron strings" and feel that he is very immature. As Sherif and Cantril (1947) have pointed out, "if the idol is a person out of the reference group, then the individual becomes a social misfit in his or her immediate surroundings." Not having an ideal to imitate is likewise bad. Many cases of problem behavior are found among those who do not have and never had an ideal with whom they could identify themselves and thus have the anchorage of security that this gives (Gough and Peterson, 1952).

6. VOCATIONAL INTERESTS

It is important to a person's success and happiness that he do the kind of work he can do well and enjoys doing. However, a too early decision of one's life work is just as serious as not deciding until it is time to go to work. Emphasis on "what are you going to do when you grow up?" is likely to force the child to make a vocational decision before he knows enough about his abilities and interests or about possible vocations in which he might fit to make a wise choice. This early choice puts a ceiling on the individual's vocational aspirations and limits the range of his interests (Pusey, 1954).

The child's vocational interests generally originate through identification with someone he admires. He decides he wants to do what his ideal does (Fagin, 1953). During the elementary-school years, the child's concepts of his future are vague, poorly defined, and fanciful. He describes the future in which getting married plays an important role. He looks forward optimistically to being on his own and having the independence that this will bring (Strang, 1954). What interest he has in money is centered mainly on the ability to earn and spend as he pleases, thus guaranteeing his independence (Prevey, 1945, 1948).

Age of Choosing. There is a steady increase in the number of vocational choices made between the ages of nine and eighteen years, when a peak occurs, owing to environmental forces which compel the individual to come to some decision about his future. As Kaplan (1946) has pointed out, "Our youngsters usually delay their vocational decisions because they are not forced to do vocational thinking until late in their school careers." Girls, as a rule, decide on their vocations later than boys because there is less pressure brought to bear on them to choose than is true of boys and there are fewer vocational choices open to them (Kaplan, 1946). Vocational interests are not well defined or stable before fifteen or sixteen years of age for most boys and girls (Fagin, 1953). While some children know as early as the sixth grade what their vocational interests are, most want to follow the parental occupation or parental wishes in this matter until they reach the mid-teens (Baxter, 1951). Professional choices, as in the case of teaching, have been found to be made earlier than decisions about factory work (Norton, 1953).

The pattern of vocational choice has been found to be very similar for the majority of children at different age levels. This pattern is as follows:

1. *Period of fantasy choices,* when the child's occupational aspirations are indiscriminate and "unreal." Instead of being governed by such occupational realities as abilities and training, the child makes fantasy attempts to play adult roles. This period lasts up to the eleventh year.

2. *Period of tentative choices,* from eleven to seventeen years, when occupational preferences are based first on likes and dislikes or interests, but later on aptitudes and capacities, and still later, on personal values and ideals.

3. *Period of realistic choices,* which occurs after the age of seventeen years, when there is consideration of occupational opportunities and other realities. (Ginzberg et al., 1951.)

Factors Influencing Choice. The young child usually accepts his parents' plans for his future as he follows other parental plans. In the early years of childhood, parents are the major influence in guiding and directing the child's vocational thinking (Kaplan, 1946). The influence of the parents is twofold. In the first place, parents put emphasis in varying degrees on jobs they think desirable. Their second area of influence is by telling children to avoid certain types of work for various reasons or by making incidental references of an unfavorable kind to the types of work they want the child to avoid. The result is that, even before the child reaches the adolescent years, the range of his vocational choice has been limited (Jahoda, 1952).

The social status of the child's family and the status parents would like to achieve for their child are important influences in the child's interest in different types of work. For the most part, parents consider social status and social prestige as more important than interest (Galler, 1951). In the case of the teaching profession, for example, upper- and upper-middle-class parents rate college teaching as best for boys, and elementary-school teaching as best for girls. Parents from the lower-middle and lower classes put less emphasis on teaching as a suitable occupation for their children (Anderson, 1954). In the case of Negro children, teaching is a favorite choice by parents for their children because of its prestige value and because of lack of competition (Harrison, 1953). Among children of the lower-income groups, vocational aspirations are increasingly away from menial work as children grow older (Goff, 1954).

In addition to parental influence, other factors that influence a child's vocational thinking are his siblings, his classmates and friends, his teachers, his relatives and adult friends of the family, and his personal or school interests. The relative importance of these factors is illustrated in Fig. 64. Children with high IQ scores choose mostly the higher occupations, while those with lower intellectual rating are more likely to choose trades, skilled labor, and clerical work (Jersild et al., 1933). The child's ideal at the time influences his vocational thinking, whether it be a parent, teacher, or movie hero (Freeston, 1939). Girls as a rule think in terms of work which will eventually lead to marriage, while boys think in terms of adventure and glamour (Gough, 1952a; Norton, 1953).

Children generally do not take into consideration their abilities for a given occupation when they select it. The choice is, as a rule, based on factors other than ability or fitness for the occupation chosen. Nor do the young choosers take into consideration whether or not there will be enough demand for the type of work they wish to do to justify their electing it as a life career. On the whole, their choices of vocation are not based on practical considerations.

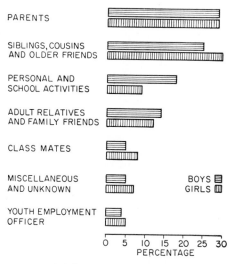

PARENTS

SIBLINGS, COUSINS
AND OLDER FRIENDS

PERSONAL AND
SCHOOL ACTIVITIES

ADULT RELATIVES
AND FAMILY FRIENDS

CLASS MATES

MISCELLANEOUS
AND UNKNOWN

YOUTH EMPLOYMENT
OFFICER

BOYS
GIRLS

0   5   10   15   20   25   30
PERCENTAGE

Fig. 64. Relative importance of different factors in vocational choice. (*From G. Jahoda, Job attitudes and job choice among secondary modern school leavers,* II, *Occupat. Psychol., London,* 1952, **26**, 206–224. *Used by permission.*)

This is well illustrated by the fact that most girls would like to be actresses or models, regardless of their looks, their poise, or their ability to appear to advantage in front of people. Being a doctor or a lawyer, an aviator or an officer in the army or the navy is the ambition of nearly every boy at some time or other. The tendency is to select a "glamour occupation," with little or no consideration for their fitness for such an occupation. This is true of Negro as well as of white children (Gray, 1944). Boys even more than girls suffer from "illusory aspirations" (Witty et al., 1941).

Changes in Vocational Interests. Fortunately, few boys and girls retain an interest in some line of work indefinitely. As they grow older, they develop new vocational interests with more and more trend toward an interest in the type of work they are capable of doing. As Lehman and Witty (1931) have pointed out, few phases of human nature are subject to such marked changes as are shown in the vocational interests and preferences of growing boys and girls. During adolescence, there is even greater shifting of vocational interests than there is in childhood, as there is a shift from unrealistic to more realistic vocational aims. Vocational interests do not, as a rule, become stabilized until late adolescence or even early adulthood (Fox, 1947; Jacobs, 1949; Somerville and Sumner, 1950; Mallinson and Crumrine, 1952; Strong, 1952, 1952a). After the age of twenty-five, vocational stability appears, owing to psychological inertia, social obligations, and limitations imposed by the individual's background (Kaplan, 1946).

While *reasonable* shifts in vocational interests are desirable to avoid putting a ceiling on the child's vocational choice at too early an age, before he actually knows what he can do or wants to do (Pusey, 1954), too much instability in this area is likely to lead to confusion, which will make a final choice difficult for the child. In elementary school, teachers can talk in general about occupations and the necessary training for them. In addition, children can be shown pictures of different vocational activities, can be given vocational-aptitude tests, and can be urged to talk to their parents and listen to adults discussing different types of work (Baxter, 1951). The following suggestions will aid the child in making a choice: (1) help him to develop an adequate self-concept; (2) provide outlets for abilities and interests to enable the child to see what he wants to do and likes to do; (3) avoid class bias; and (4) link abilities and interests with vocations (Fagin, 1953).

7. School

To a young child, going to school means "growing up." He looks forward eagerly to the time when he will have the status of a "school child" and will be able to learn to read and write. Typically, children are interested in school and what it represents during the first two grades. The life of a scholar appeals to the child, and he is challenged by what there is to learn. At this time, he likes things that distinctly belong to school more than the things school shares with life outside of school, such as games and outdoor play. The first- and second-graders usually like their teacher and may go so far as to idealize the teacher to the point where they shift affection from the mother to the teacher.

However, as the child progresses through the grades, his interest in things distinctly belonging to school and scholarship declines and he begins to complain about them. As his interest in school work declines, his interest in things that go along with school, as recess, play, and sports, increases. By the end of elementary school, he often dislikes his teacher, the school program, the rules and regulations of the school, and its physical appointments. He rebels against doing his homework and longs for the time when he can leave school (Jersild and Tasch, 1949).

By the sixth or seventh grade it has been found that children are predominantly critical of school, and approximately one out of every five is distinctly dissatisfied with school (Tenenbaum, 1944). An explanation of the unfavorable attitude toward school which is so commonly found among older children is that it is a reflection of the growing child's need for freedom and independence. It is influenced by the fact that the child has only casual contacts with the teacher out of her formal context, and this deprives him of the emotional warmth that is generally associated with interests (Harris, 1950a).

Factors Influencing Interest. There are many factors which influence the child's attitude toward school and the interest he has in different aspects of school. *Social pressures* from his parents and contemporaries are strong forces before he enters school and after he has been there. What his parents think of school and its importance in his life will largely determine the degree of interest the child has (Stendler, 1951). Later, his classmates' attitudes toward school will influence his attitude. As Harris (1950a) has pointed out, possibly the child's unfavorable attitude toward school "reflects no more than the widespread and thoroughly American characteristic of unfavorable criticism of his institutions." When it is the "thing to do" to criticize school, the child will very likely do what his contemporaries are doing.

Parental attitudes toward school, which influence so markedly the child's attitudes and degree of interest, vary according to the social class to which the family belongs. Parents from the upper-middle class are great believers in education as solutions to social problems; those from the lower-middle and upper-lower classes regard education as necessary for vocational success but are not great believers in education per se; those from the lower classes often reject school and what it stands for (Davis, 1949; Havighurst and Taba, 1949).

In a study of mothers' attitudes toward school at the first-grade level, it was found that mothers from the middle class prepared their children for school by putting emphasis on the fact that "everyone does it" and by helping the child through reading and teaching him the alphabet and how to write. Mothers from the upper classes have educational aspirations which include college, while those from the lower classes expect their children to finish high school but to go no further. The difference in educational aspiration on the part of mothers of the upper and lower classes was also shown in their attitudes toward the child's report card. Parents of the upper classes are often disappointed in their children's reports, while those from the lower classes accept the reports without reservations and often refuse to go to the school for parent-teacher conferences (Stendler, 1951). Educational aspirations on the part of parents are generally the determinant of whether or not the child will eventually go to college (Berdie, 1953).

Degree of *adjustment* plays an important role in determining the child's attitude toward school. It has been found that when children enter kindergarten under four years nine months of age, and first grade under five years nine months, they are more likely to have difficulties in adjusting to school than are children who are slightly older. Overage children likewise have adjustment problems. These problems arise mainly in the areas of social and emotional adjustments (Hamalainen, 1952). Because reading plays such an important part in the curriculum of the school child, the child who is ready to learn to read and who can, as a result, learn to read without undue effort makes better adjustments than does the child whose reading readiness is below that of his classmates. Reading readiness is not dependent upon intelligence alone but is markedly influenced by parent-child interactions, with emphasis on verbal interactions. These are generally superior in middle-class homes as compared with those of the lower classes (Milner, 1951).

The good student generally enjoys his studies and likes school better than does the poor student. He prefers his studies to extracurricular activities (Bond, 1952). A child with a very high IQ, on the other hand, is likely to become bored with school work, to learn "not to hear the insupportable drill" on things he has known for years, and to become the butt of teasing and bullying on the part of his less able classmates (Hollingworth, 1939). The child who is not so bright, on the other hand, finds learning hard, and he tries to convince himself that grades are unimportant and that he is satisfied with mediocre success (Bond, 1952). The child who lacks social acceptance and finds himself being left out of things usually learns to dislike school, even though he may be a good student. As soon as he is able to do so, he will want to leave school, not because of lack of interest in the school work but because of lack of social acceptance (Hollingshead, 1949).

And, finally, the child's interest in school is markedly influenced by his attitude toward *"work."* By the time children reach the age of ten years, they have developed a dislike for anything that might be considered work, whether it be reading matter of a more difficult type, school subjects, hobbies, or even sports, which require much practice. This antiwork attitude, which is probably related to the general attitude toward growing up, shows itself indiscriminately in all activities connected with the home or the school. Boys, even more than girls at this age, show an anti-intellectual attitude (Tyler, 1955).

Areas of Interest. Interest in *school subjects* changes as the child progresses through the grades. Children in the early grades show an interest in mathematics, art, and English, but little in nature study, natural science, geography, and local or world news. Girls show less interest in mathematics as they progress in school but a relatively stable interest in English usage, writing, and reading. Boys, on the other hand, show a stable interest in mathematics but a decline of interest in English. There is an increase in interest in nature study and natural science as children reach junior high school (Jersild and Tasch, 1949). Reasons given by students for lack of interest in certain subjects are failing to see the need for a subject, finding the subject matter uninteresting or too difficult and the instructional methods monotonous, and failure on the teacher's part to "put the subject across" (Young, 1932).

When a school subject has the reputation of being "hard," the student is likely to approach it with an unfavorable attitude (Perry, 1943). If a child makes poor grades in a subject or fails it, he inevitably dislikes it (Klein, 1939). If a school subject ties up with daily interests, it is more likely to be interesting to the child than when he can see no need for it (Congdon, 1937). That is why children become more interested in science as they grow older. It also explains their growing interest in history, especially in the case of boys (Fine, 1955).

Extracurricular activities gain in popularity as the child goes through school. There is a growing interest in sports, games, gym, and physical education. Recess periods become increasingly more popular as children grow older (Jersild and Tasch, 1949). There is also a growing interest in social clubs as children advance in school (McGehee, 1941). Social relationships play an important role in the child's interest in extracurricular activities. When children form groups and exclude others from their activities, when certain pupils run everything in the school, or when some of the pupils make fun of their classmates, the situation is likely to make a child dislike school (Jones, 1948).

Teacher-pupil relationships play a dominant role in the child's attitude toward and interest in school. While some children like their teachers, those who do not are likely to dislike school mainly because of the dislike for the teacher (Tschechtelin and Hipskind, 1940; Tenenbaum, 1944). When a child has an unfavorable attitude toward the teacher, he is likely to be maladjusted to school (Leeds, 1954). It is the teacher who determines what the social-emotional climate of the classroom will be. Even though this may vary slightly from day to day, the teacher creates an atmosphere which is generally consistent (Withall, 1952). Good parent-teacher morale exists when the teacher is aware of the status structure of the group, knows who are the leaders and popular members, and takes these factors into consideration in dealing with the class (Bogen, 1954).

There are certain things children dislike about teachers, and as a result, they develop unfavorable attitudes toward school. They are very sensitive to a teacher's fairness, and dislike teachers who have pets, who mark down a student because she does not like the student, or give unfair examinations. They dislike teachers who scold a lot; who are unduly cross, often bossy, and always "fussing at" pupils; who become angry when a child fails to understand; who give too much homework; who punish or embarrass a child in front of the class; and who are not interested in their pupils. Boys more often than girls find things to criticize in their teachers and have a poorer relationship with them than girls have (Jones, 1948; Leeds, 1954; Strang, 1954).

Children like a teacher who is friendly to her pupils, kind, patient, interested in children, understanding, and treats them as her equals (Leeds, 1954). They like a teacher who knows how to teach and who is strict, though fair (*New York Times*, 1955). While children of all socioeconomic groups expect to have the sympathy and help of their teachers when they are in trouble and, in general, a pleasant social relationship with them, children from poorer districts show a tendency to obey blindly and to be afraid of violent handling, while children from better districts are free from such pressures and fears (Biber and Lewis, 1949).

8. Appearance

The young child has little interest in his appearance. So long as he is comfortable and able to enjoy whatever activity he is engaged in, it makes little difference to him if his hair is unkempt, his nails dirty, or his clothing torn. Nor is he concerned about being slightly too thin or too fat; about having freckles on his face or crooked teeth; or about the color or texture of his skin and hair. So long as he is not so homely that other children ridicule him, he accepts his appearance as it is. For the most part, boys and girls throughout the elementary-school grades are satisfied with their appearance so far as their physical characteristics, their clothing, and their grooming are concerned (Jersild, 1952).

As children reach the end of childhood, however, they begin to take more interest in their appearance. By the fifth and sixth grades, girls show a greater concern about their looks, their clothing, and their grooming than they did when they were younger and than do boys of the same grades (Jersild, 1952). For fifth-grade girls, tidiness has a fairly high value (Tuddenham, 1951). Even though girls of this age are becoming interested in their appearance, boys of twelve years of age prefer an unkempt appearance to tidiness (Tryon, 1939). To be popular, older girls discover that they must make a good appearance, while for boys of the same age, emphasis on appearance is likely to label them as "sissies" (Bonney, 1947a; Austin and Thompson, 1948; Cannon et al., 1952). Interest in appearance is closely related to age of sexual maturing. And because girls mature earlier than boys, interest in appearance develops sooner in girls than in boys (Hurlock, 1929a; Stone and Barker, 1939; Sollenberger, 1940; Fleege, 1945a; Silverman, 1945; Ryan, 1952, 1953). Throughout the adolescent years, interest in appearance is very great. Not only is the adolescent concerned about his physique, but his concern spreads to his clothes. If he is poorly dressed, out of style, or inappropriately dressed, he feels uncomfortable and inadequate (Hurlock, 1929a; Silverman, 1945; Cobliner, 1950; Ryan, 1952, 1953).

Interest in Clothes. The baby's only interest in clothes is that they will not restrict his movements. Clothes that help to build a comfortable world for him, one in which he feels secure, are all that concern him. To a young child, clothes help to achieve independence when he can manipulate them, and they are a source of satisfaction (Read, 1950). Very early in life, the child discovers that his clothes attract attention to himself. Comments are made by adults about the newness, the color, or the style of the clothing. Playmates of his own age notice and admire his new clothes and openly

Older girls show a greater concern about their appearance than do younger children or boys. (*From Child Development, a McGraw-Hill Text-Film.*)

envy an article of clothing which they themselves do not possess. Murphy (1937) reported that three-year-olds not only noticed one another's clothes but referred to the newness, color, or any feature that was different in the clothing of other children. It is not, therefore, surprising that the little child learns the powerful effect that clothing has on others and the gratification that it gives to the wearer.

Focal Points of Interest. Studies of children's interest in clothes have revealed just what clothing means to a child. *New clothes,* which many adults dread, have a peculiar charm for the child, who wishes to wear a new garment as soon as it is bought, whether or not it is appropriate for the occasion. The child is ridiculously proud of a new garment and calls attention to it with such remarks as "See my new shoes!" The garment that is noticed and admired by others becomes especially dear to the child, but it loses its charm if it is ignored. The *first clothes* of a particular kind, especially if they are like the clothes of older children, are worn with tremendous pride. The first pocket, the first long trousers, the first kid gloves, or the first long stockings are the source of much pleasure.

Slavish conventionality in regard to clothing comes when children reach the self-conscious age, beginning around the eighth or tenth year. At this time, boys and girls want to be noticed as little as possible, and if they

A young child is humorously proud of a new garment and likes to call attention to it. (*From Child Development, a McGraw-Hill Text-Film.*)

are like others in appearance, there is less chance for them to be singled out and made conspicuous. If the child is forced to wear clothes different from those of his friends, he feels ashamed and is afraid to go out, for fear of being laughed at. This attitude becomes increasingly pronounced with each successive year until the end of early adolescence, at approximately the sixteenth year. After that, with regaining of self-confidence and a definite desire to be noticed, the adolescent swings to the opposite extreme in his attitude toward his clothing (Flaccus, 1906; Sanborn, 1927; Hurlock, 1929, 1929a; Macaulay, 1929; Silverman, 1945; Ryan, 1952).

Children under nine or ten years of age are especially interested in the *color* of their clothes. If the garment is of one of their favorite colors, they will like it, regardless of whether it is becoming or appropriate for them. The older child begins to regard color as poor taste if it is too bright or too conspicuous. In addition, he becomes more style-conscious than the young child is, and he considers the *becomingness* of the garment as well as its *appropriateness* for the occasion on which it is to be worn. Young children are especially interested in *ornamentation* of their clothes, while older children regard lines and becomingness as more important than decorations. As children approach the adolescent years, their interest in clothes is greatly influenced by adult values (Macaulay, 1929; Silverman, 1945; Pearson, 1950; Mendelsohn and Crespi, 1952; Ryan, 1952, 1953).

The child's clothes are not only a source of much pleasure to him, but they add tremendously to his attitude of self-confidence. A well-dressed child is more self-confident, better mannered, and less rowdy than a poorly dressed one. This is increasingly true as the child grows older (Young, 1938). The attitude of the social group must also be taken into consideration in evaluating the influence of clothing on the child's behavior and attitudes. What the group thinks is quickly sensed by the child and is then reflected in his attitude toward self. As Read (1950) has pointed out, "Children do like clothes and find real satisfaction in them. Bright colors or gay materials, the feel of different textures in clothing, the comfortable, familiar garment as well as the new one—these are all things that bring pleasure to the child. Clothes make a contribution to the process of growing up when they are right from his standpoint. They can help to make the man!"

Chapter 14

FAMILY RELATIONSHIPS

Changes in American life have brought about changes in family living as families break away from the Old World traditions and accept the democratic principles of American life. This has brought about a marked change in the status of women and in the relationships of men and women, husbands and wives, parents and children (Marmor, 1951). Of the many changes that have taken place, the most important are the steady decline in family size, decline of the kinship group as a family unit living under one roof, the rising predominance of the immediate family group with the weakening of ties with relatives, decline of work done in the home and increase in working wives, increase in divorce and family separations, changes in training of children in the home and increase of training in the school, shifts in recreation out of the home, increase in mobility of the family, and changes in the material milieu of the home (Gruenberg, 1947; Bossard, 1949, 1953; Young, 1953).

As Burgess (1948) has pointed out, "Never before in human history has any society been composed of so many divergent types of families. Families differ by sections of the country, by ethnic and religious groups, by economic and social classes, and by vocations. They are different according to the family life-cycle and by number and role of family members. They vary by the locus of authority within the family and by widely different styles of life." This is in direct contrast to most primitive and many civilized cultures today where there is a set pattern for family life and where the child's development is molded along rigid lines to conform to the prescribed pattern. As a result, there are no conflicts for the child, and this gives him a sense of security (MacCalman, 1950).

The rapid rate of change which exists in America today gives children many experiences which their parents never had and which their parents are often unable to understand. This is especially true of foreign-born or first-generation Americans and of those who come from rural to urban environments (Duvall and Motz, 1945; Duvall, 1946; Nye, 1950). Changes result in different values which are difficult for parents and children to agree upon (Bossard, 1954). It has made adjustment to school and neighborhood groups more difficult for the child (Bossard, 1949). Most of all, it has brought about changes and confusion regarding child-training methods (Harris, 1948; MacCalman, 1950; Nimkoff, 1950; Sussman, 1954), and it has caused tensions due to parental pessimism about their own ineptitude as parents (Hayes, 1952; Marshall, 1953).

INFLUENCE OF FAMILY RELATIONSHIPS ON CHILD

The child's attitudes and behavior are markedly influenced by the family into which he is born and in which he grows up. Because the home is the child's first environment, it sets the pattern for his attitudes toward people, things, and life in general. The child uses his parents as models for his adjustment to life. If his parents are not well adjusted, this gives the child a poor model to imitate and is likely to lead to problem behavior similar to that of his parents (Phillips, 1951). The fundamental pattern established at home is never completely eradicated, even though it may be modified and changed as the child grows older.

For many years, psychoanalysts have stressed the importance of early family experiences on the child's behavior and attitudes. According to Freud (1920), neuropathic parents who overprotect the child and smother him in affection awaken in him a "disposition for neurotic diseases." Flügel (1929) points out that too severe or too careful parents make the child rebellious, not only toward his parents but toward all adult authority. The emphasis on "momism" (Strecker, 1946) since the Second World War has stressed the psychological damage caused by maternal dominance and maternal over-protection.

The importance of family relationships in determining the child's attitudes and in setting the pattern for his behavior is seen especially clearly in cases of problem children, most of whom are the result of "problem parents." As Teagarden (1946) has pointed out, "all manner of behavior deviations can be, and often are, accounted for by the subtleties of home relationships." Children whose mothers are poorly adjusted to marriage are likely to have behavior problems (Field, 1940). Eating problems are characteristically found in children whose family situation involves domestic discord (Lurie, 1941). When family relationships are seriously disturbed, children are likely to become neurotic or delinquent (Jackson, 1950). Children with psychopathic personalities are generally found to have parents with similar personality patterns (Ingham, 1949; Morris and Nicholas, 1950). Even though the child does not fully comprehend the meaning of his parents' behavior, he "senses intuitively the psychological climate" of the home—whether or not all is well (DuBois, 1952).

The degree of adjustment children make outside the home is markedly influenced by the type of relationship they have in the home (Highberger, 1955). No one procedure, practice, technique, or way of doing things makes for good or bad adjustment on the child's part. It is the attitude toward the child—love, affection, being wanted, appreciated, trusted, and accepted as a person—that determines how well the child will adjust outside the home

(Stout and Langdon, 1950). When parental attitudes toward the child are unfavorable, as in the case of the dominant, the possessive, or the ignoring parent, the child's adjustments outside the home are likely to be poor (Shoben, 1949). Lack of affectional relationships with the child, especially during the early years of life, affects the child's personality unfavorably and interferes with the child's adjustments (Bakwin, 1949; Edmiston and Baird, 1949; Kehm, 1950; Bowlby, 1953).

Children from broken homes, or homes where parents are "emotionally divorced," develop personality patterns that interfere with good adjustments

Whether or not the young child will have eating problems will depend largely upon his relationships with his parents. (*From Child Development, a McGraw-Hill Text-Film.*)

(Haffter, 1948; Beals, 1950; Batchelor and Napier, 1953; Despert, 1953). Prolonged and repeated absence of one or both parents from the home is likely to affect the child's adjustments in proportion to the amount of absence (Riemer, 1949). Children who have been deprived of a normal home life by wars, natural disasters, industrial dislocation, and "social and psychosocial factors" are affected physically, intellectually, and emotionally (United Nations Report, 1952). Being deprived of the mother's care during the early years of life is one of the most serious factors (Mead, 1954). When parents ignore the child and devote little time to him as he grows older, his poor adjustments frequently lead to delinquency (Zucker, 1943; Wattenberg, 1950a).

In the area of social adjustments, the influence of family relationships is especially marked. The family is the most influential socializing agent. It is through family relationships, especially relationships with the parents, that the child learns to conform to group standards, mores, and traditions, and to cooperate with others (Freeman and Showel, 1953). The child develops patterns of social behavior similar to that of his parents (Bishop, 1951). How aggressive the child will be will depend largely upon the way he is treated in the home (Sears et al., 1953). Children who develop socially acceptable assertiveness come from homes where the atmosphere is democratic and where there is a happy relationship with the members of the family. Discord, severe punishment, and autocratic parental rule, on the other hand, lead to socially unacceptable assertiveness (Mummery, 1954). Prejudice on the child's part is usually associated with authoritarian and punitive child-training methods (Harris and Martin, 1950).

A definite relationship has been found between the child's status in the group and his parents' opinions regarding child-training methods. Children who are leaders have parents with outstandingly different attitudes toward their children from those parents whose children are followers or lack social acceptance. Children who are socially successful have parents who are less inclined to protect them and to prevent their developing an adequate degree of independence than are parents of children who are less successful in their social adjustments (Miles, 1946). How the child feels about adults is influenced by his relationships with his family. The nearer the child is in age to a sibling, the less friendly he is to adults. This may be explained mainly in terms of jealousy on the child's part (Koch, 1955).

In a home where parents are overanxious and concerned about their children, where discipline is inconsistent, and where there is worry, anxiety, and lack of a sense of humor, children are more emotional and more subject to temper outbursts than is true of children from homes where less tension exists on the part of the parents (Goodenough, 1931). The home atmosphere has been found to be the most important single factor in determining the child's acquisition of language. Children who have nonorganic language disorders often come from homes where there are disturbed family relationships which make the child emotionally insecure and maladjusted (McCarthy, 1954a).

Success or failure in school have been found to be related to the child's relationships with his parents and other family members. Reading ability is affected by the size of the family, the child's position in the family, and the educational level of his parents (Sheldon and Carrillo, 1952). Parents who have a college education and educational aspirations for their children generally have children who read better than do those of parents whose educational aspirations are of a lower level (Sheldon and Cutts, 1953). Lack of cultural background in the home and absence of encouragement of cultural pursuits have been found to retard the child's progress in school (Camp-bell, 1952). The influence of family relationships is not limited to success in school. The position of the child in the family and his relationship with the members of his family have been found to influence success in later life (Allen, 1955). Marital happiness of parents not only influences their chil-dren's attitudes toward marriage but also their adjustments to marriage in adult years (Terman et al., 1938; Lu, 1952a; Wallin, 1954).

How the child will react to different influences in the home and how his relationships to the various members of the family will develop will depend to a large extent upon what type of individual he is. The quiet child will be affected differently from the aggressive child by different home situations, just as the introvert will react differently from the way the extrovert would react. Because the child's reactions to family relationships depend so much on his individual make-up, it is possible in only a general way to show how different situations in the home influence the attitudes and behavior of chil-dren. Individual variations must be taken into consideration for each case.

FACTORS INFLUENCING THE CHILD'S BEHAVIOR

Relationships with people rarely remain static. As people change, their relationships with one another also change. Similarly, as the size of the group to which the individual belongs changes, so do the relationships of each member of the group with the other members. As children grow older, there is a decrease in warmth and an increase in restrictions on the part of their parents (Baldwin, 1947). The child's attitude toward his parents and siblings likewise changes. His interest in his peers increases, and he is more influenced by them than by the members of his family. He also shows a greater interest in them, and this is often resented by his family. All of these changes result in changes in family relationships as time passes.

In recent years, much attention has been given to an attempt to evaluate the different factors in the home which influence the child's attitudes and behavior. Numerous studies along these lines have been made, and the re-sults have pointed to the fact that the influence exerted by home situations and family relationships is far greater than was originally believed. While no attempt will be made to place the different factors in order of importance, as complete a survey as possible will be made of the different experimental investigations and their findings.

1. CHILD-TRAINING METHODS

The goal of all child training is to develop in the child the capacity for adjusting to the traditional roles prescribed by the cultural group to which the child's family belongs (Henry and Boggs, 1952). Children in different cultures are brought up to carry on, in their turn, their parents' manner of life (Benedict, 1949). Parents and teachers are the transmitters of the cultural ideals of their groups. These cultural ideals determine the training the child receives, and this, in turn, determines what sort of individual he will become (Bühler, 1948). Because there is no single cultural pattern in any country, there is no over-all philosophy of child training influencing parental practices. What child-rearing methods will be used will be dependent upon the parents the child has (Sewell et al., 1955).

Throughout the centuries, there have been shifts in the culturally approved child-training methods. Certain contemporary problems, as breast feeding, feeding problems, and the emotional care of children during illness were discussed as far back as the sixteenth and seventeenth centuries (Burlingham, 1951). Since the turn of this century, there has been a marked shift from rigid discipline to an understanding of the child and his needs. It is now believed that it is up to adults to meet the needs of the child. There is a shift from dogmatism to suggestions for possible alternatives (Escalona, 1949; Coughlan, 1950; Stendler, 1950; Vincent, 1951; Wolfenstein, 1953).

Parents generally use child-training methods similar to those used by their parents. Where both parents were brought up in homes that were similar in control, they are likely to reproduce in their own family the methods used by their parents. If, however, they had been brought up by different methods, there is likely to be conflict as to what method to use and a certain amount of modification of methods (Ingersoll, 1949). How the mother perceives her role as mother and the type of personality she has will markedly influence the child-training method she uses (Behers, 1954). Because there have been marked shifts in attitudes regarding child rearing in recent years, there is likely to be conflict between parents and grandparents regarding the methods to use. This leads to conflicts and interference on the part of grandparents which creates conflicts for the child (Gesell and Ilg, 1946; Thompson, 1952). When grandmothers live in the home, the mother is likely to be stricter and the grandmother more permissive than when they live in separate homes (Staples and Smith, 1954).

Before marriage, the individual's attitude toward child training is closely similar to that of his own parents (Itkin, 1952). Preparental education, however, has been found to change attitudes toward child training to greater permissiveness. The greatest resistance to change, however, occurs in areas relating to discipline, sleep, toileting, and feeding. These are the areas where child care directly interferes with the adults' own work, pleasure, or rest (Stott and Berson, 1951). This has led to confusion on the part of parents, especially when in seeking guidance they encounter differences of opinion among specialists in child training (Weinfeld, 1949; Stendler, 1950; Wolfenstein, 1953). Furthermore, because of the emphasis on the difference between the needs of the child and the adult, there are discontinuities in the training of children which make adaptation to adult life difficult for the child (Benedict, 1938).

Today, child-training methods fall roughly into two major categories, *authoritarian* and *democratic*. Authoritarian methods consist of strict rules and regulations, with severe punishment for misbehavior. Democratic methods, on the other hand, involve discussion, explanation, and reasoning with the child, with more lenient forms of punishment (Baldwin, 1949; Crist, 1953). Within these two major categories, there are variations. Strictness, for example, may range from rigid control to reasonable restraint. Democratic control may range from careful planning on the part of parents and children to extreme leniency on the parents' part (Hellersberg, 1946). The control of the child may be by the mother, the father, or both (Ingersoll, 1949). Those who are most permissive or strictest are likely to be more consistent than those between the extremes (Sewell et al., 1955). Parents who are better educated are, as a rule, more inclined to permissiveness than are those less well educated (Staples and Smith, 1954). As a rule, parents exert more control over their children when they are young than when they are approaching adolescence (Crist, 1953).

Variations in child-training methods are found within different *social groups* (Escalona, 1949). Parents from *rural* districts are, on the whole, more authoritarian in their methods than are *urban* parents (Stott, 1945). *Mothers* are usually less strict than fathers (Stott, 1940), and *younger* parents tend to be more democratic than older (Stott, 1940). *Foreign-born* parents are more authoritarian in their methods than are native-born parents. By the second generation, however, this difference is less marked (Duvall and Motz, 1945a; Green, 1946). *Social-class differences* in child training are very marked (Hoeflin, 1954). Middle-class parents are more exacting in their expectations, they begin training earlier, they supervise their children's activities more closely, and they put greater emphasis on individual achievement than do parents from the lower classes (Ericson, 1946, 1946a). With training, parents of the lower social classes have been found to shift to greater leniency in their child-care practices (Klatskin, 1952). The more *conservative* the parent, the more intolerant he is likely to be in his methods of child training (Shapiro, 1942).

2. ORDER OF BIRTH

Contrary to popular opinion, there is no "ideal position" within a family. As Goodenough and Leahy (1927) have pointed out, there probably is "no position in the family circle which does not involve, as a consequence of its own peculiar nature, certain special problems of adjustment." According to Freud (1929), the child's position in the sequence of brothers and sisters is of very great significance for the course of his later life.

Many studies have been made to determine the relative merits of different family positions. These have revealed that the long-range effects are not as pronounced as is popularly believed to be true (Wile and Noetzel, 1931; Stagner and Katzoff, 1936), though the oldest child is usually the least persistent, and the youngest the most persistent, as they grow older (Roberts, 1938). While each position provides certain emotional satisfactions and dissatisfactions for the child, the effect of the position the child has in the family constellation will be influenced by his age and sex (Sears, 1950; Bossard, 1954). Thus, to a certain extent, the advantages and disadvantages of different positions depend upon the child himself as much as upon the position he holds within the family.

Oldest Child. The law of primogeniture, favoring the first-born in accession to title, property, and wealth, is based on the supposed superiority of the first-born. However, studies of intelligence have revealed that there is a definite tendency for the intelligence quotient to increase progressively from the first-born to the later-born, at least as far as the eighth-born child (Hsiao, 1931; Steckel, 1931; Thurstone and Jenkins, 1931; Roberts, 1938). Genius, on the contrary, occurs more frequently among first-born than among later-born siblings (Cattell, 1921; Terman, 1925; Ogburn, 1927).

Studies of personality and social adjustment have revealed that the oldest child is in a position which makes successful adjustment very difficult, perhaps more difficult than for children in any other ordinal position. He is likely to experience more anxiety in nursing and weaning situations, more cautiousness about sickness and danger, and more interference at bedtime than do later-born children (Sears, 1950). He experiences a rather high-pitched relationship with his mother at the beginning which then steadily lessens in intensity, especially when a second child arrives and he is displaced by that child (Lasko, 1952). As Ashley-Montagu (1948) has pointed out, "The first-born does seem to take rather a beating. For a year or more he is emperor of the universe. Everything exists to cater to his needs. . . . Then more or less abruptly the halcyon existence is terminated, or at least considerably changed, by the eruption into it of a brother or sister. . . . Really, can one wonder that the first-born is often what parents frankly call 'a mess'!"

In addition to overprotectiveness of his parents, the first-born child is the victim of the comparative inexperience of his parents, he is likely to be expected to assume responsibilities for the care of younger children in the family, and he finds it difficult to adjust from being an only child to a non-only child (Goodenough and Leahy, 1927). Because many parents are concerned about what effects the arrival of a second child will have on the first, there is a tendency for them to encourage the continuation of the attitude of self-importance fostered when the child was an only child. As a result, the older child lords it over his younger sibling, he makes disparaging comments about the progress of the younger sibling, he encourages the younger sibling to engage in competitive activities where he is sure to emerge the victor, and he uses different attention-getting devices to claim the mother's attention (Fischer, 1952).

Parental overprotectiveness of the older child is likely to make him more conservative and less dominant and aggressive than the younger siblings (Goodenough and Leahy, 1927; Adler, 1930a; Sanford, 1943). He usually lacks self-confidence and leadership qualities, and he is easily influenced by suggestion and is very gullible. He is more dependent, more worried and excitable, has his feelings hurt more easily, and is less demonstratively affectionate than later-born siblings (Dean, 1947). Because of parental idealism, the older child often suffers from feelings of failure. This makes him worried and anxious to escape blame and leads to feelings of insecurity.

The oldest child often becomes selfish and spoiled (Ashley-Montagu, 1948). As Strauss (1951) has stressed, "He will walk constantly as if with a chip on his shoulder. This he will do because he must constantly be on his guard. He has learned from bitter experience that he may be displaced. In line with this, a general attitude of pessimism is common among first-born." A disproportionately large number of first-born children become problem children (Thurstone and Jenkins, 1931; Kawin, 1934; Wile and Jones, 1937). They are often quarrelsome and more prone to anger than younger siblings (Stratton, 1927).

Second-born Children. The second-born child is spared much of the anxiety and emotional tension his parents experienced when the first baby was born. Because his parents are more experienced in their parenthood roles, they are less likely to overprotect or baby him and they are less anxious and concerned about his welfare. As a result, the second-born child is usually less dependent than the first (Gewirtz, 1948b; Sears, 1950). In addition, the mother's attitude toward the second child is likely to be more stable than toward the first, even when the third child arrives. There is greater warmth in the mother's attitude because of the fact that she is less strained by anxiety and less influenced by the ambivalence that accompanied her loss of freedom with the arrival of the first child (Lasko, 1952). See Fig. 65.

The age difference between children is an important factor in determining how the mother treats them. When they are closely spaced, it is better for both mother and children, as she treats them more rationally, more democratically, and with more understanding. If, however, the mother is very young, the home is likely to be child-centered for the first child, but this changes when the second child arrives. The difference in treatment of the first and second child is less pronounced as the second reaches school age. In discipline, the mother is likely to be more lenient with the second than with the first child (Lasko, 1954).

Between the ages of one and two years, the second child uses the first as a pacemaker. Because he rarely can keep up to the pace set by the first, he feels inadequate (Lasko, 1952, 1954). Furthermore, to win and hold the mother's attention, the older child often makes disparaging comments about the younger and delights in engaging him in competitive activities to show his superiority over the younger. This adds to feelings of inadequacy on the part of the younger child (Fischer, 1952).

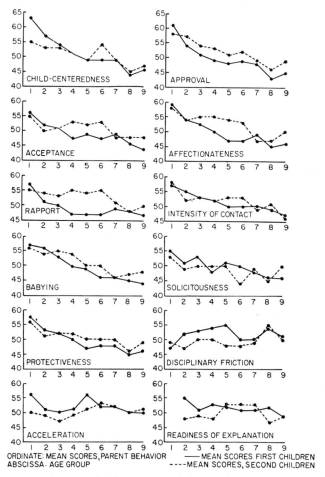

Fig. 65. Age trends in parental behavior toward first- and second-born children. (*From J. K. Lasko, Parent behavior toward first and second children, Genet. Psychol. Monogr., 1954, 49, 97–137. Used by permission.*)

Second-borns are talked to and instructed less by their mothers than are their older siblings (Lasko, 1954). In spite of this, second-borns have been found to excel first-borns on mental tests. Those with a male sibling do better than those with a female older sibling. The explanation of this is that the male "keeps the sib on his toes. It isn't that the male has greater skill or knowledge but rather that he, by the challenge he presents, stimulates or alerts his sib more than does a girl. Jealousy of him because he tends to be favored by his mother may also spark the alerting" (Koch, 1954). As a rule, second-born children are less neurotic and introverted and more fun-loving and humorous than first-borns (Cohen, 1951).

Middle Children. The middle child in a family of three or more children is apt to be somewhat neglected in favor of the first-born or the baby of the family. Like the oldest, the middle child shows some tendency toward lack of aggression, but this is far less marked than in the case of the oldest child. The middle child is rather easily influenced by suggestion; he is frequently flighty and his attention is easily distracted from the thing at hand; he shows more than the usual craving for physical demonstrations of affection; and is generally gregarious in his social attitudes. It has been found that there are more extremely unpopular children among the middle children of families than is true of children of any other ordinal position (Goodenough and Leahy, 1927). In one group of middle children, 31 per cent showed three or more negative characteristics (Winkley et al., 1951).

Youngest Child. The youngest child of a family frequently remains a baby too long. He is likely to be pampered and spoiled by the other members of the family, who continue to do things for him long after he is capable of doing them for himself. Sometimes, because he seems so much younger and less mature than the other children, there is a tendency for the family to leave the youngest child out of things and to treat him as if he did not actually fit into the family pattern of living. These two extremes of behavior —indulgence and disregard—are bound to influence the youngest child's outlook on life and, in turn, his behavior.

It is not at all unusual for older siblings to assume the role generally held by parents in the discipline of the youngest child. Older brothers and sisters "boss" him and punish him when his behavior does not come up to the standards they set. They emphasize that the youngest is spoiled, that discipline has been lax for him, that he has fewer responsibilities and enjoys more opportunities than they ever had (Bossard and Boll, 1954). The "baby" of the family, on the other hand, complains that he never has new clothes or toys, that he is the object of criticism and buck passing, and that he is pushed into the background (Bossard and Boll, 1954). As a result of this sort of treatment, the youngest child frequently becomes resentful, defiant, and irritable. He develops a "chip-on-the-shoulder" attitude which affects not only his relationships with members of the family but also with people outside the home.

According to Adler (1930a), the youngest children in families "bear unmistakable signs of the fact that they have been the youngest." He believes that they have the greatest incentive to strive to surpass other siblings. In addition, the youngest child will expect and even demand help from other members of the family. As a result, he expects that things will work out all right and that things will come his way because other people will always help him. Because his self-confidence has never been jolted by competition with a newly arrived sibling nor has he ever been dethroned, he has an advantage over other siblings. This may result in an optimistic outlook on life (Strauss, 1951).

3. ONELINESS

According to tradition, only children fall into two types, (1) the spoiled, egocentric, antisocial and, therefore, very unpopular children; and (2) the withdrawn, sensitive, nervous children, who shrink from social contacts and are overdependent on their parents. Neither type, it is obvious, is looked upon as well adjusted or is likely to make a success in life. Early studies of only children emphasized the inferiority of the only child as compared with children with siblings. G. Stanley Hall (1907) claimed that "Being an only child is a disease in itself." According to Blanton and Blanton (1927), "The only child is greatly handicapped. He cannot be expected to go through life with the same capacity for adjustment that the child reared in the family with other children has."

More recently, opinions about only children, based on the studies of only children, have changed markedly. Emphasis is now being placed on the importance of the home setting in determining whether or not being an only child is a handicap (Stott, 1940). Campbell (1934) concluded a study of only children with the statement that " 'Oneliness' per se is not the environmental spectre so widely assumed. Whatever role the mere presence or absence of siblings may play in the development of personality, its importance certainly is not crucial."

An opportunity to learn to get along with others and to adapt oneself to the social group is one of the advantages most often stressed for children with siblings. The only child, because he lacks this opportunity, is pitied. It is assumed that he will develop into a spoiled brat, who will be unpopular with his peers and frowned upon by adults. If an only child has had no preschool experience, he is confronted at school age with an adjustment problem to a group whose behavior is already unlike his. This makes adjustments difficult for him. However, children in elementary school who are only children have been found to make this adjustment successfully enough so that they are well accepted by their peers. They are more aggressive, more self-confident, more generous, more gregarious in their social interests, more independent, and more responsible than are children with siblings (Goodenough and Leahy, 1927; Fenton, 1928; Witty, 1937; Stott, 1940, 1945; Bonney, 1942a, 1944). The only child is not as likely to be "spoiled" as is the child from a two-child family (Levy, 1939).

In the case of children from town and city environments, the advantages of oneliness compensate for the disadvantages. In the case of country children, this is not the case. Because the country child is isolated, his contacts with other children, even after he reaches the school age, are rare and are likely to be limited to the times when he is in school. As a result, being an only child on a farm is somewhat of a handicap to the personal and social development of the child (Stott, 1945).

The only child develops a personality pattern distinctly different from that of children with siblings (Ashley-Montagu, 1948). He may be the victim of overprotective parents, but he is spared the personality damage that comes from sibling rivalry. During childhood, the only child shows instability of mood, he is easily excited, and his attention tends to be flighty (Goodenough and Leahy, 1927). He also shows more nervous traits than do non-only children (Fenton, 1928). As they grow older, there is little evidence that only children are more emotionally unstable than non-only children (Fenton, 1928; Carter, 1937). They are as well adjusted as children with siblings (Dyer, 1945). While only children rate slightly higher in neuroticism than do non-only children, they tend to be more self-sufficient and dominant (Thurstone and Jenkins, 1931; Campbell, 1934). As a result, they often assume leadership positions among their peers (Bossard, 1953, 1954).

While there is no evidence that an only child is brighter than a child with siblings, there is also no evidence that only children have more scholastic problems or that they are retarded academically more than are non-only children. The only child does not, however, participate voluntarily in extracurricular activities quite as much as the child with siblings (Guilford and Worcester, 1930; Hooker, 1931; Levy, 1939). Because of the widespread belief that only children are pampered and spoiled, it has been generally accepted that there are more instances of problem behavior among them than among non-only children. For the most part, the forms of problem behavior that have been found to occur more frequently among only children than among non-only, such as nail biting, crying, restlessness, and overactivity, are traceable to home factors characteristic of the environment in which there is an only child (Ward, 1930; Hooker, 1931; Winkley et al., 1951). Outside of the home, they are less troublesome (Blatz and Bott, 1927), and as they reach adolescence, they generally make better adjustments in the home than do children plagued by sibling rivalries and jealousies (Jameson, 1940; McCann, 1943; Rose, 1944, 1947, 1948).

4. FAMILY SIZE

The family is composed of a complex of interactional systems made up of the different members of the family, each of which has a bearing on the development of the personality and the behavior of each other member of the family. The larger the family, the larger the number of interactional systems. To determine how many interactional systems there will be in a given family, the following formula has been suggested:

$$2^n - n - 1$$

When, for example, there are four members in a family, there will be 11 interactional systems; when there are five members, there will be 26 interactional systems; and when there are six members, the number of interactional systems will be 57. Each relationship or interactional system has its own unique emotional quality which affects the members of the family involved in this system (Henry and Warson, 1951).

Each family group is composed of individuals of different ages and of both sexes. The masculine sex may predominate, the two sexes may be equally represented, or the family may be dominantly feminine in structure. These variations are factors of importance in influencing the behavior of each member. In addition to the members of the immediate family, there are many families where outsiders in the form of relatives, roomers, or servants become a part of the enlarged family group. These outsiders, like the members of the immediate family, influence the behavior of each individual within the group (Henry and Warson, 1951; Bossard, 1953). Even a deceased member of the family, through memories of him, can have an influence on the individuals of the family (Bossard, 1953). What role each individual plays and what influence he has is not determined by closeness of kinship but by the needs of the child and the satisfaction he derives from each. A parent, for example, may not play as important a role in the child's life as a grandparent, an older sibling, or a servant (Bossard, 1954).

Small Families. In America, the trend is toward smaller families, especially in the higher socioeconomic groups (Anderson, 1950). The small family is characterized by planning in regard to size, spacing, and child-rearing education; parenthood is intensive rather than extensive; the activities and roles of each member are individualized; there is a democratic organization with cooperation between parents and child; there are pressures on the child to live up to parental expectations; the family is under stress to achieve and get ahead; discipline of the child is by the parents, mainly the mother; and there are limited contacts within the family for each member, with the result that there are often resentments (Bossard, 1952, 1953, 1954).

The small family has been found to have definite effects on the child's development, some of which are advantageous. But he must "pay a price for this, chiefly in the form of problem-creating circumstances" (Bossard, 1954). Some of the effects are economic and social advantages for the child; more attention from his parents; early social experiences in which he is protected and the center of attention, thus leading to an exaggerated opinion of his own importance in group life; undue pressures which create or intensify emotional problems; and great impact from crises within the family because there are fewer members to share them (Bossard, 1953, 1954).

In addition, the child from the small family often does poor school work because of emotional disturbances more often than because of low-grade intelligence. While the economic status of the small family may be superior to that of the large, broken homes are more frequent, and this adds to the problems of adjustment of the child (Ellis and Beechley, 1951). In spite of some of the disadvantages of the small family, it has been found that children from small families are generally superior to those of large families (Damrin, 1949). However, a medium-sized family seems to be superior to either the large or the small family (Ellis and Beechley, 1951).

Large Families. The large family is different in almost every respect from the small family, and this affects the development of each child within the family structure, thus producing an entirely different type of individual. Large families of six or more children may be planned or not. If not planned, each member learns to accept this as a matter of fate, and this affects their attitudes toward crises. The large family is particularly vulnerable to major crises, especially illness or death of one of the parents. There is emphasis on the group rather than on the individuals who make up the family, though each member has a specialized role and specific tasks he is expected to carry out. With a large number of children, there is little opportunity for overprotection of any one child or little nagging or pressure on the child. Discipline is often carried out by older siblings who are given the role of parent-substitutes. There are few economic or social advantages for any child, especially the older children of the family (Bossard, 1952, 1953, 1954). On the other hand, children in a large family have a chance to live relatively independently from adults, and this helps to foster independence and maturity of behavior (Stöckle, 1954).

Because the pattern of life in the large family is different from that in the small family, it affects the child differently. Large-family living forces the child to adjust to the changing vicissitudes of a realistic world. As things are always happening in a large family, the child learns to adjust repeatedly to change in role, in status, and in responsibilities. As the family lives on a close margin, all members must work together, must learn to organize and submit to authority. While this fosters the development of cooperation, it also results in authoritarian rather than democratic living, and it requires specialization for each member of the family (Bossard, 1952, 1953, 1954; Bossard and Sanger, 1953). Children from large families are likely to do poorer work in school because they are less intelligent than those from smaller families. They are less likely to be emotionally disturbed or to have as many forms of problem behavior as children from small families (Ellis and Beechley, 1951).

The large family produces feelings of security for each individual. This security is emotional rather than economic, and it comes from having others available to help the individual face difficult situations and from having large numbers of his own people, especially his siblings, around. This gives five conditions which make for emotional security: someone to turn to if the child does not get enough attention and understanding from harried or indifferent parents; better understanding of his problems than he could

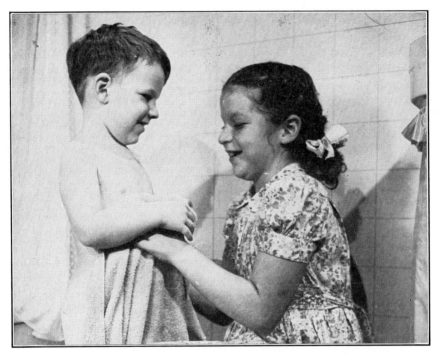

In a large family, each child learns to assume responsibilities, especially in the care of younger siblings. (*From Child Development, a McGraw-Hill Text-Film.*)

get from his parents; better teaching from siblings than from parents; little jealousy because there is little opportunity for emotional coddling; and little overdependency (Bossard and Boll, 1954).

While the home climate is often superior in a large family (Bossard and Sanger, 1953), family relationships tend to improve as the size of the family decreases. The explanations given for this are that parents of a small family can give each child more attention; children compete with each other for material possessions, and this causes a child to feel abused and resentful if the family is large and there are not enough possessions to go around; and because small families are more often planned than are large ones, each child is likely to be more welcome in a small than in a large family (Nye, 1952).

5. Sibling Relationships

The relationship of a child to his siblings will be affected by many different factors, the most important of which are the age differences of the siblings, the sex of the siblings, and the relationship that exists between the different siblings in the family and their parents. Boys, for example, react differently to brothers than they do to sisters. An older sibling is more likely to take a protective attitude toward a sibling whose age is considerably below his than toward one whose age differs from his by only a year or two. Likewise, favoritism of the parents toward one child in the family is bound to affect the reactions of the other children in the family toward that child (Bossard, 1954). Even when there is no favoritism on the part of either parent, the fact that a child *perceives* his parent's behavior as favoritism will markedly affect his attitudes toward his parents and siblings (Tryon, 1939; Stott, 1941; Kuhlen, 1952).

When a child feels that he has been mistreated, he frequently persuades another sibling to "gang up" on the sibling he believes is the parent's favorite. Or if children feel that the parent has been too harsh to a sibling who is not a favorite, they may "gang up" on the parent and present a united front of defiance. This leads to friction, resentments, and disobedience, but it serves as a means of establishing a close bond between the child and his siblings (Merry and Merry, 1950).

Among young children, sibling rivalry and jealousy are common. Hostility toward a sibling may range from slight movements to an urge to destroy by biting or crushing. As children grow older, they check some of their manifestations of hostility when they are jealous (Levy, 1936). The child will shift rapidly from one type of hostile behavior to another when jealousy is aroused. Usually, this will be directed in its more intense forms toward the parent rather than toward the child who is the object of jealousy (Anonymous, 1949). Sometimes the mother sets the stage for sibling rivalry. If a mother has not resolved her own childhood sibling rivalry, she may identify herself and her own siblings with her children and thus relieve the competitive struggles of her childhood (Hilgard, 1951).

While conflicts and rivalry are the most common forms of sibling behavior, siblings also show more favorable behavior in their relationships with one another. Among sisters, distinct patterns have been found in the behavior of younger and older sisters. Older sisters play a more aggressive role in sibling relationships than do younger sisters. When the younger sister tries to give directions to the older, this is generally met with resistance on the part of the older sister. Older sisters generally show more sympathy to a child in distress, they are more protective and willing to give, lend, help, and they are more affectionate in their relationships than are younger sisters (McFarland, 1938). The young child who has no siblings generally expresses a wish for a sibling (Gottemoller, 1943).

Sibling relationships are markedly influenced by the sex of the siblings. In the case of jealousy, there is more in girl-girl combinations than in boy-boy or in boy-girl combinations. When the combinations are of the two sexes, there is likely to be a more friendly and more protective attitude toward the sibling than in one-sex combinations (Smalley, 1930). An only girl in a sibship with all boys will either result in a tomboyish development on the girl's part or in her feeling that all men should pay her homage and treat her as a little princess, just as her brothers did (Strauss, 1951). The greater the age difference in siblings, whether they be of the same or of different sexes, the more friendly the attitude will be (Smalley, 1930).

Sibling relationships can be favorable. (*From Child Development, a McGraw-Hill Text-Film.*)

The relationship between siblings of the two sexes generally reaches a low point at the time of puberty. Throughout the gang age of childhood, when relationships between the two sexes outside the home are unfavorable, they are even more unfavorable in the home. From the construction of a "family field" consisting of different areas of behavior within the family, it is possible to trace the paths of boys and girls and thus see where their activities lie and what their social relationships with other members of the family are (Herbst, 1952). At an early age the child senses that parents, as a general rule, prefer boys to girls as far as the first-born is concerned. Even among later-born children, boys are generally given more freedom and more privileges than girls. The girl is brought up under the ever-watchful eye of her parents and must account for her absences from the home in a way that is rarely required of a boy.

As girls grow older and have an opportunity to observe affairs outside the home, they soon become aware of the social and economic advantages of being a boy. They are likely secretly or openly to rebel against their status as girls and demand rights and privileges equal to those enjoyed by their brothers. Parents tend to speed up the emancipation of their sons and retard that of their daughters (Winch, 1951). Boys are given more freedom in their personal affairs, while girls are held to a more exacting code of filial and kinship obligations (Komarovsky, 1950).

Because girls recognize society's attitude toward members of the female sex, many girls develop feelings of inferiority which affect their attitudes toward social relationships and their ability to succeed in whatever enterprises they may undertake. Other girls, to compensate for society's attitude toward them, develop an aggressive self-assertiveness and, in an attempt to establish themselves on a par with boys, frequently antagonize others. "Hybrid" feminine names, such as "Alberta" and "Paula," given to girls whose parents had earnestly wished for a boy to bear the father's name, are a constant reminder to the girls who have these names that their sex was a keen disappointment to their parents.

In spite of the fact that it is more frequently the father than the mother who is anxious that the first-born should be a boy, or that the majority of the children in the family should be boys, the father generally shows favoritism toward his daughters and acts as a strict disciplinarian toward his sons. Gardner (1947) found that fathers spent more recreation time with their daughters than with their sons. It is the mother who generally favors the boys and whose obvious preference for her sons, especially the first-born son, leads to much of the sibling rivalry that exists in many homes where there are siblings of both sexes.

6. Parent-Child Relationships

How good or poor family relationships will be depends largely upon the type of relationship that exists between the child and his parents. As Dunbar (1952) has stressed, "symbiosis," or the living together of two species of organisms in such a way that the union of the two is not disadvantageous to either but is advantageous or essential to both, can exist only if the parents and the child are aware of the fact that they are essentially different creatures. Only when this occurs can good family relationships exist. Different types of parent-child relationships are shown in Fig. 66.

The relationship of the parent to the child and of the child to the parent is in a constant state of flux, and this requires constant adjustment on the part of both. As they grow and develop, children make changing demands on their parents. Parents, in turn, demand that the child learn to conform to the standards of the home and of the social group to which the family belongs. This results in a continuous delicate interplay of psychological forces if a state of well-being in the parent-child relationship is to be maintained. Any emotional experience that disturbs the psychological equilibrium of one member of the family will bring about a disturbance in the psychological equilibrium of all members of the family (Berman, 1948).

What relationship there will be between the child and his parents will depend largely upon his parents' attitudes toward him. This will influence

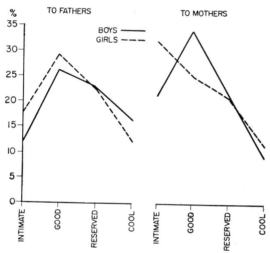

Fig. 66. Characteristic relationships of older children to their parents. (*From A. Jurovsky, The relation of older children to their parents, J. genet. Psychol., 1948, 72, 85–100. Used by permission.*)

the way they treat him, and this, in turn, will influence what the child's attitude toward his parents will be. Fundamentally, therefore, the parent-child relationship is dependent upon the parents' attitudes. These are influenced partly by *cultural values* and partly by the *personality patterns* of the parents and their *concepts* of the *role* of *parents*.

Cultural Attitudes. In recent years, there have been marked changes in attitudes toward children. Around the turn of this century, Freud (1913) contended that too much "parental tenderness" accelerates sexual maturity, "spoils" the child, and makes him unable to be satisfied with a smaller amount of love in later life.

This attitude toward too much interest in and affection for the child was echoed by many American psychologists. The one who sounded the loudest warnings was J. B. Watson (1928), who during the twenties advised parents to beware of too much mother love, because of the harmful effects on the personality development of the child as he grew older.

Now the pendulum has swung to the opposite extreme. It is agreed that mother love and affection are needed for good mental health. Too much, rather than too little, affection should be shown the child, especially during the helpless years of infancy and babyhood. One of the strongest exponents of the importance of mother love and love in general in the child's life is Ribble (1943). According to her,

> Poor relationship with the parents leads to reactions in the infant which tend to become the basis of adult personality disorders. The most important asset of the baby as he begins life is two emotionally healthy parents. His deepest need by far is the understanding care of one consistent individual, his mother. Perhaps in time we shall recognize the danger of the emotionally unhealthy personality and shall see that emotional disturbance in the parents is as dangerous as is tuberculosis or syphilis (pp. 109–110).

This emphasis on the importance of "mothering" and of early experiences in the mother-child relationship (pages 215–216) has resulted in a change in attitude toward more liberality and tolerance, with emphasis on understanding the child and his needs (Harris, 1948). From the moment of birth, infants receive more affection from their parents than was formerly believed good for them (Zachry, 1940a). When this attitude is carried to extremes and is prolonged throughout childhood into adolescence, it is likely to result in a socially and emotionally immature individual who is unfitted to make adjustments to the demands of adult life (Strecker, 1946).

Personality of Parents. Even when a general cultural attitude toward children exists, the attitude of parents toward their children is markedly influenced by their own personality patterns and their attitudes toward children as individuals. Attitudes vary from adult to adult and from time to time in the same adult (Dawe et al., 1949). The parent may be overindulgent at certain times and overstrict at others. This inconsistency of feeling, or "ambivalence," is not necessarily dependent upon the child's behavior but upon the physical and emotional condition of the parent, his memories of the way he was treated as a child in a similar situation, changes in the pattern of family living brought about by the child, the value placed upon parenthood by the members of the group to which the parent belongs, the interference of the child with the freedom and the type of work the mother enjoyed before the child's arrival, and the obstacle to parents' recreations created by the presence of a child in the home (Stott, 1939; Symonds, 1939; Stagner and Krout, 1940; Baldwin et al., 1945; Green, 1946).

The parents' attitude toward the child may be a reflection of their own *adjustment* or *maladjustment* to life and to marriage (Cole, 1954). Family happiness and unity are markedly affected by such factors as husband-wife relationships, in-law interference, money problems, or the health and personality characteristics of the parents (Pfeiffer and Scott, 1952). Among preschool children, whose life is limited mainly to the home, the attitude of the parents toward one another is more important than it is among older children. Tensions relating to affectional and ego values lying within the relationship of husband to wife have been found to have a marked influence on the child's adjustment to life (Baruch, 1937; Baruch and Wilcox, 1944). When the mother is psychotic, the child is likely to suffer more from behavior disorders than when the father is psychotic (Bender, 1937). When a mother uses her child to solve her own emotional problems, she is likely to manipulate him to suit her own needs with little consideration for his individual rights, and thus she prevents his development (Capland, 1954).

The attitude of the mother toward *motherhood* plays an important role in her relationships with her child. The arrival of a new child tends to reduce the warmth and contact between the parent and the other children and to result in a more restrictive but less effective home. During pregnancy, there is less activity in the home and less understanding of the child on the part of the mother (Baldwin, 1947a). When a woman does not want to have a child and tries to force an abortion, this leads to feelings of guilt on her part and resentments toward the child, should the abortion fail (Capland, 1954). When a woman is unhappy about her pregnancy, she is likely to experience more emotional tension and nausea than is normal, and this results in a hyperactive state of the fetus. This tension reaction often persists for many months after the infant is born (Thompson, 1942; Dunbar, 1944; Fries, 1944; Sontag, 1946; Squier and Dunbar, 1946; Wasman, 1947). A marked relationship has been found between the age of the mother and her adjustment to pregnancy. Very often, there is a resentment toward the second child, especially if the interval between the arrival of the first and second child is short (Wallin and Riley, 1950).

The attitude of the parent toward the *sex* of the child influences the pattern of parental behavior from the moment of the child's birth (Mead, 1949). In spite of the fact that many people claim that they are not greatly concerned about the sex of the child and that one sex is as good as the other (Bain, 1954), there is a tendency for parents to prefer the first child to be a boy (Dinitz et al., 1954). They also hope that a second or later-born child will be of the opposite sex (Dahlberg, 1948; Clare and Kiser, 1951; Levy and Hess, 1952). Should the child not be of the hoped-for sex, it is likely to influence the parent's attitude toward the child (Dinitz et al., 1954). While mothers try not to show favoritism toward a child of either sex (Mead, 1949), there is a tendency for them to be more severe with their daughters than with their sons (Sears et al., 1953). The father, on the other hand, differentiates his behavior toward his children from earliest childhood. He "plays up to his rough-housing little boy and pays mild courtship to his little girl, selecting gentler games" (Mead, 1949). Carry-overs of feelings from the parents' childhood experiences are likely to influence parental attitudes toward their own children. A father who, as a boy, had a deep affection for his sister is bound to reflect this feeling in his attitude toward his own children and to show greater affection for his daughters then for his sons (Macfarlane, 1941).

The *age of the child* influences his parents' attitudes toward him. The home environment of the child usually decreases in warmth and intellectual stimulation and increases in restrictiveness as the child grows older, especially when a younger sibling is born (Baldwin, 1947, 1947a). When the child rebels against parental restrictions, hostility on the parent's part increases. A comparison of parents' behavior toward three-year-olds and nine-year-olds showed that parents of nine-years-olds were less affectionate, less intellectually stimulating, less indulgent, and more restrictive than were parents of three-year-olds (Baldwin, 1945). The child's attitude toward his parents' affection likewise changes as he grows older. While the baby and young child want to be caressed, the older child will sometimes attempt to escape or will become aggressive and resist the caress by kicking, biting, or hitting (Wolfle, 1949).

The *age of the parents* is influential in determining their attitudes toward the child. Young parents are likely to take their parental responsibilities lightly, while overage parents are apt to be more nervous and less energetic than are younger parents. This causes them to be overprotective, exacting, and demanding. Should one parent be overage and the other approximately average in age, there may be a clash in interests and values between the parents regarding the child's behavior (Bossard and Boll, 1943; Bossard, 1954). The *educational level* of the parent is more important than his age. Parents of higher educational levels favor more freedom for their children, while those of lower educational levels favor more restraint (Roy, 1950).

From the moment of a child's birth, and often from the time of its conception, parents develop *ambitions* for the child, which they strive hard to have the child attain. Without taking into consideration the child's abilities or disabilities, his interests or ambitions, overambitious parents plan for his future so as to fulfill their own ambitions or to satisfy some thwarted wishes in their own lives. Parents form a concept of an idealized child, against which they compare or rate their own child. This ideal varies with the educational, social, or economic status of the parents and with their opinions on the way to train a child. There are relatively few parents, however, who do not have some ideal for their children and who do not measure their children's achievements against this ideal (Anderson, 1946).

Parental ambitions take the form of ambition for educational success, social success, or financial success (Smith, 1931). What both mothers and fathers want in their children is illustrated in Fig. 67. As may be seen from the data presented in this figure, mothers and fathers are anxious to have their sons and daughters popular with other children, bold, and daring. Quiet, sweet and babyish, submissive, and "little lady and gentlemen" behavior have less appeal for them (Radke, 1946). The father's concern about

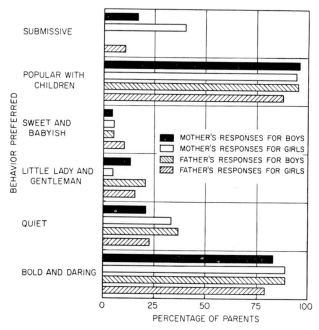

Fig. 67. Mothers' and fathers' preferences in boys' and girls' behavior. (*From M. J. Radke, The relation of parental authority to children's behavior and attitudes, University of Minnesota Press, 1946. Used by permission.*)

his children leads him to be disturbed if they lack initiative and responsibility, are disobedient, insufficiently aggressive, excitable, do poor work in school or are inadequate in athletics, and display "childish behavior." The greatest concern centers around the sons, especially the first-born son, for whom ambitions are higher than for those born later (Aberle and Naegele, 1952).

Mothers who have given up successful business or professional careers have a tendency to show demands for conformity and high standards of performance in their children similar to their own, shown in their previous work (Berger, 1948). "Planned-for" children are more subject to high expectations from their parents than are children who have not been planned for (Sloman, 1948). When mothers are mobile upward and are trying to assimilate the standards of the upper classes, they are anxious over their status. This leads to more directive and severe control over their children than is found among mothers who are more satisfied with their status (Merrill, 1946).

The child, like his parents, has certain ideals for his relationships with his parents. From the books he reads, he sets ideals for his relationships with his parents which include love, protectiveness, understanding, physical demonstrations of affection, praise and approval, sharing of work and play, fostering of independence, and administering of punishment which shows parental warmth and understanding. Because most books for children today show a strong trend toward democratic, not autocratic, family life, the child develops an ideal of this type for his own family (Fisher, 1950).

The child is well aware of what his parents expect of him, and he feels inadequate when he does not live up to their expectations (Fleege, 1945). This causes the child to be quarrelsome, disobedient, irresponsible, and to carry resentments against his parents (Smith, 1931; Stagner and Krout, 1940; Bonney, 1942a; Baldwin et al., 1945, Mueller and Mueller, 1945; Aberle and Naegele, 1952; Bossard, 1954). As a result of such attitudes, the child frequently does poor work in school or engages in fantasy and daydreaming (Smith, 1931). As Rand et al. (1942) have pointed out, "Trouble arises when the parental wish becomes selfish. When the major wish is gratification of the parental ego or a desire to live again one's own life through the child, parents rob the child of individuality and force the development of interests that are not native or dwarf capacities that should be dominant." The child who is "exploited" in order to fulfill parental ambitions often complains, whines, and feels cheated. He is precocious in dress and speech and has a compulsion to compete and a desire to excel over all others. He is a "poor sport" and, to avoid making a mistake, he avoids situations in which he is not certain of success (Martin, 1943).

Typical Parental Attitudes. Although each parent has his or her own attitude toward each child in the family and toward child-rearing methods, there are certain attitudes which are fairly universal in the American culture. These are the product of tradition, of parental teachings, and of experiences in living with children. Too often, parents approve of child behavior which makes for smooth running of the household, but show little regard for the development of the child's personality (Stogdill, 1936; Lafore, 1945). While present-day attitudes toward the child are more liberal than they were in the past, there are marked differences in attitudes among parents of different social groups (Harris, 1948).

Of the many different parental attitudes, the following are the most common.

1. *Overprotectiveness.* Parental overprotection, according to Levy (1939,

1943), consists in *excessive contact* of the parent with the child, such as fondling him excessively or sleeping with him; *prolongation of infantile care,* as nursing or bottle feeding too long, bathing and dressing when the child can do it himself; *prevention of the development of self-reliance* by supervising the child's activities too much, defending him, or solving his problems; and *lack or excess of parental control,* either by overindulgence or insistence on strict obedience. Overprotective parents allow no competing interest to interfere with their parental duties, and they reduce their other interests in life to a minimum (Bakwin, 1948). Parental overprotection, which is more commonly found among children of the more favored socio-economic groups than among those whose parents have neither the time nor the energy to "baby" them, is primarily the result of unfavorable parental attitudes toward the role the child should play in the social group.

According to Levy (1930), there are numerous causes of overprotection, the most common of which are *long period of anticipation and frustration* during which the woman's desire for a child is thwarted by sterility, mis-carriages, or the death of infants; *conditions in the child,* such as physical handicaps and illnesses that frighten the parents or that make the child less likely to survive than other children; *sexual incompatibility* between hus-band and wife; *social isolation; emotional impoverishment* in early life and an unhappy childhood; *development of dominating characteristics* from undue responsibility in childhood and continuance of this role in marriage; and *thwarted ambitions.* Sometimes mothers overprotect their children as compensations for guilt stemming from a hostile or rejecting attitude toward the child (Bakwin, 1948).

One of the most serious effects of overprotectiveness is *overdependency* on the child's part. While a baby needs continuous care, preferably by one person, during the first year of life, it is important that he should not learn to rely so much upon others emotionally that he cannot achieve independence as he grows older and is capable of achieving independence in different activities (Bender, 1950; Sears et al., 1953). If the dependency needs of the baby are not met satisfactorily, he is likely to feel insecure and afraid to be independent (Stendler, 1952). Many parents want children to turn to them for help and guidance, and as a result, they encourage the child to become overdependent. Furthermore, any major upheaval in the child's life will cause him to turn more and more to his parents for help. It is *how* the parents handle the child's dependency demands that will determine whether or not the child will become overdependent. If, for example, the methods used are inconsistent, this will encourage dependence; if the child is helped and praised for his independence, this will help to make him more independent (Stendler, 1954).

When a child is overdependent, he wants help, attention, approval, physical contact and physical proximity with others. By contrast, the child who is independent strives to overcome obstacles, he initiates his own activities, completes the activities he starts, performs routine tasks, and gains satisfaction from work (Beller, 1950). The child who is successful in his adjustments to his peers develops greater independence than does the child who makes poor social adjustments. Because he has friends and sources of satisfaction outside the home, he does not have to rely on his parents for love and security to the same extent as does the dependent child who lacks these outside sources of satisfaction (Havighurst, 1953). Even a dependent child may come to look upon his parents as tyrants and taskmasters rather than as helpers and protectors and rebel against their authority at the same time that he depends upon them for love and security (Flügel, 1929). Most children who are brought up by overprotective parents are more submissive to the father than to the mother (Kates, 1951).

Nervous tendencies, such as excitability, restlessness, and lack of concentration, are common among overprotected children (Cummings, 1944). Such children are often obese and have an immature look. Their characteristic *personality pattern* is manifested by a low level of ego strength, of aspiration, and of frustration tolerance. They show many withdrawing reactions, lack emotional control, and openly refuse responsibility. They seem to be afraid to grow up, have no confidence in their abilities, are easily influenced and dependent upon the group, and are sensitive to criticism. They either develop into typical "yes men" or openly rebel and try to be "big shots." Frequently they become rigid in their ideas of right and wrong and are unduly disturbed by wrongdoings of others (Hattwick, 1936; Martin, 1943; Bakwin, 1948; Stendler, 1952).

In *school,* the overprotected child often has difficulties. He may be accelerated in reading but is likely to have difficulties in arithmetic (Levy, 1933). He will want extra attention from the teacher, and his work will be careless in quality and lack system. When he gets along poorly in school, his parents become more attentive, and, in turn, the child does even worse work (Hattwick and Stowell, 1936). In his social adjustments, the overprotected child likewise has difficulties. He is socially immature in behavior, has no sense of responsibility, bids for attention, is selfish and spoiled, and is often quarrelsome and a troublemaker. The result is that he has many social difficulties, is usually unpopular, and rarely becomes a leader. He is often homesick when at school or with people other than his family (Hattwick and Stowell, 1936; McCann, 1941).

2. *Permissiveness.* Permissiveness is the opposite of overprotectiveness. The permissive parent is "giving" instead of "taking" from the child. He gives time, thought, and effort instead of material things; he accepts the child's early ideas and ambitions instead of foisting his own upon him; he encourages the child to play with other children; he makes the child feel accepted and strong; and he shows a tolerance and understanding of the

child's weaknesses (Martin, 1943). Permissiveness may go too far and result in indulgence. Even when casually indulgent, the parent is in general tolerant but rather haphazard in his treatment of the child (Baldwin et al., 1945).

The permissive parent recognizes that the child needs more rather than less freedom from parental restraints as he grows older. This affects the parents as well as the child. Permissive parents report that their lives are more disrupted by their children's behavior, more of their activities are dis-

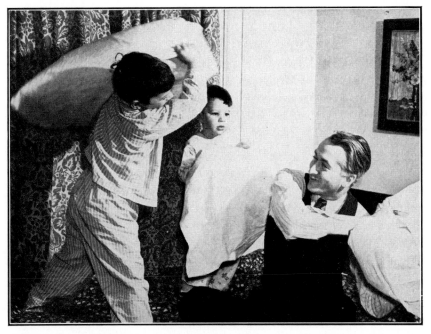

When parents are permissive, it is sometimes difficult to control their children's behavior. (*From Child Development, a McGraw-Hill Text-Film.*)

turbed by their children's noisiness, privacy is difficult to attain, it is difficult to control their children's activities, and the children offer resistance when the parents try to set any limits to their play activities. In addition, there is more damage to furniture, and the house is usually cluttered. Thus permissive parents encounter results which conflict with the traditional middle-class picture of the ideal home.

Permissiveness on the parents' part requires greater energy and expenditure of money. There are greater frustrations for the parents when their own activities are interfered with. However, if parents believe this is for the child's good, they will accept it, adjust their homes to it, and take it in stride. If, however, parents tend to hold traditional views about the role of the child, they should not try to be permissive because this will lead to too much friction with the child and too many parental frustrations (Blood, 1953). There is no question about the fact that permissiveness, if not carried to the extreme of indulgence, will lead to better parent-child relationships and a healthy family life (Martin, 1943).

Children from homes which encourage reasonable freedom for the child have been found to be resourceful, cooperative, self-reliant, and well adjusted in social situations. They show perseverance and can assume responsibilities. On the whole, they show more favorable than unfavorable behavior. When the mother is more permissive than the father, children show more favorable behavior than when the father is the more permissive parent (Grant, 1939; Read, 1945). Children who are permissively reared do not show the neurotic reactions of children with authoritarian training (Maloney, 1948). When, however, parents are indulgent, the child has a difficult time in making social adjustments. He is selfish, demanding, tyrannical, and expects constant attention, affection, and service. He responds to denials of his wishes or discipline with impatience, outbursts of temper, or assaults. He will use every device, whether coaxing, bullying, or wheedling, to get his own way, and when alone, he will be restless and unhappy (Bakwin, 1948).

3. *Rejection*. Parental rejection need not necessarily mean overt rejection of the child, as many people believe. According to Baldwin et al. (1945), rejectant behavior is characterized either by nonchalance, inertness, and a general atmosphere of unconcern for the child's welfare or by an active dominance and a conspicuous hostility in the parent's treatment of the child. Frequently, in rejection, the parent's feeling of guilt is so covered up by attempts to compensate for such an unsocial attitude that the impression is created that the parent is overprotective. As Symonds (1938) has described it, the attitude of parents who reject their children is covered with a "coating of ostensible affection and pleasant relations."

In the case of mothers, rejection of the child usually comes from the mother's unhappy adjustment to marriage (Porter, 1955). For the most part, this is caused by the emotional instability of one or both parents and their emotional immaturity. Many rejecting mothers have definitely unsatisfactory sexual relationships, or they are dissatisfied with their marriages because of the responsibilities or the clash of personalities entailed (Gleason, 1931; Newell, 1934, 1936). Rejecting fathers, on the other hand, have been found to come from homes where they were somewhat spoiled by dominating mothers. Their parents were poorly mated, quarreled frequently, and the discipline of the children was harsh and inconsistent (Symonds, 1938).

Effects of rejection. The behavior of rejected children falls into four categories: *aggressive* (attention-getting, restless, disobedient, quarrelsome, etc.); *submissive* (poor in school work, shy and seclusive, sensitive and fearful); *mixed;* and *stable.* Boys are aggressive when either or both parents' handling is consistently hostile, Girls are aggressive when either or both parents' handling is ambivalent or when the father is hostile. Girls are submissive when the fathers are protective or ambivalent, and boys when either parent is consistently protective (Newell, 1936). Children recognize their parents' lack of affection and prefer the parent of whose affection they are uncertain (Newell, 1934).

Parental rejection jeopardizes normal security feelings, undermines the child's self-esteem, and induces feelings of helplessness and frustration. This can permanently disable the child in his adjustment to life (Wolberg, 1944). Among young children who feel rejected, behavior problems in the form of enuresis, feeding difficulties, nail biting, and other nervous mannerisms are common (Fitz-Simons, 1935). As children grow older, antisocial behavior in the form of aggression, cruelty, lying, stealing, swearing, seeking attention, praise and unnecessary help, and showing off is common. They show more overt expressions of antisocial and hostile behavior with less inhibition and anxiety than do children whose parents' attitudes are more favorable (Hattwick, 1936; Martin, 1943; Cummings, 1944; Winstet, 1951).

The rejected child lacks sustained application or concentration in school and is indifferent to school work. As a result, he fails to establish desirable skills in school subjects or sports and is generally antagonistic toward society and its institutions. As a rule, a rejected child shows emotional instability. He is confused and bewildered about his plans, cannot appraise himself objectively, and is inclined to relationalize by boasting. He often feels persecuted and indulges in self-pity (Symonds, 1938, 1949). Clinical treatment of severely rejected children has been found to be less successful than it is in most other clinical cases, showing how unfavorable home influences can persist even as the child grows older (Witmer et al., 1938).

In spite of the bad features associated with parental rejection, there are some constructive values. As a result of their experiences at home, rejected children are likely to develop some form of independence, are capable of amusing themselves and of developing a special interest. They are alert, shrewd, cunning, realistic, in a hurry to grow up and to leave school. This helps them to mature socially. They like to wear mature clothes and behave in a manner characteristic of older children. When feelings of rejection persist too long, rejected children become distrustful, not overanxious to please others or to accept responsibility. Girls often become tomboys, while boys run away from school and home (Bergum, 1940; Martin, 1943).

4. *Acceptance.* Parental acceptance means an attitude on the part of parents which is characterized by a keen interest in and love for the child.

The accepting parent not only wanted the child and, in many cases planned for him, but he did not find child care a trying or difficult job. The accepting parent puts the child in a position of importance in the home and develops a relationship with the child which is characterized by emotional warmth. The following characteristics have been found in an accepting parent:

He regards his child as a person with feelings and he respects the child's right and need to express these feelings.

He does not become emotionally disturbed because the child expresses negative feelings but makes a point of accepting and returning positive feelings.

He encourages freedom of emotional expression.

He keeps communication channels open and listens with open mind to the child's side of a problem when there is a conflict.

He values the unique make-up of the child and does what he can to foster that uniqueness within the limits of healthy personality and social adjustment.

He recognizes the child's need to differentiate and separate himself from his parents and thus become an autonomous individual.

He loves his child unconditionally. (Porter, 1954.)

There are different types of parental acceptance, and these depend upon the emotional maturity of the parents. Emotionally mature parents aim at the development of an independent individual and do all they can to achieve this goal, regardless of personal sacrifices. Emotionally immature parents, by contrast, are neurotically attached to their children and try to mold them into a form to suit their own standards (Baldwin, 1948). When acceptance is accompanied by indulgence, there is a tendency for the parents to identify themselves so completely with the child that they try to live their own lives over in his. Acceptance accompanied by a democratic attitude on the parents' part, by contrast, leads to the participation of the child in family discussions and the independence of the child as a person (Baldwin et al., 1945).

Symonds (1938) has studied parents who accept their children and compared their attitudes with those of parents who reject or neglect their children. According to him, "accepting" fathers have grown up with a kindly, intelligent, friendly, hard-working father and an intelligent, non-dominating mother. The parents are compatible and happy together, wise and consistent in their discipline. "Accepting" mothers were found to have kind, intelligent, and stable fathers. They had good relationships with their mothers, brothers, and sisters. This, Symonds maintained, was as important in the homes of the mothers as it was in the case of the fathers. When the marital adjustment of parents is good, their acceptance of their children is far greater than that of parents whose marital adjustments are poor. The degree of parental acceptance is significantly related to the educational level of the parents (Porter, 1955).

The accepted child is generally socialized, cooperative, friendly, loyal, emotionally stable, and cheerful. He accepts responsibilities and cares for his own property as well as that of others. As a rule, he is honest, straight-forward, dependable, faces life confidently, and has a clear idea about his plans and ambitions for the future. He can see himself realistically and can appraise his strengths and weaknesses in an objective fashion. As Symonds (1938, 1949) has pointed out, "good citizens, good scholars, good workers, good husbands and wives, and good parents come from homes in which the children are wanted and accepted."

5. *Domination.* In every home, there is apt to be one parent who dominates the whole family. A dominating parent usually comes from a family in which one or both parents were dominating. As a child, this parent was forced into submissiveness by his own parents. Later, as a parent, he dominates his own children in much the same way as he himself was dominated. The child who is dominated by one or both par-ents has better socialized behavior than the child who is given more free-dom. He is honest, polite, and careful. But he is also likely to be shy, docile, self-conscious, submissive, and sensitive. He feels inadequate, inferior, confused, bewildered, and inhibited (Symonds, 1938, 1949). He is easily led and dominated by his family but not by his peers. As he grows older, he is likely to feel cheated, to be afraid that others will cheat him, and to develop a "sucker complex" (Martin, 1943).

6. *Submission to Child.* Just the opposite of the dominating parents are the submissive parents who give in to their children and permit them to dominate the home. The child's every wish is gratified if the parents can possibly fulfill it, even against their better judgment. The child literally bosses his parents and treats them with little or no respect. Maternal sub-missiveness in the form of overindulgence is a weakness in maternal con-trol which consists of yielding to the wishes or actions of a child or submitting to demands not ordinarily tolerated by most parents. In its active form, it consists in willfully catering to a child's whims and wishes (Levy, 1939). Parents who submit to their children generally have in-adequate personalities characterized by childishness and failure to accept responsibility. They themselves were children of submissive parents and imitate in their own behavior the behavior pattern set for them by their parents (Symonds, 1939).

Every young child is demanding and calls upon adults for help, especially when other children are present. He insists upon having the adult's full attention and upon doing things as he pleases (Ilg et al., 1949). When par-ents permit themselves to be dominated by the child, the child usually becomes disobedient and irresponsible. He defies authority and is un-manageable, aggressive, stubborn, antagonistic, and careless. At the same time, he is independent and self-confident. Frequently submissive parents cause the child to feel overconfident, self-important, and uninhibited so far as boasting is concerned (Symonds, 1939, 1949). When a mother is oversubmissive, there is a tendency for the child to be infantile in his behavior and to have a rebellious, defiant, tyrannizing attitude toward the mother (Levy, 1939).

Effect of Parental Attitudes. Parental attitudes play a role of major importance in determining the attitudes and behavior of the child. Children who become successful as they grow older are almost always those who come from homes where parental attitudes toward them have been favorable and where a wholesome relationship between parent and child existed (Miles, 1946). Such a relationship will produce a happy, friendly child who is relatively free from anxieties and is a constructive, interdependent member of the group (Martin, 1943). The emotional and social adjustments of a child from a home where parent-child relationships are superior have been found to be definitely superior to those of children from homes where family relationships were less favorable (Lewis, 1945).

A good parent-child relationship is an affectional relationship. Indications of such a relationship are the degree to which the child shows a feeling of trust and security in his parents by sharing confidences with them and by going to them for advice and help on perplexing problems; by the degree to which the child has an opportunity for self-expression and for recognition of his work and play activities; and by the degree to which the family possesses solidarity or mutual loyalty. When an affectional relationship exists between the child and his parents, the character and personality of the child will be of the type to enable him to make successful adjustments to life (Brown et al., 1946, 1947). Good parent-child relationships result in the development of a sense of responsibility on the child's part and a willingness to assume responsibilities in the home (Harris et al., 1954, 1954a).

Unsuccessful children, by contrast, are usually the product of unhealthy parental attitudes and unfavorable parent-child relationships (Miles, 1946). The child who is deprived of attention and affection from his parents is hungry for affection and wants to be part of a group. He wants to be everywhere and is afraid of missing out. Furthermore, he is overwilling to please and to do things for others. All of this is a form of compensation and an attempt to buy affection at any cost (Martin, 1943). The child whose relationships with his parents are poor may show aggression toward them in their play rather than in real life where they fear to show such aggression (Isch, 1952). As the child grows older, poor relationships with his parents are often expressed in conflicts with them (Dinkel, 1943; Lu, 1952).

While a child may have a poor relationship with one or both parents, the most damaging effects on the child come from a poor relationship with his mother. The reason for this is that the child is with his mother more than with his father, and as a result, the mother's influence is greater than the father's. There are three common types of unfavorable mother-child relationships: too close a relationship in which there is an excessive contact with the child at all levels; too distant a relationship with lack of contact with the child; and inconsistency of relationship which is close at times, then distant (Sofman, 1949). Problem behavior in children comes more often from the mother-child than from the father-child relationship (Meyer, 1950). Young children show much the same patterns of behavior in their social relationships as those they have observed in their mothers (Bishop, 1951).

7. HOME SETTING

The kind of home the child has will have a marked influence on his whole outlook on life. And the kind of home will influence the relationships the child will have with his parents, siblings, or any individuals who may live permanently or temporarily in the home. As McGuire (1952) has pointed out, "Family life has a distinct influence upon the things, persons, and ideas we perceive, upon our attachments, and upon our valuations of experiences. For this reason, variations in family background result in different learning situations. The life style of the home sets limits upon the kinds of reality testing and insights a young person may experience and upon the selection of models for identification and imitation." Of the many factors in the home setting which play roles of importance in determining the attitudes and behavior of the child, the following have been found to be the most important:

a. **Socioeconomic Status.** The pattern of family life varies according to the socioeconomic group to which the family belongs. There are marked differences in behavior patterns in families of different socioeconomic groups, as in home management, table manners, or husband-wife relations, in concepts of the roles of parents, children, and relatives, in family values, in the use of money, in social conformity, in child training and attitudes toward discipline, and in attitudes relating to family life, such as desired number of children and loyalty to the family (Bühler, 1948; Benedict, 1949; Havighurst, 1950a, 1953; Maas, 1951a; McGuire, 1952; Bossard, 1953, 1954). Certain values are held in common by mothers of different social classes, though they may not be put into practice in the same way (McGuire, 1952).

Middle-class parents regard their children with "possessive pride and hope." They emphasize social conformity to achieve status, they supervise their children closely and expect them to avoid any behavior which might bring criticism on the family. The child is encouraged to be independent at an early age as a way of "getting ahead." Education is emphasized because it is a way of "bettering themselves." This is especially true in the case of boys. The middle-class child is expected to inhibit emotional expressions and aggressions at an early age. He is given little information about sex and is severely criticized by his parents for any behavior related to sex. Because the middle-class child is wanted by his parents and is regarded as a fulfillment of their marriage, he is treated in a kindly manner, is usually brought up in a democratic home atmosphere, and is given as many advantages as his parents can afford (Davis and Dollard, 1940; Davis and Havighurst, 1946; Havighurst, 1950, 1953; Maas, 1951a; Aberle and Naegele, 1952; McGuire, 1952; Bossard, 1953, 1954). In spite of all the parental attention the middle-class child receives, the constant pressure to maintain the family status often leads to behavior problems and neurosis (Green, 1946).

The attitude of lower-class parents toward the child is that a child is the "inevitable payment for sex relations" (Bossard, 1954). This attitude does not produce the same friendly or warm relationship that characterizes the middle-class family. Children from lower-class families are given greater physical and social freedom than are those from the middle classes; they are permitted to go around the community and to movies at an earlier age; and there is little concern on the part of their parents about their education. Parental control is usually of an authoritarian type with severe punishments and little praise. Discipline is inconsistent, with loving and petting alternating with slapping to "toughen him up." The lower-class child often feels unloved, unwanted, and rejected at home and, to compensate for this, seeks companionship outside the home (Davis, 1944; Davis and Havighurst, 1946; Maas, 1951a; McGuire, 1951, 1952; Bossard, 1953, 1954).

The socioeconomic status of the family influences the type of home and the location of the home in the community. This determines to a large extent what kind of associates the child will have. Favorable or unfavorable attitudes will be developed, depending upon the kind of children the child is associated with in school and in his recreational activities. Because the social structure of our country is characterized by potential social mobility, there is always the possibility of shifting to another socioeconomic group and accepting the life style of that group. Some families are *conforming*, in that the standards of both parents agree with the social-class patterns of their group; others are *mobile*, in that both parents are oriented to a life better than theirs; others are *divergent*, in that one parent is motivated by one standard and the other parent by another standard; while still others are *declining*, in that one or both parents slip backward to the standards of a lower class (McGuire, 1952a).

The attitudes of one or both parents toward *acculturation*, or the acceptance of a new status level, will result in changes in the pattern of family life and in the attitudes and behavior of the child. When social-class continuity exists, there will be more closeness in family relationships. However, should the children move up as a result of influences outside the home and the parents remain stationary, there will be much less closeness in family relationships (Lemasters, 1954). On the other hand, should one parent be mobile and the other static, the child is likely to identify himself with the parent having the higher status, and this will lead to family friction resulting from different ideals and values (McGuire, 1952a; Bossard, 1953, 1954; Lemasters, 1954).

b. Economic Status. The economic status of the family, which frequently determines what the family social status will be, is especially important when it is markedly favorable or unfavorable. As Teagarden (1946) has pointed out, "The parental anxiety that is engendered by poverty, together with possible malnutrition and overcrowding, will in many cases cause psychic wounds." Equally unfavorable is a home setting of great wealth in which children are neglected by their parents and brought up by servants whose ignorance of child rearing and lack of interest in the children produce even more harmful effects on the child's attitudes than those suffered in homes where poverty predominates.

Aggressive personality problems, such as stealing, truancy, and running away, are more common in poor homes, while submissive personality traits, as overdependence, educational difficulties, and school maladjustments, are more often found among children coming from economically superior homes (Pisula, 1937). Jealousy has been found to increase as family income decreases (Sewall, 1930). Economic insecurity makes for emotional insecurity. Economic security, on the other hand, does not necessarily imply emotional security. Greater emotional security occurs among children from the middle-income group than from the richest groups (Meltzer, 1936). Economically favored parents deal more intelligently with their children than do less favored parents, and as a result, they have fewer behavior problems in their children (Ulton, 1936). Furthermore, parents in a favorable economic position have more time for family recreations than do those in a less favorable position (Hawkins and Walters, 1952).

c. Parental Occupations. The father's occupation has a profound influence on the child's outlook. In the early years of childhood, it is important only as it has a direct bearing on the child's welfare, such as his food, clothing, and play equipment. However, as he becomes older and begins to play with other children, the father's occupation has a cultural significance in that it gives the child social prestige or denies it. If the father's occupation is one that carries prestige, the child can bask in "reflected glory" and assimilate some of the prestige (Podolsky, 1954). The attitude of the social group, but especially of the child's peers, toward the father's occupation has a marked impact on the child (Bettelheim and Sylvester, 1950). When a child is ashamed of his father's occupation, either because of the level of work done or because of the type of clothes demanded by the work, it will affect the child's attitude toward his father, his home, and himself as an individual (Bossard, 1953, 1954).

The father's occupation affects the child indirectly in that it influences the father's standards for the child. From his experiences in work, the father knows what attitudes, skills, and qualities are essential to success in life. The father then tries to foster them in the child. Thus, standards of the occupational world "infect" the home and influence the father's role (Aberle and Naegele, 1952). Many occupations require that the father be away from home for short or long periods of time. This results in a temporary break in the family and produces a different home climate than when the family is intact. Furthermore, many occupations require shifts of residence. So long as the child is young, the major effect on him will be the break in the continuity of family life which is inevitable with residential mobility. As he becomes older, the effects will be more pronounced and more far-reaching. The child will have to adjust to a new school, to new friends, and to the mores of the new community. In addition, his parents will be preoccupied with problems arising in connection with the change and will be able to give him less time and attention than usual. During a period of adjustment to a new community, there are likely to be tension and friction in the home, and this affects every member of the family (Carrington, 1940; Landis, 1952; Bossard, 1954; Stubblefield, 1955). Family moves are often traumatic experiences for children and result in eating and sleep problems, enuresis and nightmares for young children, and in regression, daydreaming, and increased friction between siblings in older children (Stubblefield, 1955).

There are more mothers working outside the home than ever before. For the most part, they are mothers of children under ten years of age or of children who are away from home at school, college, or in homes of their own (Durand, 1948; Turner, 1952). While some mothers work because they have careers they do not want to abandon, most mothers work to supplement the family income or to support the family when the father is ill, dead, or has abandoned the family. While they are at work, they provide some care and supervision for the children, in day nurseries, with relatives or friends, or at home with an older sibling (Mohr, 1948; Bossard, 1953, 1954).

How the mother's working affects the child depends partly upon the age of the child and partly upon the provision made for the child's care while the mother works. The young child usually feels lonely and unhappy when the mother is away for the major part of the day, and different forms of discipline used by the mother and the mother substitute are confusing to him. Home duties are neglected, meals are irregular, there are few opportunities for social life and recreations with the family, and each child must assume more home duties than he would if the mother were at home. Children of working mothers often come to school late, they are not so well groomed as children whose mothers do not work, they are often inadequately fed, owing to the necessity of getting their own meals or eating at irregular times, and they are often nervous, which makes it difficult for them to concentrate, with the result that they do poor school work (Mathews, 1934; Keliher, 1943; Mohr, 1948; Bossard, 1954).

How the child feels about his mother's working depends partly upon how seriously her work interferes with his life and partly upon what his friends' mothers do (Mohr, 1948). Most children object to having their mothers work because they are lonely and feel that there is no home life when the mother is away. Furthermore, when the mother comes home from work, she is often tired and irritable, and this affects her relationships with the children (Fleege, 1945a). If the mother is engaged in work that has prestige in the eyes of the child's friends, his attitude will be different than it will be if he is ashamed of her work or the fact that she works when his friends' mothers do not. By earning money, especially if it is from a part-time job that does not keep her away from home too long or interfere too much with the child's life, the mother gains status in her child's eyes (Nye, 1952). The type of adjustment children make to their mothers' work has been found to range from quiet submission to bitter resentment (Bossard, 1953, 1954).

d. Outsiders in the Home. The presence of grandparents or other relatives in the home is bound to influence either directly or indirectly the child's behavior, depending upon the status of the relatives. Should the child's parents, for example, be living in the home of grandparents, it is frequently necessary for them to defer to the wishes of the grandparents, to ensure harmony in the home. Today, as a result of the housing shortage and the dependency of old people, there is an increasing number of grandparents living in the homes of their children. The three-generation household is a "hazardous type of family living in which the combined virtues of a diplomat, statesman, and saint are needed" (Koller, 1954).

Elderly people who have had considerable authority in the past do not find it easy to relinquish power to their children when they go to live in the home of one of their children. The children, in turn, resent an intrusion in their homes and a threat to their authority. The grandchildren are baffled by the splitting of authority among their elders (Koller, 1954). Maternal grandparents, as a rule, exert more influence than do paternal grandparents, Of the grandparents, it is usually the grandmother who exerts the greater influence. While a grandmother may assume many household responsibilities, she also tries to impose her own standards of child rearing. This leads to friction with the grandchild and feelings of resentment or inadequacy on the part of the parents. Furthermore, grandparents tend to favor their grandsons, and this does not improve family harmony

(Borden, 1946; Fried and Stern, 1948; Bossard, 1953, 1954). The disrupting influence of the grandmother comes not so much from her age as from her rigid ideas about child rearing. Because the grandfather comes in contact with the grandchildren less than the grandmother, he is a less disrupting influence in the home (Vollmer, 1937).

For the most part, grandparents are more satisfied with their relationships with the younger generation than their children or grandchildren are. They enjoy the social contacts with young people, they find such contacts more stimulating than contacts with members of their own generation, and they enjoy social contacts with the younger generations without having any real responsibilities. They bask in reflected glory when their grandchildren are successful but assume no blame for their mistakes or failures (Albrecht, 1954). For the most part, grandchildren's attitudes toward their grandparents are less favorable. They judge them in terms of the cultural stereotype of old age and attribute to them the physical and mental characteristics of old age. In this, they are influenced by their parents' attitudes toward old age (Tuckman and Lorge, 1953, 1953a, 1954; *New York Times,* 1954c; Tuckman et al., 1953).

What influence other relatives have on the child will depend largely upon how close and how frequent their contacts with the child are. In spite of the fact that children are encouraged to have feelings of loyalty toward their kinfolk, there is likely to be friction when relatives criticize the child or his parents or when they try to exert authority over the child. Friction is increased when relatives from the two sides of the family come from different socioeconomic groups. There is a tendency for the child, as he grows older and becomes aware of social-class differences, to identify himself with the relatives of the higher-class parent and to feel ashamed of the relatives of the lower-class parent (Bossard, 1953, 1954; Bossard and Boll, 1946).

Guests in the home have a marked influence on the child. The child gets new social perspectives for measuring his parents, the family status, and the pattern of family living; he learns new social roles and skills; and he acquires new interests and new information from listening to what the guests say. However, he may resent the presence of guests because it means extra work for every member of the family, it disrupts his own plans for play, and it often creates tensions with his parents who want him to make a "good impression" on the guests (Bossard, 1953, 1954). Most of the advantages and few of the disadvantages from having guests occur when the child visits in the homes of others (Bossard, 1951).

One source of trouble in many families is the mother-surrogate. While relatively few families with young children today have full-time, live-in domestic servants, many employ a baby-sitter occasionally so the parents may go out in the evenings or on holidays. Some have a part-time worker one or two days a week who may be asked to take charge of the children during the mother's absence. The presence of a servant in the home may change the climate of the home, especially when there is emphasis on the child's "acting properly" for fear of losing the servant. The baby sitter may be more lenient in her discipline than the mother, and this leads to conflicting pressures on the child and resentments toward the mother because of her strictness. On the other hand, having help with domestic duties gives the mother more free time to devote to the child and eliminates some of the tension and friction which comes when the mother is overworked (Bossard, 1953, 1954).

e. Broken Homes. When the home is broken, because of death, separation, or divorce of one of the parents, the whole pattern of family life is markedly changed. When the break is due to death, it may necessitate giving up the home and going to live with a grandparent or some other relative. There are usually financial problems when the remaining parent is the mother, and problems of care of the children when the remaining parent is the father. Should the break be caused by separation, divorce, or desertion, there is the added complication of antagonism between the parents and the shifting of the child from one parent to another. Thus it is important to note that the *type* of broken home will determine what influence it will have on the child (Nye, 1952).

Bossard (1954) has suggested seven possible effects of the broken home on the child. These are as follows: conflict is created when the child is attached to both parents; the child carries within himself the continuing awareness of the problem; the child may find restraints placed upon him which were not present when the parents were together; the child must often face the transition from a broken home to a stepchild status; the child may have to shift between two different homes and adjust to two different home climates; the child may compare his home life with that of children from unbroken homes; and the child may develop new and disturbed points of view toward both parents.

Homes that are temporarily broken by the father's absence produce stress situations for the child as well as for the parents when the father returns. A study of war-born children whose fathers were away from home when they were born and during the early part of their lives revealed that the children had more behavior problems, they were more restricted in locomotor activities, had more contacts with close relatives and fewer with other children, made poorer social adjustments outside the home and were more dependent on adults, were aggressive in a hostile form with other children, and had greater feelings of anxiety than had children who had grown up in a home where both parents were present. The distant relationship of the child with his father, when the father returned home, brought unhappiness to the child and to the father (Stolz et al., 1954).

In recent years, one out of every five marriages in the United States has been a remarriage. The presence of children often encourages remarriage to solve the problems that the broken home brings. However, remarriage brings its own problems and necessitates difficult adjustments for all, especially for the child (Bossard, 1953). How the child will adjust to the *stepparent* and the new pattern of home life created by the stepparent will be influenced by many factors. The child who has been attached to the parent who is being replaced by the stepparent will react differently from the child whose attitude toward his former parent was less favorable. Children are often introduced to the changes a stepparent brings unfairly, sometimes without any warning of the change, and this builds up resentments from the start.

Then there is the stereotype of the stepparent, especially that of the "wicked stepmother," which the child learns from his fairy tales, the movies, or from his friends. He has a mental picture of the stepmother by which he judges her in every act, and he has a tendency to misinterpret what she says or does as indications of lack of mother love. This "hangs a millstone around the neck of the stepmother and makes her role an exceedingly difficult one" (Smith, 1949). The age of the child is important in determining what adjustments he will make to a stepparent. The young child who is dependent and has few memories will generally adjust better than the older child who is less dependent and remembers his former parent better. The personality traits of the stepparent, especially the degree of confidence the stepparent has regarding his adequacy for the role, and the personality of the child, which may have been damaged during the interval between the break in the home and the appearance of the stepparent, are likewise important factors in determining the effects the stepparent will have on the child's attitudes and behavior. Because the stepmother comes in contact with the child more than does the stepfather, her influence over the child is greater than is that of the stepfather (Smith, 1945, 1949, 1955; Pfleger, 1947; Bossard, 1953, 1954).

8. Family Roles

In primitive cultures and in most civilized cultures throughout history, the role of each member of the family has been rigidly prescribed by custom, convention, and law. As a result, each child growing up in such cultures learned what role he was expected to play at different periods in his life, and he accepted these roles without question (Mead, 1939; Burgess and Locke, 1945; Tasch, 1952). In the American culture today, the roles of the different members of the family are undergoing certain changes as a result of urban life, which takes the father away from home for a major part of the day, and of the growing tendency for mothers to work outside the home (Cavan, 1953). In addition, there are differences of opinion as to how to achieve the end results prescribed by these roles. For example, there is a question about the best ways to rear a child so that he will be a "good" child, and there is a question about just what a "good" child should be. This is complicated by differences of opinion in different social classes and by the shifting of family status from one social class to another (Duvall, 1946; Havighurst, 1950a, 1953; McGuire, 1952). In Fig. 68 are shown social-class differences in concepts of a "good mother" and a "good child."

Like all other concepts, concepts of family roles are built up through personal experiences in the individual's home and in homes of relatives and friends; from observations of others; from movies, radio, television and other media of mass communication; and from reading books which deal with family life. Most books of this sort present a picture of democratic

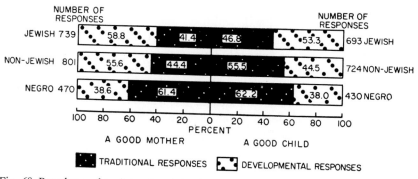

Fig. 68. Prevalence of traditional and developmental concepts of a "good mother" and a "good child" in four social classes. (*From E. M. Duvall, Conceptions of parenthood. Amer. J. Sociol., 1946, 52, 193–203. Used by permission.*)

family life which may be very contradictory to the authoritarian controls in the child's own home (Fisher, 1950). Because each individual has different learning experiences, there are likely to be different concepts of different family roles held by the various members of the same family. This leads to conflicts and tension which are especially pronounced when the child, through associations in school, develops concepts that differ markedly from those held by his parents (Havighurst, 1950a). On the other hand, there is an advantage to lack of rigidity in concepts of different roles in that it permits greater individuality and a change to meet changing circumstances (Allen, 1942; Waller and Hill, 1951).

a. Concept of Parents. To an adult, a parent is not just a person who brings a child into the world and cares for him during the helpless years of childhood. Instead, the role of the parent is to equip the child with the resources needed to meet the demands of life (Nimkoff, 1934; Murphy et al., 1937; Prevey, 1949; Breckenridge and Vincent, 1955). To do this, the child *needs* parents, but not just any kind of parents. He needs parents who will offer appropriate guidance and provide experiences in freedom and control which will help him to be ready to face life successfully (Prevey, 1949). While parenthood produces many problems, it also brings many satisfactions to the parents, especially in the form of companionship with the child and the satisfaction of watching the child grow and develop (Jersild, 1954).

"Good parents" are well-adjusted people who want the child to grow and develop (Symonds, 1949, 1949a). As a result of their training, the child is equipped to live a happy, useful life (Nimkoff, 1934). As Bain (1954) has pointed out, "Good parents are thoroughly committed to the idea that the primary business of parents is to make their children as completely independent of the parents at as early an age as possible. Parents who accept this Golden Rule will produce normal people. They will help construct a good society without which normal people cannot exist."

While all parents want to be good parents, they have different beliefs about the way to achieve this goal. Their concepts of their roles as parents influence their attitude toward the child and their methods of dealing with him (Lafore, 1945). In general, parents' concepts of their roles fall into two categories, traditional and developmental. The *traditional* concept emphasizes the authoritarian role of the parent, which stresses "making" the child conform to a pattern by instilling in the child's mind the culturally approved moral and religious values. The *developmental* concept, by contrast, emphasizes respect for the person and a permissive, growth-promoting type of guidance (Duvall, 1946; Baldwin, 1948; Elder, 1949; Escalona, 1949; Waller and Hill, 1951; Tasch, 1952; Connor et al., 1954). The traditional concept is more prevalent among the lower social classes, and the developmental among the upper classes (Duvall, 1946; Havighurst, 1950a). Parents from farms and small towns are inclined to follow the traditional concept, while city parents are more likely to follow the developmental concept (Stott, 1945).

The *child's concept of parents* is built up first from his experiences with his own parents (Stogdill, 1937). As he becomes older and comes in contact with other families through visiting in the homes of his relatives and friends (Bossard, 1951) or reads about parents in stories dealing with family life (Fisher, 1950), he is likely to change his earlier concept. The child often perceives his parent in a different light than the parent perceives himself. The parent is frequently perceived as a frustrating individual by the child, while the parent sees himself as a facilitating being (Anderson, 1946).

To most children, parents are people who do things for them and on whom the child can depend (Meltzer, 1935, 1943). Their concepts of parents are more often based on parental activities, such as the mother doing housework and the father going to work, than on the physical appearance or the personality make-up of the parents. They think of their parents in terms of the work their parents do and the time and energy devoted to their relationships with them (Finch, 1955). Having fun with their parents is an important element in their concepts of parents (Radke, 1946). To the child, a "good parent" is permissive or giving; he takes an interest in the home, the children, and the children's interests; he respects the child's individuality; and he inspires love, not fear, in the child (Sowers, 1937; Martin, 1943).

The developmental concept of parenthood emphasizes a growth-promoting type of guidance on the part of both parents. (*From Child Development, a McGraw-Hill Text-Film.*)

Children not only have definite concepts of what a mother and father should be, but they also are aware of weaknesses in parents. There are certain things of which they disapprove or which they dislike in parents. Every parent is keenly aware of the fact that sons and daughters, even before they reach the age of adolescence, become hypercritical of their parents. Frequently, however, parents do not know exactly what it is that their children dislike about them. The things which, most commonly, have been found to annoy children most in their parents' behavior are punishment, interference with their pleasures, and such parent-child conflicts. Most children, in addition, have individual "peeves" about their parents (Radke, 1946; Grace and Lohmann, 1952).

Children in urban districts are much less likely to be critical of their parents than are those in rural districts. When they do criticize, it is about more serious matters (Stott, 1945). Both boys and girls are likely to be more critical of their fathers than of their mothers. The most frequent sources of dissatisfaction with their fathers have been reported to be scolding, general irritability, swearing, poor relationships with the mother, and being away from home. Boys are more critical of their fathers than are girls. Both boys and girls feel that their fathers should give them more money, let them play more, and punish them less (Gardner, 1947).

Children not only know what they dislike in their parents, but they also have fairly definite ideas of what they would like their parents to be and what traits they would prefer to have their parents possess. They would like them to be companionable, understanding, kind, loving, affectionate, and good-natured, and to set a good example. The characteristics they regard as most important are personality traits that make their parents more interested in and sympathetic toward them (Sowers, 1937; Bossard, 1953; Hertz, 1955).

b. Concept of Mother. The *traditional* concept of the mother's role, which is held more by members of the lower than of the middle and upper classes today, is that of the authoritarian person in the child's life, who disciplines, teaches, and takes care of the children and the house with little help from the father. She may even be the provider for the family. The concept of the role of the mother in middle-class families is more *developmental* and stresses fostering the development of the child, having interests outside the home, having assistance from the father in the care of the children, and sometimes having outside help so she can do more for and with the children (Duvall, 1946; Havighurst, 1950a; Johnson, 1952; Connor et al., 1954).

The young child thinks of the mother as the person who does things for him, takes care of his physical needs with understanding, relates herself lovingly to the child, can tolerate a great deal of childish mischief, and who comes to the child's aid in time of trouble (Lerner, 1937; Meltzer, 1943; Duvall, 1946; Cederquist, 1948; Mott, 1954). The young child's concept of the mother centers mainly on her activities rather than on her appearance (Mott, 1954). As children grow older, their concepts change slightly. While they still think of the mother primarily in terms of what she does for them, they become more critical of her than they did when they were younger. This is especially true when any of her interests or activities interfere with their pleasures (Mathews, 1934; Radke, 1946; Barclay, 1953). Boys tend to idealize their mothers more than do girls and hence are less critical (Kent, 1951).

The child's concept of mother is influenced by social pressures. As Stoodley (1952) has pointed out,

As children grow up they naturally pick up ideas as to who is the "big wheel" in their family. More often than not it isn't Mother. Perhaps they go to a school where the teachers are women, but the principal is a man. Perhaps they see that the jobs they consider important are occupied mostly by men. Or perhaps they absorb the sentiment of their social milieu which associates prestige with some specific kind of expertness, whether it be that of the certified public accountant, the skilled mechanic, or the physician. Society does not associate this expertness with the mother's role. . . . Faithful to the trend of social influence, as the child orients to a competitive environment in which the prize goes to specific expertness, the mother's influence is more than likely to go into a partial and sometimes a total eclipse (p. 14).

c. Concept of Father. Traditionally, the father is the provider and the head of the house, while the mother is entrusted with the care of the house and the children. If the father teaches the child, he does so unconsciously, by his example rather than by precept. This concept is held mainly by fathers of the lower socioeconomic classes. By contrast, fathers of the middle and upper classes are holding more to the *developmental* concept of the father's role, which emphasizes understanding of and companionship with their children, consciously teaching the children and guiding their development and doing things for and with them. The father who holds to the developmental concept of his role uses more democratic forms of control over the child, less severe punishment, and is interested in helping his child to prepare for a future in keeping with the child's abilities (Duvall, 1946; Elder, 1949; Havighurst, 1950a; Johnson, 1952; Tasch, 1952; Bartemeier, 1953; Connor et al., 1954).

The concept of the role of father has been subject to greater change in recent years than has that of the mother (Tasch, 1952). Many men, especially those who are foreign-born or whose parents are foreign-born, find it difficult to accept the developmental concept (Duvall, 1946; Tasch, 1952). Because it is traditional for the father to be authoritarian in his attitudes toward the child, the man who loves his sons is often considered "soft and unmasculine." Therefore, to conform to social ideals, the father becomes strict and harsh in his treatment of his sons and, by doing so, is likely to make bullies out of them (Bartemeier, 1953). Many men feel that they are inadequate as fathers, especially in such areas as discipline, companionship with their children, and teaching of character traits (Gardner, 1943).

When a father has been separated from his children for a relatively long period of time, he is apt to feel inadequate in his role of father when he returns home. A study of the father's relationships with war-born children revealed that the father anticipated with some trepidation the problems he faced when he returned from war. These problems included adjustment to a job, to his wife, and to the first-born child who had been born during the father's absence. The strain of these adjustments simultaneously led to tensions and anxieties. Furthermore, the adjustments were complicated by differences in the husband's and wife's methods of child rearing and by disagreements with the wife's family (Stolz et al., 1954).

Most children have a fairly definite, clear-cut concept of "father," which differs markedly from their concept of "mother." According to this concept, the father is away from home more than the mother, he punishes more and harder than the mother, he knows more and is, in general, more important than the mother because he earns the money, owns more, and is the head of the family, the "boss" (Lerner, 1937; Meltzer, 1943). How the father treats the mother not only influences the child's concept of his father, but it also influences the child, indirectly, through the effect it has on the mother (Bartemeier, 1953).

d. Concept of Child. The traditional concept of a "good" child is one who respects his parents, obeys, pleases adults, shares and cooperates in the duties of the home, and is healthy and eager to learn. He will honor his parents for their unselfish devotion to him. The daughter is supposed to help in the household and play the role of provider early. The son is expected to achieve independence early and to contribute to his support in the home. This traditional concept is held more by lower-class parents than by middle and upper, and more by fathers than by mothers (Duvall, 1946; Elder, 1949; Havighurst, 1950a; Tasch, 1952; Connor et al., 1954). According to the *developmental* concept, which is held more widely by middle- and upper-class parents, the child is guided into a pattern of development suited to his innate make-up, rather than forced to conform to some socially approved ideal. The daughter is a learner with few responsibilities to the family, and the family serves her. The son, like the daughter, is dependent on the family (Duvall, 1946; Havighurst, 1950a; Connor et al., 1954).

The child's concept of his role is markedly influenced by his parents' concepts. If they think of him as a dependent, he will learn to believe that this is the child's role; if they wait on him, he will believe that a child is expected to be waited on. As is true of the parents' concept of the child, the child's concept of his role will differ according to the social class to which he belongs. Regardless of social class, however, most children hold the concept, based on their moral and religious training in the home, the school, and Sunday school, that a "good" child honors and respects his parents, is obedient to his parents' dictates, is of the sex the parents prefer, and is cooperative but never a troublemaker in the home (Stogdill, 1937; Connor et al., 1954).

9. CHILDREN'S PREFERENCE FOR PARENTS

Psychoanalysts explain the child's preference for one parent in terms of the Oedipus theory, that there is an innate, unconscious sexual desire among sons for their mothers and among daughters for their fathers. If this were true, it would mean that the child's preference was always for a parent of the opposite sex. To date, studies have not revealed this to be true. Instead, the child's attitude toward the parent is determined by the child's age, his position in the family, the way he is treated by his parents and their attitude toward him, the child's personality, cultural attitudes toward the relative importance of the mother and father, and many other factors. Thus it becomes apparent that parental preferences are learned and are influenced by the learning situation which exists for each individual child. There is no evidence of a congenital preference for either parent (Bossard, 1953).

How much time the parent spends with the child and how close the social contact of parent and child is are important in determining the child's preference for one parent. In the case of the mother whose role is traditionally that of being with the child while, traditionally, the father's role is that of the family breadwinner, there is usually greater emotional warmth for the child than in the case of the father. Furthermore, children generally play more with the mother and have more happy experiences with the mother than with the father (Jersild et al., 1933; Meltzer, 1935, 1943; Stagner and Drought, 1935; Duvall, 1937; Stogdill, 1937; Henry and Emme, 1939; Nimkoff, 1942; Rose, 1947; Bossard, 1953).

The longer the parent is separated from the child, the greater will be the child's preference for the remaining parent who takes care of him in the absence of the other parent. In the case of children born while their fathers were in the war, it was found that the child's immediate response to the father on his return was shy, withdrawing, and unresponsive behavior. The father, in turn, became critical of the child and his behavior, thus alienating the child who, in turn, rejected the father and turned even more than before to the mother for attention and affection. The attitudes of boys toward their fathers were found to be less favorable than those of girls (Stolz et al., 1954).

It is logical that the person who does most for the child should be preferred by the child. This is generally the mother. In the early years of childhood, when the child is dependent upon adults for care, the mother is unquestionably the preferred parent (Duvall, 1937, Meltzer, 1941a; Bossard, 1953). However, young children show a preference for one parent or the other in different situations. They prefer the mother in such situations as cooking, holding hands, having a bath, and reading, while the father is preferred for playing games. Girls prefer to have their mothers dress them, to sit beside their mothers and to sleep with them, and to do things to help their mothers. Boys prefer their fathers in these connections (Ammons and Ammons, 1949).

The parent who restricts the child most and punishes most is preferred less. In our culture, this is the father (Watson, 1934; Nimkoff, 1942; Havighurst, 1950a). Both boys and girls definitely prefer their father when their mother punishes them, and their mother when their father punishes them

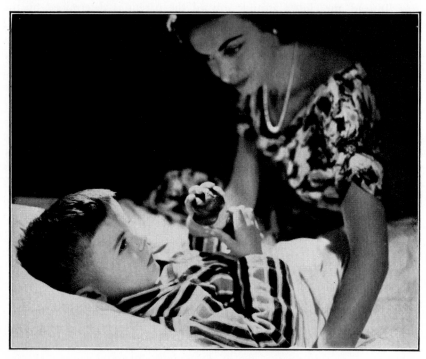

In the early years of childhood, the mother is the preferred parent because she is the one who does most for the child. (*From Child Development, a McGraw-Hill Text-Film.*)

(Ammons and Ammons, 1949). The parent who expects too much of the child and is critical of the child who does not live up to these expectations is less favored than the parent whose expectations for the child are more within the child's capacities. Mothers of planned-for children have a tendency to expect too much of their children (Sloman, 1948); so do most fathers who carry over the standards of the business world into their homes (Aberle and Naegele, 1952). Where fathers are away from home for long periods of time, as in the case of war-born children, they are more likely to be concerned about the child's behavior, such as eating, elimination, whining, thumb sucking, manners, etc., than are fathers who are with their children more constantly. This results in more severe discipline on the father's part and a withdrawal of the child from the father and attachment to the mother (Stolz et al., 1954).

While parents usually claim that they show no preference for any child, the child *senses* that there is a preference, and this affects his attitude toward the parent. The only child does not have this problem and, as a result, shows no real preference for either parent (Roberts, 1938). The youngest child in the family, or the first-born, should the child be a boy, is usually the mother's favorite. When there are boys and girls in the same family, the mother's preference is usually for the boys. As a result, it is not surprising that, at an early age, a boy begins to show a greater preference for his mother, while a girl tends to prefer the father. This tendency

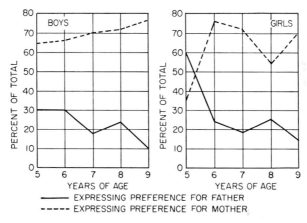

Fig. 69. Father-mother preferences of boys and girls grouped according to age. (*From M. Simpson, Parent preferences of young children, Teachers College Bureau of Publications, 1935. Used by permission.*)

grows stronger as children grow older and become more clearly aware of parental preferences (Yarnelle, 1932; Simpson, 1935; Duvall, 1937; Mott, 1937; Ammons and Ammons, 1949; Winch, 1951). Preferences of children of different ages for the father and mother are shown in Fig. 69. At all ages, but especially as children grow older, the father influences the sons more than the daughters (Brodbeck, 1954).

Back of all preferences is a reason. The child does not just happen to prefer one parent to another. In his mind, the preferred parent has an advantage over the other parent, and that advantage is generally in favor of the child. In other words, the child prefers the parent who, in one way or another, means more to him than does the parent who is not preferred. The reasons most often given by children for their preference for the mother are that they feel the mother understands them better; the mother is easier to get along with than the father; the father likes to be the "big boss"; the mother uses corporal punishment less than the father; and the mother is around more to supply the child's material wants. Furthermore, the father's attitude seems to change when children reach the age of six years, and he plays less with the children than he did when they were younger. When services are required of parents, the father is preferred for broken toys and need of money; the mother for help in case of illness, trouble in school, loss of something, or hurt feelings (Simpson, 1935; Gardner, 1947).

Chapter 15

PERSONALITY

The term "personality" comes from the Latin word *persona,* a mask that was worn by an actor while speaking or performing on the stage. The wearer of the mask revealed himself through his speech and his actions. Personality now has somewhat the same import. What a person is, how he thinks and feels, and what is included in his whole psychological make-up are, to a great extent, revealed through his behavior and his speech. Personality, then, is not one definite, specific attribute. It is, rather, the "quality of the individual's total behavior" (Woodworth, 1947). An individual's personality is the "total picture of his organized behavior, especially as it can be characterized by his fellow men in a consistent way" (Dashiell, 1949).

Personality Pattern. Personality is made up of many components, some of which are *objective,* observable, and measurable, while others are *subjective* and, therefore, less easily studied and measured. Among the objective characteristics of personality are physical characteristics, such as body size and physique, and factors in the mechanics and chemistry of his body which influence the speed and strength of his movements; aptitudes and talents, both physical and intellectual; and traits, habits, behavior patterns, and modes of action. The subjective components of personality include motives, aspirations, feelings, ideas, and attitudes regarding self, convictions, commitments, and purposes that give direction to the individual's way of thinking, feeling, and acting (Jersild, 1954).

The personality pattern is made up of "traits," or specific qualities of behavior. These consist of reactions to frustrations, ways of meeting problems, aggressive and defensive behavior, and outgrowing or withdrawing attitudes toward other people (Landis, 1954). However, the personality make-up does not consist merely of a sum of traits, but rather of traits that are organized and integrated into a pattern. The "core," or "center of gravity," of this pattern is made up of habits and attitudes fixed early in life but which may be added to and modified by the experiences of the individual (Breckenridge and Vincent, 1955). The concept of self is the picture the individual holds of himself, his abilities, his characteristics, his worth, and his relations to the world about him (Pearl, 1950; Jersild, 1951, 1954; Brownfain, 1952).

The person's image of himself as a self contains a *physical* self-image and a *psychological* self-image. The physical self-image contains the individual's concepts of his physical appearance and the importance of all parts of his body to his behavior and to the prestige they give him in the eyes of others. The psychological self-image is composed of traits that play a role of importance in his adjustments to life, such as honesty, independence, and helplessness (Anderson, 1952). The self-image, or feeling about self, is determined largely by the nature of the individual's relations with others. The self-image thus becomes a "mirror image" through which the individual's feelings about himself are influenced by the way important people in his life treat him and how they feel about him (Anderson, 1950). The role or status the individual occupies in a group or in society thus influences markedly the concept he holds of himself as an individual (Blos, 1941).

Development of Concept of Self. The individual's personality is organized around the concept of self or of selves, each of which has a definite sociocultural reference station or has resulted from the interaction of the individual and a specific sociocultural environment. The organization of these concepts of self is hierarchical. The concept of self which is acquired first (the primary concept) is the most basic. This is acquired in the family-group environment. Other concepts of self (secondary concepts) are acquired later, in other group environments outside the home. All of these concepts may be favorable or unfavorable, and they vary in importance to the general concept of self.

The primary self-concept usually influences the selection of situations in which secondary concepts of self are formed. How well integrated the primary and secondary concepts will be will depend upon the degree of continuity between the primary and secondary sociocultural environments. A child brought up in a home environment, for example, where he is the center of attention, will have to change his concept of self in environments outside the home where his status will be markedly different. The degree of integration of primary and secondary selves will, in turn, affect the degree of adjustment the individual achieves (Dai, 1952).

While concepts of self develop as a result of experiences inside the home and outside, in school, on the playground, and in any social group with which the child may be identified, the primary concepts, because they are developed first, are the most important and most basic. Thus, it is apparent, the child's home environment plays a significant role in the development of his personality. In addition, the home environment is important in maintaining ego strength. Any break in the family may have serious effects on the child's concept of self. Not the parents alone but every member of the family group contributes to the child's developing concept of self (Josselyn, 1953). This is influenced more by the relationships the child has with his parents and other family members, such as his identification with one family member or parental expectations, than by the experiences he shares with them

(Carter, 1954). Statements made by his parents, their praise or blame, all contribute to the development of a concept of self (Brown, 1954).

On this basic concept, the child develops further concepts of self related to this basic concept when his environment broadens and he comes in contact with people outside the home. How people outside the home treat him, what they say about him, and what status he achieves in the group with which he is identified are all important influences in strengthening the self-concept learned in the home environment or in modifying and changing it. As is true of the home environment, how people treat the child outside the home, and what their attitudes toward him are, are more important than

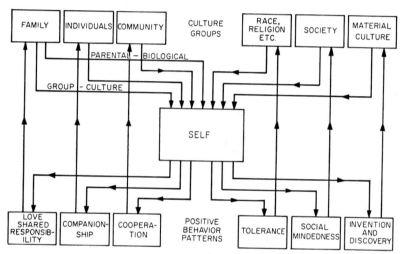

Fig. 70. The different social interactions which influence the child's concept of self. (*From F. J. Brown, Educational sociology, 2d ed., Prentice-Hall, 1954. Used by permission.*)

the experiences he shares with them (Jersild, 1951, 1954; Brown, 1954; Carter, 1954). In Fig. 70 are shown the different social influences that affect the child's concept of self. By the time the child reaches adolescence, the self-image is essentially completed though it may be revised later (Anderson, 1952).

Influence of Self-concept. A *stable* self-concept, which is dependent upon consistency of treatment in the home and continuity between the home environment and the environments outside the home (Dai, 1952), leads to far better adjustments than an unstable concept of self. The individual with a stable self-concept has a higher level of self-esteem, has fewer feelings of inferiority, is more popular with people outside the home, and shows less evidence of compensatory behavior of a defensive sort, such as shyness and withdrawing, than does the individual with a less stable self-concept (Brown-fain, 1952).

Many children, as is true of adolescents and adults, have concepts of an *idealized self,* that is, self-concepts which as individuals they would like ideally to be characteristic of them (Pearl, 1950). As a child compares himself with other children, he is often dissatisfied with the comparison and finds it difficult to accept himself as he is. He would like to be different in many or most respects from what he actually is (Fleege, 1945a; Strang, 1954). To

To make good adjustments, the child must have a realistic concept of himself and be willing to accept himself as he is, not as he would like to be or as a hero in a book. (*From Child Development, a McGraw-Hill Text-Film.*)

be well adjusted, the individual must not only have a realistic concept of himself, but of even greater importance, he must be willing to *accept* himself as he is, not as he would like to be. The self-accepting attitude consists of the ability to live fairly comfortably with one's emotions; of having confidence in one's abilities to cope with life; willingness to assume responsibilities; willingness to accept the challenge of one's abilities without overrating them or reaching for the impossible; a healthy regard for one's rights; and a regard for one's self as a worthy person, even if not perfect. Self-acceptance does not mean smug self-satisfaction, but rather the willingness to face facts and conditions of life, whether favorable or unfavorable, as candidly and as fully as possible (Jersild, 1954).

Each year, as the child's mental abilities increase, he should be able to appraise himself, his abilities and his disabilities, with greater accuracy. If this ability is accompanied by self-acceptance, it will lead to good social adjustments on the child's part. The poorly adjusted child, by comparison, either overestimates himself and finds in the group no opportunity for assuming the status he believes he deserves, or he feels inadequate because of self-perceptions and rebels against accepting the concept of himself which he realizes falls short of his ideal (Conklin, 1935; Tschechtelin, 1945; Rogers, 1947; Green, 1948; Jersild, 1954). The well-adjusted child is willing to accept criticisms because he has greater confidence in himself than the poorly adjusted child who avoids looking squarely at the fact that he is imperfect in this or that respect as criticism implies (Taylor and Combs, 1952). Children whose self-concepts are poor because of unfavorable treatment by others, as is true of Negro children, find it difficult to accept these concepts, and as a result, their self-adjustment as well as their social adjustment suffers (Dai, 1945; Anderson, 1947; Trent, 1953).

The more realistically the child can see himself, the better he will be able to judge other people accurately. The individual who shows *empathy,* or the ability to transpose himself into the thinking, feeling, and acting of another, has a level of security which makes it possible for him to afford an interest in others. As a result of this interest, he makes better social adjustments than does the individual who is self-bound because of feelings of inadequacy and insecurity (Dymond, 1950). The attitude one has toward others has been found to be closely related to the attitude one has toward one's self. Negative feelings toward self, resulting in poor self-acceptance, will be reflected in negative feelings toward others. This, in turn, will result in poor social adjustments. The more realistically the child can judge himself, the more realistically he will judge others, and this, in turn, will lead to good social adjustments (Arsenian, 1941; Sheerer, 1949; Stock, 1949; Phillips, 1951a; McIntyre, 1952; Norman, 1953; Trent, 1953; Jersild, 1954).

ADMIRED PERSONALITY TRAITS

Sooner or later, every child becomes aware of the approved personality pattern. He discovers that certain traits he has are admired, while others are criticized. This awareness has a marked effect on his concept of self and his acceptance of self (Jersild, 1954). Young children, in the preschool years, are more anxious to have the approval of adults than of their peers. For that reason, they strive to develop personality traits that will win for them the adult recognition and approval that they crave. But, as they enter school and become group-conscious, they are far more interested in winning the approval of their peers than they are of being admired by adults. As a result, the standards of socially approved personality traits change, and the child now attempts to develop those traits which his playmates will respect.

Adult Standards. A desirable personality, as characterized by adults, will include traits which are admired by adults and which will make the child's adjustment to the adult world successful. As Thorpe (1946) has emphasized, the desirable personality is characterized by "emotional stability, social maturity, and a disposition to attack problems with confidence." Because adults, typically, set adult standards for children to attain, they are disappointed when the child fails to attain the standards they admire and expect. As a result, they frequently label as "problem" behavior what is perfectly normal for the child's level of development (Jackson, 1940). Children who are considered by their classmates to be experiencing a high degree of teacher approval and a slight amount of disapproval are generally better adjusted and show more desirable personality traits than do children who fall short of their teachers' standards (deGroat and Thompson, 1949).

Children's Standards. Studies of children's friends, child leaders, and social acceptability among children (see pages 297–317) have revealed very conclusively that children have definite standards of what they like or dislike in other children. When a child possesses some of the desired personality traits, he will be popular and have a fairly wide circle of friends. If he possesses admired personality traits in a more highly developed form than his peers do, his chances of being recognized as their leader are good. But should he possess traits which are disliked, even though he may also possess some admired traits, it is very likely that he will find himself in the position of a social isolate (see pages 310–311).

As Bonney (1942) has pointed out, people are "liked or disliked not on the basis of one or two or a half dozen traits but on the basis of the impression they make as total individuals. . . . Each individual is a unique whole and is judged by the total impression he makes. He is not judged on a part-by-part or trait-by-trait basis." This, of course, means that it is possible and common for a child to have certain socially unacceptable traits and still be popular, while unpopular children may have some highly desirable traits. It depends primarily upon which are the stronger, the desirable or the undesirable, and which stand out more forcibly in the personality pattern. Bonney has emphasized this point further when he called attention to the fact that among the very popular children are some extremely unfavorable personality traits, such as being dominating or bossy; being a show-off and striving for attention; being effeminate in the case of a boy; being babyish, fighting, pouting; and dishonesty.

As children grow older, their ideals change. Personality traits which are admired in little children are now regarded as "babyish," and new traits take their place in the favor of the group. No longer is the submissive, quiet, docile child admired when he begins to play with a group of children of his own age. He must develop traits of a more aggressive sort if he wants the approval of his playmates. This frequently means the development of personality traits which are not admired by adults or are even condemned by them. With the onset of puberty and the psychological changes which accompany the physical changes occurring at that time, new standards of admired personality traits appear (Tryon, 1939).

Sex Differences in Admired Traits. Even before children reach the school age, they are aware of sex differences. For most children, this awareness comes at the age of four years. They are not only aware of their own sex, but they also learn that there are certain forms of behavior considered appropriate for their sex. Boys are more clearly aware of sex-appropriate behavior at the preschool age than are girls, while girls tend to prefer the male role to their own role more than boys prefer the female role (Rabban, 1950). Traits that are greatly admired in a boy are not admired in a girl, either by boys or girls. A boy who is sympathetic, kind, and thoughtful is admired by adults, but both boys and girls look upon him as a "sissy." The very traits that they condemn in him, however, are admired in girls, not only by other girls but also by boys. Similarly, an aggressive girl is labeled as "bossy" by other children, but an aggressive boy is admired and is likely to assume the role of leadership.

By the time children enter school, concepts of masculine and feminine personality are well established and known to children. The *typical girl* is judged to be quiet, popular, full of fun, not quarrelsome, a good sport, a "little lady," tidy, feminine, and not a show-off. The *typical boy,* by contrast, is wiggly, quarrelsome, bossy, and a show-off. He takes chances, is not bashful, is good at games, and a real boy. Thus, even in the primary grades, the pictures of a typical boy and a typical girl are almost photostats of adult concepts (Tuddenham, 1952). These concepts are illustrated in Fig. 71. To be popular, boys and girls must conform to socially approved patterns of the sex-appropriate personality pattern (Bonney, 1944a). Children of the lower socioeconomic groups are aware of appropriate sex-role patterns at an earlier age than are children of the middle and upper classes (Rabban, 1950). From twelve to fifteen years, admired traits undergo some revolutionary changes, especially in the case of girls (Tryon, 1939).

Cultural Differences. While each subcultural group has its own values for personality patterns which are used as models for individuals within that group, there are also differences in values among different cultures. A comparison of French and American children revealed that while children in both cultures developed personality patterns that were similar in major aspects, differences resulted because of the differences in values held by parents in these two cultures. For example, American children are encouraged to become independent sooner than French children who are much more dependent on their parents and adult companions; American children are encouraged to assume responsibility early, while French children learn to assume it much later; sociability is not regarded as an important goal by the French, who stress individualism, while Americans emphasize conformity as essential to social acceptance (Stendler, 1954a).

The values held by members of a cultural group are used by the adults of that group to serve as the models parents and teachers use in their child-training methods. When American and English adults were asked to state what they thought constituted a properly brought-up child, the English adults stressed suppression of impulses which are socially disturbing, self-

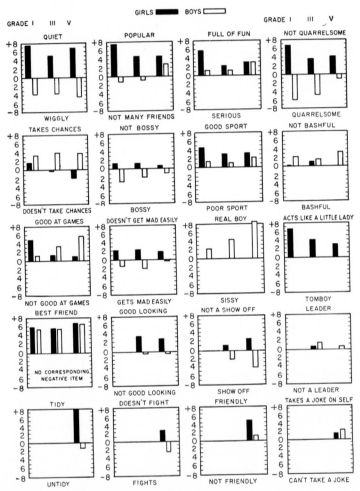

Fig. 71. Children's concepts of "masculine" and "feminine" personality traits. (*From R. D. Tuddenham, Studies in reputation. I. Sex and grade differences in school children's evaluation of their peers. IX. The diagnosis of social adjustment, Psychol. Monogr.,* 1952, **66,** No. 1, 1952. Used by permission.)

control, kindness to others, good manners, obedience, suppression of anti-social impulses, and self-reliance so that the individual will not be a burden to others. The American pattern was found to aim at a smoothly function-ing individual, equipped to get ahead with a varied armament of social skills, intelligence, geniality, good-natureness, neatness, cleanliness, honesty, trustworthiness, straightforwardness, and sociability. In the American values, stress is on adjustment to other children, while in the English values, stress is on adjustment to adults (Farber, 1951, 1953).

INDIVIDUALITY

The recognition of individual differences in personality patterns goes back at least as far as the Greeks. Hippocrates referred to four different personality "types," each with its own characteristics. Persons who manifested these characteristics were classified as the *sanguine,* or quick and active persons; the *choleric,* or strong and easily aroused persons; the *phlegmatic,* or those of a slow and stolid type; and the *melancholic,* or sad and pessimistic individuals. Today there is fairly wide acceptance of the belief that individuals cannot be classified into "types," because of the differences that exist as a result of the make-up of their personality patterns; and increasing emphasis is placed on the importance of these individual differences in personality. Furthermore, one cannot judge the personality of the child in terms of a stereotype of a given "personality type." This, however, is often done. The child is referred to as a "typical boy," a "typical brat," or a "typical grind." Often these judgments are made on the basis of first impressions, based on the child's behavior or his appearance (Asch, 1946; McKeachie, 1952). Studies have revealed that there is no syndrome of personality traits that constitutes the "artistic type" (Borg, 1952). Likewise, there are no racial types, such as the "Nordic type" or the "Mediterranean type." As Seltzer (1948) has pointed out, "For the individual, certainly, his racial characteristics for all practical purposes may be entirely ignored as an hereditary determiner of his personality." However, once a stereotype of personality has been established, it is likely to influence the individual's judgments of people who approximate this stereotype either in appearance or in behavior (Fernberger, 1948; Tuckman and Lorge, 1953).

Heredity versus Environment. As in most aspects of development, there is always the question, which is the more important for personality—heredity or environment? According to traditional views, the personality of the individual was believed to be a direct result of his heredity. This is expressed in the saying "A chip off the old block." Because people were so certain that a child was born with a personality make-up that resembled one side of the family or the other, they made little or no attempt to correct undesirable personality traits. The child was permitted to grow up with such traits becoming stronger and stronger—efforts on the part of his parents being directed toward trying to discover which side of the family was responsible for these traits, instead of putting the same energy into an attempt to correct them.

Later, with the spread of the Freudian point of view concerning the growth of personality disorders as resulting from unhealthy environmental conditions, the pendulum swung to the opposite direction, and major emphasis was placed on the role played by environment. Today, a middle-of-the-road interpretation is being accepted in place of the extreme views, which placed the whole emphasis either on heredity or on environment. It is now rather generally believed that the foundation of personality come from the maturation of hereditary traits, but that these are influenced, partly through learning in connection with direct social contacts and partly through conditioning. This point of view is expressed by Landis (1954), who holds that "Personality is dynamic, a growing entity. Psychologically, it is vested with the capacity for maturation. Except as mutilated by environment, physical traits follow their predestined course from childhood to maturity. Psychologically, it is plastic, capable of an infinite number of modifications by external stimuli. Sociologically, it is dependent on the group to provide the patterns of development, for human nature is a group project."

While changes and modifications are unquestionably brought about by environmental factors, the change is modified by the limitations of the original personality nucleus. Strong personality characteristics, which are based on hereditary traits, are not ironed out by training (Shirley, 1933a). Some traits in the personality pattern are more readily changed than others. Again, this suggests that heredity is responsible for the difference in resistance to change (Breckenridge and Vincent, 1955). Once a trait has been developed, through environmental influences, it affects not only the individual's behavior but also his interests and attitudes. This, in turn, helps to strengthen the trait and make it so deep-rooted that it will be difficult to change (Murphy, 1937; Fauquier, 1940; Banister and Ravden, 1944).

Beginnings of Individuality. At birth there are clearly discernible differences in structure and behavior (Munn, 1955). While the personality of the individual is not developed at that time, the potential qualities are there. During the first ten days of life, differences in behavior are apparent in different babies. These differences mark the beginnings of personality differences. From these variations is built up a pattern from which the individual never completely escapes (Shirley, 1933a; Bayley, 1940; Zachry, 1940a; Stagner, 1948). A month or two after birth, the baby begins to respond to other individuals, and his behavior is modified accordingly (Munn, 1955).

Because no two individuals have the same social environments, even if they have the same physical environments, they tend to exhibit increasingly different personality patterns as they grow older. Even identical twins, whose hereditary endowments are similar and whose physical environment is usually the same during the early years of life, often develop different personalities (Newman et al., 1937; Munn, 1955). At the beginning of the child's school career, various personality "types" can be distinguished. Some children are helpers who can look out for other children; some are leaders who have sufficient initiative to make suggestions and attract followers; some are maternal and care for their weaker and more helpless neighbors; some are despotic and tyrannize over others; some like to joke and make fun of others; some constantly show off; some are much-loved favorites; while some are solitary and become school failures (Bühler, 1935). Sex differences in personality are apparent as early as three years of age (Klopfer, 1939).

PERSISTENCE AND CHANGE IN PERSONALITY

Persistence of personality traits does not mean that no change occurs. It does mean, however, that there is a tendency for certain traits to remain in an unchanged, or relatively unchanged, form even in instances where training and social pressure have been operative. As Allport (1937) has stressed, the "important fact about personality is its relatively enduring and unique organization." A child who, as an infant, showed irritability would show the same trait as he grew older, even though his irritability were somewhat modified and toned down as a result of environmental pressures. Likewise, a happy, good-natured child would remain cheerful, even in the face of adversity, if persistence were characteristic of different traits. However, as Landis (1954) has pointed out, "The evidence is convincing that personality is not fixed at three months, three years, ten years, or fifty years. Personality grows and changes throughout life."

While certain personality traits change as the child passes through certain kinds of experiences, "each personality preserves a central stability, a central core or focus or 'center of gravity' which does not change. Some personalities are far more flexible than others, and change radically under radical changes in environment; others have a 'granite-like' quality which withstands the impact even of the most radical changes of environment." The center of gravity leads to stability in the personality in that it preserves a balance of traits within that personality pattern. Once this center of gravity, which is made up of habits and attitudes, is fixed, it does not change unless radical steps are taken to produce such a change (Breckenridge and Vincent, 1955).

In young children, the "core" of personality, or "center of gravity," is not well established. It can, therefore, be changed without disturbing the total personality balance. But the personality becomes less flexible as the individual grows older, because of the larger and more fixed "core" of habits and attitudes. Even though a change can be achieved, it will require more effort and pressure. Furthermore, care will have to be taken to avoid disturbing the personality balance—a problem that is not so likely to arise in younger children, in whom the personality pattern is less well fixed.

"Critical Period." Although a child remembers little of what happened in the first five years of his life, these years are, nevertheless, "critical" years in the development of his personality because it is at this time that the basic pattern of his personality is laid (Hay-Shaw, 1949). Not only are the basic personality patterns laid at this time, but many mild-to-severe personality difficulties have their origin then. As Bain (1954) has pointed out,

This is the period when mother love is perverted into "smother love," when paternal guidance swings drunkenly between anarchic gratification and tyrannical denial. This is when parents first begin to violate that fundamental principle that children are also people and hence have a right both to privacy and social interaction. The parents often want to show off the child and thus make the child into a "show-off." They expect things from him beyond his capacity and insult his intelligence because they think he doesn't know anything. They cheat and lie in his presence and then whip him for cheating and lying. They do not discipline him at all, or they discipline him too excessively. Very often they do both. The child is confused and made insecure.

What happens to personality in the early years of life is very important with respect to what sort of individual the child will grow up to be (Escalona and Leitch, 1952). Between the second and third years, the child learns to become autonomous or self-directive, or he remains dependent. If his demands for independence are not handled wisely, he will become over-dependent, or he will become hostile and willful (Havighurst, 1953). In the early years of life, the *affective index,* or pleasantly toned reactions which affect the child's outlook on life, are set. These likes and dislikes are not the result of chance attachment to an immediate experience but are the outcome of experiences with specific and closely related stimuli in the past which have become tied together into more generalized attitudes. Girls, as a rule, have more likes and pleasant attitudes than have boys (Anderson, 1952). Because growing up is not easy for a child and because he meets many frustrations to his natural impulses, he can be helped and the path can be smoothed for him if he receives the love and security he needs at home. Only under such conditions can a healthy personality pattern be established in these critical years (Hay-Shaw, 1949).

Evidence of Persistence. Mention of persistence of personality traits was made in some of the early baby biographies (Shinn, 1900, 1909; Woolley, 1925). In recent years, genetic studies of the same groups of children over a period of time have emphasized the persistence of personality patterns and have shown under what conditions changes occur. They have shown that while traits vary from year to year within a narrow range, they remain fairly consistent over a period of time. This makes it possible to formulate a prognosis of the child's future personality even as early as the first year of life. As the child grows older, predominant modes of behavior become less conspicuous. No child remains absolutely consistent with respect to predominant forms of behavior, nor are there any revolutionary changes. Shifts are always in the direction of the form of behavior that had been evident, but it is less pronounced at an earlier age (Washburn, 1929; Arrington, 1932; Bayley, 1932; Driscoll, 1933; Jersild, 1933, 1954; Stutsman, 1935; Allport,

1937; Fries, 1937; Murphy, 1937; Fries and Lewi, 1938; McGraw, 1939; Gesell and Thompson, 1941; Shirley, 1941; McKinnon, 1942; Stout and Langdon, 1953; Munn, 1955).

One of the most interesting and most extensive studies of persistence in personality traits was made on a group of 25 babies, first by Shirley (1933a) and later by Neilon (1948). During the two-year period when the babies were under constant observation and study, Shirley noted a good deal of consistency. The babies, for example, showed a decrease in irritability as they grew older. One of the babies remained consistently the most irritable of the whole group, and another, consistently the least irritable, as time went on. Modifications in their behavior likewise were noted. A baby who is fearful and screams at one year is fearful at two, but the screaming is replaced by running away.

Fifteen and a half years after Shirley made her study, Neilon (1948) matched objective measurements of personality and new personality sketches for 15 of the original 25 "Shirley babies" with the original sketches written by Shirley. The matchings were found to be easier for some of the children than for others. There was definite evidence, however, that personality similarities had persisted over this period of time and that some of the individuals were readily identifiable because of the uniqueness of their personality patterns.

With puberty changes, changes have been found to occur in the individual's personality. It is important, therefore, to determine whether patterns of personality, established during the childhood years, change as the individual emerges into adolescence, and later into adulthood, or whether the personality pattern remains much the same as it was in childhood days. Even in late adolescence, some fluctuation in traits may appear, but for the most part, early patterns are maintained (Arkin, 1933; Roberts and Fleming, 1943). In general, undesirable traits tend to be less undesirable because of the adolescent's strong desire to conform to socially approved patterns (Gesell and Thompson, 1941; McKinnon, 1942). For example, adolescents who, as children, lost their tempers, feared animals, and had nightmares tend to be emotionally unstable in adolescence; adolescents who are secretive were shy as children; and the child who was bullied by others is low in self-esteem during adolescence (Stagner, 1948).

After the individual reaches adulthood, constancy of personality traits is greater than before (Munn, 1955). Records of patients in mental hospitals have revealed that "personality characteristics of psychotic patients are stable and evidence continuous development from childhood." Those who are schizophrenic had been apathetic in childhood, while those who are excitable had been excitable in childhood (Birren, 1944). A study of six individuals, rated on 35 personality traits 50 years after their mother had recorded judgments about them in her diary, showed that there was a 70 per cent persistence of the traits after this long interval of time. However, during this period, there was a general trend toward improvement, with favorable traits improving and unfavorable ones becoming less unfavorable with age. The most stable or consistent traits proved to be affection, ambition, attractiveness, brightness, conscientiousness, sympathy, bossiness, contrariness, carelessness, irritability, jealousy, nervousness, quarrelsomeness, spunkiness, and strength of will. Less persistence was found in bravery, exactness, perseverance, quick temper, and shyness (Smith, 1952).

Explanation of Persistence. The child's personality pattern, or some dominant trait in that pattern, tends to influence the behavior of the child, and this determines what type of environment he will select. A child, for example, who is friendly selects environments in which there are others, and this constant association with others helps to increase and preserve his friendly attitude. The shy child, by contrast, seeks an environment of solitude, and this increases his shyness (Jersild, 1954). Should the child remain in an environment which fosters the development of certain personality traits for a period of time, especially during the early years of life when the personality pattern is being established, a change in environment at a later time may not be adequate to change the personality pattern. This has been illustrated in the case of adolescents who spent the early years of their lives in institutions where group routines fostered apathy, lack of ambition, restlessness, and uncontrolled emotionality. Even when placed in homes at a later age, these traits persisted because of the unfavorable self-concepts of childhood due to lack of strong anchors to specific adults and the consequent lack of affection and sense of belonging (Goldfarb, 1943, 1945).

Some individuals show more constancy in personality patterns than do others, and some traits are more constant than others. The traits that have been found to be most persistent are those associated with intelligence, physical development, and temperament; those that show the least persistence are those related to social situations, such as introversion-extroversion, attitudes, and values (Munn, 1955). Whenever there is evidence that a given trait is related either directly or indirectly to the child's hereditary endowment, it is safe to conclude that it will remain more stable over the years than a trait that has less relationship to physical or mental characteristics that are hereditary.

Changes in Personality. In spite of the fact that personality patterns remain relatively constant, there is definite evidence that changes can and do occur. As Breckenridge and Vincent (1955) have emphasized, "Personality is more fluid, or subject to change through influence of the environment than is physique or even intelligence." These changes are more frequent and more pronounced in young children than in older children and adolescents, and very much more frequent than in adults. The most variable traits tend to be those which involve social relations (Munn, 1955). Thus, the changes are, for the most part, brought about by environmental influences, primarily the pressure of social approval or disapproval. As Landis (1954) has emphasized, "Personality patterns are laid down early in life, but through guidance and understanding, these personality traits can be modified throughout life."

The change may be *quantitative,* in that there is a weakening or strengthening of a trait already present. Or it may be *qualitative,* in that a socially undesirable trait is eliminated and replaced by a socially more desirable trait. Thus *change* does not necessarily mean change to an entirely different trait, nor does it mean a completely new personality pattern. For the most part, changes consist of building upon characteristics already present, instead of the development of something new and different (Jersild, 1954). In a study of nursery-school children several years later, it was found that one child changed from predominantly "invasive" behavior at three years of age to "conforming" behavior at eight years. At both ages, he was very anxious to be noticed and accepted by other children. At first, however, his techniques were crude, while later, his techniques were more refined, and this development was reflected in more socially desirable behavior (McKinnon, 1942).

As childhood progresses, changes are generally for the better. As the child becomes increasingly aware of what is socially approved or disapproved, he tries to conform to a pattern that will win greater social acceptance (Bonney, 1942; Kuhlen and Lee, 1943). In Smith's (1952) study of individuals after a period of 50 years, it was found that in the traits in which changes did occur, there was a general trend toward improvement. Traits that, for example, were rated undesirable in childhood became less unfavorable, while traits rated as desirable in childhood became more desirable with advancing years. In general, greater improvements were made in the case of boys than in girls, and this was explained on the basis of greater social pressures on boys to improve their personalities.

Causes of Personality Changes. There is no one cause that is necessarily responsible for personality changes in the normal child. In instances when there are structural disturbances to the brain, as in the case of a brain tumor, changed personality can generally be traced directly to that one factor. But in cases of normal children, evidence points to the interaction of two or more causes that are responsible for producing changed personalities.

Fenton (1943) has classified the causes of change in personality into three major categories. These he lists as follows:

1. *Bodily or organic factors,* as food, drugs, infections, organic disorders, physical maturation and decline

2. *Factors of the social and cultural environment,* as education, recreation, social participation, etc.

3. *Factors within the individual himself,* as emotional pressures, identification with people or causes, and imitation

During the early months of life, growth and development bring about personality changes in the baby. Environmental influences at this early age are less important than they will be later, though they cannot be said to be ineffectual. The major cause of the changes that occur is maturation. This point of view is stressed by Aldrich (1947), who holds that "under normal conditions the forces of growth cause a most radical and gratifying change in personality to occur during the first 3 months of life. The compulsion and fear characteristic of the automatic, newborn stage gradually melt away until, during the third month, the baby blossoms into a smiling, cooing, pleasantly responsive individual."

As the baby grows older, his muscular development makes more complex voluntary activity possible, and this opens up new channels for personality to express itself. Should the environment obstruct the normal use of his emerging ability, Aldrich stressed, the baby will oppose those who put pressure on him. As a result, he becomes antagonistic and rebellious. An environment which fosters the development of his personality will, on the other hand, make him cooperative and responsive. And because the forces of growth are unchangeable, any adjustment in favor of producing a more desirable personality must come from the environment. A child who is difficult to work with in one situation may be easily handled in another situation. Such changes come partly from the child's advancing maturity and partly from his experiences and the environment in which he lives (Bayley, 1940).

Because social pressures become so important as the child grows older, their influence on personality becomes stronger. A child who, at home, develops an exaggerated concept of himself may, later, suffer from "esteem bankruptcy" when he discovers how far short he falls of his home-grown concept (White, 1942, 1942a, 1942b). The stronger the child's drive for social acceptance, the greater will be the chances that he will try to develop personality traits that will win for him social acceptance. Not only will he want to develop traits that are socially approved, but he will try to develop sex-approved traits for his social-class group (Tryon, 1939; Bonney, 1942; Steiner, 1953).

Control of the child's environment and direct instruction in the development of desired traits have been found to be effective in bringing about personality changes. This can be done more easily when children are young and before the pattern of their personalities is well established. To demonstrate experimentally how a socially desirable personality trait may be strengthened through training, Jack (1934) mapped out a program of training young children in such a way as to increase their self-confidence. Nonascendant, or easily dominated, children, Jack found, differed primarily from ascendant children in the degree of self-confidence they felt. The training of the nonascendant children was in three things that the ascendant children did not know—as assembling a mosaic of blocks and learning to know a storybook.

After a period of sufficient training to give the nonascendant children a feeling of self-confidence from their newly acquired skills, they were paired with ascendant children. Jack found not only that there were marked increases in their ascendancy scores but also that they attempted to dominate the ascendant children. They showed a greater interest in directing the activities of other children and in maintaining their own property rights. Not only can ascendancy behavior be increased by training, but the effects of training are *cumulative*. By increasing his self-confidence in one or more skills, he can be encouraged to try others and thus develop more ascendant behavior (Page, 1936).

Socially undesirable traits can also be weakened or eliminated. Children who showed immature reactions to failure, such as "giving up," asking for help, destructiveness, and rationalization, were given tasks graded in difficulty so that it was possible for them to see their progress and to achieve success most of the time. After a period of such training, there was marked improvement, as shown by the fact that the children showed greater interest and effort in the tasks, they depended less on adults, and the sulking, crying, and violent emotional behavior characteristic of children who have experienced too many failures disappeared (Updegraff and Keister, 1937).

Cautions in Personality Changes. In spite of the experimentally demonstrated changes that can be produced in personality traits, it is most important to bear in mind that the changes were brought about only in cases of very young children, before the personality patterns had become well established. Furthermore, how permanent these changes were and whether they carried over to everyday life situations has not been reported. Only when the child's environment remains favorable will the changes brought about in his personality be likely to become a permanent part of his personality pattern.

Of equal importance is the caution of not attempting to fit a child into a pattern to suit some adult ideal. Changing one or two personality traits that are proving to be a distinct social handicap to the child is one thing; but trying to revamp the entire personality pattern is an entirely different story. As Breckenridge and Vincent (1955) have warned,

The very stability of a central core of personality around which habits and attitudes achieve a working balance in any given personality proves to be the reason we cannot, or should not try to make over basic traits in any personality unless we have the help of highly trained specialists. To change any basic trait without due regard to the other traits, habits, and attitudes which balance this trait may be to invite disaster through a serious disturbance in the total personality balance. . . . Apparently, while the core of stability or "the integration center" is still in the early stages of formation, much in the way of change or moulding is possible without disturbance to the general balance. Even so, it is not wise to force any child into a preconceived pattern. Even very young children seem to have a certain physiologic and psychologic constitution which can be forced only so far from its original pattern without producing stresses and strains which shatter the mechanism.

FACTORS IN PERSONALITY

How much or how little influence different factors will have on the personality development of the child will depend to a large extent upon the child's ability to understand the significance of these factors in relation to himself. His concept of self is influenced by his comprehension of the attitude of the social group toward him. Should, for example, his appearance be such that he is admired by others for it, appearance would be a favorable factor in his personality development. But if he is aware of the fact that his peers do not admire his looks and that they have given him a nickname, such as "Fat Potato," which shows how they feel about his appearance, this factor will prove to be a liability in the personality pattern.

Physique

The child's body build and his personal attractiveness are either admired or disapproved of by others. The child's awareness of how people feel about his looks, his body build, and the general state of his health all influence his attitude toward self, which, in turn, is reflected in the quality of his behavior. While there is some evidence that certain personality patterns are associated with certain types of body build, there is no evidence that this relationship is due to heredity. On the other hand, there is evidence that awareness of cultural attitudes toward certain body builds is responsible for the personality patterns the individuals with these body builds develop (Bayley, 1940; Sheldon et al., 1940, 1954; Sheldon and Stevens, 1942; Munn, 1955). The effect of physique is thus indirect, rather than direct.

Every cultural group has its own standards of what is "right" or appropriate for boys and girls. In our culture, for example, the "right" size is average for the sex to slightly above in height, and average or in standard proportion to height for weight. Extreme tallness or extreme shortness and extreme stoutness or extreme thinness are regarded as "wrong" (Lockhart, 1939). However, if the child is in a group of children of his own size, there will be no effect on his concept of self, even if his size varies markedly above or below the norms for the cultural group. Only when the variation from the norm of his own group is great enough to be noticed by others will it affect the child (Scheinfeld, 1950). At an early age, children become aware of any deviation from the group norm because of the effect it has on their social relationships (Havighurst, 1953). Any nicknames that imply physical difference, such as "Fatty" or "Skinny," show how other children feel about these differences. Because this makes the child feel inadequate, it affects his personality (Sontag, 1946).

Boys with well-proportioned bodies have been found to have well-adjusted personality patterns (Seltzer, 1946); by contrast, boys with physically inferior bodies develop some compensatory form of behavior which interferes with good social adjustments, and this lack of social acceptance influences their personality development unfavorably (Dimock, 1937). Even though fat may be only temporary (Stolz and Stolz, 1951), it may make the child self-conscious, timid, retiring, slow, awkward, and incapable of holding a secure status among his peers. He is often at the mercy of more active children who tease and bully him. And because his overweight makes it impossible for him to engage in active play with other children, he becomes increasingly unsocial. This makes the child more dependent on the mother, and he develops a tendency to be immature as compared with children of the same age. Overweight leads to a "disturbance in the maturation of the total personality and a somatic compensation for thwarted creative drives" (Bruch, 1941). Only when the body build deviates enough from the approved norms to make the child feel inferior does it affect his personality (Hanley, 1951).

Racial characteristics in physical traits are likewise unimportant in their influence on personality unless they make a child feel inferior (Seltzer, 1948). However, when there is a stereotype associated with certain racial characteristics and when this stereotype is of an unfavorable sort, it does affect the child's personality. Among Negroes, light skin and other physical features approximating the Caucasian are associated with conceit and snobbishness, while dark skin is associated with low status. As a result, the light-skinned Negroes are envied, while those with dark skin are pitied. This is bound to affect the Negro child's attitude when he realizes that members of his own race feel that "black" is the worst color to be (Parrish, 1946).

PHYSICAL CONDITION

The health of the child not only influences the child's behavior at the moment, but it has long-term effects on his personality. Good health throughout childhood has a favorable influence on personality. The healthy child is able to do things without any parental restraints, he is not held back by fear that he will not be well enough to do what others do, and he feels superior to those whose health makes it impossible for them to keep up to the standards set by the group. The attitude of the family and the social group in general is so much more favorable toward a healthy child than toward a sickly one that it is certain to affect the quality of his behavior.

The child who is delicate and sickly, by contrast, comes to expect the consideration from others that he has been used to at home. He resents not being coddled by outsiders as he has been coddled by his parents. He develops timidity, and this causes him to withdraw from the activities of other children and become overdependent on his parents. Children with low energy levels, resulting from a chronic illness or malnutrition, often become shy, reserved, irritable, depressed, and unsocial (Macfarlane, 1939; Brozek et al., 1946; Guetzkow and Bowman, 1946). An irritating physical condition, such as hives or eczema, causes children to develop tempers and overactive responses (Macfarlane, 1939).

Children who suffer from *allergies* tend to have personality constellations which differ markedly from those of nonallergic children. Children with skin allergies are more emotionally unstable than those suffering from asthma, vasomotor rhinitis, or other forms of allergy (Riess and deCillis, 1940). The emotional instability of the allergic child is shown in ebb and flow which may "alternate with almost incredible swiftness and vehemence" (Rhodes, 1952). Feelings of hostility are common among allergic children. However, the allergic child more often turns the hostility against himself than against others (Miller and Baruch, 1950). There are marked changes for the better in the child's personality when the allergy is brought under control (Clarke, 1952). The older the child when he develops *diabetes,* the better able he is to control his negative emotions. The more severe the case, the more dependent the child will be, and this results in emotional instability and feelings of inadequacy from the necessary restrictions (Bennett and Johannsen, 1954).

How much effect *crippling* has on the child's personality will depend upon his attitude toward his physical disability. Because his attitudes are often unfavorable, he makes poor social adjustments, and this adds to his unfavorable attitudes toward himself (Cruickshank and Dolphin, 1949; Wenar, 1954). The age at which the crippling occurs is important. If it occurs early there is a better opportunity for the child to adjust to dependence on others than when crippling occurs later. Parents' attitudes toward the crippled child are likewise important factors in determining the child's attitude (Gates, 1946). At first, a handicapped child is realistic about his abilities and achievements. Later, he becomes frustrated by his limited achievement and sets goals beyond his capacity (Wenar, 1954).

How markedly *physical defects* influence the child's personality will depend upon how much he realizes that he is different. Children who had suffered from polio are not as much affected when their environment limits them to other children with similar handicaps as when they are with children who have no such handicaps (Phillips et al., 1948). Children who are deaf or blind develop a rigidity of personality when they are with other children whose hearing and sight are not handicaps to them (McAndrew, 1948). The child with cerebral palsy realizes in a vague way that he is different at first. Later he becomes aware of the limitations this handicap imposes on him, with the result that he may try to deny the handicap or he may feel ashamed and guilty because he is different. This is especially true when other children impress upon him that he is different (Bice, 1954).

A handicapped child in a school situation with other children who are normal may feel that the school work and social relationships compensate for many of the things the child is forced to miss and which other children enjoy, such as sports and parties. Or he may suffer from the contempt of stronger children and from feeling excluded and lonely. His attitude will be determined largely by the treatment he receives in school (Bühler, 1952). Whenever the handicapped child is treated in such a way that he feels different, his attitude toward himself will be colored by feelings of inferiority and of resentment, and this will have a marked effect on his personality (Bice, 1954).

The condition of the *endocrine glands,* or the glands of internal secretion, affects the personality development of the child. A hyperthyroid condition, for example, makes the child nervous, excited, jumpy, restless, and overactive. The opposite, a hypothyroid state, in which there is a deficiency of secretion from the thyroid glands, causes the child to be lethargic, unresponsive, depressed, dissatisfied, and distrustful.

While there is not a large amount of evidence at the present time regarding the specific effects of the different glands of the endocrine system on the personality of the child, there is a strong belief that these glands are of no small importance in the personality make-up of the child. With the physical changes which occur at puberty, there is a change in endocrine balance which is reflected in personality at that time. At any age, a marked deviation in size from the norm of the group will affect the child's personality adversely. The psychological reaction to deviations may be to compensate, to overcompensate, or to become recessive (Margolese, 1948).

CLOTHES

The influence of clothing on children and the interest children have in their clothes have already been discussed (see pages 477–479). There is no question that the child's clothes must be regarded as a factor of importance in his personality development. He is keenly aware of the attitude of others, primarily of his peers, toward his clothes. Not style alone, but compliance with the style accepted by the group to which he belongs, will be a factor of importance. This means that it is not sufficient for the child to be in style so far as current trends in fashion are concerned. What is most important is that his clothing must resemble that of the children with whom he has identified himself, even if their styles do not conform to the prevailing styles in the community. Having clothes that other children admire, envy, and imitate gives the child a feeling of importance, when he is recognized by his peers in this way. Feelings of inferiority, on the other hand, frequently develop in the child who is dressed in clothes which other children make fun of or which give him an appearance so markedly different from that of the group that he is self-conscious. As a result of these feelings of inferiority, the child develops a rejecting attitude and shows a tendency to respond in a negative fashion (Silverman, 1945). Being poorly dressed over a period of time is likely to lead to marked feelings of inadequacy, with their characteristic influence on the child's personality (Dickens, 1944).

That clothes play an important role in influencing the individual's concept of self has been emphasized by Morton (1926): "For the vast majority of the human race, clothing plays a large part in making for happiness and success. . . . Clothes help to make us self-confident, self-respecting, jolly, free or they make us self-conscious, shy, sensitive, restrained. . . . Clothes then make or mar us. They may enhance our personality or be so conspicuous as to subordinate us to them, or they may be just ordinary, nondescript, characterless." For the child, growing up is difficult because of the many adjustments he must make to the adult world. For that reason, "clothes may make growing up easier or harder. They may be a symbol of security, an extension of self, a way of identifying with someone, a means of real satisfaction" (Read, 1950).

THE CHILD'S NAME

Teagarden (1946) has pointed out that "The name that is given to a child at birth or shortly thereafter may constitute a psychological hazard." This applies not only to the child's real name but also to any nickname or name of endearment that his parents or relatives may use. When the child is old enough to play with other children, around the third year, he begins to realize the importance of his name. Names which lend themselves to distortions, names which are difficult to pronounce and are, therefore, frequently mispronounced, names that other children criticize or make fun of, names that confuse the sexes, or names which combined with others make queer initials (Charles Oliver Watson—"COW") or meanings (Ima Virginia Bird) are bound to lead to uncomfortable feelings on the part of the unfortunate who bears such a name (Mencken, 1936; Walton, 1937; Allen et al., 1941; Eagelson, 1946; Broom et al., 1955).

Preferred names are usually common names. As is true of clothing, the child likes his name to be like the names of his friends. The sound of the name is unimportant to him. For both given names and family names, the child likes names that are easy to pronounce, easy to spell, and lend themselves to nicknames that will not cause the child embarrassment. Only as the child grows older does he begin to show less liking for too common names and to prefer a name that is slightly distinctive (Walton, 1937; Allen et al., 1941; Finch et al., 1944; Eagelson, 1946; Arthaud et al., 1948). If the child's name is liked by others, it makes him feel self-important, and this reacts favorably on his concept of self.

Some children develop attitudes of superiority because of their names, while others develop attitudes of inferiority (Plottke, 1950). If the child dislikes his name, it may make him shy, retiring, sensitive and easily embarrassed (Eagelson, 1946; Merry and Merry, 1950). As the child reaches adolescence, the effect may be so great as to lead to poor school work and a withdrawal from social situations (Houston and Sumner, 1948; Savage and Wells, 1948). Children of minority groups discover that certain names awaken prejudice. They therefore try to change their names or use a nickname that will not identify them with the minority group (Schettler, 1942; Eagelson, 1946; Wells and Palwick, 1950). Name changing is more often carried out by second-generation parents than first and by those of the higher rather than of the lower socioeconomic groups. By changing their name, they hope to change their identity and thus spare themselves and their children the prejudice that their name has brought (Broom et al., 1955).

Nicknames. Most nicknames are verbal caricatures. They may come from an adaptation of the child's own name, but they almost always present a word picture of the individual. In a study of children's nicknames, Orgel and Tuckman (1935) have found that they fall into the following classifications: "pet" names, or names of endearment; nationality or place-of-birth nicknames, as "Yid" or "Dago"; names of animals, as "pig" or "cow"; distortion of the real name; nicknames from the individual's initials; nicknames from physical defects, as "Fatty" or "Skinny"; and nicknames based on personality defects, as "Sissy" or "Crybaby." The child's nickname shows him how other children feel about him (Sontag, 1946).

Most children dislike their nicknames and build up a feeling of resentment against those who use them, especially when they know that the nickname has been given as a way of making fun of the child. Too widespread use of the nickname on the part of the child's playmates may readily result in feelings of inferiority and resentment of so pronounced a form that the child will withdraw from the group and try to establish relationships with another group. Many cases of problem behavior result from the child's attempts to compensate for a nickname that makes him feel inferior (Stolz, 1940). Not all children, of course, dislike their nicknames. As they grow older, they learn to distinguish between nicknames that imply ridicule and rejection and those that imply acceptance and affection (Habbe, 1937; Finch et al., 1944; Dexter, 1949). However, the possible unfavorable effects of a nickname are so great that one must conclude that "Fortunate is the boy whose name and/or personal characteristics do not suggest humorous, bizarre nicknames to the imaginative minds of his peers" (Habbe, 1937).

INTELLIGENCE

Average intelligence makes it possible for a child to adjust with reasonable success to his environment, provided that other conditions are favorable. But even though other conditions may be favorable, very low or very high intelligence frequently prove to be a disadvantage in social adjustments.

Because of this, the personality development of the child is unfavorably influenced.

A child whose intelligence is definitely below that of other children of the same age in school or in the neighborhood group soon finds himself an outsider. He cannot keep up to the standard set by the others, either in academic work or in extracurricular activities. Because his interests are different from theirs and because he cannot understand or adjust himself to their interests, he soon develops feelings of inadequacy which force him to leave the group. As a result, he develops the personality traits generally associated with marked feelings of inferiority (Brown et al., 1952).

A very high level of intelligence likewise affects the personality development of the child, but the effect is generally far from favorable. Hollingworth (1940) has called attention to some of the special problems of personality development which are characteristic of those of very high intelligence. These are *negativism toward authority,* because the individual recognizes that authority is often irrational and erroneous in its operation; *intolerance* of those not so bright; *habits of chicanery,* which develop when very bright children try to adjust to a world that is unadapted to them; *solitary pursuits* and *companionship of older persons; self-sufficiency* and a tendency to *dominate situations.* Many of the personality characteristics of very bright children are the result of their psychological isolation due to the fact that there are rarely children of similar ability for them to associate with.

Early Experiences

Childhood experiences and the memory of these experiences as the years go by leave an indelible impression on the individual's personality. The child whose childhood has been happy has an entirely different outlook on life from that of the child whose early years have been marked by constant friction, sadness, and emotional tension. Even though conditions improve in the child's environment as he grows older, the memories of those unhappy experiences will never be completely forgotten, nor will the effect on his personality ever be entirely eradicated (Wang, 1932). How important early experiences are has been emphasized by Bartemeier (1953), who maintains that "whatever emotional damage is inflicted on a child during the period of infancy has far greater effects upon the future character development than a similar damage inflicted at a later period when the personality has become more fully organized."

The importance of early experiences to future personality development was first stressed by Freud (1920), who found that many of his adult patients had had unhappy childhood experiences. Later, frustrations that thwart some natural impulse were blamed for the trouble. Children subjected to undue thwartings during the early years of life were claimed to regress to infantile modes of behavior, to turn their interests from outer to inner spheres, and to become self-centered and reflective rather than expressive (Jung, 1928; Adler, 1930; Lewin, 1935; Horney, 1939; Frank, 1950a; Munn, 1955). However, many of the adverse effects of early experiences can be corrected, especially by psychoanalytic therapy (Alexander, 1951).

Absence of mothering and emotional privation during the early years of life have been found to influence the personality development of the child, especially in the case of institutional children who are deprived of affection over a relatively long period of time. If the deprivation is for only a short time, the effects will be less and less permanent (Goldfarb, 1943, 1945; Ribble, 1943; Kunst, 1948; Bakwin, 1949; Dashiell, 1949; Spitz, 1949). As a result of emotional deprivation during the first year of life, the baby lacks animation, is apathetic, sad, depressed, and shows signs of "mournful waiting" (Roudinesco, 1952).

Methods used in child training during the early years of life, especially those related to breast feeding, weaning, and toilet training, are believed by many to have a marked influence on the personality development of the baby and to carry this influence into adolescence or even into adult years. Contrasts have been made with methods used in America and among different primitive tribes to show that the characteristic personality patterns developed are related to the training methods used during the early years of life (Mead, 1935; Havighurst et al., 1947; Goldman, 1948; Benedict, 1949; Orlansky, 1949; Blair, 1950; Escalona et al., 1950; Newton, 1951; Purcell, 1952; Whiting and Child, 1953).

There is lack of convincing evidence to prove that the individual's personality reflects the type of care he had during the early years of life; that is, there is no definite evidence that bottle feeding produces a better personality pattern than breast feeding or that early toilet training, per se, is worse than later training so far as the personality pattern is concerned. Nor is there any definite evidence that the effects of these early experiences related to training methods carry into the adult years. On the other hand, there is ample evidence that the attitude and emotional reactions of the mother, the total cultural context of the environment in which the child grows up, and other factors in the child's total experience are far more important in determining the pattern of his personality (Dunbar, 1944; Benedict, 1949; Orlansky, 1949; Newton, 1951; Thurston and Mussen, 1951; Pattie and Cornett, 1952; Sewell, 1952; Sewell and Mussen, 1952; Munn, 1955). Babies and young children need attention, but not too much attention (Pinnau, 1950; Stone, 1954). Only when the mother's attitudes make the child feel anxious and guilty in relation to training or eating will there be any real effect on the personality (Sperling, 1951; Smock and Thompson, 1954).

The importance of parental attitude rather than the specific methods of child training have been stressed thus by Spock (1951): "The child between one and three is vulnerable, terribly vulnerable, to the attitudes of his parents. If he is regularly shamed for his accidents, accidents in the general and in the sanitary sense, he acquires a sense of shame and unworthiness. If he is excessively dominated he becomes defiant or submissive. If he is constantly warned that the parent will no longer love him unless he behaves differently, his whole personality will be poisoned with uneasiness and antagonism."

FAMILY INFLUENCES

How family relationships will affect the child will depend to a certain extent upon the child himself. Some children, for example, are more disturbed by tension within the home than are others. A child who is nervous and tense will be more upset by the attention given to a new baby than he would if he were more phlegmatic in disposition. Similarly, a healthy child will react very differently to the attention and pampering he receives as the "baby" of the family than he would if he were a delicate, sickly child. The child's concept of himself as an individual is influenced more by the nature of his relationships with the different members of the family than by the number of these relationships (Carter, 1954).

Family-life Pattern. What type of home life the child has is important to his personality development. And the type of home life is largely determined by the parents. Parents who feel insecure in their role of parenthood, because of inexperience (Kanner, 1951), who are emotionally unstable (Stott, 1945), who have unfavorable attitudes toward their children (Wallin and Riley, 1950), or who disagree about methods of child training (Koshuk, 1947) produce far less desirable home-life patterns than do more secure and more stable parents. There is a relationship between the parents' attitudes and emotions and the amount of formal education they have had. Parents with the least education have been found to be more irritable, less controlled in their emotions, and more immature in their behavior than better-educated parents (Stott, 1945). Parents with feelings of personal inadequacy are more likely to be authoritarian and restrictive in their methods of handling children than are parents who are more assured and secure (Block, 1955).

A pattern of home life in which parents and children are companionable, where cooperative and democratic relations exist, and where attempts are made to meet the needs of the child produces a well-adjusted personality in the child. This type of home provides the affectional relationships every child needs with his parents and siblings (Stott, 1939, 1939a, 1940; Brown et al., 1947; Baldwin, 1948; Graves, 1948; Beals, 1950). Homes characterized by family discord, unhappiness due to lack of affectional relations among the members, lack of interest in the children, friction among parents, and breaks due to separation, death, or divorce lead to emotional instability and poor adjustments on the child's part (Stott, 1939, 1940, 1945; McKinney, 1941; Torrance, 1945; Brown et al., 1947; Stagner, 1948; Havighurst, 1952).

There have been found to be certain forms of personality maladjustment that are closely related to certain types of unfavorable home-life patterns. Poor marital adjustment of the parents is closely associated with finickiness, overdependence, attention demanding, negativism, and temper tantrums among young children (Macfarlane, 1939). Parental rejection is related to unsocialized aggression (attacking others); parental negligence to socialized aggression (cooperative stealing and gang disturbances); parental over-protectiveness to shyness and withdrawal; and hypercritical attitudes on the parents' part to worry, anxiety, and seclusiveness (Grant, 1939; Hewitt and Jenkins, 1946).

Home Setting. Children brought up in rural areas have been found to be superior in both self-adjustment and social adjustments to children from urban areas. Children from villages are likewise superior to city children in these areas of adjustment. In general, rural children are more self-reliant, have a greater sense of personal worth, of belonging, and greater freedom from nervous symptoms and withdrawing tendencies than do children from the cities. They have greater social skills and are superior in both school and community relationships. On the whole, they receive better ratings from their teachers and fewer unfavorable ratings from their peers than do children from urban areas (Mangus, 1948).

The socioeconomic status of the family affects the child's developing personality both directly and indirectly: *directly* because it determines what social-class standards the parents will accept and what child-training methods they will use; *indirectly* because it will determine where and how the family will live. The physical environment of the home, such as size, neighborhood, general condition of the furnishings, etc., has little influence, per se, on the child's personality. However, because the type of home and the neighbor-hood in which it is located influence parental attitudes, they are important factors in the development of the child's personality. Poor surroundings and a run-down condition of the home affect parental morale, especially that of the mother, and this indirectly affects the child (Francis, 1933; Francis and Fillmore, 1934; Stott, 1945). Children from poor homes generally make poorer adjustments and have more personality problems than do children from better homes (Gesell and Lord, 1927; Stagner, 1935, 1948; Lurie et al., 1943; French and Mensh, 1948).

Membership in Minority Group. Even before the child enters school, his personality may be affected by the treatment he receives from other children as a result of his membership in a minority group. The child is well aware of the fact that he is looked down upon by other children, and he develops personality traits that are a compensation for this discrimination. He de-velops feelings of inadequacy and inferiority, he develops resentful attitudes

toward society, and he develops many forms of compensatory behavior that
further increase the discrimination against him. Each year, as he grows
older, his self-adjustment becomes poorer, and accompanying this is poorer
social adjustment (Dai, 1945; Engle, 1945; Anderson, 1947; Zeligs, 1950,
1950a).

Children from different minority groups seem to be affected in a slightly
different way by discrimination. Negro children develop a higher level of
activity, emotionality, self-awareness, sensitiveness, and competitiveness
(Goodman, 1952). They have more nervous symptoms and are more antisocial than white children (Engle, 1945). Those whose skin color is the
darkest make the poorest adjustments because they are aware of the unfavorable stereotype associated with dark skin color, and they often become
quarrelsome and vindictive (Parrish, 1946). The Jewish child is well aware
of his minority-group status by the time he is seven years old, and the
effects of this are increasingly serious with each passing year. Social restraints
result in frustrations with the accompaniment of fear, uncertainty, and
anxiety (Radke-Yarrow, 1953). By adolescence, many Jewish children develop personality patterns characterized by aggression, destructiveness, sub-
missiveness, strong rebellion, or derogation of the in-group as compensations for their frustrations (Radke-Yarrow and Lande, 1953).

Children of the Amish faith have been found to make poor social adjustments because they feel they do not "belong," that other children are
mean to them and persecute them, and that they do not have as much fun
as other children nor can they do the things they would like to do (Engle,
1945). Thus it is apparent that being a member of a minority group will
affect the personality development of the child, and this influence will be
of an unfavorable kind. The memory of unhappy childhood experiences,
when other children are "mean" to them and discriminate against them
because of their race, creed, or color, is bound to leave an indelible impression—one which will alter the child's outlook on life.

Influence of Parents. It has been pointed out that the child's personality
is the "result of the impact on him of all the conscious and unconscious expressions of parents' personalities, as well as their conscious attitudes toward children and their bringing up" (Lerner and Murphy, 1941). How
the child *perceives* his parents' attitudes is, in reality, more important than
the attitudes themselves. Children who perceive themselves as accepted have
been found to show greater ego aspirations, tenacity, and independence
from parents than do children who perceive themselves as rejected by their
parents. Girls perceive themselves as more accepted by their parents, as a
rule, than do boys (Ausubel et al., 1954).

Parental attitudes that have been found to be favorable to the development of the child's personality are characterized by understanding, love,
and interest in the child as an individual. Parental attitudes that have been

found to be unfavorable to the child's personality development are characterized by lack of emotional warmth, rejection in such subtle forms as criticism and hostility submerged under a cloak of insincere care and affection, favoritism toward a sibling, and a high degree of behavioral control (Symonds, 1938, 1949a; Shirley, 1941; Brown et al., 1947; Graves, 1948; Stout and Langdon, 1950; Cass, 1952; Rich, 1954). Lack of awareness on the mother's part of the child's needs will lead to personality problems (Cass, 1952), as will the mother's mood swings (Spitz, 1949). It is the parents' attitude toward the child and their personalities that are far more influential in the child's personality development than are the external factors of the home environment (Shirley, 1941; Lewis, 1945). This point of view is stressed by Shirley (1941): "A secure and wholesomely loved child goes forth to meet a new experience in a spirit of adventure, and comes out triumphant in his encounters with new places, new materials, and new friends, old and young. A child that is oversheltered or underloved goes forth from his home with misgivings and doubts, and gives an impression of inadequacy and immaturity in his encounter with new experiences that makes him unwelcome either in the society of adults or children" (p. 217).

The child's personality is also influenced indirectly by his parents through his tendency to imitate them and to identify himself with them (DuBois, 1952). While both boys and girls tend to identify themselves with the mother when they are young, they later identify with the parent they most admire or for whom they have a strong affectional relationship (Winch, 1951). Imitation of the parent is seen in the fact that the personality patterns of both boys and girls in early childhood more closely resemble that of the mother than of the father, owing to the more constant contacts with the mother (Roff, 1950). There are also indications of imitation in the personality disturbances of children which closely resemble those of the mother (Sperling, 1950; Phillips, 1951). Because the child's personality is so strongly influenced by his parents, Symonds (1949a) has justifiably claimed, "If an individual possesses a healthy, stable, courageous, and loving father and mother, the chances are that he will be a good student, a good worker, a good husband or wife, a good leader, and a good citizen."

Sibling Influences. The type of relationship that exists among siblings has much the same influence on the child's personality development as does his relationship with his parents (Havighurst, 1952b). *Ordinal position* has been found to have some influence on the personality development of each child. There is a tendency for the first-born child to develop a dependence on his parents, and this makes it difficult for him to adjust to others outside the home. Furthermore, he is likely to be selfish and to suffer from feelings of insecurity resulting from displacement when the second child arrived. To compensate for feelings of insecurity, he often develops tricky,

attention-getting mechanisms. The second-born child is usually better adjusted, happier, and more generous than the first-born. The "baby" of
the family, on the other hand, tends to become dependent, selfish, and
demanding (Adler, 1930; Stagner and Katzoff, 1936; Davis and Havighurst,
1946; Havighurst, 1952b; Bossard, 1953, 1954; Descombey and Roquebrune,
1953).

Size of family has been found to play an important role in the child's
personality development. Children from small families not only develop
different personality patterns than do those from large families, but on the

Good relationships among siblings helps to promote a well-adjusted personality in the
child. (*From Child Development, a McGraw-Hill Text-Film.*)

whole, the personality pattern is better (Stagner and Katzoff, 1936; Bossard,
1953, 1954). Very early in life, every child in the family acquires a specific
role which comes to be recognized not only by his family but by outsiders
as well. The larger the family group, the greater the diversity of roles. In
a large family, what role the child assumes will depend on what roles have
already been preempted by older siblings. Because no child wants to be
the exact counterpart of one of his siblings, he selects a role that will give
him recognition as an individual (Bossard and Boll, 1955).

In large families, eight main types have been identified, each of which
produces an individual personality pattern. These types are:

1. The *responsible* type who assumes direction of the other siblings and renders service to the family. This is usually the first-born.

2. The *popular* type who is sociable and well liked. This is often the second-born or the sibling who follows the responsible one. Finding most responsibility preempted, the next child tries to gain status through personal charm.

3. The *socially ambitious* type whose appeal is directed mostly to people outside the family. This is more often a girl than a boy and the third, fourth, or fifth child.

4. The *studious* type who finds recognition in the family and outside by good school work.

5. The *self-centered isolate* who is either secretive or stubbornly antisocial in his attitude toward other siblings, with an unwillingness to participate in family activities. This is usually a later-born child with an age differential between him and his siblings, or a boy after several girls, or a child with a special interest his siblings do not share.

6. The *irresponsible* type who may be in any ordinal position in the family.

7. The *sickly type* who suffers from some physical handicap or chronic illness. Some children use imaginary illness to gain attention or justify their failures. This type is generally found among the later-born.

8. The *"spoiled"* type, who is often the last-born of the family. (Bossard and Boll, 1955.)

At the opposite extreme of the large family is the family with an only child. While it is popularly believed that the only child will be "spoiled" by overprotective and doting parents and relatives and thus become selfish, self-centered, and uncooperative, this is mainly true of only children of rich parents. Among those who come from families of moderate incomes, the only child has been found to have a personality pattern that leads to good social acceptance and often to leadership status (Adler, 1930; Guilford and Worcester, 1930; Levy, 1931; Maller, 1931; Bossard, 1953, 1954). As Campbell (1934) has pointed out, "Whatever role the mere presence or absence of siblings may play in the development of personality, its importance is certainly not crucial."

SCHOOL INFLUENCES

The influence of the school in the personality development of the child is very great because the school becomes a substitute for the home and the teacher, a substitute for the mother (Rich, 1954). Once the child reaches the school age, he spends approximately one-half of his waking time in the school. That is why its "impact is second only to the home in the individual's childhood" (Bühler, 1952). To determine how much influence the school has on the individual's concept of self, Bühler (1952) asked adults to recall their school experiences. While some had happy memories, there were more unhappy than happy memories, and the former were stronger and more emotionally toned than the latter. For the most part, the unhappy memories centered around unfavorable social experiences in school due to physical or socioeconomic handicaps. Many recalled discrimination against them, others felt that they were treated as outsiders or "different" because of their abilities, while others claimed that an already existing insecurity was increased rather than helped or lessened by their school experiences. Because these memories were vivid and bitter, the experiences themselves unquestionably had great impact on the personalities of these individuals during their childhood days.

Influence of Teacher. In the early grades, the influence of the teacher is the most important single factor in the total school influence on the child's personality. Directly, the teacher affects the way the child feels about himself by the way she corrects his behavior, ignores him or his social behavior, or by the way she interprets his school work. Indirectly, she influences his personality by helping him to adjust to the group and by helping the group to adjust to him, thus influencing the degree of social acceptance he achieves (Frank and Frank, 1954). The attitude of the teacher toward her work and toward children is very important. The teacher who likes her work, understands children, and is enthusiastic about what she is teaching creates a far better school climate than does the teacher who has little interest (Laycock, 1950; Whitley, 1954).

The *personality pattern of the teacher* influences the child's personality, never the opposite (Herrick, 1945; Anderson et al., 1946; Sister Mary Amatora, 1953). The "dominative" teacher has much the same influence on the child's personality as does an authoritarian parent (Anderson and Brewer, 1945). The overdependent teacher overvalues authority and status, while the overly independent teacher is lacking in sympathy and understanding and is likely to be harsh on passive pupils (Zimmerman and Lewton, 1951). A well-adjusted teacher can do much to encourage good adjustment on the part of her pupils. As Sister Mary Amatora (1954a) has pointed out, it is "of vital importance to the development of wholesome personality in the children that they have teachers who possess well-adjusted personalities."

Maladjusted teachers, on the other hand, do not always cause maladjustments in their pupils. Sometimes a teacher who has experienced maladjustments can understand and sympathize better with pupils who are having difficulties than can well-adjusted teachers (Gladstone, 1946). Another area of influence comes from the teacher's values. Because most teachers come from middle-class homes, they tend to have middle-class values. This reinforces the values the middle-class child has learned at home. In the case of children from the lower classes, the teacher's values may be at variance with the values the child has learned at home, and this proves to be confusing to him (Havighurst, 1946, 1952).

How much influence the teacher will have on the child depends to a certain extent upon the amount of interaction there is between teacher and pupil. When the school is organized on the "homeroom plan" with a special teacher in charge, the child comes in contact more closely and more often with this teacher than when he has different teachers for different subjects (Jackson, 1953). As children grow older, they tend to become critical of their teachers, and this influences them, indirectly, as much as if they admired and imitated their teachers. The critical child picks out flaws in the teacher's personality, appearance, and behavior and tries to avoid developing similar traits. Sometimes a disliked teacher exerts an unfavorable influence on her pupils by increasing emotional tension and thus leading to quarrelsome behavior outside of school (Hart, 1934; Merry and Merry, 1950).

Grade placement and *school grades* indicate to a child how he rates as compared with his classmates. If he is in a "slow" section, he discovers that he is considered less able than children in the "fast" section. When the school has rigid grade standards, the child who cannot meet these standards successfully feels inadequate. Report cards to parents tend to increase this feeling of inadequacy and encourage competition with other children (Heffernan, 1952). The very bright child, by contrast, who meets the school standards successfully without too much effort, is likely to develop negativism toward authority and intolerance toward those who are less bright (Hollingworth, 1940). On the whole, pupils who make good grades are likely to be better adjusted because they are happier in school and have more favorable concepts of self than do pupils who make poor grades (Jersild and Tasch, 1949; Resnick, 1951).

PLAYMATES AND FRIENDS

The young child is more anxious to have the approval of his parents and other adults than of his peers. But after he has entered school and become a member of a school group, the approval of his playmates becomes more necessary to him than the approval of his parents. It is then that he turns his attention to the development of personality traits which his playmates admire, even though they may not be the ones admired by his parents. In addition, he attempts to eliminate—or at least to minimize—the intensity of undesirable personality traits which he discovers the group disapproves of and which may readily put him in the position of a social isolate.

Early social experiences are important in the development of personality. When the child, through lack of social acceptance or lack of playmates of suitable age, must play alone or depend on adult companionship, he will develop personality traits very different from those he would have developed had he had playmates of his own age. Or should he substitute imaginary playmates for real playmates, he is likely to lack self-sufficiency, and be dominant, if not actually "bossy," in situations where real children are involved (Wingfield, 1948). In addition, he will lack empathy, he is likely to be rigid, introverted, and subject to uncontrolled emotional outbursts, and

he is either self-centered and demanding in his social contacts or a "lone
wolf" who prefers to get along alone rather than have strong emotional
ties to anyone (Dymond, 1950).

By contrast, the child whose early social experiences have been satisfying
develops a sense of personal security. This, in turn, makes it possible for
him to be less self-bound and to turn his interest and attention to others. As
a result, he develops empathy in that he can transpose himself into the
thinking, feeling, and acting of others. This makes him more socially ac-

Popularity plays an important role in the development of the child's personality. (*From
Child Development, a McGraw-Hill Text-Film.*)

ceptable and more popular than the child who is self-bound (Dymond,
1950). Through his contacts with others, he learns to assess himself and
his status in the group, thus laying solid foundations for a realistic concept
of himself (Gray, 1946). The more pleasant early social experiences the
child has, the better his outlook on life will be and, in turn, the better his
social adjustments (Anderson, 1952). However, even when children are
popular with others, it does not necessarily mean that they possess desirable
personality characteristics (Alexander and Alexander, 1952).

The popularity of the child has a considerable part in the development
of his personality. Children who are accepted in the social group, who feel
that other children like and admire them, or who find themselves from time
to time in positions of leadership in their groups develop a self-confidence

and poise which are lacking in children who are social isolates. The child who is friendly and self-confident, in turn, wins more friends, and this adds to his already existing popularity. As his popularity increases, his poise, self-assurance, and leadership qualities also grow stronger. The popular child has a freer, lighter attitude, he is more relaxed, and less influenced by the opinions of others than is the unpopular child (Potashin, 1946).

Just the opposite is true for children who are unpopular. They feel inferior; they are envious of their more popular associates; they resent being ignored by their peers; they are sullen and irritable, and usually carry a chip on the shoulder; or they are ready to "fly off the handle" at the slightest provocation. This, naturally, does not add to their popularity, nor does it help them to develop the personality traits which will make them popular. Unpopular children show a degree of tension and often seem awed. They acquiesce to the popular, try to impress them by showing off, or agree impetuously with whatever the popular children may suggest. In addition, they often develop a "chip-on-the-shoulder" attitude (Potashin, 1946).

Every child, sooner or later, is well aware of how he stands with the group. This knowledge has a marked influence on his concept of self. If lack of acceptance comes through no fault of his but rather because he belongs to a minority group or comes from a lower socioeconomic status than the other children in his class, this leads to bitter resentments which color unfavorably the feelings of inadequacy which lack of popularity gives rise to (Klausner, 1953). The more accepted the child is, the more favorable will be his concept of self, and this will be reflected in behavior that reduces the social distance between him and others (Smith, 1954). With social acceptance, the concept of self improves as time passes, while lack of social acceptance leads to poorer and poorer concepts of self. The child who is socially acceptable to his peers thus has a pattern of personality development that is different from that of the child who lacks social acceptance (Havighurst, 1953).

CULTURAL INFLUENCES

Custom and tradition are of no slight significance in the personality development of the child. There are certain socially approved patterns of behavior for both boys and girls in every culture, both uncivilized and civilized. These differ from culture to culture. But in every culture, children are subjected to pressures to develop a personality pattern that will conform as closely as possible to the standards set by the culture (Malinowski, 1927; Mead, 1935, 1939, 1949; Taylor, 1948; Benedict, 1949). In America, there are three different types of cultural systems, the *general American* culture, *social-class* cultures, and *ethnic-group* cultures. Each of these has its own standards of approved personality pattern (Davis and Havighurst, 1946; Havighurst, 1952; Stendler, 1954a). Even in cultures that are nearly alike, there may be the same values, but different emphasis is placed on them. The French, for example, put more emphasis on thrift than do the Americans (Stendler, 1954a), while the British put more emphasis on self-control than do the Americans (Farber, 1951, 1953). Thus, as Stendler (1954a) has pointed out, "As cultures differ, so do the personalities embedded in those cultures."

Every cultural and subcultural group prescribes a manner of approved behavior, or a role, for each member of the group (Warren, 1949). Children are socialized by teaching them, by formal or informal means, the approved

When a child sets goals beyond his reach, he is likely to develop feelings of inadequacy and inferiority. (*From Child Development, a McGraw-Hill Text-Film.*)

ways of thinking, feeling, and behaving which are characteristic of that culture (Schoeppe, 1953). In addition, the members of the cultural group "show the new member of that group what the rewards of the game of life are and convince him that he wants these rewards" (Gillin, 1949). To be well adjusted in any cultural group, the individual must accept the approved cultural norm as his own standard. The "rugged individualist" who refuses to conform becomes a cultural misfit (LaBarre, 1949; Schoeppe, 1953). In a rapidly changing culture, as is true in America today, especially in relation to the role of women, it is difficult for parents to guide their children's development by standards that held in their own youth (Linton, 1942; Mead, 1949, 1951; Milner, 1949; Schoeppe et al., 1953). The problem is further complicated by *social mobility*. As parents improve their status in society, they must accept patterns of the new social group with which they identify themselves. This results in feelings of insecurity and anxiety on the part of the child who must adjust to a new role with this change (Bogardus, 1949; Bossard and Sanger, 1949; McGuire, 1950; Sjoberg, 1951; Ort, 1952; Prothro, 1954). The status of the individual in the cultural pattern and the influence of social mobility are shown in Fig. 72.

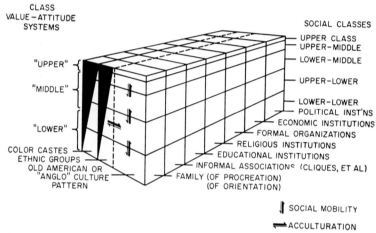

Fig. 72. Status of the individual in the cultural pattern. (*From C. McGuire, Social stratification and mobility patterns, Amer. sociol. Rev.,* 1950, **15**, 195–204. *Used by permission.*)

Basic Personality. Every social class and every cultural group produces a different basic personality. The *basic personality* is the organization of the drives and of the emotions of the individual, the deeper-lying parts of mental behavior, as compared with the more overt and visible aspects of mental behavior, as values. The basic personality includes inner feelings toward parents, members of the same or of the opposite sex, guilt, emotional reactivity, and hostility. Many of these feelings may be unconscious (Havighurst, 1952). The cultural group to which the child's parents belong sets the pattern for this basic personality, and through child rearing in the early years of life, the child adopts this pattern. The way the child is brought up is, thus, responsible for the type of personality he develops. Within a given cultural group, the personality patterns of different individuals will be similar, but will differ from those of individuals in different cultural groups because of the different social pressures from those groups (Davis and Havighurst, 1946; LaBarre, 1949; Havighurst, 1952). There is an "upper-class personality" that is distinct from a "core personality" (McArthur, 1955). In children from the lower-income groups, lack of confidence grows greater with increasing age and feelings of inadequacy become stronger. The opposite is true for children from the better-income groups (Goff, 1954).

Because the basic personality pattern is dependent not so much upon biological inheritance as upon cultural pressures, this means that it is possible to shape almost any type of personality required for successful living in that culture (LaBarre, 1949; Stendler, 1954a). The impact of culture is mediated chiefly through the family during the early years of life (Winch, 1950a; Bossard, 1954). Later, pressures from the school and the peer group supplement family pressures. From these pressures, the child learns to behave in a socially approved way for his sex group in that culture and to have attitudes which are sex-appropriate. While values may be more individual than other elements of the basic personality pattern, they are not different enough to change the personality pattern to any marked degree (Linton, 1942; Mead, 1949; Milner, 1949; Klineberg, 1953; Schoeppe et al., 1953). When boys and girls develop personality patterns that are atypical for their sex group, it is generally because the home patterns deviate from the norms of the group (Milner, 1949). This results in feelings of inadequacy on the part of the child who is different. On the other hand, the child who conforms to the approved pattern for his sex group will be happier and better adjusted (Gough, 1952a; Sherriffs and Jarrett, 1953; Trumbull, 1953).

LEVEL OF ASPIRATION

For the first few years of life, the child has no standards by which to judge his behavior. He merely knows that certain acts are right and others wrong by the reactions of adults to them (Davis and Havighurst, 1947). By the time the child is three or four years old, he begins to establish standards for himself. With each passing year, pressures from his parents, his teachers, and his peers result in making these standards more definite and specific. Often, in his hopes of winning approval and recognition, he sets his standards above his capacities (Breckenridge and Vincent, 1955). These standards become *levels of aspiration,* or the "level of future performance in a familiar task which an individual explicitly undertakes to reach" (Gruen, 1945). In establishing his levels of aspiration, the child is influenced by the ideal person with whom he has identified himself and whom he would like to be like (see pages 466–469 for a discussion of the ideal self).

The child's level of aspiration has a marked influence on his concept of self. The child may, through ignorance of his own capacities, set goals far beyond his reach. In this, he is encouraged by pressures from his parents who are anxious for him to "get ahead" (Kahl, 1953). Furthermore, he discovers that a high level of aspiration raises his prestige in his own eyes as well as in the eyes of others (Holt, 1946). Boys generally feel a greater need for achievement than do girls, and this causes them to set goals beyond their capacities (Walter and Marzolf, 1951). Negro children in nonsegregated schools likewise show higher levels of aspiration than do whites, as a form of compensation for their status in the group and in hopes of achieving status of a more desirable sort. Generally, their ambitions are unrealistic in that they are unrelated to specific abilities (Boyd, 1952).

The more the individual is deprived of things he wants, the more desirable they seem and the greater his aspiration for them. This holds true for social status as well as for individual achievement and material possessions (Marks, 1951). Level of aspiration is also influenced by past achievement. Children who are successful tend to raise their levels of aspiration. Among those who are unsuccessful, on the other hand, there is less tendency to revise their aspirations downward than to hold them constant or even to raise them (Reissman, 1953). The child whose level of aspiration is too high for his abilities becomes an "impractical idealist" who sees himself constantly as a failure; the child who sets his aspirations below his abilities lacks "ambition" and "gets nowhere" in life; while the child who "has his feet on the ground" checks his aspirations with his achievements and constantly revises his aspirations to fit more realistically into his abilities (Breckenridge and Vincent, 1953). Most children, unfortunately, fall into the first two categories.

Success and happiness in life are determined, to a large extent, by whether one feels oneself to be a success or failure. And how one feels about oneself is influenced by what one aspires to do and what one actually does (Frank, 1935). The habit of expecting too much, or too little, of what one is able to accomplish is set early in life and has a marked influence on the individual's concept of self. By adolescence, the relationship between level of aspiration and the individual's effort to achieve this aspiration is well set. Thus it becomes apparent that the child must learn early to assess his abilities realistically and must be encouraged to set levels of aspiration within the level of his ability if he is to be happy, successful, and well adjusted. Pressures from the social group to aim above his abilities lead to too high levels of aspiration, with consequent failure and feelings of inadequacy on the child's part (Frank, 1935; Breckenridge and Vincent, 1955).

The child who measures up to his own expectations feels proud and satisfied with himself and with his achievements. This is more characteristic of the intelligent and well-adjusted child who has learned to judge himself and others realistically than of the less intelligent and less well-adjusted child (Sears, 1940; Arsenian, 1942; Norman, 1953; Jersild, 1954). The child with a realistic level of aspiration may meet failure, but he will react realistically to it. When he is convinced, after repeated failure, that his level of aspiration was too high for his abilities, he will revise his level of aspiration but without feelings of anxiety, frustration, and compensation (Gruen, 1945).

By contrast, the child whose levels of aspiration have been unrealistic and who, as a result, meets constant failure may adjust his level of aspiration; he may substitute a different type of activity for the one in which he is failing; or he may take a defensive attitude, blaming others for his failure or blaming poor health or lack of training; he may shun similar situations in the future; he may become discouraged and give up; or he may substitute daydreams of success for attempts to achieve real success (Gould, 1939; Sears, 1940; Holt, 1946; Young and Yavitz, 1946; Horrocks, 1951; Jersild, 1954; Breckenridge and Vincent, 1955). Failure causes the child to be unsure of himself, with the result that he changes his level of aspiration without giving himself time to see if he might eventually reach it; he is variable and unpredictable in his performances; he will be anxious, worried, and suffer from feelings of inadequacy; and he will be submissive in his attitude toward others. All of these will contribute to poor self-concepts, with poor adjustment and unhappiness on the child's part (Gruen, 1945; Holt, 1946; Taylor and Farber, 1948; Topp, 1950, 1952).

LEVEL OF ADJUSTMENT

Adjustment means the extent to which an individual's personality functions efficiently in a world of other people. From birth to eighteen years are trying years (Topp, 1950). In the process of adjusting himself to the adult world, the child may pass through these years without undue distress, or he may experience such difficulties that the foundations will be laid for mental illness in adulthood. Which it will be will depend to a large extent upon the type of environment he has and the understanding guidance he receives from his parents and other adults with whom he is associated (Yellowlees, 1940; Warren, 1949; Jones, 1951). If he learns to be secure in the intimate relationships with his family, the child can tolerate the insecurity that comes when he tries to adjust to the world outside the home (Martin, 1951a).

As Thompson (1952) has pointed out, "Normal adjustment is a relative thing. Every child suffers some anxiety, displays some behavior that is unacceptable to others, fails to reach some goals that are extremely important to him, and experiences some periods of what he calls unhappiness. However, the child whose psychological adjustment can be considered within normal range 'bounces back' from these disappointments and depressions. He continues to orient his behavior toward goals that promise to satisfy his needs, and he adjusts his goal-setting to the social demands of his culture."

Below the age of twelve years, definite mental illness is rare. But symptoms appear at that time in ineffective adjustments to everyday life situations, such as crying, attention-getting devices, and daydreaming, which, if permitted to go unchecked, may result in serious mental illness as the child reaches maturity. No normal child is completely free from what is labeled as "problem behavior." The average number of different forms varies from four to six per child, with the frequency varying according to the age of the child (Macfarlane, 1943). A child may be quite disturbed and yet make good adjustments in school (Pilzer, 1952). Some children may be considered well adjusted by their teachers and yet be considered "problems" by their parents, and seriously disturbed by clinical workers (Harris, 1952). Boys, as a rule, suffer more from personality disturbances than do girls (Tenenbaum, 1940; Ullmann, 1952).

Personality Maladjustments. There are two major types of personality maladjustment; the first involves behavior which is satisfying to the child but socially unacceptable, while the second involves behavior which is socially acceptable but is a source of continuous, excessive, and disturbing conflict to the child (Strang, 1938). Anxiety and worry lead to neuroticism as time passes and the child develops handicapping personality disorders (Topp, 1950). Whether the child will engage in behavior which is satisfying to him and socially acceptable or whether he will behave in a socially acceptable manner, in spite of the psychological strain on him, will be characteristic of his own personality pattern and the level of adjustment he has attained (Seashore and Jensen, 1948).

There are a number of causes of personality maladjustment, of which the following have been found to be the most common:

1. Thwarting of impulses and desires which lead to a feeling of inferiority, such as feeling of guilt because of sex delinquencies or failure in school
2. Undue emotional stimulation, such as some terrible emotional shock or continued overexcitement during a long period of time
3. Bad home conditions caused by parental disagreements, parental separation, or the child's inability to rise to the level of the family's aspirations (Jordon, 1942)

There are a number of personality traits of an undesirable sort that appear in a mild form in children. At first, they appear very harmless and are frequently allowed to persist, without any real effort being made to overcome them. No single pattern is serious when viewed by itself. However, when several patterns are observable in the same child and when they seem to fit into a "personality picture," then they are significant and may be regarded as "danger signals" of future trouble. Of the many different behavior patterns that are danger signals of future trouble, the following are regarded as most serious:

Flying into fits of rage on the slightest provocation
Showing signs of excessive "worriedness" and anxiety
Frequently appearing depressed, rarely smiling or joking with others
Repeated stealing of small articles, despite severe punishment
Frequently appearing to be lost in daydreams
Showing very sensitive reactions to real or imagined slights

Excessive cruelty to younger or smaller children or animals

Abnormal anxiety about achieving perfection in any task

Frequent expression of the idea that he is being singled out for punishment more than others

Inability to avoid misbehavior even when repeatedly warned and punished

Excessive concern with physical appearance

Habit of lying on any occasion to suit some purpose

High degree of indecisiveness when relatively minor choices must be made

Hostility toward any kind of authority

Accident proneness

Repeated acts of destruction of material things

Teasing and bullying others when feeling rejected

Homesickness when away from familiar people and places

"Clowning" as a means of attracting attention to himself

Projecting blame on others and rationalizing acts when criticized

Tattling on other children to win adult attention and approval

"Sour grapes" attitude to cover up disappointment by minimizing the value of unattainable things (Rose, 1947; Seashore and Jensen, 1948; Klapp, 1949; Brenman, 1952; Topp, 1952)

Once a pattern of maladjustive behavior appears, it is likely to persist. As Bennett (1953) has pointed out,

Maladjustive behavior shows a tenacious tendency to remain maladjustive. Forms of activity that succeed in doing the individual far more harm than good remain in operation even in the face of the strongest psychotherapeutic efforts. Minor forms of maladjustive behavior become permanent fixtures in the totality of an individual's behavior and often remain throughout his lifetime. Small things, insignificant in themselves, pile up and add burdens to the day-to-day existence and drain efficiency.

Unless minor disturbances are discovered and remedial measures taken to correct them, they are likely to develop into handicapping disorders (Topp, 1950). Since most personality disturbances result from the child's environment, mainly that of the home, where adult tensions and pressures exist, the only way to eliminate the cause of the trouble would be for adults to remove the stresses from their own lives or, as Jersild (1954) facetiously suggested, "transport the children to another world."

Well-adjusted Personalities. The well-adjusted child is one whose concept of self is realistic in that what he thinks of himself agrees closely with what others think of him and with his achievements (Merry and Merry, 1950; Lawton, 1951). He enjoys a kind of inner harmony when there is a degree of integration of his intellectual and emotional capacities (Jersild, 1954). As Bain (1954) points out, he

thinks, acts, and feels according to what is expected and tolerated within his society. . . . He is both satisfied and stimulated by the life he leads. He has the habit of happiness and the habit of making and breaking habits effectively. He is neither unduly frightened by the future nor wedded to the past. . . . He has no sense of sin but he profits by experience. He has a sturdy sense of humor which laughs *with* people, not *at* them. He knows his limitations and capacities and acts accordingly. He has a fairly accurate judgment of others and of what others think of him. . . . He makes his goals and ideals consistent with his knowledge of what is possible, and he is open-minded about the "possible." He respects himself because he respects others. . . . He wants an opportunity to realize his own potentials so long as it does not prevent others from doing the same.

Children who are well adjusted come from homes that are happy places, where discipline is used for more far-reaching purposes than merely deterring wrongdoing, where responsibility is a part of the routine of life, where there is religion, where the family enjoys recreations together, and where family relationships and attitudes toward children are wholesome (Stout and Langdon, 1951). In such homes, children learn to take responsibilities on their own level, to be independent and take care of their own needs, to solve their own problems, and to be happy when alone (Stains, 1951). If children are to be well adjusted, adults must know not only how to *create* a good environment for children, but once it is created, they must know how to *maintain* it (Anderson, 1948).

HAPPINESS IN CHILDHOOD

Most adults think of childhood as a happy, carefree period of life. As Rosenzweig and Rosenzweig (1952) have pointed out, "The golden days of childhood, as they appear in the conventional reminiscence of adults, are more consistent with fantasy than with fact. The myths of all races similarly portray the childhood of man as a paradise." As a matter of fact, the child is probably no happier than the adult. While the adult is looking back longingly at his childhood and wishing he could return to it, the child is looking forward to the day when he will be "grown up" and free from the controls of adults which constantly frustrate him.

A number of studies have been made of adult memories of childhood days. These have shown that childhood is remembered as a relatively happy age, though not free from memories of unhappy experiences. Because this is a time when the individual is relatively free from worries and responsibilities, he is likely to be happier than he will be in adolescence when worries and responsibilities are piled upon him which he cannot always meet successfully (Waldfogel, 1948; Tuckman and Lorge, 1952). As the babyhood years are years of dependency, there is a feeling of being all-powerful and the center of attention. This is very satisfying to the baby and makes him happy. Only physical discomforts and pain, from illness or injury, and occasional corporal punishment, will make him unhappy (Thompson and Witryol, 1948).

After the child is four years old, there are many memories of unfulfilled wishes, unsolved problems, unpleasant incidents, of being forced to do things he did not want to do, and of punishments that he often considered unjustified (Thompson and Witryol, 1948; Waldfogel, 1948; Smith, 1952a). At this time, home and family are very important in determining the child's happiness (Barschak, 1951). No longer is the child omnipotent, as he was in babyhood, and he now meets new environmental obstacles constantly, as well as new demands that he assume responsibilities formerly assumed by others.

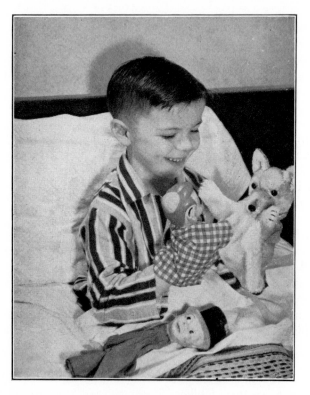

Childhood should be a happy age if the child is to develop into a well-adjusted individual. (*From Child Development, a McGraw-Hill Text-Film.*)

When the child goes to school, he meets not only more environmental obstacles and demands from adults, but he also comes in competition with other children in school work and in play. How well he can meet these demands and competition will determine how happy he will be. Adults report many memories of feelings of inadequacy and insecurity at this age (Thompson and Witryol, 1948; Waldfogel, 1948; Winker, 1949; Bühler, 1952; Jersild, 1954a). Family and home are less important factors in the child's happiness now than they were earlier, though friction with family members and feelings of guilt when parental expectations are not met contribute to the child's unhappiness (Waldfogel, 1948; Wall, 1948; Barschak, 1951). Success in school work and popularity with peers are now more important than home relationships in determining how happy or unhappy the older child will be (Watson, 1930; Thompson and Witryol, 1948; Bühler, 1952). As the child approaches adolescence, these factors become even more important than earlier and result in more unhappy experiences (Thompson and Kepler, 1945; Winker, 1949; Bühler, 1952).

Happiness and Adjustment. Happiness in childhood comes mostly from human relationships (Justin, 1950). However, these relationships must be satisfactory to the child if they are to bring him happiness. For the young child, pleasant relationships with his family will make him happy, while for the older child, his relationships with people outside the home are more essential to his happiness than are relationships with the family (Jersild and Tasch, 1949; Barschak, 1951). The child soon discovers that pleasant relationships with others depend more upon his adjustment to them than upon their adjustment to him. He must fit into the socially approved pattern of the group if he is to be an accepted member of it.

The child whose personality pattern has been developed along lines approved by the group has, therefore, a far better chance for successful social adjustments than has the child whose personality is atypical for the group. While he might make good adjustments in a cultural group where certain of his outstanding traits were admired, he will not make good adjustments to the group with which he is associated unless he conforms to the pattern of that group (Tuddenham, 1952). In addition, the child must have a realistic concept of himself if he is to be well adjusted and socially acceptable. He must be aware of his own qualities and achievements as well as of his weaknesses and failures (Jersild and Tasch, 1949; Jersild, 1954). Thus, only when the child has a realistic concept of self which will enable him to adjust successfully to the people with whom he comes in contact can he hope to have a happy childhood.

BIBLIOGRAPHY

Abbe, M.: 1950. Ideal personalities of pupils and teachers judged by pupils. *Jap. J. Psychol.*, **20**, 37–43.

Aberle, D. F., and K. D. Naegele: 1952. Middle-class fathers' occupational roles and attitudes toward children. *Amer. J. Orthopsychiat.*, **22**, 366–378.

Abernethy, E. M.: 1936. Relationships between mental and physical growth. *Monogr. Soc. Res. Child Develpm.*, **1**, No. 7.

Abt, I., A. Adler, and P. Bartelme: 1929. The relationship between the onset of speech and intelligence. *J. Amer. med. Ass.*, **93**, 1351–1353.

Ackerman, N. W., and M. Jahoda: 1950. *Anti-Semitism and emotional disorder.* New York: Harper.

Adams, S.: 1932. A study of the growth of language between two and four years. *J. juv. Res.*, **16**, 269–277.

Adler, A.: 1930. *Problems of neurosis.* New York: Cosmopolitan Book Corp.

———: 1930a. *The education of children.* New York: Greenberg.

Albrecht, R.: 1954. The parental responsibilities of grandparents. *Marriage Fam. Living,* **16**, 201–204.

Aldrich, C. A.: 1947. The pediatrician looks at personality. *Amer. J. Orthopsychiat.*, **17**, 571–574.

———: 1948. On the subject of orderly or lawful behavior. *Pediatrics*, **1**, 725–732.

———, M. A. Norval, C. Knop, and F. Venegas: 1946. The crying of newly born babies. IV. A follow-up study after additional nursing care had been provided. *J. Pediat.*, **28**, 665–670.

———, C. Sung, and C. Knop: 1945. The crying of newly born babies. I. The community phase. *J. Pediat.*, **26**, 313–326.

———, ———, and ———: 1945a. The crying of newly born babies. II. The individual phase. *J. Pediat.*, **27**, 89–96.

———, ———, and ———: 1945b. The crying of newly born babies. III. The early home period. *J. Pediat.*, **27**, 429–435.

Alexander, F.: 1951. The dynamics of personality development. *Soc. Casework,* **32**, 139–143.

Alexander, T.: 1951. Certain characteristics of the self as related to affection. *Child Develpm.*, **22**, 285–290.

Alexander, T., and M. Alexander: 1952. A study of personality and social status. *Child Develpm.*, **23**, 207–213.

Alexandria, Sister M.: 1946. Personality adjustment and leadership. *Education,* **66**, 584–590.

Allen, F. H.: 1942. *Psychotherapy with children.* New York: Rinehart.

Allen, I.: 1948. Facial growth in children five to eight years of age. *Hum. Biol.*, **20**, 109–145.

Allen, I. M.: 1947. Defect of the speech function in childhood. *New Zealand med. J.,* **46**, 297–307.

Allen, L., L. Brown, L. Dickinson, and K. C. Pratt: 1941. The relation of first name preferences to their frequency in the culture. *J. soc. Psychol.*, **14**, 279–293.

Allen, P. J.: 1952. The leadership pattern. *Amer. sociol. Rev.*, **17**, 93–96.

———: 1955. Childhood backgrounds of success in a profession. *Amer. sociol. Rev.,* **26**, 186–190.

Allen, R. M.: 1951. A longitudinal study of six Rorschach protocols of a three-year-old child. *Child Develpm.,* **22**, 61–69.

Allport, G. W.: 1937. *Personality: a psychological interpretation.* New York: Holt.

———, J. M. Gillespie, and J. Young: 1948. The religion of the postwar college student. *J. Psychol.,* **25**, 3–33.

——— and B. M. Kramer: 1946. Some roots of prejudice. *J. Psychol.,* **22**, 1–39.

Alm, I.: 1953. The long-term prognosis for prematurely born children: a follow-up study of 999 premature boys born in wedlock and of 1002 controls. *Acta paediatr. Stockh.,* **42**, Suppl. 94.

Almy, M. C.: 1949. Children's experiences prior to first grade and success in beginning to read. *Teach. Coll. Contr. Educ.,* No. 954.

Alpert, A.: 1941. The latency period. *Amer. J. Orthopsychiat.,* **11**, 126–132.

Alschuler, R. H., and L. A. Hattwick: 1943. Easel painting as an index of personality in preschool children. *Amer. J. Orthopsychiat.,* **13**, 615–625.

——— and ———: 1947. Understanding children through their painting. *Understanding the Child,* **16**, 98–101.

——— and ———: 1947a. *Painting and personality.* Chicago: University of Chicago Press.

Altmann, M., E. Knowles, and H. D. Bull: 1941. A psychosomatic study of the sex cycle in women. *Psychosom. Med.,* **3**, 199–225.

Altus, G. T.: 1953. W.I.S.C. patterns of a selective group of bilingual school children. *J. genet. Psychol.,* **83**, 241–248.

Amatora, Sister Mary: 1952. Can elementary school children discriminate certain traits in their teachers? *Child Develpm.,* **23**, 75–80.

———: 1953. Guiding the child's personality potential to fruitful fulfillment. *Education,* **74**, 156–163.

———: 1954. Contrasts in boys' and girls' judgments in personality. *Child Develpm.,* **25**, 51–61.

———: 1954a. Similarity in teacher and pupil personality. *J. Psychol.,* **37**, 45–50.

Amen, E. W.: 1941. Individual differences in apperceptive reaction: a study of the response of preschool children to pictures. *Genet Psychol. Monogr.,* **23**, 319–385.

——— and N. Renison: 1954. A study of the relationship between play patterns and anxiety in young children. *Genet. Psychol. Monogr.,* **50**, 3–41.

Ames, L. B.: 1937. The sequential patterning of prone progression in the human infant. *Genet. Psychol. Monogr.,* **19**, 409–460.

———: 1939. Some relationships between stair-climbing and prone progression. *J. genet. Psychol.,* **54**, 313–325.

———: 1940. The constancy of psycho-motor tempo in individual infants. *J. genet. Psychol.,* **57**, 445–450.

———: 1941. Motor correlates of infant crying. *J. genet. Psychol.,* **59**, 239–247.

———: 1945. Free drawing and completion drawing: a comparative study of preschool children. *J. genet. Psychol.,* **66**, 161–165.

———: 1946. The development of the sense of time in the young child. *J. genet. Psychol.,* **68**, 97–125.

———: 1948. Postural and placement orientation in writing and block behavior: developmental trends from infancy to age ten. *J. genet. Psychol.,* **73**, 45–52.

———: 1949. Development of interpersonal smiling responses in the preschool years. *J. genet. Psychol.,* **74**, 273–291.

———: 1949a. *Bilaterality. J. genet. Psychol.,* **75**, 45–50.

——: 1952. The sense of self of nursery school children as manifested by their verbal behavior. *J. genet. Psychol.,* **81,** 193–232.

—— and F. L. Ilg: 1951. Developmental trends in writing behavior. *J. genet. Psychol.,* **79,** 28–46.

—— and J. Learned: 1946. Imaginary companions and related phenomena. *J. genet. Psychol.,* **69,** 147–167.

—— and ——: 1948. The development of verbalized space in the young child. *J. genet. Psychol.,* **72,** 63–84.

Ames, R. T.: 1952. The accuracy of Negro and white children's predictions of teachers' attitudes toward Negro students. *J. Negro Educ.,* **21,** 125–135.

Ames, V. C., and C. D. Flory: 1944. Physical growth from birth to maturity. *Rev. educ. Res.,* **14,** 427–437.

Ammons, R. B.: 1950. Reactions in projective doll-play interview of males two to six years of age to differences in skin color and facial features. *J. genet. Psychol.,* **76,** 323–341.

—— and H. S. Ammons: 1949. Parent preferences in young children's doll-play interviews. *J. abnorm. soc. Psychol.,* **44,** 490–505.

Anastasi, A., M. Cohen, and D. Spatz: 1948. A study of fear and anger in college students through the controlled diary method. *J. genet. Psychol.,* **73,** 243–249.

—— and F. A. Cordova: 1953. Some effects of bilingualism upon the intelligence test performance of Puerto Rican children in New York City. *J. educ. Psychol.,* **44,** 1–19.

—— and R. D'Angelo: 1952. A comparison of Negro and white preschool children in language development and Goodenough draw-a-man I.Q. *J. genet. Psychol.,* **81,** 147–165.

—— and deJésus, C.: 1953. Language development and non-verbal I.Q. of Puerto Rican preschool children in New York City. *J. abnorm. soc. Psychol.,* **48,** 357–366.

—— and J. P. Foley: 1936. An analysis of spontaneous drawings by children in different cultures. *J. appl. Psychol.,* **20,** 689–726.

Anders, S. F.: 1955. Religious behavior in church families. *Marriage Fam. Living,* **17,** 54–57.

Anderson, C. M.: 1950. *Saints, sinners, and psychiatry.* Philadelphia: Lippincott.

——: 1952. The self-image: a theory of the dynamics of behavior. *Ment. Hyg., N.Y.,* **36,** 227–244.

Anderson, F. N., and N. V. Scheidemann: 1933. A study of triplets. *Genet. Psychol. Monogr.,* **14,** 93–176.

Anderson, H. H.: 1936. Domination and integration in the social behavior of young children in an experimental play situation. *Proc. 2nd Biennial Meeting, Soc. Res. Child Develpm.,* pp. 27–29.

——: 1937. Domination and integration in the social behavior of young children in an experimental play situation. *Genet. Psychol. Monogr.,* **19,** 343–408.

——: 1939. Domination and social integration in the behavior of kindergarten children and teachers. *Genet. Psychol. Monogr.,* **21,** 287–385.

—— and H. M. Brewer: 1945. Studies of teachers' classroom personalities. *Appl. Psychol. Monogr.,* **1,** No. 6.

——, ——, and M. F. Reed: 1946. Studies in teachers' classroom personalities. *Appl. Psychol. Monogr.,* No. 11.

Anderson, J. E.: 1939. The development of spoken language. *38th Yearb. nat. Soc. Stud. Educ.,* pp. 211–224.

——: 1942. The contribution of child development to psychology. *J. consult. Psychol.,* **6,** 128–134.

————: 1946. Parents' attitudes on child behavior: a report of three studies. *Child Develpm.*, **17**, 91–97.

————: 1948. Personality organization in children. *Amer. Psychologist*, **3**, 409–416.

————: 1949. *The psychology of development and personality adjustment.* New York: Holt.

————: 1952. The relation of attitude to adjustment. *Education*, **73**, 210–218.

Anderson, W. A.: 1943. The family and individual social participation. *Amer. sociol. Rev.*, **8**, 420–424.

————: 1950. *Marriages and families of university graduates.* Ithaca, N.Y.: Cornell University Press.

Anderson, W. E.: 1947. The personality characteristics of 153 Negro pupils, Dunbar High School, Okmulgee, Oklahoma. *J. Negro Educ.*, **16**, 44–48.

Anderson, W. F.: 1954. Attitudes of parents of differing socio-economic status toward the teaching profession. *J. educ. Psychol.*, **45**, 345–352.

Anonymous, 1949. Ambivalence in first reactions to a sibling. *J. abnorm. soc. Psychol.*, **44**, 541–548.

Anthony, S.: 1940. *The child's discovery of death.* New York: Harcourt, Brace.

Antonov, A. N.: 1947. Children born during the siege of Leningrad in 1942. *J. Pediat.*, **30**, 250–259.

Appel, M. H.: 1942. Aggressive behavior in nursery school children and adult procedures in dealing with such behavior. *J. exp. Educ.*, **11**, 185–199.

Ariamov, E. A.: 1948. Fantasy and lying in childhood. *Semia i Shkola*, **11**, 16–19.

Arkin, E.: 1933. The problem of the stability of the human organism. *J. genet. Psychol.*, **42**, 229–236.

Arlitt, A. H.: 1911. The effect of alcohol on the intelligent behavior of the white rat and its progeny. *Psychol. Monogr.*, **26**, No. 4.

Arrington, R. E.: 1932. Interrelations in the behavior of young children. *Child Develpm. Monogr.*, No. 8.

————: 1939. Time-sampling studies of child behavior. *Psychol. Monogr.*, **51**, No. 2.

Arsenian, S.: 1937. Bilingualism and mental development. *Teach. Coll. Contr. Educ.*, No. 712.

————: 1941. A further study of the Gleeton Interest Inventory. *Occupations*, **20**, 94–99.

————: 1942. Own estimates and objective measurement. *J. educ. Psychol.*, **33**, 291–302.

————: 1945. Bilingualism in the post-war world. *Psychol. Bull.*, **42**, 65–86.

Arthaud, R. L., A. N. Hohneck, C. H. Ramsey, and K. C. Pratt: 1948. The relation of family name preferences to their frequency in the culture. *J. soc. Psychol.*, **28**, 19–37.

Asch, S. E.: 1946. Forming impressions of personality. *J. abnorm. soc. Psychol.*, **41**, 258–290.

ASHA Committee on the Midcentury White House Conference: 1952. Speech disorders and speech correction. *J. Speech Hearing Disorders*, **17**, 129–137.

Ashley-Montagu, M. F.: 1948. Sex order of birth and personality. *Amer. J. Orthopsychiat.*, **18**, 351–353.

Austin, M. C., and G. G. Thompson: 1948. Children's friendships: a study of the bases on which children select and reject their best friends. *J. educ. Psychol.*, **39**, 101–116.

Austin, T. R., and R. B. Sleight: 1951. Aesthetic preference for isosceles triangles. *J. appl. Psychol.*, **35**, 340–341.

Ausubel, D. P.: 1950. Negativism as a phase of ego development. *Amer. J. Orthopsychiat.*, **20**, 796–805.

————: 1951. Prestige motivation of gifted children. *Genet. Psychol. Monogr.*, **43**, 53–117.

———, E. E. Balthazar, I. Rosenthal, L. S. Blackman, S. H. Schpoont, and J. Welkowitz: 1954. Perceived parent attitudes as determinants of children's ego structure. *Child Develpm.,* **25,** 173–183.

———, H. M. Schiff, and E. B. Gasser: 1952. A preliminary study of developmental trends in sociopathy: accuracy of perception of own and others' sociometric status. *Child Develpm.,* **23,** 111–128.

Axline, V. M.: 1947. *Play therapy.* Boston: Houghton Mifflin.

———: 1951. Observing children at play. *Teach. Coll. Rec.,* **52,** 358–363.

Ayer, M. E., and R. G. Bernreuter: 1937. A study of the relationship between discipline and personality traits in little children. *J. genet. Psychol.,* **50,** 165–170.

Bach, G. R.: 1945. Young children's play fantasies. *Psychol. Monogr.,* **59,** No. 2.

Bagby, P. H.: 1953. Culture and the causes of culture. *Amer. Anthrop.,* **55,** 535–554.

Bahm, A. J.: 1946. Humanism: a religion for scientists. *Sci. Mon., N.Y.,* **62,** 310–315.

Bailey, Sister Agnes Therese: 1946. Aggression in infancy and early childhood. *Cath. educ. Rev.,* **44,** 421–429.

Bain, R.: 1954. Making normal people. *Marriage Fam. Living,* **16,** 27–31.

Baker, J. N.: 1943. The press and crime. *J. crim. Law Criminol.,* **33,** 463–467.

Bakwin, H.: 1947. The emotional status at birth. *Amer. J. Dis. Child.,* **74,** 373–376.

———: 1948. "Pure mother" overprotection. *J. Pediat.,* **33,** 788–794.

———: 1949. Emotional deprivation in infants. *J. Pediat.,* **35,** 512–521.

———: 1950. Lateral dominance. *J. Pediat.,* **36,** 385–391.

——— and R. M. Bakwin: 1951. Discipline in children. *J. Pediat.,* **39,** 623–634.

——— and T. W. Patrick: 1944. The weight of Negro infants. *J. Pediat.,* **24,** 405–407.

Bakwin, R. M.: 1953. The comics. *J. Pediat.,* **42,** 633–635.

——— and H. Bakwin: 1952. Cluttering. *J. Pediat.,* **40,** 393–396.

Baldridge, M.: 1949. Three decades of language study. *Childh. Educ.,* **26,** 117–124.

Baldwin, A. L.: 1945. Differences in parent behavior toward three- and nine-year-old children. *J. Pers.,* **15,** 143–165.

———: 1947. Changes in parent behavior during childhood. *Amer. Psychologist,* **2,** 425–426.

———: 1947a. Changes in parent behavior during pregnancy. *Child Develpm.,* **18,** 29–39.

———: 1948. Socialization and the parent-child relationship. *Child Develpm.,* **19,** 127–136.

———: 1949. The effect of the home environment on nursery-school behavior. *Child Develpm.,* **20,** 49–61.

———, J. Kalhorn, and F. H. Breese: 1945. Patterns of parent behavior. *Psychol. Monogr.,* **58,** No. 3.

Baldwin, B. T.: 1922. The relation between mental and physical growth. *J. educ. Psychol.,* **13,** 193–203.

——— and B. L. Wellman: 1928. The pegboard as a means of analyzing form perception and motor control in young children. *J. genet. Psychol.,* **35,** 389–414.

Baley, S.: 1948. Color, form, and size perception in the preschool child. *Psychol. Abstr.,* No. 248.

Banham, K. M.: 1950. The development of affectional behavior in infancy. *J. genet. Psychol.,* **76,** 283–289.

———: 1951. Senescence and the emotions: a genetic theory. *J. genet. Psychol.,* **78,** 175–183.

———: 1952. Obstinate children are adaptable. *Ment. Hyg., N.Y.,* **36,** 84–89.

Banister, H., and M. Ravden: 1944. The environment and the child. *Brit. J. Psychol.,* **35,** 82–87.

Bankston, H. S.: 1954. Gaining emotional maturity through group discussion. *Understanding the Child*, **23**, 25–26.

Barclay, D.: 1953. How girls judge mother's role. *New York Times,* June 21.

Barker, L. S., M. Schoggen, P. Schoggen, and R. G. Barker: 1952. The frequency of physical disability in children: a comparison of sources of information. *Child Develpm.*, **23**, 215–226.

Barker, R. G., T. Dembo, and K. Lewin: 1943. Frustration and regression. *In* R. G. Barker, J. S. Kounin, and H. F. Wright, *Child behavior and development.* New York: McGraw-Hill.

——, J. S. Kounin, and H. F. Wright: 1943. *Child behavior and development.* New York: McGraw-Hill.

Barnes, E.: 1902. The prettiest thing. *Stud. in Educ.*, **2**, 180–194.

Barnhart, E. N.: 1942. Developmental stages in compositional construction on children's drawings. *J. exp. Educ.*, **11**, 156–184.

Baron, D.: 1951. Personal-social characteristics and classroom social status: a sociometric study of fifth and sixth grade girls. *Sociometry*, **14**, 32–43.

Barschak, E.: 1951. A study of happiness and unhappiness in the childhood and adolescence of girls in different cultures. *J. Psychol.*, **32**, 173–215.

Bartemeier, L.: 1953. The contribution of the father to the mental health of the family. *Amer. J. Psychiat.*, **110**, 277–280.

Bartlett, E. R., and D. B. Harris: 1935. Personality factors in delinquency. *Sch. & Soc.*, **43**, 653–656.

Baruch, D. W.: 1937. A study of reported tension in interparental relationships as coexistent with behavior adjustment in young children. *J. exp. Educ.*, **6**, 187–204.

——: 1941. Aggression during doll play in a preschool. *Amer. J. Orthopsychiat.*, **11**, 252–260.

—— and J. A. Wilcox: 1944. A study of sex differences in preschool children's adjustments coexistent with interparental tensions. *J. genet. Psychol.*, **64**, 281–303.

Batchelor, I. R. C., and M. Napier: 1953. Broken homes and attempted suicide. *Brit. J. Delinqu.*, **4**, 99–108.

Battin, T. C.: 1953. The use of the diary and survey method involving the questionnaire technique to determine the impact of television on school children in regard to viewing habits and formal and informal education. *Speech Monogr.*, **20**, 135–136.

Baumgarten, F., and M. Tramer: 1943. Kinderzeichnungen in vergleichend psychologischer Beleuchtung. *Z. Kinderpsychiat.*, **9**, 161–220.

Bavelas, A.: 1942. A method for investigating individual and group ideology. *Sociometry*, **5**, 371–377.

Baxter, L. C.: 1951. Vocational guidance for elementary school pupils. *Elem. Sch. J.*, **51**, 343–345.

Bayer, L. M., and M. M. Snyder: 1950. Illness experience of a group of normal children. *Child Develpm.*, **21**, 93–120.

Bayley, N.: 1932. Study of the crying of infants during mental and physical tests. *J. genet. Psychol.*, **40**, 306–329.

——: 1933. Mental growth during the first three years. A developmental study of 61 children by repeated tests. *Genet. Psychol. Monogr.*, **14**, 1–92.

——: 1935. The development of motor abilities during the first three years. *Monogr. Soc. Res. Child Develpm.*, **1**, 1–26.

——: 1936. Growth changes in the cephalic index during the first five years of life. *Hum. Biol.*, **8**, 1–18.

——: 1940. *Studies in the development of young children.* Berkeley: University of California Press.

———: 1943. Size and body build of adolescents in relation to rate of skeletal maturing. *Child Develpm.*, **14**, 51–90.

———: 1944. The emotions of children: their development and modification. *Childh. Educ.*, **21**, 156–160.

———: 1946. Tables for predicting adult height from skeletal age and present height. *J. Pediat.*, **28**, 49–64.

———: 1951. Some psychological correlates of somatic androgyny. *Child Develpm.*, **22**, 47–60.

———: 1954. Some increasing parent-child similarities during the growth of children. *J. educ. Psychol.*, **45**, 1–21.

——— and F. C. Davis: 1935. Growth changes in bodily size and proportions during the first three years. *Biometrika*, **27**, 26–87.

——— and A. Espenschade: 1944. Motor development from birth to maturity. *Rev. educ. Res.*, **14**, 381–382.

——— and S. R. Pinnau: 1952. Tables for predicting adult height from skeletal age: revised for use with the Greulich-Pyle Hand Standards. *J. Pediat.*, **40**, 423–441.

Bayton, J. A.: 1946. Personality and prejudice. *J. Psychol.*, **22**, 59–65.

Beach, V., and M. H. Bressler: 1944. Phases in the development of children's painting. *J. exp. Educ.*, **13**, 1–4.

Beals, L.: 1950. A study of certain factors and their relationship to the personal adjustment of children. *Sch. & Soc.*, **72**, 55–57.

Bean, C. H.: 1932. An unusual opportunity to investigate the psychology of language. *J. genet. Psychol.*, **40**, 181–202.

Beasley, W. C.: 1933. An investigation of related problems in the vision of newborn infants. *Psychol. Bull.*, **30**, 626.

Beaver, A. P.: 1932. The initiation of social contacts by preschool children. *Child Develpm. Monogr.*, No. 7.

Becker, M. G., and C. P. Loomis: 1948. Measuring rural, urban, and farm and non-farm cleavages in a rural consolidated school. *Sociometry*, **11**, 246–261.

Beckey, R. E.: 1942. A study of certain factors related to retardation of speech. *J. Speech Hearing Disorders*, **7**, 233–249.

Beekman, E.: 1947. What high-school seniors think of religion. *Relig. Educ.*, **42**, 333–337.

Beeler, S.: 1953. Angry girls—behavior control by girls in latency. *Smith Coll. Stud. soc. Work*, **23**, 205–226.

Behers, M. L.: 1954. Child rearing and the character structure of the mother. *Child Develpm.*, **25**, 225–238.

Bell, G. B., and H. E. Hall: 1954. The relationship between leadership and latency. *J. abnorm. soc. Psychol.*, **49**, 156–157.

Bell, J.: 1943. Psychological aspects of dental treatment of children. Madison: *J. exp. Educ.*, p. 87.

Bell, J. E.: 1952. Perceptual development and the drawings of children. *Amer. J. Orthopsych:at.*, **22**, 386–393.

Beller, E. K.: 1949. Two attitude components of younger boys. *J. soc. Psychol.*, **29**, 139–151.

———: 1950. Dependency and independence in young children. *Amer. Psychologist*, **5**, 293.

Belogianis, D., K. Kymer, A. J. Lukes, and J. B. Geisel: 1944. Positive techniques in the classroom. *Elem. Sch. J.*, **44**, 594–601.

Benda, C. E.: 1943. Prevention of mental deficiency from the viewpoint of neuropathology: with special reference to the frequency and significance of birth injuries. *Amer. J. ment. Def.*, **48**, 33–45.

———: 1949. Prenatal maternal factors in mongolism. *J. Amer. med. Ass.*, **139**, 979–985.

———: 1954. Psychopathology of childhood. In L. Carmichael, *Manual of child psychology*, 2d ed. New York: Wiley, pp. 1115–1161.

———, M. J. Farrell, and C. E. Chipman: 1951. The inadequacy of present-day concepts of mental deficiency and mental illness in child psychiatry. *Amer. J. Psychiat.*, **107**, 721.

Bender, I. E., and A. H. Hastorf: 1950. The perception of persons: forecasting another person's responses on three personality scales. *J. abnorm. soc. Psychol.*, **45**, 556–561.

Bender, J. F.: 1944. Do you know someone who stutters? *Sci. Mon., N.Y.*, **49**, 221–223.

Bender, L.: 1937. Behavior problems in the children of psychotic and criminal parents. *Genet. Psychol. Monogr.*, **19**, 229–339.

———: 1944. The psychology of children's reading and the comics. *J. educ. Sociol.*, **18**, 223–231.

———: 1950. Anxiety in disturbed children. *In* P. H. Hoch and J. Zubin, *Anxiety*. New York: Grune & Stratton.

——— and R. S. Lourie: 1941. The effect of comic books on the ideology of children. *Amer. J. Orthopsychiat.*, **11**, 540–550.

——— and S. Paster: 1941. Homosexual trends in children. *Amer. J. Orthopsychiat.*, **11**, 730–743.

——— and P. Schilder: 1936. Aggressiveness in children. *Genet. Psychol. Monogr.*, **18**, 410–525.

——— and B. F. Vogel: 1941. Imaginary companions of children. *Amer. J. Orthopsychiat.*, **11**, 56–65.

Benedict, R.: 1938. Continuities and discontinuities in cultural conditioning. *Psychiatry*, **1**, 161–167.

———: 1949. Child rearing in certain European countries. *Amer. J. Orthopsychiat.*, **19**, 342–350.

Benjamin, H.: 1932. Age and sex differences in the toy preferences of young children. *J. genet. Psychol.*, **41**, 417–429.

Bennett, E. M.: 1953. A socio-cultural interpretation of maladjustive behavior. *J. soc. Psychol.*, **37**, 19–26.

——— and D. E. Johannsen: 1954. Psychodynamics of the diabetic child. *Psychol. Monogr.*, **68**, No. 11.

Benton, A. L.: 1940. Mental development of prematurely born children. *Amer. J. Orthopsychiat.*, **10**, 719–746.

Berdie, R. F.: 1953. Why don't they go to college? *Personnel Guid. J.*, **31**, 352–356.

Berenda, R. W.: 1950. *Influence of the group on the judgments of children: an experimental investigation*. New York: King's Crown.

Berger, I. L.: 1948. Psychopathologic attitudes of frustrated previously employed mothers toward their offspring. *J. nerv. ment. Dis.*, **108**, 241–249.

Bergum, M.: 1940. Constructive values associated with rejection. *Amer. J. Orthopsychiat.*, **10**, 312–326.

Berman, S.: 1948. Adjustment of parents to children in the home. *J. Pediat.*, **32**, 66–77.

Bernard, J.: 1946. Human fetal reactivity to tonal stimulation. *Amer. Psychologist*, **1**, 256.

——— and L. W. Sontag: 1947. Fetal reactivity to tonal stimulation: a preliminary report. *J. genet. Psychol.*, **70**, 205–210.

——— and ———: 1951. Fetal reactivity to sound. *In* W. Dennis, *Readings in child psychology*. New York: Prentice-Hall, pp. 15–19.

Bernarda, M.: 1949. Wat den Kenjonge mensen over den dood. *Vlaam. Opvoedk. Fijdschr.,* **30,** 32–40.

Berne, E. V.: 1930. An experimental investigation of social behavior patterns in young children. *Univ. Ia. Stud. Child Welf.,* **4,** No. 3.

Bernstein, M. E.: 1948. Recent changes in the secondary sex ratio of the upper social strata. *Hum. Biol.,* **20,** 182–194.

———: 1952. Studies in the human sex ratio. II. The proportion of unisexual siblings. *Hum. Biol.,* **24,** 35–43.

———: 1953. Parental age and sex ratio. *Science,* **118,** 448–449.

Beskow, B.: 1949. Mental disturbances in premature children at school age. *Acta Paediat.,* **37,** 125–149.

Beswick, R. C., R. Warner, and J. Warkany: 1949. Congenital anomalies following maternal rubella. *Amer. J. Dis. Child.,* **78,** 334–338.

Bettelheim, B., and E. Sylvester: 1950. Notes on the impact of parental occupation: some cultural determinants of symptom choice in emotionally disturbed children. *Amer. J. Orthopsychiat.,* **20,** 785–795.

Betts, G. H.: 1934. The religious ideas of children. *Christian Century,* May 9.

Biber, B., and C. Lewis: 1949. An experimental study of what young school children expect from their teachers. *Genet. Psychol. Monogr.,* **40,** 3–97.

Bice, H. V.: 1954. Some factors that contribute to the concept of self in the child with cerebral palsy. *Ment. Hyg., N.Y.,* **38,** 120–131.

Biddulph, L. G.: 1954. Athletic achievement and the personal and social adjustment of high school boys. *Res. Quart. Amer. Ass. Hlth phys. Educ.,* **25,** 1–7.

Biehler, R. F.: 1954. Companion choice behavior in the kindergarten. *Child Develpm.,* **25,** 45–50.

Bird, C., E. D. Monachesi, and H. Hurdick: 1952. Studies of group tensions. IV. The effect of parental discouragement of play activities upon the attitudes of white children toward Negroes. *Child Develpm.,* **23,** 295–306.

Birren, J. E.: 1944. Psychological examinations of children who later became psychotic. *J. abnorm. soc. Psychol.,* **39,** 84–96.

Bishop, B. M.: 1951. Mother-child interaction and the social behavior of children. *Psychol. Monogr.,* **65,** No. 11.

Blair, G. M.: 1950. Personality and social development. *Rev. educ. Res.,* **20,** 375–389.

Blanchard, B. E.: 1947. A social acceptance study of transported and non-transported pupils in a rural secondary school. *J. exper. Educ.,* **15,** 291–303.

Blanton, M. G.: 1917. The behavior of the human infant during the first thirty days of life. *Psychol. Rev.,* **24,** 456–483.

Blanton, S.: 1929. Speech disorders. *Ment. Hyg., N.Y.,* **13,** 740–753.

Blanton, S., and M. G. Blanton: 1927. *Child guidance.* New York: Appleton-Century-Crofts.

Blatz, W. E.: 1938. *The five sisters.* New York: Morrow.

———, K. D. Allin, and D. A. Millichamp: 1936. *A study of laughter in the nursery school child.* Toronto: University of Toronto Press.

——— and E. A. Bott: 1927. Studies in mental hygiene of children. I. Behavior of public school children—a description of method. *J. genet. Psychol.,* **34,** 552–582.

———, ———, and D. A. Millichamp: 1935. *The development of emotion in the infant.* Toronto: University of Toronto Press, Child Develpm. Ser., No. 4.

———, S. N. F. Chant, and M. D. Salter: 1937. *Emotional episodes in the child of school age.* Toronto: University of Toronto Press, Child Develpm. Ser., No. 9.

———, M. I. Fletcher, and M. Mason: 1937. Early development in spoken language of the Dionne quintuplets. *In* W. E. Blatz, *Collected studies of the Dionne quintuplets.* Toronto: University of Toronto Press, Child Develpm. Ser., No. 16.

Block, J.: 1955. Personality characteristics associated with father's attitudes toward child-rearing. *Child Develpm.*, **26**, 41–48.

Blonsky, P. P.: 1929. Früh- und Spätjahrkinder. *Jb. Kinderheiltk.*, **124**, 115–135.

———: 1932. Schönheit und Unschönheit. *Arch. ges. Psychol.*, **85**, 529–558.

Blood, R. O.: 1953. Consequences of permissiveness for parents of young children. *Marriage Fam. Living*, **15**, 209–212.

Blos, P.: 1941. *The adolescent personality*. New York: Appleton-Century-Crofts.

Blum, L. H.: 1952. Pediatric practice and the science of child development. *Nerv. Child*, **9**, 233–241.

——— and A. Dragositz: 1947. Finger painting: the developmental aspect. *Child Develpm.*, **18**, 88–105.

Blumer, H.: 1933. *Movies and conduct*. New York: Macmillan.

——— and P. M. Hauser: 1933. *Movies, delinquency, and crime*. New York: Macmillan.

Boas, F.: 1935. The tempo of growth of fraternities. *Proc. nat. Acad. Sci.*, **21**, 413–419.

Bodman, F., M. MacKinlay, and K. Sykes: 1950. The social adaptation of institution children. *Lancet*, **258**, 173–176.

Body, M. K.: 1955. Patterns of aggression in the nursery school. *Child Develpm.*, **26**, 3–11.

Bogardus, E. S.: 1948. The social distance differential. *Sociol. soc. Res.*, **32**, 882–887.

———: 1949. Cultural pluralism and acculturation. *Sociol. soc. Res.*, **34**, 125–129.

Bogen, I.: 1954. Pupil-teacher rapport and the teacher's awareness of status structure within the group. *J. educ. Sociol.*, **28**, 104–114.

Boland, J. L.: 1951. Type of birth as related to stuttering. *J. Speech Hearing Disorders*, **16**, 40–43.

Bon, I. R., and D. C. Lopez: 1953. Preferences in colors and illustrations of elementary school children of Puerto Rico. *J. educ. Psychol.*, **44**, 490–496.

Bond, J. A.: 1952. Analysis of factors affecting scholarship of high school pupils. *J. educ. Res.*, **46**, 1–16.

Bonney, M. E.: 1942. A study of social status on the second grade level. *J. genet. Psychol.*, **60**, 271–305.

———: 1942a. A study of the relation of intelligence, family size, and sex differences with mutual friendships in the primary grades. *Child Develpm.*, **13**, 79–100.

———: 1943. Personality traits of socially successful and socially unsuccessful children. *J. educ. Psychol.*, **34**, 449–472.

———: 1944. Relationships between social success, family size, socioeconomic home background, and intelligence among school children in grades III to V. *Sociometry*, **7**, 26–39.

———: 1944a. Sex differences in social success and personality traits. *Child Develpm.*, **15**, 63–79.

———: 1946. A sociometric study of the relationship of some factors to mutual friendships on the elementary, secondary, and college levels. *Sociometry*, **9**, 21–47.

———: 1947. Sociometric study of agreement between teacher judgments and student choices. *Sociometry*, **10**, 133–146.

———: 1947a. Popular and unpopular children: a sociometric study. *Sociometry Monogr.*, No. 9.

———: 1951. A sociometric study of the peer acceptance of rural students in three consolidated high schools. *Educ. Admin. Superv.*, **11**, 234–240.

———: 1954. Choosing between the sexes on a sociometric measurement. *J. soc. Psychol.*, **39**, 99–114.

Bookwalter, K. W.: 1952. The relationship of body size and shape to physical performance. *Res. Quart. Amer. phys. Educ. Ass.*, **23**, 271–279.

Borden, B.: 1946. The role of grandparents in children's behavior problems. *Smith Coll. Stud. soc. Work,* **17,** 115–116.

Borg, W. R.: 1952. Personality characteristics of a group of college art students. *J. educ. Psychol.,* **43,** 149–156.

Bose, R. G.: 1929. Religious concepts of children. *J. relig. Educ.,* **24,** 831–837.

Bossard, J. H. S.: 1949. Social change in the United States. *Ann. Amer. Acad. pol soc. Sci.,* **265,** 69–79.

——: 1951. Process in social weaning: a study of childhood visiting. *Child Develpm.,* **22,** 211–220.

——: 1952. The large family system—a research report. *Amer. sociol. Rev.,* **17,** 3–9.

——: 1953. *Parent and child.* Philadelphia: University of Pennsylvania Press.

——: 1954. *The sociology of child development,* rev. ed. New York: Harper.

—— and E. S. Boll: 1943. *Family situations.* Philadelphia: University of Pennsylvania Press.

—— and ——: 1946. The immediate family and the kinship group—a research report. *Social Forces,* **24,** 379–384.

—— and ——: 1954. Security in the large family. *Ment. Hyg., N.Y.,* **38,** 529–544.

—— and ——: 1955. Personality roles in the large family. *Child Develpm.,* **26,** 71–78.

—— and W. P. Sanger: 1949. Social mobility and the child: a case study. *J. abnorm. soc. Psychol.,* **44,** 266–271.

—— and ——: 1953. The large family system—a research report. *Amer. sociol. Rev.,* **17,** 3–9.

Boston, M. V.: 1939. Some factors related to the expression of fear in a group of average and superior children. *Smith Coll. Stud. soc. Work,* **10,** 106–107.

Bousfield, W. A., and W. D. Orbison: 1952. Ontogenesis of emotional behavior. *Psychol. Rev.,* **59,** 1–7.

Bowlby, J.: 1953. Some pathological processes set in train by early mother-child separation. *J. ment. Sci.,* **99,** 265–272.

Bowles, G. T.: 1932. *New types of old Americans at Harvard and eastern women's universities.* Cambridge: Harvard Univ. Press.

Bowles, H.: 1937. A study of nurses' attitudes toward the behavior problems of children under hospital care. *Child Develpm.,* **8,** 282–288.

Boyd, E.: 1935. The growth of the surface area of the human body. *Univ. Minn., Inst. Child Welf. Monogr.,* No. 10.

Boyd, G. F.: 1952. The levels of aspiration of white and Negro children in a non-segregated elementary school. *J. soc. Psychol.,* **36,** 191–196.

Boynton, M. A., and F. L. Goodenough: 1930. The posture of nursery school children during sleep. *Amer. J. Psychol.,* **42,** 270–278.

Boynton, P. L.: 1936. The vocational preferences of school children. *J. genet. Psychol.,* **49,** 411–425.

——: 1936a. The wishes of elementary school children. *Peabody J. Educ.,* **13,** 165–174.

——: 1940. The relationship of hobbies to personality characteristics of school children. *J. exp. Educ.,* **8,** 363–367.

——: 1941. The relationship between children's tested intelligence and their hobby participation. *J. genet. Psychol.,* **58,** 353–362.

—— and J. C. Boynton: 1938. *Psychology of child development.* Minneapolis: Educ. Publishers.

—— and F. A. Ford: 1933. The relationship between play and intelligence. *J. appl. Psychol.,* **17,** 294–301.

—— and J. D. Wang: 1944. Relation of the play interests of children to their economic status. *J. genet. Psychol.*, **64**, 129–138.

Brackett, C. W.: 1933. Laughing and crying in preschool children. *J. exp. Educ.*, **2**, 119–126.

——: 1934. Laughing and crying in preschool children. *Child Develpm. Monogr.*, No. 14.

Bradley, N. C.: 1947. The growth of the knowledge of time in children of school age. *Brit. J. Psychol.*, **38**, 67–78.

Breckenridge, M. E., and E. L. Vincent: 1955. *Child development*, 3d ed. Philadelphia: Saunders.

Brenman, M.: 1952. On teasing and being teased: the problem of "moral masochism." *Psychoanal. Stud. Child*, **7**, 264–285.

Brian, C. R., and F. L. Goodenough: 1929. The relative potency of color and form perception at various ages. *J. exp. Psychol.*, **12**, 197–213.

Bridges, K. M. B.: 1929. The occupational interests and attention of four-year-old children. *J. genet. Psychol.*, **36**, 551–570.

——: 1930. A genetic theory of the emotions. *J. genet. Psychol.*, **37**, 514–527.

——: 1931. *Social and emotional development of the pre-school child*. London: Kegan Paul.

——: 1933. A study of social development in early infancy. *Child Develpm.*, **4**, 36–49.

Brieland, D.: 1952. A variation of the "guess who" technique for the study of the adjustment of children. *J. educ. Res.*, **45**, 385–390.

Britt, S. H.: 1949. *Social psychology of modern life*, rev. ed. New York: Rinehart.

Brodbeck, A. J.: 1954. Learning theory and identification. IV. Oedipal motivation as a determinant of conscious development. *J. genet. Psychol.*, **84**, 219–227.

—— and O. C. Irwin: 1946. The speech behavior of infants without families. *Child Develpm.*, **17**, 145–146.

Brody, D. S.: 1950. A genetic study of sociality patterns of college women. *Educ. psychol. Measmt*, **10**, 513–520.

Bromberg, W.: 1938. The meaning of time for children. *Amer. J. Orthopsychiat.*, **18**, 142–147.

Bronfenbrenner, U. A.: 1944. Constant frame of reference for sociometric research. *Sociometry*, **7**, 40–75.

Bronstein, I. R., S. Wexler, A. W. Brown, and L. J. Halpern: 1942. Obesity in childhood. *Amer. J. Dis. Child.*, **63**, 238–251.

Broom, L., H. P. Beem, and V. Harris: 1955. Characteristics of 1,107 petitioners for change of name. *Amer. sociol. Rev.*, **20**, 33–39.

Brotherton, D. A., J. M. Read, and K. C. Pratt: 1948. Indeterminate number concepts. II. Application by children to determinate number groups. *J. genet. Psychol.*, **73**, 209–236.

Brown, A. W., J. W. Morrison, and G. B. Couch: 1946. The influence of affectional family relationships on personality and character. *Amer. Psychologist*, **1**, 252.

——, ——, and ——: 1947. Influence of affectional family relationships on character development. *J. abnorm. soc. Psychol.*, **42**, 422–428.

Brown, D. G., and W. L. Lowe: 1951. Religious beliefs and personality characteristics of college students. *J. soc. Psychol.*, **33**, 103–129.

Brown, F.: 1948. What American men want to know about sex. *J. soc. Psychol.*, **27**, 119–125.

Brown, F. J.: 1954. *Educational sociology*, 2d ed. New York: Prentice-Hall.

Brown, L. P., H. D. Gates, E. L. Nolder, and B. Van Fleet: 1952. Personality characteristics of exceptional children and their mothers. *Elem. Sch. J.*, **52**, 286–290.

Brown, W. H., and V. C. Morris: 1954. Social acceptance among "Texas" children. *Understanding the Child*, **23**, 56–60.

Brownell, W. A., and G. Hendrickson: 1950. How children learn information conceptions and generalizations. *49th Yearb. nat. Soc. Stud. Educ.*, Pt. 1, pp. 92–128.

Brownfain, J. J.: 1952. Stability of the self-concept as a dimension of personality. *J. abnorm. soc. Psychol.*, **47**, 597–606.

Brownfield, E. D.: 1953. Communication-key to dynamics of family interaction. *Marriage Fam. Living*, **15**, 316–319.

Brownstone, C.: 1940. Why children's secret language. *Parents Mag.*, May 30–31.

Brozek, J., H. Guetzkow, and A. Keys: 1946. A study of personality of normal young men maintained on restricted intakes of vitamins of the B complex. *Psychosom. Med.*, **8**, 98–109.

Bruce, M.: 1941. Animism vs. evolution in the concept of "alive." *J. Psychol.*, **12**, 81–90.

Bruch, H.: 1939. Studies in obesity in childhood. I. Physical growth and development of obese children. *Amer. J. Dis. Child.*, **58**, 457–484.

———: 1940. Obesity in childhood. IV. Energy-expenditure in obese children. *Amer. J. Dis. Child.*, **60**, 1082–1109.

———: 1941. Obesity in childhood and personality development. *Amer. J. Orthopsychiat.*, **11**, 467–474.

———: 1941a. Obesity in relation to puberty. *J. Pediat.*, **19**, 365–375.

———: 1943. Food and emotional security. *Nerv. Child*, **3**, 165–173.

——— and G. Touraine: 1940. Obesity in childhood. V. The family frame of obese children. *Psychosom. Med.*, **2**, 141–206.

Brumbaugh, F. N.: 1939. *Stimuli which cause laughter in children*. Unpublished Ph.D. dissertation, New York University.

——— and F. T. Wilson: 1940. Children's laughter. *J. genet. Psychol.*, **57**, 3–29.

Bruner, J. S., and R. Tagiuri: 1954. The perception of people. *In* G. Lindzey, *Handbook of social psychology*. Cambridge, Mass.: Addison-Wesley, Vol. II, pp. 634–654.

Bryan, E. S.: 1930. Variations in the responses of infants during first ten days of postnatal life. *Child Develpm.*, **1**, 56–77.

Bryan, F. E.: 1953. How large are children's vocabularies? *Elem. Sch. J.*, **54**, 210–216.

Bryngelson, B.: 1935. Sidedness as an etiological factor in stuttering. *J. genet. Psychol.*, **47**, 204–217.

——— and T. Clark: 1933. Left-handedness and stuttering. *J. Hered.*, **24**, 387–390.

——— and B. Rutherford: 1937. A comparative study of laterality of stutterers and non-stutterers. *J. Speech Disorders*, **2**, 12–16.

Buck, R. C.: 1952. Acquaintance positions in the group. *Sociol. soc. Res.*, **37**, 33–36.

Bühler, C.: 1927. Die ersten sozialen Verhaltungsweisen des Kindes. *Quellen u. Stud. z. Jugendkd.*, **5**, 1–102.

———: 1930. *The first year of life*. New York: Day.

———: 1932. Jugentagebuch und Lebenslauf. Zwei Mädchentagebücher mit einer Einleitung. *Quellen u. Stud. z. Jugendkd.*, **9**, 1–261.

———: 1935. *From birth to maturity*. London: Routledge.

———: 1939. *The child and his family*. New York: Harper.

———: 1948. The influence of cultural ideology on child training. *J. child Psychiat.*, **1**, 239–246.

———: 1952. School as a phase of human life. *Education*, **73**, 219–222.

——— and H. Hetzer: 1928. Das erste Verständnis von Ausdruck im ersten Lebensjahr. *Zsch. f. Psychol.*, **107**, 50–61.

Bühler, K.: 1930. *The mental development of the child*. New York: Harcourt, Brace.

Burge, I. C.: 1952. Some aspects of handedness in primary school children. *Brit. J. educ. Psychol.*, **22**, 45–51.

Burgess, E. W.: 1948. The family in a changing society. *Amer. J. Sociol.*, **53**, 417–422.

—— and H. J. Locke: 1945. *The family.* New York: American Book.

Burke, B. S.: 1949. Relations of maternal nutrition to condition of infant at birth: study of siblings. *J. Nutrit.*, **38**, 453–467.

——, V. A. Beal, S. B. Kirkwood, and H. C. Stuart: 1943. Nutrition studies during pregnancy. *Amer. J. Obstet. Gynaec.*, **46**, 38–52.

——, S. S. Stevenson, J. Worcester, and H. G. Stuart: 1949. Nutrition studies during pregnancy. V. Relation of maternal nutrition to condition of infant at birth. *J. Nutrit.*, **38**, 453–467.

Burlingham, D. T.: 1949. The relationship of twins to each other. *In* A. Freud, H. Hartmann, and E. Kris, *The psychoanalytical study of the child.* New York: International Universities Press, pp. 57–72.

——: 1951. Precursors of some psychoanalytic ideas about children in the sixteenth and seventeenth centuries. *In* R. S. Eissler, A. Freud, H. Hartmann, and E. Kris, *The psychoanalytic study of the child.* New York: International Universities Press, pp. 244–254.

——: 1952. *Twins.* New York: International Universities Press.

—— and A. Freud: 1949. *Kriegskinder.* London: Imago.

Buswell, M. M.: 1953. The relationship between the social structure of the classroom and the academic success of pupils. *J. exp. Educ.*, **22**, 37–52.

Butterworth, R. F., and G. G. Thompson: 1951. Factors related to age-grade trends and sex differences in children's preferences for comic books. *J. genet Psychol.*, **78**, 71–96.

Buxbaum, E.: 1949. The role of a second language in the formation of ego and superego. *Psychoanal. Quart.*, **18**, 279–289.

Cahn, P.: 1949. The role of play in the development of fraternal relationships of an older brother. *Sauvegarde*, **4**, 40–52.

Caille, R. K.: 1933. Resistant behavior of preschool children. *Child Develpm. Monogr.*, No. 11.

Caldwell, O. W., and B. L. Wellman: 1926. Characteristics of school leaders. *J. educ. Res.*, **14**, 1–13.

Campbell, A. A.: 1934. The personality adjustment of only children. *Psychol. Bull.*, **31**, 193–203.

Campbell, E. H.: 1939. The social-sex development of children. *Genet. Psychol. Monogr.*, **21**, 461–552.

Campbell, W. J.: 1952. The influence of home environment on the educational progress of selective secondary school children. *Brit. J. educ. Psychol.*, **22**, 89–100.

Cannon, K. L., R. Staples, and I. Carlson: 1952. Personal appearance as a factor in social acceptance. *J. Home Econ.*, **44**, 710–713.

Capland, G.: 1954. The disturbance of the mother-child relationship by unsuccessful attempts at abortion. *Ment. Hyg., N.Y.*, **38**, 67–80.

Capon, N. B.: 1945. The assessment of health in children. *Arch. Dis. Child.*, **20**, 54,

Cappe, J.: 1947. Les manifestations artistiques chez l'enfant. *Nouv. Rev. Pédag.*, **3**, 89–93.

Caprio, F. S.: 1950. A study of some psychological reactions during pre-pubescence to the idea of death. *Psychiat. Quart.*, **24**, 495–505.

Carithers, H. A.: 1951. Mother-pediatrician relationship in the neonatal period. *J. Pediat.*, **38**, 654–660.

Carlson, H. B.: 1934. Attitudes of undergraduate students. *J. soc. Psychol.*, **5**, 202–213.

Carmichael, L.: 1954. The onset and early development of behavior. *In* L. Carmichael, *Manual of child psychology*, 2d ed. New York: Wiley, pp. 60–187.

Carpenter, J., and P. Eisenberg: 1938. Some relationships between family background and personality. *J. Psychol.*, **6**, 115–136.

Carrel, A.: 1935. *Man the unknown*. New York: Harper.

Carrington, E. M.: 1940. The family in a changing social order. *Educ. Forum*, **4**, 191–197.

Carroll, J. B.: 1938. Diversity of vocabulary and the harmonic series law of word-frequency distribution. *Psychol. Rec.* **2**, 377–386.

————: 1939. Determining and numerating adjectives in children's speech. *Child Develpm.*, **10**, 215–229.

Carrothers, J. E.: 1947. Left-handedness among school pupils. *Amer. School Board J.*, **114**, 17–19.

Carter, D. C.: 1954. The influence of family relationships and family experience on personality. *Marriage Fam. Living*, **16**, 212–215.

Carter, H. D.: 1940. Ten years of research of twins: contributions to the nature-nurture problem. *39th Yearb. nat. Soc. Stud. Educ.*, No. 1, 235–255.

Carter, W. P.: 1937. *The only child in the family: a comparison with other orders of birth*. Ph.D. dissertation, University of Chicago.

Case, A.: 1921. Children's ideas of God. *Relig. Educ.*, **16**, 143–146.

Cass, L. K.: 1952. An investigation of parent-child relationships in terms of awareness, identification, projection, and control. *Amer. J. Orthopsychiat.*, **22**, 305–313.

Cassel, R. N., and R. G. Saugstad: 1952. Level of aspiration and sociometric distance. *Sociometry*, **15**, 318–325.

Castner, B. M.: 1932. The development of fine prehension in infancy. *Genet. Psychol. Monogr.*, **12**, 105–194.

Catalano, F. L., and D. McCarthy: 1954. Infant speech as a possible predictor of later intelligence. *J. Psychol.*, **38**, 203–209.

Cattell, J. McK.: 1921. *American men of science*. New York: Science Press.

Cattell, P.: 1940. *The measurement of intelligence in infants and young children*. New York: Psychological Corporation.

Cavan, R. S.: 1953. *The American family*. New York: Crowell.

Cavanaugh, J. R.: 1949. The comics war. *J. crim. Law Criminol.*, **40**, 28–35.

Cederquist, H. T.: 1948. The "good mother" and her children. *Smith Coll. Stud. soc. Work*, **19**, 1–26.

Centers, B.: 1950. Social-class identification of American youth. *J. Pers.*, **18**, 290–302.

Centers, R.: 1949. *The psychology of social classes*. Princeton: Princeton University Press.

Challman, R. C.: 1932. Factors influencing friendships among preschool children. *Child Develpm.*, **3**, 146–158.

Chaney, B., and M. B. McGraw: 1932. Reflexes and other motor activities in newborn infants: a report of 125 cases as a preliminary study of infant behavior. *Bull. neurol. Inst., N.Y.*, **2**, 1–56.

Chapin, P. S.: 1950. Sociometric stars as isolates. *Amer. J. Sociol.*, **56**, 263–267.

Charters, W. W.: 1933. *Motion pictures and youth*. New York: Macmillan.

Chen, H. P., and O. C. Irwin: 1946. Infant speech vowels and consonant types. *J. Speech Hearing Disorders*, **11**, 27–29.

Chevaleva-Janovskaja, E.: 1927. Les groupements spontanés d'enfants à l'âge préscholaire. *Arch. de Psychol.*, **20**, 219–233.

Child, I. L.: 1940. The relation between measures of infantile animism and neuroticism. *J. abnorm. soc. Psychol.*, **35**, 453–456.

————, E. H. Potter, and E. M. Levine: 1946. Children's textbooks and personality development. *Psychol. Monogr.*, **60**, No. 3.

Chittenden, G. E.: 1942. An experimental study in measuring and modifying assertive behavior in young children. *Monogr. Soc. Res. Child Develpm.*, **7**, No. 1.

Christensen, A. H.: 1952. A quantitative study of personality dynamics in stuttering and nonstuttering siblings. *Speech Monogr.*, **19**, 144–145.

Chyatte, C., and D. F. Schaeffer: 1951. Prejudice verbalizations among children. *J. educ. Psychol.*, **42**, 421–431.

Clare, J. E., and C. V. Kiser: 1951. Social and psychological factors affecting fertility. XIV. Preference for children of a given sex in relation to fertility. *Milbank mem. Fund Quart.*, **29**, 421–473.

Clark, E. J.: 1951. Teacher reactions toward objectionable pupil behavior. *Elem. Sch. J.*, **51**, 446–449.

Clark, K. B.: 1953. Race prejudice and children. *Child*, **17**, 113–115.

———— and M. K. Clark: 1939. The development of consciousness of self and the emergence of racial identification in Negro preschool children. *J. soc. Psychol.*, **10**, 591–599.

———— and ————: 1940. Skin color as a factor in racial identification of Negro preschool children. *J. soc. Psychol.*, **11**, 159–169.

———— and ————: 1950. Emotional factors in racial identification and preference in Negro children. *J. Negro Educ.*, **19**, 341–350.

Clark, R. A., and C. McGuire: 1952. Sociographic analysis of sociometric valuations. *Child Develpm.*, **23**, 129–140.

Clark, W. H.: 1952. Sex differences and motivation in the urge to destroy. *J. soc. Psychol.*, **36**, 167–177.

Clark, W. R.: 1939. Radio listening activities of children. *J. exp. Educ.*, **8**, 44–48.

————: 1940. Radio listening habits of children. *J. soc. Psychol.*, **11**, 131–149.

Clarke, F. M.: 1939. A developmental study of the bodily reaction of infants to an auditory startle stimulus. *J. genet. Psychol.*, **55**, 415–427.

Clarke, T. W.: 1952. Allergy and the "problem child." *Nerv. Child*, **9**, 278–281.

Coast, L. C.: 1939. A study of the knowledge and attitudes of parents of preschool children. *Univ. Ia. Stud. Child Welf.*, **17**, 157–181.

Cobb, H. V.: 1954. Role-wishes and general wishes of children and adolescents. *Child Develpm.*, **25**, 161–171.

Cobliner, W. J.: 1950. Feminine fashion as an aspect of group psychology: analysis of written replies received by means of a questionnaire. *J. soc. Psychol.*, **31**, 283–289.

Coffin, T. E.: 1948. Television's effect on leisure-time activities. *J. appl. Psychol.*, **32**, 550–558.

Cohen, F.: 1951. Psychological characteristics of the second child as compared with the first. *Indian J. Psychol.*, **26**, 79–84.

Cohen, J. T., and J. E. Anderson: 1931. Note on the eruption of the permanent teeth in a group of subnormal children, including an observation on the frequency of congenitally missing laterals. *J. genet. Psychol.*, **39**, 270–284.

Colby, M. G., and J. B. Robertson: 1942. Genetic studies of abstraction. *J. comp. Psychol.*, **33**, 385–401.

Cole, L.: 1954. *Psychology of adolescence*, 4th ed. New York: Rinehart.

Coleman, J. C., and J. E. McCalley: 1948: Nail-biting among college students. *J. abnorm. soc. Psychol.*, **43**, 517–525.

Colm, H.: 1951. Help and guidance as discipline for pre-adolescents. *Nerv. Child*, **9**, 131–138.

Congdon, N. A.: 1937. Differences in the achievement in geography, civics and history, and general science of teachers-college entrants from different sections of the country and from rural and urban populations. *J. exp. Educ.*, **5**, 274–277.

Conklin, E. S.: 1935. *Principles of adolescent psychology.* New York: Holt.

Conn, J. H.: 1939. Factors influencing development of sexual attitudes and awareness in children. *Amer. J. Dis. Child.*, **58**, 738–745.

——: 1940. Children's reactions to the discovery of genital differences. *Amer. J. Orthopsychiat.*, **10**, 747–754.

——: 1940a. Sexual curiosity of children. *Amer. J. Dis. Child.*, **60**, 1110–1119.

——: 1941. The treatment of fearful children. *Amer. J. Orthopsychiat.*, **11**, 744–751.

——: 1948. Children's awareness of the origin of babies. *J. child Psychiat.*, **1**, 140–178.

——: 1951. Children's awareness of sex differences. II. Play attitudes and game preferences. *J. child Psychiat.*, **2**, 82–99.

—— and L. Kanner: 1940. Spontaneous erections in early childhood. *J. Pediat.*, **16**, 337–340.

—— and ——: 1947. Children's awareness of sex differences. *J. child Psychiat.*, **1**, 3–57.

Connor, R., T. B. J. Johannis, and J. Waters: 1954. Parent-adolescent relationships. *J. Home Econ.*, **46**, 183–191.

Cook, W. M.: 1931. Ability of children in color discrimination. *Child Develpm.*, **2**, 303–320.

Cooke, J. V.: 1948. Antibody formation in early infancy against diphtheria and tetanus toxoids. *J. Pediat.*, **33**, 146–149.

Cooper, O. A.: 1942. Discussion on the relationship between speech disorders and personality defects in children, and how stuttering may unfavorably affect children's personality development. *J. Pediat.*, **21**, 418–421.

Cooper, W. M.: 1950. Parental delinquency. *Phylon*, **11**, 269–273.

Cordeau, R.: 1953. The "golden section" in the drawings of children. *Enfance*, **6**, 147–151.

Cornelius, R.: 1949. Games minus competition. *Childh. Educ.*, **26**, 77–79.

Corner, G. W.: 1944. *Ourselves unborn.* New Haven: Yale Univ. Press.

Coughlan, R.: 1950. How to survive parenthood. *Life Mag.*, June 26.

Cousinet, R.: 1951. Investigation on what students think of play and work. *J. Psychol. norm. path.*, **44**, 556–568.

Cramer, M. W.: 1950. Leisure-time activities of economically privileged children. *Sociol. soc. Res.*, **34**, 444–450.

Crane, A. R.: 1951. A note on preadolescent gangs. *Australian J. Psychol.*, **3**, 43–46.

——: 1952. Preadolescent gangs: a topological interpretation. *J. genet. Psychol.*, **81**, 113–123.

Cressey, P. G., and F. M. Thrasher: 1934. *Boys, movies, and city streets.* New York: Macmillan.

Crist, J. R.: 1953. High-school dating as a behavior system. *Marriage Fam. Living*, **15**, 23–28.

Crudden, C. H.: 1937. Reactions of newborn infants to thermal stimuli under constant tactual conditions. *J. exp. Psychol.*, **20**, 350–370.

Cruickshank, W. M.: 1951. The relation of physical disability to fear and guilt feelings. *Child Develpm.*, **22**, 291–298.

—— and J. E. Dolphin: 1949. The emotional needs of crippled and noncrippled children. *J. except. Child*, **16**, 33–40.

Crump, E. B., C. Wilson-Webb, and M. P. Pointer: 1952. Prematurity in the Negro infant. *Amer. J. Dis. Child*, **83**, 463–474.

Cummings, J. D.: 1944. The incidence of emotional symptoms in school children. *Brit. J. educ. Psychol.,* **14,** 151–161.

Cunningham, R.: 1951. *Group behavior of boys and girls.* New York: Teach. Coll. Bur. Publ.

Dahlberg, G.: 1948. Do parents want boys or girls? *Acta Genetica et Statistica Medica,* **1,** 163–167.

——: 1952. Die tendez zu Zwillingsgeburten. *Acta Genet. med. Gemellolog.,* **1,** 80–88.

Dahlke, H. O.: 1953. Determinants of sociometric relations among children in the elementary school. *Sociometry,* **16,** 327–338.

Dai, B.: 1945. Some problems of personal development among Negro children. *Proc. Inst. Child Res. Quart., Woods Schs.,* **12,** 67–105.

——: 1952. A socio-psychiatric approach to personality organization. *Amer. sociol. Rev.,* **17,** 44–49.

Dale, E.: 1935. *Attendance at motion pictures and the contents of motion pictures.* New York: Macmillan.

Dale, J.: 1950. Seasonal variations in growth of the composite preschool child. *Med. J. Australia,* **2,** 281–285.

Damann, V. T.: 1941. Developmental changes in attitude as one factor determining energy output in a motor performance. *Child Develpm.,* **12,** 241–246.

Damrin, D. E.: 1949. Family size and sibling age, sex, and position as related to certain aspects of adjustment. *J. soc. Psychol.,* **29,** 93–102.

Darcy, N. T.: 1952. The performance of bilingual Puerto Rican children on verbal and nonverbal tests of intelligence. *J. educ. Res.,* **45,** 499–506.

Dashiell, J. F.: 1917. Children's sense of harmonies in colors and tones. *J. exp. Psychol.,* **2,** 466–475.

——: 1949. *Fundamentals of general psychology,* 3d ed. Boston: Houghton, Mifflin.

Davenport, C. B.: 1932. The growth of the human foot. *Amer. J. phys. Anthrop.,* **17,** 167–211.

——: 1940. Post-natal development of the head. *Proc. Amer. phil. Soc.,* No. 83.

Davis, A.: 1941. American status systems and the socialization of the child. *Amer. sociol. Rev.,* **6,** 345–356.

——: 1944. Socialization and adolescent personality. *43d Yearb. nat. Soc. Stud. Educ.,* Pt. 1, pp. 198–216.

——: 1949. *Social-class influences upon learning.* Cambridge: Harvard University Press.

—— and J. Dollard: 1940. *Children of bondage.* Washington: American Council on Education.

—— and R. J. Havighurst: 1946. Social class and color differences in child rearing. *Amer. sociol. Rev.,* **11,** 698–710.

—— and ——: 1947. *Father of the man.* Boston: Houghton, Mifflin.

Davis, C. M.: 1939. Results of the self-selection of diets by young children. *Canad. med. Ass. J.,* **41,** 257–261.

Davis, D. C.: 1952. Comparative studies of the growth and development of premature and full-term children with special reference to oral communication. *Speech Monogr.,* **19,** 114–115.

Davis, D. M.: 1939. The relation of repetitions in the speech of young children to certain measures of language maturity and situational factors. Part I. *J. Speech Disorders,* **4,** 303–318.

——: 1940. The relation of repetitions in the speech of young children to certain measures of language maturity and situational factors. Part II. *J. Speech Disorders,* **5,** 235–241.

Davis, E. A.: 1932. The form and function of children's questions. *Child Develpm.,* **3,** 57–74.

——: 1937. Development in the use of proper names. *Child Develpm.,* **8,** 270–272.

——: 1937a. Mean sentence length compared with long and short sentences as a reliable measure of language development. *Child Develpm.,* **8,** 69–79.

——: 1937b. *The development of linguistic skills in twins, singletons with siblings and only children from age five to ten years.* Minneapolis: University of Minnesota Press.

——: 1939. Accuracy versus error as a criterion in children's speech. *J. educ. Psychol.,* **30,** 365–371.

Davis, H. V., R. R. Sears, H. C. Miller, and A. J. Brodbeck: 1948. Effects of cup, bottle, and breast feeding on oral activities of newborn infants. *Pediatrics,* **2,** 549–558.

Davis, M. E.: 1955. Factors favoring fertility. *In* M. Fishbein and E. W. Burgess, *Successful marriage,* 2d ed. New York: Doubleday, pp. 232–242.

Davitz, J. R.: 1955. Social perception and sociometric choice of children. *J. abnorm. soc. Psychol.,* **50,** 173–176.

Dawe, H. C.: 1934. An analysis of two hundred quarrels of preschool children. *Child Develpm.,* **5,** 139–157.

——, D. Ekern, and H. Berger: 1949. Differences in adult contacts with children, *J. Home Econ.,* **41,** 87–88.

Dawson, G. E.: 1900. Children's interest in the Bible. *Ped. Sem.,* **7,** 151–178.

Dawson, M. A.: 1937. Children's preferences for conversational topics. *Elem. Sch. J.,* **37,** 429–437.

Day, E. J.: 1932. The development of language in twins and single children. I. A comparison of twins and single children. *Child Develpm.,* **3,** 179–199.

——: 1932a. The development of language in twins. II. The development of twins: their resemblances and differences. *Child Develpm.,* **3,** 298–316.

Dayhaw, L. T.: 1953. Guiding handedness in the development of the child. *Education,* **74,** 196–199.

Dean, D. A.: 1947. *The relation of ordinal positions to personality in young children.* M.A. thesis. Iowa City: State University of Iowa.

DeBoer, J. J.: 1939. Radio and children's emotions. *Sch. & Soc.,* **50,** 369–373.

deGroat, A. F., and G. G. Thompson: 1949. A study of the distribution of teacher approval and teacher disapproval among sixth-grade pupils. *J. exp. Educ.,* **18,** 57–75.

Delman, L.: 1935. The order of participation of limbs in responses to tactual stimulation of the newborn infant. *Child Develpm.,* **6,** 98–109.

Dempsey, D.: 1954. And after TV fades, there remains the magic of a book. *New York Times,* Nov. 14.

Denhoff, E.: 1954. The physically handicapped child and the nursery school. *Except. Child,* **20,** 202–208.

Dennis, W.: 1934. A description and classification of the responses of the newborn infant. *Psychol. Bull.,* **31,** 5–22.

——: 1934a. The age at walking of children who run on all fours. *Child Develpm.,* **5,** 92–93.

——: 1935. A psychologic interpretation of the persistence of the so-called Moro reflex. *Amer. J. Dis. Child.,* **50,** 888–893.

——: 1935a. The effect of restricted practice upon the reaching, sitting, and standing of two infants. *J. genet. Psychol.,* **47,** 17–32.

————: 1935b. Laterality of function in early infancy under controlled developmental conditions. *Child Develpm.,* **6,** 242–252.

————: 1935c. An experimental test of two theories of social smiling in infants. *J. soc. Psychol.,* **6,** 214–221.

————: 1936. A biography of baby biographies. *Child Develpm.,* **7,** 71–73.

————: 1938. Historical notes on child animism. *Psychol. Rev.,* **45,** 257–266.

————: 1938a. Infant development under conditions of restricted practice and of minimum social stimulation: a preliminary report. *J. genet. Psychol.,* **53,** 149–157.

————: 1939. Is infant behavior appreciably affected by cultural influences? *Psychol. Bull.,* **36,** 598–599.

————: 1940. Does culture appreciably affect patterns of infant behavior? *J. soc. Psychol.,* **12,** 305–317.

————: 1940a. Infant reactions to resistance: an evaluation of Watson's theory. *Trans. N.Y. Acad. Sci.,* **2,** 202–218.

————: 1941. Infant development under conditions of restricted practice and minimum social stimulation. *Genet. Psychol. Monogr.,* **23,** 143–189.

————: 1941a. Effect of pubertas praecox on the age at which onset of walking occurs. *Amer. J. Dis. Child.,* **61,** 951–957.

————: 1942. Piaget's questions applied to a child of known environment. *J. genet. Psychol.,* **60,** 307–320.

————: 1943. Is the newborn infant's repertoire learned or instinctive? *Psychol. Rev.,* **50,** 330–337.

————: 1943a. On the possibility of advancing and retarding the motor development of infants. *Psychol. Rev.,* **50,** 203–218.

————: 1943b. Animism and related tendencies in Hopi children. *J. abnorm. soc. Psychol.,* **38,** 21–36.

————: 1951. *Readings in child psychology.* New York: Prentice-Hall.

————: 1953. Animistic thinking among college and university students. *Sci. Mon., N.Y.,* **76,** 247–250.

———— and M. G. Dennis: 1937. Behavioral development in the first year as shown by forty biographies. *Psychol. Rec.,* **1,** 349–361.

———— and ————: 1938. Infant development under conditions of restricted practice and a minimum of social stimulation: a preliminary report. *J. genet. Psychol.,* **53,** 149–157.

———— and ————: 1940. Cradles and cradling practices of the Pueblo Indians. *Amer. Anthrop.,* **42,** 107–115.

———— and ————: 1940a. The effect of cradling practices upon the onset of walking in Hopi children. *J. genet. Psychol.,* **56,** 77–86.

Descombey, J., and G. Roquebrune: 1953. Childhood personality and sibling relationships. *Enfance,* **6,** 329–368.

Desenberg, B. N.: 1947. Home sex education and monogamy. *Marriage Fam. Living,* **9,** 89–92.

Despert, J. L.: 1942. *Preliminary report on children's reactions to the war, including a critical survey of the literature.* Cornell University Medical College, New York: Payne Whitney Nursing School.

————: 1946. Anxiety, phobias, and fears in young children: with special reference to prenatal, natal, and neonatal factors. *Nerv. Child,* **5,** 8–24.

————: 1946a. Psychosomatic study of stuttering children. I. Social, physical, and psychiatric findings. *Amer. J. Orthopsychiat.,* **16,** 100–113.

————: 1949. Sleep in pre-school children: a preliminary study. *Nerv. Child,* **8,** 8–27.

————: 1952. Suicides and depression in children. *Nerv. Child,* **9,** 378–389.

———: 1953. *Children of divorce*. Garden City, N.Y.: Doubleday.

Deutsche, J. M.: 1937. *The development of children's concepts of causal relations*. Minneapolis: University of Minnesota Press.

Dexter, E. S.: 1949. Three items related to personality: popularity, nicknames, and homesickness. *J. soc. Psychol.*, **30**, 155–158.

Dickens, D.: 1944. Social participation as a criterion for determining scientific standards in clothing. *Rural Sociol.*, **9**, 341–349.

Dickenson, J. R., and H. S. Lewin: 1951. The role of discipline in modern education. *Nerv. Child*, **9**, 122–124.

Dickinson, R. L.: 1955. Anatomy and physiology of the sex organs. *In* M. Fishbein and E. W. Burgess, *Successful marriage*, 2d ed. New York: Doubleday, pp. 67–87.

Dickson, V. E.: 1932. Behavior difficulties that baffle teachers. *J. juv. Res.*, **16**, 93–101.

Dillon, M. S.: 1934. Attitudes in children toward their own bodies and those of other children. *Child Develpm.*, **5**, 165–176.

Dimock, H. S.: 1937. *Rediscovering the adolescent*. New York: Association Press.

Ding, G. F., and A. T. Jersild: 1932. A study of the laughing and smiling of preschool children. *J. genet. Psychol.*, **40**, 452–472.

Dingwall, M.: 1949. Maintenance of mental health. III. Going to school the second five years. *Ment. Hlth, London*, **9**, 31–33.

Dinitz, S., R. R. Dynes, and A. C. Clarke: 1954. Preferences for male or female children: traditional or affectional? *Marriage Fam. Living*, **16**, 128–134.

Dinkel, R. M.: 1943. Parent-child conflict in Minnesota families. *Amer. sociol. Rev.*, **8**, 412–419.

Disher, D. R.: 1933. An experimental study of the reactions of new-born infants to olfactory stimuli. *Psychol. Bull.*, **30**, 582.

Dixon, J. C.: 1949. Concept formation and emergence of contradictory relations. *J. exp. Psychol.*, **39**, 144–149.

Dockeray, F. C.: 1934. Differential feeding reactions of newborn infants. *Psychol. Bull.*, **31**, 747.

Doering, C. W., and M. F. Allen: 1942. Data on the eruption and caries of the deciduous teeth. *Child Develpm.*, **13**, 113–129.

Dolger, L., and J. Ginandes: 1946. Children's attitude toward discipline as related to socio-economic status. *J. exp. Educ.*, **15**, 161–165.

Doll, E. A., W. M. Philps, and R. T. Melcher: 1932. *Mental deficiency due to birth injuries*. New York: Macmillan.

Dollard, J., L. W. Doob, N. E. Miller, O. H. Mowrer, and R. R. Sears: 1939. *Frustration and aggression*. New Haven: Yale University Press.

Doob, L. W.: 1948. *Public opinion and propaganda*. New York: Holt.

Dorcus, R. M., and G. W. Shaffer: 1945. *Textbook of abnormal psychology*. Baltimore: Williams & Wilkins.

Dorkey, M., and E. W. Amen: 1947. A continuation study of anxiety reactions in young children by means of a projective technique. *Genet. Psychol. Monogr.*, **35**, 139–186.

Douglass, H. R.: 1925. The development of number concept in children of preschool and kindergarten ages. *J. exp. Psychol.*, **8**, 443–470.

Dow, P., and R. Torpin: 1939. Placentation studies: correlations between size of sac, area of placenta, weight of placenta, and weight of baby. *Hum. Biol.*, **11**, 248–258.

Downie, N. M.: 1953. A comparison between children who have moved with those who have been in continuous residence on various factors of adjustment. *J. educ. Psychol.*, **44**, 50–53.

Dreizen, S., C. Currie, J. Gilley, and T. D. Spies: 1953. The effect of nutritive failure on the growth patterns of white children in Alabama. *Child Develpm.*, **24**, 189–202.

Drillien, C. M.: 1948. Studies in prematurity. IV. Development and progress of the prematurely born child in the preschool period. *Arch. Dis. Child.*, **23**, 69–83.

Driscoll, G. P.: 1933. The developmental status of the preschool child as a prognosis of future development. *Child Develpm. Monogr.*, No. 13.

Drought, A.: 1929. A survey of studies in experimental aesthetics. *J. educ. Res.*, **20**, 97–102.

Drucker, A. J., H. T. Christensen, and H. H. Remmers: 1952. Some background factors in sociosexual modernism. *Marriage Fam. Living*, **14**, 334–337.

DuBois, F. S.: 1952. The security of discipline. *Ment. Hyg., N.Y.*, **36**, 353–372.

Dudley, D., D. Duncan, and E. Sears: 1932. A study of the development of motor coordination in an infant between the ages of 58 and 67 weeks. *Child Develpm.*, **3**, 82–86.

Dudycha, G. J., and M. M. Dudycha: 1933. Adolescent memories of preschool experiences. *J. genet. Psychol.*, **42**, 468–480.

—— and ——: 1941. Childhood memories: a review of the literature. *Psychol. Bull.*, **38**, 669–681.

Duggins, O. H., and M. Trotter: 1950. Age changes in head hair from birth to maturity. II. Medulation in hair of children. *Amer. J. phys. Anthrop.*, **8**, 399–415.

Dukes, W. F.: 1955. Psychological studies of values. *Psychol. Bull.*, **52**, 24–50.

Dunbar, F.: 1944. Effect of the mother's emotional attitude on the infant. *Psychosom. Med.*, **6**, 150–159.

——: 1952. Symbiosis of parent and child. *Amer. J. Orthopsychiat.*, **22**, 809–824.

Duncan, M. H.: 1949. Home adjustment of stutterers versus non-stutterers. *J. Speech Hearing Disorders*, **14**, 255–259.

Dunham, E. C., and H. Thoms: 1945. Effects of severe rickets in early childhood on skeletal development in adolescence. *Amer. J. Dis. Child.*, **69**, 339–345.

Dupertuis, C. W., and N. B. Michael: 1953. Comparison of growth in height and weight between ectomorphic and mesomorphic boys. *Child Develpm.*, **24**, 203–214.

Durand, J. D.: 1948. *The labor force in the United States: 1896–1960.* New York: Social Science Research Council.

Durost, W. N.: 1932. Children's collecting activity related to social factors. *Teach. Coll. Contr. Educ.*, No. 537.

Dusenberry, L.: 1952. A study of the effects of training in ball throwing by children ages three to seven. *Res. Quart. Amer. phys. Educ. Ass.*, **23**, 9–14.

Duvall, E. M.: 1937. Child-parent social distance. *Sociol. soc. Res.*, **21**, 458–463.

——: 1946. Conceptions of parenthood. *Amer. J. Sociol.*, **52**, 193–203.

——: 1954. *The effect of TV on the family and child life.* Nashville: Report of the Second National Conference on Family Life of the Methodist Church.

—— and A. B. Motz: 1945. Age and education as factors in school experience and personal-family adjustments. *Sch. Rev.*, **53**, 413–421.

—— and ——: 1945a. Attitudes of second-generation daughters to family living. *J. consult. Psychol.*, **9**, 281–286.

Dyer, D. T.: 1945. Are only children different? *J. educ. Psychol.*, **36**, 297–302.

Dymond, R. F.: 1949. A scale for the measurement of empathic ability. *J. consult. Psychol.*, **13**, 228–233.

——: 1950. Personality and empathy. *J. consult. Psychol.*, **14**, 343–350.

——, A. S. Hughes, and V. L. Raabe: 1952. Measurable changes in empathy with age. *J. consult. Psychol.*, **16**, 202–206.

Dysinger, W. S., and C. A. Ruckmick: 1933. *The emotional responses of children to the motion-picture situation.* New York: Macmillan.

Eagelson, O. W.: 1946. Students' reactions to their given names. *J. soc. Psychol.,* **23,** 187–195.

Eaton, M. T.: 1944. *A survey of the achievement in social studies of 10,220 sixth grade pupils in 464 schools in Indiana.* Indiana University, Bulletin 20.

Eberhart, J. C.: 1942. Attitudes toward property: a genetic study by the paired-comparison rating of offenses. *J. genet. Psychol.,* **60,** 3–35.

Eblis, J. H., F. F. Tisdall, and W. A. Scott: 1941. The influence of prenatal diet on the mother and child. *J. Nutrit.,* **22,** 515–526.

Edelston, H.: 1943. Separation anxiety in young children: a study of hospital cases. *Genet. Psychol. Monogr.,* **28,** 3–95.

Edmiston, R. W., and F. Baird: 1949. The adjustment of orphanage children. *J. educ. Psychol.,* **40,** 482–488.

Eisenberg, A. L.: 1936. *Children and radio programs.* New York: Columbia University Press.

Ekholm, E., and K. Niemineva: 1950. On prenatal changes in the relative weights of the human adrenals, the thymus, and the thyroid gland. *Acta paediat., Stockh.,* **39,** 67–86.

Elder, R. A.: 1949. Traditional and developmental conceptions of fatherhood. *Marriage Fam. Living,* **11,** 98–100.

Elias, L. J.: 1949. *High school youth look at their problems.* Pullman, Wash.: State College of Washington.

Elkine, D.: 1928. De l'orientation de l'enfant d'âge scolaire dans les relations temporelles. *J. de Psychol.,* **25,** 425–429.

Elkish, P.: 1952. Significant relationships between the human figure and the machine in the drawings of boys. *Amer. J. Orthopsychiat.,* **22,** 79–85.

Ellingson, R. J., and D. B. Lindsley: 1949. Brain waves and cortical development in newborn and young infants. *Amer. Psychologist,* **4,** 248–249.

Elliott, M. H.: 1942. Patterns of friendship in the classroom. *Prog. Educ.,* **18,** 383–390.

Ellis, A., and R. M. Beechley: 1951. A comparison of child guidance clinic patients coming from large, medium, and small families. *J. genet. Psychol.,* **79,** 131–144.

—— and E. W. Fuller: 1950. The sex, love, and marriage questions of senior nursing students. *J. soc. Psychol.,* **31,** 209–216.

Ellis, R. W. B.: 1951. Assessment of prematurity by birth weight, crown-rump length, and head circumference. *Arch. Dis. Child.,* **26,** 411–422.

England, A. O.: 1946. Non-structural approach to a study of children's fears. *J. clin. Psychol.,* **2,** 364–368.

Engle, T. L.: 1945. Personality adjustments of children belonging to two minority groups. *J. educ. Psychol.,* **36,** 543–560.

English, O. S., and G. H. J. Pearson: 1945. *Emotional problems of living.* New York: Norton.

Ephron, B. K.: 1953. *Emotional difficulties in reading.* New York: Julian Press.

Ericson, M. C.: 1946. Child-rearing and social status. *Amer. J. Sociol.,* **52,** 190–192.

——: 1946a. Social status and child-rearing practices. *Amer. Psychologist,* **1,** 239–240.

Erikson, E. H.: 1951. Sex differences in the play configurations of preadolescents. *Amer. J. Orthopsychiat.,* **21,** 667–692.

Erwin, D.: 1934. An analytical study of children's sleep. *J. genet. Psychol.,* **45,** 199–226.

Escalona, S. K.: 1945. Feeding disturbances in very young children. *Amer. J. Orthopsychiat.,* **15,** 76–80.

——: 1949. A commentary upon some recent changes in child-rearing practices. *Child Develpm.,* **20,** 157–162.

—— and M. Leitch: 1952. Early phases of personality development. *Monogr. Soc. Res. Child Develpm.,* **17,** No. 1.

————, R. R. Sears, and G. W. Wise: 1950. Approaches to a dynamic theory of development. I. Relation of cup feeding in infancy to thumbsucking, and the oral drive. *Amer. J. Orthopsychiat.,* **20,** 123–138.

Espenschade, A.: 1940. Motor performance in adolescence. *Monogr. Soc. Res. Child Develpm.,* **5,** No. 1.

Estvan, F. J.: 1952. The relationship of social status, intelligence, and sex of ten- and eleven-year-old children to an awareness of poverty. *Genet. Psychol. Monogr.,* **46,** 3–60.

Evans, M. E.: 1944. Illness history and physical growth. *Amer. J. Dis. Child.,* **68,** 390–394.

Everitt, V., and M. Potgieter: 1952. Food habits and well-being of school children. *Elem. Sch. J.,* **52,** 344–350.

Evry, H.: 1952. TV murder causes bad dreams. *Film World,* **8,** 247.

Fagin, B.: 1953. Guiding the vocational interests of the child. *Education,* **74,** 171–179.

Fahs, S. L.: 1932. Should Peggy and Peter pray? *Relig. Educ.,* **27,** 596–605.

————: 1950. The beginnings of mysticism in children's growth. *Relig. Educ.,* **45,** 139–147.

Fairbanks, G.: 1942. An acoustical study of the pitch of infant hunger wails. *Child Develpm.,* **13,** 227–238.

Farber, M. L.: 1951. English and Americans: a study of national character. *J. Psychol.,* **32,** 241–249.

————: 1953. English and Americans: values in the socialization process. *J. Psychol.,* **36,** 243–250.

Farrell, M.: 1953. Understanding of time relations of five-, six-, and seven-year-old children of high I.Q. *J. educ. Res.,* **46,** 587–594.

Fasten, N.: 1946. Multiple human births. *Hygeia,* **24,** 756–757, 796.

————: 1950. The myth of prenatal influences. *Hygeia,* **27,** 42–43.

Faunce, D. F., and J. A. Beegle: 1948. Cleavages in a relatively homogeneous group of rural youth. *Sociometry,* **11,** 207–216.

Fauquier, W.: 1940. The attitudes of aggressive and submissive boys toward athletics. *Child Develpm.,* **11,** 115–128.

Fea, H. R.: 1953. Interrelationships among materials read, written, and spoken by pupils of the fifth and sixth grades. *J. educ. Psychol.,* **44,** 159–174.

Fearing, F.: 1947. Influence of the movies on attitudes and behavior. *Ann. Amer. Acad. pol. soc. Sci.,* **254,** 70–79.

Federal Security Agency Report: 1950. *Estimated number of deaths and death rates for specified causes, United States,* 1950. Washington: National Office of Vital Statistics.

Feifel, H., and I. Lorge: 1950. Quantitative differences in the vocabulary responses of children. *J. educ. Psychol.,* **41,** 1–18.

Felder, J. G.: 1932. Some factors determining the nature and frequency of anger and fear outbreaks in preschool children. *J. juv. Res.,* **16,** 278–290.

Feldman, S.: 1941. Origins of behavior and man's life-career. *Amer. J. Psychol.,* **54,** 53–63.

Fenton, J. C.: 1925. *A practical psychology of babyhood.* Boston: Houghton Mifflin.

Fenton, N.: 1928. The only child. *J. genet. Psychol.,* **35,** 546–556.

————: 1943. *Mental hygiene and school practice.* Stanford University, Calif.: Stanford University Press.

Ferguson, L. W.: 1941. The cultural genesis of masculinity and femininity. *Psychol. Bull.,* **38,** 584–585.

Ferguson, R. G.: 1954. Some developmental factors in childhood aggression. *J. educ. Res.,* **48,** 15–27.

Fernberger, S. W.: 1948. Persistence of stereotype sex differences. *J. abnorm. soc. Psychol.*, **43**, 97–101.

Fialkin, H. N., and R. O. Beckman: 1938. The influence of month of birth on the intelligence test scores of adults. *J. genet. Psychol.*, **52**, 203–211.

Field, M.: 1940. Maternal attitudes found in twenty-five cases of children with behavior primary disorders. *Amer. J. Orthopsychiat.*, **10**, 293–311.

Fields, S. J.: 1953. Discrimination of facial expression and its relation to personal adjustment. *J. soc. Psychol.*, **38**, 63–71.

Finch, H. M.: 1955. Young children's concepts of parent roles. *J. Home Econ.*, **47**, 99–103.

Finch, M., H. Kilgren, and K. C. Pratt: 1944. The relation of first name preferences to age of judges or to different although overlapping generations. *J. soc. Psychol.*, **20**, 249–264.

Fine, B.: 1955. Children most interested in science. *New York Times*, July 10.

Finley, C. B.: 1946. Age-grade progression in social attitudes and their predictive value. *Amer. Psychologist*, **1**, 445–446.

Fischer, A. E.: 1952. Sibling relationships with special reference to the problems of the second-born. *J. Pediat.*, **40**, 254–259.

Fisher, H. H.: 1950. Family life in children's literature. *Elem. Sch. J.*, **50**, 516–520.

Fisher, M. S.: 1934. Language patterns of preschool children. *Genet. Psychol. Monogr.*, No. 15.

Fisher, R. L.: 1951. Preferences of different age and socioeconomic groups in instrumental musical situations. *J. soc. Psychol.*, **33**, 147–152.

Fisher, S. C.: 1948. Relationships in attitudes, opinions, and values among family members. *Univ. Calif. Publ. in Culture and Soc.*, **2**, 29–100.

Fishman, J. A.: 1952. Degree of bilingualism in a Yiddish school and leisure-time activities. *J. soc. Psychol.*, **36**, 155–165.

Fite, M. D.: 1940. Aggressive behavior in young children and children's attitudes toward aggression. *Genet. Psychol. Monogr.*, **22**, 151–319.

Fitz-Simons, M. J.: 1935. *Some parent-child relationships.* New York: Teachers College Bureau of Publications.

Flaccus, L. W.: 1906. Remarks on the psychology of clothes. *Ped. Sem.*, **13**, 61–83.

Fleege, U. H.: 1945. Movies as an influence in the life of the modern adolescent. *Cath. educ. Rev.*, **43**, 336–352.

———: 1945a. *Self-revelation of the adolescent boy.* Milwaukee: Bruce Publishing Co.

Flory, C. D.: 1936. Osseous development in the hand as an index of skeletal development. *Monogr. Soc. Res. Child Develpm.*, **1**, No. 3.

Flügel, J. C.: 1929. *The psychoanalytic study of the family.* London: International Psychoanalytical Library, No. 3.

Fogler, S.: 1953. Progress report on TV. *Elem. Sch. J.*, **53**, 513–516.

Forbes, H. S., and H. B. Forbes: 1927. Fetal sense reaction: hearing. *J. comp. Psychol.*, **7**, 353–355.

Forest, I., A. E. Watson, and M. H. Appel: 1934. Nursery school quarrels. *Childh. Educ.*, **10**, 314–318.

Forlano, G., and J. W. Wrightstone: 1955. Measuring the quality of social acceptability within a class. *Educ. psychol. Measmt.*, **15**, 127–136.

Forshay, A. W.: 1951. The teacher and children's social attitudes. *Teach. Coll. Rec.*, **52**, 287–296.

Foster, J. C., F. L. Goodenough, and J. E. Anderson: 1928. The sleep of young children. *J. genet. Psychol.*, **35**, 201–218.

Foster, S.: 1927. A study of the personality make-up and social setting of fifty jealous children. *Ment. Hyg., N.Y.*, **11**, 53–77.

Fox, J. F.: 1934. Leisure-time social backgrounds in a suburban community. *J. educ. Sociol.,* **7**, 493–503.

Fox, W. M.: 1947. The stability of measured interests. *J. educ. Res.,* **41**, 305–310.

Fraisse, P., and P. Vautrey: 1952. Perception of space, of speed, and of time in the five-year old child. *Enfance,* **5**, 1–20.

Francis, C. C.: 1939. Factors influencing appearance of centers of ossification during early childhood. *Amer. J. Dis. Child.,* **57**, 817–830.

Francis, K. V.: 1933. A study of the means of influence of socio-economic factors upon the personality of children. *J. juv. Res.,* **17**, 70–77.

—— and E. A. Fillmore: 1934. The influence of environment upon the personality of children. *Univ. Ia. Stud. Child Welf.,* **9**, No. 2.

Frank, J.: 1942. The people in the comics. *Prog. Educ.,* **19**, 28–31.

——: 1944. What's in the comics? *J. educ. Sociol.,* **18**, 214–222.

Frank, J. D.: 1935. Individual differences in certain aspects of the level of aspiration. *Amer. J. Psychol.,* **47**, 119–128.

Frank, L. K.: 1944. The adolescent and the family. *43d Yearb. nat. Soc. Stud. Educ.,* pp. 240–254.

——: 1948. What families do for the nation. *Amer. J. Sociol.,* **53**, 471–473.

——: 1949. This is the adolescent. *Understanding the Child,* **18**, 65–69.

——: 1950. The concept of maturity. *Child Develpm.,* **21**, 21–24.

——: 1950a. Genetic psychology and its prospects. *In Symposium on genetic psychology in honor of the sixtieth anniversary of Clark University, Worcester, Mass.,* April 20.

—— and M. H. Frank: 1954. Teachers' attitudes affect children's relationships. *Education,* **75**, 6–12.

—— and R. E. Hartley: 1951. Play and personality formation in preschool groups. *Personality,* **1**, 149–161.

Frederiksen, N.: 1942. The effects of frustration on negativistic behavior of young children. *J. genet. Psychol.,* **61**, 203–226.

Freeman, H. A.: 1931. First graders' religious ideas. *Sch. & Soc.,* **34**, 733–735.

Freeman, H. E., and M. Showel: 1953. The role of the family in the socialization process. *J. soc. Psychol.,* **37**, 97–101.

Freeston, P. M.: 1939. Vocational interests of elementary-school children. *Occup. Psychol., Lond.,* **13**, 223–237.

Freidson, E.: 1953. Adult discontent: an aspect of children's changing taste. *Child Develpm.,* **24**, 39–49.

French, J. E.: 1952. Children's preferences for pictures of varied complexity of pictorial pattern. *Elem. Sch. J.,* **53**, 90–95.

French, R. L., and I. N. Mensh: 1948. Some relationships between interpersonal judgments and socioeconomic status in a college group. *Sociometry,* **11**, 335–345.

French, T., J. G. Miller, and D. Riesman: 1950. Psychoanalysis and ethics. *Univ. Chicago Round Table,* No. 638, 1–12.

Frenkel-Brunswik, E.: 1946. Studies of social discrimination in children. *Amer. Psychologist,* **1**, 456.

——: 1948. A study of prejudice in children. *Hum. Rel.,* **1**, 295–306.

——: 1951. Patterns of social and cognitive outlook in children and parents. *Amer. J. Orthopsychiat.,* **21**, 543–558.

—— and J. Havel: 1953. Prejudice in the interviews of children. I. Attitudes toward minority groups. *J. genet. Psychol.,* **82**, 91–136.

Freud, A., and D. T. Burlingham: 1944. *Infants without families.* New York: International Universities Press.

Freud, S.: 1913. *The interpretation of dreams*. London: G. Allen.

———: 1920. *A general introduction to psychoanalysis*. New York: Boni.

———: 1929. *Introductory lectures on psychoanalysis*. London: G. Allen.

———: 1936. *The problem of anxiety*. New York: Norton.

Fried, E. G., and K. Stern: 1948. The situation of the aged within the family. *Amer. J. Orthopsychiat.*, **17**, 142–181.

Friedman, A.: 1951. Observations in a play group of young children. *Ind. psychol. Bull.*, **9**, 25–30.

Friedman, K. C.: 1944. Time concepts of elementary-school children. *Elem.. Sch. J.*, **44**, 337–342.

———: 1944a. Time concepts of junior and senior high school pupils and of adults. *Sch. Rev.*, **52**, 233–238.

Fries, M. E.: 1937. Factors in character development, neuroses, psychoses, and delinquency. *Amer. J. Orthopsychiat.*, **17**, 142–181.

———: 1941. Mental hygiene in pregnancy, delivery, and the puerperium. *Ment. Hyg., N.Y.*, **25**, 221–236.

———: 1944. Psychosomatic relationship between mother and infant. *Psychosom. Med.*, **6**, 159–162.

——— and B. Lewi: 1938. Interrelated factors in development. *Amer. J. Orthopsychiat.*, **8**, 726–752.

Froe, O. D.: 1953. The negative concept in discipline and its relation to rapport in counseling. *Educ. Admin. Superv.*, **39**, 470–477.

Fuller, A. P.: 1931. The origin of parental attitudes toward discipline. *Smith Coll. Stud. soc. Work*, **1**, 402.

Fuller, E. M.: 1948. Injury-prone children. *Amer. J. Orthopsychiat.*, **18**, 708–723.

Furfey, P. H.: 1926. *The gang age*. New York: Macmillan.

———: 1927. Some factors influencing the selection of boys' chums. *J. appl. Psychol.*, **11**, 47–51.

———: 1930. *The growing boy*. New York: Macmillan.

———: 1931. Case studies in developmental age. *Amer. J. Orthopsychiat.*, **1**, 292–297.

Galler, E. H.: 1951. Influence of social class on children's choice of occupations. *Elem. Sch. J.*, **51**, 439–445.

Gamble, M. A.: 1951. The viewers' views on classroom TV. *Educ. Screen*, **30**, 226–227.

Gardner, G. E.: 1944. A factor in the sex education of children. *Ment. Hyg., N.Y.*, **28**, 55–63.

———: 1952. What about the aggressive child? *The Child*, **16**, 146–149, 155–156.

Gardner, L. P.: 1943. A survey of attitudes and activities of fathers. *J. genet. Psychol.*, **63**, 15–53.

———: 1947. An analysis of children's attitudes toward fathers. *J. genet. Psychol.*, **70**, 3–28.

Garrison, K. C.: 1951. *Psychology of adolescence*, 4th ed. New York: Prentice-Hall.

———: 1952. *Growth and development*. New York: Longmans.

Garth, T. R., and E. P. Porter: 1934. The color preferences of 1,032 young children. *Amer. J. Psychol.*, **46**, 448–451.

Garvey, C. R.: 1939. *The activity of young children during sleep*. Minneapolis: University of Minnesota Press.

Gates, A. I.: 1949. Reading in the elementary school. *48th Yearb. nat. Soc. Stud. Educ.*, Pt. II.

——— and A. W. Scott: 1931. Characteristics and relations of motor speed and dexterity among young children. *J. genet. Psychol.*, **39**, 423–454.

────── and G. A. Taylor: 1926. An experimental study of the nature of improvement resulting from practice in a motor function. *J. educ. Psychol.*, **27**, 226–236.

Gates, G. S.: 1923. An experimental study of the growth of social perception. *J. educ. Psychol.*, **14**, 449–461.

──────: 1925. A preliminary study of a test for social perception. *J. educ. Psychol.*, **16**, 452–457.

Gates, M. F.: 1946. A comparative study of some problems of social and emotional adjustment of crippled and non-crippled boys and girls. *J. genet. Psychol.*, **60**, 219–244.

Gatewood, M. C., and A. P. Weiss: 1930. Race and sex differences in new-born infants. *J. genet. Psychol.*, **38**, 31–49.

Geisel, G. B.: 1945. Discipline reconsidered. *Sch. & Soc.*, **62**, 193–195.

──────: 1951. Discipline viewed as a developmental need of the child. *Nerv. Child*, **9**, 115–121.

Geleerd, E. R.: 1945. Observations on temper tantrums in children. *Amer. J. Orthopsychiat.*, **15**, 238–246.

Gellermann, L. W.: 1933. Form discrimination in chimpanzees and two-year-old children. *J. genet. Psychol.*, **42**, 1–50.

Gerver, J. M., and R. Day: 1950. Intelligence quotients of children who have recovered from erythroblastosis fetalis. *J. Pediat.*, **36**, 342–349.

Gesell, A.: 1928. *Infancy and human growth.* New York: Macmillan.

──────: 1929. Maturation and infant behavior pattern. *Psychol. Rev.*, **36**, 307–319.

──────: 1930. *The guidance of mental growth in infant and child.* New York: Macmillan.

──────: 1933. The individual in infancy. *In* C. Murchison, *The foundations of experimental psychology.* Worcester: Clark University Press, pp. 628–661.

──────: 1933a. The mental growth of prematurely born infants. *J. Pediat.*, **2**, 676–680.

──────: 1939. Reciprocal neuromotor interweaving: a principle of development evidenced in the pattern of infant behavior. *J. comp. Neurol.*, **70**, 161–180.

──────: 1941. The genesis of behavior in fetus and infant: the growth of the mind from the standpoint of developmental morphology. *Proc. Amer. phil. Soc.*, **84**, 471–488.

──────: 1946. Behavior aspects of the care of the premature infant. *J. Pediat.*, **29**, 210–212.

──────: 1949. Growth potentials of the human infant. *Sci. Mon., N.Y.*, **68**, 252–256.

──────: 1949a. The developmental aspect of child vision. *J. Pediat.*, **35**, 310–317.

──────: 1952. Developmental pediatrics. *Nerv. Child*, **9**, 225–227.

──────: 1954. The ontogenesis of infant behavior. *In* L. Carmichael, *Manual of child psychology*, 2d ed. New York: Wiley, pp. 335–373.

────── et al.: 1940. *The first five years of life.* New York: Harper.

────── and C. S. Amatruda: 1941. *Developmental diagnosis: normal and abnormal child development*, 2d ed. New York: Hoeber.

────── and ──────: 1945. *The embryology of behavior.* New York: Harper.

────── and L. B. Ames: 1940. The ontogenetic organization of prone behavior in human infancy. *J. genet. Psychol.*, **56**, 247–263.

────── and ──────: 1946. The development of directionality in drawing. *J. genet. Psychol.*, **68**, 45–61.

────── and ──────: 1947. The infant's reaction to his mirror image. *J. genet. Psychol.*, **70**, 141–154.

────── and ──────: 1947a. The development of handedness. *J. genet. Psychol.*, **70**, 155–175.

—— and H. M. Halverson: 1936. The development of thumb opposition in the human infant. *J. genet. Psychol.,* **48,** 339–361.

—— and F. L. Ilg: 1937. *The feeding behavior of infants: a pediatric approach to the mental hygiene of early life.* Philadelphia: Lippincott.

—— and ——: 1943. *Infant and child in the culture of today.* New York: Harper.

—— and ——: 1946. *The child from five to ten.* New York: Harper.

—— and ——: 1949. *Child development.* New York: Harper.

—— and E. E. Lord: 1927. A psychological comparison of nursery-school children from homes of low and high economic status. *J. genet. Psychol.,* **34,** 339–356.

—— and H. Thompson: 1929. Learning and growth in identical twins: an experimental study by the method of co-twin control. *Genet. Psychol. Monogr.,* **6,** 1–123.

—— and ——: 1934. *Infant behavior, its genesis and growth.* New York: McGraw-Hill.

—— and ——: 1938. *The psychology of early growth.* New York: Macmillan.

—— and ——: 1941. Twins T and C from infancy to adolescence: a biogenetic study of individual differences by the method of co-twin control. *Genet. Psychol. Monogr.,* **24,** 3–121.

Gewirtz, J. L.: 1948. Studies in word fluency. I. Its relation to vocabulary and mental age in young children. *J. genet. Psychol.,* **72,** 165–176.

——: 1948a. Studies in word fluency: II. Its relation to eleven items of child behavior. *J. genet. Psychol.,* **72,** 177–184.

——: 1948b. *Dependent and aggressive interaction in young children.* Ph.D. dissertation, Iowa City: University of Iowa.

Gibb, C. A.: 1947. The principles and traits of leadership. *J. abnorm. soc. Psychol.,* **42,** 267–284.

Gibson, J. R., and T. McKeown: 1951. Observation on all births (23,970) in Birmingham, 1947. III. Survival. *Brit. J. soc. Med.,* **5,** 177–183.

—— and ——: 1952. Observations on all births (23,970) in Birmingham, 1947. VI. Birth weight, duration of gestation, and survival related to sex. *Brit. J. soc. Med.,* **6,** 150–152.

—— and ——: 1952a. Observations on all births (23,970) in Birmingham, 1947. VII. Effect of changing family size on infant mortality. *Brit. J. soc. Med.,* **6,** 183–187.

Giddings, G.: 1934. Child's sleep—effect of certain foods and beverages on sleep motility. *Amer. J. pub. Health,* **24,** 609–614.

——: 1939. Motility of school children during sleep. *Amer. J. Physiol.,* **127,** 480–485.

Giesecke, M.: 1936. The genesis of hand preference. *Monogr. Soc. Res. Child Develpm.,* **1,** No. 5.

Gilbert, M. S.: 1939. *Biography of the unborn.* Baltimore: Williams & Wilkins.

Gilliland, A. R.: 1953. Changes in religious beliefs of college students. *J. soc. Psychol.,* **37,** 113–116.

—— and D. W. Humphreys: 1943. Age, sex, method, and interval as variables in times estimation. *J. genet. Psychol.,* **63,** 123–130.

Gillin, J.: 1949. Personality formation from the cultural point of view. *In* C. Kluckholm and H. Murray, *Personality in nature, society, and culture.* New York: Knopf.

Gilmer, B. von H.: 1933. An analysis of the spontaneous responses of the newborn infant. *J. genet. Psychol.,* **42,** 391–405.

Ginzberg, E., J. W. Ginzberg, S. Axelrod, and J. L. Herma: 1951. *Occupational choice.* New York: Columbia University Press.

Gladstone, R.: 1946. Do maladjusted teachers cause maladjustment? A review. *J. except. Child,* **15,** 65–70.

Glaser, K., A. H. Parmelee, and E. B. Plattner: 1950. Growth pattern of prematurely born infants. *Pediatrics (Springfield)*, **5**, 130–144.

Glasner, P. J.: 1949. Personality characteristics and emotional problems in stutterers under the age of five. *J. Speech Hearing Disorders*, **14**, 135–138.

Gleason, M. C.: 1931. A study of attitudes leading to the rejection of the child by the mother. *Smith Coll. Stud. soc. Work*, **1**, 407.

Glueck, S., and E. T. Glueck: 1950. *Unravelling juvenile delinquency*. New York: Commonwealth Fund.

Goff, R. G.: 1954. Some educational implications of the influence of repetition on aspiration levels of minority group children. *J. exp. Educ.*, **23**, 179–184.

Goff, R. M.: 1949. Problems and emotional difficulties of Negro children. *Teach. Coll. Contr. Educ.*, No. 960.

———: 1950. Problems and emotional difficulties of Negro children due to race. *J. Negro Educ.*, **19**, 152–158.

Goldfarb, W.: 1943. Infant rearing and problem behavior. *Amer. J. Orthopsychiat.*, **13**, 249–265.

———: 1945. Effects of psychological deprivation in infancy and subsequent stimulation. *Amer. J. Psychiat.*, **102**, 18–33.

Goldman, F.: 1948. Breast feeding and character formation. *J. Pers.*, **17**, 83–103.

Goldschmidt, W.: 1950. Social class in America—a critical review. *Amer. Anthrop.*, **52**, 483–498.

Goldstein, K.: 1948. *Language and language disturbances*. New York: Grune & Stratton.

Goldstein, M. S.: 1939. Development of the head in the same individuals. *Hum. Biol.*, **11**, 197–219.

Golein, E. S.: 1954. Forming impressions of personality. *J. Pers.*, **23**, 65–67.

Goodenough, F. L.: 1926. *Measurement of intelligence by drawings*. Yonkers, N.Y.: World.

———: 1931. *Anger in young children*. Minneapolis: University of Minnesota Press.

———: 1954. The measurement of mental growth in childhood. *In* L. Carmichael, *Manual of child psychology*, 2d ed. New York: Wiley, pp. 459–491.

——— and D. B. Harris: 1950. Studies in the psychology of children's drawings. II. 1928–1949. *Psychol. Bull.*, **47**, 369–433.

——— and A. M. Leahy: 1927. The effect of certain family relationships upon the development of personality. *J. genet. Psychol.*, **34**, 45–71.

——— and R. C. Smart: 1935. Interrelationships of motor abilities in young children. *Child Develpm.*, **6**, 141–153.

——— and M. A. Tinker: 1930. A comparative study of several methods of measuring speed of tapping in children and adults. *J. genet. Psychol.*, **38**, 145–160.

Goodman, M. E.: 1951. The education of children and youth to live in a multi-racial society. *J. Negro Educ.*, **19**, 399–407.

———: 1952. *Race awareness in young children*. Cambridge, Mass.: Addison-Wesley.

Gordon, H. C., and B. J. Novack: 1950. I.Q. and month of birth. *Science*, **112**, 62–63.

Gordon, L. V.: 1952. Personal factors in leadership. *J. soc. Psychol.*, **36**, 245–248.

Gorer, G.: 1948. *The American people*. New York: Norton.

Gottemoller, R.: 1943. The sibling relationships of a group of young children. *Nerv. Child*, **2**, 268–277.

Gough, H. G.: 1952. Identifying psychological femininity. *Educ. psychol. Measmt*, **12**, 427–439.

———: 1952a. On making a good impression. *J. educ. Res.*, **46**, 33–42.

———, D. B. Harris, and W. E. Martin: 1950. Mothers' child-training preferences and children's ethnic attitudes. *Amer. Psychologist*, **5**, 467.

——, ——, ——, and M. Edwards: 1950. Children's ethnic attitudes. I. Relationship to certain personality factors. *Child Develpm.*, **21**, 83–91.

—— and D. R. Peterson: 1952. The identification and measurement of predispositional factors in crime and delinquency. *J. consult. Psychol.*, **16**, 207–212.

Gould, H. N., and M. P. Gould: 1932. Age of first menstruation in mothers and daughters. *J. Amer. med. Ass.*, **98**, 1349–1352.

Gould, R.: 1939. An experimental analysis of "level of aspiration." *Genet. Psychol. Monogr.*, **21**, No. 1.

Grace, H. A., and J. J. Lohmann: 1952. Children's reactions to stories depicting parent-child conflict situations. *Child Develpm.*, **23**, 61–74.

Graham, V., T. A. Jackson, and L. Long: 1944. Generalization of the concept of middleness. *J. genet. Psychol.*, **65**, 227–237.

Grant, E. I.: 1939. The effect of certain factors in the home environment upon child behavior. *Univ. Ia. Stud. Child Welf.*, **17**, 63–94.

Graves, C. C.: 1948. Factors in the development and growth of children's personalities. *J. Iowa Stud. med. Soc.*, **38**, 437–439.

Gray, H.: 1948. Prediction of adult stature. *Child Develpm.*, **19**, 167–175.

Gray, J. S.: 1946. *Psychology in human affairs.* New York: McGraw-Hill.

Gray, S.: 1944. The vocational preferences of Negro school children. *J. genet. Psychol.*, **64**, 239–247.

——: 1944a. The wishes of Negro school children. *J. genet. Psychol.*, **64**, 225–237.

Gray, W. S.: 1947. The social effects of reading. *Sch. Rev.*, **55**, 269–277.

Green, A. W.: 1946. The middle-class male child and neuroses. *Amer. sociol. Rev.*, **11**, 31–41.

Green, E. H.: 1933. Friendships and quarrels among preschool children. *Child Develpm.*, **4**, 237–252.

——: 1933a. Group play and quarreling among preschool children. *Child Develpm.*, **4**, 302–307.

Green, G. H.: 1948. Insight and group adjustment. *J. abnorm. soc. Psychol.*, **43**, 49–61.

Greenaway, E.: 1954. Reading standards raised by television. *New York Times*, Nov. 4.

Greenberg, P. J.: 1932. Competition in children: an experimental study. *Amer. J. Psychol.*, **44**, 221–248.

Greenberg, R. G., and A. H. Bryan: 1951. Methodology in the study of physical measurements of school children, I. *Hum. Biol.*, **23**, 160–179.

Greenblatt, E. L.: 1950. Relationship of mental health and social status. *J. educ. Res.*, **44**, 193–204.

Greenhill, I. P.: 1955. The birth of the baby. *In* M. Fishbein and E. W. Burgess, *Successful Marriage*, 2d ed. Garden City: Doubleday, pp. 255–266.

Greenstein, J.: 1954. Effect of television upon elementary school grades. *J. educ. Res.*, **48**, 161–176.

Gregg, A.: 1928. An observational study of laughter of three-year-old children. Unpublished master's thesis. New York: Columbia University Library.

Griffiths, W.: 1952. *Behavior difficulties of children as perceived and judged by parents, teachers, and children themselves.* Minneapolis: University of Minnesota Press.

Grigsby, O. J.: 1932. An experimental study of development of concepts in preschool children as evidenced by their expressive ability. *J. exp. Educ.*, **1**, 144–162.

Gronlund, N. E.: 1950. The accuracy of teachers' judgments concerning the sociometric status of sixth grade pupils, I. *Sociometry*, **13**, 197–225.

——: 1950a. The accuracy of teachers' judgments concerning the sociometric status of sixth grade pupils, II. *Sociometry*, **13**, 329–357.

Gross, M. M.: 1946. The effect of certain types of motivation on the "honesty" of children. *J. educ. Res.,* **40,** 133–140.

Grossmann, B., and J. Wrighter: 1948. The relation between selection-rejection and intelligence, social status, and personality amongst sixth-grade children. *Sociometry,* **11,** 346–355.

Groves, E. R.: 1940. *The family and its social functions.* Philadelphia: Lippincott.

Gruelich, W. W.: 1950. The rationale of assessing the developmental status of children from roentgenograms of the hand and wrist. *Child Develpm.,* **21,** 33–44.

Gruen, E. W.: 1945. Levels of aspiration in relation to personality factors in adolescents. *Child Develpm.,* **16,** 181–188.

Gruenberg, S. M.: 1944. The comics as a social force. *J. educ. Sociol.,* **18,** 204–213.

———: 1947. Changing conceptions of the family. *Ann. Amer. Acad. pol. soc. Sci.,* **251,** 128–136.

Gruesser, Sister M. J.: 1950. Categorical valuations of Jews among Catholic parochial school children. *Cath. Univ. Amer. Stud. Sociol..* **34,** 1–169.

Guanella, F. M.: 1934. Block building activities of young children. *Arch. Psychol., N.Y.,* No. 174.

Guetzkow, H. S., and P. H. Bowman: 1946. *Men and hunger.* Elgin, Ill.: Brethren Publishing Co.

Guilford, R. B., and D. A. Worcester: 1930. A comparative study of the only child. *J. genet. Psychol.,* **38,** 411–426.

Gutteridge, M. V.: 1939. A study of motor achievements of young children. *Arch. Psychol., N.Y.,* No. 244.

Guttmacher, A. F.: 1955. Miscarriages and abortions. *In* M. Fishbein and E. W. Burgess, *Successful marriage,* 2d ed. Garden City, N.Y.: Doubleday, pp. 195–206.

Habbe, S.: 1937. Nicknames of adolescent boys. *Amer. J. Orthopsychiat.,* **7,** 371–377.

Hacker, F. J., and E. R. Geleerd: 1945. Freedom and authority in adolescence. *Amer. J. Orthopsychiat.,* **15,** 621–630.

Haffter, C.: 1948. *Kinder aus Geschiedenen Ehen.* Bern: Haus Huber.

Hagman, E. P.: 1933. The companionships of preschool children. *Univ. Ia. Stud. Child Welf.,* **7,** No. 4.

Hagman, S. R.: 1932. A study of fears of children of preschool age. *J. exp. Psychol.,* **1,** 110–130.

Hahn, E.: 1948. Analysis of the content and form of speech of first grade children. *Quart. J. Speech,* **34,** 361–366.

Hahn, E. F.: 1943. *Stuttering: significant theories and therapies.* Stanford, Calif.: Stanford University Press.

Hall, G. S.: 1891. The contents of children's minds on entering school. *Ped. Sem.,* **1,** 139–173.

———: 1907. *Aspects of child life and education.* Boston: Ginn.

Halverson, H. M.: 1931. An experimental study of prehension in infants by means of systematic cinema records. *Genet. Psychol. Monogr.,* **10,** 107–286.

———: 1933. The acquisition of skill in infancy. *J. genet. Psychol.,* **43,** 3–48.

———: 1940. Genital and sphincter behavior of the male infant. *J. genet. Psychol.,* **56,** 95–136.

———: 1941. Variations in pulse and respiration during different phases of infant behavior. *J. genet. Psychol.,* **59,** 259–330.

———: 1942. The differential effects of nudity and clothing on muscular tonus in infancy. *J. genet. Psychol.,* **61,** 55–67.

Hamalainen, A. E.: 1952. Kindergarten-primary entrance age in relation to later school adjustment. *Elem. Sch. J.,* **12,** 406–411.

Hanley, C.: 1951. Physique and reputation of high-school boys. *Child Develpm.*, **22**, 247–260.

Hanlon, C. R., J. B. Butchart, and P. R. Kempf: 1949. Injuries in childhood. *J. Pediat.*, **34**, 688–698.

Harding, V. S. V.: 1952. A method of evaluating osseous development from birth to 14 years. *Child Develpm.*, **23**, 247–271.

———: 1952a. Time schedule for the appearance and fusion of a second center of ossification of the calcaneus. *Child Develpm.*, **23**, 181–184.

Hardy, M. C.: 1937. Social recognition at the elementary school age. *J. soc. Psychol.*, **8**, 365–384.

———: 1938. Frequent illness in childhood, physical growth and final size. *Amer. J. phys. Anthrop.*, **23**, 241–260.

———, H. H. Boyle, and A. L. Newcomb: 1941. Physical fitness of children from different economic levels in Chicago. *J. Amer. med. Ass.*, **117**, 2154–2161.

Hare, A. P.: 1952. A study of interaction and consensus in different sized groups. *Amer. sociol. Rev.*, **17**, 261–267.

Harms, E.: 1943. The development of humor. *J. abnorm. soc. Psychol.*, **38**, 351–369.

———: 1944. The development of religious experience in children. *Amer. J. Sociol.*, **50**, 112–122.

Harris, A. J.: 1952. What is a "normal" child? *J. teach. Educ.*, **3**, 58–61.

Harris, D. B.: 1948. Social change in the beliefs of adults concerning parent-child relationships. *Amer. Psychologist*, **3**, 264.

———: 1950. Behavior ratings of post-polio cases. *J. consult. Psychol.*, **14**, 381–385.

———: 1950a. How children learn interests. *49th Yearb. nat. Soc. Stud. Educ.*, Pt. 1. pp. 129–135.

———: 1954. How student-teachers identify responsibility in children. *J. educ. Psychol.*, **45**, 233–239.

———, K. E. Clark, A. M. Rose, and F. Valasek: 1954. The measurement of responsibility in children. *Child Develpm.*, **25**, 21–28.

———, ———, ———, and ———: 1954a. The relationship of children's home duties to an attitude of responsibility. *Child Develpm.*, **25**, 29–33.

———, H. G. Gough, and W. E. Martin: 1950. Children's ethnic attitudes. II. Relationship to parental beliefs concerning child training. *Child Develpm.*, **21**, 169–181.

——— and E. S. Harris: 1946. A study of fetal movements in relation to mother's activity. *Hum. Biol.*, **18**, 221–237.

——— and W. E. Martin: 1950. Mothers' child-training preferences and children's ethnic attitudes. *Amer. Psychologist*, **5**, 467.

Harris, E. K.: 1946. The responsiveness of kindergarten children to the behavior of their fellows. *Monogr. Soc. Res. Child Develpm.*, **11**, No. 2.

Harris, H. S.: 1933. *Bone growth in health and disease.* London: Oxford University Press.

Harris, I. D., L. Rapoport, and M. A. Rynerson: 1950. Observations on asthmatic children. *Amer. J. Orthopsychiat.*, **20**, 490–505.

Harrison, E. C.: 1953. A study of vocational attitudes. *J. Negro Educ.*, **22**, 471–475.

Harrison, M. L.: 1934. The nature and development of concepts of time among young children. *Elem. Sch. J.*, **34**, 507–514.

Harrower, M. R.: 1934. Social status and the moral development of the child. *Brit. J. educ. Psychol.*, **1**, 75–95.

Hart, F. W.: 1934. *Teachers and teaching.* New York: Macmillan.

Hartley, E. L., and D. C. Krugman: 1948. Note on children's social role perception. *J. Psychol.*, **26**, 399–405.

——, M. Rosenbaum, and S. Schwartz: 1948. Children's use of ethnic frames of reference. *J. Psychol.*, **26**, 367–386.

Hartley, R. E.: 1946. Sociability in preadolescence. *Teach. Coll. Contr. Educ.*, No. 918.

——: 1952. *Growing through play: experiences of Teddy and Bud.* New York: Columbia University Press.

——, L. K. Frank, and R. M. Goldensen: 1952. *Understanding children's play.* New York: Columbia University Press.

Hartshorne, H., and E. Lotz: 1932. *Case studies of present-day religious teachings.* New Haven: Yale University Press.

—— and M. A. May: 1927. Testing the knowledge of right and wrong. *Relig. Educ. Ass. Monogr.*, **1**, 47–48.

—— and ——: 1928. *Studies in deceit.* New York: Macmillan.

—— and ——: 1928a. *Studies in the nature of character.* New York: Macmillan.

—— and ——: 1929. *Studies in service and self-control.* New York: Macmillan.

——, ——, and F. K. Shuttleworth: 1930. *Studies in the nature of character.* III. *Studies in the organization of character.* New York: Macmillan.

Hattendorf, K. W.: 1932. A study of the questions of young children concerning sex: a phase of an experimental approach to parent education. *J. soc. Psychol.*, **3**, 37–64.

Hattwick, B. W.: 1936. Interrelations between the preschool child's behavior and certain factors in the home. *Child Develpm.*, **7**, 200–226.

—— and M. Stowell: 1936. The relation of parent over-attentiveness to children's work habits and social adjustments in kindergarten and the first six grades of school. *J. educ. Res.*, **30**, 169–176.

Hattwick, L. A.: 1940. Group life of the young child. *J. educ. Sociol.*, **14**, 205–216.

—— and M. K. Sanders: 1938. Age differences in behavior at the nursery school level. *Child Develpm.*, **9**, 27–47.

Hattwick, L. H.: 1937. Sex differences in behavior of nursery school children. *Child Develpm.*, **8**, 343–355.

Havighurst, R. J.: 1946. Child development in relation to community social structure. *Child Develpm.*, **17**, 85–90.

——: 1950. *Developmental tasks and education.* New York: Longmans.

——: 1950a. Social class differences and family life education at the secondary level. *Marriage Fam. Living*, **12**, 133–135.

——: 1952. Social class and basic personality structure. *Sociol. soc. Res.*, **36**, 355–363.

——: 1952a. The function of successful discipline. *Understanding the Child*, **21**, 35–38.

——: 1953. *Human development and education.* New York: Longmans.

——, R. G. Kuhlen, and C. McGuire: 1947. Personality development. *Rev. educ. Res.*, **17**, 333–344.

——, M. Z. Robinson, and M. Dorr: 1946. The development of the ideal self in childhood and adolescence. *J. educ. Res.*, **40**, 241–257.

—— and H. Taba: 1949. *Adolescent character and personality.* New York: Wiley.

Hawkes, G. R.: 1952. A study of personal values of elementary school children. *Educ. psychol. Measmt*, **12**, 654–663.

Hawkins, H., and J. Walters: 1952. Family recreation activities. *J. Home Econ.*, **44**, 623–626.

Hay-Shaw, C.: 1949. Maintenance of mental health. II. The first five years. *Ment. Hlth, London*, **9**, 3–6.

Hayes, D. T.: 1952. Freedom and fears in the family today. *Understanding the Child*, **21**, 39–44.

Hayes, M. L., and M. E. Conklin: 1953. Intergroup attitudes and experimental change. *J. exp. Educ.*, **22**, 19–36.

Hazlitt, V.: 1930. Children's thinking. *Brit. J. Psychol.,* **20,** 354–361.

Healy, F., and A. F. Bronner: 1936. *New light on delinquency and its treatment.* New Haven: Yale University Press.

Heathers, G.: 1953. Emotional dependence and independence in a physical threat situation. *Child Develpm.,* **24,** 169–179.

———: 1954. The adjustment of two-year-olds in a novel social situation. *Child Develpm.,* **25,** 147–158.

Heffernan, H.: 1952. The organization of the elementary school and the development of a healthy personality. *J. elem. Educ.,* **20,** 129–153.

Heisler, F.: 1948. A comparison between those elementary school children who attend moving pictures, read comic books, and listen to serial radio programs to an excess with those who indulge in these activities seldom or not at all. *J. educ. Res.,* **48,** 182–190.

Hellersberg, E. F.: 1946. Food habits of adolescents in relation to family training and present adjustment. *Amer. J. Orthopsychiat.,* **16,** 34–51.

Hellman, M.: 1943. The phase of development concerned with the erupting of permanent teeth. *Amer. J. Orthod. Oral Surg.,* **29,** 507–526.

Henry, J., and J. W. Boggs: 1952. Child-rearing, culture, and the natural world. *Psychiatry,* **15,** 261–271.

——— and S. Warson: 1951. Family structure and psychic development. *Amer. J. Orthopsychiat.,* **21,** 59–73.

Henry, L. K., and E. E. Emme: 1939. The home-adjustment inventory: an attitude scale for personal procedures. *Psychol. Bull.,* **36,** 630.

Herbst, P. G.: 1952. The measurement of family relationships. *Hum. Rel.,* **5,** 3–35.

Herrick, V. E.: 1945. Teachers' classroom personalities. *Elem. Sch. J.,* **46,** 126–129.

Hertz, R. F.: 1955. 100,000 children tell how children should behave. *This Week Mag.,* July 24.

Hess, J. H., G. J. Mohr, and P. F. Bartelme: 1934. *The physical and mental growth of prematurely born children.* Chicago: University of Chicago Press.

Hetzer, H.: 1930. Das gross-sprecherische Kind. *Päd. Warte,* **37.**

——— and B. Reindorf: 1928. Development of language and the social environment. *Child Develpm. Abstr.,* No. 2, p. 380.

——— and B. H. Tudor-Hart: 1927. Die frühesten Reaktionen auf die menschliche Stimme. *Quellen und Studien,* **5,** 103–124.

Hewitt, L. E., and R. L. Jenkins: 1946. *Fundamental patterns of maladjustment: the dynamics of their origin.* Springfield, Ill.: State of Illinois.

Hicks, J. A.: 1930. The acquisition of motor skill in young children. *Child Develpm.,* **1,** 90–105.

———: 1930a. The acquisition of motor skill in young children. II. The influence of specific and of general practice on motor skill. *Child Develpm.,* **1,** 292–297.

———: 1931. The acquisition of motor skill in young children: an experimental study of the effects of practice in throwing at a moving target. *Univ. Ia. Stud. Child Welf.,* No. 4, 80.

——— and F. D. Stewart: 1930. The learning of abstract concepts of size. *Child Develpm.,* **1,** 195–203.

Highberger, R.: 1955. The relationship between maternal behavior and the child's early adjustment to nursery school. *Child Develpm.,* **26,** 49–61.

Hightower, P. R.: 1930. Biblical information in relation to character conduct. *Univ. Ia. Stud. Charact.,* **3,** No. 2.

Hildreth, G.: 1936. Developmental sequences in name writing. *Child Develpm.,* **7,** 291–303.

———: 1944. The simplification tendency in reproducing designs. *J. genet. Psychol.*, **64**, 329–333.

———: 1948. Manual dominance in nursery school children. *J. genet. Psychol.*, **72**, 29–45.

———: 1949. The development and training of hand dominance. I. Characteristics of handedness. *J. genet. Psychol.*, **75**, 197–220.

———: 1949a. The development and training of hand dominance. II. Developmental tendencies in handedness. *J. genet. Psychol.*, **75**, 221–254.

———: 1949b. The development and training of hand dominance. III. Origins of handedness and lateral dominance. *J. genet. Psychol.*, **75**, 255–275.

———: 1949c. Reading progress in the early primary period. 48*th Yearb. nat. Soc. Stud. Educ.*, Pt. II, pp. 54–92.

———: 1950. The development and training of hand dominance. IV. Developmental problems associated with handedness. *J. genet. Psychol.*, **76**, 39–100.

———: 1950a. The development and training of hand dominance. V. Training of handedness. *J. genet. Psychol.*, **76**, 101–144.

Hilgard, J. R.: 1932. Learning and maturation in preschool children. *J. genet. Psychol.*, **41**, 36–56.

———: 1933. The effect of early and delayed practice on memory and motor performances studied by the method of co-twin control. *Genet. Psychol. Monogr.*, **14**, 493–567.

———: 1951. Sibling rivalry and social heredity. *Psychiatry*, **14**, 375–385.

Hill, D. S.: 1930. Personification of ideals by urban children. *J. soc. Psychol.*, **1**, 379–393.

Hill, G. E.: 1935. The ethical knowledge of delinquent and nondelinquent boys. *J. soc. Psychol.*, **6**, 107–114.

———: 1943. Relation of children's interests in comic strips to the vocabulary of these strips. *J. educ. Psychol.*, **34**, 48–54.

——— and M. E. Trent: 1940. Children's interests in comic strips. *J. educ. Res.*, **34**, 30–36.

Hill, M. C., and B. C. McCall: 1950. Social stratification in "Georgia Town." *Amer. sociol. Rev.*, **15**, 721–729.

Hirota, K.: 1951. Experimental studies of competition. *Jap. J. Psychol.*, **21**, 70–81.

Hirsch, N. D. M.: 1939. Relationship between interest, ability, and self-estimated ability among maladjusted boys. *J. abnorm. soc. Psychol.*, **34**, 395–399.

Hoch, P. H., and J. Zubin: 1949. *Psychosexual development.* New York: Grune & Stratton.

Hoeflin, R.: 1954. Child-rearing practices and child care resources used by Ohio farm families with preschool children. *J. genet. Psychol.*, **84**, 271–297.

Hofstaetter, P. R.: 1951. The rate of maturation and the cephalization coefficient: a hypothesis. *J. Psychol.*, **31**, 271–280.

Holaday, P. W., and C. D. Stoddard: 1933. *Getting ideas from the movies.* New York: Macmillan.

Hollander, E. P., and W. B. Webb: 1955. Leadership, fellowship, and friendship: an analysis of peer nominations. *J. abnorm. soc. Psychol.*, **50**, 163–167.

Hollingshead, A. DeB.: 1949. *Elmtown's youth.* New York: Wiley.

Hollingworth, H. L.: 1928. *Mental growth and decline.* New York: Appleton-Century-Crofts.

———: 1949. *Psychology and ethics.* New York: Ronald.

Hollingworth, L. S.: 1926. *Gifted children, their nature, and nurture.* New York: Macmillan.

————: 1939. What we know about the early selection and training of leaders. *Teach. Coll. Rec.,* **40,** 575–592.

————: 1940. Personality and adjustment as determiners and correlates of intelligence. *39th Yearb. nat. Soc. Stud. Educ.,* pp. 271–275.

————: 1942. *Children above 180 I.Q.* Yonkers, N.Y.: World.

Holmes, F. B.: 1935. An experimental study of the fears of young children. *Child Develpm. Monogr.,* No. 20, Pt. III.

————: 1936. An experimental investigation of a method of overcoming children's fears. *Child Develpm.,* **7,** 6–30.

Holmes, T. C.: 1932. Comprehension of some sizes, shapes, and positions by young children. *Child Develpm.,* **3,** 269–273.

Holt, R. R.: 1946. Level of aspiration: ambition or defense. *J. exp. Psychol.,* **36,** 398–416.

Honzik, M. P.: 1951. Sex differences in the occurrence of materials in the play constructions of preadolescents. *Child Develpm.,* **22,** 15–35.

Hooker, D.: 1951. The development of behavior in the human fetus. *In* W. Dennis, *Readings in child psychology.* New York: Prentice-Hall, pp. 1–14.

Hooker, H. F.: 1931. A study of the only child at school. *J. genet. Psychol.,* **39,** 122–126.

Hopkins, J. W.: 1947. Height and weight of Ottawa elementary school children of two socioeconomic strata. *Hum. Biol.,* **19,** 68–82.

Hopkins, L. A.: 1949. Rubella-deafened infants: comparison of a group of rubella-deafened children with a group of hereditarily deaf children and their sibs. *Amer. J. Dis. Child.,* **78,** 182–200.

Horne, B. M., and C. C. Philles: 1942. A comparative study of the spontaneous play activities of normal and mentally defective children. *J. genet. Psychol.,* **61,** 33–46.

Horney, K.: 1939. *New ways in psychoanalysis.* New York: Norton.

————: 1951. On feeling abused. *Amer. J. Psychoanal.,* **11,** 5–12.

Horowitz, E. L.: 1935. Spatial localization of the self. *J. soc. Psychol.,* **6,** 379–387.

Horowitz, R. E.: 1939. Racial aspects of self-identification in nursery school children. *J. Psychol.,* **7,** 91–99.

————: 1943. A pictorial method for study of self-identification in preschool children. *J. genet. Psychol.,* **62,** 135–148.

Horrocks, J. E.: 1951. *The psychology of adolescence.* Boston: Houghton Mifflin.

———— and M. E. Buker: 1951. A study of the friendship fluctuations of preadolescents. *J. genet. Psychol.,* **78,** 131–144.

———— and G. G. Thompson: 1946. A study of the friendship fluctuations of rural boys and girls. *J. genet. Psychol.,* **69,** 189–198.

Hoult, T. F.: 1949. Comic books and juvenile delinquency. *Sociol. soc. Res.,* **33,** 279–284.

Houston, T. J., and F. C. Sumner: 1948. Measurements of neurotic tendency in women with uncommon given names. *J. gen. Psychol.,* **39,** 289–292.

Howard, P. J., and C. H. Morrell: 1952. Premature infants in later life: study of intelligence and personality of 22 premature infants at ages 8 to 19 years. *Pediatrics,* **9,** 577–584.

Howard, R. W.: 1934. *A developmental study of triplets.* Ph.D. thesis. Minnesota: University of Minnesota.

————: 1946. Intellectual and personality traits of a group of triplets. *J. Psychol.,* **21,** 25–36.

————: 1946a. The language development of a group of triplets. *J. genet. Psychol.,* **69,** 181–188.

————: 1947. The developmental history of a group of triplets. *J. genet. Psychol.,* **70,** 191–204.

Howells, W. W.: 1948. Birth order and body size. *Amer. J. phys. Anthrop.*, **6**, 449–460.

———: 1949. Body measurements in the light of familial influence. *Amer. J. phys. Anthrop.*, **7**, 101–108.

Hsiao, H. H.: 1931. The status of the first-born with special reference to intelligence. *Genet. Psychol. Monogr.*, **9**, 1–118.

Huang, I.: 1943. Children's conceptions of physical causality: a critical summary. *J. genet. Psychol.*, **63**, 71–121.

——— and Y. J. Chen: 1936. Social function of children's language. *Chung Hua educ. Rev.*, **23**, 69–94.

——— and H. W. Lee: 1943. Experimental analysis of child animism. *J. genet. Psychol.*, **63**, 71–121.

——— and ———: 1945. Experimental analysis of child animism. *J. genet. Psychol.*, **66**, 69–74.

Huff, R. L.: 1927. Percept content of school children's minds. *J. genet. Psychol.*, **34**, 129–143.

Hughes, M. A., and L. Stockdale: 1940. The young child and graphic expression. *Childhood Educ.*, **16**, 307–314.

Hughes, M. M.: 1945. Learning new ways of behaving. *Childhood Educ.*, **22**, 125–131.

Hull, C. L.: 1920. Quantitative aspects of the evolution of concepts. *Psychol. Monogr.*, **28**, No. 123.

Hulson, E. L.: 1930. An analysis of the free play of ten four-year-old children through consecutive observations. *J. juv. Res.*, **14**, 188–208.

Humphrey, M. E.: 1951. Consistency of hand usage. *Brit. J. educ. Psychol.*, **21**, 214–225.

Hunt, J. McV., and R. L. Solomon: 1942. The stability and some correlations of group status in a summer-camp group of young boys. *Amer. J. Psychol.*, **55**, 33–45.

Hunt, W. A.: 1939. "Body jerk" as a concept in describing infant behavior. *J. genet. Psychol.*, **55**, 215–220.

——— and F. M. Clarke: 1937. The startle pattern in children and identical twins. *J. exp. Psychol.*, **21**, 259–362.

———, ———, and E. B. Hunt: 1936. Studies of the startle pattern. IV. Infants. *J. Psychol.*, **2**, 339–352.

Huntington, E.: 1938. *Season of birth: its relation to human abilities.* New York: Wiley.

Hurley, B. J.: 1949. The handicapped child as a person. *Understanding the Child*, **18**, 9.

Hurlock, E. B.: 1924. The value of praise and reproof as incentives for children. *Arch. Psychol., N.Y.*, No. 71.

———: 1925. An evaluation of certain incentives used in school work. *J. educ. Psychol.*, **16**, 145–159.

———: 1927. The use of group rivalry as an incentive. *J. abnorm. soc. Psychol.*, **22**, 278–290.

———: 1927a. A study of self-ratings by children. *J. appl. Psychol.*, **11**, 490–502.

———: 1929. *The psychology of dress.* New York: Ronald.

———: 1929a. Motivation in fashion. *Arch. Psychol., N.Y.*, No. 111.

———: 1943. *Modern ways with children.* New York: Whittlesey.

——— and M. Burstein: 1932. The imaginary playmate: a questionnaire study. *J. genet. Psychol.*, **41**, 380–392.

——— and L. C. McDonald: 1934. Undesirable behavior traits in junior-high-school students. *Child Develpm.*, **5**, 278–290.

——— and S. Sender: 1930. The "negative phase" in relation to the behavior of pubescent girls. *Child Develpm.*, **1**, 325–340.

——— and J. L. Thomson: 1934. Children's drawings: an experimental study of perception. *Child Develpm.*, **5**, 127–138.

Hurme, V. O.: 1948. Standards of variation in the eruption of the first six permanent teeth. *Child Develpm., 19,* 213–231.

Ilg, F. L., and L. B. Ames: 1950. Developmental trends in reading behavior. *J. genet. Psychol., 76,* 291–312.

——— and ———: 1951. Developmental trends in arithmetic. *J. genet. Psychol., 79,* 3–28.

———, J. Learned, A. Lockwood, and L. B. Ames: 1949. The three-and-a-half-year-old. *J. genet. Psychol., 75,* 21–31.

Iliff, A., and V. A. Lee: 1952. Pulse rate, respiration rate, and body temperature of children between two months and eighteen years. *Child Develpm., 23,* 237–245.

Illingworth, R. S.: 1951. Sleep problems in the first three years. *Brit. med. J., 1,* 722–728.

———, C. C. Harvey, and S-Y. Gin: 1949. Relation of birth weight to physical development in childhood. *Lancet, 247,* 598–602.

———, ———, and G. H. Jawett: 1950. The relation of birth weight to physical growth: a statistical study. *Arch. Dis. Child., 25,* 380–388.

Ingalls, T. H.: 1950. Congenital deformities not inherited. *New York Times,* Dec. 20.

Ingersoll, H. L.: 1949. A study of the transmission of authority patterns in the family. *Genet. Psychol. Monogr., 38,* 225–302.

Ingham, H. V.: 1949. A statistical study of family relationships in psychoneurosis. *Amer. J. Psychiat., 106,* 91–98.

Irwin, O. C.: 1930. The amount and nature of activities of newborn infants under constant external stimulating conditions during the first ten days of life. *Genet. Psychol. Monogr., 8,* No. 1, 1–92.

———: 1932. Infant responses to vertical movements. *Child Develpm., 3,* 167–169.

———: 1932a. The amount of motility of seventy-three infants. *J. comp. Psychol., 14,* 415–428.

———: 1932b. The distribution of the amount of motility in young infants between two nursing periods. *J. comp. Psychol., 14,* 429–445.

———: 1932c. The latent time of body startle in infants. *Child Develpm., 2,* 104–107.

———: 1933. Motility in young infants. I. Relation to body temperature. *Amer. J. Dis. Child., 45,* 531–533.

———: 1941. Effect of strong light on the body activity of newborns. *J. comp. Psychol., 32,* 233–236.

———: 1941a. Research on speech sounds for the first six months of life. *Psychol. Bull., 38,* 277–285.

———: 1942. The developmental status of speech sounds of ten feebleminded children. *Child Develpm., 13,* 29–39.

———: 1947. Development of speech during infancy: curve of phonemic frequencies. *J. exp. Psychol., 37,* 187–193.

———: 1947a. Consonant sounds according to manner of articulation. *J. Speech Hearing Disorders, 12,* 402–404.

———: 1948. Infant speech: development of vowel sounds. *J. Speech Hearing Disorders, 13,* 31–34.

———: 1948a. Infant speech: the effect of family occupational status and of age on sound frequencies. *J. Speech Hearing Disorders, 13,* 320–323.

———: 1948b. Infant speech: speech sound development of sibling and only infants. *J. exp. Psychol., 38,* 600–602.

———: 1951. Infant speech: consonantal position. *J. Speech Hearing Disorders, 16,* 159–161.

——— and H. P. Chen: 1941. A reliability study of speech sounds observed in the crying of newborn infants. *Child Develpm., 12,* 351–368.

—— and ——: 1943. Speech sound elements during the first years of life: a review of the literature. *J. Speech Hearing Disorders*, **8**, 109–121.

—— and ——: 1946. Development of speech during infancy: curve of phonemic types. *J. exp. Psychol.*, **36**, 431–436.

—— and T. Curry: 1941. Vowel elements in the crying vocalizations of infants under ten days of age. *Child Develpm.*, **12**, 99–109.

—— and L. A. Weiss: 1934. Differential variations in the activity and crying of the newborn infant under different intensities of light: a comparison of observational with polygraph findings. *Univ. Ia. Stud. Child Welf.*, **9**, No. 4, 139–147.

—— and ——: 1934a. The effect of clothing on the general and vocal activity of the newborn infant. *Univ. Ia. Stud. Child Welf.*, **9**, No. 4, 165–175.

Isaacs, S.: 1940. Temper tantrums in early childhood in their relation to internal objects. *Int. J. Psychoanal.*, **21**, 280–293.

——, S. C. Brown, and R. H. Thonless: 1941. *The Cambridge Evacuation Survey*. London: Methuen.

Isch, M. J.: 1952. Fantasied mother-child interaction in doll play. *J. genet. Psychol.*, **81**, 233–258.

Itkin, W.: 1952. Some relationships between intrafamily attitudes and preparental attitudes toward children. *J. genet. Psychol.*, **80**, 221–252.

Jack, L. M.: 1934. An experimental study of ascendant behavior in preschool children. *Univ. Ia. Stud. Child Welf.*, **9**, No. 3.

Jackson, J.: 1953. A statistical analysis of an alumni survey. *J. genet. Psychol.*, **82**, 215–234.

Jackson, L.: 1950. Emotional attitudes toward the family of normal, neurotic, and delinquent children. *Brit. J. Psychol.*, **41**, 173–185.

Jackson, V. D.: 1940. The measurement of social proficiency. *J. exp. Educ.*, **8**, 422–474.

Jacobs, R.: 1949. Stability of interests at the secondary school level. *Educ. Rec. Bull.*, **52**, 83–87.

Jahoda, G.: 1952. Job attitudes and job choice among secondary modern school leavers, II. *Occup. Psychol., London*, **26**, 206–224.

James, H. E. O.: 1943. Adolescent leisure. *Lancet*, **244**, 504.

James, W.: 1890. *The principles of psychology*. New York: Holt.

Jameson, S. G.: 1940. Adjustment problems of university girls because of parental patterns. *Sociol. soc. Res.*, **24**, 262–271.

Jeans, P. C.: 1950. Feeding of healthy infants and children. *J. Amer. med. Ass.*, **142**, 806–813.

Jenkins, L. M.: 1930. A comparative study of motor achievements of children at five, six, and seven years of age. *Teach. Coll. Contr. Educ.*, No. 414.

Jennings, H.: 1937. Structure of leadership-development and sphere of influence. *Sociometry*, **1**, 99–143.

Jennings, H. C.: 1930. *The biological basis of human nature*. New York: Norton.

Jennings, H. H.: 1944. *Leadership and isolation*. New York: Longmans.

Jensen, K.: 1932. Differential reactions in newborn infants. *Genet. Psychol. Monogr.*, **12**, 361–479.

——: 1939. The social studies. *38th Yearb. nat. Soc. Stud. Educ.*, Pt. 1, 325–360.

Jersild, A. T.: 1932. Training and growth in the development of children. *Child Develpm. Monogr.*, **10**, 1–73.

——: 1933. The constancy of certain behavior patterns in young children. *Amer. J. Psychol.*, **45**, 125–129.

——: 1936. Research in the development of children. *Teach. Coll. Rec.*, **38**, 132–138.

——: 1939. Music. *38th Yearb. nat. Soc. Stud. Educ.*, 135–151.

————: 1948. Children's fears. *J. nat. Educ. Ass.*, **37**, 212–213.

————: 1951. Self-understanding in childhood and adolescence. *Amer. Psychologist*, **6**, 22–26.

————: 1952. *In search of self*. New York: Teachers College Bureau of Publications.

————: 1954. *Child psychology*, 4th ed. New York: Prentice-Hall.

————: 1954a. Emotional development. *In* L. Carmichael, *Manual of child psychology*, 2d ed. New York: Wiley, pp. 833–917.

———— and S. F. Bienstock: 1935. Development of rhythm in young children. *Child Develpm. Monogr.*, No. 22.

———— and M. D. Fite: 1939. The influence of nursery school experience on children's social adjustments. *Child Develpm. Monogr.*, No. 25.

————, B. Goldman, and J. J. Loftus: 1941. A comparative study of the worries of children in two school situations. *J. exp. Educ.*, **9**, 323–326.

———— and F. B. Holmes: 1935. Children's fears. *Child Develpm. Monogr.*, No. 20.

———— and ————: 1935a. Methods of overcoming children's fears. *J. Psychol.*, **1**, 75–104.

———— and ————: 1935b. Some factors in the development of children's fears. *J. exp. Educ.*, **4**, 133–141.

———— and F. V. Markey: 1935. Conflicts between preschool children. *Child Develpm. Monogr.*, No. 21.

————, ————, and C. L. Jersild: 1933. Children's fears, dreams, wishes, daydreams, likes, dislikes, pleasant and unpleasant memories. *Child Develpm. Monogr.*, No. 12.

———— and M. M. Meigs: 1943. Children and war. *Psychol. Bull.*, **40**, 541–573.

———— and R. Ritzman: 1938. Aspects of language development: the growth of loquacity and vocabulary. *Child Develpm.*, **9**, 243–259.

———— and R. J. Tasch: 1949. *Children's interests and what they suggest for education*. New York: Teachers College Bureau of Publications.

————, E. S. Woodyard, and C. del Solar: 1949. *Joys and problems of child rearing*. New York: Teachers College Bureau of Publications.

John, E.: 1941. A study of the effects of evacuation and air-raids on children of preschool age. *Brit. J. educ. Psychol.*, **11**, 173–182.

Johnson, B. J.: 1928. Changes in muscular tension in coordinated hand movements. *J. exp. Psychol.*, **11**, 329–341.

————: 1936. Variations in emotional responses of children. *Child Develpm.*, **7**, 85–94.

Johnson, H. M.: 1933. *The art of block building.* New York: Day.

Johnson, J. O.: 1950. *A study of the social position of mentally handicapped children in regular grades*. Ph.D. thesis. Urbana, Ill.: University of Illinois.

Johnson, L.: 1932. Children's reading interests as related to sex and grade in school. *Sch. Rev.*, **11**, 257–272.

Johnson, M. W.: 1935. The effect on behavior of variation in the amount of play equipment. *Child Develpm.*, **6**, 56–68.

Johnson, P. P.: 1952. Conceptions of parenthood held by adolescents. *J. abnorm. soc. Psychol.*, **47**, 783–789.

Johnson, W.: 1942. A study of the onset and development of stuttering. *J. Speech Hearing Disorders*, **7**, 251–257.

———— and V. Bissell: 1940. Iowa hand usage dextrality quotients of one hundred high school students. *J. educ. Psychol.*, **38**, 148–151.

————, S. F. Brown, J. F. Curtis, C. W. Edney, and J. Keaster: 1948. *Speech handicapped children*. New York: Harper.

———— and D. Duke: 1940. Revised Iowa hand usage dextrality quotients of six-year-olds. *J. educ. Psychol.*, **31**, 45–52.

Jolles, I.: 1952. A study of the validity of some hypotheses for the qualitative interpretation of the H-T-P for children of elementary school age. I. Sexual identification. *J. clin. Psychol.*, **8**, 113–118.

Jones, H.: 1951. Maintenance of mental health. *Ment. Hlth, Lond.*, **10**, 40–42.

Jones, H. E.: 1939. Relationships in physical and mental development. *Rev. educ. Res.*, **9**, 91–110.

————: 1943. *Development in adolescence.* New York: Appleton-Century-Crofts.

————: 1946. Skeletal maturing as related to strength. *Child Develpm.*, **17**, 173–185.

————: 1949. *Motor performance and growth.* Berkeley, Calif.: University of California Press.

————: 1954. The environment and mental development. *In* L. Carmichael, *Manual of child psychology*, 2d ed. New York: Wiley, pp. 631–696.

———— and H. H. Hsiao: 1928. A preliminary study of intelligence as a function of birth order. *J. genet. Psychol.*, **35**, 428–433.

———— and M. C. Jones: 1928. A study of fear. *Childhood Educ.*, **5**, 136–143.

Jones, M. C.: 1924. A laboratory study of fear: the case of Peter. *J. genet. Psychol.*, **31**, 308–315.

————: 1924a. The elimination of children's fear. *J. exp. Psychol.*, **7**, 382–390.

————: 1926. The development of early behavior patterns in young children. *J. genet. Psychol.*, **33**, 537–585.

————: 1948. Adolescent friendships. *Amer. Psychologist*, **3**, 352.

Jones, T. D.: 1939. The development of certain motor skills and play activities in young children. *Child Develpm. Monogr.*, No. 26.

Jones, V.: 1936. *Character and citizenship training in the public school.* Chicago: University of Chicago Press.

————: 1954. Character development in children—an objective approach. *In* L. Carmichael, *Manual of child psychology*, 2d ed New York: Wiley, pp. 781–832.

Jordon, A. M.: 1942. *Educational psychology*, 3d ed. New York: Holt.

Josselyn, I. M.: 1953. The family as a psychological unit. *Soc. Casework*, **34**, 336–344.

Jung, C. G.: 1928. *Contributions to analytical psychology.* New York: Harcourt, Brace.

Jurovsky, A.: 1948. The relation of older children to their parents. *J. genet. Psychol.*, **72**, 85–100.

Justin, F.: 1932. A genetic study of laughter provoking stimuli. *Child Develpm.*, **3**, 114–136.

————: 1950. Home training in human values. *J. Home Econ.*, **47**, 722.

Kahl, J. A.: 1953. Educational and occupational aspirations of "common man" boys. *Harv. educ. Rev.*, **23**, 186–203.

Kahn, E., and L. W. Simmons: 1940. Problems of middle age. *Yale Rev.*, **29**, 349–363.

Kahn, H. A.: 1951. Changing causes of death in childhood. *Pub. Hlth Rep.*, **66**, 1246–1247.

Kallman, F. J., and G. Sander: 1949. Twin studies in senescence. *Amer. J. Psychiat.*, **106**, 29–36.

Kambouropoulon, P.: 1926. Individual differences in the sense of humor. *Amer. J. Psychol.*, **37**, 268–278.

Kanner, L.: 1942. *Child psychiatry.* Springfield, Ill.: Charles C. Thomas.

————: 1951. Emotional cultural impacts on contemporary motherhood. *J. child Psychiat.*, **2**, 168–175.

Kaplan, L.: 1952. The annoyances of elementary school teachers. *J. educ. Res.*, **45**, 649–665.

Kaplan, O. J.: 1946. Age and vocational choice. *J. genet. Psychol.*, **68**, 131–134.

Karlin, I. W., A. C. Youtz, and L. Kennedy: 1940. Distorted speech in young children. *Amer. J. Dis. Child.*, **59**, 1203–1218.

Kasatkin, N. I., and A. M. Levikova: 1935. On the development of early conditioned reflexes and differentiations of auditory stimuli in infants. *J. exp. Psychol.,* **18,** 1–19.

Kasser, E.: 1945. The growth and decline of a child's slang vocabulary at Mooseheart: a self-contained community. *J. genet. Psychol.,* **66,** 129–137.

Kastein, S.: 1947. The chewing method of treating stuttering. *J. Speech Hearing Disorders,* **12,** 195–198.

Katcher, A., and M. M. Levin: 1955. Children's conceptions of body size. *Child Develpm.,* **26,** 103–110.

Kates, S. L.: 1951. Suggestibility, submission to parents and peers, and extrapunitiveness, intropunitiveness, and impunitiveness in children. *J. Psychol.,* **31,** 233–241.

Katz, E.: 1940. The relationship of I.Q. to height and weight from three to five years. *J. genet. Psychol.,* **57,** 65–82.

———: 1944. *Children's preferences for traditional and modern paintings.* New York: Teachers College Bureau of Publications.

Katz, S. E., and F. S. Breed: 1922. The color preferences of children. *J. appl. Psychol.,* **6,** 255–266.

Kawin, E.: 1934. *Children of pre-school age.* Chicago: University of Chicago Press.

Kehm, F. S.: 1950. Family life education—future tense? *J. educ. Res.,* **43,** 601–613.

Keister, M. E.: 1950. Relation of mid-morning feeding to behavior of nursery school children. *J. Amer. diet. Ass.,* **26,** 25–29.

Keliher, A. V.: 1943. Expect this from children when mothers work. *Prog. Educ.,* **20,** 335–337.

Kellogg, W. N.: 1941. A method for recording the activity of the human fetus *in utero,* with specimen results. *J. genet. Psychol.,* **51,** 307–326.

——— and B. M. Eagleson: 1931. The growth of social perceptions in different racial groups. *J. educ. Psychol.,* **22,** 367–375.

Kelting, L. S.: 1934. An investigation of the feeding, sleeping, crying, and social behavior of infants. *J. exp. Educ.,* **3,** 97–106.

Kenderdine, M.: 1931. Laughter in the preschool child. *Child Develpm.,* **2,** 228–230.

Kent, D. P.: 1951. Subjective factors in mate selection—an exploratory study. *Sociol. soc. Res.,* **35,** 391–398.

Kent, E.: 1949. A study of maladjusted twins. *Smith Coll. Stud. soc. Work,* **19,** 63–77.

Kepler, H.: 1934. Distribution of aggressive and submissive behavior among two hundred problem children. *Smith Coll. Stud. soc. Work,* **4,** 167–168.

Kernstetter, L. M.: 1944. Exploring the environment in a classroom situation. *Sociometry,* **9,** 149–150.

Kestenberg, J. S.: 1946. Early fears and early defenses. *Nerv. Child,* **5,** 56–70.

Keston, M. J., and I. M. Pinto: 1955. Possible factors influencing musical preferences. *J. genet. Psychol.,* **86,** 101–113.

Key, C. B., M. R. White, W. P. Honzig, A. B. Heiney, and D. Erwin: 1936. The process of learning to dress among nursery-school children. *Genet. Psychol. Monogr.,* **18,** 67–163.

Kidd, J. W.: 1951. An analysis of social rejection in a college men's residence hall. *Sociometry,* **14,** 226–234.

Kimmins, C. W.: 1928. *The springs of laughter.* London: Methuen.

Kingsbury, D.: 1946. Feet for the future. *Parents' Mag.,* **21,** 34, 104–105.

Kingsley, A., and E. L. Reynolds: 1949. The relation of illness patterns in children to ordinal position in the family. *J. Pediat.,* **35,** 17–23.

Kinney, E. E.: 1953. A study of peer group acceptability at the fifth grade level in a public school. *J. educ. Res.,* **47,** 57–64.

Kinsey, A. C., W. B. Pomeroy, and C. E. Martin: 1948. *Sexual behavior in the human male*. Philadelphia: Saunders.

——, ——, ——, and P. H. Gebhard: 1953. *Sexual behavior in the human female*. Philadelphia: Saunders.

Kirkendall, L. A.: 1948. Sex problems of adolescents. *Marr. Hyg.*, **1**, 205–208.

Klapp, O. E.: 1949. The fool as a social type. *Amer. J. Sociol.*, **55**, 157–162.

Klatskin, E. H.: 1952. Shifts in child care practices in three classes under an infant care program of flexible methodology. *Amer. J. Orthopsychiat.*, **22**, 52–61.

Klausner, S. Z.: 1953. Social class and self-concept. *J. soc. Psychol.*, **38**, 201–205.

Klein, A.: 1939. Failure and subjects liked and disliked. *High Point*, **21**, 22–25.

Klein, E. T.: 1950. Abnormal pressure habits. *Dent. Surv.*, **6**, 1081.

Klein, H.: 1946. The family and dental disease. IV. Dental disease experienced in parents and offspring. *J. Amer. dent. Ass.*, **33**, 735–743.

——, C. E. Palmer, and M. Kramer: 1937. Studies on dental caries. II. The use of the normal probability curve for expressing the age distribution of eruption of the permanent teeth. *Growth*, **1**, 385–394.

——, ——, and J. W. Knutson: 1938. Studies on dental caries. *Pub. Hlth Rep.*, **53**, 751–765.

Kleitman, N.: 1939. *Sleep and wakefulness*. Chicago: University of Chicago Press.

Klineberg, O.: 1953. Cultural factors in personality adjustment of children. *Amer. J. Orthopsychiat.*, **33**, 465–471.

Klingensmith, S. W.: 1953. Child animism: what the child means by "alive." *Child Develpm.*, **24**, 51–61.

Klopfer, B.: 1939. Personality differences between boys and girls in early childhood. *Psychol. Bull.*, **36**, 538.

Knauber, A. J.: 1931. A study of the art ability found in very young children. *Child Develpm.*, **2**, 66–71.

Knehr, C. A., and A. Sobel: 1949. Mental ability of prematurely born children at early school age. *J. Psychol.*, **27**, 355–361.

Knopf, I. J., and T. W. Richards: 1952. The child's differentiation in sex as reflected in drawings of the human figure. *J. genet. Psychol.*, **81**, 99–112.

Koch, H. L.: 1933. Popularity in preschool children: some related factors and a technique for its measurement. *Child Develpm.*, **4**, 164–175.

——: 1935. An analysis of certain forms of so-called "nervous habits" in young children. *J. genet. Psychol.*, **46**, 139–170.

——: 1944. A study of some factors conditioning the social distance between the sexes. *J. soc. Psychol.*, **20**, 79–107.

——: 1946. The social distance between certain racial, nationality, and skin pigmentation groups in select populations of American school children. *J. genet. Psychol.*, **68**, 63–95.

——: 1954. The relation of "primary mental abilities" in five- and six-year-olds to sex of child and characteristics of his sibling. *Child Develpm.*, **25**, 209–223.

——: 1955. The relation of certain family constellation characteristics and the attitudes of children toward adults. *Child Develpm.*, **26**, 13–40.

Koenig, F. G.: 1953. Improving the language abilities of bilingual children. *Except. Child*, **14**, 183–186.

Koffka, K.: 1925. *The growth of the mind*. New York: Harcourt.

Koller, M. R.: 1954. Studies of three-generation households. *Marriage Fam. Living*, **16**, 203–206.

Komarovsky, M.: 1946. Cultural contradictions and sex roles. *Amer. J. Sociol.*, **52**, 184–189.

———: 1950. Functional analysis of sex roles. *Amer. sociol. Rev.*, **15**, 508–516.

Korner, A. F.: 1947. *Some aspects of hostility in young children.* Ph.D. thesis. New York: Columbia University.

Koshuk, R. P.: 1947. Developmental records of 500 nursery school children. *J. exp. Educ.*, **16**, 134–148.

Krall, V.: 1953. Personality characteristics of accident-repeating children. *J. abnorm. soc. Psychol.*, **48**, 99–107.

Krogman, W. M.: 1939. Facing facts of face growth. *Amer. J. Orthod. Oral Surg.*, **25**, 279–284.

———: 1948. A handbook of the measurement and interpretation of height and weight in the growing child. *Monogr. Soc. Res. Child Develpm.*, **13**, No. 3.

Kuhlen, R. G.: 1952. *The psychology of adolescent development.* New York: Harper.

——— and M. Arnold: 1944. Age differences in religious beliefs and problems during adolescence. *J. genet. Psychol.*, **65**, 291–300.

——— and B. J. Lee: 1943. Personality characteristics and social acceptability in adolescence. *J. educ. Psychol.*, **34**, 321–340.

——— and G. G. Thompson: 1952. *Psychological studies of human development.* New York: Appleton-Century-Crofts.

Kuhlmann, F.: 1922. *A handbook of mental tests.* Baltimore: Warwick & York.

Kunst, M. S.: 1948. A study of thumb- and finger-sucking in infants. *Psychol. Monogr.*, **62**, No. 3.

LaBarre, W.: 1949. The age period of cultural fixation. *Ment. Hyg., N.Y.*, **33**, 209–221.

Lacey, J. I., and K. M. Dallenbach: 1939. Acquisition by children of the cause-effect relationship. *Amer. J. Psychol.*, **52**, 103–110.

Lafore, G. G.: 1945. Practices of parents in dealing with preschool children. *Child Develpm. Monogr.*, No. 31.

Laing, A.: 1939. The sense of humour in childhood and adolescence. *Brit. J. educ. Psychol.*, **9**, 201.

Laird, D. A., and H. Drexel: 1934. Experimenting with foods and sleep. *Amer. J. Dietet. Ass.*, **10**, 89–97.

Landis, C., et al.: 1940. *Sex in development.* New York: Hoeber.

Landis, J. T.: 1954. Personality—a 1954 view. *J. Home Econ.*, **46**, 459–462.

Landis, P. H.: 1951. Marriage preparation in two generations. *Marriage Fam. Living*, **13**, 155–156.

———: 1952. *Adolescence and youth: the process of maturing.* New York: McGraw-Hill.

Landreth, C.: 1941. Factors associated with crying in young children in the nursery school and the home. *Child Develpm.*, **12**, 81–97.

——— and B. C. Johnson: 1953. Young children's responses to a picture and inset test designed to reveal reactions to persons of different skin color. *Child Develpm.*, **24**, 63–80.

Langford, L. M., and O. W. Alm: 1954. A comparison of parent judgments and child feelings concerning the self adjustment and social adjustment of twelve-year-old children. *J. genet. Psychol.*, **85**, 39–46.

Lantagne, J. E.: 1950. An analysis of the health interests of 3,000 secondary school children. *Res. Quart. Amer. phys. Educ. Ass.*, **21**, 34–39.

Lantz, H.: 1949. Religious participation and social orientation of 1,000 university students. *Sociol. soc. Res.*, **33**, 285–291.

Lark-Horovitz, B.: 1937. On art appreciation of children. I. Preference of picture subjects in general. *J. educ. Res.*, **31**, 118–137.

————: 1938. On art appreciation of children. II. Portrait preference study. *J. educ. Res.*, **31**, 572–598.

————: 1939. On art appreciation of children. III. Textile pattern preference study. *J. educ. Res.*, **33**, 7–35.

Lasko, J. K.: 1952. Parent-child relationships: report from the Fels Research Institute. *Amer. J. Orthopsychiat.*, **22**, 300–304.

————: 1954. Parent behavior toward first and second children. *Genet. Psychol. Monogr.*, **49**, 97–137.

Lasswell, H. D.: 1948. *Power and personality*. New York: Norton.

Latif, I.: 1934. The physiological basis of linguistic development and the ontogeny of meaning. I. *Psychol. Rev.*, **41**, 55–85.

————: 1934a. The physiological basis of linguistic development and of the ontogeny of meaning. II. *Psychol. Rev.*, **41**, 153–156.

Laughlin, F.: 1953. *A study of the peer status of sixth and seventh grade children*. Ph.D. thesis. New York: Teachers College.

Lawton, G.: 1938. Fears: their cause and prevention. *Child Develpm.*, **9**, 151–159.

————: 1943. *New goals for old age*. New York: Columbia University Press.

————: 1951. *Aging successfully*. New York: Columbia University Press.

Laycock, S. R.: 1950. Effect of the teacher's personality on the behavior of pupils. *Understanding the Child*, **19**, 50–55.

Lazar, M.: 1937. *Reading interests, activities, and opportunities of bright, average, and dull pupils*. New York: Teachers College Bureau of Publications.

Lazarsfeld, P. F., and F. N. Stanton: 1944. *Radio research*. New York: Duell, Sloane, & Pearce.

Leal, M. A.: 1929. *Physiological maturity in relation to certain characteristics of boys and girls*. Philadelphia: University of Pennsylvania Press.

Lederer, R. K.: 1939. An exploratory investigation of handed status in the first two years of life. *Univ. Ia. Stud. Child Welf.*, **16**, No. 2.

Lee, M. A. M.: 1932. A study of emotional instability in nursery school children. *Child Develpm.*, **3**, 142–145.

Lee, M. R.: 1952. Background factors related to sex information and attitudes. *J. educ. Psychol.*, **43**, 467–485.

Leeds, C. H.: 1954. Teacher behavior liked and disliked by pupils. *Education*, **75**, 29–37.

Lehman, H. C.: 1926. A comparison of the play activities of town and country children. *J. genet. Psychol.*, **33**, 455–476.

————: 1928. The child's attitude toward the dog versus the cat. *J. genet. Psychol.*, **35**, 62–72.

———— and T. H. Anderson: 1927. Social participation versus solitariness in play. *J. genet. Psychol.*, **34**, 278–298.

———— and P. A. Witty: 1927. Periodicity and play behavior. *J. educ. Psychol.*, **18**, 115–118.

———— and ————: 1927a. *The psychology of play activities*. New York: A. S. Barnes.

———— and ————: 1928. A study of play in relation to intelligence. *J. appl. Psychol.*, **12**, 369–397.

———— and ————: 1928a. Some compensatory mechanisms of the Negro. *J. abnorm. soc. Psychol.*, **23**, 28–37.

———— and ————: 1928b. Some compensatory mechanisms of the Negro. *J. abnorm. soc. Psychol.*, **23**, 28–37.

———— and ————: 1931. A study of vocational attitudes in relation to pubescence. *Amer. J. Psychol.*, **43**, 93–101.

Lemasters, E. E.: 1954. Social class mobility and family integration. *Marriage Fam. Living*, **16**, 226–232.

Leonard, A.: 1952. Toys for toddlers. *Today's Health*, December, 42–43, 60.

Leonard, E. A.: 1920. A parent's study of children's lies. *J. genet. Psychol.*, **27**, 105–135.

Leopold, W. F.; 1949. Speech development of a bilingual child. *Northw. Univ. Stud. Human.*, **3**, No. 18.

Lerner, E.: 1937. *Constraint areas and the moral judgment of children.* Menasha, Wis.: Banta.

—— and L. B. Murphy: 1941. Methods for the study of personality in young children. *Monogr. Soc. Res. Child Develpm.*, **6**, No. 4.

Leroy, A.: 1950. Dessins en transparence et niveau de développement. *Enfance*, **3**, 276–287.

——: 1951. Representation of perspective in the drawings of children. *Enfance*, **4**, 286–307.

Leuba, C.: 1933. An experimental study of rivalry in young children. *J. comp. Psychol.*, **16**, 367–378.

——: 1941. Tickling and laughter: two genetic studies. *J. genet. Psychol.*, **58**, 201–209.

Leuba, J. H.: 1916. *The belief in God and immortality.* Boston: Sherman, French.

Levinson, E. D.: 1949. Fetal defects following rubella in the pregnant mother. *McGill med. J.*, **18**, 183–198.

Levy, D. M.: 1928. Fingersucking and accessory movements in early infancy. *Amer. J. Psychiat.*, **7**, 881–918.

——: 1930. Paper on maternal overprotection. *Amer. J. Psychiat.*, **9**, 904.

——: 1933. Relation of maternal overprotection to school grades and intelligence tests. *Amer. J. Orthopsychiat.*, **3**, 26–34.

——: 1936. Hostility patterns in sibling rivalry experiments. *Amer. J. Orthopsychiat.*, **6**, 183–257.

——: 1937. Studies in sibling rivalry. *Res. Monogr. Amer. Orthopsychiat. Ass.*, No. 2.

——: 1939. Maternal overprotection. *Psychiatry*, **2**, 563–568.

——: 1943. *Maternal overprotection.* New York: Columbia Univ. Press.

—— and A. Hess: 1952. Problems in determining maternal attitudes toward newborn infants. *Psychiatry*, **15**, 273–286.

—— and S. H. Tulchin: 1925. The resistant behavior of infants and children during mental tests. *J. exp. Psychol.*, **6**, 304–322.

Levy, J.: 1931. A quantitative study of behavior problems in relation to family constellation. *Amer. J. Psychiat.*, **10**, 637–654.

Lewin, H. S.: 1953. Facts and fears about the comics. *Nation's Schools*, **52**, 46–48.

Lewin, K.: 1935. *Dynamic theory of personality.* New York: McGraw-Hill.

—— and P. Grable: 1945. Conduct, knowledge, and acceptance of new values. *J. soc. Issues*, **1**, 53–64.

——, R. Lippitt, and R. K. White: 1939. Patterns of aggressive behavior in experimentally created "social climates." *J. soc. Psychol.*, **10**, 271–299.

Lewis, M.: 1931. How parental attitudes affect the problem of lying in children. *Smith Coll. Stud. soc. Work*, **1**, 403–404.

Lewis, M. M.: 1951. *Infant speech: a study of the beginnings of language.* 2d ed. New York: Humanities Press.

Lewis, S. J.: 1933. The proper time to start orthodontic treatment. *Amer. J. dent. Ass.*, **20**, 693–707.

—— and I. G. Lehman: 1929. Observations on growth changes of the teeth and dental arches. *Dent. Cosmos*, **71**, 5.

Lewis, W. D.: 1945. Influence of parental attitudes on children's personal inventory scores. *J. genet. Psychol.*, **67**, 195–201.

Lézine, I.: 1951. Researches on the stages of taking consciousness of self in young twins. *Enfance*, **4**, 35–49.

Ligon, E. M.: 1939. *Their future is now.* New York: Macmillan.

Lindgren, H. C.: 1952. The development of a scale of cultural idealization based on the California Test of Personality. *J. educ. Psychol.*, **43**, 81–91.

Lindzey, G., and S. Rogolsky: 1950. Prejudice and identification of minority group membership. *J. abnorm. soc. Psychol.*, **45**, 37–55.

Ling, B. C.: 1941. Form discrimination as a learning cue in infants. *Comp. Psychol. Monogr.*, **17**, No. 2.

Link, H. C.: 1944. The definition of social effectiveness and leadership through measurement. *Educ. psychol. Measmt*, **4**, 57–67.

Linton, R.: 1942. Age and sex categories. *Amer. sociol. Rev.*, **7**, 589–603.

Lippitt, R.: 1941. Popularity among preschool children. *Child Develpm.*, **12**, 305–332.

——— and R. K. White: 1947. An experimental study of leadership and group life. *In* T. M. Newcomb, *Readings in social psychology.* New York: Holt, pp. 315–330.

Lippman, H. S.: 1927. Certain behavior responses in early infancy. *J. genet. Psychol.*, **34**, 424–440.

Liu, C. H.: 1950. *The influence of cultural background on the moral judgments of children.* Ph.D. thesis. New York: Columbia University.

Lockhart, E. G.: 1930. The attitudes of children toward certain laws. *Relig. Educ.*, **25**, 144–149.

———: 1930a. The attitude of children toward law. *Univ. Ia. Stud. Charact.*, **3**, No. 1.

———: 1939. *Improving your personality.* Chicago: Walton.

Loeb, N.: 1941. *The educational and psychological significance of social acceptability and its appraisal in an elementary school setting.* Ph.D. thesis. Toronto: University of Toronto.

Lombard, O. M.: 1950. Breadth of bone and muscle by age and sex in childhood. *Child Develpm.*, **21**, 229–239.

Long, A.: 1941. Parents' reports of undesirable behavior in children. *Child Develpm.*, **12**, 43–62

Long, L.: 1940. Conceptual relationships in children: the concept of roundness. *J. genet. Psychol.*, **57**, 289–315.

———: 1941. Size discrimination in children. *Child Develpm.*, **12**, 247–254.

——— and L. Welch: 1941. The development of the ability to discriminate and match numbers. *J. genet. Psychol.*, **59**, 377–387.

——— and ———: 1942. Influence of levels of abstractness on reasoning. *J. Psychol.*, **13**, 41–59.

Loomis, C. P., W. B. Baker, and C. Proctor: 1949. The size of the family as related to social success of children. *Sociometry*, **12**, 313–320.

Lord, F. E.: 1941. A study of spatial orientation of children. *J. educ. Res.*, **34**, 481–505.

Lourie, N. V.: 1951. Discipline: a consistent, non-punitive concept. *Child Welfare*, **30**, 3–6.

Lu, Y. C.: 1952. Parental role and parent-child relationships. *Marriage Fam. Living*, **14**, 294–297.

———: 1952a. Parent-child relationships and marital roles. *Amer. sociol. Rev.*, **17**, 357–361.

Lucio, W. H., and C. D. Mead: 1939. An investigation of children's preferences for modern pictures. *Elem. Sch. J.*, **39**, 678–689.

Lund, F. H.: 1940. Intelligence and emotionality. *39th Yearb. nat. Soc. Stud. Educ.*, Pt. 1, 282–285.

———, E. R. Yeomans, and E. A. Geigs: 1946. Health indices in relation to age, sex, race, and socioeconomic status. *J. soc. Psychol.*, **24**, 111–117.

Lund, S. E. T.: 1933. Psycho-biological study of a set of identical girl triplets. *Hum. Biol.*, **5**, 1–34.

Lundström, R.: 1952. Rubella during pregnancy: its effect on prenatal mortality, the incidence of congenital abnormalities and immaturity. *Acta paediat., Stockh.,* **41,** 583–594.

Lurie, L. A., S. Levy, F. M. Rosenthal, and O. R. Lurie: 1943. Environmental influences. *Amer. J. Orthopsychiat.,* **13,** 150–161.

Lurie, O. R.: 1941. Psychological factors associated with eating difficulties in children. *Amer. J. Orthopsychiat.,* **11,** 452–466.

Lyness, P. I.: 1951. Patterns in the mass communications tastes of the young audience. *J. educ. Psychol.,* **42,** 449–467.

———: 1952. The place of the mass media in the lives of boys and girls. *Journalism Quart.,* **29,** 43–54.

Lynip, A. W.: 1951. The use of magnetic devices in the collection and analysis of the preverbal utterances of an infant. *Genet. Psychol. Monogr.,* **44,** 221–262.

Maas, H. S.: 1951. Personal and group factors in leaders' social perception. *J. abnorm. soc. Psychol.,* **45,** 54–63.

———: 1951a. Some social class differences in the family systems and group relations of pre- and early adolescents. *Child Developm.,* **22,** 145–152.

Macaulay, E.: 1929. Some notes on the attitude of children to dress. *Brit. J. med. Psychol.,* **9,** 150–158.

——— and S. H. Watkins: 1926. An investigation into the development of the moral conceptions of children. *Forum Educ.,* **4,** 13–33, 92–108.

MacCalman, D. R.: 1950. A psychiatrist looks at the newborn. *Practitioner,* **164,** 65–70.

MacClenathan, R. H.: 1934. Teachers and parents study children's behavior problems. *J. educ. Sociol.,* **7,** 325–333.

Maccoby, E. E.: 1951. Television: its impact on school children. *Publ. Opin. Quart.,* **15,** 421–444.

MacDonald, M., C. McGuire, and R. J. Havighurst: 1949. Leisure activities and the socio-economic status of children. *Amer. J. Sociol.,* **54,** 505–519.

Macfarlane, J. W.: 1938. Studies in child guidance. *Monogr. Soc. Res. Child Develpm.,* **3,** No. 6.

———: 1938a. Family influences on children's personality development. *Childhood Educ.,* **15,** 55–59.

———: 1939. The relation of environmental pressures to the development of the child's personality and habit patterning. *J. Pediat.,* **15,** 142–154.

———: 1941. Inter-personal relationships within the family. *Marriage Fam. Living,* **3,** 25–31.

———: 1943. Study of personality development. *In* R. G. Barker, J. S. Kounin, and H. F. Wright, *Child behavior and development.* New York: McGraw-Hill, Chap. 18.

Machover, K.: 1949. *Personality projection in the drawing of the human figure.* Springfield, Ill.: Charles C Thomas.

MacKenzie, B. K.: 1948. The importance of contact in determining attitudes toward Negroes. *J. abnorm. soc. Psychol.,* **43,** 417–441.

Mackie, R. P.: 1948. Crippled children in school. *U.S. Office Educ. Bull.,* No. 5.

MacLean, A. H.: 1930. The idea of God in Protestant religious education. *Teach. Coll. Contr. Educ.,* No. 410.

MacLeod, R. B.: 1951. The place of phenomenological analysis in social psychological theory. *In* J. H. Rorher and M. Sherif, *Social psychology at the crossroads.* New York: Harper.

Maddock, E.: 1947. A collection and analysis of conversational patterns of children. *Speech Monogr.,* **14,** 214–215.

Mahler, M. S.: 1945. Ego psychology applied to behavior patterns. *In* N. Lewis, *Modern trends in child psychiatry*. New York: International Universities Press, Chap. 6.

Malinowski, B.: 1927. *The father in primitive psychology*. New York: Norton.

Mallay, H.: 1935. A study of some of the techniques underlying the establishment of successful social contacts at the preschool level. *J. genet. Psychol.*, **47**, 431–457.

Maller, J. B.: 1929. Cooperation and competition. *Teach. Coll. Contr. Educ.*, No. 384.

———: 1930. Character growth and Jewish education. *Relig. Educ.*, **25**, 627–630.

———: 1931. Size of family and personality. *J. soc. Psychol.*, **2**, 3–27.

———: 1937. Juvenile delinquency in New York: a summary of a comprehensive report. *J. Psychol.*, **3**, 1–25.

Mallinson, G. G., and W. M. Crumrine: 1952. An investigation of the stability of interests of high-school students. *J. educ. Res.*, **45**, 369–383.

Malone, A. J., and M. Massler: 1952. Index of nail-biting in children. *J. abnorm. soc. Psychol.*, **47**, 193–202.

Maloney, J. C.: 1948. Authoritarianism and intolerance. *Int. J. Psychoanal.*, **29**, 236–239.

Malter, M. S.: 1952. The content of current comic magazines. *Elem. Sch. J.*, **52**, 505–510.

Mangus, A. R.: 1948. Personality adjustments of rural and urban children. *Amer. sociol. Rev.*, **13**, 566–575.

Manwell, E. M., and S. L. Fahs: 1951. *Consider the children—how they grow*, rev. ed. Boston: Beacon Press.

Margolese, M. S.: 1948. Mental disorders in childhood due to endocrine disorders. *Nerv. Child*, **7**, 55–77.

Marinho, H.: 1942. Social influence in the formation of enduring preferences. *J. abnorm. soc. Psychol.*, **37**, 448–468.

Markey, F. V.: 1935. Imaginative behavior of preschool children. *Child Develpm. Monogr.*, No. 18.

Marks, R. W.: 1951. The effect of probability, desirability, and "privilege" on the stated expectations of children. *J. Pers.*, **19**, 332–351.

Marmor, J.: 1951. Psychological trends in American family relationships. *Marriage Fam. Living*, **13**, 145–147.

Marquis, D. P.: 1931. Can conditioned responses be established in the newborn infant? *J. genet. Psychol.*, **39**, 479–492.

———: 1941. Learning in the neonate: the modification of behavior under three feeding schedules. *J. exp. Psychol.*, **29**, 263–282.

———: 1943. A study of frustration in newborn infants. *J. exp. Psychol.*, **32**, 123–138.

Marshall, E. I.: 1937. A review of American research on seasonal variation in stature and body weight. *J. Pediat.*, **10**, 819–831.

Marshall, J.: 1953. Children in the present world situation. *Amer. J. Orthopsychiat.*, **23**, 454–464.

Martin, A. R.: 1943. A study of parental attitudes and their influence upon personality development. *Education*, **63**, 596–608.

Martin, K. L.: 1952. Handedness: A review of the literature on the history, development, and research of laterality preference. *J. educ. Res.*, **45**, 527–533.

Martin, M. H.: 1951. Some reactions of preschool children to discipline. *Nerv. Child*, **9**, 125–130.

Martin, W. E.: 1951. Qualitative expressions in young children. *Genet. Psychol. Monogr.*, **44**, 147–219.

———: 1951a. Identifying the insecure child. I. The Wolff Security Test. *J. genet. Psychol.*, **78**, 217–232.

———: 1954. Learning theory and identification. III. The development of values in children. *J. genet. Psychol.*, **84**, 211–217.

Mason, B. D.: 1952. Leadership in the fourth grade. *Sociol. soc. Res.,* **36,** 239–245.

Massler, M., and B. S. Savara: 1950. Natal and neonatal teeth. *J. Pediat.,* **36,** 349–359.

———, I. Schour, and H. G. Poucher: 1941. Developmental patterns of the child as reflected in the calcification pattern of the teeth. *Amer. J. Dis. Child,* **62,** 33–67.

——— and T. Suher: 1951. Calculation of "normal" weight in children. *Child Develpm.,* **22,** 75–94.

Matheny, W. D., and H. V. Meredith: 1947. Mean body size of Minnesota schoolboys of Finnish and Italian ancestry. *Amer. J. phys. Anthrop.,* **5,** 343–355.

Mathews, S. M.: 1934. The effect of mothers' out-of-home employment upon children's ideas and attitudes. *J. appl. Psychol.,* **18,** 116–136.

Maudry, M., and M. Nekula: 1939. Social relations between children of the same age during the first two years of life. *J. genet. Psychol.,* **54,** 193–215.

Maxfield, K. E., and H. A. Fjeld: 1942. The social maturity of the visually handicapped preschool child. *Child Develpm.,* **13,** 1–27.

Maxwell, C. H., and W. P. Brown: 1948. The age-incidence of defects in school children: their changing health status. *J. sch. Hlth.,* **18,** 65–80.

Maybury, M. W.: 1952. Selection of materials by nursery school children of superior mental intelligence. *J. educ. Res.,* **46,** 17–31.

Mayer, A. J., and R. V. Marks: 1954. Differentials in infant mortality by race, economic level, and cause of death for Detroit: 1940 to 1950. *Hum. Biol.,* **26,** 145–155.

Mayo, S. C.: 1950. Age profiles of social participation in rural areas of Wake County, North Carolina. *Rural Sociol.,* **15,** 242–251.

McAndrew, M. C.: 1948. Rigidity and isolation: a study of the deaf and the blind. *J. abnorm. soc. Psychol.,* **43,** 476–494.

McAndrew, Sister M. B.: 1943. An experimental investigation of young children's ideas of causality. *Stud. Psychol. Psychiat. Cathol. Univ. Amer.,* **6,** No. 2.

McArthur, C.: 1955. Personality differences between middle and upper classes. *J. abnorm. soc. Psychol.,* **50,** 247–254.

McCann, W. H.: 1941. Nostalgia: a review of the literature. *Psychol. Bull.,* **38,** 165–182.

———: 1943. Nostalgia: a descriptive and comparative study. *J. genet. Psychol.,* **62,** 97–104.

McCarthy, D.: 1929. A comparison of children's language in different situations and its relation to personality traits. *J. genet. Psychol.,* **36,** 583–591.

———: 1930. *The language development of the preschool child.* Minneapolis: University of Minnesota Press.

———: 1947. The psychologist looks at the teaching of English. *Indep. Sch. Bull.,* **5,** 3–11.

———: 1952. Organismic interpretation of infant vocalization. *Child Develpm.,* **23,** 273–280.

———: 1952a. Factors that influence language growth: home influences. *Elem. Eng.,* **29,** 421–428, 440.

———: 1953. Some possible explanations of sex differences in language development and disorders. *J. Psychol.,* **35,** 155–160.

———: 1954. Language development. *In* L. Carmichael, *Manual of child psychology,* 2d ed. New York: Wiley, pp. 492–630.

———: 1954a. Language disorders and parent-child relationships. *J. Speech Hearing Disorders,* **19,** 514–523.

McCarty, S. A.: 1924. *Children's drawings: a study of interest and abilities.* Baltimore: Williams & Wilkins.

McCaskill, C. L., and B. L. Wellman: 1938. A study of common motor achievements at the preschool age. *Child Develpm.,* **9,** 141–150.

McConnon, K.: 1935. *The situation factor in the language responses of nursery school children.* Ph.D. thesis. Minneapolis: University of Minnesota.

McCurry, W. H., and O. C. Irwin: 1953. A study of word approximations in the spontaneous speech of infants. *J. Speech Hearing Disorders,* **18,** 133–139.

McDonagh, E. C.: 1950. Television and the family. *Sociol. soc. Res.,* **35,** 113–122.

McDougall, W.: 1923. *An introduction to social psychology.* Boston: J. W. Luce.

McFarland, M. B.: 1938. Relationships between young sisters as revealed by their overt responses. *Child Develpm. Monogr.,* No. 24.

McGehee, W.: 1941. Change in interest with change in grade status of elementary school children. *J. educ. Psychol.,* **33,** 151–156.

McGinnis, J. M.: 1930. Eye-movements and optic nystagmus in early infancy. *Genet. Psychol. Monogr.,* **8,** 321–430.

McGraw, M. B.: 1931. A comparative study of a group of Southern white and Negro infants. *Genet. Psychol. Monogr.,* **10,** 1–105.

——: 1932. From reflex to muscular control in the development of an erect posture and ambulation in the human infant. *Psychol. Bull.,* **29,** 652–653.

——: 1932a. From reflex to muscular control in the assumption of an erect posture and ambulation in the human infant. *Child Develpm.,* **3,** 291–297.

——: 1935. *Growth: a study of Johnny and Jimmy.* New York: Appleton-Century-Crofts.

——: 1939. Later development of children specially trained during infancy: Johnny and Jimmy at school age. *Child Develpm.,* **10,** 1–19.

——: 1939a. Swimming behavior of the human infant. *J. Pediat.,* **15,** 485–490.

——: 1940. Neural maturation as exemplified in achievement of bladder control. *J. Pediat.,* **16,** 580–590.

——: 1940a. Neuromuscular development of the human infant as exemplified in the achievement of erect locomotion. *J. Pediat.,* **17,** 747–771.

——: 1940b. Suspension grasp behavior of the human infant. *Amer. J. Dis. Child.,* **60,** 799–811.

——: 1941. Development of the plantar response in healthy infants. *Amer. J. Dis. Child.,* **61,** 1215–1221.

——: 1941a. Neural maturation as exemplified in the changing reactions of the infant to pin prick. *Child Develpm.,* **12,** 31–42.

—— and K. W. Breeze: 1941. Quantitative studies in the development of erect locomotion. *Child Develpm.,* **12,** 267–303.

—— and A. P. Weinbach: 1936. Quantitative measures in studying development of behavior patterns. (Erect locomotion.) *Bull. neurol. Inst., N.Y.,* **4,** 563–572.

McGuire, C.: 1950. Social stratification and mobility patterns. *Amer. sociol. Rev.,* **15,** 195–204.

——: 1951. Family background and community patterns. *Marriage Fam. Living,* **13,** 160–164.

——: 1952. Family life in lower and middle class homes. *Marriage Fam. Living,* **14,** 1–6.

——: 1952a. Conforming, mobile, and divergent families. *Marriage Fam. Living,* **14,** 109–115.

——: 1953. Family and age-mates in personality formation. *Marriage Fam. Living,* **15,** 17–23.

—— and R. A. Clark: 1952. Age-mate acceptance and indices of peer status. *Child Develpm.,* **23,** 141–154.

McHugh, G.: 1944. Autistic thinking as a transitory phenomenon of childhood. *Child Develpm.,* **15,** 89–98.

McIntyre, C. J.: 1952. Acceptance by others and its relation to acceptance of self and others. *J. abnorm. soc. Psychol.,* **47,** 624–625.

McKay, J. B., and M. B. Fowler: 1941. Some sex differences observed in a group of nursery school children. *Child Develpm.,* **12,** 75–79.

McKeachie, W. J.: 1952. Lip stick as a determiner of first impressions of personality: an experiment for the general psychology course. *J. soc. Psychol.,* **36,** 241–244.

McKee, J. P., and F. B. Leader: 1955. The relationship of socioeconomic status and aggression to the competitive behavior of preschool children. *Child Develpm.,* **26,** 135–142.

McKee, P.: 1949. Reading programs in grades IV through VIII. 48*th Yearb. nat. Soc. Stud. Educ.,* Pt. II, pp. 127–146.

McKellar, P., and R. Harris: 1952. Radio preferences of adolescents and children. *Brit. j. educ. Psychol.,* **22,** 101–113.

McKeown, T., and C. R. Lowe: 1951. The sex ratio of stillbirths related to cause and duration of gestation. *Hum. Biol.,* **23,** 41–60.

McKinney, F.: 1941. *Psychology of personal adjustment.* New York: Wiley.

McKinnon, K. M.: 1942. Consistency and change in behavior manifestations. *Child Develpm. Monogr.,* No. 30.

Mead, A. R.: 1951. What schools can do to improve social attitudes. *Educ. Leadership,* **9,** 183–187.

Mead, M.: 1932. An investigation of the thought of primitive children with special reference to animism. *J. Royal Anthrop. Instit.,* **62,** 173–190.

——: 1935. *Sex and temperament in three primitive societies.* New York: Morrow.

——: 1939. *From the South Seas.* New York: Morrow.

——: 1949. *Male and female.* New York: Morrow.

——: 1951. The impact of culture on personality development in the United States today. *Understanding the Child,* **20,** 17–18.

——: 1954. Some theoretical considerations on the problem of mother-child separation. *Amer. J. Orthopsychiat.,* **24,** 471–483.

Meier, N. C.: 1939. The graphic and allied arts. 38*th Yearb. nat. Soc. Stud. Educ.,* pp. 175–184.

Meister, D.: 1949. A comparative study of figure-ground discrimination in preschool children and adults. *J. genet. Psychol.,* **74,** 311–323.

Melcher, R. T.: 1937. Development within the first two years of infants prematurely born. *Child Develpm.,* **8,** 1–14.

Mellinger, B. E.: 1932. *Children's interest in pictures.* New York: Teachers College Bureau of Publications.

Meltzer, H.: 1935. Children's attitudes to parents. *Amer. J. Orthopsychiat.,* **5,** 244–265.

——: 1936. Economic security and children's attitudes to parents. *Amer. J. Orthopsychiat.,* **6,** 590–608.

——: 1937. Anger adjustments in relation to intelligence and achievement. *J. genet. Psychol.,* **50,** 63–82.

——: 1941. Children's thinking about nations and races. *J. genet. Psychol.,* **58,** 181–199.

——: 1941a. Sex differences in parental preference patterns. *Character & Pers.,* **10,** 114–128.

——: 1943. Sex differences in children's attitudes to parents. *J. genet. Psychol.,* **62,** 311–326.

Melville, A. H.: 1912. An investigation of the function and use of slang. *Ped. Sem.,* **19,** 94–100.

Mencken, H. L.: 1936. *The American language,* 2d ed. New York: Knopf.

Mendelsohn, H., and I. Crespi: 1952. The effect of autistic pressuure and institutional structure on preferences in a choice situation. *J. soc. Psychol.,* **36,** 109–123.

Mengert, W. F.: 1948. Fetal and neonatal mortality, causes and prevention. *Amer. J. Obstet. Gynaec.,* **55**, 660–668.

Menzies, H. F.: 1946. Children in day nurseries with special reference to the child under two years. *Lancet,* **251**, 499–501.

Meredith, H. V.: 1935. The rhythm of physical growth. *Univ. Ia. Stud. Child Welf.,* **11**, No. 3.

———: 1938. Bodily changes in adolescence. *Hygeia,* **16**, 832–834, 927–929.

———: 1941. Stature and weight of children of the United States. *Amer. J. Dis. Child.,* **62**, 909–932.

———: 1944. The stature of Toronto children half a century ago and today. *Hum. Biol.,* **16**, 126–131.

———: 1946. Physical growth from birth to two years. II. Head circumference. *Child Develpm.,* **17**, 1–61.

———: 1946a. Order and age of eruption for the deciduous dentition. *J. dent. Res.,* **25**, 43–66.

———: 1948. Body size in infancy and childhood: a comparative study on data from Okinawa, France, South Africa, and North America. *Child Develpm.,* **19**, 179–195.

———: 1950. Birth order and body size. II. Neonatal and childhood materials. *Amer. J. phys. Anthrop.,* **8**, 195–225.

———: 1951. Relation between socioeconomic status and body size of boys seven to ten years of age. *Amer. J. Dis. Child.,* **82**, 707–709.

——— and A. W. Brown: 1939. Growth in body weight during the first ten days of postnatal life. *Hum. Biol.,* **11**, 24–77.

——— and S. S. Culp.: 1951. Body form in childhood: ratios quantitatively describing four slender-to-stocky continua on boys four to eight years of age. *Child Develpm.,* **22**, 3–14.

——— and M. S. Goldstein: 1952. Studies of the body size of North American children of Mexican ancestry. *Child Develpm.,* **23**, 91–110.

——— and E. M. Meredith: 1950. Annual increment norms for ten measures of physical growth on children four to eight years of age. *Child Develpm.,* **21**, 141–147.

——— and ———: 1953. The body size and form of present-day white elementary children residing in West-Central Oregon. *Child Develpm.,* **24**, 83–102.

——— and P. R. Sherbina: 1951. Body form in childhood: ratios quantitatively describing three slender-to-stocky continua on girls four to eight years of age. *Child Develpm.,* **22**, 275–283.

Merrill, B.: 1946. A measurement of mother-child interaction. *J. abnorm. soc. Psychol.,* **41**, 37–49.

Merry, F. K.: 1943. Temper tantrums. *In* H. M. Rivlin and H. Schueler, *Encyclopedia of modern education.* New York: Philosophical Library, pp. 821–822.

——— and R. V. Merry, 1950. *The first two decades of life.* New York: Harper.

Métraux, R. W.: 1950. Speech profiles of the preschool child, 18 to 54 months. *J. Speech Hearing Disorders,* **15**, 37–53.

Meyer, B. M.: 1950. The unique role of woman as therapist in psychiatry. *Med. Wom. J.,* **57**, 18–23.

Meyer, C. T.: 1947. The assertive behavior of children as related to parent behavior. *J. Home Econ.,* **39**, 77–80.

Meyer, E.: 1940. Comprehension of spatial relations in preschool children. *J. genet. Psychol.,* **57**, 119–151.

Meyers, C. E.: 1944. The effect of conflicting authority on the child. *Univ. Ia. Stud. Child Welf.,* **20**, 31–98.

Midcentury Conference Report: 1951. *Midcentury Conference report on children and youth: fact-finding report.* Raleigh, N.C.: Health Publications Institute.

Middleton, C. E., and F. C. Sumner: 1953. Season of birth as related to seasonal preference and personality traits. *J. Psychol.*, **36**, 423–425.

Mikell, R. F.: 1953. Normal growth and development of children with visual handicap. *New Outlook for the Blind*, **47**, 91–96.

Miles, K. A.: 1946. Relationship between certain factors in the home background and the quality of leadership shown by children. Reported by J. E. Anderson, Parents' attitudes on child behavior: a report of three studies. *Child Develpm.*, **17**, 91–97.

Miller, A. M.: 1930. *Children and the movies*. Chicago: University of Chicago Press.

Miller, H., and D. W. Baruch: 1950. A study of hostility in allergic children. *Amer. J. Orthopsychiat.*, **20**, 506–519.

Millichamp, D. A.: 1953. Another look at play. *Bull. Inst. Child Stud., Toronto*, **15**, No. 4, 1–13.

Mills, C. A.: 1950. Temperature influence over human growth and development. *Hum. Biol.*, **22**, 71–74.

Milner, E.: 1949. Effects of sex role and social status on early adolescent personality. *Genet. Psychol. Monogr.*, **40**, 231–325.

————: 1951. A study of the relationship between readiness in grade one school children and patterns of parent-child interaction. *Child Develpm.*, **22**, 95–112.

Minkowski, M.: 1921. Sur les mouvements, des réflexes, et les réactions musculaires du foetus humain de 2 à 5 mois et leurs relations avec le système nerveux foetal. *Rev. Neurol.*, **37**, 1104–1118, 1235–1250.

————: 1921a. Über Bewegungen und Reflexe des menschlichen Foetus während der ersten Hälfte seiner Entwicklung. *Schweiz. Arch. Neurol. Psychiat.*, **8**, 148–151.

————: 1922. Über fruhzeitige Bewegungen, Reflexe und muskulare Reactionem beim menschlichen Fötus und ihre Bezeihungen zur fötalen Nerven und Muskel System. *Schweiz. med. Wschr.*, **52**, 721–724, 751–755.

————: 1924. Zum gegenwartigen Stand der Lehre von den Reflexen in Entwicklingsgeschichtlicher und der anatomischphysiologisher Bezeihung. *Schweiz. Arch. Neurol. Psychiat.*, **15**, 239–259.

————: 1928. Neurobiologische Studien am menschlichen Foetus. *Handb. biol. Arb. Meth.*, **5**, 511–618.

————: 1928a. Über die elektrische Erregbarkeit der fötalen Muskulatur. *Schweiz. Arch. Neurol. Psychiat.*, **22**, 64–71.

Mirenva, A. N.: 1935. Psychomotor education and the general development of preschool children: experiments with twin controls. *J. genet. Psychol.*, **46**, 433–454.

Missildine, W. H.: 1946. The emotional background of thirty children with reading disabilities with emphasis on its coercive elements. *Nerv. Child*, **5**, 263–272.

———— and P. J. Glasner: 1947. Stuttering: a reorientation. *J. Pediat.*, **31**, 300–305.

Mitchell, A. H.: 1949. The effect of radio programs on silent reading achievement of ninety-one sixth grade students. *J. educ. Res.*, **42**, 460–470.

Mitchell, E. D., and B. S. Mason: 1948. *The theory of play*, rev. ed. New York: A. S. Barnes.

Mitchell, J. C.: 1943. Do virtues and vices change? *Sch. & Soc.*, **57**, 111–112.

Mitchell, M. A.: 1949. The relationship of reading to social acceptability of sixth grade children. *Teach. Coll. Contr. Educ.*, No. 953.

Mohr, G. J.: 1948. Psychosomatic problems in childhood. *Child Develpm.*, **19**, 137–142.

———— and N. Bartelme: 1930. Mental and physical development of children prematurely born. *Amer. J. Dis. Child.*, **40**, 1000–1015.

Mohr, J.: 1948. Home-making problems of working women. *Smith Coll. Stud. soc. Work*, **19**, 27–62.

Moll, A.: 1923. *The sexual life of the child*. New York: Macmillan.

Moncur, J. P.: 1951. Environmental factors differentiating stuttering children from nonstuttering children. *Speech Monogr.,* **18,** 312–325.

———: 1952. Parental domination in stuttering. *J. Speech Hearing Disorders,* **17,** 155–165.

———: 1955. Symptoms of maladjustment differentiating young stutterers from non-stutterers. *Child Develpm.,* **26,** 91–96.

Moore, J. E.: 1937. A test of eye-hand coordination. *J. appl. Psychol.,* **21,** 668–672.

Moore, J. K.: 1948. Speech content of selected groups of orphanage and non-orphanage preschool children. *J. exp. Educ.,* **16,** 122–133.

Moreno, J. L.: 1934. *Who shall survive?* Washington: Nervous and Mental Disease Publishing Co.

———: 1947. Changes in sex groupings of school children. *In* T. M. Newcomb and E. L. Hartley, *Readings in social psychology.* New York: Holt, pp. 383–387.

Morgan, D.: 1955. Television versus reading. *Wilson Library Bull.,* **26,** 327.

Morgan, H. G.: 1946. Social relationships of children in a war-boom community. *J. educ. Res.,* **40,** 271–286.

Morgan, J. J. B.: 1942. *Child psychology,* 3d ed. New York: Rinehart.

——— and S. S. Morgan: 1944. Infant learning as a developmental index. *J. genet. Psychol.,* **65,** 271–289.

Morgan, S. S., and J. J. B. Morgan: 1944. An examination of the development of certain adaptive behavior patterns in infants. *J. Pediat.,* **25,** 168–177.

Morley, D. E.: 1952. A ten-year survey of speech disorders among university students. *J. Speech Hearing Disorders,* **17,** 25–31.

Morris, W. W., and A. L. Nicholas: 1950. Intra-family personality configurations among children with primary behavior disorders and their parents: a Rorschach investigation. *J. clin. Psychol.,* **6,** 309–319.

Morton, G. M.: 1926. Psychology of dress. *J. Home Econ.,* **18,** 584–586.

Mott, S. M.: 1937. Mother-father preference. *Character & Pers.,* **5,** 302–304.

———: 1954. Concept of mother—study of four- and five-year-old children. *Child Develpm.,* **25,** 99–106.

Mouztakas, C. E.: 1955. Emotional adjustment and the play therapy process. *J. genet. Psychol.,* **86,** 79–99.

Mudge, E. L.: 1923. *The God-experience.* Cincinnati: Caxton.

Mueller, J. H., and K. H. Mueller: 1945. Socioeconomic backgrounds and campus success. *Educ. psychol. Measmt,* **3,** 143–152.

Muhsam, F. V.: 1947. Correlation in growth. *Hum. Biol.,* **19,** 260–269.

———: 1951. Correlation of height and weight in early childhood. *Lancet,* **261,** 1021.

Mullen, F. A.: 1948. Truancy and classroom disorder as symptoms of personality problems. *Amer. Psychologist,* **3,** 360.

———: 1950. Truancy and classroom disorder as symptoms of personality problems. *J. educ. Psychol.,* **41,** 97–109.

Mummery, D. V.: 1947. An analytical study of ascendant behavior of preschool children. *Child Develpm.,* **18,** 40–81.

———: 1950. A comparative study of the ascendant behavior of Northern and Southern nursery school children. *Child Develpm.,* **21,** 183–196.

———: 1954. Family backgrounds of assertive and non-assertive children. *Child Develpm.,* **25,** 63–80.

Munn, N. L.: 1955. *The evaluation and growth of human behavior.* New York: Houghton Mifflin.

——— and B. B. Steining: 1931. The relative efficiency of form and background in the child's discrimination of visual patterns. *J. genet. Psychol.,* **39,** 73–90.

Murphy, D. P., M. E. Shirlock, and E. A. Doll: 1942. Microcephaly following maternal pelvic irradiation for the interruption of pregnancy. *Amer. J. Roentgenology and*
———: 1951. Children's ideas on the origin of illness. *Hlth. Educ. J.,* **9,** 6–12.

Murphy, G.: 1947. *Personality.* New York: Harper.

———, L. B. Murphy, and T. M. Newcomb: 1937. *Experimental social psychology,* rev. ed. New York: Harper.

Murphy, L. B.: 1937. *Social behavior and child personality.* New York: Columbia University Press.

Mussen, P. H.: 1950. Some personality and social factors related to changes in children's attitudes toward Negroes. *J. abnorm. soc. Psychol.,* **45,** 423–441.

———: 1953. Differences between the TAT responses of Negro and white boys. *J. consult. Psychol.,* **17,** 373–376.

Muste, M. J., and D. F. Sharpe: 1947. Some influential factors in the determination of aggressive behavior in preschool children. *Child Develpm.,* **18,** 11–28.

Myers, R. G.: 1949. Same sexed families. *J. Hered.,* **40,** 260–270.

———: 1949a. War and post-war experience in regard to the sex ratio at birth in various countries. *Hum. Biol.,* **21,** 257–259.

NABRAT Report: 1954. *Children and television—some opinions.* Los Angeles: Nat. Ass. for Better Radio and Television.

Nagy, M. H.: 1948. The child's theories concerning death. *J. genet. Psychol.,* **73,** 3–27.

———: 1950. Children's theories concerning the origin of diseases. *In Proceedings and papers of the 12th International Congress of Psychology at Edinburgh.* London: Oliver & Boyd, pp. 96–97.

———: 1951. Children's ideas on the origin of illness. *Hlth Educ. J.,* **9,** 6–12.

———: 1953. Children's birth theories. *J. genet. Psychol.,* **83,** 217–226.

———: 1953a. Children's conceptions of some bodily functions. *J. genet. Psychol.,* **83,** 199–216.

———: 1953b. The representation of "germs" by children. *J. genet. Psychol.,* **83,** 227–240.

National Office of Vital Statistics Report: 1947. Infant mortality by race and by urban and rural areas, U.S., each division and state. *Special Reports* (Washington), **27,** No. 4.

Nedelsky, R.: 1952. The teacher's role in the peer group during middle childhood. *Elem. Sch. J.,* **52,** 325–334.

Neel, J. V.: 1953. The effect of exposure to the atomic bombs on pregnancy termination in Hiroshima and Nagasaki: Preliminary report. *Science,* **118,** 537–541.

Neiburgs, H. E.: 1947. Gestational changes in the vaginal epithelium and their relation to the sex of the foetus. *Amer. J. Obstet. Gynaec.,* **54,** 653–656.

——— and R. B. Greenblatt: 1949. Specific estrogenic and androgenic smears in relation to the fetal sex during pregnancy. *Amer. J. Obstet. Gynaec.,* **57,** 356–363.

Neilon, P.: 1948. Shirley's babies after fifteen years: a personality study. *J. genet. Psychol.,* **73,** 175–186.

Neisser, E. G.: 1951. *Brothers and sisters.* New York: Harper.

Nestrick, W. V.: 1939. Constructional activities of adult males. *Teach. Coll. Contr. Educ.,* No. 780.

Neugarten, B. L.: 1946. Social class and friendship among school children. *Amer. J. Sociol.,* **51,** 305–313.

Neustadt, R., and A. Myerson: 1940. Quantitative sex hormone studies in homosexuality. *Amer. J. Psychiat.,* **97,** 524–551.

New York Times: 1954. Infant blindness linked to oxygen. Sept. 23.

———: 1954a. Stomach-slumber by babies decried. Dec. 8.

———: 1954b. TV-watching habits of students studied. Jan. 2.

————: 1954c. New version for Mother Goose. Apr. 30.

————: 1955. Pupils like teachers who know their trade. May 15.

————: 1955a. Child's I.Q. linked to mother's diet. Mar. 17.

Newberry, H.: 1941. The measurement of three types of fetal activity. *J. comp. Psychol.*, **32**, 521–530.

Newcomb, T. M.: 1950. Role behaviors in the study of individual personality and of the group. *J. Pers.*, **18**, 273–289.

Newell, H. W.: 1934. The psychodynamics of maternal rejection. *Amer. J. Orthopsychiat.*, **4**, 387–401.

————: 1936. A further study of maternal rejection. *Amer. J. Orthopsychiat.*, **6**, 576–589.

Newhall, S. M.: 1937. Identification by young children of differently oriented visual forms. *Child Develpm.*, **8**, 105–111.

Newman, H. H.: 1940. *Multiple births. Twins, triplets, quadruplets, and quintuplets.* New York: Doubleday.

————, F. N. Freeman, and K. J. Holzinger: 1937. *Twins: a study of heredity and environment.* Chicago: University of Chicago Press.

Newsweek Magazine: 1950. Medical report, Jan. 23.

Newton, N. R.: 1951. The relationship between infant feeding experience and later behavior. *J. Pediat.*, **38**, 28–30.

Nimkoff, M. F.: 1934. *The child.* Philadelphia: Lippincott.

————: 1942. The child's preference for father or mother. *Amer. sociol. Rev.*, **7**, 517–524.

————: 1950. What do modern inventions do to family life? *Ann. Amer. Acad. pol. soc. Sci.*, **272**, 53–58.

Noback, C. R.: and J. G. Robertson: 1951. Sequences of appearance of ossification centers in the human skeleton during the first five prenatal months. *Amer. J. Anat.*, **89**, 1–28.

Norman, R. D.: 1953. The interrelationships among acceptance-rejection, self-other identity, insight into self, and realistic perception of others. *J. soc. Psychol.*, **37**, 205–235.

Northway, M. L.: 1943. Social relationships among preschool children. Abstracts and interpretations of three studies. *Sociometry*, **6**, 429–433.

————: 1943a. Children with few friends. *School*, **32**, 380–384.

————: 1944. Outsiders. *Sociometry*, **7**, 10–25.

————: 1946. Sociometry and some challenging problems of social relationships. *Sociometry*, **9**, 187–198.

————, E. B. Frankel, and R. Potastin: 1947. Personality and sociometric status. *Sociomet. Monogr.*, No. 11.

Norton, J. L.: 1953. Patterns of vocational interest development and actual job choice. *J. genet. Psychol.*, **82**, 235–262.

Norval, M. A.: 1946. Sucking response of newly born babies at breast. *Amer. J. Dis. Child.*, **71**, 41–44.

————: 1947. Relationship of weight and length of infants at birth to the age at which they begin to walk. *J. Pediat.*, **30**, 676–679.

———— and R. L. J. Kennedy: 1949. Illnesses within the first year of life. *J. Pediat.*, **35**, 43–48.

————, ————, and J. Berkson: 1951. Biometric studies of the growth of children of Rochester, Minnesota. *Hum. Biol.*, **23**, 273–301.

Nowlis, V.: 1952. A search for significant concepts in a study of parent-child relationships. *Amer. J. Orthopsychiat.*, **22**, 286–299.

Nye, I.: 1950. Adolescent-parent adjustment—socioeconomic level as a variable. *Rural Sociol.*, **15**, 334–339.

————: 1952. Adolescent-parent adjustment: age, sex, sibling number, broken homes, and employed mothers as variables. *Marriage Fam. Living,* **14,** 327–332.

Oakden, E. C., and M. Sturt: 1922. The development of the knowledge of time in children. *Brit. J. Psychol.,* **12,** 309–336.

Oakes, M. E.: 1947. Children's explanations of natural phenomena. *Teach. Coll. Contr. Educ.,* No. 926.

O'Brien, C. C.: 1953. The role of music in guiding the child. *Education,* **73,** 1–6.

Ogburn, W. F.: 1927. Our social heritage. *Survey Graphic,* **59,** 277–279, 341–343.

Olmstead, R. W., and E. B. Jackson: 1950. Self-demand feeding in the first week of life. *Pediatrics,* **6,** 396–401.

Olney, E. E., and H. M. Cushing: 1935. A brief report of the responses of preschool children to commercially available pictorial materials. *Child Develpm.,* **6,** 52–55.

Olson, W. C.: 1930. *Problem tendencies in children: a method for their measurement and description.* Minneapolis: University of Minnesota Press.

————: 1949.*Child development.* Boston: Heath.

Omwake, L.: 1939. Factors influencing the sense of humor. *J. soc. Psychol.,* **10,** 95–104.

————: 1942. Humor in the making. *J. soc. Psychol.,* **15,** 265–279.

Ordan, H.: 1945. *Social concepts and the child's mind.* New York: King's Crown.

Orgel, S. Z., and J. Tuckman: 1935. Nicknames of institutional children. *Amer. J. Orthopsychiat.,* **5,** 276–285.

Orlansky, H.: 1949. Infant care and personality. *Psychol. Bull.,* **46,** 1–48.

Ort, R. S.: 1952. A study of role-conflicts as related to class level. *J. abnorm. soc. Psychol.,* **47,** 425–432.

Osborne, E. G.: 1937. *Camping and guidance.* New York: Association Press.

Page, M. L.: 1936. The modification of ascendant behavior in preschool children. *Univ. Ia. Stud. Child Welf.,* **12,** No. 3.

Palmer, C. E.: 1936. The relation of body size to sickness in elementary school children. *Amer. J. phys. Anthrop.,* **21,** 22–29.

Palmer, M. F.: 1940. The speech development of normal children. *J. Speech Disorders,* **5,** 185–188.

Parrish, C. H.: 1946. Color names and color notions. *J. Negro Educ.,* **15,** 13–20.

Parsons, T.: 1942. Age and sex in the social structure of the United States. *Amer. sociol. Rev.,* **7,** 604–616.

————: 1947. Certain primary sources and patterns of aggression in the social structure of the western world. *Psychiatry,* **10,** 167–187.

Parten, M. B.: 1932. Social participation among preschool children. *J. abnorm. soc. Psychol.,* **27,** 243–269.

————: 1932a. Leadership among preschool children. *J. abnorm. soc. Psychol.,* **27,** 430–440.

————: 1933. Social play among preschool children. *J. abnorm. soc. Psychol.,* **28,** 136–147.

Partridge, E. D.: 1934. Leadership among adolescent boys. *Teach. Coll. Contr. Educ.,* No. 608.

Pasamanick, B.: 1946. A comparative study of the behavioral development of Negro infants. *J. genet. Psychol.,* **69,** 3–44.

Pattie, F., and S. Cornett: 1952. Unpleasantness of early memories and maladjustment of children. *J. Pers.,* **20,** 315–321.

Pearl, D.: 1950. Ethnocentrism and the self-concept. *J. soc. Psychol.,* **40,** 137–147.

Pearl, R.: 1930. *Alcohol: biological aspects.* In Encyclopedia of the Social Science. New York: Macmillan.

Pearson, L. H.: 1950. Teen-agers' preferences in clothes. *J. Home Econ.,* **42,** 801–802.

Peatman, J. G., and I. Greenspan: 1935. The reliability of a questionnaire on superstitious beliefs of elementary school children. *J. abnorm. soc. Psychol.*, **30**, 208–221.

—— and R. A. Higgons: 1940. Development of sitting, standing, and walking of children reared with optimal pediatric care. *Amer. J. Orthopsychiat.*, **10**, 88–110.

—— and ——: 1942. Relation of infant's weight and body build to locomotor development. *Amer. J. Orthopsychiat.*, **12**, 234–240.

Peiper, A.: 1924. Beiträge zur Sinnes-Physiologie der Frühgeburt. *Jb. Kinderheilk.*, **104**, 195–200.

Peller, L. E.: 1952. Models of children's play. *Ment. Hyg., N.Y.*, **36**, 66–83.

People's League of Health: 1942. Interim report, nutrition of expectant and nursing mothers. *Lancet*, **2**, 10–12.

Perry, W. M.: 1943. Influence of student dreads upon attitudes toward school subjects. *J. exp. Educ.*, **12**, 48–63.

Peterson, R. C., and L. L. Thurstone: 1932. The effect of a motion picture film on children's attitudes toward Germans. *J. educ. Psychol.*, **23**, 241–246.

Peterson, W. F.: 1936. Report in *New York Times*, Nov. 18.

Pfeiffer, M. S., and D. D. Scott: 1952. Factors in family happiness and unity. *J. Home Econ.*, **44**, 413–414.

Pfleger, J.: 1947. "The wicked stepmother" in a child guidance clinic. *Smith Coll. Stud. soc. Work*, **17**, 159–184.

Phillips, E. L.: 1951. Parent-child similarities in personality disturbances. *J. clin. Psychol.*, **7**, 188–190.

——: 1951a. Attitudes toward self and others: a brief questionnaire report. *J. consult. Psychol.*, **15**, 79–81.

——, I. R. Berman, and H. B. Hanson: 1948. Intelligence and personality factors associated with poliomyelitis among school-age children. *Monogr. Soc. Res. Child Develpm.*, **12**, No. 2.

Philp, A. J.: 1940. Strangers and friends as competitors and co-operators. *J. genet. Psychol.*, **57**, 249–258.

Phipps, M. J.: 1949. Some factors influencing what children know about human growth. *Amer. Psychologist*, **4**, 79–81.

Piaget, J.: 1926. *The language and thought of the child.* New York: Harcourt Brace.

——: 1929. *The child's conception of the world.* New York: Harcourt Brace.

——: 1930. *The child's conception of physical causality.* New York: Harcourt Brace.

——: 1932. *The moral judgment of the child.* New York: Harcourt Brace.

Pigors, P.: 1935. *Leadership or domination.* Boston: Houghton Mifflin.

Pile, W. J.: 1951. A study of the correlation between dementia praecox and the month of birth. *Virginia med. Monthly*, **78**, 438–440.

Pilzer, E.: 1952. Disturbed children who make a good school adjustment. *Smith Coll. Stud. soc. Work*, **22**, 103–210.

Pinnau, S. R.: 1950. A critique on the articles of Margaret Ribble. *Child Develpm.*, **21**, 203–228.

Pintner, R.: 1931. Intelligence and month of birth. *J. appl. Psychol.*, **15**, 149–154.

—— and G. Forlano: 1933. The influence of month of birth on intelligence quotients. *J. educ. Psychol.*, **24**, 561–584.

—— and ——: 1934. The birth month of eminent men. *J. appl. Psychol.*, **18**, 178–188.

—— and ——: 1939. Season of birth and intelligence. *J. genet. Psychol.* **54**, 353–358.

—— and ——: 1943. Season of birth and mental differences. *Psychol. Bull.*, **40**, 25–35.

——, ——, and H. Freedman: 1937. Personality and attitudinal similarity among classroom friends. *J. appl. Psychol.*, **21**, 48–65.

—— and G. Lev: 1940. Worries of school children. *J. genet. Psychol.*, **56**, 67–76.

—— and J. B. Maller: 1937. Month of birth and average intelligence among different ethnic groups. *J. genet. Psychol.*, **50**, 91–107.

Piret, R.: 1940. Recherches génétiques sur le comique. *Acta psychol.* (*Hague*), **5**, 103–192. (Abstracted in *Psychol. Abstr.*, 1944, **18**, No. 2324.)

Pistor, F.: 1939. Measuring the time concepts of children. *J. educ. Res.*, **33**, 293–300.

——: 1940. How time concepts are acquired by children. *Educ. Method*, **20**, 107–112.

Pisula, C.: 1937. Behavior problems of children from high and low socio-economic groups. *Ment. Hyg., N.Y.*, **21**, 452–456.

Pitje, G. M.: 1951. Sex education among the Pedi. *Int. J. Sexol.*, **4**, 212–216.

Plaut, J. S.: 1941. Negativism: its treatment and its implications. *Amer. J. Dis. Child.*, **61**, 358–368.

Plottke, P.: 1950. The child and his name. *Indiv. psychol., Bull.*, **8**, 150–157.

Podolsky, E.: 1952. Horrors. *Calif. Parent-Teacher J.*, December, p. 23.

——: 1953. The first six years. *Understanding the Child*, **22**, 71–72.

——: 1953a. How the child reacts to his physical defects. *Ment. Hyg., N.Y.*, **37**, 581–584.

——: 1954. The father's occupation and the child's emotions. *Understanding the Child*, **23**, 22–25.

Pope, B.: 1953. Socio-economic contrasts in children's peer culture values. *Genet. Psychol. Monogr.*, **48**, 157–220.

——: 1953a. Prestige values in contrasting socioeconomic groups of children. *Psychiatry*, **16**, 381–385.

Portenier, L.: 1943. The psychological field as a determinant of the behavior and attitudes of preschool children. *J. genet. Psychol.*, **62**, 327–333.

Porter, B. M.: 1954. Measurement of parental acceptance of child. *J. Home Econ.*, **46**, 176–182.

——: 1955. The relationship between marital adjustment and parental acceptance of children. *J. Home Econ.*, **47**, 157–164.

Potashin, R.: 1946. A sociometric study of children's friendships. *Sociometry*, **9**, 48–70.

Potgieter, M., and V. Everitt: 1950. A study of children's eating habits. *J. Home Econ.*, **42**, 363–366.

Potter, E. L.: 1948. Reproductive histories of the mothers of 322 infants with erythroblastosis. *Pediatrics*, **2**, 369–381.

——: 1955. Pregnancy. *In* M. Fishbein and E. W. Burgess, *Successful marriage*, 2d ed. New York: Doubleday, pp. 243–254.

Pratt, K. C.: 1930. Note on the relation of temperature and humidity to the activity of young infants. *J. genet. Psychol.*, **36**, 480–484.

——: 1932. A note upon the relation of activity of sex and race in young infants. *J. soc. Psychol.*, **3**, 118–120.

——: 1934. Generalization and specificity of the plantar response in newborn infants: the reflexogenous zone. *J. genet. Psychol.*, **44**, 265–300; **45**, 22–38, 371–389.

——: 1934a. The effects of repeated auditory stimulation upon the general activity of newborn infants. *J. genet. Psychol.*, **44**, 96–116.

——: 1945. A study of the "fears" of rural children. *J. genet. Psychol.*, **67**, 179–194.

——: 1954. The neonate. *In* L. Carmichael, *Manual of child psychology*, 2d ed. New York: Wiley, pp. 215–291.

——, A. K. Nelson, and K. H. Sun: 1930. *The behavior of the newborn infant.* Columbus: Ohio State University Press.

Pressey, S. L.: 1946. Changes from 1923 to 1943 in the attitudes of public school and university students. *J. Psychol.*, **21**, 173–188.

—— and F. P. Robinson: 1944. *Psychology and the new education.* New York: Harper.

Preston, M. I.: 1940. Physical complaints without organic basis. *J. Pediat.,* **17,** 279–304.

——: 1941. Children's reactions to movie horrors and radio crime. *J. Pediat.,* **19,** 147–168.

Prevey, E. E.: 1945. A quantitative study of family practices in training children in the use of money. *J. educ. Psychol.,* **36,** 411–428.

——: 1948. Developing good habits in the use of money. *J. Home Econ.,* **38,** 79–81.

——: 1949. Children need parents. *Childhood Educ.,* **25,** 206–209.

Preyer, W.: 1937. Embryonic motility and sensitivity. *Monogr. Soc. Res. Child Develpm.,* **2,** No. 6.

Pritchard, E., and R. O'jemann: 1941. An approach to the measurement of insecurity. *J. exp. Educ.,* **10,** 114–118.

Probst, C. A.: 1931. A general information test for kindergarten children. *Child Develpm.,* **2,** 81–95.

Prothro, E. T.: 1954. Cross-cultural patterns of national stereotypes. *J. soc. Psychol.,* **40,** 53–59.

Prugh, D. G., E. M. Staub, H. H. Sands, R. M. Kirschbaum, and E. A. Lonihan: 1953. A study of the emotional reactions of children and families to hospitalization and illness. *Amer. J. Orthopsychiat.,* **23,** 70–106.

Punke, H. H.: 1936. Leisure-time attitudes and activities of high-school children. *Sch. & Soc.,* **43,** 884–888.

——: 1950. Neglected social values of prolonged human infancy. *Sch. & Soc.,* **71,** 369–372.

Purcell, K.: 1952. Memory and psychological security. *J. abnorm. soc. Psychol.,* **47,** 433–440.

Pusey, N. M.: 1954. Stress on job choice decried by Dr. Pusey in education panel. *New York Times,* Jan. 21.

Rabban, M.: 1950. Sex-role identification in young children in two diverse social groups. *Genet. Psychol. Monogr.,* **42,** 81–158.

Radke, M. J.: 1946. *The relation of parental authority to children's behavior and attitudes.* Minneapolis: University of Minnesota Press.

—— and J. Sutherland: 1949. Children's concepts and attitudes about minority and majority American groups. *J. educ. Psychol.,* **40,** 449–468.

——, ——, and P. Rosenberg: 1950. Racial attitudes of children. *Sociometry,* **13,** 154–171.

—— and H. G. Trager: 1950. Children's perceptions of the social roles of Negroes and whites. *J. Psychol.,* **29,** 3–33.

——, ——, and H. Davis: 1949. Social perceptions and attitudes of children. *Genet. Psychol. Monogr.,* **40,** 327–447.

Radke-Yarrow, M.: 1953. Developmental changes in the meaning of minority group membership. *J. educ. Psychol.,* **44,** 82–101.

—— and B. Lande: 1953. Personality correlates of differential reactions to minority group belonging. *J. soc. Psychol.,* **38,** 253–272.

——, H. J. Trager, and J. Miller: 1952. The role of parents in the development of children's ethnic attitudes. *Child Develpm.,* **23,** 13–53.

Ramsey, G. V.: 1943. The sex information of younger boys. *Amer. J. Orthopsychiat.,* **13,** 347–352.

——: 1943a. The sexual development of boys. *Amer. J. Psychol.,* **56,** 217–233.

——: 1953. Studies of dreaming. *Psychol. Bull.,* **50,** 432–455.

Rand, W., M. E. Sweeny, and E. L. Vincent: 1942. *Growth and development of the young child.* Philadelphia: Saunders.

Rank, O.: 1929. *The trauma of birth.* New York: Harcourt Brace.

——: 1932. *Modern education: a critique of its fundamental ideas.* New York: Knopf.

Rankin, M.: 1944. *Children's interests in library books of fiction.* New York: Teachers College Bureau of Publications.

Rapp, G. W., and G. C. Richardson: 1952. A salivary test for prenatal sex determination. *Science,* **115,** 265.

—— and ——: 1952a. New test reported for sex prediction. *New York Times,* Mar. 8.

Rarick, G. L., and R. McKee: 1949. A study of twenty third-grade children exhibiting extreme levels of achievement on tests of motor proficiency. *Res. Quart. Amer. Ass. Hlth,* **20,** 142–152.

Ratcliff, G. D.: 1950. Miscarriage. *Woman's Home Companion,* November, 42–75.

Ray, W. S.: 1932. A preliminary report on a study of fetal conditioning. *Child Develpm.,* **3,** 175–177.

Razran, G.: 1950. Ethnic dislikes and stereotypes: a laboratory study. *J. abnorm. soc. Psychol.,* **45,** 7–27.

Read, K. H.: 1945. Parents' expressed attitudes and children's behavior. *J. consult. Psychol.,* **9,** 95–100.

——: 1950. Clothes help build personality. *J. Home Econ.,* **42,** 348–350.

Reardon, H., J. L. Wilson, and B. Graham: 1951. Physiological deviations of the premature infant. *Amer. J. Dis. Child.,* **81,** 99–138.

Recreation Survey: 1954. Recreational interests and needs of high-school youth. *Recreation,* **47,** 43–46.

Redfield, J.: 1937. A preliminary report of dark adaptation in young infants. *Child Develpm.,* **8,** 263–269.

——: 1939. The light sense in newborn infants. *Univ. Ia. Stud. Child Welf.,* **16,** 107–145.

Reece, L. H.: 1954. The play needs of children aged 6 to 12. *Marriage Fam. Living,* **16,** 131–134.

Reeves, W. R.: 1931. Report of Committee on street play. *J. educ. Sociol.,* **4,** 607–618.

Reichard, S., M. Schneider, and D. Rapaport: 1944. The development of concept formation in children. *Amer. J. Orthopsychiat.,* **14,** 156–161.

Reichenberg-Hackett, W.: 1950. The geo sign test: a semistructural drawing situation utilized as a screening test for adjustment. *Amer. J. Orthopsychiat.,* **20,** 578–594.

——: 1953. Changes in Goodenough drawings after a gratifying experience. *Amer. J. Orthopsychiat.,* **23,** 501–517.

Reissman, L.: 1953. Levels of aspiration and social class. *Amer. sociol. Rev.,* **18,** 233–242.

Remmers, H. H., M. S. Myers, and E. M. Bennett: 1951. Purdue Survey. *Purdue Opin. Panel,* **10,** No. 3.

Renshaw, S., V. L. Miller, and D. P. Marquis: 1933. *Children's sleep.* New York: Macmillan.

Resnick, J.: 1951. A study of some relationships between high-school grades and certain aspects of adjustment. *J. educ. Res.,* **44,** 321–333.

Reuss, C. F.: 1954. Research findings on the effects of modern-day religion on family life. *Marriage Fam. Living,* **16,** 221–225.

Reynard, M. C., and F. C. Dockeray: 1939. The comparison of temporal intervals in judging depth of sleep in newborn infants. *J. genet. Psychol.,* **55,** 103–120.

Reynolds, E. L.: 1943. Degree of kinship and pattern of ossification. *Amer. J. phys. Anthrop.,* **1,** 405–416.

——: 1949. The fat/bone index as a sex-differentiating characteristic. *Hum. Biol.,* **21,** 199–204.

—— and T. Asakawa: 1948. The measurement of obesity in childhood. *Amer. J. phys. Anthrop.,* **6,** 475–486.

—— and P. Grote: 1948. Sex differences in the distribution of tissue components in the human leg from birth to maturity. *Anat. Rec.,* **102,** 45–53.

—— and L. W. Sontag: 1944. Seasonal variation in weight, height, and appearance of ossification centers. *J. Pediat.,* **24,** 524–535.

Reynolds, G. R.: 1942. The child's slant on the comics. *Sch. Exec.,* **62,** 17–36.

Reynolds, M. M.: 1928. Negativism of preschool children. *Teach. Coll. Contr. Educ.,* No. 288.

—— and H. Mallay: 1933. The sleep of young children. *J. genet. Psychol.,* **43,** 322–351.

Rhodes, I. G.: 1952. Allergic causes of emotional disturbances in children. *Nerv. Child,* **9,** 369–377.

Ribble, M. A.: 1943. *The rights of infants.* New York: Columbia University Press.

——: 1944. Infantile experience in relation to personality development. *In* J. McV. Hunt, *Personality and the behavior disorders.* New York: Ronald, pp. 621–651.

Ricciuti, E. A.: 1951. Children and radio: a study of listeners and non-listeners to various types of radio programs in terms of selected ability, attitudes, and behavior measures. *Genet. Psychol. Monogr.,* **44,** 69–143.

Rice, C.: 1931. Eye and hand movements in the training of perception. *Child Develpm.,* **2,** 30–48.

Rich, G. G.: 1954. Childhood as a preparation for delinquency. *J. educ. Sociol.,* **27,** 404–413.

Richards, T. W.: 1935. Gross metabolic changes characteristic of the activity of the neonate. *Child Develpm.,* **6,** 231–241.

——: 1936. The importance of hunger in the bodily activity of the neonate. *Psychol. Bull.,* **33,** 817–835.

——: 1936a. The relationship between bodily and gastric activity of newborn infants. *Hum. Biol.,* **8,** 369–386.

—— and H. Newberry: 1938. Can performance on test items at six months postnatally be predicted on the basis of fetal activity? *Child Develpm.,* **9,** 79–86.

——, ——, and R. Fallgatter: 1938. Studies in fetal behavior: II. Activity of the human fetus *in utero* and its relation to other prenatal conditions, particularly the mother's basal metabolic rate. *Child Develpm.,* **9,** 69–72, 79–86.

Ricketts, A. F.: 1934. A study of the behavior of young children in anger. *Univ. Ia. Stud. Child Welf.,* **9,** No. 3, 161–171.

Riemer, M. D.: 1949. The effect on character development of prolonged or frequent absence of parents. *Ment. Hyg., N.Y.,* **33,** 293–297.

Riess, B. F., and O. deCillis: 1940. Personality differences in allergic and non-allergic children. *J. abnorm. soc. Psychol.,* **35,** 104–113.

Riley, J. W., F. V. Cantwell, and F. Ruttiger: 1949. Some observations on the social effects of television. *Publ. Opin. Quart.,* **13,** 223–234.

Rinsland, H. D.: 1945. *A basic vocabulary of elementary school children.* New York: Macmillan.

Roberts, C. S.: 1938. Ordinal position and its relationship to some aspects of personality. *J. genet. Psychol.,* **53,** 173–213.

Roberts, K. E., and V. V. Fleming: 1943. Persistence and change in personality patterns. *Monogr. Soc. Res. Child Develpm.,* **8,** No. 3.

Robertson, G. G.: 1940. Nausea and vomiting in pregnancy. *Lancet,* **251,** 336–341.

Robinow, M., M. Johnston, and M. Anderson: 1943. Feet of normal children. *J. Pediat.,* **3,** 141–149.

Rockwood, L. D., and M. E. N. Ford: 1945. *Youth, marriage, and parenthood*. New York: Wiley.

Roe, V., and R. Milisen: 1942. The effect of maturation upon defective articulations in elementary grades. *J. Speech Hearing Disorders*, **7**, 37–50.

Roff, M.: 1950. Intra-family resemblances in personality characteristics. *J. Psychol.*, **30**, 199–227.

Rogers, C. R.: 1947. The organization of personality. *Amer. Psychologist*, **2**, 358–368.

———: 1948. Role of self-understanding in the prediction of behavior. *J. consult. Psychol.*, **12**, 174–186.

Rose, A. A.: 1944. Insecurity feelings in adolescent girls. *Nerv. Child*, **4**, 46–59.

———: 1947. A study of homesickness in college freshmen. *J. soc. Psychol.*, **26**, 185–203.

———: 1948. The homes of homesick girls. *J. child Psychiat.*, **1**, 181–189.

——— and B. K. Stavrianos: 1943. Sex differences in the perceptual attitude of children. *J. Psychol.*, **16**, 129–143.

Rose, B. M.: 1930. Some traits associated with sibling jealousy in problem children. *Smith Coll. Stud. soc. Work*, **1**, 364–376.

Rose, M. S.: 1940. *Feeding the family*. 4th ed. New York: Macmillan.

Rosen, S.: 1952. Effects of emotional disturbances on social skills. *Counseling*, **10**, 6–7.

Rosenthal, S.: 1952. A fifth grade classroom experiment in fostering mental health. *J. child Psychiat.*, **2**, 302–329.

Rosenzweig, S.: 1954. Babies are taught to cry: an hypothesis. *Ment. Hyg., N.Y.*, **38**, 81–84.

——— and E. L. Mirmow: 1950. The validation of trends in the Children's Form of the Rosenzweig Picture-Frustration Study. *J. Person.*, **18**, 306–314.

——— and L. Rosenzweig: 1952. Aggression in problem children and normals as evaluated by the Rosenzweig Picture-Frustration Study. *J. abnorm. soc. Psych.*, **47**, 683–688.

Ross, B. M.: 1930. Some traits associated with sibling jealousy in problem children. *Smith Coll. Stud. soc. Work*, **1**, 364–376.

Roudinesco, J.: 1952. Severe maternal deprivation and personality development in early childhood. *Understanding the Child*, **21**, 104–108.

Roy, K.: 1950. Parents' attitude toward their children. *J. Home Econ.*, **42**, 652–653.

Royster, L. T.: 1936. Body type of Negro children. *Arch. Pediat.*, **53**, 259–262.

Rubinov, O.: 1933. The course of man's life—a psychological problem. *J. abnorm. soc. Psychol.*, **28**, 206–215.

Rudisill, M.: 1952. Children's preferences for color versus other qualities in illustrations. *Elem. Sch. J.*, **52**, 444–451.

Ruja, H.: 1948. The relation between neonate crying and the length of labor. *J. genet. Psychol.*, **73**, 53–55.

Rusk, H. A.: 1955. "Is the baby normal?" *New York Times*, May 1.

Russell, D. H.: 1949. *Children learn to read*. Boston: Ginn.

———: 1949a. Reading and child development. *48th Yearb. nat. Soc. Stud. Educ.*, Pt. II, 10–32.

———: 1953. The development of thinking processes. *Rev. educ. Res.*, **23**, 137–145.

Russell, R. W.: 1940. Studies in animism: II. The development of animism. *J. genet. Psychol.*, **56**, 353–366.

———: 1940a. Studies in animism. IV. An investigation of concepts allied to animism. *J. genet. Psychol.*, **57**, 83–91.

——— and W. Dennis: 1939. Studies in animism. I. A standardized procedure for the investigation of animism. *J. genet. Psychol.*, **55**, 389–400.

———, ———, and F. E. Ash: 1940. Studies in animism. III. Animism in feeble-minded subjects. *J. genet. Psychol.*, **57**, 57–63.

Rust, M. M.: 1931. The effect of resistance on intelligence test scores of young children. *Child Develpm. Monogr.*, No. 6.

Ryan, M. E.: 1949. Social adjustment of kindergarten children ten years later. *Smith Coll. Stud. soc. Work*, **19**, 138–139.

Ryan, M. S.: 1952. Psychological effects of clothing. I. Survey of the opinions of college girls. *Cornell Univ. Agr. Exp. Sta. Bull.*, No. 882.

———: 1953. Psychological effects of clothing. II. Comparison of college students with high-school students, rural and urban students, boys and girls. *Cornell Univ. Agr. Exp. Sta. Bull.*, No. 900.

Sadger, J.: 1941. Preliminary study of the psychic life of the fetus and primary germ. *Psychoanal. Rev.*, **28**, 327–358.

Salber, E. J., and E. S. Bradshaw: 1953. Weight of Bantu babies in the first ten days of life. *Brit. J. soc. Med.*, **7**, 154–159.

——— and ———: 1954. The effect of birth weight and time of first feed on the weight of Bantu babies in the first 10 days of life. *Hum. Biol.*, **26**, 156–171.

Sanborn, H. C.: 1927. The function of clothing and bodily adornment. *Amer. J. Psychol.*, **38**, 1–20.

Sanders, J.: 1932. Similarity in triplets. *J. Hered.*, **23**, 225–234.

Sandin, A. A.: 1944. Social and emotional adjustments of regularly promoted and non-promoted pupils. *Child Develpm. Monogr.*, No. 32.

Sandman, E. S.: 1952 A study of sociometry on the kindergarten level. *J. educ. Sociol.*, **25**, 410–422.

Sanford, F. H.: 1942. Speech and personality. *Psychol. Bull.*, **39**, 811–845.

———: 1949. Some characteristics of the follower which influence leadership phenomena. *Amer. Psychologist*, **4**, 262–263.

Sanford, R. N.: 1943. Physique, personality and scholarship. *Monogr. Soc. Res. Child Develpm.*, **8**, No. 1.

Sarbin, T. R.: 1952. A preface to a psychological analysis of the self. *Psychol. Rev.*, **59**, 11–22.

Sargent, H.: 1945. Projective methods: their origins, theory, and application in personality research. *Psychol. Bull.*, **42**, 257–293.

Savage, B. M., and F. L. Wells: 1948. A note on singularity in given names. *J. soc. Psychol.*, **27**, 271–272.

Scammon, R. E.: 1930. *The measurement of the body in childhood. In* J. A. Harris et al., *The measurement of man.* Minneapolis: Univ. Minnesota Press, pp. 173–216.

———: 1942. Developmental anatomy. *In* J. P. Schaeffer, *Morris' anatomy.* 10th ed. New York: Blakiston.

——— and L. A. Calkins: 1929. *The development and growth of the external dimensions of the human body in the foetal period.* Minneapolis: University of Minnesota Press.

Schacter, M., and S. Cotte: 1951. A study of the mental development of premature infants. *Pediatrics*, **40**, 955.

Schall, L., M. H. Lurie, and G. Keleman: 1951. Embryonic hearing organs after maternal rubella. *Laryngoscope*, **61**, 99–112.

Schaltenbrand, C.: 1928. The development of human motility and motor disturbances. *Arch. Neurol. Psychiat. (Chicago)*, **20**, 720–730.

Scheinfeld, A.: 1943. *Women and men.* New York: Harcourt Brace.

———: 1950. *The new you and heredity.* Philadelphia: Lippincott.

Schettler, C.: 1942. Does your name identify you? *Social Forces*, **21**, 172–176.

Schilder, P., and D. Wechsler: 1934. The attitudes of children toward death. *J. genet. Psychol.*, **45**, 406–451.

Schmeidler, G. R.: 1941. The relation of fetal activity to the activity of the mother. *Child Develpm.*, **12**, 63–68.

Schoeppe, A.: 1953. Sex differences in adolescent socialization. *J. soc. Psychol.*, **38**, 175–185.

———, E. A. Haggard, and R. J. Havighurst: 1953. Some factors affecting sixteen-year-olds' success in five developmental tasks. *J. abnorm. soc. Psychol.*, **48**, 42–52.

Schuessler, K., and A. L. Strauss: 1950. A study of concept learning by scale analysis. *Amer. sociol. Rev.*, **15**, 752–762.

Schulman, M. J., and R. J. Havighurst: 1947. Relations between ability and social status in a midwestern community. IV. Size of vocabulary. *J. educ. Psychol.*, **38**, 437–442.

Schwartz, E. E.: 1949. Statistics of juvenile delinquency in the United States. *Ann. Amer. Acad. pol. soc. Sci.*, **261**, 9–20.

Scott, L. F.: 1953. A study of children's TV interests. *Calif. J. educ. Res.*, **4**, 162–164.

———: 1954. Social attitudes of children revealed by responses to television programs. *Calif. J. secon. Educ.*, **22**, 176–179.

Scott, R. B., W. Cardoza, W. Warrick, A. D. Smith, and M. R. DeLilly: 1950. Growth and development of Negro infants. III. Growth during the first year of life as observed in private pediatric practice. *J. Pediat.*, **37**, 885–893.

———, M. E. Jenkins, and R. P. Crawford: 1950. Growth and development of Negro infants. I. Analysis of birth weights of 11,818 newborn infants. *Pediatrics*, **6**, 425–431.

Seagoe, M. V.: 1931. The child's reactions to the movies. *J. juv. Res.*, **15**, 169–180.

———: 1933. Factors influencing the selection of associates. *J. educ. Res.*, **27**, 32–40.

———: 1952. Some current research in television for children. *Calif. J. educ. Res.*, **3**, 151–153.

———: 1952a. Children's television habits and preferences. *Quart. Film, Radio, Telev.*, **6**, 143–152.

Sears, P. S.: 1940. Levels of aspiration in academically successful and unsuccesful children. *J. abnorm. soc. Psychol.*, **35**, 498–536.

———: 1951. Doll play aggression in normal young children: influence of sex, age, sibling status, father's absence. *Psychol. Monogr.*, **65**, No. 6.

Sears, R. R.: 1950. Ordinal position in the family as a psychological variable. *Amer. sociol. Rev.*, **15**, 397–401.

———: 1951. Effects of frustration and anxiety on fantasy aggression. *Amer. J. Orthopsychiat.*, **51**, 498–505.

———, J. W. M. Whiting, V. Nowlis, and P. S. Sears: 1953. Some child-rearing antecedents of aggression and dependency in young children. *Genet. Psychol. Monogr.*, **47**, 135–234.

Seashore, H. C., and A. Bavelas: 1942. A study of frustration in children. *J. genet. Psychol.*, **61**, 279–314.

Seashore, R. H., and L. D. Eckerson: 1940. The measurement of individual differences in general English vocabularies. *J. educ. Psychol.*, **31**, 14–38.

——— and W. Jensen: 1948. Personality classification. *Sci. Mon., N.Y.*, **66**, 472–474.

Seegers, J. C., and R. H. Seashore: 1949. How large are children's vocabularies? A discussion. *Elem. Sch. J.*, **26**, 181–194.

Seham, M., and O. Schey: 1934. The influence of the environment on health and function. *Child Develpm.*, **5**, 177–196.

Seidl, J. C. G.: 1937. *The effect of bilingualism on the measurement of intelligence.* Ph.D. thesis. New York: Fordham University.

Seils, L. G.: 1951. The relationship between measures of physical growth and gross motor performance of primary-grade school children. *Res. Quart. Amer. phys. Educ. Ass.*, **22**, 244–260.

Seltzer, C. C.: 1946. Body disproportions and dominant personality traits. *Psychosom. Med.*, **8**, 75–97.

———: 1948. Phenotype patterns of racial reference and outstanding personality traits. *J. genet. Psychol.*, **72**, 221–248.

Sewall, M.: 1930. Two studies in sibling rivalry. I. Some causes of jealousy in young children. *Smith Coll. Stud. soc. Work*, **1**, 6–22.

Seward, B., and D. B. Harris: 1951. The reading ease, human interest value, and thematic content of St. Nicholas Magazine. *J. educ. Psychol.*, **42**, 153–165.

Seward, G. H.: 1944. Sex roles in post-war planning. *J. soc. Psychol.*, **19**, 167–185.

———: 1946. *Sex and the social order*. New York: McGraw-Hill.

Sewell, W. H.: 1952. Infant training and the personality of the child. *Amer. J. Sociol.*, **58**, 150–159.

——— and P. H. Mussen: 1952. The effects of feeding, weaning, and scheduling procedures on childhood adjustment and the formation of oral symptoms. *Child Develpm.*, **23**, 185–191.

———, ———, and C. W. Harris: 1955. Relationships among child training practices. *Amer. sociol. Rev.*, **20**, 137–148.

Shaffer, L. F.: 1930. *Children's interpretations of cartoons*. New York: Teachers College Bureau of Publications.

Shalter, A.: 1951. A survey of student reading. *Eng. J.*, **40**, 271–273.

Shapiro, M. B.: 1942. Some correlates of opinion on the upbringing of children. *Brit. J. Psychol.*, **43**, 141–149.

Sheerer, E. T.: 1949. An analysis of the relationship between acceptance of and respect for self and acceptance of and respect for others in 10 counseling cases. *J. consult. Psychol.*, **13**, 169–175.

Sheldon, W. D., and L. Carrillo: 1952. Relation of parents, home, and certain developmental characteristics to children's reading ability. *Elem. Sch. J.*, **52**, 262–270.

——— and W. C. Cutts: 1953. Relation of parents, home, and certain developmental characteristics to children's reading ability. II. *Elem. Sch. J.*, **53**, 517–521.

Sheldon, W. H., and S. S. Stevens: 1942. *The varieties of temperament*. New York: Harper.

———, ———, and W. B. Tucker: 1940. *Varieties of human physique*. New York: Harper.

———, ———, and ———: 1954. *Atlas of man*. New York: Harper.

Sheridan, M. D.: 1945. The child's acquisition of speech. *Brit. med. J.*, **1**, 707–709.

Sherif, M.: 1948. *An outline of social psychology*. New York: Harper.

——— and H. Cantril: 1947. *The psychology of ego-involvements*. New York: Wiley.

Sherman, M., and I. C. Sherman: 1925. Sensori-motor responses in infants. *J. comp. Psychol.*, **5**, 53–68.

——— and ———: 1929. *The process of human growth*. New York: Norton.

———, ———, and C. D. Flory: 1936. Infant behavior. *Comp. Psychol. Monogr.*, **12**, 1–107.

Sherriffs, A. C., and R. F. Jarrett: 1953. Sex differences in attitudes about sex differences. *J. Psychol.*, **35**, 161–168.

Sherrill, L. G.: 1939. *The opening doors of childhood*. New York: Macmillan.

Shinn, M. W.: 1900. *The biography of a baby*. Boston: Houghton Mifflin.

———: 1909. *Notes on the development of a child*. Berkeley: University Press.

Shipley, W. C., P. E. Dallman, and B. A. Steel: 1947. The influence of size on preferences for rectangular proportions in children and adults. *J. exp. Psychol.*, **37**, 330–336.

Shirley, M. M.: 1931. A motor sequence favors the maturation theory. *Psychol. Bull.*, **28**, 204–205.

———: 1931a. *The first two years.* Minneapolis: University of Minnesota Press, Vol. 1.

———: 1933. *The first two years.* Minneapolis: University of Minnesota Press, Vol. 2.

———: 1933a. *The first two years.* Vol. 3. *Personality manifestations.* Minneapolis: University of Minnesota Press.

———: 1938. Common content in the speech of preschool children. *Child Develpm.*, **9**, 333–346.

———: 1938a. Development of immature babies during the first two years. *Child Develpm.*, **9**, 347–360.

———: 1939. A behavior syndrome characterizing prematurely born children. *Child Develpm.*, **10**, 115–128.

———: 1941. The impact of the mother's personality on the young child. *Smith. Coll. Stud. soc. Work*, **12**, 15–64.

——— and L. Poyntz: 1945. Children's emotional responses to health examinations. *Child Develpm.*, **16**, 89–95.

Shoben, E. J.: 1949. The assessment of parental attitudes in relation to child adjustment. *Genet. Psychol. Monogr.* **39**, 101–148.

Shock, N. W.: 1944. Physiological aspects of development. *Rev. educ. Res.*, **14**, 413–426.

———: 1947. Physiological factors in development. *Rev. educ. Res.*, **17**, 362–370.

Shull, C. A.: 1940. A study of suitability of motion picture theatre programs to the needs of the child. *J. educ. Sociol.*, **13**, 274–279.

Shuttleworth, F. K.: 1949. The adolescent period: a graphic atlas. *Monogr. Soc. Res. Child Develpm.*, **14**, No. 1.

Silverman, S. S.: 1945. Clothing and appearance: their psychological implications for teen-age girls. *Teach. Coll. Contr. Educ.*, No. 912.

Simmons, K.: 1944. The Brush Foundation Study of child growth and development: II. Physical growth and development. *Monogr. Soc. Res. Child Develpm.*, **9**, No. 1.

Simpson, M.: 1935. *Parent preferences of young children.* New York: Teachers College Bureau of Publications.

Singer, A.: 1951. Certain aspects of personality and their relation to certain group modes and constancy of friendship choice. *J. educ. Res.*, **45**, 33–42.

Sirkin, J., and W. F. Lyons: 1941. A study of speech defects in mental deficiency. *Amer. J. ment. Def.*, **46**, 74–80.

Sjoberg, G.: 1951. Are social classes in America becoming more rigid? *Amer. sociol. Rev.*, **16**, 775–783.

Skeels, H. M., R. Updegraff, B. L. Wellman, and H. M. Williams: 1938. A study of environmental stimulation: an orphanage preschool project. *Univ. Ia. Stud. Child. Welf.*, **15**, No. 4.

Slater, E., R. Beckwith, and L. Behnke: 1939. Studies from the Center for Research in Child Health and Development, School of Public Health, Harvard University. II. Types, levels, and irregularities of response to a nursery school situation of forty children observed with special reference to the home environment. *Monogr. Soc. Res. Child Develpm.*, **4**, No. 21.

Slavson, S. R.: 1951. Authority, restraint and discipline in group therapy with children. *Nerv. Child*, **9**, 187–195.

Sloman, S. S.: 1948. Emotional problems in "planned for" children. *Amer. J. Orthopsychiat.*, **18**, 523–528.

Smalley, R. E.: 1930. The influence of differences in age, sex and intelligence in determining the attitudes of siblings toward each other. *Smith Coll. Stud. soc. Work,* **1**, 23–40.

Smith, C. A.: 1947. Effects of maternal undernutrition upon the newborn infant in Holland (1944–1945). *J. Pediat.,* **30**, 229–243.

Smith, G. H.: 1950. Sociometric study of best-liked and least-liked children. *Elem. Sch. J.,* **51**, 77–85.

——: 1954. Personality scores and the personal distance effect. *J. soc. Psychol.,* **39**, 57–62.

Smith, H.: 1931. Families with ambitions unsuitable for the children. *Smith Coll. Stud. soc. Work,* **1**, 406.

Smith, J. J.: 1941. Religious development of children. *In* C. E. Skinner and P. L. Harriman, *Child psychology*. New York: Macmillan, pp. 273–298.

Smith, J. M.: 1936. The relative brightness values of three lines for newborn infants. *Univ. Ia. Stud. Child Welf.,* **12**, 93–140.

Smith, M. E.: 1926. An investigation of the development of the sentence and the extent of vocabulary in young children. *Univ. Ia. Stud. Child Welf.,* **3**, No. 5.

——: 1931. A study of five bilingual children from the same family. *Child Develpm.,* **2**, 184–187.

——: 1932. The preschool child's use of criticism. *Child Develpm.,* **3**, 137–141.

——: 1933. Grammatical errors in the speech of preschool children. *Child Develpm.,* **4**, 183–190.

——: 1933a. The influence of age, sex, and situation on the frequency, form and function of questions asked by preschool children. *Child Develpm.,* **4**, 201–213.

——: 1935. A study of some factors influencing the development of the sentence in preschool children. *J. genet. Psychol.,* **46**, 182–212.

——: 1935a. A study of the speech of eight bilingual children of the same family. *Child Develpm.,* **6**, 19–25.

——: 1939. Some light on the problem of bilingualism as found from a study of the progress in mastery of English among preschool children of non-American ancestry in Hawaii. *Genet. Psychol. Monogr.* **21**, 119–284.

——: 1949. Measurement of vocabularies of young bilingual children in both of the languages used. *J. genet. Psychol.,* **74**, 305–310.

——: 1952. A comparison of certain personality traits as rated in the same individuals in childhood and fifty years later. *Child Develpm.,* **23**, 159–180.

——: 1952a. Childhood memories compared with those of adult life. *J. genet. Psychol.,* **80**, 151–182.

——, G. Lecker, J. W. Dunlap, and E. E. Cureton: 1930. The effect of race, sex, and environment on the age at which children walk. *J. genet. Psychol.,* **38**, 489–498.

Smith, M. K.: 1940. Measurement of size of vocabulary of children from 6 to 18 years of age (school grades 1 to 12). *Psychol. Bull.,* **37**, 581.

——: 1941. Measurement of the size of general English vocabulary through the elementary grades and high school. *Genet. Psychol. Monogr.,* **24**, 311–345.

Smith, S.: 1931. Influence of illness during the first two years on infant development. *J. genet. Psychol.,* **39**, 284–287.

——: 1939. Age and sex differences in children's opinions concerning sex differences. *J. genet. Psychol.,* **54**, 17–25.

Smith, W. C.: 1945. The stepchild. *Amer. sociol. Rev.,* **10**, 237–242.

——: 1949. The stepmother. *Sociol. soc. Res.,* **33**, 342–347.

——: 1955. Remarriage and the stepchild. *In* M. Fishbein and E. W. Burgess, *Successful marriage*, 2d ed. New York: Doubleday, pp. 328–349.

Smock, C. D., and G. G. Thompson: 1954. An inferred relationship between early childhood conflicts and anxiety responses in adult life. *J. Pers.*, **23**, 88–98.

Sofman, A.: 1949. Clinical manifestations of poor mother-child relationships. *Smith Coll. Stud. soc. Work*, **19**, 107–108.

Sollenberger, R. T.: 1940. Some relationships between the urinary excretion of male hormone by maturing boys and their expressed interests and attitudes. *J. Psychol.*, **9**, 179–189.

Somerville, A. W., and F. C. Sumner: 1950. The persistence of vocational preferences in successful individuals. *J. Psychol.*, **30**, 77–80.

Sontag, L. W.: 1940. Effect of fetal activity on the nutritional state of the infant at birth. *Amer. J. Dis. Child.*, **60**, 621–630.

——: 1941. The significance of fetal environmental differences. *Amer. J. Obstet. Gynaec.*, **42**, 996–1003.

——: 1946. Some psychosomatic aspects of childhood. *Nerv. Child*, **5**, 296–304.

—— and L. Lipford: 1943. The effect of illness and other factors on the appearance pattern of skeletal epiphyses. *J. Pediat.*, **23**, 391–409.

—— and T. W. Richards: 1938. Studies in fetal behavior. I. Fetal heart rate as a behavioral indicator. *Monogr. Soc. Res. Child Develpm.*, **3**, No. 4.

—— and R. F. Wallace: 1933. An apparatus for recording fetal movement. *Amer. J. Psychol.*, **45**, 517–519.

—— and ——: 1934. Preliminary report of the Fels Fund: study of fetal activity. *Amer. J. Dis. Child.*, **48**, 1050–1057.

—— and ——: 1935. The movement response of the human fetus to sound stimuli. *Child Develpm.*, **6**, 253–256.

—— and ——: 1935a. The effect of cigaret smoking during pregnancy upon the fetal heart rate. *Amer. J. Obstet. Gynaec.*, **29**, 77–82.

—— and ——: 1936. Changes in the rate of the human fetal heart in response to vibratory stimuli. *Amer. J. Dis. Child.*, **51**, 583–589.

—— and J. Wines: 1947. Relation of mothers' diets to status of their infants at birth and in infancy. *Amer. J. Obstet. Gynaec.*, **54**, 994–1003.

Sowers, A.: 1937. Parent-child relationships from the child's point of view. *J. exp. Educ.*, **6**, 205–231.

Spector, S. I.: 1953. Climate and social acceptability. *J. educ. Sociol.*, **27**, 108–114.

Spelt, D. K.: 1948. The conditioning of the human fetus in utero. *J. exp. Psychol.*, **38**, 338–346.

Spencer, W. P.: 1955. Heredity: facts and fallacies. *In* M. Fishbein and E. W. Burgess, *Successful marriage*, 2d ed. New York: Doubleday, pp. 217–231.

Sperling, M.: 1950. Children's interpretation and reaction to the unconscious of their mothers. *Intern. J. Psychoanal.*, **31**, 36–41.

——: 1951. The neurotic child and his mother: a psychoanalytic study. *Amer. J. Orthopsychiat.*, **21**, 351–364.

Spiegel, L. A.: 1950. The child's concept of beauty: a study in concept formation. *J. genet. Psychol.*, **77**, 11–23.

Spiegelman, M., C. Terwilliger, and F. Fearing: 1952. The content of the comic strips: a study of a mass medium of communication. *J. soc. Psychol.*, **35**, 37–57.

Spiker, C. C., and O. C. Irwin: 1949. The relationship between I.Q. and indices of infant speech sound development. *J. Speech Hearing Disorders*, **14**, 335–343.

Spitz, R. A.: 1949. The role of ecological factors in emotional development in infancy. *Child Develpm.*, **20**, 145–155.

——: 1951. Purposive grasping. *Personality*, **1**, 141–148.

—— and K. M. Wolf: 1946. The smiling response: a contribution to the ontogenesis of social relations. *Genet. Psychol. Monogr.*, **34**, 57–125.

Spock, B.: 1951. What we know about the development of healthy personalities in children. *Understanding the Child*, **20**, 2–9.

——: 1953. *Baby and child care*. New York: Pocket Books.

Spoerl, D. T.: 1944. The academic and verbal adjustment of college-age bilingual students. *J. genet. Psychol.*, **64**, 139–157.

Sprague, E. M.: 1929. *Conversational contacts of nineteen nursery school children*. Unpublished master's essay. New York: Columbia University.

Spriestersbach, D. C., and J. F. Curtis: 1951. Misarticulation and discrimination of speech sounds. *Quart. J. Speech*, **37**, 483–491.

Springer, D. V.: 1950. Awareness of racial differences by preschool children in Hawaii. *Genet. Psychol. Monogr.*, **41**, 215–270.

——: 1951. Development of concepts related to the clock as shown in young children's drawings. *J. genet. Psychol.*, **79**, 47–54.

——: 1952. Development in young children of an understanding of time and the clock. *J. genet. Psychol.*, **80**, 83–96.

——: 1953. National-racial preferences of fifth-grade children in Hawaii. *J. genet. Psychol.*, **83**, 121–136.

Springer, N. N.: 1938. The influence of general social status on the emotional stability of children. *J. genet. Psychol.*, **53**, 321–328.

Squier, R., and F. Dunbar: 1946. Emotional factors in the course of pregnancy. *Psychosom. Med.*, **8**, 161–175.

Stagner, R.: 1935. Economic status and personality. *Sch. & Soc.*, **42**, 551–552.

——: 1948. *Psychology of personality*, 2d ed. New York: McGraw-Hill.

——: 1952. Personality development. *Rev. educ. Res.*, **22**, 459–474.

—— and N. Drought: 1935. Measuring children's attitudes toward their parents. *J. educ. Psychol.*, **26**, 169–176.

—— and E. Katzoff: 1936. Personality as related to birth order and family size. *J. appl. Psychol.*, **20**, 340–346.

—— and M. A. Krout: 1940. A correlation study of personality development and structure. *J. abnorm. soc. Psychol.*, **35**, 339–355.

Stains, K. B.: 1951. Developing independence in children. *Understanding the Child*, **20**, 49.

——: 1954. The beginnings of dishonesty. *Understanding the Child*, **23**, 55.

Staker, A. M.: 1948. Changes in social status of elementary school pupils. *Educ. Res. Bull.*, **27**, 157–159.

Staples, R., and H. Conley: 1949. The use of color in the finger painting of young children. *Child Develpm.*, **20**, 201–212.

—— and G. W. Smith: 1954. Attitudes of grandmothers and mothers toward child-rearing practices. *Child Develpm.*, **25**, 91–97.

Steckel, M. A.: 1931. Intelligence and birth order in family. *In* L. L. Thurstone and R. L. Jenkins, *Order of birth, parentage, and intelligence*. Chicago: University of Chicago Press.

Steiner, I. D.: 1953. Some social values associated with objectively and subjectively defined social class membership. *Social Forces*, **31**, 327–332.

Steiner, M., and W. Pomerance: 1951. Studies in prematurity. IV. Influence of fetal maturity on weight lag period. *Pediatrics*, **8**, 513–517.

Stendler, C. B.: 1949. *Children of Brasstown*. Urbana: University of Illinois Press.

——: 1949a. A study of some socio-moral judgments of junior high school children. *Child Develpm.*, **20**, 15–28.

———: 1950. Sixty years of child training practices: revolution in the nursery. *J. Pediat.*, **36**, 122–134.

———: 1951. Social class differences in parental attitude toward school at Grade 1 level. *Child Develpm.*, **22**, 37–46.

———: 1952. Critical periods in socialization and overdependency. *Child Develpm.*, **23**, 3–12.

———: 1954. Possible causes of overdependency in young children. *Child Develpm.*, **25**, 127–146.

———: 1954a. The learning of certain secondary drives by Parisian and American children. *Marriage Fam. Living*, **16**, 195–200.

———, D. Damrin, and A. C. Haines: 1951. Studies in cooperation and competition. I. The effects of working for group and individual rewards on the social climate of children's groups. *J. genet. Psychol.*, **79**, 173–197.

——— and N. Young: 1950. The impact of beginning first grade upon socialization as reported by mothers. *Child Develpm.*, **21**, 241–260.

——— and ———: 1951. Impact of first grade entrance upon the socialization of the child: changes after eight months of school. *Child Develpm.*, **22**, 113–122.

Stengel, E.: 1947. A critical and psychological study of echo reactions. *J. men. Sci.*, **93**, 598–612.

Stern, W.: 1930. *Psychology of early childhood*. New York: Holt.

Stewart, A. H., I. H. Weiland, A. R. Leider, C. A. Mangham, T. H. Holmes, and H. S. Ripley: 1954. Excessive infant crying (colic) in relation to parent behavior. *Amer. J. Psychiat.*, **110**, 687–694.

Stiebling, H. K.: 1943. *Adequacy of American diets*. Chicago: American Medical Association.

Stiles, F. S.: 1950. Developing an understanding of human behavior at the elementary school level. *J. educ. Res.*, **43**, 516–524.

Stock, D.: 1949. An investigation into the interrelations between the self-concept and feelings directed toward other persons and groups. *J. consult. Psychol.*, **13**, 176–180.

Stockard, C. R.: 1931. *The physical basis of personality*. New York: Norton.

Stöckle, O.: 1954. The family with many children and its significance for social education. *Heilpädag. Werkbl.*, **23**, 144–149.

Stocks, P.: 1952. Recent statistics of multiple births in England and Wales. *Acta Genet. med. Gemellolog.*, **1**, 8–12.

Stogdill, R. M.: 1936. Experiments in the measurement of attitudes toward children: 1899–1935. *Child Develpm.*, **7**, 31–36.

———: 1937. Survey of experiments of children's attitudes toward parents: 1894–1936. *J. genet. Psychol.*, **51**, 293–303.

———: 1948. Personal factors associated with leadership: a survey of the literature. *J. Psychol.*, **25**, 35–71.

Stolz, H. R.: 1940. Shorty comes to terms with himself. *Prog. Educ.*, **17**, 405–411.

——— and L. M. Stolz: 1951. *Somatic development of adolescent boys*. New York: Macmillan.

Stolz, L. M., et al.: 1954. *Father relations with war-born children*. Stanford: Stanford University Press.

Stone, C. P., and R. G. Barker: 1937. Aspects of personality and intelligence in postmenarcheal and premenarcheal girls of the same chronological age. *J. comp. Psychol.*, **23**, 439–455.

——— and ———: 1939. The attitudes and interests of premenarcheal and postmenarcheal girls. *J. genet. Psychol.*, **54**, 27–71.

Stone, L. J.: 1954. A critique of studies of infant isolation. *Child Develpm.*, **25**, 9–20.

Stoodley, B. H.: 1952. Mother role as focus of some family problems. *Marriage Fam. Living,* **14,** 13–16.

Stott, D. H.: 1950. *Delinquency and human nature.* Fife, Scotland: Carnegie United Kingdom Trust.

Stott, L. H.: 1939. Personality development in farm, small-town, and city children. *Univ. Nebr. Agr. Exp. Sta. Res. Bull.,* No. 114.

———: 1939a. Some family life patterns and their relation to personality development in children. *J. exp. Educ.,* **8,** 148–160.

———: 1940. General home setting as a factor in the study of the only versus the non-only child. *Charact. & Pers.,* **8,** 156–162.

———: 1940a. Parental attitudes of farm, town, and city parents in relation to certain personality adjustments in their children. *J. soc. Psychol.,* **11,** 325–339.

———: 1941. Parent-adolescent adjustment, its measurement and significance. *Charact. & Pers.,* **10,** 140–150.

———: 1945. Research in family life in Nebraska. *J. Home Econ.,* **37,** 80–83.

——— and M. P. Berson: 1951. Some changes in attitudes resulting from a preparental education program. *J. soc. Psychol.,* **34,** 191–202.

Stouffer, G. A. W.: 1952. Behavior problems of children as viewed by teachers and mental hygienists. *Ment. Hyg., N.Y.,* **36,** 271–283.

Stoughton, M. L., and A. M. Ray: 1946. A study of children's heroes and ideals. *J. exp. educ.,* **15,** 156–160.

Stout, I. W., and G. Langdon: 1950. A study of the home life of well-adjusted children. *J. educ. Sociol.,* **23,** 442–460.

——— and ———: 1951. A study of the home life of well-adjusted children in three areas of the United States. *J. educ. Sociol.,* **25,** 67–85.

——— and ———: 1953. A report on follow-up interviews with parents of well-adjusted children. *J. educ. Sociol.,* **26,** 434–442.

Strang, R.: 1938. Guidance in personality development. *37th Yearb. nat. Soc. Stud. Educ.,* Pt. 1, pp. 197–228.

———: 1943. Why children read the comics. *Elem. Sch. J.,* **43,** 336–342.

———: 1951. *An introduction to child study,* 3d ed. New York: Macmillan.

———: 1954. How children and adolescents view their world. *Ment. Hyg., N.Y.,* **38,** 28–33.

Stratton, S. M.: 1927. Anger and fear: their probable relation to each other, to intellectual work, and to primogeniture. *Amer. J. Psychol.,* **39,** 125–140.

Strauss, A. L.: 1951. The animism controversy: reexamination of Huang-Lee data. *J. genet. Psychol.,* **78,** 105–113.

———: 1952. The development and transformation of monetary meanings in the child. *Amer. sociol. Rev.,* **17,** 275–286.

———: 1954. The development of conceptions of rules in children. *Child Develpm.,* **25,** 193–208.

——— and K. Schuessler: 1951. Socialization, logical reasoning, and concept development in the child. *Amer. sociol. Rev.,* **16,** 514–523.

Strauss, B. V.: 1951. The dynamics of ordinal position effects. *Quart. J. Child Beh.,* **3,** 133–145.

Strayer, L. C.: 1930. Language and growth: the relative efficacy of early and deferred vocabulary training, studied by the method of co-twin control. *Genet. Psychol. Monogr.,* **8,** 209–319.

Strecker, E. A.: 1946. *Their mothers' sons.* Philadelphia: Lippincott.

Strickland, R. G.: 1951. *The language arts in the elementary school.* Boston: Heath.

Strong, E. K.: 1952. Interest scores while in college of occupations engaged in 20 years later. *Educ. psychol. Measmt,* **11**, 335–348.

———: 1952a. Permanence of interest scores over 22 years. *J. appl. Psychol.,* **35**, 89–91.

Stuart, H. C., and E. H. Sobel: 1946. The thickness of the skin and subcutaneous tissue by age and sex in childhood. *J. Pediat.,* **28**, 646.

Stubblefield, R. L.: 1955. Children's emotional problems aggravated by family moves. *Amer. J. Orthopsychiat.,* **25**, 120–126.

Stubbs, E. M.: 1934. The effect of the factors of duration, intensity, and pitch of sound stimuli on the responses of newborn infants. *Univ. Ia. Stud. Child Welf.,* **9**, No. 4.

——— and O. C. Irwin: 1933. Laterality of leg movements of four newborn infants. *Child Develpm.,* **4**, 358–359.

Stutsman, R.: 1935. Constancy in personality trends. *Psychol. Bull.,* **32**, 701–702.

Sullenger, T. E., L. H. Parke, and W. K. Wallin: 1953. The leisure time activities of elementary school children. *J. educ. Res.,* **46**, 551–554.

Sussman, M. B.: 1954. Family continuity: selective factors which affect relationship between families at generational levels. *Marriage Fam. Living,* **16**, 112–120.

Svendsen, M.: 1934. Children's imaginary companions. *Arch. Neurol. Psychiat.,* **39**, 985–999.

Swanson, C. E., and R. L. Jones: 1951. Television owning and its correlates. *J. appl. Psychol.,* **35**, 352–357.

Swanson, R., and A. L. Benton: 1955. Some aspects of the genetic development of right-left discrimination. *Child Develpm.,* **26**, 123–133.

Sweet, C.: 1946. Enuresis: a psychologic problem of childhood. *J. Amer. med. Ass.,* **132**, 279–281.

Symonds, P. M.: 1937. Changes in sex differences in problems and interests of adolescents with increasing age. *J. genet. Psychol.,* **50**, 83–89.

———: 1938. A study of parental acceptance and rejection. *Amer. J. Orthopsychiat.,* **8**, 679–688.

———: 1939. A study of parental dominance and submission. *Psychol. Bull.,* **36**, 540–541.

———: 1946. *The dynamics of human adjustment.* New York: Appleton-Century-Crofts.

———: 1949. *The dynamics of parent-child relationship.* New York: Teachers College Bureau of Publication.

———: 1949a. Essentials of good parent-child relations. *Teach. Coll. Rec.,* **50**, 528–538.

——— and H. F. Daringer: 1930. Studies in the learning of English expression. IV. Sentence structure. *Teach. Coll. Rec.,* **32**, 50–64.

Taft, R.: 1955. The ability to judge people. *Psychol. Bull.,* **52**, 1–23.

Takahashi, E.: 1954. The sex ratio of neonatal deaths in Japan. *Hum. Biol.,* **26**, 133–142.

Tarwater, J. W.: 1953. Self-understanding and the ability to predict anothers' response. *Marriage Fam. Living,* **15**, 126–128.

Tasch, R. J.: 1952. The role of the father in the family. *J. exp. Educ.,* **20**, 319–361.

Taylor, C., and A. W. Combs: 1952. Self-acceptance and adjustment. *J. consult. Psychol.,* **16**, 89–91.

——— and G. G. Thompson: 1955. Age trends in preferences for certain facial proportions. *Child Develpm.,* **26**, 97–102.

Taylor, E. A.: 1952. Some factors relating to social acceptance in eighth grade classrooms. *J. educ. Psychol.,* **43**, 257–272.

Taylor, J. H.: 1934. Innate emotional responses in infants. *Ohio State Univ. Contr. Psychol.: Stud. Infant Behav.,* **12**, 69–93.

—— and I. E. Farber: 1948. The effect of failure and success as a function of ascendancy and submission. *Amer. Psychologist*, **3**, 361.

Taylor, K. W.: 1942. Educating parents in wartime. *Understanding the Child*, **11**, 8–13.

Taylor, L.: 1945. The social adjustment of the only child. *Amer. J. Sociol.*, **51**, 227–232.

Taylor, W. S.: 1948. Basic personality in orthodox Hindu culture patterns. *J. abnorm. soc. Psychol.*, **43**, 3–12.

Teagarden, F. M.: 1946. *Child psychology for professional workers*, rev. ed. New York: Prentice-Hall.

Templin, M. C., and M. D. Steer: 1939. Studies of growth of speech in preschool children. *J. Speech Hearing Disorders*, **4**, 71–77.

Tenenbaum, S.: 1940. Uncontrolled expressions of children's attitudes toward school. *Elem. Sch. J.*, **40**, 670–678.

——: 1944. Attitudes of elementary school children to school teachers and classmates. *J. appl. Psychol.*, **28**, 134–141.

Ter Keurst, A. J.: 1939. Comparative differences between superstitious and non-superstitious children. *J. exp. Educ.*, **7**, 261–267.

Terman, L. M.: 1922. *The measurement of intelligence*. Boston: Houghton Mifflin.

——: 1925, 1926, 1930. *Genetic studies of genius*. Stanford: Stanford University Press, 3 vols.

——, P. Buttenwieser, L. W. Ferguson, and W. B. Johnson: 1938. *Psychological factors in marital happiness*. New York: McGraw-Hill.

—— and M. Lima: 1927. *Children's reading*. New York: Appleton-Century-Crofts.

—— and M. A. Merrill: 1937. *Measuring intelligence*. Boston: Houghton Mifflin.

—— and M. H. Oden: 1947. *The gifted child grows up*. Stanford: Stanford University Press.

Thevaos, D. G.: 1951. *The influence of sematic variation on word difficulty with consequent effects on vocabulary estimates and frequency-difficulty variations*. Ed.D. thesis. New York: Teachers College.

Thomas, R. M.: 1951. Effects of frustration on children's paintings. *Child Develpm.*, **22**, 123–132.

Thompson, G. G.: 1946. The effect of chronological age on aesthetic preferences for rectangles of different proportions. *J. exp. Psychol.*, **36**, 50–58.

——: 1952. *Child psychology*. Boston: Houghton Mifflin.

—— and J. E. Horrocks: 1947. A study of the friendship fluctuations of urban boys and girls. *J. genet. Psychol.*, **70**, 53–63.

—— and M. O. Kepler: 1945. A study of the production of pleasant and unpleasant items as related to adolescent development. *J. educ. Psychol.*, **36**, 535–542.

—— and S. L. Witryol: 1948. Adult recall of unpleasant experiences during three periods of childhood. *J. genet. Psychol.*, **72**, 111–123.

Thompson, H.: 1943. The modifiability of play behavior with special reference to attentional characteristics. *J. genet. Psychol.*, **62**, 165–188.

——: 1954. Physical growth. *In* L. Carmichael, *Manual of child psychology*. 2d ed. New York: Wiley, pp. 292–334.

Thompson, L. J.: 1942. Attitudes of primiparae as observed in a prenatal clinic. *Ment. Hyg., N.Y.*, **26**, 243–256.

Thoms, H.: 1954. New wonders of conception. *Woman's Home Companion*, November 7–8, 100–103.

Thorndike, R. L.: 1941. Words and the comics. *J. exp. Educ.*, **10**, 110–113.

——: 1941a. *Comparative study of children's reading interests*. New York: Teachers College Bureau of Publications.

—— and F. Henry: 1940. Differences in reading interests related to differences in sex and intelligence level. *Elem. Sch. J.*, **40**, 751–763.

Thorpe, L. P.: 1946. *Child psychology and development.* New York: Ronald.

Thrasher, F. M.: 1927. *The gang.* Chicago: University of Chicago Press.

——: 1949. The comics and delinquency: cause or scapegoat. *J. educ. Sociol.*, **23**, 195–205.

Thrum, M. E.: 1935. The development of concepts of magnitude. *Child Develpm.*, **6**, 120–140.

Thurston, J. R., and P. H. Mussen: 1951. Infant feeding gratification and adult personality. *J. Pers.*, **19**, 419–458.

Thurstone, L. L.: 1931. Influence of motion pictures on children's attitudes. *J. soc. Psychol.*, **2**, 291–305.

—— and R. L. Jenkins: 1929. Birth order and intelligence. *J. educ. Psychol.*, **20**, 641–652.

—— and ——: 1931. *Order of birth, parentage, and intelligence.* Chicago: University of Chicago Press.

Todd, J.: 1943. Preferences of children for modern and older paintings. *Elem. Sch. J.*, **44**, 223–251.

Todd, T. W.: 1937. *Atlas of skeletal maturation* (*hand*). St. Louis: Mosby.

——: 1938. The record of metabolism imprinted on the skeleton. *Amer. J. Orthodontics oral Surg.*, **24**, 811–816.

Tolstrup, K.: 1953. On psychologenic obesity in children. *Acta paediat. Stockh.*, **42**, 289–304.

Topp, R. F.: 1950. Behavior difficulties in childhood as portents of future emotional disorders. *Elem. Sch. J.*, **51**, 196–200.

——: 1952. Preadolescent behavior patterns suggestive of emotional malfunctioning. *Elem. Sch. J.*, **52**, 340–343.

Torrance, P.: 1945. The influence of the broken home on adolescent adjustment. *J. educ. Sociol.*, **18**, 359–364.

Townsend, E. A.: 1951. A study of copying ability in children. *Genet. Psychol. Monogr.*, **43**, 3–51.

Trainham, G., and J. C. Montgomery: 1946. Self-demand feeding for babies. *Amer. J. Nursing*, **46**, 767–770.

Traxler, A. E.: 1945. The relationship between vocabulary and general achievement in the elementary school. *Elem. Sch. J.*, **45**, 331–333.

Trent, R.: 1953. *The correlates of self-acceptance among Negro children.* Ed.D. thesis. New York: Teachers College.

Trotter, M., and O. H. Duggins: 1948. Age changes in head hair from birth to maturity. I. Index and size of hair of children. *Amer. J. phys. Anthrop.*, **6**, 489–505.

Troup, E., and O. P. Lester: 1942. The social competence of identical twins. *J. genet. Psychol.*, **60**, 167–175.

Trumbull, R.: 1953. A study of relationships between factors of personality and intelligence. *J. soc. Psychol.*, **38**, 161–173.

Tryon, C. M.: 1939. Evaluation of adolescent personality by adolescents. *Monogr. Soc. Res. Child Develpm.*, **4**, No. 4.

Tschechtelin, Sister Mary A.: 1945. Self-appraisal of children. *J. educ. Res.*, **39**, 26–32.

—— and Sister M. J. Hipskind: 1940. Measuring the attitudes of elementary school children toward their teachers. *J. educ. Psychol.*, **31**, 195–203.

Tuckman, J., and I. Lorge: 1952. The best years of life: a study in ranking. *J. Psychol.*, **34**, 137–149.

—— and ——: 1953. When does old age begin and a worker become old? *J. Geront.*, **8**, 483–488.

—— and ——: 1953a. "When aging begins" and stereotypes about aging. *J. Geront.*, **8**, 489–492.

—— and ——: 1954. Old people's appraisal of adjustment over the life span. *J. Pers.*, **22**, 417–422.

——, ——, and G. A. Spooner: 1953. The effect of family environment on attitudes toward old people and the older worker. *J. soc. Psychol.*, **38**, 207–218.

Tuddenham, R. D.: 1951. Studies in reputation. III. Correlates of popularity among elementary school children. *J. educ. Psychol.*, **42**, 257–276.

——: 1952. Studies in reputation. I. Sex and grade differences in school children's evaluations of their peers. II. The diagnosis of social adjustment. *Psychol. Monogr.*, **66**, No. 1.

Tudor-Hart, B. E.: 1926. Are there cases in which lies are necessary? *J. genet. Psychol.*, **33**, 586–641.

Turner, E., and M. B. Eyre: 1940. A study of the emotional stability in elementary school students in grades four to eight. *Psychol. Bull.*, **37**, 595.

Turner, R. H.: 1952. Children and women's work, *Social. soc. Res.*, **36**, 377–381.

Turner, W. D.: 1948. Altruism and its measurement in children. *J. abnorm. soc. Psychol.*, **43**, 502–516.

Tyler, L. E.: 1951. The relationship of interests to abilities and reputation among first grade children. *Educ. psychol. Measmt*, **11**, 255–264.

——: 1955. The development of "vocational interests": I. The organization of likes and dislikes in ten-year-old children. *J. genet. Psychol.*, **86**, 33–34.

Ugurel-Semin, R.: 1952. Moral behavior and moral judgments of children. *J. abnorm. soc. Psychol.*, **47**, 463–474.

Ullmann, C. A.: 1952. Identification of maladjusted school children. *Pub. Hlth Monogr.*, No. 7.

Ulton, P.: 1936. A study of parent-child relationships. *Center. Res. Child Develpm. Monogr.*, **1**, No. 4.

United Nations Report: 1952. *Children deprived of normal home life.* New York: United Nations.

United Nations Report: 1953. Games of childhood same around world. *New York Times*, May 24.

Updegraff, R.: 1930. The visual perception of distance in young children and adults: a comparative study. *Univ. Ia. Stud. Child Welf.*, **4**, No. 4.

——: 1933. The correspondence between handedness and eyedness in young children. *J. genet. Psychol.*, **42**, 490–492.

——: 1942. The young child in wartime. *Nat. Parent-Teacher*, **36**, 40–41.

—— and E. K. Herbst: 1933. An experimental study of the social behavior in young children by certain play materials. *J. genet. Psychol.*, **42**, 372–391.

—— and M. E. Keister: 1937. A study of children's reactions to failure and an experimental attempt to modify them. *Univ. Ia. Stud. Child Welf.*, **13**, No. 4.

Usdin, G. L., and M. L. Weil: 1952. Effect of apnea neonatorum on intellectual development. *Pediatrics*, **9**, 387–394.

Valentine, C. W.: 1942. *The psychology of early childhood.* Cleveland: Sherwood Press.

Valentine, W. L., and L. Wagner: 1934. Relative arm motility in the newborn infant, I. *Ohio State Univ. Contr. Psychol.*, **12**, 53–68.

Van Alstyne, D.: 1929. *The environment of three-year-old children: factors related to intelligence and vocabulary tests.* New York: Teachers College Bureau of Publications.

———: 1932. *Play behavior and choice of play materials of preschool children.* Chicago: University of Chicago Press.

Vance, T. F., and L. T. McCall: 1934. Children's preferences among play materials as determined by the method of paired comparisons of pictures. *Child Develpm.,* **5,** 267–277.

Vander Werf, L.: 1951. Words never tell us. *Understanding the Child,* **20,** 50–53.

Van Dorn, V., and F. Mayfarth: 1949. Religious nurture and childhood education. *Relig. Educ.,* **44,** 141–148.

Van Dusen, C. R.: 1939. An anthropometric study of the upper extremities of children. *Hum. Biol.,* **11,** 277–284.

Variot, G., and J. Gotcu: 1927. Le début de la marche bipède chez le jeune enfant dans ses rapports avec l'âge et la taille. *Bull. et Mém. de la Soc. d'Anthrop. de Paris,* **8,** 17–23.

Vernon, M. D.: 1948. The development of imaginative construction in children. *Brit. J. Psychol.,* **39,** 102–111.

Vicery, F. E.: 1946. Adolescent interests in social problems. *J. educ. Res.,* **40,** 309–315.

Vinacke, W. E.: 1951. The investigation of concept formation. *Psychol. Bull.,* **48,** 1–31.

———: 1954. Concept formation in children of school age. *Education,* **74,** 527–534.

Vincent, C. E.: 1951. Trends in infant care ideas. *Child Develpm.,* **22,** 199–209.

Volberding, E.: 1948. Out-of-school behavior of eleven-year-olds. *Elem. Sch. J.,* **48,** 432–441.

Vollmer, H.: 1937. The grandmother: a problem in child rearing. *Amer. J. Orthopsychiat.,* **7,** 378–382.

———: 1946. Jealousy in children. *Amer. J. Orthopsychiat.,* **16,** 660–671.

Vosk, M.: 1953. Correlates of prejudice. *Rev. educ. Res.,* **23,** 353–361.

Voss, M. D.: 1936. A study of conditions affecting the functioning of the art appreciation process at the child level. *Psychol. Monogr.,* **48,** 1–39.

Wagner, I. F.: 1938. The body jerk of the neonate. *J. genet. Psychol.,* **52,** 65–77.

———: 1938a. A note on the hiccough of the neonate. *J. genet. Psychol.,* **52,** 233–234.

Wagoner, L. C., and E. M. Armstrong: 1928. The motor control of children as involved in the dressing process. *J. genet. Psychol.,* **35,** 84–97.

Waldfogel, S.: 1948. The frequency and affective character of childhood memories. *Psychol. Monogr.,* **62,** No. 4.

Wall, W. D.: 1948. Happiness and unhappiness in childhood and adolescence of a group of women students. *Brit. J. Psychol.,* **38,** 191–208.

Wallenstein, N.: 1937. Character and personality of children from broken homes. *Teach. Coll. Contr. Educ.,* No. 721.

Waller, W., and R. Hill: 1951. *The family: a dynamic interpretation.* New York: Dryden.

Wallin, P.: 1950. Cultural contradictions and sex roles: a repeat study. *Amer. sociol. Rev.,* **15,** 288–293.

———: 1954. Marital happiness of parents and their children's attitude to marriage. *Amer. sociol. Rev.,* **19,** 20–23.

——— and R. P. Riley: 1950. Reactions of mothers to pregnancy and adjustment of offspring in infancy. *Amer. J. Orthopsychiat.,* **20,** 616–622.

Wallis, R. S.: 1954. The overt fears of Dakota Indian children. *Child Develpm.,* **25,** 185–192.

Walter, L. M., and S. S. Marzolf: 1951. The relation of sex, age, and school achievement to levels of aspiration. *J. educ. Psychol.,* **42,** 285–292.

Walton, W. E.: 1936. Empathic responses in children. *Psychol. Monogr.,* **48,** 40–67.

———: 1937. The affective value of first names. *J. appl. Psychol.,* **21,** 369–409.

Wang, C. K. A.: 1932. The significance of early personal history for certain personality traits. *Amer. J. Psychol.*, **44**, 768–774.

Ward, A.: 1930. The only child. *Smith Coll. Stud. soc. Work*, **1**, 41–65.

Warden, C. J., and A. Cohen: 1931. A study of certain incentives applied under school-room conditions. *J. genet. Psychol.*, **39**, 320–327.

Warkany, J.: 1944. Congenital malformations induced by maternal nutritional deficiency. *J. Pediat.*, **25**, 476–480.

Warner, W. L.: 1949. *Democracy in Jonesville: a study of quality and inequality.* New York: Harper.

—— and P. S. Lunt: 1941. *The social life of a modern community.* New Haven: Yale Univ. Press.

Warren, R. L.: 1949. Cultural, personal, and situational roles. *Sociol. soc. Res.*, **34**, 104–111.

Washburn, A.: 1950. Human growth. *In Education for psychiatric social work.* New York: American Association of Psychiatric Social Workers, pp. 138–150.

Washburn, R. W.: 1929. A study of the smiling and laughing of infants in the first year of life. *Genet. Psychol. Monogr.*, **6**, 397–535.

——: 1932. A scheme for grading the reactions of children in a new social situation. *J. genet. Psychol.*, **40**, 84–99.

Wasman, H. S.: 1947. Psychological factors involved in normal pregnancy. *Univ. Toronto med. J.*, **25**, No. 2, 51–61.

Watson, G.: 1930. Happiness among adult students of education. *J. educ. Psychol.*, **21**, 79–109.

——: 1934. A comparison of the effects of lax versus strict home training. *J. soc. Psychol.*, **5**, 102–105.

Watson, J. B.: 1925. *Behaviorism.* New York: People's Institute Publishing Co.

——: 1925a. What the nursery has to say about instincts. *J. genet. Psychol.*, **32**, 293–327.

——: 1928. *Psychological care of infant and child.* New York: Norton.

—— and R. Raynor: 1920. Conditioned emotional reactions *J. exp. Psychol.*, **3**, 1–4.

—— and R. R. Watson: 1921. Studies in infant psychology. *Sci. Mon., N.Y.*, **13**, 493–515.

Wattenberg, W. W.: 1950. Church attendance and juvenile misconduct. *Sociol. soc. Res.*, **34**, 195–202.

——: 1950a. Family recreations and delinquency. *Focus*, **29**, 6–9.

Weathers, G. R.: 1954. Children up late for TV, a study shows. *New York Times*, Dec. 3.

Wechsler, D.: 1950. Intellectual development and psychological maturity. *Child Develpm.*, **21**, 45–50.

Weech, A. A., and R. V. D. Campbell: 1941. The relation between the development of behavior and the pattern of physical growth. *Child Develpm.*, **12**, 237–240.

Weider, A., and P. A. Noller: 1950. Objective studies of children's drawings of the human figure. I. sex awareness and socioeconomic level. *J. clin. Psychol.*, **6**, 319–325.

Weinfeld, G. F.: 1949. Opinions of pediatricians on certain problems of infant care. *Arch. Pediat.*, **66**, 266–270.

Welch, L.: 1938. A preliminary study of the interaction of conflicting concepts of children between the ages of 3 and 5 years. *Psychol. Rec.*, **2**, 439–459.

——: 1939. The development of size discrimination between the ages of 12 and 40 months. *J. genet. Psychol.*, **55**, 243–268.

——: 1939a. The span of generalization below the two-year age level. *J. genet. Psychol.*, **58**, 269–297.

———: 1939b. The development of discrimination of form and area. *J. Psychol.*, **7**, 37–54.

———: 1940. A preliminary investigation of some aspects of the hierarchical development of concepts. *J. gen. Psychol.*, **22**, 359–378.

——— and L. Long: 1940. The higher structural phases of concept formation. *J. Psychol.*, **9**, 59–95.

——— and ———: 1940a. A further investigation of the higher structural phases of concept formation. *J. Psychol.*, **10**, 211–220.

——— and ———: 1943. Comparison of the reasoning ability of two age groups. *J. genet. Psychol.*, **62**, 63–76.

Welford, A. T.: 1946. An attempt at an experimental approach to the psychology of religion. *Brit. J. Psychol.*, **36**, 55–73.

Wellman, B. L.: 1937. Motor achievement of preschool children. *Childh. Educ.*, **13**, 311–316.

———, I. M. Case, I. G. Mengert, and D. E. Bradbury: 1931. Speech sounds of young children. *Univ. Ia. Stud. Child Welf.*, **5**, No. 2.

Wells, C. A., and T. J. Lynch: 1954. The amount of free reading engaged in by intermediate grade pupils who have viewed television for one year or more. *J. educ. Res.*, **47**, 473–477.

Wells, F. L., and H. R. Palwick: 1950. Note on usage of male personal names. *J. soc. Psychol.*, **31**, 291–294.

Wells, J., and G. Arthur: 1939. Effect of foster-home placement on the intelligence ratings of children of feeble-minded parents. *Ment. Hyg., N.Y.*, **23**, 277–285.

Wenar, C.: 1954. The effects of a motor handicap on personality. II. The effects on integrative ability. *Child Develpm.*, **25**, 287–294.

Wenger, M. A.: 1936. An investigation on conditioned responses in human infants. *Univ. Ia. Stud. Child Welf.*, **12**, 8–90.

Werner, H., and E. Kaplan: 1950. Development of word meaning through verbal context: an experimental study. *J. Psychol.*, **29**, 251–257.

——— and ———: 1950a. The acquisition of word meanings: a developmental study. *Monogr. Soc. Res. Child Develpm.*, **51**, No. 1.

Wesselhoeft, C.: 1949. Rubella (German measles) and congenital deformities. *New Eng. med. J.*, **240**, 258–261.

Wetzel, N. C.: 1944. Growth. *In* O. Glasser, *Medical physics*. Chicago: The Year Book Publishers.

———: 1948. The role of the grid technique in a physical fitness program. *Med. Women's J.*, **55**, 19–37.

Wheeler, L. R., and V. D. Wheeler: 1945. Differences in religious ideas and attitudes of children who go to church and those who never attend. *Relig. Educ.*, **40**, 149–161.

Whipple, G.: 1953. Appraisal of the interest appeal of illustration. *Elem. Sch. J.*, **53**, 262–269.

White, M. A., and H. M. Williams: 1939. The approach-withdrawal pattern in the social behavior of young children. *J. genet. Psychol.*, **54**, 73–84.

White, R. W.: 1942. The personality of Joseph Kidd. I. History of an adolescent crisis in development of ego structure. *Charact. & Pers.*, **11**, 183–208.

———: 1942a. The personality of Joseph Kidd. II. Psychological appraisal at eighteen and a half years. *Charact. & Pers.*, **11**, 309–338.

———: 1942b. The personality of Joseph Kidd. III. Three years of ego reconstruction. *Charact. & Pers.*, **11**, 339–360.

Whiting, J. W. M., and I. L. Child: 1953. *Child training and personality: a cross cultural study*. New Haven: Yale University Press.

Whitley, H. E.: 1954. Mental health problems in the classroom. *Understanding the Child*, 23, 98–103.

Whitley, M. T.: 1929. Children's interest in collecting. *J. educ. Psychol.*, 20, 249–261.

Wickens, D. D., and C. Wickens: 1940. A study of conditioning in the neonate. *J. exp. Psychol.*, 26, 94–102.

Wickman, E. K.: 1929. *Children's behavior and teacher's attitudes.* New York: Commonwealth Fund.

Widdowson, E. M.: 1951. Mental contentment and physical growth. *Lancet*, 260, 1316–1318.

Wieder, G. S.: 1954. Group procedures modifying attitudes of prejudice in the college classroom. *J. educ. Psychol.*, 45, 332–344.

Wiese, M. J., and S. G. Cole: 1946. A study of children's attitudes and the influence of a commercial motion picture. *J. Psychol.*, 21, 151–171.

Wiggam, A. E.: 1941. Do brains and character go together? *Sch. & Soc.*, 54, 261–265.

Wile, I. S., and R. Davis: 1941. The relation of birth to behavior. *Amer. J. Orthopsychiat.*, 11, 320–334.

—— and A. B. Jones: 1937. Ordinal position and the behavior disorders of young children. *J. genet. Psychol.*, 51, 61–63.

—— and E. Noetzel: 1931. A study of birth order and behavior. *J. soc. Psychol.*, 2, 52–71.

Wiley, J. H.: 1951. A scale to measure parental attitudes toward certain aspects of children's behavior. *Speech Monogr.*, 18, 132–133.

Wilkins, W. L.: 1952. Social peers and parents. *Education*, 73, 234–237.

Williams, A. M.: 1939. Children's choices in science books. *Child Develpm. Monogr.*, No. 27.

Williams, H. M.: 1937. An analytical study of language achievement in preschool children. *Univ. Ia. Stud. Child Welf.*, 13, No. 2, 9–18.

Williams, J. R., and R. B. Scott: 1953. Growth and development of Negro infants. II. Motor development and its relationship to child rearing practices in two groups of Negro infants. *Child Develpm.*, 24, 103–121.

Williams, R. M., and M. L. Mattson: 1942. The effect of social groupings upon the language of preschool children. *Child Develpm.*, 13, 233–245.

Wilson, C. O.: 1931. *A study of laughter situations among young children.* Lincoln, Nebr.

Wilson, F. T.: 1938. Verbally expressed wishes of children and college women students. *J. Psychol.*, 5, 91–105.

——: 1939. Expressed wishes of elderly persons, college men, and birthday wishes of first grade children. *J. genet. Psychol.*, 55, 81–101.

——: 1939a. Birthday wishes of first grade children. *J. genet. Psychol.*, 55, 319–352.

——: 1941. Reading interests of young children. *J. genet. Psychol.*, 58, 363–389.

——: 1943. Stories that are liked by young children. *J. genet. Psychol.*, 63, 55–69.

——: 1943a. Young children's favorite stories and characters, and their reasons for liking them. *J. genet. Psychol.*, 63, 157–164.

Wilson, L. A.: 1955. The influence of a child purpose upon the perseverance of young children. *J. exp. Educ.*, 23, 353–358.

Winch, R. F.: 1950. Some data bearing on the Oedipus hypothesis. *J. abnorm. soc. Psychol.*, 45, 481–489.

——: 1950a. The study of personality in the family setting. *Social Forces*, 28, 310–316.

——: 1951. Further data and observations on the Oedipus hypothesis: the consequence of an inadequate hypothesis. *Amer. sociol. Rev.*, 16, 784–795.

Wingfield, A. H., and P. Sandiford: 1928. Twins and orphans. *J. educ. Psychol.*, 19, 410–423.

Wingfield, R. C.: 1948. Bernreuter personality ratings of college students who recall having had imaginary playmates during childhood. *J. child Psychiat.*, **1**, 90–94.

Winker, J. B.: 1949. Age trends and sex differences in the wishes, identifications, activities, and fears of children. *Child Develpm.*, **20**, 191–200.

Winkley, R., K. Jackson, O. A. Faust, M. F. Murray, and E. G. Cermak: 1951. Emotional reactions and behavior of children in the home. *J. Pediat.*, **38**, 476–481.

Winstet, B.: 1951. The use of a controlled play situation in determining certain effects of maternal attitudes on children. *Child Develpm.*, **22**, 299–311.

Wishik, S. M.: 1950. The importance of "timing" in child health supervision. *Child Develpm.*, **21**, 51–60.

Withall, J.: 1952. Assessment of the social-emotional climate experienced by a group of seventh graders as they moved from class to class. *Educ. psychol. Monogr.*, **12**, 440–451.

Withey, R. A.: 1952. The role of religion in higher education. *Sch. & Soc.*, **76**, 257–261.

Witmer, H., and R. Kotinsky: 1953. *Personality in the making. Fact finding report of the Midcentury White House Conference on Children and Youth.* New York: Harper.

Witmer, H., et al.: 1938. The outcome of treatment of children rejected by their mothers. *Smith Coll. Stud. soc. Work*, **8**, 187–234.

Witryol, S. L.: 1950. Age trends in children's evaluation of teacher-approved and teacher-disapproved behavior. *Genet. Psychol. Monogr.*, **41**, 271–326.

—— and G. G. Thompson: 1953. A critical review of the stability of social acceptability scores obtained with the partial-rank-order and the paired-comparison scales. *Genet. Psychol. Monogr.*, **48**, 221–260.

Wittenberg, R. M., and J. Berg: 1952. The stranger in the group. *Amer. J. Orthopsychiat.*, **22**, 89–97.

Witty, P. A.: 1931. A study of deviates in versatility and sociability of play interests *Teach. Coll. Contr. Educ.*, No. 470.

——: 1937. Only and intermediate children in the senior high school. *J. exp. Educ.*, **6**, 180–186.

——: 1941. Children's interest in reading the comics. *J. exp. Educ.*, **10**, 100–104.

——: 1941a. Reading the comics—a comparative study. *J. exp. Educ.*, **10**, 105–109.

——: 1951. Television and the educative process. *Sch. & Soc.*, **74**, 369–372.

——: 1951a. Television and the high school student. *Education*, **72**, 242–251.

——: 1952. Children's interest in comics, radio, motion pictures, and TV. *Educ. Admin. Superv.*, **38**, 138–147.

——: 1954. Children change video favorites. *New York Times*, Jan. 11.

——: 1954a. Comparative studies of interest in TV. *Educ. Admin. Superv.*, **40**, 321–335.

——: 1955. Comics, television, and our children. *Today's Health*, February, pp. 18–21.

——, and A. Coomer: 1943. Activities and preferences of a secondary-school group. *J. educ. Psychol.*, **34**, 65–76.

——, ——, and D. McBean: 1946. Children's choices of favorite books: a study conducted in ten elementary schools. *J. educ. Psychol.*, **37**, 266–278.

——, S. Garfield, and W. G. Brink: 1941. A comparison of the vocational interests of Negro and white high-school students. *J. educ. Psychol.*, **32**, 124–132.

—— and D. Kopel: 1939. *Reading and the educative process.* Boston: Ginn.

—— and D. Moore: 1945. Interest in reading the comics among Negro children. *J. educ. Psychol.*, **36**, 303–308.

——, E. Smith, and A. Coomer: 1942. Reading the comics in grades VII and VIII. *J. educ. Psychol.*, **33**, 173–182.

Wolberg, L. R.: 1944. The character structure of the rejected child. *Nerv. Child*, **3**, 74–88.

Wolf, T. H.: 1938. The effect of praise and competition on the persisting behavior of kindergarten children. *Instit. Univ. Minn. Press, Child Welf. Monogr. Ser.*, No. 15.

Wolfenstein, M.: 1946. The impact of a child's story on mothers and children. *Monogr. Soc. Res. Child Develpm.*, **11**, No. 1.

———: 1951. A phase in the development of children's sense of humor. *In* R. S. Eissler, *The psychoanalytic study of the child.* New York: International Universities Press, pp. 336–350.

———: 1953. Trends in infant care. *Amer. J. Orthopsychiat.*, **33**, 120–130.

———: 1954. Children's understanding of jokes. *Psychoanal. Stud. Child*, **8**, 162–176.

Wolfenstein, M. T.: 1950. A developmental study of children's fantasies about moral problems: II. Conceptions of "goodness." *Amer. Psychologist*, **5**, 304–305.

Wolff, E., and L. M. Bayer: 1952. Psychosomatic disorders of childhood and adolescence. *Amer. J. Orthopsychiat.*, **22**, 510–521.

Wolff, M.: 1947. *The personality of the preschool child.* New York: Grune & Stratton.

Wolfle, H. M.: 1949. The import of the caress in modern child psychology. *Amer. Psychologist*, **4**, 249.

Wolman, B.: 1951. Spontaneous groups of children and adolescents in Israel. *J. soc. Psychol.*, **34**, 171–182.

Woodruff, A. D.: 1945. Personal values and religious background. *J. soc. Psychol.*, **22**, 141–147.

Woodworth, R. S.: 1941. *Heredity and environment: a critical survey of recently published material on twins and foster children.* New York: Social Science Research Council.

——— and D. G. Marquis: 1947. *Psychology*, 5th ed. New York: Holt.

Woofter, A. C.: 1940. Preliminary survey on relation of physical defects to scholastic standing. *Child Develpm. Abstr.*, **14**, No. 150.

Woolley, H. T.: 1925. Agnes: a dominant personality in the making. *J. genet. Psychol.*, **32**, 569–598.

Worbois, G. M.: 1942. Language development of children of two different rural environments. *Child Develpm.*, **13**, 175–180.

Worcester, J., and O. M. Lombard: 1948. Predictability of leg length. *Child Develpm.*, **19**, 159–166.

Wrenn, C. G.: 1949. Student discipline in a college. *Educ. psychol. Measmt*, **9**, 625–633.

Wright, B. A.: 1942. Altruism in children and the perceived conduct of others. *J. abnorm. soc. Psychol.*, **37**, 218–233.

Wright, M. E.: 1943. The influence of frustration upon the social relations of young children. *Charact. & Pers.*, **12**, 111–122.

Yankauer, A.: 1950. The relationship of fetal and infant mortality to residential segregation. *Amer. sociol. Rev.*, **15**, 644–648.

Yarnelle, E. C.: 1932. The relation of children's preferences to the preferences and attitudes of their parents. *Smith Coll. Stud. soc. Work*, **2**, 376–377.

Yedinack, J. G.: 1949. A study of the linguistic functioning of children with articulation and reading disabilities. *J. genet. Psychol.*, **74**, 23–59.

Yellowlees, H.: 1940. The problem of adolescence. *Lancet*, **238**, 233–235.

Young, F. E.: 1938. *Clothing the child.* New York: McGraw-Hill.

Young, F. M.: 1932. Cause for loss of interest in high-school subjects as reported by 631 college students. *J. educ. Res.*, **25**, 110–115.

———: 1941. An analysis of certain variables in a developmental study of language. *Genet. Psychol. Monogr.*, **23**, 3–141.

———: 1942. Certain social indices in the language of preschool subjects. *J. genet. Psychol.*, **61**, 109–123.

———: 1942a. Development as indicated by a study of pronouns. *J. genet. Psychol.*, **61**, 125–134.

Young, K.: 1953. What strong family life means to our society. *Soc. Casework*, **34**, 323–329.

Young, P. T., and J. A. Yavitz: 1946. Activities in which college students experience success and failure and those in which they wish to be more successful. *J. soc. Psychol.*, **24**, 131–148.

Zachry, C. B.: 1940. *Emotion and conduct in adolescence.* New York: Appleton-Century-Crofts.

———: 1940a. The child's emotional and social adjustment. *Proc. 6th Conf. on Educ. and Except. Child, Child Res. Clinic Woods Sch.*, pp. 8–15.

Zazzo, R.: 1948. Images du corps et conscience de soi. *Enfance*, **1**, 29–43.

Zeleny, L. D.: 1949. Social leadership. *Sociol. soc. Res.*, **33**, 431–436.

———: 1951. Status and role among fifth-grade school children. *Sociol. soc. Res.*, **35**, 425–427.

Zeligs, R.: 1939. Children's worries. *Sociol. soc. Res.*, **24**, 22–32.

———: 1941. Environmental factors annoying to children. *Sociol. soc. Res.*, **25**, 549–556.

———: 1942. Children's wishes. *J. appl. Psychol.*, **26**, 231–240.

———: 1942a. *Glimpses into child life.* New York: Morrow.

———: 1945. Social factors annoying to children. *J. appl. Psychol.*, **29**, 75–82.

———: 1948. Children's intergroup attitudes. *J. genet. Psychol.*, **72**, 101–110.

———: 1950. Reasons given by children for their intergroup attitudes. *J. genet. Psychol.*, **76**, 145–161.

———: 1950a. Intergroup attitudes of Gentile, Jewish, and Apache Indian children, *J. educ. Psychol.*, **41**, 243–248.

———: 1950b. Children's concepts and stereotypes of Dutch, French, Italian, Mexican, Russian, and Negro. *J. educ. Res.*, **43**, 367–375.

———: 1950c. The meaning of democracy to sixth-grade children. *J. genet. Psychol.*, **76**, 263–281.

———: 1950d. Children's concepts and stereotypes of Polish, Irish, Finn, Hungarian, Bulgarian, Dane, Czechoslovakian, Hindu, and Filipino. *J. genet. Psychol.*, **77**, 73–83.

———: 1951. Your child's good-will depends on you. *J. Negro Educ.*, **20**, 32–38.

———: 1952. Children's concepts and stereotypes of Norwegian, Jew, Scotch, Canadian, Swedish, and American Indian. *J. educ. Res.*, **45**, 349–360.

———: 1953. Children's concepts and stereotypes of Turk, Portuguese, Roumanian, Arab, Chinese, French-Canadian, Mulatto, South American, Hawaiian, and Australian. *J. genet. Psychol.*, **83**, 171–178.

———: 1954. Races and nationalities most and least liked by children. *J. educ. Res.*, **48**, 1–14.

———: 1955. Children's concepts and stereotypes of American, Greek, English, German, and Japanese. *J. educ. Sociol.*, **28**, 360–368.

Zimmerman, K. A., and E. Lewton: 1951. Teacher personality in school relationships. *Educ. Leadership*, **8**, 422–428.

Zintz, M. V.: 1951. Academic achievement and social and emotional adjustment of handicapped children. *Elem. Sch. J.*, **51**, 502–507.

Zorbaugh, H.: 1944. The comics—there they stand. *J. educ. Sociol.*, **18**, 196–203.

———: 1949. What adults think of the comics as reading for children. *J. educ. Sociol.*, **23**, 225–235.

Zucker, H.: 1943. The emotional attachment of children to their parents as related to standards of behavior and delinquency. *J. Psychol.*, **15**, 31–40.

Zyve, C. I.: 1927. Conversations among children. *Teach. Coll. Rec.*, **29**, 46–61.

VISUAL BIBLIOGRAPHY

The visual aids listed below and on the following pages can be used to illustrate and supplement much of the material in this book. For the convenience of users the films have been grouped by chapters, but since many of the films deal with various aspects of child development, we recommend that they be reviewed before use in order to determine their suitability for particular groups or units of study.

Motion pictures and filmstrips are included in the following list, the character of each being indicated by the self-explanatory abbreviations "MP" and "FS." Immediately following this identification is the name of the producer and, if different, the distributor. Abbreviations are used for these names and are identified in the list of sources at the end of the bibliography. Unless otherwise indicated, the motion pictures are 16-mm sound black-and-white films and the filmstrips are 35-mm silent black-and-white. The length of motion pictures is given in minutes (min), that of filmstrips in frames (fr).

Most of the films can be borrowed or rented from state and local film libraries, and users should consult *A Directory of 2660 16mm Film Libraries,* available for 50 cents from the Government Printing Office, Washington 25, D.C.

While this bibliography is reasonably comprehensive, film users should also examine the latest annual editions and supplements of *Educational Film Guide* and *Filmstrip Guide,* published by the H. W. Wilson Co., New York. These *Guides,* standard reference books, are available in most school, college, and public libraries. Certain specialized catalogs will also be useful, namely:

Selected Films for Mental Health Education. National Association for Mental Health, New York 16.

Motion Pictures on Child Life. Children's Bureau, U.S. Department of Health, Education, and Welfare, Washington 25, D.C.

Psychological Cinema Register. Pennsylvania State University, University Park, Pa.

The following three series of films are especially recommended for portraying visually and dramatically the concepts explained in this book.

1. *Child Development* (MP-FS series, McGraw). Nine motion pictures and five filmstrips with the following titles. Each is described under its appropriate chapter, as noted below.

Principles of Development (Chap. 1)
Child Care and Development (Chap. 1)
Heredity and Prenatal Development (Chap. 2)
Children's Emotions (Chap. 7)
Social Development (Chap. 8)
Children's Play (Chap. 10)
Children's Fantasies (Chap. 13)
Sibling Relations and Personality (Chap. 14)
Sibling Rivalries and Parents (Chap. 14)

2. *Ages and Stages* (MP series, CNFB/McGraw). Four motion pictures, color or black and white, with the following titles and descriptions:

He Acts His Age (15 min). Survey of typical behavior patterns of children from ages one to fifteen, demonstrating that as children grow their interests, activities, and emotions change.

The Terrible Twos and Trusting Threes (22 min). A study of child behavior at two and three years, showing what to expect from youngsters of these ages, and suggesting how parents can deal constructively with their problems.

The Frustrating Fours and Fascinating Fives (22 min). Portrays characteristic patterns of a four-year-old boy, from imaginative craftsmanship to inconsistent destructiveness, and the changes that occur as he grows into a five-year-old.

From Sociable Six to Noisy Nine (22 min). Portrays characteristic patterns of behavior exhibition by children from six to nine, and constructive efforts of parents to understand and guide these children.

3. *Adolescent Development* (MP-FS series, McGraw). Five motion pictures that, while not directly related to the foregoing text, illustrate later stages in development toward adulthood.
Titles are:

The Meaning of Adolescence (16 min)
Physical Aspects of Puberty (19 min)
Age of Turmoil (20 min)
Social-Sex Attitudes in Adolescence (22 min)
Meeting the Needs of Adolescents (19 min)

CHAPTER 1. PRINCIPLES OF DEVELOPMENT

Child Care and Development (MP, McGraw, 17 min). Explains the habits of daily physical care that ensure a happy, healthy child. Covers good habits of eating, sleeping, and bathing, the wearing of proper clothing, and outdoor exercise. (Follow-up filmstrip, 45 fr, available.)

Child Development (MP series, EBF, 11 min each). Ten films, with the following self-descriptive titles, produced at the Yale University Clinic of Child Development with the collaboration of Dr. Arnold Gesell.

Baby's Day at Forty-eight Weeks
Baby's Day at Twelve Weeks
Behavior Patterns at One Year
Early Social Behavior
From Creeping to Walking
Growth of Infant Behavior: Early Stages
Growth of Infant Behavior: Later Stages
Learning and Growth
Posture and Locomotion
Thirty-six Weeks Behavior Day

Dr. Spock (MP, MOT/McGraw, 27 min). Presents the theories and practices of Dr. Spock and his suggestions to parents for dealing with children from infancy to age six.

Embryology of Human Behavior (MP, AAMC/IFB, 28 min color). Explains that a child grows in accordance with certain universal laws and at the same time develops as an individual. Traces the patterning processes of behavior.

Life Begins (MP, EBF, 60 min). Pictures 24 years of clinical practice and research on problems of infancy at the Yale University Clinic of Child Development under the direction of Dr. Arnold L. Gesell.

Life with Baby (MP, MOT/McGraw, 18 min). Shows how children grow mentally and physically. A popular version and condensation of the Gesell Child Development Series.

Principles of Development (MP, McGraw, 17 min). Outlines the fundamentals of child growth and development and considers the variables which make each child different from every other one. (Follow-up filmstrip available.)

CHAPTER 2. PRENATAL DEVELOPMENT

All My Babies (MP, Col U Press, 55 min). Story of Mary Cooley, a midwife, from the time she takes a case until the baby is taken to its first Well Baby Clinic.

Genetics and Behavior (MP, PCR, 16 min silent color or black and white). Documents the thesis that the structure which limits behavior is inherited, but not behavior itself. Showings restricted to professional personnel.

Heredity (MP, EBF, 11 min). Explains with animated charts and animal picturization the Mendelian laws of inheritance.

Heredity and Family Environment (MP, McGraw, 9 min). Portrays by pictorial examples and explains through psychological interpretations the meanings of heredity and environment and their relationship.

Heredity and Prenatal Development (MP, McGraw, 21 min). Discusses cell growth and heredity, describes fertilization of ovum and traces development of fetus until delivery, considers development of physical functions of newborn, and stresses connection between physical and emotional sensitivity. (Follow-up filmstrip available.)

Human Reproduction (MP, McGraw, 20 min). Explains the human reproductive systems and the process of conception, pregnancy, and childbirth. Describes the anatomy, physiology, and functions of the male and female reproductive organs and illustrates, by animated drawings, the body mechanisms of delivery. (Follow-up filmstrip, 30 fr, available.)

In the Beginning (MP, USDA, 17 min). Shows by means of time-lapse cinematography the ovulation, fertilization, and early development of the mammalian (rabbit) egg.

Prenatal Care (MP, Med Film, 23 min). Portrays three women in normal pregnancy through the ninth-month period, and explains recommended exercise, clothing, and diet during this time.

CHAPTER 3. THE NEWBORN INFANT

Care of the Newborn Baby: The Nurse's Role in Instructing the Parents (MP, USOE/UWF, 31 min). Nurse's functions and duties in teaching parents to care for newborn babies; what the nurse can do in the home, clinic, and hospital; and how to hold, dress, bathe, and feed a baby. (Follow-up filmstrip, 93 fr, available.)

Childbirth: Normal Delivery (MP, Cited, 16 min color). Gives a close-up of the actual birth of a baby. Photographed under medical supervision. Distribution restricted to medical schools, hospitals, nursing and educational institutions, and lectures or showings under medical supervision.

Postnatal Care (MP, Med Film, 12 min). Shows a mother in her hospital room doing exercises, caring for her baby, nursing the baby, etc., and discusses the father's relationship to the new family situation.

Studies of the Psychoanalytic Research Project on Problems in Infancy (MP, NYU). Series of eleven films, all but one silent, documenting various aspects of infant behavior.

Anxiety: Its Phenomenology in the First Year of Life (20 min)
Birth and the First Fifteen Minutes of Life (10 min)
Genesis of Emotions (30 min)
Grasping (20 min)
Grief (30 min)
Motherlove (20 min)
Psychogenic Diseases in Infancy: An Attempt at Their Classification (20 min)
Shaping the Personality: The Role of Mother-Child Relations in Infancy (30 min)
The Smile of the Baby (30 min sound)
The Smiling Response (20 min)
Somatic Consequences of Emotional Starvation in Infants (30 min)

CHAPTER 4. PHYSICAL GROWTH

Anthropometric Measurements of Children (MP, Calif U, 10 min). Describes the methods used in securing anthropometric measurements of young children for purposes of research. Devised for use by students of child development.

Human Growth (MP, Brown, 19 min color). A mixed group of seventh-grade students view and discuss a film which traces human growth and development of the organism from mating through pregnancy and birth, then from infancy through childhood, and adolescence to adulthood. Emphasizes male and female structural development.

CHAPTER 5. MOTOR DEVELOPMENT

Development of Locomotion (MP, Calif U, 10 min silent). Depicts developmental sequences in a series of children from six to fifteen months of age. Gives examples of various methods of locomotion.

Growth of Adaptive Behavior (MP, EBF, 15 min silent). Traces the development of motor coordination through a child's first five years.

Growth of Motor Behavior (MP, EBF, 15 min silent). Traces the development of motor control from birth to age five, showing the transition from uncoordinated activity to complex controlled movements of eyes, hands, trunk, and legs.

Large Muscle Motor Skills of Four Year Olds (MP, Calif U, 10 min silent color). Through individual sequences showing running, balancing, jumping, pedaling, pumping, kicking, throwing, catching and bouncing, hitting and punching, pushing and pulling, climbing, suspending own weight, tumbling, and guiding a wagon, indicates the types and levels of large muscle motor skills that are characteristic of children of this age.

Study in Human Development (MP, PCR, four parts, each 17–19 min silent). Film studies documenting developmental changes in manipulation, posture, locomotion, motor skills, social behavior from birth to five years of age. Titles are:

Six to Thirty Weeks
Forty-two Weeks to Fifteen Months
Nineteen Months to Two Years and Eight Months
Three Years to Five Years

CHAPTER 6. DEVELOPMENT OF SPEECH

Good Speech for Gary (MP, USC/McGraw, 22 min color or black and white). Explains some of the more common speech defects in young children and shows modern teaching methods being used to help children overcome these defects.

Report on Donald (MP, Minn U, 20 min). Reviews the history of a college freshman to explain how and why he developed a severe speech block, and shows how the clinic at the university helps him gain control over his speech.

CHAPTER 7. EMOTIONAL DEVELOPMENT

Angry Boy (MP, MHFB/IFB, 32 min). Tells the story of emotional disturbances engendered by family tensions. Tommy, a preadolescent boy, is caught stealing. At a child-guidance clinic, a psychiatric team traces his disturbances to their basic causes, and is able to help him.

Children's Emotions (MP, McGraw, 22 min). Discusses the major emotions of childhood—fear, anger, jealousy, curiosity, joy—and points out what the parent can do to lessen fears and promote the child's happiness and natural development. (Follow-up filmstrip available.)

Fears of Children (MP, MHFB/IFB, 30 min). Parent-child situation in which the mother tends to coddle her five-year-old son and the father expects too much of him. Explains how the conflict magnifies the child's fears.

First as a Child (MP, Va Health/IFB, 22 min). Case history of a crippled child from the public health nurse's first visit to his home through diagnosis, treatment, and after-care. Points out the necessary consideration given to the child's emotional troubles.

Judging Emotional Behavior (MP, Churchill, 20 min). A motion-picture test designed to measure the sensitivity of individuals to the emotions of others. Ten sequences are shown in which two people react as if certain events described by a narrator were happening to them.

CHAPTER 8. SOCIAL DEVELOPMENT

Martha Belongs (MP, Wisc U, 12 min color). Emphasizes the early contacts of a baby with her own family and the need of an infant to have opportunities to develop at her own pace and to have freedom for exercise. Points up natural opportunities for sex education of older children in the family.

Social Development (MP, McGraw, 16 min). Offers an analysis of social behavior at different age levels and the reasons underlying the changes in behavior patterns as the child develops. (Follow-up filmstrip available.)

CHAPTER 9. SOCIAL ADJUSTMENTS

Children Growing Up with Other People (MP, BIS/UWF, 30 min). Shows how youngsters emerge from their early involuntary dependence into self-reliant members of their respective family, school, and other groups.

Guidance Problem for School and Home (MP, TC, 18 min). Depicts the problem of Danny, a second-grade child who has poor social adjustment and is not doing well in school. Shows how conferences between the teacher and his mother help solve the problem.

The Quiet One (MP, Film Doc/Athena, 67 min). Tells the story of Donald Peters, a mentally retarded Negro boy, who is an only child and the victim of a disrupted home in the Harlem district of New York City, and of his treatment at the Wiltwyck School at Esopus, N.Y.

CHAPTER 10. PLAY

The Child at Play (MP, TC, 18 min). Shows the nature of children's spontaneous play as reviewed in a one-way-vision room by depicting the unrestrained play activity of a three-year-old child and youngsters of various ages.

Children's Play (MP, McGraw, 27 min). Shows how play differs at various age levels, describes some different forms of play, and emphasizes the need for playtime.

Understanding Children's Play (MP, NYU, 10 min). How adults can understand and help children through observation of their use of toys and toy materials.

Your Children's Play (MP, BIS/McGraw, 20 min). Gives examples of play behavior of one- to eight-year-olds, and emphasizes the need for parents to understand the reasons for such behavior patterns,

CHAPTER 11. DEVELOPMENT OF UNDERSTANDING

Children Learning by Experience (MP, BIS/UWF, 40 min). Develops the themes that all children want to learn, enjoy practicing simple skills, strive to understand the world about them, learn some things at secondhand, and learn a great many things through play and imagination.

Experimental Studies of Children's Learning (MP, Calif U, 13 min color silent). Laboratory processes used in measuring rates of learning by children.

CHAPTER 13. SOME CHILDHOOD INTERESTS

Children's Fantasies (MP, McGraw, 21 min). Explores the reasons for a child's fantasies and explains how they develop and how children can be affected by them.

CHAPTER 14. FAMILY RELATIONSHIPS

Baby Meets His Parents (MP, EBF, 11 min). Points out how differences in personality can be accounted for, not only by heredity, but also by the human relationships and environmental factors experienced during the first years of life.

David and His Family (FS, YAF, 30 fr). Story of a young boy's life at home with a new baby brother, and how he adjusts himself to this situation.

David's Bad Day (FS, YAF, 36 fr). Shows the personality problems created by the advent of a baby brother in a family, and how the parents recognize and solve them.

The Family (MP, USIA/UWF, 20 min). Shows how the daily problems of a family are solved when each member understands the needs and desires of others, and the family faces its problems together.

Family Circles (MP, CNFB/McGraw, 31 min). Portrays, through three dramatized situations, the interplay between home and school influences, and how family attitudes affect children's success in school.

Head of the House (MP, USIA/UWF, 40 min). Depicts the emotional problems of a young boy, his rebellion against parental controls, particularly his father's repressive discipline, and his gradual development into a potential juvenile delinquent. Shows the assistance of a community social worker and a neighborhood welfare house in bringing about development of better understanding between father and son.

The Lonely Night (MP, MHFB, 62 min). Story of a young woman's journey out of the dark hours of emotional disturbance. Shows the process of psychiatric treatment candidly and completely, and the kind of family life that can help build emotional strength.

Preface to a Life (MP, USPHS, 29 min). Parental influence on a child's developing personality, illustrated by a series of episodes showing the effects of an overly solicitous mother and an overly demanding father; and, in contrast, the healthy childhood resulting when both parents accept their child as an individual.

Sibling Relations and Personality (MP, McGraw, 22 min). Demonstrates through a series of case studies the relationships children have with brothers and sisters during their developmental years.

Sibling Rivalries and Parents (MP, McGraw, 11 min). Describes the reasons for rivalry among brothers and sisters, its various manifestations, and parental means of holding natural friction to a minimum.

CHAPTER 15. PERSONALITY

A Character Neurosis with Depressive and Compulsive Trends in the Making: Life History of Mary from Birth to Fifteen Years (MP, NYU, 60 min silent). Film record of a girl with superior biological capacity, an active congenital-activity type who develops, during her fifteen years, a neurosis through interaction with those in her environment.

Infants Are Individuals (MP, EBF, 15 min). Demonstrates that individuality and personality are apparent in youngsters from their earliest day. Shows how certain behavior patterns disclosed in infancy persist into later life.

Personality Development (MP, EBF). Series of four films with the following titles and running times:

    Answering the Child's Why (13 min)
    Baby Meets His Parents (11 min)
    Helping the Child to Accept the Do's (11 min)
    Helping the Child to Face the Don'ts (11 min)

Shyness (MP, CNFB/McGraw, 23 min). Portrays the lonely existence of a shy adult, and illustrates the causes of shyness through studies of three children. Explains the reasons for shyness and how this problem may be overcome.

Studies of Normal Personality Development (MP, NYU). Series of 10 films produced by the Department of Child Study at Vassar College.

    Balloons: Aggression and Destructive Games (20 min)
    Finger Painting (22 min color)
    Frustration Play Techniques (35 min)
    A Long Time to Grow. Part 1: Two- and Three-year-olds in Nursery School (35 min)
    A Long Time to Grow. Part 2: Four- and Five-year-olds in School (35 min)
    Meeting Emotional Needs in Childhood: The Groundwork of Democracy (33 min)
    Pay Attention (30 min)
    Preschool Incidents. Part 1: When Should Grownups Help? (13 min)
    Preschool Incidents. Part 2: And Then Ice Cream (10 min)
    Preschool Incidents. Part 3: When Should Grownups Stop Fights? (15 min)

Symbols of Expression (MP, PCR, 26 min silent). Attempts to demonstrate that an individual's drawings, "doodlings," art productions, dance forms, signatures, or writings embody "key symbols" of his personality.

This Is Robert: A Study of Personality Growth in a Pre-school Child (MP, NYU, 75 min). Traces the development of an aggressive but appealing child from his early nursery school days to his first year in a public school.

Unity of Personality (MP, PCR, 18 min silent). Demonstrates similarities of expressive behavior characteristics of five individuals with very different personalities. The behavior patterns shown include gestures, facial movements, handwriting, handling objects, athletic activities, and walking gaits.

MAIN SOURCES OF FILMS

AAMC—American Association of Medical Colleges, 185 N. Wabash St., Chicago 1.

Athena—Athena Films, Inc., 165 W. 46th St., New York 19.

BIS—British Information Services, 30 Rockefeller Plaza, New York 20.

Brown—E. C. Brown Trust, 220 S.W. Alder St., Portland 4, Ore.

CNFB—Canadian National Film Board, 1270 Avenue of the Americas, New York 20.

Calif U—University of California, Berkeley, Calif.

Churchill—Churchill-Wexler Film Productions, 801 N. Seward St., Los Angeles 38.

Cited—Cited Films, 30 Rockefeller Plaza, New York 20.

Col U Press—Columbia University Press, Center for Mass Communication, 413 W. 117th St., New York 27.

EBF—Encyclopaedia Britannica Films, Inc., 1150 Wilmette Ave., Wilmette, Ill.

IFB—International Film Bureau, 57 E. Jackson Blvd., Chicago 4.

MHFB—Mental Health Film Board, Inc., 166 E. 38th St., New York 16.

MOT—March of Time, New York (Films distributed by McGraw-Hill Book Co.)

McGraw—McGraw-Hill Book Co., Inc., Text-Film Dept., 330 W. 42nd St., New York 36.

Med Film—Medical Films, Inc., 116 Natoma St., San Francisco 5.

Minn U—University of Minnesota, Minneapolis 14, Minn.

NYU—New York University Film Library, 26 Washington Pl., New York 3.

PCR—Psychological Cinema Register, Pennsylvania State University, University Park, Pa.

TC—Teachers College, Columbia University, 525 W. 120th St., New York 27.

USC—University of Southern California, Los Angeles.

USDA—U.S. Department of Agriculture, Washington 25, D.C.

USIA—U.S. Information Agency, Washington 25, D.C. (Films distributed in the U.S. by United World Films)

USOE—U.S. Office of Education, Washington 25, D.C. (Films distributed by United World Films)

USPHS—U.S. Public Health Service, Washington 25, D.C.

Va Health—Virginia Department of Health, Richmond, Va.

UWF—United World Films, Inc., 1445 Park Ave., New York 29.

Wisc U—University of Wisconsin, Madison, Wis.

YAF—Young America Films, Inc., 18 E. 41st St., New York.

NAME INDEX

Abbe, M., 467, 577
Aberle, D. F., 503, 504, 514, 516, 528, 577
Abernethy, E. M., 169, 577
Abt, I., 169, 577
Ackerman, N. W., 290, 577
Adams, S., 204, 577
Adler, A., 488, 490, 555, 560, 561, 577
Albrecht, R., 518, 577
Aldrich, C. A., 89, 90, 91, 173, 177, 210, 405, 546, 577
Alexander, F., 555, 577
Alexander, M., 564, 577
Alexander, T., 249, 564, 577
Alexandria, Sister M., 304, 577
Allen, F. H., 521, 577
Allen, I., 110, 116, 577
Allen, I. M., 210, 577
Allen, L., 552, 577
Allen, M. F., 124, 597
Allen, P. J., 303, 484, 577, 578
Allen, R. M., 272, 578
Allport, F. H., 183
Allport, G. W., 290, 390, 391, 396, 446, 449, 451, 453, 541, 542, 578
Alm, I., 99, 100, 101, 103, 578
Alm, O. W., 317, 621
Almy, M. C., 339, 578
Alpert, A., 458, 460, 461, 578
Alschuler, R. H., 399, 578
Altmann, M., 36, 578
Altus, G. T., 213, 578
Amatora, Sister Mary, 396, 458, 562, 578
Amatruda, C. S., 210, 604
Amen, E. W., 236, 323, 328, 367, 578, 597
Ames, L. B., 10, 13, 14, 16, 90, 146, 147, 151, 156, 157, 158, 160–163, 175, 204, 246, 248, 265, 300, 332, 334, 375, 385, 386, 388–392, 402, 578, 579, 604, 615
Ames, R. T., 395, 579
Ames, V. C., 114, 579
Ammons, H. S., 528, 529, 579
Ammons, R. B., 290, 396, 397, 528, 529, 579

Anastasi, A., 193, 209, 212, 213, 579
Anders, S. F., 452, 579
Anderson, C. M., 564, 579
Anderson, F. N., 66, 579
Anderson, H. H., 279, 287, 436, 562, 579
Anderson, J. E., 98, 105, 125, 153, 193, 502, 522, 532, 533, 542, 573, 579, 592
Anderson, T. H., 258, 622
Anderson, W. A., 258, 493, 580
Anderson, W. E., 535, 558, 580
Anderson, W. F., 470, 580
Anthony, S., 453, 580
Antonov, A. N., 68, 580
Appel, M. H., 274, 276, 580
Ariamov, E. A., 431, 580
Arkin, E., 543, 580
Armstrong, E. M., 156, 655
Arnold, M., 379, 446, 448–450, 453, 621
Arrington, R. E., 204, 205, 542, 580
Arsenian, S., 213, 535, 569, 580
Arthaud, R. L., 552, 580
Arthur, G., 6, 657
Asakawa, T., 113, 640
Asch, S. E., 539, 580
Ashley-Montagu, M. F., 487, 488, 492, 580
Austin, M. C., 298, 302, 313, 476, 580
Austin, T. R., 398, 580
Ausubel, D. P., 272, 273, 289, 307, 315, 316, 375, 377, 391, 394, 396, 405, 412, 415, 432, 436, 558, 580, 581
Axline, V. M., 322, 323, 581
Ayer, M. E., 427, 581

Bach, G. R., 323, 581
Bagby, P. H., 294, 581
Bahm, A. J., 446, 581
Bailey, Sister A. T., 276, 581
Bain, R., 263, 501, 522, 542, 572, 581
Baird, F., 482, 599
Baker, J. N., 438, 581
Bakwin, H., 95, 114, 164–166, 201, 215,

671

SUBJECT INDEX